SEVENTH EDITION

Accounting Theory

Dedicated to
Joel, Chris, Ethan, and Bianca;
Josh; and Cheri;
and in loving memory of Barbara and Coco.
And to Glenda, Cambria, and Tim;
and Joan, Tom, and Frank.

SEVENTH EDITION

Accounting Theory

Conceptual Issues in a Political and Economic Environment

HARRY I. WOLK
Drake University

JAMES L. DODD
Drake University

JOHN J. ROZYCKI
Drake University

SAGE Publications

Los Angeles • London • New Delhi • Singapore

For information:

Sage Publications, Inc.
2455 Teller Road
Thousand Oaks, California 91320
E-mail: order@sagepub.com

Sage Publications India Pvt. Ltd.
B 1/I 1 Mohan Cooperative
 Industrial Area
Mathura Road, New Delhi 110 044
India

Sage Publications Ltd.
1 Oliver's Yard
55 City Road
London EC1Y 1SP
United Kingdom

Sage Publications Asia-Pacific
 Pte. Ltd.
33 Pekin Street #02-01
Far East Square
Singapore 048763

Printed in the United States of America

Library of Congress Cataloging-in-Publication Data

Wolk, Harry I.
Accounting theory: Conceptual issues in a political and economic environment/Harry I. Wolk, James L. Dodd, John J. Rozycki. — 7th ed.
     p. cm.
Includes bibliographical references and index.
ISBN 978-1-4129-5345-0 (cloth)
     1. Accounting. I. Dodd, James L., 1947– II. Rozycki, John J. III. Title.

HF5625.W64 2008
657—dc22   2007023766

This book is printed on acid-free paper.

07   08   09   10   11   10 9 8 7 6 5 4 3 2 1

Acquisitions Editor:	Al Bruckner
Editorial Assistant:	MaryAnn Vail
Production Editor:	Diane S. Foster
Copy Editor:	Tony Moore
Typesetter:	C&M Digitals (P) Ltd.
Proofreader:	Dennis Webb
Cover Designer:	Bryan Fishman
Marketing Manager:	Nichole M. Angress

Contents

Preface

We are now embarked on our journey into a new century, not to mention a new millennium. Due to advancing technology, the world is undergoing rapid change and is becoming smaller: Capital can be sent instantly virtually anywhere in the world by a quick computer keystroke; mergers and acquisitions routinely unite firms in different countries. Some nations are newly and rapidly developing, other nations have reemerged from recently fallen empires, and still other nations are forming supranational groups such as the European Union (EU) and the Association of Southeast Asia Nations (ASEAN). In this dynamic political and economic atmosphere, accounting is facing new challenges and must keep up.

Accounting and its end product—financial statements—play an extremely important role on the economic side of this dynamic world economy. The accounting profession is working to make financial statements more transparent and more informative as well as attempting to limit accounting "shenanigans" by, among other means, the Sarbanes-Oxley Act of 2002. Meanwhile, we are attempting to bring about harmonization or convergence between Financial Accounting Standards of the United States and International Financial Reporting Standards of the International Accounting Standards Board.

These and other events make it clear that the accounting profession certainly cannot take things for granted. It is a great time to be entering the accounting profession, on either the public or private side or in the related discipline of finance. We have every confidence that today's students can contribute to solving our many problems and adding to our knowledge inventory. We hope that this book will play a small part in this process.

Objectives and Features of the 7th Edition

This book is intended for one-semester accounting theory courses at either the senior or graduate levels. At the graduate level, the book is appropriate for courses in MBA programs with accounting concentrations and for MS programs in accounting. It would also be appropriate for graduate programs in finance that stress financial statement analysis. However, there is much innovation going on in accounting and finance programs. For example, at our university, many of the elements of accounting theory from the first half of the book are introduced at the start of the undergraduate intermediate accounting sequence. Individual chapters in the last half of the text then supplement specific accounting topics as the courses develop (a three-course series is now used, covering what has previously been called intermediate and advanced accounting).

Not only is the text flexible in terms of possible courses in which it can be used, but in addition, the extensive footnoting makes it possible to use the text at either the graduate or undergraduate level.

Although the subject matter of the 7th edition of *Accounting Theory* is certainly technical, we have attempted to make it as clear and interesting as possible. The book provides a comprehensive survey and analysis of the underlying theory elements in the first half of the book and their application to the financial statements and important accounting events and transactions in the second half.

In both parts of the book, we provide very extensive review and discussion of the accounting literature coming from both American and other journals from the English-speaking world. Given the close relationship between accounting and finance, our discussion also reflects our forays into the finance literature as well. Technical points and issues are frequently supplemented by real-world examples coming from sources such as *The Wall Street Journal*. This should lead to a richer understanding of financial accounting and its applications.

All chapters of the book have been updated, many very extensively. We provide a solid entry into our sister discipline of finance, particularly in Chapters 8 and 13. Chapter 8, in fact, provides an excellent introduction to the empirical literature in accounting and how it relates to finance. In addition, many chapters provide connections between Financial Accounting Standards and International Financial Reporting Standards. Convergence between the two is also discussed in Chapter 10.

The abundant list of references and footnotes, and the extensive end-of-chapter questions, essays, and cases, make the text very flexible for use at either the graduate or undergraduate level.

Acknowledgments

Over the years we have received many valuable reviews, critiques, and comments from reviewers of the current and previous editions. From these reviewers of *Accounting Theory*, we would like to thank the following individuals:

James Bannister
University of Hartford

Patricia Carver
Bellarmine College

Mike Bitter
Stetson University

James Robert Duncan
Ball State University

Rafik Z. Elias, DBA, CPA
California State University, Los Angeles

Bob Fahnestock
The University of West Florida

Janey Forney
Piedmont College

Louella Moore
Arkansas State University

Bob Russ, CPA, PhD
Northern Kentucky University

Zane Swanson
Emporia State University

Michael Tyler, PhD
Barry University

Clark M. Wheatley, PhD, CPA
Florida International University

Wilcox, William
Bradley University

We would also like to thank Teresa Beed of the University of Montana for allowing us to use her excellent test bank for our end-of-chapter materials. With this 7th edition we lose one author but gain another. We thank Michael G. Tearney of the University of Kentucky for his contributions to six editions of this book. Coming aboard is John J. Rozycki, finance professor at Drake, who has already established himself as an important member of our authorship team. From Sage Publications we wish to thank, in particular, Al Bruckner, MaryAnn Vail, Nichole Angress, Diane Foster, and Tony Moore. They have been a pleasure to work with. As usual, we would like to thank our typist, Ginger Wheeler, for her usual fine job of getting us from the 6th to the 7th edition. Finally, we also received many useful insights from current and previous users of the book, as well as from other interested parties. We greatly appreciate all of their efforts.

1

An Introduction to Accounting Theory

Learning Objectives

After reading this chapter, you should be able to:

- Understand the meaning of accounting theory and why it is an important topic.
- Understand the relationship between accounting theory and policy making.
- Understand what measurement is and its role in accounting.
- Gain insight into the principal valuation systems in accounting.

Although accounting has not been called the "dismal science," it is frequently viewed as a dry, cold, and highly analytical discipline with very precise answers that are either correct or incorrect. Nothing could be further from the truth. To take a simple example, assume that two enterprises that are otherwise similar are valuing their inventory and cost of goods sold using different accounting methods. Firm A selects LIFO and Firm B selects FIFO, giving totally different but equally correct answers.

However, one might say that a choice among inventory methods is merely an "accounting construct": The type of "games" accountants play that are of interest to them but have nothing to do with the "real world." Once again this would be totally incorrect. The LIFO versus FIFO argument has important income tax ramifications, resulting—under LIFO—in a more rapid write-off of current inventory costs against revenues (assuming rising inventory prices), which generally means lower income taxes. Thus an accounting construct has an important "social reality": how much income tax is paid.[1]

Income tax payments are not the only social reality that accounting numbers affect. Here are some other examples:

1. Income numbers can be instrumental in evaluating the performance of management, which can affect salaries and bonuses and even whether individual management members will retain their jobs.

2. Income numbers and various balance sheet ratios can affect dividend payments.

3. Income numbers and balance sheet ratios can affect the firm's credit standing and, therefore, the cost of capital.

4. Different income numbers might affect the price of the firm's stock if the stock is publicly traded and the market cannot "see through" the accounting methods that have been used.

Since it is the case that accounting numbers have important social consequences, why is it the case that we cannot always measure "economic reality" accurately? Different perceptions exist of economic reality. For example, we may say on the one hand that the value of an asset may be equal to the amount paid for it in markets in which the asset would ordinarily be acquired, or, on the other hand, some may see an asset's value represented by the amount the firm could acquire by selling the asset. These two values are not the same. The former value is called *replacement cost* or *entry value*, and the latter is called *exit value* (these are not the only possible value choices). Both values are discussed in the appendix to this chapter and in Chapter 14. Exit values are usually lower than entry values because the owning enterprise does not generally have the same access to buyers as firms that regularly sell the asset through ordinary channels. Hence, there is a valuation choice between exit and entry values. Suppose, however, that we take the position that both of these valuations have merit but they are not easy to measure because market quotations may not be available and users may not understand what these valuations mean. Hence, a third choice may arise: historical cost. While entry and exit values represent some form of economic reality, the unreliability of the measurements may lead some people to opt for historical cost on the grounds that users understand it better than the other two approaches and measurement of the historical cost number may be more reliable.

The question we have just been examining, the choice among accounting values including historical cost, falls within the realm of accounting theory. There are, however, other issues that arise in this example, both implicit and explicit:

1. For what purposes do users need the numbers (e.g., evaluating management's performance, evaluating various aspects of the firm's credit standing, or even using the accounting numbers as an input for predicting how well the enterprise will do in the future)?[2]

2. How costly might it be to generate the desired measurement?

The choice among the different types of values, as well as the related issues, falls within the domain of accounting theory. The term *accounting theory* is actually quite mysterious. There are many definitions throughout the accounting literature of this somewhat elusive term. *Accounting theory* is defined here as the basic assumptions, definitions, principles, and concepts—and how we derive them—that underlie accounting rule making by a legislative body. Accounting theory also includes the reporting of accounting and financial information. There has been and will continue to be extensive discussion and argumentation as to what these basic assumptions, definitions, principles, and concepts should be; thus, accounting theory is never a final and finished product. Dialogue always continues, particularly as new issues and problems arise. As the term is used here, it applies to financial accounting and not to managerial or governmental accounting. *Financial accounting* refers to accounting information that is used by investors, creditors, and other outside parties for analyzing management performance and decision-making purposes.[3]

We interpret the definition of accounting theory broadly. Clearly, the drafting of a conceptual framework that is supposed to provide underlying guidance for the making of accounting rules falls within the coverage of accounting theory. Analyzing accounting rules to see how they conform to a conceptual framework or other guiding principles likewise falls within the accounting theory realm. While the actual practice of accounting is generally of less theoretical interest, questions such as why firms choose particular methods when choice exists (the LIFO versus FIFO question, for example) *are* of theoretical interest because we would like to know the reasons underlying the choice. In a pragmatic sense, one can say that accounting theory is concerned with improving financial accounting and statement presentation, although conflict may exist between managers and investors, among other groups, relative to the issue of what improves financial statements, because their interests are not exactly the same.

We can also examine the types of topics, issues, and approaches discussed as part of accounting theory. In addition to conceptual frameworks and accounting legislation, accounting theory includes concepts (e.g., realization and objectivity), valuation approaches (discussed in Appendix 1-A), and hypotheses and theories. Hypotheses and theories are based on a more formalized method of investigation and analysis of subject matter used in academic disciplines such as economics and other social sciences employing research methods from philosophy, mathematics, and statistics. This newer and more formal approach to the development of accounting theory is a relatively recent innovation in our field and permeates much of the accounting research going on today. Researchers are attempting to analyze accounting data for explaining or predicting phenomena related to accounting, such as how users employ accounting information or how preparers choose among accounting methods.[4]

Formalized analyses and investigation of accounting data are discussed in Chapter 2. The results of the research process are published in books and academic and professional journals devoted to advancing knowledge of financial accounting as well as of other branches of accounting, such as cost and management accounting, auditing, taxes, and systems. Various facets of accounting theory are discussed throughout this book.

We begin by briefly examining the relationship between accounting theory and the institutional structure of accounting. One of the objectives of this book is to assess the influence of accounting theory on the rule-making process. Hence, the approach adopted here is concerned with the linkages (and often the lack thereof) between accounting theory and the institutions charged with promulgating the rules intended to improve accounting practice. Closely related to accounting theory is the process of measurement. *Measurement* is the assignment of numbers to properties or characteristics of objects. Measurement and how it applies to accounting are introduced in this chapter and appear throughout the text. The appendix to the chapter briefly illustrates the principal valuation approaches to accounting.

These valuation methods are concerned with the measurement of economic phenomena. They are discussed in more depth in Chapter 14, but they are also referred to in the intervening chapters on accounting theory.

Accounting Theory and Policy Making

The relationship between accounting theory and the standard-setting process must be understood within its wider context, as shown in Exhibit 1.1. We caution that Exhibit 1.1 is extremely simplistic. Economic conditions have an impact on both political factors and accounting theory. Political factors, in turn, also have an effect on accounting theory. For example, after Statement of Financial Accounting Standards (SFAS) No. 96 on income tax allocation appeared in 1987, several journal articles as well as corporate preparers of financial statements severely criticized it. Eventually, political factors (see the following discussion) such as the costliness and difficulty of implementing SFAS No. 96 led to its replacement by SFAS No. 109. Despite its simplicity, Exhibit 1.1 is a good starting point for bringing out how ideas and conditions eventually coalesce into policy-making decisions that shape financial reporting.

Bodies such as the FASB and the SEC, which have been charged with making financial accounting rules, perform a policy function. This policy function is also called *standard setting* or *rule making* and specifically refers to the process of arriving at the pronouncements issued by the FASB or SEC. The inputs to the policy-making function come from three main (although not necessarily equal) sources: Economic factors, political factors, and accounting theory.

Exhibit 1.1   The Financial Accounting Environment

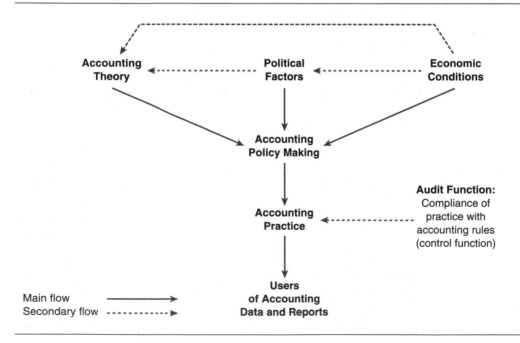

The best example of an economic factor would be the steep inflation of the 1970s, which was undoubtedly the catalyst that led the FASB to force the disclosure of information concerning price changes, is a classic example of an *economic condition* that impinged on policy making. Another example of an economic factor would be the acceleration of mergers and acquisitions.

The term *political factors* refers to the effect on policy making of those who would be subject to the resulting rules or regulations. Included in this category would be auditors, who are responsible for assessing whether the rules have been followed; preparers of financial statements, represented by organizations such as Financial Executives International (FEI); and investors, represented by organizations such as the CFA Institute and the public itself, who might be represented by governmental groups such as Congress or by departments or agencies of the executive branch of government, such as the Securities and Exchange Commission (SEC).[5]

In addition, the management of major firms and industry trade associations are important political components of the policy-making process. Although it has been important to give voice to those who are affected by accounting rule making, it should be remembered that political factors may subvert the standard-setting process. One example of this has been the *special purpose entity* (SPE). SPEs, as the name implies, are arrangements whereby the firm and an outside equity investor jointly own an entity that may largely be a shell enterprise. SPEs allow firms to "park" liabilities on the SPE's balance sheet if the outside equity investor owns as little as 3% of the SPE. Leaving the liability off its own balance sheet improves the firm's debt–equity ratio and, in general, gives the firm's balance sheet what we might call a facelift. The FASB's initial attempt to solve the SPE problem failed because of political interference by the then Big Five public accounting firms. However, owing to public pressure resulting from the Enron debacle, the FASB has begun again to address this problem (see Chapter 18).

Accounting theory is developed and refined by the process of accounting research. Accounting professors mainly carry out research, but many individuals from policy-making organizations, public accounting firms, and private industry also play an important role in the research process.

Standards and other pronouncements of policy-making organizations are interpreted and put into practice at the organizational level. Hence, the output of the policy level is implemented at the accounting practice level. Of course we have now entered an era when failures of large publicly traded companies (e.g., Enron, WorldCom) are going to have a significant impact on financial accounting standards, auditing rules, and institutional structures of organizations such as the FASB and the SEC.[6] Many of these issues will be discussed in Chapters 3, 12, and 17, among others.

Users consist of many groups and include actual and potential shareholders and creditors as well as the public at large. It is important to remember that users not only employ financial statements and reporting in making decisions, but they are also affected by the policy-making function and its implementation at the accounting practice level.

All facets of the accounting theory and policy environment are important and are considered in this book. Our principal focus is on that part of the track running between accounting theory and the accounting policy function.

The Role of Measurement in Accounting

Measurement is an important aspect of accounting theory. Larson views measurement separately from theory owing to the technicalities and procedures of the measurement process itself.[7] However, the process of measurement is so integral to accounting theory that it cannot easily be separated from it.

Measurement is defined as the assignment of numbers to the attributes or properties of objects being measured, which is exactly what accountants do. Objects themselves have numerous attributes or properties. For example, assume a manufacturing firm owns a lathe. The lathe has properties such as length, width, height, and weight. If we eliminate purely physical attributes (because accounting measures are made in monetary units), there are still several others to which values could be assigned. These would include historical cost, replacement cost of the lathe in its present condition, selling price (exit value) of the lathe in its present condition, and present value of the future cash flows that the lathe will help to generate. Attributes or properties are particular characteristics of objects that we measure. It should be clear that we do not measure objects themselves but rather something that might be termed the dollar "numerosity" or "how-muchness" that relates to a particular attribute of the object.

Direct and Indirect Measurements

If the number assigned to an object is an actual measurement of the desired property, it would be called a *direct measurement*. However, this does not necessarily mean that it is accurate. An *indirect measurement* of a desired attribute is one that must be made by roundabout means. For example, assume that we want to measure the replacement cost of ending inventory for a retail concern. If the inventory is commonly sold, we could determine the replacement cost of the inventory by multiplying the current wholesale price per unit for each inventory type by the quantity held and adding these amounts for all inventory types. This would be a direct measurement. Assume that our retail establishment has a silver fox coat in its inventory, a type of coat no longer commonly fashionable because of societal changes (animal rights activism, for example). Assume the coat originally cost the firm $1,000 when acquired, and we estimate that it could be sold now for only $600. If the normal markup for fur coats was 20% on cost, we would estimate the replacement cost to be $500 ($600 ÷ 1.2 = $500). This would be an indirect measurement. Direct measures are usually preferable to indirect measures.

Assessment and Prediction Measures

Another way of categorizing measurements is to classify them as assessment or prediction measures. Assessment measures are concerned with particular attributes of objects. They can be either direct or indirect. Prediction measures, on the other hand, are concerned with factors that may be indicative of conditions in the future.[8] Hence, there is a functional relationship between the predictor (prediction measure) and the future condition. For example, income of a present period might be used as a predictor of dividends for the following period. By the same token, income is basically an assessment measure because it indicates how well the firm did during the period. Another example of an assessment measure involves marketable securities carried at market value. The measurement assesses how much cash would be generated if the securities were sold.

The Measurement Process

Several elements are brought together in the measurement process. Even when a direct assessment measure is used, that does not mean there is only one absolutely correct measure. A simple measure of this type, such as a count of cash, depends on several factors:

- The object itself
- The attribute being measured
- The measurer
- Counting or enumerating operations
- Instruments available for the measuring task
- Constraints affecting the measurer

Objects themselves and their attributes differ vastly in type and complexity. How much cash does a small retail firm have? What is the size of the grape harvest in the Napa Valley during the current year? How many cubic inches of topsoil did Iowa lose in 2007? The measurers themselves might have different qualifications. An ambitious junior accountant and a clerk who is somewhat shaky in arithmetic and not overly concerned about the job could bring markedly different talents to a measuring task. Counting and enumerating operations vary from simple arithmetic in a cash count to statistical sampling in inventory valuation. Instruments used by the measurer could include everything from a personal computer to a hand calculator to pencil and paper, and the most obvious constraint would be time. Clearly, even a direct assessment measure is not as simple a matter as might first be thought.

Types of Measurements

Nominal Scale

The relationship between the measuring system itself and the attributes of the objects being measured determines the type of measurement.[9] The simplest type of measuring system is the nominal scale. A nominal scale is nothing more than a basic classification system, a system of names. Assume that all the students at a university come from Massachusetts, Connecticut, or Rhode Island. If we wish to classify students by state, a 1 might be assigned to Massachusetts students, a 2 to those from Connecticut, and a 3 to Rhode Islanders. In this example, the numbering system serves no other purpose than to classify by state. The same purpose could be achieved by the assignment of a different number for the state of origination—as long as the assignment of numbers to students is done consistently in accordance with the new nominal scale. A chart of accounts provides a good example of nominal classification in accounting.

Ordinal Scale

Next in the order of measurement rigor is the ordinal scale. Numerals assigned in ordinal rankings indicate an order of preference. However, the degree of preference among ranks is not necessarily the same. Assume that three candidates are running for office. A voter's ranking might be Abel first, Baker second, and Charles third. However, the voter may see a virtual toss-up between Abel and Baker, either of whom is vastly preferable to Charles. In accounting, current assets and current liabilities are listed in the order of liquidity in the balance sheet, which is an ordinal ranking.

Interval Scale

In interval scales, unlike ordinal rankings, the change in the attribute measured among assigned numbers must be equal. The Fahrenheit temperature scale is an example. The increase in warmth from 9° to 10° is the same as that from 19° to 20° or any other increase in temperature of 1°.

Ratio Scale

Like the interval scale, the ratio scale assigns equal value to the intervals between assigned numbers, but it also has an additional feature. In the ratio scale, the zero point must have a unique quality. In the Fahrenheit scale, for example, it does *not*. The zero point on a Fahrenheit thermometer does not imply absence of temperature. Therefore, we cannot say that 8° is twice as warm as 4°; furthermore, 8° divided by 4° is not "equal" to 16° divided by 8°. Using a ratio scale type of measurement in accounting is at least possible because the zero point implies nothingness in terms of dollar amounts. Thus, in accounting, both $100,000 of current assets divided by $50,000 of current liabilities and $200,000 of current assets divided by $100,000 of current liabilities indicate twice as much current assets as current liabilities. This is possible only because of the uniqueness of the zero point in accounting.

Quality of Measurements

In attempting to analyze the worth of a measure, several qualities might be considered. Since measurers and their skills, tools, and measuring techniques are so important, we might consider agreement among measurers, in the statistical sense, as one criterion.

Intuitively, it would be very appealing to users if they knew that the numbers would be the same no matter which accountant prepared them. This is exactly the way Ijiri and Jaedicke view *objectivity*. They define it as the degree of consensus among measurers in situations in which a given group of measurers having similar instruments and constraints measure the same attribute of a given object.[10] Objectivity is then defined as

$$V = \frac{1}{N} \sum_{i=1}^{n} (x_i - \bar{x})^2 \tag{1.1}$$

where

n = the number of measurers in the group

x_i = measurement of the ith measurer

$\bar{x}$ = mean of all x_i for all measurers involved

In Equation 1.1, Ijiri and Jaedicke have used the statistical measure of variance as a means of quantifying the degree of agreement among measurers. The closer each x_i is to $\bar{x}$, the more objective is the measure and the smaller V will be. A comparison among competing measures in terms of objectivity could thus be made by comparing the Vs in controlled experiments.[11]

In the case of prediction measures, an obvious criterion is how well the task of prediction is accomplished. Assume that users of accounting data for a particular firm presume that dividends are equal to 50% of the income of the preceding period. This can be stated as

$$D_{j2} = (0.50 I_{j1}) \qquad (1.2)$$

where

$$D_{j2} = \text{dividends of firm } j \text{ for period 2}$$

$$I_{j1} = \text{income of firm } j \text{ for period 1}$$

Very often the predictor—the right-hand term in Equation 1.2—cannot be known because users are diverse and make predictions in vastly different ways. In these cases, how well the prediction is accomplished cannot be quantified. Where it can be, a measure of predictive ability—called *bias* by Ijiri and Jaedicke—can be determined by the following equation:

$$B = (\bar{x} - x^*)^2 \qquad (1.3)$$

where

$$x^* = \text{the value the predictor should have been, given}$$
$$\text{the actual value of what was predicted and the}$$
$$\text{predictive model—such as Equation 1.2—of users}$$

While objectivity (verifiability) and bias (usefulness) have been formally demonstrated here, a standard-setting agency such as the Financial Accounting Standards Board has to cope with these issues and the related trade-offs between them.[12] For example, in SFAS No. 87 the Board switched from basing pension expense on current salaries to future salaries. Part of the reasoning underlying the change was that predictions of cash flows would be enhanced (usefulness) by using future salaries even though the previous method of basing pension expense on current salaries would be more objective. Trade-offs of this type arise quite frequently for standard setters.

Two other qualities that are pertinent to both assessment and prediction measures are timeliness and the cost constraint.[13] In terms of financial accounting, *timeliness* means that financial statement data—which are aggregations of many measurements—should be up-to-date and ready for quarterly announcements of earnings as well as for annual published financial statement purposes and SEC filings if the firm's stock is publicly traded (the 10-K and 10-Q requirements of the SEC). Oftentimes, the need for information on a timely basis may conflict with the cost constraint problem.

It is easy to lose sight of the fact that data are costly to produce. Many costs (e.g., computer information systems and accounting staffs) are fixed. More precise or accurate measurements, as well as more timely measures, involve expending additional resources. Timeliness and costliness must be considered in the policy-setting process, if not in theory formulation.

We will be referring again to problems of measurement throughout this text; however, we must make one observation immediately. Many of the measurements in traditional financial accounting are of neither the assessment nor the prediction variety. Historical cost depreciation and LIFO inventory valuations are numbers that admittedly do not represent any real attributes. Whether these are really measurements is not the primary issue. The important question is whether measurements made by totally arbitrary methods have utility for users.

Sterling refers to methods such as LIFO and FIFO as calculations rather than measurements if they do not correspond—that is, attempt to simulate or come as close as possible—to the measurement of real phenomena or attributes.[14] For example, LIFO and FIFO measures of cost of goods sold and inventories are simply cost flow calculations, which are concerned with dividing or allocating historical costs between asset and expense categories. They are not concerned with the measurement of such *real economic phenomena* as the replacement cost of the ending inventory and the inventory that has been sold. The distinction between measurements and calculations is important and should be kept in mind throughout this book.

Plan of This Book

After this relatively brief introduction to accounting theory, we view in Chapter 2 the relation between accounting theory and accounting research. In Chapter 3, the institutional history of the accounting standard-setting bodies in the United States, including current developments, is discussed. Chapter 4 completes the first part of the text by discussing why standard-setting in accounting by an outside body is necessary as opposed to a laissez faire situation in which companies make their own accounting rules subject to the possible policing by the securities and capital markets.

Chapters 5, 6, and 7 are concerned with underlying theoretical approaches to standard setting. Chapter 5 discusses the first real attempt by a standard-setting body to employ a theoretical approach to accounting rule making, an attempt that failed but nevertheless provided an important learning experience for accounting regulation. Chapter 6 discusses the search for the objectives of the standard-setting process. Finally, the culmination of the theoretical search, the conceptual framework of the FASB, is discussed in Chapter 7.

In Chapter 8, we discuss the usefulness of accounting information to investors and creditors. Chapter 9 concentrates on two very important theoretical considerations: (1) how much uniformity should be applied to booking similar transactions by different enterprises and (2) utilizing disclosure in financial statements. Important issues of international accounting, including convergence between FASB and International Financial Reporting Standards (IFRSs) are discussed in Chapter 10. Thereafter, specific IFRSs are discussed in the appropriate chapters.

Chapters 11, 12, and 13 cover the three major financial statements: balance sheet, income statement, and statement of cash flows. Chapter 14 discusses theoretical approaches to accounting for changing prices, including the new standard on fair value measurement, SFAS No. 157.

Chapters 15 through 18 cover specific transaction areas within accounting. Chapter 15 is concerned with income tax allocation; Chapter 16 with pensions and other postretirement benefits; Chapter 17 with leases; and Chapter 18 with intercorporate equity investments. In these chapters and the preceding three chapters on financial statements, we attempt to apply, wherever possible, theoretical criteria discussed in the first part of the book. Also, we conclude appropriate chapters with a short section called Improving Accounting Standards. These are brief summations of ways to improve transparency and disclosure in financial statements. By *transparency* we mean attempts to apply what have been called *accounting principles* as opposed to *accounting rules*. Accounting principles refer to consistent theoretical approaches in various transaction areas, as opposed to accounting rules, which are often quite involved and are intended to allow enterprises to avoid the real economic substance of these transactions. A supplementary chapter on oil and gas accounting is available in the Instructor's Resource Manual.

Summary

While accounting theory has many definitions, it is defined here as the basic rules, definitions, principles, and concepts that underlie the drafting of accounting standards and how they are derived. We also include appropriate hypotheses and theories. From a pragmatic standpoint, the purpose of accounting theory is to improve financial accounting and reporting.

The relationship between accounting theory and policy making (the establishment of rules and standards) shows accounting theory to be one of the three major inputs into the standard-setting process, the others being political factors and economic conditions. There are numerous and complex interrelationships among these three inputs, but Exhibit 1.1 provides a useful basic understanding of the process.

In our discussion, we view measurement as an integral part of accounting theory. Accounting theory is ultimately concerned with what information is needed by users, whereas measurement is involved with what is being measured and how it is being measured. The latter obviously has an important effect on the former. As a result, there are often trade-offs between verifiability and the usefulness of the numbers being generated by the measurement process. The costliness and timeliness of the information are other important considerations underlying the measurement process.

There are four types of measurements: nominal, ordinal, interval, and ratio scale. Accounting has the potential to be in the ratio scale category. Meaningful comparisons may thus be made among similar accounting measurements for different firms. However, many so-called measurements in accounting are simply calculations in which no meaningful attempt is made to make them correspond to real economic phenomena.

Appendix 1-A briefly illustrates and discusses the principal valuation approaches to accounting. These include historical costs, general price level, exit- and entry-value models of current value accounting, and discounted cash flows.

Appendix 1-A: Valuation Systems

Over the years, many debates in accounting have centered on the issue of valuation of accounts appearing in the balance sheet and income statement. We believe that many other theoretical issues should precede any attempt to come to grips with the valuation question. However, a basic familiarity with valuation systems enriches the theoretical discussion in this chapter and sets the table for later chapters. Consequently, an extremely simple example will be used to illustrate five valuation systems that have been extensively discussed in the literature. Using a simple example is a way to make clear the assumptions and workings of the valuation methods while holding aside, for the moment, many difficult problems that will surface later. The main aspects of each system will be discussed and critiqued here.

Much more will be said in Chapter 14 on issues of valuation. Let it be said, however, that even though inflation, at the time of writing, is not particularly excessive—although it is always a concern—we are in the midst of a ferment in which we are moving from historical costing to more value-oriented approaches.

The Simple Company

1. Simple Company was formed on December 30, 2005, by stockholders who invested a total of $90,000 in cash.

2. The owners operate the company and receive no salary for their services.

3. On December 31, 2005, the owners acquired for $90,000, cash, a machine that provides a service customers pay for in cash.

4. The machine has a life of three years with no salvage value.

5. All services provided by this machine occur on the last day of the year.

6. No other assets are needed to run the business, nor are there any other expenses aside from depreciation.

7. Dividends declared equal income for the year.

8. The remaining cash is kept in a checking account that does not earn interest.

9. The general price index stands at 100 on December 31, 2005. It goes up to 105 on January 1, 2007, and 110 on January 1, 2008.

10. Budgeted revenues and actual revenues are the same. They are $33,000 for 2006, $36,302 for 2007, and $39,931 for 2008.

11. Replacement cost for a new asset of the same type increases to $96,000 on January 1, 2007, and $105,000 on January 1, 2008.

12. Net realizable value of the asset is $58,000 on December 31, 2006, and $31,000 on December 31, 2007. It has no value on December 31, 2008.

13. Simple Company is dissolved on December 31, 2008. All cash is distributed among the owners.

14. There are no income taxes.

The balance sheet for Simple Company after acquiring its fixed asset is shown in Exhibit 1.2.

Exhibit 1.2   Simple Company Balance Sheet

Balance Sheet December 31, 2005			
Fixed assets	$90,000	Capital stock	$90,000

Valuation Approaches to Accounting for the Simple Company

Historical Cost

Throughout the financial history of the United States, historical costing has been the orthodoxy in published financial statements. But severe inflationary periods in this country as well as in many other nations of the industrial and third worlds has led to an extensive search for a viable alternative either to replace historical costing or serve as a supplement to it. In a period of rising prices, attributes measured by historical costing methods generally have limited relevance to economic reality. The major exception to this is accounts that are either receivable or payable in cash during the short run, such as accounts receivable and payable, as well as cash itself.

The presumed saving graces of historical costing are that its valuation systems are both more objectively determinable and better understood than are competing valuation systems. However, the objectivity issue is by no means to be taken for granted. Even in our simple example, sum-of-the-years'-digits or fixed-percentage-of-declining-balance depreciation (among other methods) might have been selected to create a different balance sheet. In addition, factoring in estimated depreciable life and salvage could also produce different results. The understandability of historical costing is largely a function of familiarity. The introduction of new valuation methods obviously requires familiarizing users with their underlying assumptions and limitations.

Historical costing has also been defended as more suitable as a means for distributing income among capital providers, officers and employees, and taxation agencies because it is not based on hypothetical opportunity cost figures. Hence, the presumption is that there would be less conflict among competing groups over the distribution of income. However, this argument is by no means conclusive. As with depreciation, methods selected for income measurement can be easily disputed. Furthermore, opportunity cost valuations may be hypothetical in one sense, but they are surely far more indicative of economic valuation than are historical costs.

Income statements and balance sheets under historical costing are summarized in Exhibit 1.3. Balance sheets on December 31, 2008, in Exhibits 1.3 through 1.7 are prior to final dissolution.

Exhibit 1.3   Simple Company

Income Statements–Historical Costs

	2006	2007	2008	Total
Revenues	$33,000	$36,302	$39,931	$109,233
Depreciation	30,000	30,000	30,000	90,000
Net income	$3,000	$6,302	$9,931	$19,233

Balance Sheet as of December 31

	2006	2007	2008
Cash	$30,000	$60,000	$90,000
Fixed asset (net)	60,000	30,000	
Total assets	$90,000	$90,000	$90,000
Capital stock	$90,000	$90,000	$90,000
Total equities	$90,000	$90,000	$90,000

General Price-Level Adjustment

Financial statements based on historical costing combine dollars that were expended or received at different dates. For example, a balance sheet on December 31, 2000, would add together cash that is on hand at that date with the book value of a building that was acquired in, say, 1960. It is, of course, very well known that a 1960 dollar had considerably greater purchasing power than a 2000 dollar. Consequently, there is a very serious additivity problem under historical costing because dollars of different purchasing power are added to or subtracted from each other. The additivity issue is an aspect of measurement theory.

One possible response to this problem is general price-level adjustment. This refers to the purchasing power of the monetary unit relative to all goods and services in the economy. Obviously, the measurement of this phenomenon is a considerable task. Adjustment is accomplished by converting historical cost dollars by an index such as the Consumer Price Index compiled by the Department of Labor. This index is not really broad enough, as its name implies, to be a true general price index, but it has been advocated as a meaningful substitute.

Except for monetary assets and liabilities—every item receivable or payable in a specific and unalterable number of dollars as well as cash itself—all amounts in financial statements adjusted for price levels would be restated in terms of the general purchasing power of the dollar at a given date, either as of the financial statement date itself or the average purchasing power of the dollar during the current year. Assume, for example, that land was purchased on January 1, 1970, for $50,000 when the general price index stood at 120. On December 31, 2000—the balance sheet date—the general price index stands at 240. The transformation to bring forward the historical cost is accomplished in the following manner:

$$\$50,000 \left(\frac{240}{120}\right) = \$100,000 \tag{1.4}$$

Since it takes twice as many dollars to buy the same general group of goods and services in 2000 as in 1970, the general price-level adjusted cost of the land is, likewise, twice the historical cost.

Adjustments of this type restore the additivity of the dollar amounts on the 2000 statements. However, we must stress one very important point: In no way should the $100,000 figure be construed as the value of the land on December 31, 2000. The historical cost of the land has been merely brought forward or adjusted so that it is expressed in terms that are consistent with the purchasing power of 2000 dollars. Consequently, some individuals see price-level adjustment as a natural extension of the historical cost approach rather than as a separate valuation system.

Exhibit 1.4 shows income statements and balance sheets using general price-level adjustments. Footnotes to the income statements show the calculations for general price-level adjusted depreciation. Purchasing power loss on monetary items is an element that arises during inflation when holdings of monetary assets exceed monetary liabilities. Calculating the purchasing power loss is very similar to the adjustment for changing price levels. In the Simple Company case, the cash holding prior to the price-level change is multiplied by a fraction consisting of the general price-level index *after* change in the numerator divided by the general price-level index *before* change in the denominator. The unadjusted amount of cash is then deducted to arrive at the purchasing power loss.

Although a purchasing power loss is certainly real, it is totally different from other losses and expenses, which represent actual diminutions in the firm's assets of either an unproductive or productive nature. Purchasing power losses do not result in a decrease in monetary assets themselves but rather in a decline in their purchasing power when the general price-level index increases. Consistent with the will-o'-the-wisp nature of the loss, if an entry were booked, it would take the following form:

Purchasing Power Loss	XXX	
Retained Earnings		XXX

The direct effect in the accounts is thus negligible even though a very real type of loss has occurred. Calculations for purchasing power losses on monetary assets are shown below the income statements in Exhibit 1.4.

Current Value Systems

Current value, as the term implies, refers to attempts to assign to financial statement components numbers that correspond to some existing attribute of the elements being

Exhibit 1.4   Simple Company

Income Statements–General Price-Level Adjustment

	2006	2007	2008	Total
Revenues	$33,000	$36,302	$39,931	$109,233
Depreciation[a,b]	30,000	31,500	33,000	94,500
Operating income	$3,000	$4,802	$6,931	$14,733
Purchasing power loss[c,d]	–	**1,500**	**3,000**	**4,500**
Net income	$3,000	$3,302	$3,931	$10,233

Balance Sheet as of December 31

	2006	2007	2008
Cash	$30,000	$63,000	$99,000
Fixed asset (net)	60,000	31,500	
Total assets	$90,000	$94,500	$99,000
Capital stock[e,f]	$90,000	$94,500	$99,000
Total equities	$90,000	$94,500	$99,000

a $\text{Depreciation}_{2007} = \$30,000 \times \dfrac{105}{100} = \$31,500$

b $\text{Depreciation}_{2008} = \$30,000 \times \dfrac{110}{100} = \$33,000$

c $\text{Purchasing power loss}_{2007} = \left(\$30,000 \times \dfrac{105}{100}\right) - \$30,000 = \$1,500$

d $\text{Purchasing power loss}_{2008} = \left(\$63,000 \times \dfrac{110}{105}\right) - \$63,000 = \$3,000$

e $\text{Capital stock}_{2007} = \$90,000 \times \dfrac{105}{100} = \$94,500$

f $\text{Capital stock}_{2008} = \$90,000 \times \dfrac{110}{100} = \$99,000$

measured. There are two valuation systems that fall into the current value category: exit value (very similar to *net realizable value*) and replacement cost (also called *entry value*). As we shall see, entirely different purposes and philosophies underlie each system.

Exit Valuation. This approach is primarily oriented toward the balance sheet. Assets are valued at the net realizable amounts that the enterprise would expect to obtain for them if they were disposed of in the normal course of operations rather than in a bona fide liquidation. Hence, the method is frequently referred to as a process of *orderly liquidation*.[15] Liabilities would be similarly valued at the amounts it would take to pay them off as of the statement date. The income statement for the period would be equal to the change in the net realizable value of the firm's net assets occurring during the period, excluding the effect of capital transactions. Expenses for such elements as depreciation represent the decline in net realizable value of fixed assets during the period.

The benefit of this system, as proponents of exit-value accounting see it, is the relevance of the information it provides. With this approach, the balance sheet becomes a huge statement of the net liquidity available to the enterprise in the ordinary course of operations. It thus portrays the firm's adaptability, or the ability to shift its presently existing resources into new opportunities. A point in the system's favor is that all of the measurements are additive because valuations are at the same time point for the balance sheet (and for the same period of time on the income statement) and measure the same attribute. But the principal criticism of exit valuation also involves the same question of relevance: How useful are net realizable value measurements for fixed assets if the firm intends to keep and utilize the great bulk of them for revenue production purposes in the foreseeable future? As will be seen in Chapter 14, a variant of the exit-value approach is used for fair value measurement purposes in SFAS No. 157.

Exhibit 1.5 shows exit-value income statements and balance sheets. As previously noted, depreciation amounts represent the decline in net realizable value of the fixed asset occurring during each period.

Replacement Cost, or Entry Value. As the name implies, this system uses current replacement cost valuations in financial statements. Both replacement cost and exit values are current market values. Replacement cost will usually be higher for two reasons: First, selling an asset that a firm does not ordinarily market usually results in a lower price than a regular dealer would be able to obtain. The automobile market provides a good example. If a person buys a new car and immediately decides to sell it, he or she usually cannot recover full cost because of limited access to the buying side of the market. Second, "tearing out" and other disposal costs are deducted from selling price in determining net realizable values. Hence, the two different markets can result in significantly different current values.

Exhibit 1.5   Simple Company

Income Statements–Exit Valuation

	2006	2007	2008	Total
Revenues	$33,000	$36,302	$39,931	$109,233
Depreciation	32,000	27,000	31,000	90,000
Net income	$ 1,000	$ 9,302	$ 8,931	$ 19,233

Balance Sheet as of December 31

	2006	2007	2008
Cash	$32,000	$59,000	$90,000
Fixed asset (net)	58,000	31,000	
Total assets	$90,000	$90,000	$90,000
Capital stock	$90,000	$90,000	$90,000
Total equities	$90,000	$90,000	$90,000

Replacement cost is ideally measured where market values are available for similar assets. This is often the case for acquired merchandise inventories and stocks of raw materials that will be used in the production process. However, market values are often unavailable for such unique fixed assets as land, buildings, and heavy equipment specially designed for a particular firm. The same is true even for used fixed assets that are not unique, although secondhand markets often exist for these assets. These same considerations of measurement difficulty, however, also apply to the exit valuation system.

In the absence of firm market prices, either appraisal or specific index adjustment can estimate replacement cost. Cost constraints may inhibit the use of appraisals, but there are specific indexes applicable to particular segments of the economy—for example, machinery and equipment used in the steel industry. Indexes are essentially averages, and if calculated for too wide a segment of the economy, they may not be good representations of replacement cost.

Replacement cost income statements and balance sheets appear in Exhibit 1.6. When replacement costs changed, depreciation was calculated by taking one-third of the new cost. Current value depreciation is a much more complex phenomenon to measure in practice. The holding gain adjustment on the balance sheet offsets the excess depreciation above historical cost.

The principal argument used to justify the replacement cost system over exit values is that if the great majority of the firm's assets were not already owned, it would be economically justifiable to acquire them. On the other hand, fixed assets are sold mainly when they become obsolete or their output is no longer needed. But advocates of the replacement cost school of thought disagree on some important points. The main disagreement concerns interpretation of holding gains and losses, the differences between replacement cost of assets and their

Exhibit 1.6   Simple Company

Income Statements–Replacement Cost

	2006	2007	2008	Total
Revenues	$33,000	$36,302	$39,931	$109,233
Depreciation	30,000	32,000	35,000	97,000
Net income	$3,000	$4,302	$4,931	$12,233

Balance Sheet as of December 31

	2006	2007	2008
Cash	$30,000	$62,000	$97,000
Fixed asset (net)	60,000	32,000	
Total assets	$90,000	$94,000	$97,000
Capital stock	$90,000	$90,000	$90,000
Holding gain adjustment		4,000	7,000
Total equities	$90,000	$94,000	$97,000

historical costs. The point at issue is whether these gains and losses should be run through income or closed directly to capital. We should also note that replacement cost and exit valuation can be combined with general price-level adjustment to provide a more complete analysis of inflationary effects on the firm.

Discounted Cash Flows

Of the systems discussed, only the discounted cash flow approach is a purely theoretical method with virtually no operable practicability on a statement-wide basis.[16] In this system, valuation of assets is a function of discounted cash flows and income is measured by the change in the present value of cash flows arising from operations during the period. Thus, both asset valuation and income measurement are anchored to future expectations.

In Exhibit 1.7, the internal rate of return of the asset is found by discounting the future cash flows at the rate that will make them just equal the cost of the asset (10% in this case). Thereafter, income is equal to 10% of the beginning-of-period asset valuation and

Exhibit 1.7   Simple Company

Income Statements and Discounted Cash Flows					
Income statement	*2006*	*2007*	*2008*	*Total*	*Change*
Revenue	$33,000	$36,302	$39,931	$109,233	
Depreciation	24,000	29,702	36,298	90,000	
Net income (10% of beginning-of-period asset value)	$9,000	$6,600	$3,633	$19,233	
Beginning-of-period asset value	$90,000	$66,000	$36,298		
Calculation of present values (PV)					
Revenue	$33,000	$36,302	$39,931		
Discount factor	×0.9091	×0.8264	×0.7513		
PV as of Dec. 31, 2005	$30,000	$30,002	$30,001	$90,002	
Revenue	$33,000	$36,302	$39,931		
Discount factor	×1.0000	×0.9091	×0.8264		
PV as of Dec. 31, 2006[a]	$33,000	$33,002	$33,001	$99,003	$9,000
Revenue	$33,000	$36,302	$39,931		
Discount factor	×1.0000	×1.0000	×0.9091		
PV as of Dec. 31, 2007	$33,000	$36,302	$36,301	$105,603	$6,600
Revenue	$33,000	$36,302	$39,931		
Discount factor	×1.0000	×1.0000	×1.0000		
PV as of Dec. 31, 2008	$33,000	$36,302	$39,931	$109,233	$3,630

[a] $1 rounding error for the change in total present values.

depreciation is "plugged" to bring about this result. Income is also equal to the change in the present value of the cash flows measured at the beginning and end of the period.

In a real situation, the method would be virtually impossible to apply because many assets contribute jointly to the production of cash flows, so individual asset valuation could not be determined. Also, the future orientation of asset valuation and income determination leads to very formidable estimation problems, which would undoubtedly reduce objectivity in terms of the degree of consensus among measurers.

Because of the insuperable measurement problems, the discounted cash flow approach can be implemented only for a very restricted group of assets and liabilities: those whose interest and principal payments are directly stipulated or can be imputed. An alternative approach for other assets, whereby assets of the firm would be valued in terms of those attributes assumed to approximate most closely their discounted cash flow in terms of their expected usage, has been advocated.[17] A mixed bag of discounted cash flows, net realizable values, and replacement costs would result.

QUESTIONS

1. What does the term "social reality" mean and why are accounting and accounting theory important examples of it?

2. Why do the value choices (entry value, exit value, and historical cost) fall within the domain of accounting theory?

3. Of the three inputs to the accounting policy-making function, which do you think is the most important?

4. How can political factors be an input into accounting policy making if the latter is concerned with governing and making the rules for financial accounting?

5. Is accounting theory, as the term is defined in this text, exclusively developed and refined through the research process?

6. What type of measurement is the measurement of objectivity in Equation 1.1: nominal, ordinal, interval, or ratio scale?

7. The measurement process itself is quite ordinary and routine in virtually all situations. Comment on this statement.

8. Can assessment measures be used for predictive purposes?

9. A great deal of interest is generated each week during the college football and college basketball seasons by the ratings of the teams by the Associated Press and United Press International. Sports writers or coaches are polled on what they believe are the top 25 teams in the country. Weightings are assigned (25 points for each first place vote, 24 for each second place vote, . . . one for each 25th

place vote) and the results are tabulated. The results appear as a weekly listing of the top 25 teams in the nation. Do you think that these polls illustrate the process of measurement? Discuss.

10. Accounting practitioners have criticized some proposed accounting standards on the grounds that they would be difficult to implement because of measurement problems. They therefore conclude that the underlying theory is inappropriate. Assuming that the critics are correct about the implementational difficulties, would you agree with their thinking? Discuss.

11. Some individuals believe that valuation methods proposed by a standard-setting body such as FASB should be based on those measurement procedures having the highest degree of objectivity as defined by Equation 1.1. Thus, some assets might be valued on the basis of replacement cost and others on net realizable value. Do you see any problems with this proposal? Discuss.

12. What type of measurement scale (nominal, ordinal, interval, or ratio scale) is being used in the following situations?

Musical scales

Insurance risk classes for automobile insurance

Numbering of pages in a book

A grocery scale

A grocery scale deliberately set 10 pounds too high

Assignment of students to advisers, based on major

13. If general price-level adjustment is concerned with the change over time of the purchasing power of the monetary unit, why is it not considered a current-value approach?

14. How do entry- and exit-value approaches differ?

15. Why is discounted cash flow extremely difficult to implement in the accounts?

16. How do measurement and calculation in accounting differ from each other? Give three examples of each.

17. Are issues of costliness and timeliness as they pertain to accounting standards part of accounting theory?

18. Do you think that changes brought about in accounting standards by failures of publicly traded companies such as Enron should be classified under political factors or economic decisions? Support your position.

19. Political factors are an adverse influence upon the accounting standard-setting function. Discuss this statement.

20. Did the 21st century begin on January 1, 2000?

21. Do you think that the color-coded terrorist threat system instituted by the Department of Homeland Security involves a measurement system? Explain.

22. Since the FASB makes the standards that are used by business and industry, they make accounting theory. Comment on this statement.

CASES, PROBLEMS, AND WRITING ASSIGNMENTS

1. Assume that three accountants have been selected to measure the income of a firm under two different income measurement systems. The results for the first income system (M1) were incomes of $3,000, $2,600, and $2,200. Under the second system (M2), results were $5,000, $4,000, and $3,000. Assume that users of accounting data believe that dividends of a year are equal to 75% of income determined by M1 for the previous year. Users also believe that dividends of a year are equal to 60% of income determined by M2 for the previous year. Actual dividends for the year following the income measurements were $3,000. Determine the objectivity and bias of each of the two measurement systems for the year under consideration. On the basis of your examination, which of the two systems would you prefer?

2. J & J Enterprises is formed on December 31, 2000. At that point, it buys one asset costing $2,487. The asset has a three-year life with no salvage value and is expected to generate cash flows of $1,000 on December 31 in the years 2001, 2002, and 2003. Actual results are exactly the same as plan. Depreciation is the firm's only expense. All income is to be distributed as dividends on the three dates mentioned. Other information:
- The price index stands at 100 on December 31, 2000. It goes up to 104 and 108 on January 1, 2002 and 2003, respectively.
- Net realizable value of the asset on December 31 in the years 2001, 2002, and 2003 is $1,500, $600, and $0, respectively.
- Replacement cost for a new asset of the same type is $2,700, $3,000, and $3,300 on the last day of the year in 2001, 2002, and 2003, respectively.
- Revenue is $1,000 per year, the internal rate of return is 10%, and all cash flows are received (and distributed) on December 31.

Required:

Income statements for the years 2001, 2002, and 2003 under:

Historical costing

General price-level adjustment

Exit valuation

Replacement cost

Discounted cash flows

3. Objectivity (also called "verifiability") and bias (usefulness) are two extremely important characteristics of accounting. Discuss each of the following situations in terms of how you believe they would affect objectivity and bias.
   a. The latest standard on troubled debt restructuring, SFAS No. 114, calls for newly restructured receivables to be discounted at the original or historical discount rate. Two board members disagreed with the majority position because they thought the discount rate should be the current discount rate, given the terms of the note and the borrower's credit standing.
   b. SFAS No. 115 requires marketable equity securities to be carried at fair value (market value). Its predecessor, SFAS No. 12, required marketable equity securities to be carried at lower-of-cost-or-market.

    c. Assume that a new standard would allow only FIFO in inventory and cost-of-goods-sold accounting with weighted average and LIFO being eliminated (you may ignore income tax effects).

4. Accounting theory has several different definitions and approaches. Using Hendriksen and van Breda (1992, chap. 1) and Belkaoui (1993, chap. 3), list and briefly discuss these definitions and approaches. From the perspective of a professional accountant, evaluate these approaches in terms of their usefulness.

5. What theoretical issues are involved in Statement of Financial Accounting Standards No. 2, which calls for expensing research and development costs?

6. Read "The Margins of Accounting" by Peter Miller in The European Accounting Review (Vol. 7, No. 4, 1998). What is Miller's main point? Discuss the examples he uses to illustrate his main point including those pertaining to management accounting. What do you think the significance of his article is for understanding accounting?

CRITICAL THINKING AND ANALYSIS

1. Is accounting theory really necessary for the making of accounting rules? Discuss.

2. Every fall, *U.S. News and World Report* comes out with a much awaited ranking of American colleges and universities (you may have even used it yourself). Although there has been much criticism of the methodology that the magazine employs as well as some "fudging" of the numbers by universities in their response to the questionnaire, this report represents what the chapter calls a "social reality." What is meant by "social reality" and why does this college and university ranking provide a good analogy for accounting?

3. Accounting rule making should only be concerned with information for investors and creditors. Discuss this statement.

Notes

1. *For a brilliant discussion of accounting constructs and their relation to social reality, see Mattessich (1991) and (1995, pp. 41–58).*

2. *Potter (2005) discusses a fairly sizable segment of the accounting literature that is concerned with the effects of accounting standards on society as a whole but that generally has been outside the considerations of standard-setting bodies. This literature involves accounting as a sociological phenomenon.*

3. *Richardson (2002) discusses the dominance of financial accounting over managerial accounting within a Canadian context. We would simply say that cost accounting (costs of products and services appearing within published financial statements) must be subject to financial accounting standards. It would come under the scope of accounting theory. Managerial accounting (the use of data by management for planning and control purposes) need not be subject to financial accounting rules. Hence, it would not be under the domain of accounting theory.*

4. *Although many new ideas are coming into accounting, its roots are ancient. Pacioli, a 15th-century Italian monk, is generally credited with documenting the double-entry bookkeeping system. However, archeological evidence indicates that the roots of accounting may go as far back as 8000 B.C. in the form of clay tokens*

tracking quantities of grain or cattle, which may have marked transactions between individuals. Indeed this crude accounting may well have not only preceded both written language and abstract counting systems but may also have been an impetus that triggered their development. For further details, see Mattessich (1995, pp. 15–40).

5. *CFA Institute awards the Chartered Financial Analyst® charter (CFA®), which is a globally recognized designation for individual investment professionals.*

6. *Time magazine in 2002 gave three women, two of whom were trained in accounting, their Persons of the Year Award (which frequently goes to head-of-state types). Cynthia Cooper, a Mississippi State University accounting major, was the head of internal auditing at WorldCom who reported to the audit committee that several billion dollars of expense were improperly capitalized. Sherron Watkins, a vice president at Enron and a University of Texas accounting major, reported on Enron's accounting shenanigans to the late Kenneth Lay, Enron's board chairman, who did nothing.*

7. *Larson (1969).*

8. *Chambers (1968, p. 246) does not believe that prediction measures should fall within the scope of measurement theory.*

9. *Excellent coverage of this topic is given by Mattessich (1964, pp. 57–74).*

10. *Ijiri and Jaedicke (1966). Objectivity, prior to the Ijiri and Jaedicke paper, referred to the quality of evidence underlying a measurement. In the statistical sense developed by Ijiri and Jaedicke, the word verifiability has tended to supplant objectivity.*

11. *Objectivity tests have been applied by McDonald (1968) and Sterling and Radosevich (1969). Both studies used standard deviation of alternative measurements rather than the variance of Equation 1.1.*

12. *Ijiri and Jaedicke (1966, p. 481) combine the objectivity and bias measures into one formula. Objectivity and bias together add up to the reliability of the measure ($R = V + B$).*

13. *McDonald (1967, pp. 676–677).*

14. *Sterling (1989, p. 85).*

15. *Chambers (1991) provides an excellent summary and defense of exit valuation.*

16. *See Devine (1999, p. 219) for a discussion of replacement cost as a proxy or substitute for discounted cash flows.*

17. *For more detail, see Staubus (1967). Rosenfield (2003) does not believe that present value of future cash flows are a viable measurement for assets. Instead, he sees them as future events that do not yet exist, in contrast to presently existing costs and values.*

References

Belkaoui, Ahmed (1993). *Accounting Theory,* 3rd ed. Dryden Press.

Chambers, Raymond J. (April 1968). "Measures and Values: A Reply to Professor Staubus," *Accounting Review,* pp. 239–247.

———— (December 1991). "Metrical and Empirical Laws in Accounting," *Accounting Horizons,* pp. 1–15.

Devine, Carl Thomas (1999). *Essays in Accounting Theory: A Capstone.* Garland.

Hendriksen, Eldon, and Michael van Breda (1992). *Accounting Theory,* 5th ed. Richard D. Irwin.

Ijiri, Yuji, and Robert Jaedicke (July 1966). "Reliability and Objectivity of Accounting Methods," *Accounting Review,* pp. 474–483.

Larson, Kermit (January 1969). "Implications of Measurement Theory on Accounting Concept Formulation," *Accounting Review,* pp. 38–47.

Mattessich, Richard (1964). *Accounting and Analytical Methods.* Richard D. Irwin.

———— (1991). "Social Reality and the Measurement of its Phenomena," *Advances in Accounting* 9: pp. 3–17.

———— (1995). *Critique of Accounting: Examination of the Foundations and Normative Structure of an Applied Science.* Quorum Books.

McDonald, Daniel (October 1967). "Feasibility Criteria for Accounting Measures," *The Accounting Review*, pp. 662–679.

———— (Spring 1968). "A Test Application of the Feasibility of Market Based Measures in Accounting," *Journal of Accounting Research*, pp. 38–49.

Potter, Bradley (October 2005). "Accounting as a Social and Institutional Practice: Perspectives to Enrich our Understanding of Accounting Change," *Abacus*, pp. 265–289.

Richardson, Alan J. (December 2002). "Professional Dominance: The Relationship Between Financial Accounting and Managerial Accounting, 1926-1986," *Accounting Historians Journal*, pp. 91–121.

Rosenfield, Paul (June 2003). "Presenting Discounted Future Cash Receipts and Payments in Financial Statements," *Abacus*, pp. 233–249.

Staubus, George (October 1967). "Current Cash Equivalent for Assets: A Dissent," *The Accounting Review*, pp. 650–661.

Sterling, Robert R. (Spring 1989). "Teaching the Correspondence Concept," *Issues in Accounting Education*, pp. 82–93.

Sterling, Robert R., and Raymond Radosevich (Spring 1969). "A Valuation Experiment," *Journal of Accounting Research*, pp. 90–95.

2

Accounting Theory and Accounting Research

Learning Objectives

After reading this chapter, you should be able to:

- Understand the meaning of scientific method and the difference between deductive and inductive reasoning.
- Gain insights into the nature of positive accounting research.
- See how accounting fits into the art-versus-science dichotomy.
- Understand the main directions of accounting research.

Chapter 1 mentioned that valuation models such as those illustrated in Appendix 1-A, as well as more formalized methods of investigation, are important elements that can add to accounting theory. The process of investigating phenomena—affecting the rules, definitions, concepts, and principles of accounting—consists of the formal methods of deductive and inductive reasoning. The investigatory process itself is called research. Its use in accounting results in our field being referred to as an academic discipline.

Accounting has been an academic discipline in colleges and universities for more than 100 years. One of the characteristics associated with an academic discipline is the publication of the ideas it generates in magazines (which academics prefer to call *journals,* a particularly appropriate name for the discipline of accounting). Although there are numerous viewpoints about the appropriate content of and approach used in carrying out accounting research, what is particularly interesting for our purposes is the increase in the use of the scientific method in the published research on accounting theory.

In this chapter, we first examine the scientific method and how it relates to accounting research. The term refers to the formal procedures used to derive the laws and principles that govern the so-called hard scientific disciplines, such as physics and chemistry. As applied to accounting, scientific method involves analyzing the behavior of rule makers, preparers, auditors, and the users of accounting information, as well as the behavior of security prices. The role and meaning of theory to a given discipline are affected by whether the discipline is a science. Therefore, we need to consider the questions of whether accounting is, or can be, a science and of the relation of art to science. An important segment of accounting theory derives from the research process.[1] Therefore, the chapter concludes by examining the main directions of current accounting research as well as some other influences affecting accounting research.

Accounting Research and Scientific Method

Theories attempt to explain relationships or predict phenomena. Although accounting theory embraces a wide range of philosophical viewpoints, we are particularly concerned in this chapter with the formally developed theories that have been derived from the research process.

In terms of scientific method, a theory is, first of all, nothing more than sentences.[2] It must contain a basic set of premises (also called assumptions or postulates). The premises may be self-evident or they may be constructed so that they can be tested by statistical inference, in which case they are usually called hypotheses. Some of the terms in premises may be undefined, but other terms may need precise definitions. The words *debit* and *credit* are so well understood by accountants that no definition is necessary. However, the word *liabilities,* as used in a theory, needs to be carefully defined because several different conceptions of it exist. In the narrowest sense, liabilities can be defined legally—amounts presently due other parties for goods, services, or other consideration already received. However, the definition can be extended to include future cash disbursements for estimated income tax liabilities—straight-line depreciation is used for published financial statement purposes, and accelerated depreciation is used for tax purposes (a legal liability does not exist in this situation). Finally, a theory contains a set of conclusions derived from the premises. The conclusions can be determined either by deduction or induction.

Research Approaches

Deductive Reasoning

A deductive system is one in which logical reasoning is employed to derive one or more conclusions from a given set of premises. Empirical data are not analyzed in purely deductive systems. A simple example of a deductive system would be as follows:

Premise 1:   A horse has four legs.

Premise 2:   John has two legs.

Conclusion 1: John is not a horse.

In this simple case, only one conclusion can be derived from the premises. In a more complex system, more than one conclusion can be derived. However, conclusions must not be in conflict with one another. Notice that no other conclusion relative to John could possibly be reached from the given premises.

Of course, if we were applying this theory to a real being named John, as opposed to analyzing the logic of a set of sentences, we would have to see and, if necessary, examine John to determine his status. At this point we would be in the inductive realm—because we would be judging the theory not simply by its internal logic but rather by observing the evidence itself. For example, John might be a horse that had two legs amputated. Assuming that the reasoning is valid, only questioning premises or conclusions empirically can challenge a deductive theory.

Accounting and economic theorists have developed different income models by means of deductive reasoning. The main source of a firm's income is an increase in wealth resulting from operations during the period. *Income* has often been defined as the maximum amount that can be distributed to owners while still leaving the firm as well-off at the end of a period as it was at the beginning of the period.[3] Income thus is conditional, in the definitional sense, on maintaining intact the firm's capital at the beginning of the period. This concept is known as *capital maintenance*. Beginning with the basic premise, capital maintenance, there are at least three different ways to approach "well-offness" in capital maintenance terms. If we assume that the dollar is stable, historical cost income measurement is appropriate and capital maintenance is ascertained in unadjusted dollars. In a period of inflation, if we desire to take into account the shrinking general purchasing power of the dollar, revenues and expenses can be measured by restating historical cost figures by appropriate general price-level adjustments. Similarly, income measured by calculating expenses in terms of current replacement costs can be geared to a physical capacity concept of capital maintenance.

Some deductive approaches to accounting theory have used formalized axioms as the premises of a system from which various rules of accounting can be derived. By formalized axioms, we mean a set of terms rigorously defined according to the rules and terminology of symbolic logic.[4] Formalized deductive approaches (sometimes called analytical/deductive methods) have not met with a great deal of success in accounting theory. This is owing to a limited understanding of symbolic techniques as well as a lack of agreement on the fundamental premises of financial accounting. General deductive reasoning, however, remains extremely important in accounting theory and policy making.

Inductive Reasoning

Inductive reasoning examines or tests data, usually a sample from a population, and makes inferences about the population.[5] If an individual were testing a pair of dice to see whether they were loaded, he or she might throw each die 100 times in order to check that all sides come up approximately one-sixth of the time. Accounting researchers gather data through many methods and sources. These include questionnaires sent to practitioners or other appropriate parties, laboratory experiments involving individuals in simulation exercises, numbers from published financial statements, and prices of publicly traded securities.

In a complex environment such as the business world, a good inductive theory must carefully specify the problem that is under examination. The research must be based on a hypothesis that is capable of being tested. The process includes selecting an appropriate sample from the population under investigation, gathering and scrutinizing the needed data, and employing the requisite tools of statistical inference to test the hypothesis.

One of the criticisms of early inductive or empirical research in accounting was that the relationships expressed were mechanistic. For example, empirical tests were made on the relationship between security prices and changes in accounting methods. However, the question of why standard setters or financial managers chose particular alternatives largely remained unanswered. Empirical research that posits relations between earnings and security prices, attempts to answer the question of why particular standards are selected by policy makers, or asks why management selects the particular accounting alternatives it chooses has been called positive accounting research.[6] *Positive accounting research* attempts to explain behavioral relationships in accounting. It attempts to describe "what is" without making any value judgments as to how things should be, although the researcher must make value judgments, as subsequent sections will demonstrate.

Many examples of inductively derived theories are present in the accounting literature. Watts and Zimmerman, for example, explored the question of how corporate management responds to new standards proposed by the Financial Accounting Standards Board (FASB); the Board invites written responses from interested parties to exposure drafts of proposed new standards.[7] One of their premises was that management acts in its own self-interest; for example, increasing personal compensation through bonus arrangements if reported net income increases. However, this is not necessarily the case in very large firms, if they are subject to antitrust action or regulation because of their dominant market position. In these firms, it may be in management's best long-run interests to have standards that result in lower reported net income. As a result, Watts and Zimmerman hypothesized that management has more incentive to favor standards that lower reported net income when the firm is subject to political pressure. They examined responses to the Board's exposure draft requiring general price-level adjusted income calculations in corporate annual reports (the exposure draft was eventually withdrawn). Their findings tended to corroborate the hypothesis that the proposal was supported by larger firms that would have lower income as a result of general price-level adjustment. Similarly, those larger firms that would have higher income using general price-level adjustment tended to be against the proposal.

Several other comments are in order relative to Watts and Zimmerman's study. Their premise concerned potential management reactions to accounting rules that could either increase or reduce income, but the exposure draft on general price-level accounting concerned a supplementary measurement of income rather than the primary measurement using historical cost. The exposure draft would have required the publication by most firms of general price-level-adjusted income statements in addition to the primary historical cost statements. Their study concerned whether general price-level-adjusted income was higher or lower than historical cost income. Hence, it appears to have been a very reasonable test of the question of how management reacts to standards that are perceived to increase or decrease a secondary measurement of income relative to the primary reported income number itself.

However, several other aspects of the study do raise important issues. Solomons, for example, has stated that Watts and Zimmerman's evidence is rather flimsy because it involves a relatively small number of firms (52), a single accounting issue, and a single point in time (the year 1973). Solomons has also noted (from an unpublished study by William Lanen and Meir Schneller) that many of the firms that lobbied in favor of general price-level-adjusted income when that technique appeared to give a lower reported income were not availing themselves of existing techniques. These include accelerated depreciation and LIFO, which would have reduced reported income as well as income taxes in the LIFO case.[8] The possibility of measurement error also exists relative to the situations in which general price-level-adjusted income for 1973 would have been lower than reported historical cost income.

Furthermore, of the nine largest firms that would have had lower general price-level-adjusted income relative to reported historical cost income in 1973, two lobbied against the proposed standard, which certainly raises questions about the predictive use of the hypothesis.[9] Moreover, three other firms (Union Carbide, Continental Oil, and International Harvester) also lobbied against the proposed standard even though their general price-level-adjusted income was lower than reported historical cost income for 1973. Since these firms ranked between 22 and 34 in the Fortune 500 for 1973, it appears that the premise—large firms would be in favor of standards that decrease income—would be applicable only to a very small handful of very large firms (although there were anomalies here as noted earlier). We raise these criticisms of Watts and Zimmerman simply to show that empirical research in an area involving human behavior is subject to many interpretations and must be used in an extremely guarded and careful fashion if inferences relative to the standard-setting process are to be drawn from the research. There are, however, still other problems with Watts and Zimmerman's research, which will be considered shortly.

Normative and Descriptive Theories

In addition to the deductive or inductive classifications, theories may also be categorized as normative (prescriptive) or descriptive. *Normative theories* employ a value judgment: Contained within them is at least one premise saying that this is the way things *should* be. For example, a premise stating that accounting reports should be based on net realizable value measurements of assets would indicate a normative system. By contrast, *descriptive theories* attempt to find relationships that actually exist. The Watts and Zimmerman study is an excellent example of a descriptive theory applied to a particular situation.

Deductive systems are often normative although mathematics and symbolic logic are deductive systems that are value free. Inductive approaches usually attempt to be descriptive. These characteristics derive from the nature of the deductive and inductive methods. The deductive method is basically a closed, nonempirical system; its conclusions are based strictly on its premises. The inductive approach, because it tries to find and explain real-world relationships, is, conversely, in the descriptive realm by its very nature.

However, there is the question of whether empirical research can, in fact, be value free (neutral) in its findings because implicit value judgments underlie the form and content of the research itself.[10] This point has also been made by Gunnar Myrdal, the famed Swedish economist, who is quoted by Mattessich:

Questions must be asked before answers can be given. The questions are an expression of our interest in the world, they are at bottom valuations. Valuations are thus necessarily involved already at the stage when we observe facts and carry on theoretical analysis, and not only at the stage when we draw political inferences from facts and valuations.[11]

Watts and Zimmerman do concede that from the perspective of both researcher and user, values do indeed underlie research.[12] Furthermore, Christenson has discussed the fact that positive research is not concerned with accounting issues per se but rather with the behavior of those who prepare and use accounting data—accountants, management, and users. The choice of issues to be addressed certainly involves values as Myrdal has so forcefully stated. Even though positive research is concerned with a different type of issue—behavioral relationships—than conventional accounting research, this does not necessarily mean that it is value free. An example of the difficulty of maintaining a value-free orientation is provided in a list of "positive" questions provided by a positive researcher. One entry on this list:

Why has the accounting profession been *cursed* [italics added] with a strong authoritative bias—resulting in the establishment of professional bodies such as the Committee on Accounting Procedure (CAP), Accounting Principles Board (APB), and the FASB to rule on "generally accepted accounting techniques"?[13]

This question certainly contains strong biases of its own. A value judgment is obviously involved in asking whether standard-setting bodies have or have not been successful. While empirical research attempts to be descriptive, it is virtually impossible for investigators to be totally neutral as they attempt to determine "what is."[14] Recognition of this fact by researchers might well improve the nature and findings of descriptive theories.[15]

Finally, on the output side, one of the purposes of positive research is to satisfy "information demand" by managers, auditors, users (financial analysts and creditors), and standard setters.[16] These groups look to positive research to maximize their own welfare.[17] The assumption—which is really a tautology—that individuals act in their own best self-interest appears to be the principal underlying postulate of positive accounting research. Hence, it is highly unlikely that positive researchers themselves could be free of their own underlying postulate.

Global and Particularistic Theories

A more sharply defined difference between deductive and inductive systems is that the former are sometimes global (macro) in content, whereas the latter are usually particularistic (micro). Where the premises of deductive systems are total or all-encompassing in nature, their conclusions must be sweeping. Within the context of accounting, examples of the global approach are the theories that advocate one type of valuation system for all accounts, as illustrated in Appendix 1-A. Inductive systems, because they are grounded in real-world phenomena, can realistically focus on only a small part of the relevant environment. In other words, inductive research tends to examine rather narrowly defined questions and problems. Again, the Watts and Zimmerman (1978) paper provides a representative example of the particularistic scope of inductive theory.

Many individuals (Nelson, for example) see global theories of accounting at an impasse.[18] The *Statement on Accounting Theory and Theory Acceptance* (1977) of the American Accounting Association regarded the conflict among global accounting theories as unresolvable at that particular time.[19] Caplan saw the future direction of accounting research in inductive theory because it could shed light on particular questions.[20] Nevertheless, there continue to be important advocates of normative approaches.[21] In fact, the distinction between deductive and inductive research is simply not clear-cut.

Complementary Nature of Deductive and Inductive Methods

The deductive–inductive distinction in research, although a good concept for teaching purposes, often does not apply in practice. Far from being either/or competitive approaches, deduction and induction are complementary in nature and are often used together.[22] Hakansson, for example, suggested that the inductive method can be used to assess the appropriateness of the set of originally selected premises in a primarily deductive system.[23] Obviously, changing the premises can change the logically derived conclusions. The research process itself does not always follow a precise pattern. Researchers often work backward from the conclusions of other studies by developing new hypotheses that appear to fit the data. They then attempt to test the new hypotheses.

The methods used by the greatest detective in all literature, Sherlock Holmes, renowned for his extraordinary powers of deductive reasoning, provide an excellent example of the complementary nature of deductive and inductive reasoning. In one of Holmes's cases, Silver Blaze, a famous racehorse, mysteriously disappeared when its trainer was murdered. One element of the case was that the watchdog did not bark when the horse disappeared. Dr. Watson, Holmes's somewhat slow-witted sidekick, saw nothing unusual about the dog not barking. Holmes, however, immediately deduced that the horse was taken from the stable by someone from the household rather than by an outsider. Thus, his list of suspects was immediately narrowed. Holmes was also keenly aware of induction: He systematically observed elements that would increase his knowledge and perceptions. Extensive studies of such diverse items as cigar ashes, the influence of various trades upon the form of the hand, and the uses of plaster of paris for preserving hand and footprints added considerable depth to his deductive abilities.

In a not dissimilar fashion, inductive research in accounting can help to shed light on relationships and phenomena existing in the business environment. This research, in turn, can be useful in the policy-making process in which deductive reasoning helps to determine rules that are to be prescribed. Hence, it should be clear that inductive and deductive methods can be used together and are not mutually exclusive approaches despite the impossibility of keeping inductive research value free.

Is Accounting an Art or a Science?

Both the rule-making structure and the practice of accounting occasionally raise the question of whether accounting is an art or a science. At least one author (in the 1940s) perceived it as a science.[24] However, he did not really set up criteria for defining a science, except his own particular prejudices in terms of valuation issues. Somewhat later, another author maintained that accounting was very closely related to the liberal arts.[25] Accounting itself was seen as a "practical art." However, that author did not present any real criteria for distinguishing between an art and a science. Certainly we can see that discussing accounting in terms of scientific method and the role of measurement theory in accounting potentially places accounting within the scientific domain.

In an important article and a follow-up book, Sterling has attempted to clarify the position of accounting relative to science.[26] He points out that the arts rely heavily on the personal interpretations of practitioners. For example, one painter might represent a model as having three eyes, whereas another painter might use the conventional two eyes—and a green nose—to represent the same subject. In science, however, he argues that there should be a relatively high amount of agreement among practitioners about the phenomena being observed and measured (notice the relationship of Sterling's definition of a science to the concept of measurement).

Sterling believes that accounting, as presently practiced, is far closer to an art than a science—owing to the way accountants define problems. In the case of depreciation, for example, a great deal of latitude is allowed in our measurements (if that is even the appropriate word) in selecting a depreciation method as well as deciding on an estimated number of years of life and a salvage value. The result is a low degree of verifiability, as well as the fact that no real attribute of the asset or the related expense calculation emerges except for the vague concepts unamortized historical cost and depreciation expense. A scientific approach, on the other hand, would strive to institute rigorous measurement procedures resulting in economically meaningful attributes, such as replacement cost or net realizable value of the asset or other elements being measured. The intention would be to provide information useful for either predictive or assessment purposes. These objectives are not being well served under our present rules.

Whether rigidly specified measurement procedures can be instituted to bring about a high degree of consensus among measurers in accounting is, of course, an extremely important question. However, scientists do not always come up with uniform measurements or interpretations of what they are measuring. Three examples from other disciplines should help to clarify this point.

Econometrics

One of the principal functions of econometricians (literally, "economic measurers") is predicting gross domestic product and related variables, such as the percentage of unemployment. There are several large models that have been constructed in an attempt to predict these variables. The models employ hundreds of simultaneous equations that must be solved by computer to generate the predictions. However, considerable disagreement exists among the models, and their predictions are often far from accurate when the actual results are tabulated. A further complicating factor is that the predictions interact with the results because many large corporations, as well as the federal government, use the services of econometric forecasters, which, of course, influence their actions. Nevertheless, the term *economic science* has been used to describe what econometricians do, although some may dispute the characterization.

Climatology

Although the computer has become an invaluable tool for scientific research, it has been unable to penetrate the mysteries and eliminate the controversies of the greenhouse effect in climatology.

These estimates, which have been used to great effect by environmentalists, are based on computer simulations of future climate change, or, as they are called in the trade, General Circulation Models. In fact, every greenhouse forecast—every dire prediction of dangerous heat waves, droughts, flooding, radically shifting weather patterns, and the like—is the result of computers attempting to model the myriad factors that influence climate change . . . the body of the report, which was written and reviewed by climate scientists, raises all kinds of doubts about the models' reliability. Climate modeling is a difficult and expensive proposition, and modelers themselves are the last to claim that their computers give them much predictive power.

And for good reason. The General Circulation Models attempt to mimic our climate system by using a mathematical simulation of the earth and its oceans and atmosphere. Unfortunately, the mechanisms of our climate are extremely complicated. Take cloud cover, one of the most obvious factors in climate change. Clouds create a problem for the greenhouse models because their influence far outweighs any possible effect of man-made emissions. It is nearly impossible to predict what kinds of clouds will form, or even whether they will serve to enhance or diminish global warming. Depending on your assumptions, you can have the model arrive at pretty much whatever answer you want.[27]

Again, computers are extremely useful, but model building, as in the case of climatology, may be no better than the assumptions used by the researcher.

Human Anthropology

Going further afield, we take an example from human anthropology, which is concerned with the study of ancient people and their forebears. In the mid-1970s, an almost complete female skeleton (but without the skull) was discovered in a remote desert in Ethiopia. The skeleton of this species, named *Australopithecus afarensis* (the skeleton itself is affectionately and unscientifically known as "Lucy" because its discoverers jubilantly played "Lucy in the Sky with Diamonds" and other Beatles' songs after the discovery was made). Lucy has been subjected to many scientific measurements, including carbon dating, which put her age at approximately 3,500,000 years. In addition, careful scrutiny of the structure of the leg and thigh bones indicated that the creature walked upright like humans rather than with the shambling gait of members of the ape family.

Nevertheless, a huge controversy surrounded this species, *Australopithecus afarensis*. Some anthropologists, particularly its discoverers, maintained that it was a true ancestor of the line that eventually became humankind. Other anthropologists, though, thought that the species was not a true progenitor of humans. Fortunately, more scientific evidence has been found. Early in 1994 it was announced that the skull of a large male of the same species as Lucy was found about a mile from where she was discovered. While the argument still has not been decided, the evidence is now much stronger that *Australopithecus afarensis* is indeed a genuine forebear of humankind. Scientific reasoning and assessment of evidence can be a slow and painstaking process with definitive answers not easily forthcoming.

Summary of Accounting as a Science

These three examples demonstrate that science is not always exact and scientists do not always agree on the results of their work. Bearing this in mind, we can say, along with Sterling, that accounting has the potential to become a science, an outcome that should be pleasing to all involved. However, accounting is largely concerned with the human element, which is less controllable than the physical phenomena measured in the natural sciences. Consequently, we can expect accounting, along with economics and other social sciences, to be less precise in its measurements and predictions than the natural sciences.[28]

Directions in Accounting Research

The approaches discussed below represent particular orientations or directions of accounting research. They represent a significant change over the purely normative research of two generations ago.

The Decision-Model Approach

The *decision-model approach* asks what information is needed for making decisions. From this point of view, financial statements based on entry values, exit values, and discounted cash flows qualify as useful possibilities (see Appendix 1-A). This approach does not ask what information users want but rather concentrates on what information is useful for particular decisions. Thus, its orientation is normative and deductive. A premise underlying this research is that decision makers may need to be taught how to use this information if they are unfamiliar with it.[29]

There are many adherents of this school advocating a range of valuation possibilities. Chambers and Sterling advocate the exit-value approach because the selling price of assets is relevant to the decision of keeping or disposing of assets.[30] Also, aggregated exit values of all assets provide a measure of total liquidity available to the enterprise. Bell is a current-value advocate who favors the usage of deprival value for assets. *Deprival value* is the lower of (a) replacement cost or (b) the recoverable amount that is the higher of net realizable value or present value.[31] Solomons is likewise a deprival-value advocate who is also a vigorous defender of the need for a conceptual framework grounded in recognition and measurement criteria that uphold current value attributes because of their usefulness in decision making.[32]

The work of several other important accounting theoreticians also falls into the decision-model approach, even though their valuation orientation does not assume as primary a position as with Chambers, Sterling, Bell, and Solomons. Ijiri is a strong advocate of the stewardship function, which is concerned with the accountability of management (whom Ijiri refers to as the "accountor") and owners or accountees. Ijiri is an advocate of historical costing with adjustment for the change in the purchasing power of the monetary unit (general price-level adjustment).[33] Mattessich has long been an advocate of rigorous axiomatic methods for determining a general theory of accounting that could then be used for determining specific information needs of users.[34] Finally, Staubus has been an advocate of accounting measurements that simulate discounted cash flows as closely as possible to facilitate decision making by investors.[35]

The normative nature of the decision-model approach has led some advocates of newer theoretical approaches to declare that the decision-model approach is nonscientific. However, Mattessich has very clearly demonstrated that value-laden assumptions are a necessary aspect of goal-oriented (means-ends) activities, such as the administrative sciences (which include accounting).[36] In other words, scientific method and the resulting approaches just discussed can be utilized in activities that have desired ends, as opposed to, for example, the natural sciences, which attempt to describe the natural world. Although not as dominating a force as it used to be prior to the rise of empirical research in accounting, the decision-model approach is still an important focus of research in accounting.

The two major decisions embraced by the decision-model approach are (1) enabling the user to better predict future cash flows and (2) analyzing the efficiency and effectiveness of management (stewardship). Perhaps the decision-model school, of all the research orientations, accords most closely with the standard-setting function itself, including the derivation of conceptual frameworks. The decision-model approach and standard-setting function are clearly normative types of operations. Decision-model issues and concerns closely parallel those of standard setters, although the latter must also cope with the politics of the regulatory process.

Capital Markets Research

A significant amount of empirical (inductive) research has shown that prices of publicly traded securities react rapidly and in an unbiased manner to new information, although this finding has recently come under challenge. Whether immediate or gradual, over time, market prices eventually reflect all publicly available information. This proposition, which stems principally from the discipline of finance, is known as the efficient-markets hypothesis (EMH). In addition, return on a security is a function of risk: volatility of the security's return relative to the volatility of the entire securities market. This insight has led to a very significant increase in emphasis on diversifying investment portfolios rather than attempting to "beat" the market on an individual security basis. The EMH has some potentially significant implications for accounting (criticisms of the EMH are discussed in Chapter 8). For example, because information is rapidly reflected in security prices, the impetus for increased disclosure with less concern for choice among accounting alternatives has grown stronger.[37]

However, while disclosure is very important, including numbers in the body of the financial statements is preferable to footnote disclosure. Since the EMH states that the return of a security is based on its risk, other research has attempted to assess the relationship between accounting-based measures of risk (financial statement ratios, for example) and market-based risk measures.[38] The effect of accounting policy choices on security prices has also been extensively tested. Other examples of capital markets research are discussed in Chapter 8.

Capital markets research is difficult to do because researchers must specify the parameters and research design very carefully. Parameters (number and type of firms examined and time period[s] selected) and research design can affect the results of the particular study. Furthermore, subsequent researchers may interpret the results of previous research too broadly, generalizing what may not be applicable to the population as a whole.[39]

Behavioral Research

Behavioral research is another important area of investigation. The main concern of behavioral research is how users of accounting information make decisions and what information they need. Notice that this approach is descriptive, whereas the decision-model approach is normative. Much of this research uses laboratory subjects, often students, in carefully controlled experimental situations.

McIntyre, for example, attempted to find out whether replacement cost information is more useful than historical cost information in evaluating actual annual rate of return.[40] In other words, this approach seeks to understand what information is selected and how it is processed. Four middle-sized firms in the tire and rubber industry were analyzed over a three-year period. McIntyre's subjects were graduate and undergraduate students. Some students received replacement cost financial statements, others received historical cost statements, and still others received both. The subjects were asked to select the firm that would produce the highest actual annual rate of return during the three years. Actual annual rate of return was defined as

$$r = \frac{1}{n} \frac{(\Delta M + D)}{M} \tag{2.1}$$

where

$n =$ length of the assumed holding period in years

$D =$ dividends received during the holding period

$M =$ market value of the stock at the beginning of the holding period

$\Delta M =$ change in the market value of the stock during the holding period

Although there were considerable qualifications, McIntyre's findings failed to show any advantage to users of replacement cost financial statements. But the question of how representative McIntyre's student subjects were relative to the broad population of real decision makers is a problem that pervades virtually all behavioral research employing student subjects in laboratory experiments.

Behavioral research grew in popularity from approximately the mid-1960s until the mid-1970s when it declined in popularity and then gained in popularity again in the mid-1990s.[41] The decline in this research in the mid-1970s has been attributed to the growing importance of the EMH, mentioned previously. Under this hypothesis, as long as an investor is properly diversified, portfolio returns would be commensurate with the risk undertaken and the market could not be beaten. As a result, there was little perceived need for studies of the sort undertaken by McIntyre. However, by the mid-1990s enough questions about the EMH had arisen to result in a resurgence of interest in behavioral research.

Behavioral research has been divided into two types: behavioral and experimental.[42] Behavioral research involves individual judgments in a single-person setting. Experimental research is interactive, involving more than one person and taking into account the effect of the decision of one person (or group) on the decisions of other persons (or groups).

Behavioral research in the financial accounting area embraces many issues. These include how managers and auditors prepare accounting and financial information, how users interpret financial statements and information, and the effect of individual decisions upon the market.[43]

Agency Theory

Agency theory (also called contracting theory) is now an extremely important type of accounting research. It arose as a result of the perceived separation of interests in the modern corporation between management and ownership interests that were outside of the corporation and not involved in management decisions. The Watts and Zimmerman (1978) study previously discussed is the first major agency theory work done in accounting. Agency theory studies may be deductive or inductive and are a special example of behavioral research, although the roots of agency theory lie in finance and economics rather than in psychology and sociology. Its underlying assumption, as we have discussed, is that individuals act in their own best self-interest, which may, at times, conflict with the enterprise's best interests. Another important assumption of agency theory is that the enterprise is the locus or intersection point for many contractual-type relationships that exist among management, owners, creditors, and government. As a result, agency theory is concerned with the various costs of monitoring and enforcing relations among these various groups.[44]

The audit, for example, can be viewed as an instrument for ensuring that the firm's financial statements have been subject to a certain amount of external scrutiny. In addition, the statements themselves—presuming an unqualified opinion—are assumed to meet the criterion of being in accordance with generally accepted accounting principles. The audit, therefore, attempts to give assurances to outsiders, such as owners and creditors, about the governance of the enterprise by management. Of course, recent events in the corporate world have considerably shaken the public's confidence in the audit.

Many agency relationships between parties are defined or governed by accounting numbers. These include bond covenants, management compensation contracts, and firm size. Bond covenants frequently prescribe the maximum level of ratios such as debt-to-equity, violation of which can lead to technical default.[45] The tighter the debt to equity constraint, the more likely that management will choose accounting alternatives that will increase income. Research has shown that lenders set bond covenants tightly so that they serve as a "trip wire" relative to violations occurring.[46] Hence, violations can be relatively frequent, but they are not necessarily signs of financial distress.[47] Nevertheless, some borrowers are willing to pay higher interest rates to acquire more flexibility in the setting of debt covenants.[48]

In the case of management compensation contracts, management will likely attempt to choose methods that will increase income and also increase bonuses. Our previous discussion of positive accounting research noted the presumed linkage between very large firm size and governmental interference, which could lead to the choice of income-lowering alternatives. As a result, the choice of accounting methods by firms may be influenced by their effect on agency contracts.[49]

One hypothesis of agency theory is that management attempts to maximize its own welfare by minimizing the various agency costs arising from monitoring and contracting. Notice that this is not quite the same as saying that management attempts to maximize the value of the firm. Although management tries to maximize its compensation, it must do so within the framework of increasing net income, return on investment, or similar accounting measures while also attempting to positively change the firm's security price. Hence, minimizing contracting costs refers to not negatively disrupting the delicate relationship between accounting-based measures of performance and not getting qualified opinions on audits.

While the main management drive will usually be toward improving performance, management may also attempt to choose accounting rules that maximize income immediately rather than over time, such as in the case of the investment tax credit (see Chapter 3), in order to maximize its own compensation. Stock options (Chapters 3 and 12) provide an important example of management interests not being aligned with stockholder interests. In these and similar cases, management actions may not always be in the best interests of stockholders. This is sometimes called opportunistic behavior or moral hazard. The audit, as an example of minimizing agency costs, would be an example of efficient contracting. Difficulties exist relative to correlating accounting method choice with efficient contracting purposes, hence examples of it in the accounting literature are infrequently encountered and often misspecified.[50]

Other assumptions about the nature of the firm compete with the agency theory assumption that the firm is the locus or nexus for many contractual types of relationships. Chambers, for example, has described the firm as "a temporary coalition of participants in unstable equilibrium."[51] Chambers's coalition view sees the firm—even though it is an artificial entity—playing a stronger role vis-à-vis the various participants than it does under agency theory, where the firm per se has virtually no role. In the coalition view, income as a measurement of the economic performance of the firm and economically viable measures of assets and liabilities are important functions of accounting and should be the primary considerations of standard-setting agencies. No such viewpoint exists in agency theory. The point is not that agency theory is either "right" or "wrong"; theories such as agency theory and the coalition view are both partial descriptions of the workings and interrelationships of the firm and its constituent participants.

Other questions have been raised about agency theory. For example, since self-interest is such a paramount assumption of agency theory, individuals exposed to it may act in accordance with the assumption making it, in effect, a self-fulfilling prophecy.[52] Also, the simplicity of the assumptions underlying agency theory research ignore the complexity of business and social relationships.[53]

Various competing theories and viewpoints may bring important insights to accountants, auditors, users, and standard setters. No individual approach should be deemed superior to all others, for important contributions may come from any and all sources. Furthermore, while important adherents of agency theory research insist that the results are positive and descriptive and cannot be used for policy purposes (clearly a value judgment), there is no reason why standard setters should not use the results of agency theory research if the results are deemed to be valid and useful.[54]

Information Economics

Accountants are becoming increasingly conscious of the cost (and benefits) of producing accounting information. This has led to a relatively new field of inquiry for accounting researchers: *information economics*. Information economics research is usually analytical/ deductive in nature. With the exception of cash flow accounting, alternatives to the historical cost accounting model would, prima facie, appear to impose additional information production costs upon firms. Whether the benefits of alternative information sets or larger information sets are worth their costs is an important question. The nature of this problem has been succinctly stated by Beaver and Demski:

> The crux of the argument on behalf of accrual accounting rests on the premise that (1) reported income under accrual accounting conveys more information than a less ambitious cash flow-oriented accounting system would, (2) accrual accounting is the most efficient way to convey this additional information, and, as a corollary, (3) the "value" of such additional information system exceeds its "cost."[55]

Information economics has recently included agency theory assumptions and situations in its analysis. This is because risk sharing between principal and agent is closely connected with the issue of whether both sides have full information or whether information asymmetry exists in which one party (usually the agent) has more information than the other party.[56] The objective of the information theory analysis is to determine how optimal contractual arrangement incentives and risk sharing can be negotiated.[57] This research has also shown the importance of the stewardship function of accounting (evaluating the performance of management is extremely important relative to determining managerial incentives and rewards).

Critical Accounting

Critical accounting is that branch of accounting theory that views accounting as having a pivotal role in adjudicating conflicts between the corporation and social constituencies such as labor, consumers, and the general public.[58] It is thus directly concerned with the active social role of accountants. Critical accounting coalesced from an amalgamation of two other areas of accounting that developed in the 1960s: public interest accounting and social accounting.[59]

Public interest accounting was concerned with doing pro bono (free) work of a tax and financial advisory nature for individuals, groups, and small businesses who were unable to pay for these services. *Social accounting* pertained to attempts to measure and bring onto corporate income statements the costs of externalities, such as pollution, which are a detriment to society but were costless to the instigating party (at least until the enactment of air and water pollution standards). Critical accounting is much broader than public interest accounting and social accounting (which it still embraces). Furthermore, it is the intention of critical accounting researchers to move the field from the fringes occupied by public interest accounting and social accounting into the mainstream of accounting research (and action) interests by adopting "a conflict-based perspective."[60]

Critical accounting differs in one major respect from all of the other research areas previously discussed: The other research directions presume a sharp separation between the researcher and his or her field of investigation. For example, positive accounting researchers and behaviorists believe that they are simply reporting on the behavior of subjects that they are examining. Even admittedly normative researchers, such as those in the decision-model school, see a reality that is independent from them. Thus, their work is involved with finding the most useful way to report on the operations and wealth of business and other entities. Critical accounting researchers, however, believe that in viewing and investigating reality, they also help to shape that reality. For example, Chua has stated:

> Given this mutually interactive coupling between knowledge and the human, physical world, the production of knowledge is circumscribed by man-made rules or beliefs which define the domains of knowledge, empirical phenomena, and the relationship between the two. . . . Epistemological [the study of how to determine knowledge] assumptions decide what is to count as acceptable truth by specifying the criteria and process of assessing truth claims.[61]

Tinker presents an interesting example from astronomy to illustrate the problem perceived by critical accountants.[62] He discusses the planet Uranus. All of the other research schools would say that the planet is an entity that is independent of us. Critical accountants would say that we are interpreting reality even by our naming the planet "Uranus." Moreover, our attempts to scientifically describe Uranus are circumscribed by what our instruments can tell us, which is always subject to later refinement and reinterpretation. Venus—another example—has an extremely hot surface and is often described as being "unfriendly" and "hostile" even though it is an inanimate object.[63] Chua has neatly described this predicament:

> Critical philosophers accept that the standards by which a scientific explanation is judged adequate are temporal context-bound notions. Truth is very much in the process of being hammered out and is grounded in social and historical practices. There are no theory-independent facts that can conclusively prove or disprove a theory.[64]

Furthermore, when we go beyond mere measurements—which are tentative, possibly incorrect, and subject to the limitations of our measuring instruments and our underlying theories—our word descriptions take over, which encase the very reality that we are attempting to describe.

It is because we interpret our own reality and cannot stay neutral that critical accountants believe that accounting should more strongly emphasize the attempt to solve broad societal problems. As might be suspected, some of their strongest attacks have been aimed at agency theory and the contention of the value-free nature of this type of research. In critical accounting research, there is less emphasis on mathematical and statistical models and more on historical explanation.[65]

These are some of the main directions of current accounting research. Some may be more promising than others, but we believe that all approaches are capable of contributing to our knowledge and providing important insights to the policy process. Sterling (1979b) and May and Sundem (1976) have also expressed a similar view.[66] Many of these approaches will be discussed throughout the text.

A Scientific Revolution in Accounting?

As should be obvious from this discussion of the many viewpoints in accounting research, it is a field that is presently in a considerable state of flux. Some have predicted a scientific revolution in accounting because of dissatisfaction with the existing paradigm.[67] A *paradigm* is a shared problem-solving view among members of a science or discipline. In accounting, the shared paradigm has been historical costing, which is based on the concepts of realization and matching and other important tenets, such as conservatism, going concern, accounting entity, and time period.[68] The inability of historical costing to cope with the problems of financial reporting during the 1970s in the wake of severe inflation caused a great deal of dissatisfaction. The effects of inflation at that time, combined with the concurrent development of empirical research in accounting as well as other research perspectives, led some to envision the possible development of a new paradigm in accounting.

We are now at a point at which there appears to be an evolutionary movement toward a wider use of current values (now called fair value, discussed in Chapter 14). Whether this constitutes a "scientific revolution" at this time is debatable. However, if the paradigm is applied just to accounting research as opposed to accounting practice, then a better case can be made that we have had a paradigm shift in accounting because of the rise, in particular, of capital market and agency theory research. These are now the predominant forms of research in accounting.[69] The many new research approaches and outlooks in accounting make this an exciting time to be involved with financial accounting. Only time will tell whether a new valuation model or other type of paradigm will emerge as our new orthodoxy.

Summary

One important avenue for the development of accounting theory is through research. In reasoning from premises (assumptions) to conclusions, results can be determined either deductively (logically reasoning from premises to conclusions) or inductively (by gathering data to support or refute the hypothesis). Deductive reasoning is generally normative, and, ideally, inductive reasoning is purely descriptive (although findings derived from inductive reasoning cannot be totally value free or neutral). Deductive and inductive reasoning are, however, complementary. Clearly, accounting policy making is normative since it is concerned with prescribing choices among accounting methods and requiring particular disclosures.

Whether accounting is an art or a science is a recurring question. In the realm of art, practitioners rather freely use individual interpretations when plying their craft. Science is more rigorous; practitioners should have a relatively high amount of consensus when measuring the same phenomena. There can, however, be strong disagreements in science. Accounting appears to be closer to an art than a science today because there is much free choice in selecting accounting methods, and rigorous measurement of phenomena by accountants is presently not a part of our discipline.

Accounting research has taken many directions, including the decision-model approach, capital market research, behavioral research, agency theory, information economics, and critical accounting perspectives. Our viewpoint is that all these approaches are potentially valuable in terms of adding to our knowledge about accounting and its environment, although the decision-model approach is the closest to the standard-setting function.

QUESTIONS

1. Do you think that the work of a policy-making organization such as the FASB or the SEC is normative (value-judgment oriented) or positive (oriented toward value-free rules)? Discuss.

2. An individual who was appraising accounting education had the following premises (assumptions):
   a. Accounting professors used to do more consulting with accounting practitioners than they do today.
   b. Accounting professors have become more interested in research that is abstract and not necessarily practical.
   He, therefore, concluded that accounting students are not as well prepared to enter the accounting profession as they used to be. Which type of reasoning was the individual using? What is your assessment of his conclusion?

3. In 1936, the United States was still suffering from the Great Depression. During the presidential election campaign, an extensive survey of voter attitudes was undertaken to find out whether the public preferred the incumbent, Franklin Delano Roosevelt, or the challenger, Alf Landon. The sample was gathered randomly from telephone book listings throughout the country. A preference was found for Alf Landon; however, Roosevelt won reelection by a huge landslide. What type of research was being conducted? Why do you think it failed to make an accurate prediction?

4. In accounting, deductive approaches are generally normative. Why do you think this is the case?

5. A frequent argument is that inductive reasoning is value free because it simply investigates empirical evidence. Yet some charge that it is not value free. What do you think is the basis for this charge?

6. Several years ago an author stated that corporate income could be scientifically ascertained, but any type of adjustment for inflation would be pure folly because measurements would tend to become very subjective. Do you agree with the author's appraisal? Comment in detail.

7. Of the four disciplines in the following list, which do you think qualify as sciences and which do not? State your reasons very carefully.
   a. Law
   b. Medicine
   c. Cosmetology
   d. Accountancy

8. Several occupations within two of the aforementioned disciplines are listed here. Which do you think come closest to being scientific?
   a. Accounting researcher
   b. Chief accountant for an industrial firm
   c. Medical researcher
   d. Doctor (general practitioner)

9. What are some of the pitfalls of empirical research?

10. If Watts and Zimmerman are correct that managers of very large firms oppose accounting standards that would raise their income and favor those that would lower it, what policy implications would this have for a standard-setting organization such as the FASB?

11. What is the major difference in orientation between positive accounting theory and more overtly normative theories, such as the valuation approaches discussed in Chapter 1?

12. For a discipline to become a science, the results of experiments and research must be exact. Do you agree with this statement? Discuss.

13. Why, in practical terms, is it impossible to separate deductive and inductive approaches to theoretical reasoning?

14. What is the relationship among scientific method, accounting research, and accounting policy making?

15. What are the two principal underlying assumptions of agency theory (positive accounting research)? Critique their role in constructing a theory of accounting.

16. The "uncertainty principle" of the famous physicist Werner Heisenberg states that physical phenomena cannot be precisely measured because the very act of measuring affects the phenomenon being measured. Which of the directions of accounting research discussed in the chapter does Heisenberg's uncertainty principle relate to most closely?

17. Why do you think the term "deprival value" was used to name a specific type of replacement cost?

18. Of the following decision-model advocates discussed in the chapter (Chambers, Sterling, Solomons, Bell, and Ijiri), which one stands out as most unlike the others?

19. What is the difference between "accounting theory" and "accounting research?"

20. Why does the decision-model orientation to research accord more closely with the standard-setting function than any of the other research directions?

21. If there has been a paradigm shift (scientific revolution) in accounting research, but not in accounting practice, what may this signify?

22. In accounting behavioral research, student subjects have been frequently used as proxies for real-world decision makers. Does this lead to any potential problems?

23. Why do you think that ethnographic research (footnote 65) would be difficult to apply to organizations such as the SEC and FASB?

CASES, PROBLEMS, AND WRITING ASSIGNMENTS

1. Agency theory takes the view that the corporation is the locus or nexus of many competing and conflicting interests. List as many of these conflicting groups as you can and discuss in detail the nature of their conflicts with other groups.

2. Using the article by Colin Lyas ("Philosophers and Accountants") in *Philosophy* (January 1984, pp. 99–110), discuss and compare Sterling's scientific approach to standard setting with the judicial or jurisprudential approach of Stamp.

CRITICAL THINKING AND ANALYSIS

1. How can accounting move more toward becoming a science rather than an art? Discuss.

Notes

1. *Searcy and Mentzer (2003) give a broad overview of the entire research process, including the different types of research, research methodology, and the research process itself.*

2. *Scientific method cannot be precisely defined and restricted to a given set of rules or procedures. See AAA (1972, pp. 403–406). For more on accounting and scientific method, see Mattessich (1984).*

3. *Hicks (1961, p. 172).*

4. *For an incisive review of this literature, see Willett (1987).*

5. *Deductive reasoning prevailed over the inductive form from the time of Ancient Greece down through the Middle Ages. One of the individuals most responsible for shifting emphasis to inductive reasoning was the famous Elizabethan statesman and scholar, Sir Francis Bacon. See Eiseley (1962).*

6. *Discussions of positive research in accounting and a critique of previous empirical work appear in Watts and Zimmerman (1986 and 1990).*

7. *Watts and Zimmerman (1978).*

8. *Solomons (1986, pp. 239–241).*

9. *McKee, Bell, and Boatsman (1984) found statistical biases in Watts and Zimmerman's analysis that led them to question the explanatory power and predictive ability of the Watts and Zimmerman hypothesis.*

10. *Tinker, Merino, and Neimark (1982); and Christenson (1983).*

11. *Mattessich (1978, p. 236).*

12. *Watts and Zimmerman (1990, p. 146).*

13. *As quoted in Christenson (1983, p. 4). Sterling (1990) is also very forceful about the point that one cannot study a discipline by studying the behavior of those who practice the discipline. Hence, Sterling sees positive research being concerned with the sociology of accounting rather than with the mainstream focus on income determination and wealth measurement. In answer to this criticism, Watts and Zimmerman (1990, p. 147) maintain that chemical actions and reactions can occur independently of chemists, but accounting does not happen without the presence of accountants.*

14. *Schreuder (1984, pp. 216–218) discusses the view of Max Weber, the noted sociologist, that scientific statements are devoid of normative content and therefore cannot be used for justifying policies. This is an ideal position that appears to cut off pure descriptive research from the policy-making domain. It may thus be a mixed blessing that inductive research cannot be hermetically sealed and kept free from contamination by value judgments!*

15. *For a brilliant essay on the pervasiveness of values, see Devine (1985). Devine does note that the separation of facts from values should, insofar as possible, be attempted. The question of values engaged Watts and Zimmerman (1979) in another journal article. In this paper, they attempted to show that accounting theories provide "excuses" for particular political purposes. Since this outcome buttressed their own claim for providing "value-free" theories, the question arises as to whether they would have wanted to publish any other "finding." Peasnall and Williams (1986), in refuting Watts and Zimmerman, make a reasonably good case that the leading academic journals attempt to publish research that is largely value free (to the extent that this is possible).*

16. *Watts and Zimmerman (1986, p. 340).*

17. *Ibid. (p. 3).*

18. *Nelson (1973, p. 16).*

19. *AAA (1977).*

20. *Caplan (1972, pp. 437–443).*

21. *See Hakansson (1969) and Mattessich (1995).*

22. *See Carnap (1951, pp. 199–202) and Rudner (1966, p. 66). Bell, who is sharply critical of much empirical work, nevertheless sees a complementary relationship between empirical work and normative questions and issues that must ultimately be decided on what can be called a logico-deductive basis (Bell, 1987).*

23. *Hakansson (1969, p. 37).*

24. *Kelley (1948).*

25. *Cullather (1959).*

26. *Sterling (1975 and 1979b).*

27. *Salmon (1993, p. 26). See Shapiro (2006) for an updated view of this problem.*

28. *See Stamp (1981) for an extended discussion of this point. Stamp advocates a theoretical grounding of accounting in a system similar to the judicial processes of the law rather than science. Under the legal approach, precedent could be used to determine circumstances in which different accounting methods might be employed. Accounting judgment would play a stronger role in the Stamp judicial approach to accounting as opposed to Sterling's scientific orientation. See Lyas (1984) for a comparison of Stamp and Sterling. The judicial (jurisprudential) approach will surface again in Chapter 7.*

29. *This is strongly implied in Sterling (1979a, pp. 354–357).*

30. *Chambers (1991) and Sterling (1979b, pp. 117–124).*

31. *Bell (1993, p. 284).*

32. *Solomons, (1986, pp. 158–163).*

33. *Ijiri (1981).*

34. *Mattessich (1972), (1993), and (1995). For an in-depth critique of the Mattessich system, see Archer (1998).*

35. *Staubus (1977). Staubus's more recent work is concerned with prescribed accounting methods as simulations of market value. See Staubus (1985 and 1986). Salvary (1992) focuses on "recoverable cost" as a general characteristic of extant accounting rules and methods.*

36. *Mattessich (1978, pp. 42–48).*

37. *See Beaver (1973).*

38. *For example, see Beaver, Kettler, and Scholes (1970) and Bildersee (1975).*

39. *See the very interesting article by Bamber, Christensen, and Gaver (2000).*

40. *McIntyre (1973). For an extended critique of McIntyre's research design, see Dyckman (1975).*

41. *Libby, Bloomfield, and Nelson (2002, pp. 775–776).*

42. *Kachelmeier and King (2002, p. 219).*

43. *Libby, Bloomfield, and Nelson (2002).*

44. *See Watts (1977) for more on agency relationships and the role of audited financial statements in an unregulated economy. Bricker and Chandar (2000) believe that more attention should be paid in agency theory research to the ownership role of financial intermediaries such as pension funds and mutual funds. These institutions have begun to play a more active role vis-a-vis management. Financial institution/owners were responsible for removing board chairmen at General Motors, American Express, and IBM in the early 1990s. Of course Enron and other scandals revealed that boards of directors were often very passive and compliant to management. Bricker and Chandar also see financial institutions more concerned with managerial outcomes, such as share price and price-earnings ratios, as opposed to company operations per se.*

45. *Generally speaking, the presence of debt covenants can affect security prices when earnings announcements are made. Hence, there is both an earnings effect and a debt covenant effect to earning announcements. The debt covenant effect will be greater the closer the firm is to violating the debt covenant. See Core and Schrand (1999).*

46. *Dichev and Skinner (2002).*

47. *Expedia, Inc., the online travel company, had a debt covenant requiring it to maintain owners' equity of at least $5.25 billion. A decline in operating cash flows during the third quarter of 2006 led to goodwill impairment, which, in turn, led to a debt covenant violation. The violation did not cause a default; hence, it is an example of the milder type of violation. See Rapoport (2006, p. C3).*

48. *Beatty, Ramesh, and Weber (2002).*

49. *Proponents of agency theory are generally advocates against accounting regulation on the grounds that the contracting and monitoring mechanisms will result in acceptable accounting alternatives being selected, which means that the cost of accounting regulation exceeds its benefits. See Watts and Zimmerman (1986, pp. 156–178), for example. Tinker (1988, pp. 169–170) makes the point that agency theory can be used as a basis for justifying accounting regulation. Armstrong (1991, p. 10) attacks the foundations of agency theory because he sees the possibility of the incentive and monitoring mechanisms leading to a withdrawal of autonomy and trust by management, resulting in a lack of identity between management and owners.*

50. *See Holthausen (1990, p. 211). Holthausen also discusses the information perspective, in which management might attempt to signal information about future cash flows (see Chapters 4 and 9 for more on signaling).*

51. *Chambers (1990, p. 16).*

52. *Cohen and Holder-Webb (2006).*

53. *Ibid.*

54. *For an excellent discussion of the dichotomy of agency theory and its positive orientation and the restriction of it from prescriptive purposes, see Whittington (1987).*

55. *Beaver and Demski (1979, p. 43).*

56. *For a summary of this literature, see Mattessich (1993, pp. 195–199).*

57. *Ibid. (p. 198).*

58. *Neimark (1988, p. ix).*

59. *Neimark (1986, p. ix).*

60. *Tinker, Lehman, and Neimark (1991, p. 30).*

61. *Chua (1986, p. 604).*

62. *Tinker (1988, pp. 166–167).*

63. *English composer Gustav Holst wrote a popular suite called "The Planets." Uranus is perceived in Holst's music as a clever magician or conjurer. Holst's depictions of the planets are also closely connected to astrology, a totally unscientific field.*

64. *Chua (1986, p. 620).*

65. *Somewhat related to critical accounting theory is the field of* ethnographic research *as it is applied to accounting. This research method involves extensive observation of organizations and the individuals within them to determine the interpretation and role of accounting within the organization. One of the problems of ethnographic research is that researchers bring their own biases to each investigation. Hence, there are limitations to the generalizability of research results. While ethnographic research has largely been in the management accounting realm, it could, in theory at least, be extended to the workings of organizations such as the SEC and FASB. From a geographical perspective, ethnographic research has largely been performed by European researchers. For more background on ethnographic research, see Dey (2002). Ethnographic research falls under the umbrella of qualitative research. See Denzin and Lincoln (2000).*

66. *Sterling (1979b, p. 53); May and Sundem (1976).*

67. *The nature of scientific revolutions and dissatisfaction with existing paradigms is described in the very influential work of Thomas S. Kuhn (1970).*

68. *Wells has been a strong proponent of the Kuhnian view applied to accounting (Wells, 1976).*

69. *See Bamber, Christensen, and Gaver (2000) for a recent discussion of the potential paradigm shift in accounting. Reiter and Williams (2002) make the case that capital markets research and agency theory have pushed aside other research approaches by, among other methods, controlling access to leading journals. They also see something of a "cabal" among the universities having the perceived leading doctoral programs in accounting.*

References

American Accounting Association (1972). "Report of the Committee on Research Methodology in Accounting," *Accounting Review Supplement*, 399–520.

———— (1977). *Statement on Accounting Theory and Theory Acceptance*. American Accounting Association.

Archer, Simon (Autumn 1998). "Mattessich's Critique of Accounting: A Review Article," *Accounting and Business Research*, pp. 297–316.

Armstrong, Peter (1991). "Contradiction and Social Dynamics in the Capitalist Agency Relationship," *Accounting, Organizations and Society* (Vol. 16, No. 1), pp. 1–25.

Bamber, Linda S., T. E. Christensen, and K. M. Gaver (2000). "Do We Really Know What We Think We Know? A Case of Seminal Research and its Subsequent Overgeneralization," *Accounting, Organizations and Society* (Vol. 25, No. 2), pp. 103–129.

Beatty, Ann, K. Ramesh, and J. Weber (June 2002). "The Importance of Accounting Changes in Debt Contracts: The Cost of Flexibility in Covenant Calculations," *Journal of Accounting and Economics*, pp. 205–227.

Beaver, William (August 1973). "What Should Be the FASB's Objectives?" *Journal of Accountancy*, pp. 49–56.

Beaver, William, and Joel Demski (January 1979). "The Nature of Income Measurement," *Accounting Review*, pp. 38–46.

Beaver, William, Paul Kettler, and Myron Scholes (October 1970). "The Association Between Market Determined and Accounting Determined Risk Measures," *Accounting Review*, pp. 654–682.

Bell, Philip W. (Spring 1987). "Accounting as a Discipline for Study and Practice: 1986," *Contemporary Accounting Research*, pp. 338–367.

——— (February 1993). "Establishing Guidelines for Financial Reporting," *Accounting Enquiries*, pp. 262–306.

Bildersee, John (January 1975). "The Association Between a Market-Determined Measure of Risk and Alternative Measures of Risk," *Accounting Review*, pp. 81–98.

Bricker, Robert, and N. Chandar (2000). "Where Berle and Means Went Wrong: A Reassessment of Capital Market, Agency and Financial Reporting," *Accounting, Organizations and Society* (Vol. 25, No. 6), pp. 529–554.

Caplan, Edward (1972). "Accounting Research as an Information Source for Theory Construction," *Accounting Review Supplement*, pp. 437–444.

Carnap, Rudolf (1951). *The Nature and Application of Inductive Logic*. Chicago: University of Chicago Press.

Chambers, R. J. (1990). "Positive Accounting Theory and the PA Cult" (unpublished manuscript).

——— (December 1991). "Metrical and Empirical Laws in Accounting," *Accounting Horizons*, pp. 1–15.

Christenson, Charles (January 1983). "The Methodology of Positive Accounting," *Accounting Review*, pp. 1–22.

Chua, Wai Fong (October 1986). "Radical Developments in Accounting Thought," *Accounting Review*, pp. 601–632.

Cohen, Jeffrey, and L. Holder-Webb (February 2006). "Rethinking the Influence of Agency Theory in the Accounting Academy," *Issues in Accounting Education*, pp. 17–30.

Core, John E., and C. M. Schrand (1999). "The Effect of Accounting-Based Debt Covenants on Equity Valuation," *Journal of Accounting and Economics* (Vol. 27, No. 1), pp. 1–34.

Cullather, James (October 1959). "Accounting: Kin to the Humanities," *Accounting Review*, pp. 525–527.

Denzin, Norman K., and Yvonna S. Lincoln (2000). *Handbook of Qualitative Research*. Thousand Oaks, CA: Sage.

Devine, Carl T. (1985). "Description, Phenomenology, and Value-Free Science," in *Essays in Accounting Theory, Vol. V, Studies in Accounting Research #22*. American Accounting Association, pp. 1–16.

Dey, Colin (2002). "Methodological Issues: The Use of Critical Ethnography as an Active Research Methodology," *Accounting, Auditing & Accountability Journal* (Vol. 15, No. 1), pp. 106–121.

Dichev, Illia, and D. Skinner (September 2002). "Large-Sample Evidence on the Debt Covenant Hypothesis," *Journal of Accounting Research*, pp. 1091–1123.

Dyckman, Thomas R. (October 1975). "The Effects of Restating Price-Level Changes: A Comment," *Accounting Review*, pp. 796–808.

Eiseley, Loren (1962). *Francis Bacon and the Modern Dilemma*. University of Nebraska Press.

Hakansson, Nils (Spring 1969). "Normative Accounting Theory and the Theory of Decision," *International Journal of Accounting*, pp. 33–48.

Hicks, John R. (1961). *Value and Capital*, 2nd ed. Oxford University Press.

Holthausen, Robert (1990). "Accounting Method Choice: Opportunistic Behavior, Efficient Contracting and Information Perspectives," *Journal of Accounting and Economics* (Vol. 12, No. 1), pp. 207–218.

Ijiri, Yuji (1981). *Historical Cost Accounting and its Rationality*. The Canadian Certified General Accountants' Research Foundation.

Kachelmeier, Steven, and R. King (September 2002). "Using Laboratory Experiments to Evaluate Accounting Policy Issues," *Accounting Horizons*, pp. 219–232.

Kelley, Arthur (April 1948). "Definitive Income Determinations: The Measurement of Corporate Income on an Objective Scientific Basis," *Accounting Review*, pp. 148–153.

Kuhn, Thomas S. (1970). *The Structure of Scientific Revolutions*. University of Chicago Press.

Libby, Robert, R. Bloomfield, and M. Nelson (November 2002). "Experimental Research in Financial Accounting," *Accounting, Organizations and Society*, pp. 775–810.

Lyas, Colin (January 1984). "Philosophers and Accountants," *Philosophy*, pp. 99–110.

Mattessich, Richard (July 1972). "Methodological Preconditions and Problems of a General Theory of Accounting," *Accounting Review*, pp. 469–487.

——— (1978). *Instrumental Reasoning and Systems Methodology*. D. Reidel.

——— (1984). "The Scientific Approach to Accounting," in *Modern Accounting Research: History, Survey, and Guide*. The Canadian Certified General Accountants' Research Foundation, pp. 1–19.

——— (1993). "Paradigms, Research Traditions and Theory Nets of Accounting," in *Philosophical Perspectives on Accounting: Essays in Honour of Edward Stamp*, eds. M. J. Mumford and K. V. Peasnall. Routledge, pp. 177–220.

——— (1995). *Critique of Accounting: Examination of the Foundations and Normative Structure of an Applied Science*. Quorum Books.

May, Robert, and Gary Sundem (October 1976). "Research for Accounting Policy: An Overview," *Accounting Review*, pp. 747–763.

McIntyre, Edward (July 1973). "Current-Cost Financial Statements and Common-Stock Investment Decisions," *Accounting Review*, pp. 575–585.

McKee, A. James, Jr., Timothy B. Bell, and James R. Boatsman (October 1984). "Management Preferences Over Accounting Standards: A Replication and Additional Tests," *Accounting Review*, pp. 647–659.

Neimark, Marilyn (1986). "Marginalizing the Public Interest in Accounting" (editorial), *Advances in Public Interest Accounting* (Vol. 1), pp. ix–xiv.

——— (1988). "Preface," *Advances in Public Interest Accounting* (Vol. 2), pp. ix–x.

Nelson, Carl (1973). "A Priori Research in Accounting," in *Accounting Research 1960–1970: A Critical Evaluation*, eds. N. Dopuch and L. Revsine. University of Illinois, pp. 3–19.

Peasnall, K. V., and D. J. Williams (September 1986). "Ersatz Academics and Scholar-Saints: The Supply of Financial Accounting Research," *Abacus*, pp. 121–135.

Rapoport, Michael (2006). "Expedia Might Trip Debt Covenant," *Wall Street Journal* (October 12), p. C3.

Reiter, Sara Ann, and P. Williams (2002). "The Structure and Progressivity of Accounting Research: The Crisis in the Academy Revisited," *Accounting, Organizations and Society* (Vol. 27, No. 6), pp. 575–607.

Rudner, Richard (1966). *Philosophy of Social Science*. Prentice Hall.

Salmon, Jeffrey (July 1993). "Greenhouse Anxiety," *Commentary*, pp. 25–28.

Salvary, Stanley C. W. (February 1992). "Recoverable Cost: The Basis of a General Theory of Accounting Measurement," *Accounting Enquiries*, pp. 233–273.

Schreuder, Hein (1984). "Positively Normative (Accounting) Theories," in *European Contributions to Accounting Research*, eds. A. G. Hopwood and H. Schreuder. VU Uitgeverij/Free University Press, pp. 213–231.

Searcy, DeWayne, and J. Mentzer (2003). "A Framework for Conducting and Evaluating Research," *Journal of Accounting Literature*, pp. 130–167.

Shapiro, Kevin (September 2006). "Global Warming: Apocalypse Now?," *Commentary*, pp. 42–47.

Solomons, David (1986). *Making Accounting Policy*. Oxford, UK: Oxford University Press.

Stamp, Edward (Spring 1981). "Why Can Accounting Not Become a Science Like Physics?" *Abacus*, pp. 13–27.

Staubus, George (1977). *Making Accounting Decisions*. Scholars Book Company.

———— (January 1985). "An Induced Theory of Accounting Measurement," *Accounting Review*, pp. 53–75.

———— (Spring 1986). "The Market Simulation Theory of Accounting Measurement," *Accounting and Business Research*, pp. 117–132.

Sterling, Robert R. (September/October 1975). "Toward a Science of Accounting," *Financial Analysts Journal*, pp. 28–36.

———— (1979a). *Theory of the Measurement of Enterprise Income*. Scholars Book Company.

———— (1979b). *Toward a Science of Accounting*. Scholars Book Company.

———— (September 1990). "Positive Accounting: An Assessment," *Abacus*, pp. 97–135.

Tinker, Tony (1988). "Panglossian Accounting Theories: The Science of Apologizing in Style," *Accounting, Organizations and Society* (Vol. 13, No. 2), pp. 165–190.

Tinker, Tony, Cheryl Lehman, and Marilyn Neimark (1991). "Falling Down the Hole in the Middle of the Road: Political Quietism in Corporate Social Reporting," *Accounting, Auditing & Accountability Journal* (Vol. 4, No. 2), pp. 28–54.

Tinker, Tony, Barbara Merino, and Marilyn Neimark (1982). "The Normative Origins of Positive Theories: Ideology and Accounting Thought," *Accounting, Organizations and Society* (Vol. 7, No. 2), pp. 167–200.

Watts, Ross L. (April 1977). "Corporate Financial Statements, a Product of the Market and Political Processes," *Australian Journal of Management*, pp. 33–75.

Watts, Ross, L., and Jerold L. Zimmerman (January 1978). "Toward a Positive Theory of the Determination of Accounting Standards," *Accounting Review*, pp. 112–134.

———— (April 1979). "The Demand for and Supply of Accounting Theories: The Market for Excuses," *The Accounting Review*, pp. 273–305.

———— (1986). *Positive Accounting Theory*. Prentice Hall.

———— (1990). "Positive Accounting Theory: A Ten Year Perspective," *Accounting Review* (January 1990), pp. 131–156.

Wells, M. C. (July 1976). "A Revolution in Accounting Thought?" *Accounting Review*, pp. 471–482.

Whittington, Geoffrey (Autumn 1987). "Positive Accounting: A Review Article," *Accounting and Business Research*, pp. 327–336.

Willett, R. J. (Spring 1987). "An Axiomatic Theory of Accounting Measurement," *Accounting and Business Research*, pp. 155–171.

3

Development of the Institutional Structure of Financial Accounting

Learning Objectives

After reading this chapter, you should be able to:

- Understand the historical background and development of accounting standard setting in the United States.
- Understand how the Financial Accounting Standards Board (FASB) differs from its two predecessors.
- Understand the institutional problems facing the FASB.
- Appreciate the complexity of the standard-setting process.
- Understand how the liability crisis in public accounting is being modified.
- Grasp the significance of the Sarbanes-Oxley bill and other current developments in accounting.

In Chapter 1, we described the role of accounting theory in the standard-setting process. In this chapter, we focus on major events that have led to the present institutional arrangements for the development of accounting standards in the United States. In Chapter 10, we will briefly examine the standard-setting process in other English-speaking countries as well as attempts to establish uniform accounting standards on an international basis.

In the United States prior to 1930, accounting was largely unregulated. The accounting practices and procedures used by a firm were generally considered confidential. Thus, one firm had little knowledge about the procedures followed by other companies. Obviously, the result was a considerable lack of uniformity in accounting practices among companies, both from year to year and within the same industry. Bankers and other creditors, who were the primary users of financial reports, provided the only real direction in accounting practices. Bank and creditor pressure was aimed primarily at the disclosure of cash and near-cash resources that could be used for repayment of debt.

The emphasis on debt-paying ability can be traced back to the social and economic conditions in the United States prior to the end of World War I. The American public typically did not invest large sums in the corporate sector until the 1920s. When the federal government made lump-sum payments for the retirement of Liberty Bonds, the public suddenly had large amounts of available cash. Private corporations were expanding, and both they and government leaders encouraged the public to invest in American business. A "people's capitalism" concept took hold, and the number of individual shareholder investors rapidly increased. Unfortunately, financial reporting lagged behind investor needs, so reports continued to be prepared primarily for the needs of creditors.[1]

Not until the stock market crash of 1929 did shareholder investors begin to question whether accounting and reporting practices were adequate to assess investments. The realization that financial reports were based on widely varying accounting practices and were frequently misleading to current and prospective investors led to the first of three distinct periods in the development of accounting standards:

- The formative years (1930–1946)
- The postwar period (1946–1959)
- The modern period (1959–present)[2]

Before investigating these three periods, we will briefly survey the development of accounting in the United States prior to 1930.

Accounting in the United States Prior to 1930

By the 1880s, it had become clear that accounting was an important instrument in America for conducting business.[3] An organization calling itself the American Association of Public Accountants was formed in 1886 with 10 members. In 1896, this organization plus another group—The Institute of Bookkeepers and Accountants—were both behind the successful passage in New York State of the law that created the professional designation of "Certified Public Accountant." By 1913, 31 states had passed laws providing for the issuance of Certified Public Accountant (CPA) certificates. However, there was little uniformity among the various states regarding the requirements needed to earn the CPA.

Another significant accomplishment of the association was the founding of the *Journal of Accountancy* in 1905. This publication continues to be an important professional journal to the present day.

The early work of the association also included the appointment of a committee on terminology, which resulted in a list of terms and definitions that was adopted in 1915. More terms were defined in various issues of the *Journal of Accountancy*, resulting in the 1931 publication of a 126-page book containing the definitions.

A huge boon to the growing accounting profession was Congress's enactment of the income tax law in 1913. Another impetus to the profession occurred in 1917 with the entry of the United States into World War I. The specific issue involving public accounting was military contracts in which manufacturers were to be reimbursed on a cost-plus basis.

The American Institute of Accountants (AIA) was formed in 1916 from the old American Association of Public Accountants (the name was changed to the American Institute of Certified Public Accountants [AICPA] in 1957). The new group became a national organization. Its creation was not intended to replace state societies but rather to complement them. It sought to increase uniformity and standardization in qualifications and requirements for membership.

Meanwhile, a second organization—the American Society of Certified Public Accountants—formed in 1921. Whereas the AIA took a unified national outlook relative to issues such as examinations and qualifications, the American Society was more concerned with maintaining power in the various states. Rivalry between these two organizations was very heated. Largely by pressure from the New York State Society, the two organizations combined in 1936, maintaining the name of the older group.

During the rivalry between these two organizations, the AIA was the clear leader in the area of promulgating technical materials. As far back as 1918, the institute, in cooperation with the Federal Trade Commission (FTC), published a pamphlet entitled "Approved Methods for the Preparation of Balance Sheet Statements." The document was published in the *Federal Reserve Bulletin* and was considered by that body to provide the minimum standards for conducting a balance sheet audit. The pamphlet was later revised in 1929 under the general direction of the Federal Reserve Board. The document dealt mainly with auditing procedures, but financial accounting matters were, of necessity, discussed.

Another factor leading to an increased demand for auditing services as well as significant questions about the practice of accounting was the onset of the Great Depression in 1929. Questions arose as to whether accounting practices led to poor investment decisions by business, but the case has never been proven.[4] However, the Depression and the election of Franklin D. Roosevelt to the presidency in 1932 and the enactment of the New Deal legislation led to enormous changes in accounting, producing the first of the three distinct periods in the development of accounting standards.

Formative Years, 1930–1946

As a result of the stock market crash, the period from 1930 to 1946 influenced accounting practices in the United States extensively.

NYSE/AICPA Agreement

In 1930, the AICPA (we will use this acronym even though the name was not changed until 1957) began a cooperative effort with the New York Stock Exchange (NYSE) that eventually led to the preparation of one of the most important documents in the development of accounting rule making.[5] The AICPA's Special Committee on Cooperation with the Stock Exchange worked closely with the NYSE's Committee on Stock List to develop accounting principles to be followed by all companies listed on the exchange. The NYSE was concerned that listed companies were using a large variety of undisclosed accounting practices. Initially, the AICPA thought that the best solution was a dual approach: (a) education of users of accounting reports regarding the reports' limitations and (b) improvement of reports to make them more informative to users. Ultimately, the AICPA's committee suggested the following general solution to the NYSE committee:

The more practical alternative would be to leave every corporation free to choose its own methods of accounting within . . . very broad limits . . . , but require disclosure of the methods employed and consistency in their application from year to year. . . . Within quite wide limits, it is relatively unimportant to the investor which precise rules or conventions are adopted by a corporation in reporting its earnings if he knows what method is being followed and is assured that it is followed consistently from year to year. . . . [6]

The AICPA's committee prepared a formal draft of "five broad accounting principles" that was approved by the NYSE's committee on September 22, 1932. This document represented the first formal attempt to develop "generally accepted accounting principles" (GAAP). In fact, the AICPA's committee coined the phrase "accepted principles of accounting." The first five principles were later incorporated as Chapter 1 of *Accounting Research Bulletin* (ARB) 43. The joint effort of the NYSE and AICPA had a profound influence on accounting policy making in the United States during the next 50 years. Reed K. Storey described it this way:

The recommendations [all aspects of the original NYSE/AICPA document] were not fully implemented, but the basic concept which permitted each corporation to choose those methods and procedures which were most appropriate for its own financial statements within the basic framework of "accepted accounting principles" became the focal point of the development of principles in the United States.[7]

Formation of the SEC

Congress created the Securities and Exchange Commission (SEC) in 1934. The SEC's defined purpose was (and still is) to administer the Securities Act of 1933 and the Securities and Exchange Act of 1934. The two acts were the first national securities legislation in the United States. The 1933 act regulates the issuance of securities in interstate markets; the 1934 act is primarily concerned with the trading of securities. The 1933 and 1934 acts conferred on the SEC both broad and specific authority to prescribe the form and content of financial information filed with the SEC.

The SEC initially allowed the accounting profession to set accounting principles without interference. However, statements made by the SEC in 1937 and 1938 indicated that it was growing impatient with the profession. In December 1937, SEC commissioner Robert Healy addressed the American Accounting Association (AAA): "It seems to me, that one great difficulty has been that there has been no body which had the authority to fix and maintain standards [of accounting]. I believe that such a body now exists in the Securities and Exchange Commission."[8]

Finally, on April 25, 1938, the message the SEC was sending the profession became quite clear. The SEC issued Accounting Series Release (ASR) No. 4, which said:

In cases where financial statements filed with the Commission . . . are prepared in accordance with accounting principles for which there is no substantial authoritative support, such financial statements will be presumed to be misleading or inaccurate despite disclosures contained in the certificate of the accountant or in footnotes to the statements provided the matters are material. In cases where there is a difference of opinion between the Commission and the registrant as to the proper principles of accounting to be followed, disclosure will be accepted in lieu of correction of the financial statements themselves only if the points involved are such that there is substantial authoritative support for the practices followed by the registrant and the position of the Commission has not previously been expressed in rules, regulations, or other official releases of the Commission, including the published opinions of its chief accountant.9

The implicit message was that unless the profession established an authoritative body for the development of accounting standards, the SEC would determine acceptable accounting practices and mandate methods to be employed in reports filed with it.

Committee on Accounting Procedure, 1936–1946

In 1933, the AICPA formed the Special Committee on Development of Accounting Principles, but this committee accomplished very little and was subsequently replaced by the Committee on Accounting Procedures (CAP) in 1936, which also was relatively inactive until 1938. However, in 1938, prompted primarily by the SEC's new policy embodied in ASR 4, the CAP was expanded from 7 to 21 members and became much more active.

The CAP originally wanted to develop a comprehensive statement of accounting principles that would serve as a general guide to the solution of specific practical problems. However, most felt it would take at least five years to develop such a statement and by that time the SEC undoubtedly would have lost its patience. Thus, the CAP decided to adopt a policy of attacking specific problems and, whenever possible, recommending preferred methods of accounting.[10]

The CAP, acting in response to ASR 4, began in 1939 to issue statements on accounting principles that, prima facie, had "substantial authoritative support." During the two-year period of 1938 to 1939, it issued 12 Accounting Research Bulletins (ARBs). The CAP was cognizant of the SEC looking over its shoulder and frequently consulted with the SEC to determine whether proposed ARBs would be acceptable to the commission.[11]

The SEC was initially satisfied with the accounting profession's efforts to establish accounting principles. However, it had always let it be known that it was prepared to take over the rule-making process if the profession lagged. The following quotation from the commission's 1939 report to Congress clearly indicates its position:

> One of the most important functions of the Commission is to maintain and improve the standards of accounting practices. . . . the independence of the public accountant must be preserved and strengthened and standards of thoroughness and accuracy protected. I [Chairman Jerome N. Frank] understand that certain groups in the profession [CAP] are moving ahead in good stride. They will get all the help we can give them so long as they conscientiously attempt that task. That's definite. But if we find that they are unwilling or unable . . . to do the job thoroughly, we won't hesitate to step in to the full extent of our statutory powers.[12]

Not all accounting constituents were happy with the way accounting rules were being developed during this period. Members of the American Accounting Association (AAA) favored a deductive approach to the formulation of accounting rules—as opposed to the predominantly informal inductive approach employed by the CAP. Regarding the first four ARBs, the editor of *The Accounting Review* wrote:

> It is unfortunate that the four pamphlets thus far published give no evidence of extensive research or of well-reasoned conclusions. They reflect, on the other hand, a hasty marshaling of facts and opinions, and the derivation of temporizing rules to which it is doubtless hoped that a professional majority will subscribe. As models of approach in a field already heavily burdened with expedients and dogmatism, they leave much to be desired.[13]

This formative era did not produce a comprehensive set of accounting principles. However, it did make two very important contributions. First, accounting practices, especially in terms of uniformity, improved significantly. Second, the private sector was firmly established as the source for accounting policy making in the United States.[14] When World War II began, the development of accounting rules slowed down significantly. During the war years, the CAP dealt almost exclusively with accounting problems involving war transactions. Of the 13 ARBs issued between January 1942 and September 1946, 7 dealt with war-related problems and 3 with terminology.

Postwar Period, 1946–1959

An even greater economic boom occurred in the postwar period than in the 1920s. Industry required massive amounts of capital in order to expand. The expansion, in turn, created more jobs and more money in the economy. At the encouragement of stock exchanges, industry began to actively tap money available from the public. In 1940, there were an estimated 4 million stockholders in the United States. By 1952, the number had grown to 7 million; by 1962, the number reached 17 million. Thus, a large portion of the American public had a direct financial interest in listed corporations.

Corporate financial reports were an important source of information for financial decisions. Thus, financial reports and the accounting rules used to prepare them received wide attention. For the first time, accounting policy making became an important topic in the financial press. The primary problem was one of uniformity or comparability of reported earnings among different companies. The financial press and the SEC brought increasingly heavy pressure to bear on the accounting profession to eliminate different methods of accounting for similar transactions that significantly affected reported net income.

ARB 32 and the SEC

The CAP was busy during the postwar period. In total, 18 ARBs were issued from 1946 to 1953. Although the committee had been quite successful in eliminating many questionable accounting practices of the 1930s, the strategy created a new set of problems during the late 1940s and early 1950s. While eliminating suspect accounting practices, the CAP failed to make positive recommendations for general accounting principles. As a result, there was an oversupply of "good" accounting principles. Many alternative practices continued to flourish because there was no underlying accounting theory. This situation led to conflicts between the CAP and the SEC.

The most publicized conflict dealt with the all-inclusive income statement versus current operating performance. The CAP felt that utilizing current operating performance would enhance comparability of earnings reports among companies and among years for the same company. Any extraordinary gains and losses, it pointed out, are excluded from net income under the current operating performance concept. Consequently, it issued ARB 32 recommending that concept. Upon issuance of ARB 32, the SEC chief accountant wrote: "The Commission has authorized the staff to take exception to financial statements, which appear to be misleading, even though they reflect the application of ARB 32."[15]

In 1950, in an amendment to Regulation S-X, the SEC proposed use of the all-inclusive concept. This proposal was in direct conflict with ARB 32. Subsequently, the CAP and the SEC reached a compromise agreement regarding ARB 32 in which extraordinary items (called special items) would be the last items on the income statement.[16] Thus, the CAP maintained its prominent role in policy making. However, it was definitely subject to oversight by the SEC.

The Price-Level Problem

By the end of 1953, the accounting profession became increasingly concerned with accounting under conditions of changing price levels. The profession turned its attention almost entirely to this problem. As a result, for approximately three years little, if any, progress was made regarding the development of accounting principles. The main thrust of the price-level debate dealt with depreciation charges. Depreciation charges based on historical costs did not accurately measure the attrition of fixed-asset values in terms of current purchasing power. The result was an overstatement of reported net income. In general, the profession finally decided that to reflect changes in purchasing power would confuse users of financial statements. As a result, it shelved the price-level debate for many years and directed its attention again to the development of standards of financial accounting.

Closing Years of the CAP

The years from 1957 to 1959 represented a period of transition in the development of accounting standards in the United States. Criticism of the CAP increased, and even pillars of the accounting establishment were disapproving of its operations. Finally, a president of the AICPA, Alvin R. Jennings, called for a new approach to the development of accounting principles.

During the middle and late 1950s, interest in the development of accounting principles was growing both within and outside the profession. Unfortunately, much of this interest took the form of negative criticism directed toward the CAP. Financial executives and accounting practitioners in the smaller firms complained that they were not given an adequate hearing to express their opinions on proposed ARBs. Many felt that the CAP worked too slowly on pressing issues and refused to take unpopular positions on controversial topics. Leonard Spacek, managing partner of Arthur Andersen & Co., shocked the accounting profession with these remarks:

> The partners of our firm believe that the public accounting profession is not in important respects carrying its public responsibility in the certification of financial statements at the present time. We believe that the profession's existence is in peril. Until the profession establishes within its framework (a) the premise of an accepted accounting principle, (b) the principles of accounting that meet those premises, and (c) a public forum through which such principles of accounting may be determined, our firm is dedicated to airing in public the major shortcomings of the profession.[17]

Spacek seemed to be calling for the profession to prepare a comprehensive statement of basic accounting principles. In this he was not alone. In 1957, the AAA had published a statement of underlying concepts and definitions in which it at least attempted a deductive approach.[18] From its very inception, the CAP had discarded a formalized deductive approach because it was too time consuming. In fact, the committee had devoted its time to solving specific problems by prescribing rules on a piecemeal basis—without developing fundamental principles of financial accounting, much less a comprehensive theory.

A New Approach

Alvin R. Jennings delivered a historic speech in 1957 at the AICPA's annual meeting. He suggested a reorganization of the AICPA to expedite development of accounting principles. Jennings emphasized the need for research as part of this process. In other words, he called for a conceptual approach to replace the piecemeal method that had been followed for 20 years by the CAP. The accounting profession was ready to consider Jennings's new approach. The AICPA appointed a Special Committee on Research Program, which finished its report in less than a year. This report became the "articles of incorporation" for the Accounting Principles Board (APB) and the Accounting Research Division. The report emphasized the importance of research in establishing financial accounting standards:

> Adequate accounting research is necessary in all of the foregoing [establishing standards]. Pronouncements on accounting matters should be based on thorough-going independent study of the matters in question, during which consideration is given to all points of view. For this an adequate staff is necessary. . . . Research reports or studies should be carefully reasoned and fully documented. They should have wide exposure to both the profession and the public.[19]

The CAP was heavily criticized, perhaps deservedly so, but it represented the profession's first sustained attempt to develop workable financial accounting rules. It issued a total of 51 ARBs during its existence. One of these, ARB Opinion No. 43, represented a restatement and revision of the first 42 bulletins. Significant parts of ARB Opinion 43 remain in force to this day. Throughout the CAP's life, ARBs were increasingly recognized as authoritative and had a pronounced effect on accounting practice.

Modern Period, 1959 to the Present

The "charter" that created the APB and the Accounting Research Division called for a two-pronged approach to the development of accounting principles. The research division was to be semiautonomous. It had its own director, who had authority to publish the findings of the research staff, and was to be exclusively devoted to the development of accounting principles with no responsibilities to the technical committees of the AICPA. In establishing what research projects to undertake, the director of research had to confer with the chairman of the APB. If the two disagreed, the APB as a whole determined which projects the research division would undertake. Results of the projects of the research division would be published in the form of Accounting Research Studies (ARSs). These studies would present detailed documentation, all aspects of particular problems, and recommendations or conclusions. At the outset, two projects were called for in the special committee's report: (1) the "basic postulates of accounting" and (2) a "fairly broad set of coordinated accounting principles" based on the postulates.

In form, the APB was very similar to the CAP. It had from 18 to 21 members, all of whom were members of the AICPA. They represented large and small CPA firms, academe, and private industry. The hope was that the APB's opinions would be based on the studies of the research division. A two-thirds majority was required for the issuance of an opinion, and disclaimers of dissenting members were to be published.

Early Years of the APB

The early years of the APB were characterized by failure and doubt. Research studies called for in the original charter were not accepted by the profession, and controversy surrounding the investment tax credit resulted in a serious challenge by large CPA firms to the board's authority.

ARSs 1 and 3

ARS 1, *The Basic Postulates of Accounting*, by Maurice Moonitz, published in 1961, did not initially generate much reaction, favorable or unfavorable, from either the APB or the profession. Apparently, everyone was awaiting the publication of the companion study on principles before passing judgment. ARS 3, *A Tentative Set of Broad Accounting Principles for Business Enterprises*, by Robert Sprouse and Moonitz, appeared in April 1962. To say the least, this study provoked criticism from all areas. In fact, following the publication of the text of the study, 9 of the 12 members of the project advisory committees on the postulates and principles studies issued personal comments. Only one of the comments was positive. APB Statement 1 expressed the APB's views of the study. The statement said, in part: "The Board believes, however, that while these studies [1 and 3] are a valuable contribution to accounting thinking, they are too radically different from present generally accepted accounting principles for acceptance at this time."[20]

By issuing that statement, the APB seriously weakened the dual approach to the development of accounting standards.

Investment Tax Credit

In November 1962, the issuance of APB Opinion No. 2, which dealt with the investment tax credit, caused another problem. The profession as a whole was divided on how to account for the investment tax credit. Two alternatives existed: (1) recognizing the tax benefit in the year received, designated the flow-through method, and (2) recognizing the tax benefit over the life of the related asset, called the deferral method. The board chose not to commission a research study on the subject and issued APB Opinion No. 2, which opted for the deferral method. Almost immediately, three large CPA firms made it known that they would not require their clients to follow the opinion. Furthermore, in January 1963, the SEC issued ASR 96, which allowed registrants to employ either the flow-through or deferral methods. Obviously, these large CPA firms and the SEC had challenged the APB's authority. As a result, APB Opinion No. 4 was issued, which permitted the use of either method.

This successful challenge caused the binding authority of APB opinions to be questioned in the press for several years. Finally, in late 1964 the AICPA's council (the organization's governing body) declared the authority of APB opinions in an appendix to APB Opinion No. 6. It unanimously agreed that departures from APB opinions must be disclosed in financial statements audited by a member of the AICPA. If the independent accountant concluded that a method being employed had substantial authoritative support, even though it was not contained in a specific accounting principle, this support must be disclosed in footnotes or the auditor's report. Furthermore, the auditor must, if possible, disclose the effect of the departure. If the principle employed did not have *substantial authoritative support*, the auditor must qualify the opinion, give an adverse opinion, or disclaim the opinion.[21] Thus, as 1964 drew to a close, the authoritative nature of APB opinions had been established. However, the two-pronged approach to the development of accounting principles had yet to be implemented.

The Embattled APB

From 1965 to 1967, further criticisms of the board appeared in the press. The "high-profile" period for the accounting profession had arrived. The diversity of accounting practices was discussed in *Barron's, Business Week, Dun's Review, Forbes, Fortune,* the *New York Times,* and the *Wall Street Journal.* Despite the public controversy, the APB compiled an impressive list of accomplishments.

During this period, the APB issued seven opinions, including at least three that were noteworthy. Accounting for the employer's cost of pension plans successfully utilized the desired approach embodied in the charter. ARS 8, *Accounting for the Cost of Pension Plans,* by Ernest L. Hicks, reviewed the arguments for and against various accounting alternatives and the practical problems of each. APB Opinion No. 8 used this research study as a source document. Not only did APB Opinion No. 8 represent the first real application of the two-pronged approach, but it also received unanimous approval from the board.

Also adopted unanimously by the board was APB Opinion No. 9, which dealt with the areas of extraordinary items and earnings per share. This opinion eliminated the wide diversity in existing practices for handling extraordinary items. Also, it approved the all-inclusive concept of the income statement.

In another controversial area, income tax allocation, the dual approach was again employed. ARS 9, *Interperiod Allocation of Corporate Income Taxes,* by Homer Black, was used as a source of information in the deliberations of the board. Although controversial, APB Opinion No. 11, which required comprehensive income tax allocation, did significantly curtail alternative procedures in practice. Thus, by the close of 1967, the board had finally demonstrated it could function in a meaningful manner.

ARS 7 and APB Statement 4

When the accounting profession failed to accept ARS 1 and ARS 3, another research study was commissioned. Its objectives were to discuss the basic concepts of accounting principles and summarize existing acceptable principles and practices. For this purpose, ARS 7, *Inventory of Generally Accepted Accounting Principles for Business Enterprises,* by Paul Grady, was successful. Although the study was well received by the profession, it fell short of the original task assigned to the board in 1958 by the Special Committee on Research Program. Grady codified existing pronouncements (over 50% of the study was reproductions of pronouncements) and then tried to derive the profession's existing structure of principles. The study blended inductive and deductive approaches because it took existing pronouncements and then attempted to deduce accounting principles from the body of accepted pronouncements.

Possibly because of the failure of the APB to accomplish its original task on accounting principles, the Special Committee of the Accounting Principles Board recommended that "at the earliest possible time" the board should set forth the purposes and limitations of financial statements, determine acceptable accounting principles, and define "generally accepted accounting principles."[22]

To accomplish this task, a committee worked for five years to produce APB Statement 4, *Basic Concepts and Accounting Principles Underlying Financial Statements of Business Enterprises,* which was approved by the APB in 1970. The statement had two purposes:

(1) to provide a foundation for evaluating present accounting practices, for assisting in solving accounting problems, and for guiding the future development of financial accounting; and (2) to enhance understanding of the purposes of financial accounting, the nature of the process and the forces which shape it, and the potential and limitations of financial statements in providing needed information.[23]

APB Statement 4 covered many of the same topics included in ARS 7, but it went beyond that study (as Chapter 6 will show). The statement had no authoritative standing, however. Being an APB *statement,* as opposed to an *opinion,* "it is binding on no one for any purpose whatsoever."[24] Thus, the APB failed in its original charge to set forth the basic postulates and broad principles of accounting, at least in any binding and coherent manner.

Continuing Criticism

Criticism of the standard-setting process continued and was dual in nature: (a) exposure for tentative APB opinions was too limited and occurred too late in the process and (b) the problems with business combinations showed the standard-setting process was too long and subject to too many outside pressures that were not appropriately channeled into the formulation process.

In response to considerable criticism of the exposure process, the APB initiated several important changes that have been carried forward to the Financial Accounting Standards Board (FASB). It introduced public hearings in 1971 and circulated discussion memorandums to interested parties several months prior to the drafting of proposed opinions. These memoranda discussed all aspects of the particular accounting problem and invited interested parties to send written comments as well as to voice their views at the public hearing. After the public hearing, outlines of the proposed opinion were distributed to interested parties for "mini-exposure" to determine initial reaction to the proposed opinion. Following that stage, an official exposure draft of the proposed opinion was widely distributed throughout the profession and comments were requested. Ultimately, the opinion required at least a two-thirds favorable vote of the board to be issued. The broadened exposure process prior to issuance of an accounting standard allowed interested parties to be involved in the standard-setting process and tended to alleviate criticism, other than that of timeliness, of the APB.

The controversy over business combinations and goodwill was the most time consuming and extensively discussed problem the APB faced. In 1963, it published ARS 5, *A Critical Study of Accounting for Business Combinations,* by Arthur Wyatt; ARS 10, *Accounting for Goodwill,* by George Catlett and Norman Olson, appeared in the latter part of 1968. Both of these studies reached conclusions that were at variance with existing accounting principles. ARS 5 concluded that pooling-of-interests accounting should be discontinued and that goodwill may have two components—one with limited life requiring periodic amortization, the other with unlimited life to be carried forward indefinitely to future periods. ARS 10 concluded that goodwill does not qualify as an asset and should be immediately subtracted from stockholders' equity upon completion of the combination.

Business combinations and goodwill received more publicity and discussion than any other subject taken up by the APB. News publications such as *Time* and *Newsweek* had several articles on the subject. Three congressional committees and the Federal Trade Commission (FTC), as well as the SEC, concerned themselves with the merger accounting problem.[25]

A brief review of the various drafts of the proposed opinion on business combinations and goodwill indicates the difficulty in establishing accounting principles on this subject. The initial draft opinion, in July 1969, proposed that pooling of interests should be eliminated and goodwill should be amortized over a period no longer than 40 years. In February 1970, another draft opinion allowed pooling of interests when a 3-to-1 size test was met and also required amortization of goodwill over a maximum of 40 years. The APB was unable to obtain a two-thirds majority on the draft. Finally, in June 1970, a two-thirds majority agreed to allow pooling of interests with a 9-to-1 size test and goodwill amortization restricted to the 40-year maximum. However, when the APB met again in July, one member changed his vote. Thus, the board was again at an impasse. Finally, the business combination and goodwill subjects were split into two opinions: APB Opinion No. 16 on business combinations, eliminating the size test for a pooling of interests, passed 12 to 6; APB Opinion No. 17 on goodwill, requiring amortization over a maximum of 40 years, passed 13 to 5.

The difficulty of arriving at definitive standards of accounting for business combinations and goodwill was certainly in part responsible for the decision to begin a comprehensive review of the procedures for establishing accounting principles. In April 1971, the AICPA formed two special study groups. One group, The Study Group on Establishment of Accounting Principles, was chaired by Francis M. Wheat, a former SEC commissioner and a long-time critic of the accounting profession. The second group, The Study Group on the Objectives of Financial Statements, was chaired by Robert M. Trueblood, a prominent CPA and managing partner of Touche Ross & Co.

The Wheat and Trueblood Committee Reports

The Wheat Committee completed its report in March 1972. It called for significant changes in the establishment of financial accounting standards. The report made the following recommendations:

The establishment of a Financial Accounting Foundation. This foundation would have 9 trustees whose principal duties would be to appoint members of the FASB and raise funds for its operation.

The establishment of the FASB. The Board would have seven full-time members and would establish standards of financial reporting.

The establishment of the Financial Accounting Standards Advisory Council. This Council, with 20 members, would consult with the FASB for establishing priorities and task forces as well as reacting to proposed standards.[26]

The AICPA's council accepted the recommendations in June 1972; the FASB became a reality on July 1, 1973.

The Trueblood Committee (also called the Study Group) did not complete its report until October 1973, after the formation of the FASB. The report identified several objectives of financial statements but did not make any suggestions regarding implementation. It concluded with the following statement:

The Study Group concludes that the objectives developed in this report can be looked upon as attainable in stages within a reasonable time. Selecting the appropriate course of action for gaining acceptance of these objectives is not within the purview of the Study Group. However, the Study Group urges that its conclusions be considered as an initial step in developing objectives important for the ongoing refinement and improvement of accounting standards and practices.[27]

The FASB subsequently considered the Trueblood Committee's report in its conceptual framework project.

The FASB: An Overview

The charge to the newly formed FASB was different in one important respect from that given to the APB in 1959. Whereas the APB was to work toward standard setting with a two-pronged approach, the new FASB, although it had a research division, was to establish standards of financial accounting and reporting in the most efficient and complete manner possible. Thus, the FASB was not required to stipulate the postulates and principles of accounting as an underlying framework. Perhaps a trade-off between "efficiency" and "completeness" was intended. Ironically, FASB Statements are more thoroughly researched than prior standards of either the

CAP or the APB. The FASB also launched the conceptual framework project, a major attempt to provide a "constitution" for the standard-setting function.

Mechanics of Operations

The structure for establishing financial accounting standards has been modified somewhat since the FASB's founding in 1973. The modifications were the result of recommendations made by the Structure Committee of the Financial Accounting Foundation (FAF) in 1977. Exhibit 3.1 diagrams the organizational structure and its relationship to its constituency.

The FAF's Board of Trustees consists of 16 members, 11 members nominated by eight organizations: the AAA, AICPA, CFA Institute, Financial Executives International (FEI), Government Finance Officers Association, Institute of Management Accountants (IMA), Securities Industry Association, and National Association of State Auditors, Comptrollers and Treasurers. An additional five members come from at-large nominations. The Trustees approve all member additions and are responsible for oversight, administration, and finances of the FASB and the Governmental Accounting Standards Board (GASB).

The FASB includes seven members, each serving five-year terms. Any individual member can serve a maximum of two terms. During their terms of office, board members must maintain complete independence. This applies not only to other employment arrangements (past, present, or future) but also to investments. "There must be no conflict, real or apparent, between the members' private interest and the public interest."[28] The background requirement for board members is simply knowledge of accounting, finance, and business and concern for the public interest. In March 1979, for the first time the Board had a majority of members with backgrounds primarily in areas other than public accounting.

The Financial Accounting Standards Advisory Council (FASAC) is instrumental in the establishment of financial accounting standards. It is also appointed by the Board of Trustees. The FASAC advises the FASB on its operating and project plans, agenda and priorities, and appointment of task forces, as well as on all major or technical issues.

The standard-setting procedure starts with the identification of a problem. A task force is then formed to explore all aspects of the problem. It produces a discussion memorandum identifying all issues and possible solutions, which is widely circulated to interested parties. The FASB then convenes a public hearing during which interested parties may make their views known to the Board. Subsequently, an exposure draft of the final standard is issued and written comments are requested. After consideration of written comments, either another exposure draft is issued (if significant changes are deemed necessary) or the Board takes a final vote. A normal 4-to-3 majority vote is required for passing new standards.

However, do not assume that the FASB standard-setting procedure is cut-and-dried. Johnson and Swieringa have given an extensively detailed discussion of the process involving SFAS No. 115 on accounting for marketable securities.[29] To say the least, the process was highly political. Adding to the complexity was the intertwining of the marketable securities project with the financial instruments project (marketable securities are a subset of financial instruments). Johnson and Swieringa traced the sequence of events, which went from 1986 through issuance of the standard in 1993 to the issuance of the implementation guide in 1995, a total of 111 events.[30] Putting it further into perspective, the FASB devoted 11,000 staff hours to the

Exhibit 3.1   The Structure of the Board's Constituency Relationships

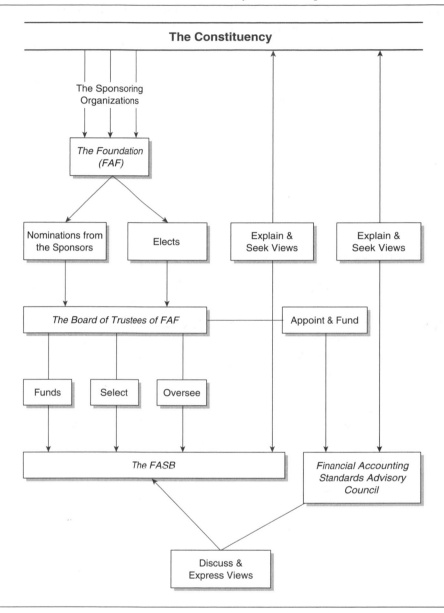

project between 1990 and 1994. Not only were the FASB and FASAC involved but also the SEC, the Federal Home Loan Bank Board, and the chairman of the Board of Governors of the Federal Reserve System, as well as several other government agencies. Among the issues involved were not only how marketable securities should be accounted for but also the scope of the securities that would be covered by the standard, and whether financial institutions would be subject to the standard. Hence, a highly charged political atmosphere surrounded the project.

Kinney made some very trenchant observations about the process involving SFAS No. 115.[31] First, the FASB process developed in the 1970s may not be capable of dealing with the more complex environment of the 1990s and beyond.[32] For example, financial markets are now globalized, communication is virtually instantaneous, deregulation erodes differences between financial institutions making them more competitive, and information technology makes it possible to assess risks of both financial assets and financial liabilities leading to better possibilities of determining current valuations on both sides of the balance sheet. Second, the more complex environment may well have a detrimental effect on the typical financial statements generated under GAAP.[33] For example, some nonfinancial measures may correlate more closely with security prices than financial measures such as income. Third is the issue of how adaptable the conceptual framework (Chapter 7) is to newly emerging types of businesses and business situations and transactions (how this document might be amended and extended may become an important consideration in the relatively near future).[34]

Assessment of the FASB

The FASB has been subject to extensive scrutiny over the years. Even though the SEC has allowed the accounting profession to set standards, the fact remains that the SEC has the legal authority to establish standards whenever it chooses. Both the CAP and the APB made important progress in eliminating poor accounting practices and in standardizing existing practices, but they were not successful in developing a theoretical basis for standard setting. In the early years of the FASB's existence, it too was criticized. Some said it issued too many pronouncements, while others complained that not enough had been issued. Some critics said the Board was too conceptual in its approach, but others said it had ignored research and accounting theory. Furthermore, some felt the FASB did not have a significant effect on financial reporting, although others maintained that changes had been too radical.

With all this in mind, a comprehensive review of the Board was undertaken by the Structure Committee of the Board of Trustees of the FAF in late 1976. The basic charge of the committee was to "make recommendations to the Board of Trustees regarding any changes in the basic structure of the FASB and the FASAC."[35] The committee's report included 17 major findings. It found overwhelming support for maintaining the standard-setting process in the private sector and for the FASB as the right body to discharge that responsibility. Regarding the standard-setting process, the committee found that:

1. The process of establishing a new accounting standard requires careful consideration of the views of all elements of the constituency.

2. The process requires research to assess the possible effects of a proposed standard.

3. A successful standard cannot be imposed by the standard setter; it must be assimilated by the constituency.

4. The assimilation process may require an educational effort to demonstrate the overall value of the proposed new standard.[36]

Since 1977, as a result of the various findings of the Structure Committee, significant changes have occurred. Basically, these changes have increased the involvement of the constituency. Meetings of the FASB, FASAC, the Foundation, and task forces are now open to the public. Additionally, the Board publishes a weekly news bulletin, *Action Alert*.[37] Furthermore, the Board has made greater use of available resources outside the FASB staff as well as of task forces. As a result, the Board has become sensitive to the potential economic consequences of proposed standards prior to issuance.

The FASB has been quite productive when compared with its predecessors. It has issued more than 159 Statements of Financial Accounting Standards as of June 2007, as well as numerous interpretations and technical bulletins. If a philosophical trend can be inferred from these standards, it would be that there is a move to "clean up the balance sheet." This has resulted in a more conservative balance sheet with immediate, as opposed to delayed, recognition of events on the income statement. In addition, between 1978 and 1985 the FASB issued six Statements of Financial Accounting Concepts and a seventh in 2000. These statements constitute the *conceptual framework*, a document that is intended to provide a theoretical underpinning for the assessment of accounting standards and practices. (Chapter 7 takes a critical look at the conceptual framework.) Exhibit 3.2 summarizes some areas of difference among the FASB, the APB, and the CAP. The FASB, in our opinion, has been more successful than its two predecessors. Nevertheless, despite its accomplishments, the FASB once again came under severe attack.

Evolution of FASB's Power

Several organizations have attempted to restrict or constrict the FASB's legislative powers. When responsibility for standard setting was transferred from the AICPA to the FASB in 1972, the AICPA established the Accounting Standards Executive Committee (AcSEC) to perform a liaison function between the AICPA and the FASB. This committee responds to discussion memoranda, invitations to comment, and exposure drafts and prepares issue papers for the FASB that can add a subject to the Board's agenda.

AcSEC issues two types of pronouncements: Statements of Position (SOP) and Industry Accounting Guides (Guides). Generally, SOPs and Guides deal with more narrow, specialized subjects than FASB Statements.

In Statement of Auditing Standards No. 69 issued in 1992, SOPs and Guides are considered to be just below FASB Statements, APB Opinions, and extant CAP research bulletins in the hierarchy of generally accepted accounting principles (GAAP) for nongovernmental entities.

Unlike FASB Statements, neither the SOPs nor the Guides are considered mandatory accounting standards under the AICPA's Rule 203 of the Rules of Conduct, but the FASB has embarked on a program (see Statement of Financial Accounting Standards [SFAS] No. 32) to incorporate the majority of the SOPs and Guides in FASB Statements. SOPs, however, are becoming broader in scope and may affect many industries. For example, SOP 92-3, *Accounting for Foreclosed Assets,* affects all reporting entities except those already using current value for foreclosed assets.[38] In addition to its pronouncements, AcSEC periodically prepares *Issue Papers* covering various accounting practice problems that frequently cause a

Exhibit 3.2   Comparing the CAP, APB, and FASB

Characteristic	CAP	APB	FASB
Organizational independence	Part of AICPA	Part of AICPA	Separate from AICPA; six sponsoring organizations
Independence of members	Other full-time employer	Other full-time employer	Full-time employee of FASB, usually CPA firm
Breadth of membership	Must be CPA	Must be CPA	Need not be CPA; members have come from public accounting, government, industry, securities firms, academe
Due process	Little if any	Very limited, although it became broader toward the end of its existence	More extensive and brought into the process (open hearing and replies to exposure draft for example); can lead to problems of "democratic paralysis" (see Chapter 4)
Theoretical document supporting standards	Not attempted	Postulates and principles failed; neither ARS No. 7 nor APB Statement No. 4 were particularly successful	Conceptual framework completed more successful than APB efforts
Use of research	Very limited	Main use was in ARSs	More extensive than its predecessors, discussion memorandums search the literature; the FASB has commissioned several research studies

subject to be added to the FASB's agenda. Among the standards that have come up through the AcSEC route are SFAS No. 61, *Accounting for Title Plant;* SFAS No. 63, *Financial Reporting by Broadcasters;* and SFAS No. 65, *Accounting for Certain Mortgage Banking Activities.* AcSEC work that has not yet become embodied in FASB Standards is designated "preferable accounting principles" in SFAS Nos. 32 and 83, which justify accounting changes in accordance with APB Opinion No. 20.

If fairly narrow industry-type standards have become the province of AcSEC, another group—the Emerging Issues Task Force (EITF)—created in 1984, has concerned itself with highly technical issues, such as financial instruments, which may affect firms in virtually every industry. The EITF has also been concerned with specialized problems of financial institutions. Members of this group consist of senior technical partners of the major firms and the chief accountant of the SEC. The EITF does not have any formal authority, but its consensus views may well be de facto GAAP.[39] One fear is that the EITF may establish excessively complicated and complex standards such as those of the Internal Revenue Code, which might result in rule-dominated practice that could erode professionalism.[40]

A further challenge to the FASB's standard-setting powers has come from the Government Accounting Standards Board (GASB), created by the FAF in 1984 to deal with municipal accounting. Unfortunately, its responsibilities overlap with those of the FASB, resulting in an old-fashioned turf battle. Separately issued general-purpose financial statements of such entities as hospitals, colleges and universities, and pension plans are supposed to use FASB standards except where the GASB has issued a particular standard covering a specific type of entity or a precise economic practice or activity. As a result of this overlap, GASB standards tend to "muscle out" particular FASB standards for governmental entities. The situation became intolerable for both private and public industries that had previously used FASB standards and preferred to continue to do so. However, some public-sector organizations wanted the dispute settled on the basis of public versus private ownership and threatened to withdraw support of FAF if it was not.[41] A tentative compromise has largely agreed to this system. In addition, separately issued general-purpose financial statements of colleges and universities, health care organizations, and gas and electric utilities are to be subject to FASB standards unless governing boards of public-sector organizations in these categories decide to be governed by GASB standards.[42]

The AcSEC and EITF were established to solve the problems of particular industries as well as to address narrow technical issues; the GASB establishes a different jurisdiction. Two prominent business organizations aimed a much more direct blow at the essence of the way the FASB operates. The FASB, as a separate organization with its own staff and board members, could be neutral in a way that its predecessors could not be. But in July 1985, the Financial Executives International (FEI) and the Accounting Principles Task Force of the Business Roundtable (an organization comprising the chief executive officers of most major American corporations) urged a stronger business representation on the FASB itself and among the trustees of the FAF. The major complaints seemed to be the cost of preparing standards (e.g., SFAS No. 96) and the difficulty of understanding them (e.g., SFAS Nos. 33 and 96). Additional FASB members (one to two members) now come from business under the Board's present composition, although the business "takeover" attempt appears to have been effectively parried. Nevertheless, the concerns of business may not have fallen on deaf ears. Indeed, in 1990 the FAF changed the vote required to pass a standard from 4-to-3 back to 5-to-2. This may have been a sign of improvement in FASB operations. If a standard can pass by only a 4-3 margin (as has frequently been the case), it may well indicate that part or all of the standard should be carefully reconsidered.[43] Nevertheless, in 2002 the FASB once again switched back to a 4-to-3 required margin for passing standards.[44]

However, make no mistake about it: The FASB has been under strong attack. The pressure was intensified by the FASB's attempt to attribute an expense to incentive-type stock options, which has, in particular, upset small growth-oriented, high-technology firms. However, the FASB eventually prevailed in this argument with the passage of SFAS Nos. 123 and 123R.

We do not think that the FASB will be meet extinction. However, the SEC has clearly increased its influence by providing the funding. The next step would be a public-sector takeover by the SEC or a body designated by and subservient to the SEC. The FASB will quite likely survive, but the effects of continuing accounting scandals may well limit its independence, morphing it into a quasi-governmental agency.

While not related to these challenges to the FASB, it is worthwhile to note what causes public firms to oppose and lobby against proposed standards. Elbannan and McKinley discuss factors that lead firms to lobby against proposed FASB standards while still operating within the prescribed rules.[45] Their framework is complementary to agency theory studies that stress opposition arising mainly from financial and economic consequences. They posit that standards creating perceived uncertainty in the prediction of future variables and those producing high information processing costs incite the corporate resistance efforts.

Congressional Investigations

We have described challenges to the FASB's legislative authority that have arisen from dissatisfaction with the standard-setting process. Another source of pressure has been the congressional investigation of the auditing profession and the standard-setting apparatus. Two congressional subcommittee reports circulated in late 1976 and early 1977 were highly critical. Congressman John E. Moss was chairman of a subcommittee whose report was particularly critical of the diversity of existing generally accepted accounting principles. The report of the Senate subcommittee, chaired by Senator Lee Metcalf, was directed toward the institutional structure of financial accounting. The report was critical of the concentration of power by the FASB, SEC, AICPA, and the "Big Eight" (now "Big Four") CPA firms. In essence, the report called for government regulation of the entire profession. Following public hearings, the report was modified significantly to allow standard setting to remain in the private sector.

Many organizational changes have occurred because of these congressional investigations. The principal purpose of these changes has been to:

strengthen the auditing process and the independence of auditors,

assure compliance with high standards of performance not only of individual CPAs but also of CPA firms under an effective self-regulatory system,

assure greater participation by public representatives in the affairs of the profession,

establish distinctions between public and smaller nonpublic companies for purposes of applying technical standards, and

enhance the overall effectiveness of the profession in serving public needs.[46]

Furthermore, the SEC must now include a specific section on the accounting profession in its annual report to Congress. In general, since the time of the congressional investigations, these reports have been complimentary to the profession in terms of standard setting and self-governance. The allegation of undue influence over the FASB by the then Big Eight public accounting firms has yet to be substantiated by concrete evidence.[47] Brown's research did, however, show a similarity of responses by seven of the Big Eight firms to 12 discussion memoranda of the FASB appearing between October 1974 and December 1977.[48]

Such similarity assuredly shows a general agreement on issues, but absolutely nothing more in terms of the possibility of collusion. It is interesting to note that the resulting FASB Statements appeared to be evenly split in terms of "closeness" between the attestors (the then Big Eight firms) and the preparers of financial statements (as evidenced by corporate respondents and interest groups).[49]

Congress continued to scrutinize the public accounting profession. A subcommittee of the House of Representatives, chaired by Congressman John D. Dingell, was concerned with the laxity of auditors in detecting and disclosing fraud. Because of this concern, the National Commission on Fraudulent Financial Reporting (Treadway Commission) was formed in 1985. Its recommendations were to increase the auditor's responsibility for detecting fraudulent financial reporting. The resulting Private Securities Litigation Reform Act of 1995 required that the audit include procedures designed to give reasonable assurance that illegal acts that would materially affect financial statements will be detected.[50]

If illegal acts are detected and they are consequential, the auditors must report this to the audit committee. If corrective action is not taken and the board of directors does not inform the SEC, the auditor should report the situation to the SEC and consider resigning from the engagement.[51] Liability, however, may still exist for the auditor if the quantity or timeliness of information disclosure is inadequate.

Despite increasing regulation of the auditor's responsibilities, within CPA firms the importance of the audit function relative to the management consulting function steadily declined throughout the 1990s. As business failures increased, the SEC began questioning whether consulting fees were compromising the auditor's independence and adversely affecting the public's interests. The profession strongly resisted. As Shaun O'Malley, retired chairman of the former Price Waterhouse LLP summed it up, "There's never been a case where an audit failure in any way related to nonaudit services."[52] Of course, subsequent corporate accounting scandals and SEC-mandated public disclosure of fees paid to the firm's auditor showed the potential financial risk to the auditor if it were to say no to its client. The idea that the audit firm has the integrity to stand its ground even though it may be biting the hand that feeds it is admirable. However, in practice, the potential loss of revenues totaling millions of dollars evidently encouraged a rationalization that aggressive, sometimes fraudulent, accounting was not of sufficient materiality to warrant a less than unqualified audit opinion. Following a series of high-profile scandals (e.g., Enron, Arthur Andersen, WorldCom, Tyco), Congress responded with near emergency-like legislation producing one of the most significant reform packages since FDR's New Deal—the Sarbanes-Oxley Public Company Accounting Reform and Investor Protection Act of 2002 (SOX).[53]

Sarbanes-Oxley Act (SOX)

SOX established the Public Company Accounting Oversight Board (PCAOB), a private-sector regulatory body overseen by the SEC. The PCAOB is responsible for registering public accounting firms, setting audit standards, inspecting registered accounting firms, and enforcing compliance with SOX. The AICPA's Auditing Standards Board (ASB) no longer sets the standards for auditing, attestation, and quality control. The PCAOB must consult with professional groups such as the ASB, but it has full authority to establish the standard as it deems necessary. SOX replaced peer review with inspection by the PCAOB, another step away from self-management by the profession. These changes prompted the AICPA to rethink its role in this new regulatory structure.

In addition to establishment of the PCAOB, SOX more clearly defined auditor independence, record retention requirements, audit committee roles in corporate governance, CEO and CFO certifications of financial statements, and penalties for noncompliance.[54] This basket of far-reaching regulations was intended to restore public confidence lost in the 1990s and early 2000s owing to financial abuse stemming from major scandals.

The emphasis on short-term profitability led to dysfunctional behaviors by management and an eventual blemish on the accounting profession. In addition to the emphasis on short-term profitability, the audit committees and corporate boards of directors—particularly compensation committees—failed to assert themselves.

On the surface, SOX appears to affect the auditing profession alone; statutory authority for setting financial accounting and reporting standards for publicly held companies remained with the SEC. However, for 30+ years, the SEC had relegated these responsibilities to the FASB, a private sector, independent organization. A subtle but important SOX-related change concerns the FASB budget; the majority of its funding ($20+ million per year) originally came from private-sector contributions. SOX now requires that FASB funding be like PCAOB funding, originating from fee assessments on public companies and accountants, not contributions. The change increases FASB's independence from the constituents it serves but increases its dependence on the SEC for approval of its budget. For the past two decades, the accounting profession and the government have strongly advocated the importance of the FASB as an independent regulatory body. However, current rhetoric and laws are inconsistent. For better or worse, the FASB lost a significant amount of independence from the SEC with SOX's passage. Now, the SEC controls the FASB's funding via the budgetary process. As a result of SOX, the FASB can no longer assess operating fees from corporations and public accountants.[55]

SOX implementation became the immediate focus of public companies and CPA firms. An unrelenting stream of financial restatements and news of corporate malfeasance initially muffled frustrations of actually implementing the new law. Absent guidance on materiality guidelines, arguments arose questioning the cost benefit of Section 404, the requirement that public companies review and assess their internal controls. The compliance costs for small companies raised the question, "Can one size fit all?" The presumed exodus of initial public offerings (IPO) from the U.S. to foreign exchanges was argued to result from the overly burdensome regulatory requirements of SOX. Conversions of public companies to private ownership further bolstered the argument that the law had gone too far. Rather than viewing SOX-related compliance costs as an investment to bring previously underfunded internal controls up-to-date, business clamored to alter the law despite the voices of former prominent regulators, Paul Volcker (chairman of the Federal Reserve, 1979–1987) and Arthur Levitt, Jr. (SEC chairman, 1993–2001).[56] Eventually, regulators yielded to an easing of the rules, rationalizing that monetary savings warranted the revision.[57] Despite the onerous costs presumably brought about by SOX, Thomson Financial finds American securities markets robust relative to initial public offerings by foreign firms.[58]

International Convergence

Currently, a single set of accounting standards does not exist in all capital markets; U.S. GAAP is not universally accepted in all countries. The term "harmonization" was used for many years to reflect this international objective, but "convergence" is the currently accepted term in use. In 2002, the International Accounting Standards Board (IASB) and FASB formally announced their intention to pursue "convergence." This will be covered in Chapter 10.

The Liability Crisis in Public Accounting

The liability crisis in public accounting has been an extremely important problem facing the entire profession. There has been tremendous pressure to turn the audit into a fraud-detection mechanism with the situation mentioned earlier of requiring the auditor to report to the SEC, in the case of publicly traded companies, if management and the board of directors do not act appropriately. Certainly, auditors are entitled to some share of the blame for cutting corners on audits in attempts to reduce costs as a result of "lowball" bidding on audits as well as supervisory inefficiencies and poor judgment. Schuetze has also leveled some charges against the standard-setting function in terms of ambiguity concerning revenue recognition rules and overly complex definitions of accounting elements.[59]

Doubtless, both auditors and standard setters share some part of the blame.[60] Nevertheless, there have been some inherent problems in the legal system, combined with the fact that auditors are viewed as having very "deep pockets," that have led to some reform in the most important part of the previously mentioned Private Securities Litigation Reform Act (PSLRA) of 1995.

Prior to PSLRA, auditors in both federal and state cases were subject to joint and several liability for damages suffered by third parties who relied on the financial statements of firms attested to by CPAs. Joint and several liability means that one party can be stuck with more than its proportionate share of the judgment caused by its actions. Narayanan gives the following graphic example of joint and several liability in which a girl was hurt in a bumper car accident at Walt Disney World.

	Responsibility	*Damages Paid*
Plaintiff (girl)	14%	
Boyfriend	85%	
Walt Disney World	1%	86%

The boyfriend had no financial resources, so Walt Disney World was assigned 86% of the damages even though its responsibility was determined to be only 1% of the blame for the accident.[61]

This part of the PSLRA has put what appears to be a brake on federal court actions against auditors because of limitations set against the use of joint and several liability. Joint and several liability is not applicable unless the defendant "knowingly violates security laws."[62] In its place would be proportionate liability, which restricts liability to each defendant's proportionate share of the damages based on the judge's or jury's assessment of the individual's share of the damages.

One possible result of the PSLRA is that litigation against auditors may be shifted from federal courts to state courts.[63] However, some states are putting their own limitations on joint and several liability and moving toward proportionate liability except where the defendants knowingly engaged in fraud.[64]

Current Role of the AICPA

The AICPA no longer has exclusive authority in the private sector for promulgating auditing rules. SOX has relegated the Auditing Standards Board to a role of advising the PCAOB before it sets standards for auditing, attestation, and quality control. As audit firms became advocates for their clients rather than protecting public interests, and the AICPA campaigned for a broader certification that deemphasized a CPA's auditing responsibilities, it relinquished its role as police officer for self-regulation. Post-SOX, the AICPA has been working to regain the public confidence lost during corporate debacles of the 2000s and attempting to find its niche within the new accounting standard-setting and reporting structure.

The AICPA has clearly lost power over the years with standard setting relegated to the FASB and PCAOB. One way to regain some power would be for the AICPA to become the standard-setting body for smaller firms (referred to as "baby GAAP" in private companies). There has been some question whether this differentiation should be small firms versus large firms or public versus privately owned firms. In either event, such a division would add complexity to the standard-setting process, especially if two standards-setting bodies were involved. Consequently, any distinction between small and large firms to avoid costs or complexity should be done exclusively by the FASB, the official standard-setting body. However, a recent collaboration between the AICPA and FASB proposes that the AICPA participate in a separate standard-setting process for private companies.[65] It is puzzling as to why the FASB would want to give up this standard-setting authority. Even more troubling is the fact that the AICPA would be the representative of the privately owned firms. This proposal appears to be a very dangerous one. It is not a matter of different requirements for private versus public firms but rather the advocacy position that privately held firms would gain.

The AICPA still has an important role to curb what has been called "shopping for accounting principles," which involves increasing competition among auditing firms to land clients. As the phrase implies, greater numbers of clients have tried to find an auditor who will either lowball its bid to secure a client or will go along with a questionable accounting method that the client desires to employ.[66]

The opinion-shopping problem may have, in fact, led auditors to support totally outlandish positions, according to the former chief accountant of the SEC.[67] Among other examples mentioned, he discusses an airline that overhauled aircraft engines and mainframes. The costs were to be amortized over the future benefit period. However, the airline, aided and abetted by its auditor (two of them, in fact), attempted to classify the portion of the deferred charge that would be written off over the following year as a current asset. In light of these types of problems, the AICPA has been attempting to strengthen professional standards of conduct and rules of performance and behavior.[68] Hence, the AICPA formed the AICPA Special Committee on Financial Reporting in 1991 with the charge of recommending what additional information management should provide for users and the extent to which auditors should report on this information.

Current Role of the SEC

The SEC has statutory authority to set accounting standards for public companies. It has, as a matter of policy, been supportive of private-sector standard setting in general and the FASB in particular.[69] In ASR 150, the SEC stated that financial statements based on accounting practices for which there is no substantial authoritative support will be presumed to be misleading. For the first time, accounting standards set in the private sector were formally recognized as having substantial authoritative support. Prior to ASR 150, this support was informal.

The SEC and FASB have had differences of opinion; generally, however, their relationship has been cordial and mutually beneficial. There have been instances in which the SEC pressed for greater attention to specific issues, but the FASB argued that resource constraints prevented it from addressing the SEC's concerns. The new fees-imposed funding required by SOX may provide the necessary resources to adequately address "hot issues" and bring the two organizations closer together. Also, given the public's growing distrust of financial statements, especially in light of the number of restatements, the FASB will likely become more conservative and more sensitive to the public's interest. So, the likelihood of significant differences between the SEC and the FASB is relatively small. Given that the SEC now funds the FASB, the FASB has become more of a quasi-governmental body than a purely private sector one. Furthermore, the SEC is putting pressure on the FASB to exert more control over appointment of new members of the Board, including the opportunity to nominate new members. Whether this leads to increased politicization of the standard-setting process, only time will tell.

Another aspect of SEC operations involves electronic filing of financial data with the SEC via "EDGAR" (Electronic Data Gathering, Analysis, and Retrieval System). Most public domestic companies began filing electronically in 1996. While some problems have occurred, the program appears to be quite successful. A related development involves corporate reporting via the Internet. Research has found wide variation in timeliness of corporate information presented on the Internet.[70] Some enterprises provide up-to-date information such as monthly sales, whereas others may present outdated information such as two-year-old financial statements. Financial reporting on the Internet will surely become much more important in coming years.

Other Groups

At least three professional associations other than the AICPA have an interest in the standard-setting process in the United States today: the AAA, the FEI, and the IMA.

The AAA has been concerned with accounting standards for many years. From 1936 to 1957, it sponsored several statements on accounting principles. In 1966, a committee appointed two years earlier to develop an integrated statement on basic accounting theory published *A Statement of Basic Accounting Theory*. Parts of this statement subsequently appeared in APB Statement 4, which has become significant in the development of the FASB's conceptual framework project. An AAA committee issued a report calling for a special commission to study the organizational structure for establishing accounting standards at about the same time the Wheat Committee was being formed. Owing to the formation of the Wheat Committee, the AAA never formed its commission, but the initial committee report reflects the AAA's obvious interest in the development of accounting standards. Zeff has observed that the AAA has played a more important role than is generally acknowledged at crucial turning points in the standard-setting process.[71] Today, the AAA sponsors various research studies on accounting problems. These *Studies in Accounting Research*, of which there have been 33 to date, represent a significant contribution to the development of accounting theory. AAA subcommittees also respond to FASB exposure drafts.

The FEI's technical committee on corporate reporting reviews all FASB discussion memorandums and exposure drafts and develops the official FEI position, which is communicated to the FASB. FEI also frequently participates in FASB public hearings. In addition, the FEI formed the Financial Executives Research Foundation specifically to fund various research projects in accounting and related areas. Numerous projects have been published to date.

Since its formation in 1919, the IMA has conducted research and published reports in the cost and managerial accounting areas. Recently, it has become more interested in external financial reporting and, as a consequence, formed its Committee on Accounting and Reporting Concepts. This committee responds to various FASB projects.

In addition to the three professional groups with an interest in accounting standards, an increasingly important organization is the International Accounting Standards Board, which will be examined in greater detail in Chapter 10. The Norwalk Agreement of 2002 formally established plans for the FASB and IASB to pursue convergence of international and U.S. accounting standards. Clearly, the IASB's role in establishing standards is growing.

Summary

We have recounted a brief history of the three financial accounting policy-making bodies that have existed in the United States since 1930. Prior to that year, published accounting information was largely unregulated in this country.

As a result of cooperation between the AICPA and NYSE, work on drafting accounting principles was begun. A major impetus was, of course, the creation of the SEC, which was given the power by Congress to prescribe accounting principles. As a result, the CAP was formed, and most of the responsibility for the policy-making function has remained in the private sector. In its existence, the CAP issued a total of 51 ARBs, the most famous being ARB 43. Toward the close of its existence, the CAP was increasingly criticized because it attempted to solve problems on a piecemeal basis without a coherent, underlying theory.

The APB was conceived with high optimism. Opinions were to be based on in-depth research studies, which, in turn, were to be grounded in a set of underlying postulates and principles: In other words, the deductive approach was to come into flower. Unfortunately, the rejection of ARS 3, the broad principles study, virtually put an end to the formalized deductive approach—despite the publication of the conservative ARS 7, which attempted to extract principles from existing rules. Despite considerable progress on many fronts, the very shaky start of the APB, combined with its own institutional weaknesses and its fumbling of the business combination issue led to the body's demise.

The work of two important committees, one concerned with the organization of a new body and the other with the objectives of financial accounting, preceded the formation of the FASB. Board members were granted much greater independence, and the organization itself was separate from the AICPA. The FASB appears to have weathered a great deal of criticism leveled at it in its early years; however, the SOX Act of 2002 significantly changed how the FASB will operate in the future. Financially independent of accounting firms and corporations, but more closely aligned with the SEC, the FASB's very existence is suspect unless it restores the public's confidence in the accounting profession. Everyone appears to want the FASB to succeed, but the laws are in place to make movement to 100% government regulation relatively simple, if the FASB fails.

The liability crisis in public accounting, a huge problem for the entire profession, may be mitigated by moving from joint and several liability toward proportionate liability. This has largely occurred at the federal level through the Private Securities Litigation Reform Act of 1995, and it is just beginning to be felt in state securities law changes.

QUESTIONS

1. How did the APB pave the way for the FASB?

2. In what ways does the FASB differ most markedly from its two predecessors?

3. What is the weakness of Grady's approach in arriving at principles in ARS 7?

4. Do you think that the nonbinding status of the FASB's Statements of Financial Accounting Concepts (like that of APB Statement 4) is a good idea or not?

5. Discuss the significance of the SEC's ASR 150.

6. What has been the SEC's role in the evolution of the rule-making process? How has that role changed since the passage of SOX?

7. What were the politics that led to the demise of both the CAP and the APB?

8. The FASB's standard-setting procedure is a fairly narrow, cut-and-dried approach to developing accounting standards. Evaluate this statement.

9. Should constituents have input into the FASB decisions, or should the FASB neutrally and independently set standards?

10. Explain how the role and form of research used by the APB and FASB differ.

11. What is the importance of the FAF and FASAC to the success of the FASB?

12. The three attempts at standard setting in the private sector (CAP, APB, and FASB) have all dealt with the need for a theoretical foundation. Why were the CAP and the APB unsuccessful at this endeavor?

13. Can any overall trend be detected in FASB pronouncements? Explain and cite examples to substantiate your opinion.

14. In terms of financial reporting in the future, do you expect greater refinement of measurements appearing in the body of the financial statements or increasing disclosure with less effort directed toward refinement of measurements?

15. How has Sarbanes-Oxley of 2002 affected FASB's jurisdiction and independence?

16. In late 1990s, the "Wyden Amendment" was stricken from the Crime Bill passed by Congress. The amendment would have required reporting by auditors on internal controls. Letters sent by FEI members opposing the amendment were instrumental in its defeat. The AICPA supported the amendment. From an agency theory perspective, why do you think the AICPA supported the amendment and the FEI was against it? Explain.

17. Since the FASB is independent from the AICPA, the latter is no longer concerned with standard setting and related issues. Evaluate this statement.

18. What is the relationship between the National Commission on Fraudulent Financial Reporting and the Private Securities Litigation Reform Act of 1995?

19. What is the difference between joint and several liability and proportionate liability?

CASES, PROBLEMS, AND WRITING ASSIGNMENTS

1. During its long tenure, the CAP produced a total of 51 ARBs. While the CAP was in existence, another committee, the Committee on Terminology of the American Institute of Accountants (the previous name of the AICPA), prepared certain definitions. Assess their definitions of assets and liabilities (see Chapter 11 for the definitions). Do you see any problems with one committee preparing rules and another making definitions?

2. Read Chapter 15 of ARB 43 on unamortized discount, issue cost, and redemption premium on bonds refunded. Why do you think these issues concerned the committee? What were the two

acceptable alternatives for dealing with the costs of any issue? Why would the definition of assets be helpful in analyzing a situation of this type? Are there any other situations that might be somewhat analogous to the bond redemption situation? (ARB 43 should be available in your university's library.)

3. Read "FASB Response to SEC Study on Arrangements with Off-Balance Sheet Implications, Special Purpose Entities, and Transparency of Filings by Issuers" (Feb. 2006). How would you frame the tenor of the FASB's response. To what extent does it agree with the SEC's study?

4. Five so-called broad principles of accounting were prepared by the AICPA's Special Committee on Cooperation with the Stock Exchange and approved by the NYSE's Committee on Stock List in 1932. They were to be followed by all firms listed on the exchange. Subsequently, these principles (along with a sixth item) were codified as Chapter 1 of ARB 43 and are printed here.

   a. Unrealized profit should not be credited to income account of the corporation, either directly or indirectly, through the medium of charging against such unrealized profits amounts that would ordinarily fail to be charged against income account. Profit is deemed to be realized when a sale in the ordinary course of business is effected, unless the circumstances are such that the collection of the sale price is not reasonably assured. An exception to the general rule may be made in respect of inventories in industries (such as the packing-house industry) in which owing to the impossibility of determining costs it is a trade custom to take inventories at net selling prices, which may exceed cost.

   b. Capital surplus, however created, should not be used to relieve the income account of the current or future years of charges that would otherwise fail to be made there against. This rule might be subject to the exception that where, upon reorganization, a reorganized company would be relieved of charges that would require to be made against income if the existing corporation were continued, it might be regarded as permissible to accomplish the same result without reorganization provided the facts were as fully revealed to and the action as formally approved by the shareholders as in reorganization.

   c. Earned surplus of a subsidiary company created prior to acquisition does not form a part of the consolidated earned surplus of the parent company and subsidiaries; nor can any dividend declared out of such surplus properly be credited to the income account of the parent company.

   d. While it is perhaps in some circumstances permissible to show stock of a corporation held in its own treasury as an asset, if adequately disclosed, the dividends on stock so held should not be treated as a credit to the income account of the company.

   e. Notes or accounts receivable due from officers, employees, or affiliated companies must be shown separately and not included under a general heading such as notes receivable or accounts receivable.

   f. If capital stock is issued nominally for the acquisition of property and it appears that at about the same time, and pursuant to a previous agreement or understanding, some portion of the stock so issued is donated to the corporation, it is not permissible to treat the par value of the stock nominally issued for the property as the cost of that property. If stock so donated is subsequently sold, it is not permissible to treat the proceeds as a credit to surplus of the corporation.

Now listed here are two principles from ARS 7 as well as some additional comments. This study was done under the auspices of the APB and was published in 1965.

Principle B-1. In case there are two or more classes of stock, account for the equity capital invested for each and disclose the rights and preferences to dividends and to principal in liquidation.

Principle B-4. Retained earnings should represent the cumulative balance of periodic earnings less dividend distributions in cash, property, or stock, plus or minus gains and losses of such magnitude as not to be properly included in periodic earnings. The entire amount may be presumed to be unrestricted as to dividend distributions unless restrictions are indicated in the financial statements.

This principle is closely parallel to the definition of earned surplus in Accounting Terminology Bulletin No. 1, paragraph 34, which follows:

The balance of net profits, income, gains, and losses of a corporation from the date of incorporation (or from the latest date when a deficit was eliminated in a quasi-reorganization) after deducting distributions therefrom to shareholders and transfers therefrom to capital stock or capital surplus accounts.

Terms such as "principles of accounting" have been used frequently since 1932. Describe what you think the principles might be. Do any of the principles coming from ARB 43, Chapter 1, or ARS 7 qualify as principles as you have construed them? How similar are these two partial groups of principles?

CRITICAL THINKING AND ANALYSIS

1. Why have management consulting operations created problems for the public accounting industry? How has SOX affected these problems?

2. The FASB and AICPA are considering the addition of "baby GAAP" for private companies. Take a position and argue why two GAAPs should or should not exist.

3. What role should the AICPA assume in the possible development of "baby GAAP" standards?

Notes

1. *Bedford (1970, pp. 69–70).*
2. *Storey (1964, pp. 3–8).*
3. *Much of the information for this section was gleaned from Edwards (1978), Zeff (1972), Carey (1969 and 1970), and Previts and Merino (1998).*
4. *See Ray (1960). The questions have arisen again in relation to cost accounting practices by American industry. For an interesting discussion, see Boer (1994).*
5. *Zeff (1972, p. 119).*
6. *American Institute of Accountants (1934, p. 9).*
7. *Storey (1964, p. 12).*
8. *Healy (1938, p. 5).*
9. *SEC (1938, p. 5).*
10. *Zeff (1972, pp. 135–137).*
11. *Ibid. (p. 139).*

12. *SEC (1939, p. 121).*

13. *Kohler (1939, p. 319).*

14. *Storey (1964, p. 5).*

15. *King (1947, p. 25).*

16. *This conflicted with ARB 35, which called for extraordinary items to be in the surplus statement (Statement of Retained Earnings). See Zeff (1972, pp. 157–158).*

17. *Spacek (1957, p. 21).*

18. *AAA (1957, pp. 1–12).*

19. *AICPA (1958, pp. 62–63).*

20. *APB (1962).*

21. *Although the term* substantial authoritative support *is not defined in APB Opinion No. 6, it has developed a meaning over the years that encompasses—in addition to pronouncements of rule-making bodies and the SEC—opinions of regulatory commissions, provided they do not conflict with statements from other sources, recognized textbooks, leading CPAs, and practices that are commonly followed by business. See Grady (1965, p. 16).*

22. *The CPA Letter (1965, p. 3).*

23. *CPA Letter (1970, p. 1).*

24. *Moonitz (1974, p. 22).*

25. *Zeff (1972, p. 213).*

26. *AICPA (1972, pp. 69–82).*

27. *Ibid. (p. 66).*

28. *AICPA (1972, p. 72).*

29. *Johnson and Swieringa (1996). For an explication of how the FASB approaches standard-setting issues, see Reither (1997).*

30. *Ibid. (pp. 172–177).*

31. *Kinney (1996).*

32. *Ibid. (pp. 181–182).*

33. *Ibid. (p. 183).*

34. *Ibid. (p. 184).*

35. *FAF (1977, p. 55).*

36. *Ibid. (p. 18).*

37. *Action Alert is available as an electronic notification service from FASB. Free subscription to the service is available on FASB's Web site: www.fasb.org.*

38. *Rodda (1993, p. 70).*

39. *Wishon (1986, p. 96).*

40. *Dyckman (1988, pp. 26–27).*

41. *Kirk (1989, p. 108).*

42. *Ibid.*

43. *Dopuch and Sunder (1980, p. 19) were unhappy with the change to the 4-to-3 vote. Sunder (1988) saw the problem as bureaucratic pressure on the FASB to produce standards because of the relatively large size of its staff and the scope of its operations, as well as the fact that a sizable portion of its revenues stemmed from the sale of standards, interpretations, and other official documents.*

44. *Pasewark (2002) shows that the 4-to-3 vote, not surprisingly, leads to a passage of more standards in a shorter period of time than the 5-to-2 supermajority.*

45. *Elbannan and McKinley (2006).*

46. *AICPA (1978, p. 15).*

47. *See Meyer (1974), Rockness and Nikolai (1977), McEnroe and Nikolai (1983), and Moody and Flesher (1986).*

48. *Brown (1981, pp. 240–241).*

49. *Ibid. (p. 243). Brown noted (p. 241) that the FASB's position appeared to be closest to the Financial Analysts' Federation, a group representing user interests.*

50. *King and Schwartz (1997, p. 101).*

51. *Ibid. (p. 103).*

52. *Schroeder (2000).*

53. *Miller and Pashkoff (2002).*

54. *Ibid. (p. 36).*

55. *Burns (2003).*

56. *Volcker and Levitt (2004).*

57. *Scannell and Solomon (2006).*

58. *Ball (2007, p. C3).*

59. *Schuetze (1993, p. 88, and 1991, pp. 115–116).*

60. *It should be borne in mind that major public accounting firms act as consultants to law firms engaged in litigation against other major public accounting firms. To some extent, public accounting firms are on both sides of the liability issue, although consultant's fees are far below judgment claims.*

61. *Narayanan (1994, p. 40).*

62. *King and Schwartz (1997, p. 94). There is also a minimum wealth and loss condition in which the defendant would still be joint and severally liable even in the absence of knowingly violating security laws. This occurs if the plaintiff's net worth is less than $200,000 and losses suffered exceed 10% of his or her net worth.*

63. *Cloyd, Frederickson, and Hill (1998).*

64. *Palmrose (1997). Illinois enacted legislation against joint and several liability in negligence cases in which the auditor is responsible for less than 25% of the total damages. In Texas, joint and several liability applies only when the defendant is responsible for more than 50% of the damages.*

65. *Financial Accounting Standards Board (2006).*

66. *Sack (1985).*

67. *Schuetze (1994).*

68. *See Anderson and Ellyson (1986) and Connor (1986).*

69. *For more on the relationship between the SEC and the FASB, see Sprouse (1987).*

70. *Ashbaugh, Johnstone, and Warfield (1999).*

71. *Zeff (1984).*

References

Accounting Principles Board (1962). "Statement by the Accounting Principles Board," *Statement No. 1.* Accounting Principles Board.

American Accounting Association (1957). *Accounting and Reporting Standards for Corporate Financial Statements and Preceding Statements and Supplements.* American Accounting Association.

American Institute of Accountants (1934). *Audits of Corporate Accounts.* American Institute of Accountants.

American Institute of Certified Public Accountants (December 1958). "Report of Council of the Special Committee on Research Program," *Journal of Accountancy,* pp. 62–68.

———— (1972). *Establishing Financial Accountants Standards: Report of the Study on Establishment of Accounting Principles*. American Institute of Certified Public Accountants.

———— (1978). *Report of Progress: The Institute Acts on Recommendations for Improvements in the Profession*. American Institute of Certified Public Accountants.

Anderson, George D., and R. C. Ellyson (September 1986). "Restructuring Professional Standards: The Anderson Report," *Journal of Accountancy*, pp. 92–104.

Ashbaugh, Hollis, K. Johnstone, and T. Warfield (September 1999). "Corporate Reporting on the Internet," *Accounting Horizons*, pp. 241–257.

Ball, Yvonne (February 20, 2007). "Do Tough Rules Deter Foreign IPO Listings in U.S.?," *Wall Street Journal*, p. C3.

Bedford, Norton (1970). *The Future of Accounting in a Changing Society*. Stipes.

Boer, Germain (January 1994). "Five Modern Management Accounting Myths," *Management Accounting*, pp. 22–27.

Brown, Paul R. (Spring 1981). "A Descriptive Analysis of Select Input Bases of the Financial Accounting Standards Board," *Journal of Accounting Research*, pp. 232–246.

Burns, Judith (2003). "FASB Recognition Stalled Amid Fight Over Control," *Dow Jones Newswires*, accessed via the *Wall Street Journal Online*, February 23, 2003.

Carey, John L. (1969). *The Rise of the Accounting Profession: From Technician to Professional 1896–1936*, Vol. 1. American Institute of Certified Public Accountants.

———— (1970). *The Rise of the Accounting Profession: To Responsibility and Authority 1937–1969*, Vol. 2. American Institute of Certified Public Accountants.

Cloyd, C. Bryan, J. R. Frederickson, and J. W. Hill (Summer 1998). "Independent Auditor Litigation: Recent Events and Related Research," *Journal of Accounting and Public Policy*, pp. 121–142.

Connor, Joseph E. (July 1986). "Enhancing Public Confidence in the Accounting Profession," *Journal of Accountancy*, pp. 76–83.

The CPA Letter (June 1965). "Accounting Principles: Committee Identifies the Major Professional Considerations," pp. 3–4.

———— (November 1970) . "APB Approves Fundamental Statements," p. 1.

Dopuch, Nicholas, and Shyam Sunder (January 1980). "FASB's Statements on Objectives and Elements of Financial Accounting: A Review," *Accounting Review*, pp. 1–21.

Dyckman, Thomas R. (1988). "Credibility and the Formulation of Accounting Standards Under the Financial Accounting Standards Board," *Journal of Accounting Literature*. pp. 1–30.

Edwards, James Don (1978). *History of Public Accounting in the United States*. University of Alabama Press.

Elbannan, Mohamed, and William McKinley (October 2006). "A Theory of the Corporate Decision to Resist FASB Standards: An Organization Theory Perspective," *Accounting, Organizations & Society*, pp. 601–622.

Financial Accounting Foundation (1977). *The Structure of Establishing Financial Accounting Standards: Report of the Structure Committee, the Financial Accounting Foundation*. Financial Accounting Foundation.

Financial Accounting Standards Board (2006). *Financial Accounting Series, Invitation to Comment: Enhancing the Financial Accounting and Reporting Standard-Setting Process for Private Companies*, June 8, 2006.

Grady, Paul (1965). "Inventory of Generally Accepted Accounting Principles for Business Enterprises," *Accounting Research Study No. 7*. American Institute of Certified Public Accountants.

Healy, Robert E. (March 1938). "The Next Step in Accounting," *Accounting Review*, pp. 1–9.

Johnson, L. Todd, and R. Swieringa (June 1996). "Anatomy of an Agenda Decision: Statement No. 115," *Accounting Horizons*, pp. 149–179.

King, Earle C. (1947). "SEC May Take Exception to Financial Statements Reflecting Application of Bulletin No. 32" (Letter to Carmen G. Blough dated December 11, 1947), *Journal of Accountancy* (January 1948), p. 25.

King, Ronald R., and R. Schwartz (March 1997). "The Private Securities Litigation Reform Act of 1995: A Discussion of Three Provisions," *Accounting Horizons*, pp. 92–106.

Kinney, William R., Jr. (June 1996). "What Can Be Learned From the FASB's Process for SFAS No. 115," *Accounting Horizons*, pp. 180–184.

Kirk, Donald J. (December 1989). "Jurisdictional Conflicts and Conceptual Differences," *Accounting Horizons*, pp. 107–113.

Kohler, Eric L. (September 1939). "Theories and Practice," *Accounting Review*, pp. 316–321.

McEnroe, John E., and Loren A. Nikolai (March 1983). "Voting Patterns of Big Eight Representatives in Setting Accounting and Auditing Standards," *Journal of Business Research*, pp. 77–89.

Meyer, Philip E. (Spring 1974). "The APB's Independence and Its Implications for the FASB," *Journal of Accounting Research*, pp. 188–196.

Miller, Richard I., and Paul H. Pashkoff (October 2002). "Regulations Under the Sarbanes-Oxley Act," *Journal of Accountancy*, pp. 33–36.

Moody, Sharon M., and Dale L. Flesher (Fall 1986). "Analysis of FASB Voting Patterns: Statements Nos. 1–86," *Journal of Accounting, Auditing & Finance*, pp. 319–330.

Moonitz, Maurice (1974). "Obtaining Agreement on Standards in the Accounting Profession," in *Studies in Accounting Research #8*. American Accounting Association.

Naranyan, V. G. (1994). "An Analysis of Auditor Liability Rules," *Studies in Accounting, Financial Disclosure, and the Law, 1994* (Supplement to *Journal of Accounting Research*), pp. 39–59.

Palmrose, Zoe-Vonna (Winter 1997). "Audit Litigation Research: Do the Merits Matter? An Assessment and Directions for Future Research," *Journal of Accounting and Public Policy*, pp. 355–378.

Pasework, William (2002). "The Effect of Imposed Voting Requirements on FASB Decisions," *Journal of Accounting, Auditing and Finance* (Vol. 15, No. 1), pp. 75–97.

Previts, Gary J., and Barbara D. Merino (1998). *A History of Accountancy in the United States: The Cultural Significance of Accounting*. Ohio State University Press.

Ray, Delmas D. (1960). *Accounting and Business Fluctuations*. University of Florida Press.

Reither, Cheri (December 1997). "How the FASB Approaches a Standard-Setting Issue," *Accounting Horizons*, pp. 91–104.

Rockness, Howard O., and Loren A. Nikolai (Spring 1977). "An Assessment of APB Voting Patterns," *Journal of Accounting Research*, pp. 154–167.

Rodda, Arleen (February 1993). "AcSEC Update: Financial Accounting," *Journal of Accountancy*, pp. 67–70.

Sack, Robert J. (October 1985). "Commercialism in the Profession: A Threat to Be Managed," *Journal of Accountancy*, pp. 125–134.

Scannell, Kara, and Deborah Solomon (2006). "Business Wins Its Battle to Ease a Costly Sarbanes-Oxley Rule," *Wall Street Journal* (November 10), pp. A1–A14.

Schroeder, Michael (2000). "SEC Probes Andersen for Conflict of Interest," *Wall Street Journal* (August 25), p. C1.

Schuetze, Walter (June 1991). "Keep It Simple," *Accounting Horizons*, pp. 113–117.

——— (June 1993). "The Liability Crisis in the U.S. and Its Impact on Accounting," *Accounting Horizons*, pp. 88–91.

———— (March 1994). "A Mountain or a Molehill?" *Accounting Horizons*, pp. 69–75.

Securities and Exchange Commission (1938). "Administrative Policy on Financial Statements," *Accounting Series Release No. 4*. SEC.

————. (1939). Fifth Annual Report Fiscal Year Ended June 30, 1939. Government Printing Office.

Spacek, Leonard (1957). "Professional Accountants and Their Public Responsibility," in *A Search for Fairness in Financial Reporting to the Public*. Arthur Andersen & Co. (1969), pp. 17–26.

Sprouse, Robert T. (December 1987). "The SEC-FASB Partnership," *Accounting Horizons*, pp. 92–95.

Storey, Reed K. (1964). *The Search for Accounting Principles—Today's Problems in Perspective*. American Institute of Certified Public Accountants.

Sunder, Shyam (1988). "Political Economy of Accounting Standards," *Journal of Accounting Literature*, pp. 31–41.

Volcker, Paul, and Arthur Levitt, Jr. (June 14, 2004). "In Defense of Sarbanes-Oxley," *Wall Street Journal*, p. A16.

Wishon, Keith (June 1986). "Plugging the Gaps in GAAP: The FASB's Emerging Issues Task Force," *Journal of Accountancy*, pp. 96–105.

Zeff, Stephen A. (1972). *Forging Accounting Principles in Five Countries*. Stipes.

———— (July 1984). "Some Junctures in the Evolution of the Process of Establishing Accounting Principles in the U.S.A.: 1917–1972," *The Accounting Review*, pp. 447–468.

4

The Economics of Financial Reporting Regulation

Learning Objectives

After reading this chapter, you should be able to:

- Understand theoretical arguments that favor laissez faire (unregulated) financial reporting.
- Understand counterarguments in favor of regulating the financial reporting process.
- Understand key terms in the regulation argument such as *public goods* and *signaling*.
- Appreciate both the political and economic nature of the regulatory process and the important role of *due process* in regulatory deliberations and policy making.
- Identify the economic consequences of accounting standards on the various parties affected by the standard-setting process.

Financial reporting for publicly listed companies has been regulated in the United States since the 1930s, when Congress empowered the Securities and Exchange Commission (SEC) to regulate financial reporting. The SEC is a federal agency, funded by the federal government and accountable to the United States Congress, which has statutory oversight of the actions of the SEC. However, as noted in Chapter 3, the SEC has allowed accounting policy-making power to remain in the private sector; first with the American Institute of Certified Public Accountants (AICPA), which operated the Committee on Accounting Procedure (CAP) and the Accounting Principles Board (APB), and then with the Financial Accounting Standards Board (FASB). However, the SEC has always maintained regulatory oversight of the private-sector bodies.

Even though financial reporting is a regulated activity and is likely to continue as such, arguments to the contrary occasionally arise, leading to questions about the costs and benefits of regulation. As such, it is useful to evaluate the arguments both for and against formal regulation. Such an evaluation helps us understand the nature of accounting regulation and some of the consequences that flow from it. Arguments for unregulated markets are presented first, followed by arguments for regulated markets. At the conclusion of the first two sections, we assess the merits of the two arguments. Because regulation does exist and is likely to continue, we examine next the nature of regulatory decision making and its influence on parties affected by regulation. This examination aids in understanding how the regulatory process works. Finally, we discuss the economic consequences of accounting regulation.

The Case for Unregulated Markets for Accounting Information

Several different arguments support the case for unregulated markets. The arguments all relate to the incentives for a firm to report information about itself to owners and to the capital market in general. Agency theory explains why incentives exist for voluntary reporting to owners. Wider voluntary reporting to the capital market is explained by *signaling theory* and competitiveness in the capital markets. Finally, it is argued that any information not reported voluntarily could be obtained through private contracting. The arguments supporting unregulated markets for accounting information are largely deductive in nature. Since we live in a regulated environment, empirical tests of the free market position would be quite difficult.

Agency Theory

Agency theory (Chapter 2) predicts and explains the behavior of parties involved with the firm. In law, an agent is a person employed to represent another person's interests. The economic theory of agency builds on the legal concept of agency. Agency theory conceives of the firm itself as a nexus (intersection) of agency relationships and seeks to understand organizational behavior by examining how parties to agency relationships within the firm maximize their own utility.

One of the major agency relationships is between the management group and the owners of the firm. Managers are hired by the owners of a firm to administer the firm's activities, thus establishing an agency relationship. Goals of managers and owners may not be in perfect agreement. It is easy to see how the utility-maximizing behavior of managers could be in conflict with ownership interests. Owners are interested in maximizing return on investment and security prices, while managers have a wider range of economic interests (e.g., compensation) and psychological needs (e.g., prestige). Because of this potential conflict, owners are motivated to contract with managers in such a way as to minimize conflict between the goals of the two groups. Costs are incurred in monitoring agency contracts with management, and these costs, the argument goes, reduce managers' compensation. Therefore, managers have an incentive to keep the costs low by not being in conflict with owners.

Agency theory highlights a conflict between owners and managers that is mitigated to some extent by financial reporting. Routine financial reporting is one means by which owners can monitor employment contracts with their managers. Notice that it is the manager who is providing the information for his or her own evaluation. Accountants refer to this traditional type of reporting as *stewardship,* or accountability to the owners of the firm. Agency theory has also been used to explain the demand for audits. The auditor functions as an independent verifier of financial reports submitted by managers to owners.[1] The historical development of both financial reporting and auditing supports the agency theory argument.[2]

Minimizing agency monitoring costs is an economic incentive for managers to report accounting results reliably to the ownership.[3] The incentive comes from the fact that managers are judged and rewarded, at least in part, by how well they report. Good reporting will enhance the reputation of a manager, and a good reputation should result in higher compensation because agency monitoring costs are minimized if owners perceive that accounting reports are reliable.

Competitive Capital Markets and Signaling Incentives

Agency theory provides a framework for analyzing financial reporting incentives between managers and owners. *Signaling theory* explains why firms have an incentive to report voluntarily to the capital market even if there were no mandatory reporting requirements; firms compete with one another for scarce risk capital, and voluntary disclosure is necessary to compete successfully in the market for risk capital.[4] The ability of the firm to raise capital will be improved if the firm has a good reputation with respect to financial reporting. In addition, good reporting would lower a firm's cost of capital because there is less uncertainty about firms that report more extensively and reliably; therefore, there is less investment risk and a lower required rate of return.

Incentives would exist to prepare a prospectus voluntarily when raising capital and to report regularly to maintain continued investor interest in the firm. Companies that perform well have a strong incentive to report their operating results. Competitive pressures would also force other companies to report even if they did not have good results. A failure to report would be interpreted as bad news. Companies with neutral news would be motivated to report their results to avoid being suspected of having poor results. This would leave only firms with bad news not reporting. Such a situation would also force "bad news" firms to disclose results to maintain credibility in the capital market.

This economic incentive to report (even bad news) is at the heart of the signaling theory argument for voluntary financial reporting. There is *information asymmetry* between the firm and outsiders because insiders know more about a company and its future prospects than outsiders (investors) do. Given this situation of information uncertainty, outsiders will protect themselves by offering a lower price for the company. However, the value of the company can be increased if the firm voluntarily reports (signals) private information about itself that is credible and that reduces outsider uncertainty about the firm's future prospects. A growing body of theoretical and empirical research supports these arguments about the incentives for voluntary (as opposed to mandated) financial disclosures.[5] Research on the signaling effect of management earnings forecasts, which are voluntary disclosures, reveals two signaling aspects: (1) the surprise of the income numbers forecast and (2) the surprise attributable to the earnings forecast itself.[6] Of the two, surprisingly enough, the researchers found that the forecast surprise per se was the more important of the two signaling elements. Other recent research has focused on standards where a long phase-in period is present such as Statement of Financial Accounting Standards (SFAS) No. 106 on other postretirement benefits (Chapter 16).[7] Early adoption is generally interpreted as "good news," whereas late adoption generally indicates "bad news." Using analytical research, Frantz hypothesizes that where accounting alternatives exist (straight-line versus accelerated depreciation, for example), "good news" is signaled by taking the lower income choice and "bad news" is signaled by taking the higher income alternative.[8] In the former case, firms are signaling that they have good future earnings and cash flow prospects, hence the chances of breaching debt covenants are relatively low. In the latter case, the higher income signals the market that the enterprise cannot take the chance of violating its debt covenants.

Some empirical evidence exists that SEC reporting requirements were not a significant improvement over the voluntary reporting existing prior to the 1933 and 1934 acts. One study concluded that the SEC's prospectus requirements have not significantly affected the quality of securities offered for public subscription.[9] Another study examined voluntary annual reporting prior to the Securities Exchange Act of 1934, which required the 10-K annual report.[10] The basic conclusion in the second study was that the reporting requirements mandated by the SEC were already being met on a voluntary basis. This finding says nothing about the quality or usefulness of the disclosures, but it supports the argument that voluntary disclosure will occur in a competitive capital market.

In another study relative to accounting information supplied in unregulated markets, Barton and Waymire (hereinafter B and W) found that the quality of financial reporting improves with managers' incentives to supply higher quality financial information.[11] Their main concern involves whether higher quality financial reporting lowered investor losses during the 1929 crash and not the issue of regulated versus unregulated financial reporting. Nevertheless, their study does have pertinence to the regulation issue.

B and W used a sample of 540 firms during October 1929, the month of the stock market crash and four years *prior* to the establishment of the SEC. For "quality" of reporting, they used three factors: transparency, accounting conservatism, and the use of an external audit. Proxies (representatives) for transparency included variables such as *separate* disclosure of sales, cost of sales, and depreciation on the income statement and *separate* disclosures of fixed assets, intangibles, and reserves on the balance sheet. Accounting conservatism was represented by low intangible asset values, since it was relatively easy to overstate them and thus, in turn, overstate asset values.

Three of the managerial incentives to supply better financial information in 1929, selected by B and W, include: leveraging effects, the presence of alternative uses of financial information, and the issuance of equity capital. *Leveraging effects* refers to the proportion of debt in the capital structure. The presence of alternative sources of financial information considers such information stemming from the firm's dividend policy (the greater the presence of alternative sources of financial information, the lower the quality of financial reporting). The issuance of equity capital refers to undergoing the scrutiny of the equity capital markets, which should bring about better financial reporting. In their overall results, B and W found positive correlations between quality of financial reporting and managers' incentives to supply quality financial reporting.[12]

While B and W's analysis show some incentives to supply higher quality financial reporting in the absence of regulation, one very important point must be made: The overall quality of financial information at that time was extremely poor. For example, only 25.6% of firms showed cost of sales separately and only one-third of firms showed earned surplus (retained earnings) separately (their Table 3). In the absence of accounting regulation, it is certainly difficult to conclude how much overall improvement in financial reporting would have been made in unregulated circumstances. Furthermore, management incentives to supply higher quality financial information, as selected by B and W, appear to be related to competitive issues rather than to strictly managerial ones. (One may question if the management incentives selected by B and W for 1929 were in fact appropriate for that era.)

Arguments in Favor of Private Contracting Opportunities

A third argument in favor of unregulated markets is the presumption that anyone who genuinely desires information about a firm can obtain it. Any party can privately contract for information with the firm itself, with the firm's owners, or indirectly with information intermediaries, such as stock analysts. If information were truly desired beyond that which is publicly available and free of charge, private individuals can buy the desired information. In this way, market forces should result in the optimal allocation of resources to the production of information.

An examination of the stock market reveals that people are indeed willing to contract privately for information. The securities market is as much a market for information as it is a market for securities. Investor newsletters available only by subscription are a good example of paying for private information. A somewhat less formal purchase of information is the use of brokerage firms for investment advice, although this source has been compromised.[13] The cost of investment advice is implicit in commission rates.

Because of private opportunities to contract for additional information, the argument is that market intervention in the form of mandatory disclosure rules is both unnecessary and undesirable. In this view, the demand for information is optimally met when market forces determine the production (supply) and disclosure of accounting information. Indeed, an SEC commissioner has argued that the mandatory disclosure system may not be an effective route for transmission of information to the capital markets and that it serves no purpose to force-feed the investment community with information it does not want.[14] It remains for the SEC to implement a major program for the deregulation of disclosure.[15] However, in today's market atmosphere we would not expect this to occur.

The Case for Regulated Markets for Accounting Information

Market regulation can be justified on the grounds that it is in the public interest. In this context, two reasons are normally used to defend regulation. One reason is the possibility of a failure in the free market system, referred to as *market failure*, and which results in a suboptimal allocation of resources. Natural monopolies, such as those that occur in the utilities industry, are an example of market failures requiring regulatory intervention to prevent undersupply and monopoly pricing. The second reason is the possibility that free markets are contrary to social goals. For example, it can be argued that free markets do not communicate enough relevant information to the security markets, resulting in managers and other insiders having information that is not available to shareholders. In addition, the information that would be available in unregulated markets might not provide enough comparability among firms. A philosophical justification of the standard-setting process—called *codification*—is based on evolutionary improvement of accounting standards in an open and democratic society.

Market Failures

Market failure has led to several arguments favoring regulation. The arguments concern the firm as a monopoly supplier of information, the failure of financial reporting to prevent frauds and bankruptcies, and the public-good nature of accounting information and financial reporting.

The Firm as a Monopoly Supplier of Information

One argument is that market failure occurs because the firm is a monopoly supplier of information about itself. This situation creates the opportunity for restricted production of information and monopolistic pricing if the market is unregulated. Mandatory disclosure would result in more information and a lower cost to society than would be achieved in an unregulated market. Since the firm is a monopoly, it enjoys economies of scale in the production of firm-specific information. However, being a monopoly producer, the firm could underproduce (underreport) information and charge monopolistic prices. The potential for this situation exists in the utilities industry. The regulatory solution in the utilities industry is to permit monopolistic production but to regulate prices.

With accounting regulation, the argument is that it is better to force mandatory reporting rather than to have individuals competing to buy information privately and at monopolistic prices. In other words, mandatory public disclosure is a cost-effective method of getting firm-specific information to those demanding it. It is a waste of resources for everyone to be buying the same private information about firms.

The production costs of mandatory reporting requirements may be quite small since most of the basic information is produced as a byproduct of internal accounting systems.[16] If marginal information production costs are low, then the social costs associated with mandatory financial reporting requirements may be small. And, as previously noted, mandatory public disclosures could save investors money if the alternative is private contracting. The argument is very appealing, though lacking in empirical verification. If the production costs are not low, however, then who bears the cost of producing free public disclosure? Companies will either absorb or pass on regulation costs to consumers; therefore, the owners of the company or the firm's consumers will be subsidizing the information costs. This raises the issue of who bears the costs of financial reporting regulation.

Failures of Financial Reporting and Auditing

The criticisms of accounting practice and the standard-setting process, reviewed in Chapter 3, generally have focused on the alleged low quality of financial reporting, even under regulation. The reasons cited for this are poor accounting and auditing standards, too much management flexibility in the choice of accounting policies, and occasional laxity by auditors. Corporate fraud undetected by auditors and corporate failures not signaled in advance by either financial statements or audit reports are cited as evidence that the financial reporting system is failing to protect the public interest.[17] The argument is that more and better regulation is necessary to raise the quality of financial reporting to protect the public from frauds and failures rather than no regulation.

A capitalist economy relies on a competitive private-sector capital market. Information is an important part of the capital market infrastructure. Good financial reporting is essential to create investor confidence in the fairness of the capital market so that savings will be channeled into productive investments. In addition, good information leads to better investment decisions and capital allocation, both of which are socially beneficial. The corollary is that bad financial reporting has the opposite effect. Advocates of regulation question if companies can really be trusted to report fully and accurately. In fact, the competitive nature of the capital market could even induce misleading reporting, at least by some companies during the short term. Therefore, regulation of accounting is both necessary and in the public interest to prevent some companies from bad or misleading reporting. This is a counterargument to the notion that a competitive capital market produces good voluntary reporting through signaling incentives.

This type of criticism raises important questions about the value of accounting information and can serve as an impetus for reviewing accounting and auditing standards. It can also be a catalyst for discussing the quantity and quality of mandatory accounting and auditing that would be in the public interest as well as the amount of regulation needed to achieve these goals. While there have been a flurry of recent corporate financial reporting failures, it should be stressed that accounting regulation is not going to prevent all frauds and failures; risk in investments cannot be eliminated no matter how much accounting and auditing is required. Risk is something that inherently exists in investments. Increased regulation of financial reporting may reduce the likelihood of undetected frauds and failures, but it can never totally eliminate them.

Finally, any argument favoring expanded regulation must also consider the costs of regulation. In all control or regulatory systems, there exists a point where the marginal benefits from more control are less than the marginal costs. It is by no means clear if benefits exceed costs under existing requirements, let alone under potentially expanded regulation.

Accounting as a Public Good

Market failures can also occur with what are called public goods. *Public goods* are commodities that, once produced, can be consumed without reducing the opportunity for consumption by others.[18] This condition exists because of the *soft property rights* associated with such goods. Examples of pure public goods are radio signals and highways. In the case of radio signals, National Public Radio (NPR) has stations licensed to universities that are heard by the public on FM frequencies. These stations now attempt to raise a significant amount of their operating budget from their listening public, an obviously fair arrangement. While generally successful, the public goods problem has to be overcome because the signal is available without cost to everyone who owns a radio within the listening area. By contrast, private goods possess *hard property rights* so that nonpurchasers are, by definition, excluded from consuming the good.

Public goods are underproduced in a free market owing to what are called externalities. An *externality* exists if a producer is unable to internalize (or impose) production costs on all users of the good. In slightly less technical language, the effect of an externality is that the producer of a public good has a limited incentive to produce it because all consumers cannot be charged for the good. The people who consume public goods without paying for them are called *free riders*. True market demand for public goods is not revealed in the marketplace because free riders are able to use the goods at no cost. The result is that production is less than true market demand. Underproduction of public goods is regarded as a market failure because producers are not motivated to meet the real demand for public goods. The only way in which production can be increased is through regulatory intervention. Inevitably, the cost of free riders must be borne by society as a whole if production is subsidized to meet true demand for public goods.

It appears that accounting information is a public good.[19] It can be freely passed from person to person; each person can consume the content of the information without restricting it for later users. There are two aspects of regulated financial reporting that may give rise to social value (externalities) not privately captured. The first is increased comparability of accounting numbers across firms; the second is an increase in confidence in the securities market. Both operate to reduce information risk in the capital market and should, as a result, benefit society through a lower required return on risky investments.

However, if accounting information is a public good, a company would not have a strong incentive to produce and sell accounting information about itself. In a free market, the opportunities to contract privately for firm-specific information would be restricted, and thus the heart of one argument supporting unregulated markets would be seriously challenged. The outcome would be an underproduction of accounting information in an unregulated market. Intervention in the form of mandatory reporting requirements is considered necessary to ensure that the demand for accounting information is met.

Social Goals

Another reason supporting regulation of financial reporting is that society may want to achieve certain goals that may not be met by a free market, even if there is no market failure.

This approach is also justified by a public-interest argument and inevitably involves a normative judgment about how society should allocate its resources.

Widely available and costless information is an assumption of the economic model of perfect competition. Fairness of the capital market is a public-interest type of argument. It assumes that the stock market will be fair only if all potential investors have equal access to the same information. This situation is referred to as *information symmetry* and is a laudable goal because the more widely information is distributed, the more competitive the capital market will be. The SEC has always been concerned with what might be termed fair reporting and the protection of investors. Regulation of insider trading is an application of the information symmetry philosophy. Such regulation attempts to prevent those with unfair access to private information from taking advantage of it. This behavior, it is argued, undermines investor confidence in the fairness of the capital market.

Another social goal, in addition to information symmetry, is comparability. *Comparability* (Chapter 5) refers to reliability of financial statements when making evaluations using financial statements on an interfirm basis. For example, if one firm uses FIFO and another uses LIFO, it would be difficult to compare their current ratios unless an adjustment was made to put their inventories on a similar basis. Problems of lack of comparability are not easy to solve, but an attempt to move in that direction is discussed in Chapter 9.

The Codificational Justification of Standard Setting

In an important monograph published by the American Accounting Association (AAA), Gaa has provided a meaningful justification of financial reporting regulation and the standard-setting process.[20] *Codification* refers to a pragmatic approach to improving accounting standards over time. This function occurs in an environment permeated by such problems as managers having interests that do not totally coincide with those of shareholders (the agency theory problem), underproduction of accounting information because it is a public good, the lack of information symmetry, and the lack of comparability. Gaa's concern is not with the output of the FASB in the form of standards, concepts, interpretations, and the like, but rather with the underlying rationality of the standard-setting process itself.

The *codificational* viewpoint (the term used in the philosophical literature) is not only rational but also evolutionary in the sense that the system is expected to improve over time. It thus works best in a relatively open and democratic society rather than in authoritarian societies. Given that financial accounting can be improved by regulation that binds all of the players (publicly owned enterprises), one can generally expect a rational—but not necessarily perfect—response from regulating bodies such as the CAP, APB, and FASB. When viewed from the codificational standpoint, members of an organization such as the FASB are expected to have "the ability, the opportunity, and the desire to make a correct decision (or at least, not the desire not to)."[21]

Accounting standards developed in a codificational milieu would not necessarily be correct in terms of deductive logic. Instead, the standards would be evaluated on the basis of whether they performed their intended function well—for example, whether they lead to the provision of information to users at a reasonable cost. If the standards do not work, they should be or at least could be amended. The codificational approach is thus pragmatic, because perfecting the standards is for all intents and purposes impossible.

Codification provides a good idea of what can be expected when democratic societies attempt to resolve difficult distributional problems (how benefits are distributed among competing groups). On the other hand, codification can be viewed as a banal rationalization of the status quo even though, by definition, it assumes that there will be institutional improvements over time in dealing with problems. We will have more to say about the codificational viewpoint in relation to the FASB's conceptual framework project in Chapter 7.

Comparing Regulated and Unregulated Markets

In spite of the fact that accounting is regulated, very little is really known about the costs and benefits of regulation. This means that the pro-regulation arguments as well as arguments for unregulated markets are also largely deductively reasoned rather than empirically researched. In short, it is impossible to accept either argument as correct. What follows is an attempt to assess the merits of the two arguments and to compare them on points at which they address the same issues.

One of the arguments for regulation is that firms are monopolistic suppliers of information about themselves. Prima facie, this could be viewed as a market failure. Since the firm is a monopolistic supplier of information about itself, it may be cheaper for society to require mandatory free disclosure than to have individual investors privately contracting for the same information and paying monopolistic prices.

The free-market counterargument to this is that, owing to competitive pressure for capital, firms have an incentive to report information voluntarily about themselves. Because individuals have alternative investment opportunities, companies are not really able to impose monopolistic prices. They have incentives to report freely in order to attract capital and to lower their cost of capital by being perceived as a good reporting firm. The argument is that where there is perceived information risk owing to poor quality reporting, investors penalize such companies by requiring a higher rate of return to compensate for the extra risk they think they are taking.

Pro-regulators counter that the competitive nature of the capital market provides an incentive for misleading reporting, at least in the short term. The implication is that managers of companies may not pay the penalty for poor or misleading reporting and for this reason may be tempted to manipulate reporting in the short term. However, if this were true, it would also indicate that owners have not developed good mechanisms for monitoring agency contracts with managers, which may well be the case.

There are, of course, problems that have arisen in financial reporting that have occurred under regulation. A major aspect of these problems involves the auditing function, which would occur under both regulated and unregulated financial reporting. In addition, there is pressure on the standard-setting process itself. How to alleviate this pressure is one of the most important issues that the accounting profession faces today.

Another argument against regulation is that information not voluntarily disclosed by the firm could be obtained through private contracting. However, the viability of private contracting opportunities is questionable because of the public-good nature of accounting information and the free-rider problem.

Finally, it can be argued that mandatory reporting is desirable on social grounds because it creates fairness in the capital market, a more level playing field for all. The more information that is public, the less wealth transfers between those who have information and those who do not. It is this same principle that is behind insider-trading regulations.

The arguments for and against regulation represent deliberate extremes. In reality, voluntary disclosure would probably be substantial for the reasons already cited. Yet there is merit in mandating accounting policies. For example, standardization of accounting policies may lead more quickly to better financial reporting among companies than would occur in an unregulated market. Mandatory public reporting also enhances the fairness of the capital market and may reduce the total cost to society of acquiring the information. Since most regulated information is produced as a byproduct of the firm's accounting system, regulatory costs to the firm appear to be low while benefits to society are probably substantial. If regulation is preferred, the codification philosophy justifies the *process* of standard setting, although it does not guarantee that the output of the process is—or even could be—optimal.

Much of the economic argument against regulation maintains that there are incentives for voluntary reporting. However, the focus of accounting regulation is not on mandatory reporting per se; it is on improving the quality of reported information. Accounting regulation is mainly concerned with refining and unifying the rules of recognition and measurement used in the preparation of financial statements. An important implication is that accounting regulation requires a theoretical foundation, given that it is mainly the quality of information that is being regulated. As was discussed in Chapter 3, the lack of a theoretical foundation was directly responsible for the collapse of both the Committee on Accounting Procedure (CAP) and the Accounting Principles Board (APB) as standard-setting bodies. By contrast, the FASB has developed a conceptual framework as the theoretical foundation for standard setting.

The arguments both for and against accounting regulation are persuasive but not conclusive. While we recognize that the regulatory process has inherent problems, our personal bias is in favor of accounting regulation because we believe that the benefits exceed the costs.

Imperfections of Accounting Regulation

Assuming that the benefits of accounting regulation exceed its costs, it is still impossible to know if resources are used to maximize the social welfare, or even to achieve optimality in the more restrictive sense of Pareto-optimality.[22] Accounting regulation can be justified if there is a market failure (as in the case of public goods) or if the free market produces a result incompatible with social goals. Ironically, though, accounting regulation cannot provide an optimal solution to certain problems of financial reporting. This is the paradox of regulation.

Economists have concluded that it is impossible to derive regulatory policies that will knowingly maximize the social welfare. This somewhat gloomy conclusion is the subject of Arrow's well-known *Impossibility Theorem*.[23] Once the free-market pricing system is abandoned, there is no way of determining aggregate social preferences. If the pricing system is working, aggregate social preferences are revealed through supply–demand equilibria, and resources are allocated according to market prices. There is no comparable rule in a regulated market, and for this reason it is difficult to evaluate the benefits of accounting regulation. Because of this paradox, it is also impossible to know if accounting regulation is producing the optimal quantity and quality of financial reporting.[24]

Economists argue that public goods supplied in regulated markets tend to be overproduced. This contrasts with underproduction in unregulated markets and gives rise to a second paradox of regulation. The reason for overproduction is that demand is higher than it would be in a market situation because public goods supplied under regulation are normally subsidized (or even costless) goods. Users demand high quantities of information because the good is costless to them. Since accounting information has public-good characteristics, there is a very real danger that overproduction of accounting information occurs in a regulated market. For example, users of accounting information, such as financial analysts, arguably have an insatiable demand for free information about firms.

In determining accounting policy, the FASB could easily be deceived about the demand for new or alternative accounting policies since users do not pay directly for it. There is some evidence that the FASB is cognizant of the overproduction problem or what is called *standards overload,* particularly as it affects smaller, nonpublicly traded companies. However, to date, the only relief has been the exemption of some closely held firms from supplemental disclosures.

The tendency for overproduction in regulated markets can be avoided only if a pricing system can be imposed on public goods, creating nonpurchasers who are effectively excluded from consuming the good.[25] Cable television is an example of how this imposition can be accomplished with television signals. The key is to strengthen property rights over the good so that nonpurchasers are excluded from freely consuming the good. One means of doing this in accounting might be to file company reports with the SEC and charge users for copies of the information. If accounting information were purchased in this manner, there would be incentives for users *not* to pass on the information to free riders. In this way, demand for the information could be determined, and production costs could be recovered from the actual users of accounting information. The electronic filing system at the SEC (EDGAR; see Chapter 3) might be the beginning of a technology that will facilitate the creation of property rights over financial reports enabling the charging of access fees to users.

By contrast, the present disclosure system imposes costs on companies rather than on users. Assuming that firms recover the costs indirectly through product pricing, the users of accounting information are being subsidized by the users of the firms' products. This consequence of regulation is subject to criticism on the grounds of fairness.

In summary, the negative consequences of regulating accounting, given its public-good nature, are (a) a potential overallocation of social resources to the production of free publicly available accounting information and (b) a wealth transfer from nonusers to users of accounting information. A wealth transfer occurs because users receive the benefits of free accounting information, while nonusers implicitly incur the production costs. However, there would also be social costs for *not* regulating financial reporting if there are market failures or if other socially desirable goals are unmet by free markets. All we can do is to keep the institutional process of accounting standard setting as unbiased as possible and to rely on the evolutionary nature of the codificational justification of accounting rule making. Next, we examine the political nature of the regulatory process itself.

The Regulatory Process

Regulation is essentially a political activity. This is neither intended as a criticism, nor is it surprising, even though regulation is undertaken in the public interest. However, it is unclear exactly what is meant by public interest. Since social welfare cannot be measured (the Impossibility Theorem), there are no criteria for determining what policy will maximize the public interest. Consequently, the notion of public interest is best understood in a political context and with reference to the particular creation and redistribution of income and wealth being advocated. What this means is that there is no way of determining optimal accounting regulation and that regulation will be the outcome of a political as much as an economic process.

Not surprisingly, economic self-interest models have been used for analyzing political and regulatory behavior. In a regulated market, individuals or groups who have any stake in the market will be motivated to lobby for their vested interests, to form coalitions with other parties to further strengthen their influence, and generally to try to influence the political system to their advantage.

The Political Nature of Regulation

The democratic tradition in the United States means that due process is an important ingredient in the regulatory process. In setting policy, *due process* means that a regulatory agency seeks to involve all affected parties in the deliberations; this is important in maintaining the legitimacy of the regulatory process. In other words, people affected by regulation have an opportunity to have input into the regulatory decision-making process. The due-process tradition goes back to one of the first federal agencies, the Interstate Commerce Commission.[26] It has even been suggested that a regulatory body's method of operation, which includes the principle of due process, is more important to its own political survival than the actual decisions it makes.

Some members of the accounting profession believe that accounting policy setting should be neutral and apolitical.[27] The more widely held view, however, is that accounting policy is inevitably political because of its negotiated nature.[28] In reflecting back on Chapter 3, it is easy to see why both the CAP and the APB failed as regulatory bodies. These two AICPA committees were regulatory bodies, but they lacked the necessary political structure to ensure their survival. For one thing, they had only a weak mandate to regulate financial reporting. Until the issue of Accounting Series Release (ASR) 150 in 1973, the SEC did not officially endorse private-sector standard setting.[29] What existed was an informal alliance in which the SEC tacitly accepted accounting standards as acceptable for SEC filings. Occasionally, though, the SEC would challenge a specific standard. The investment tax credit, discussed in Chapter 3, produced such a situation. Because of this arrangement, the AICPA's authority to regulate was very weak.

From the SEC's perspective, the arrangement prior to ASR 150 provided security and flexibility. By permitting self-regulation in the private sector, the SEC was shielded from the politics of actually setting accounting policy except when it was expedient to do so. In a sense, the SEC was in a position to use the private sector as a scapegoat if Congress were to challenge the work of the SEC.[30]

The other fatal characteristic of the AICPA committees was the closed-door nature of policy setting. There appeared to be no due process in the determination of accounting and disclosure rules. Although some informal fact gathering and solicitation of the views of interested parties undoubtedly occurred, it was not until late in the life of the APB that formal due-process procedures were implemented. The lack of due process, or at least the *apparent* lack of due process, sometimes led to a low level of acceptance by affected parties. Ironically, the accounting profession thought a closed-door approach was good because it insulated policy making from outside influence. It believed at the time that accounting policy was primarily a process of identifying the true and correct normative accounting methods. In hindsight, this seems naive, but accounting researchers and policy makers clung strongly to this conviction through the 1960s.

From a regulatory viewpoint, the FASB is functioning much more successfully than did earlier regulatory bodies. Its standards were endorsed by the SEC in ASR 150. Due process has been adopted as standard procedure in debating and developing accounting policy. As with the legal system, decision making under due process is extremely slow, but this is the nature of democratic politics. Arrow refers to this tendency as *democratic paralysis*.[31] Regulation under a system of due process *is* slow, but the achieving of consensus is what gives legitimacy to the regulation. The problems of the FASB alluded to in Chapter 3 stem from the costliness of implementing standards and, in some cases, their lack of understandability. The mechanism for due process, however, is firmly established in the organizational structure of the FASB, although the line between due process and behind-the-scenes politicking, as in the case of stock options, can be breached.

Regulatory Behavior

Capture theory and the *life-cycle theory* of regulation both argue that the group being regulated eventually comes to use the regulatory process to promote its own self-interest.[32] When this occurs, the regulatory process is considered captured. The life-cycle theory of regulation argues that a regulatory agency goes through several distinct phases. Although it starts out in the public interest, regulation later becomes an instrument for protecting the regulated group. The regulated parties and the regulatory agency come to see that their interests converge. It becomes very difficult for a regulator to remain truly independent because survival of the regulatory agency itself may depend on how well the policies are accepted by the group being regulated. What often happens is that the regulatory body protects the regulated group from competition. This behavior was observed in older regulatory agencies before they deregulated—such as the Interstate Commerce Commission, which regulates land transportation; the Federal Aviation Agency, which regulates air transportation; and the Federal Communications Commission, which regulates radio and television licenses. This behavior, by both the regulator and the regulated parties, is explained by the self-interest theory of political behavior.

Capture theory and the life-cycle theory have been applied to the regulation of accounting. From 1976 to 1978, the United States Congress investigated the allegation that accounting regulation had been captured by the Big Eight group of accounting firms.[33] As the predominant auditors of publicly listed corporations, this group has a large stake in the regulation game. In addition, prior to the FASB, accounting regulation was done primarily by AICPA subcommittees, which were undoubtedly heavily influenced by the Big Eight accounting firms. With the implementation of the independent FASB, however, the capture theory argument lost at least some of its validity. At the time of the congressional hearings, the FASB had been in operation for several years.

Some changes were made in response to the congressional hearings—for example, restructuring of the AICPA to lessen Big Eight dominance and to increase self-regulation by the AICPA.[34] However, the status quo in accounting regulation survived the scrutiny of Congress partly because capture theory and the life-cycle theory are less applicable to financial reporting. The number of parties directly affected by accounting regulation is much larger and more diverse than in traditional regulated industries. Studies of submissions to the FASB found that even the Big Eight group of accounting firms did not have a unified viewpoint, and the group did not dominate policy at the FASB.[35] These studies concluded that decision making at the FASB is pluralistic. Auditors and the other parties affected by accounting regulation; companies that must comply with regulations; and free riders, who use the costless information for investment analyses, have a divergence of interests, which places the accounting regulator in a more naturally neutral posture than is possible in other regulated industries.[36]

Behavior of Companies, Auditors, and Free Riders

Let's examine the three groups affected by accounting regulation—companies, auditors, and free riders—in greater detail. Management of companies can be expected to respond to regulatory proposals that will affect either the companies or itself personally. All accounting regulation imposes some amount of production cost on firms. One could argue, a priori, that there would be a natural tendency for management to oppose new disclosures or rules that will impose a cost on the firm. On the other hand, some rules may cause specific firms to increase reported net income. Management could have an incentive to support those new proposals that would positively affect reported income and that might increase its own compensation (especially when employment contracts use accounting numbers for bonuses). However, one study found the opposite result. Large regulated companies supported proposed accounting rules that would lower reported net income.[37] The suggested reason was that the self-interest of this type of company was to minimize political costs, such as the possibility of future regulatory intervention, and that lower book profits were consistent with this goal. So, even within the management group there is likely to be a range of reactions to accounting policy proposals.

Auditors are concerned with the auditing implications of financial reporting rules. It would be naive to think the opinion of large public accounting firms is not seriously considered in accounting policy deliberations. Many public accounting firms maintain regular liaison with FASB personnel and routinely attend policy hearings at the FASB. Auditors could be expected to support regulation that reduces the riskiness of audits—for example, rules that clarify or standardize financial reporting. Auditors have tended to oppose proposed policies that would expand the audit function into subjective areas, such as supplemental disclosures of inflation accounting data and profit forecasts.[38] The reason for this opposition is fairly obvious. If more subjective information is required, the auditor will incur a greater risk in auditing the information, which would increase the possibility of litigation. Assuming that auditors are risk averse, they would prefer to avoid such risky ventures, if possible.

By far the most serious problem arising from auditor behavior involves capture of auditors by auditees (the companies that they audit). This has arisen as a result of large management consulting contracts that auditors have entered into with auditees. The public accounting firm thus becomes an advocate for the auditee in the management consulting contract. Unfortunately, management consulting fees generally dwarf auditing fees, although the latter are hardly negligible. Sarbanes-Oxley, however, is bringing about a separation between auditing and management consulting.

One possible solution to the auditor–auditee problem has been proposed by Ronen. He suggests the creation of *financial statement insurance*, which would be paid by the auditee to an outside insurance company. This insurance would cover both insurance payments to shareholders as a result of misrepresentation in financial statements and also auditor fees. In turn, the insurance carrier would select and pay the auditor. Furthermore, amount of coverage and premium would be published, with those firms having higher coverage and relatively lower premiums looking best. Notice that the principal–agent relation is changed from firm and auditor to insurance carrier and auditor. If the insurance carrier selects a "lowball" auditor, it increases the risk of having to pay shareholders for subpar audits. Ronen's proposal deserves very careful consideration.[39]

Finally, free riders, such as financial analysts, may also try to influence the outcome of accounting policy deliberations. Analysts have a strong motivation to demand new accounting information that they can incorporate into investment research and newsletters. As information intermediaries, they can make money simply by summarizing public information for investors who do not have time to sift through it themselves. The lobbying behavior of free riders needs to be watched closely by the FASB because free riders do not have the direct economic interests in information production that management and auditors have. Because of this, responding to their pressure could easily result in an overproduction situation. It is politically difficult to deal with free riders because they can claim to be acting in the public interest by making the capital market fairer and more competitive through free public reporting. Although this argument has merit, it ignores the question of information production costs and who pays for accounting regulation.

The danger of bowing to pressures from special-interest groups has been noted.[40] Accounting policy making should not serve special-interest groups to the detriment of society as a whole. When regulation is dominated by special interests, its mandate no longer exists because the regulation process has been captured by a vested-interest group.

Accounting regulation is likely to continue, and so it is important to understand the nature of regulatory processes. The majority of accounting regulations deal with financial statement refinement and standardization of practices rather than with expanded disclosure per se. This may mean that the overproduction problem is exaggerated by the critics of regulation.

Economic Consequences of Accounting Policy

Clearly the accounting rule-making process is a political process in which the various constituencies lobby for their positions. While the standard-setting agency should be neutral among competing groups in terms of providing information that is useful for helping to predict cash flows and to assess managerial performance (Chapter 7), standard setting often results in benefiting one group at the expense of another. That is, accounting policy is not simply a matter of economic efficiency or optimality. It also affects income and wealth distribution (who gets what), and this is necessarily a social and political issue that transcends accounting.

The FASB does, in a limited way, recognize this problem. It considers the *economic conse-quences* of proposed accounting policies, which have been defined as "The impact of account-ing reports on . . . business, government, unions, investors, and creditors."[41] The FASB is very sensitive to producer costs and whether there are sufficient benefits (to external users) to warrant the imposition of new, costly accounting standards. Indeed, in the late 1970s the FASB began commissioning economic consequences studies to aid in assessing the effects of proposed standards on firms.[42] Unfortunately, these studies have focused primarily on firms, their stockholders, and financial analysts. Other parties, such as creditors, consumers, employees, and even governments, have not been factored into the cost–benefit calculus of financial reporting regulation. Consequently, it is not surprising that such broader questions as the desirability of corporate social responsibility accounting have not been seriously consid-ered.[43] Corporate responsibility reporting is advocated by those who believe that society as a whole has a legitimate (though necessarily pluralistic) interest in corporate behavior, and that the corporation should be made accountable for its behavior over a wide range of activities, including employee and community relations, pollution controls, and compliance with federal laws such as the Occupational Health and Safety Act and the Environmental Protection Act.

The FASB only considers costs in the narrowest of senses, producer costs, and benefits are thought of primarily in terms of the information needs of the stock market. An example of this orientation to economic consequences can be seen in the so-called standards-overload issue discussed earlier in the chapter.[44] Smaller, nonpublicly listed firms (and their auditors) argue that accounting standards are formulated mainly for larger, publicly traded firms that can afford the costs of accounting regulation and for the benefit of financial analysts who investi-gate these firms. For smaller, nonpublic firms, the compliance costs are disproportionately higher and the benefits smaller since the firms' securities are not traded. The FASB is sensitive to the issue and has suspended two disclosure-oriented standards, SFAS Nos. 14 and 69, for smaller, nonpublic firms. However, the FASB has consistently rejected the argument for differential recognition, measurement, and disclosure rules and has reaffirmed the need for one basic set of accounting standards for all firms.[45] However, this issue has again arisen in regard to SFAS No. 150 on mandatorily redeemable preferred stock (Chapter 11). The issue of separate standards for smaller firms being set by the AICPA was raised in Chapter 3.

Research into economic consequences has also focused narrowly on stockholders and managers of firms. One extensive body of research (reviewed in Chapter 8) examines the effects of accounting policies and changes in policies on stock prices. Another extensive body of research has investigated whether the choice of accounting methods or management's preference for certain accounting methods is related to accounting-based contracts—in particular, restrictive covenants in debt agreements that require the maintenance of certain levels of working capital, leverage, or interest-coverage ratios. Another accounting-based contract relates to manager compensation, and here it has been hypothesized that managers choose accounting methods that maximize their compensation under these contracts. The suggestion is that these contract-based incentives create a preference for income-increasing accounting methods.[46] This line of research has been useful in drawing attention to the ways in which accounting data can be used. Nevertheless, its focus is on a very limited aspect of the total social costs and benefits of financial reporting and the regulation of financial reporting. In conclusion, we have not really come to grips yet with enumerating the social costs and benefits of financial reporting.

Summary

The arguments for and against financial reporting regulation force us to consider why we regulate, who benefits, and who pays the costs. These are important questions to pose of any regulatory process. Since regulation is a matter of public interest, the benefits of regulation should clearly be in the public interest and should exceed costs. However, certain individuals benefit directly, while others incur the cost. An analysis of the economic consequences of regulation helps to evaluate these benefits and costs and their fairness. Economic consequences involve the impact of accounting regulation upon affected parties such as management, shareholders, creditors, government, and unions in terms of who gains and who loses in particular regulatory situations.

Regulation is a political process, and self-interest may motivate individuals and groups to participate in it. This places the regulator in the role of weighing sometimes conflicting positions and trying to determine what is in the best interests of society as a whole. Due process and neutrality are critical to regulatory success if the regulation is to retain the support of both the regulated parties and society generally. All these objectives are difficult for a regulatory agency to accomplish, and there is always the danger that vested-interest groups may capture the regulatory process and divert it to private ends.

The rationale or justification for regulation rests on the public-interest argument. However, a paradox exists. There is no way of determining optimal regulatory policies that maximize the social welfare or the public interest. The best that regulators can do is to try to determine that a net benefit exists—that is, an excess of benefits over costs. Benefits are difficult to identify and measure, although there is evidence that accounting information is useful to investors. (This research is examined in Chapter 8.) Furthermore, the regulatory purpose is subject to democratic paralysis and "capture" of the regulation process by those who are being regulated. Costs are somewhat easier to quantify. There is some reason to believe that regulation costs are low because most of the information contained in financial reports is produced as a byproduct of firms' accounting systems. Overall, then, there is reason to believe that accounting regulation produces a net benefit to society.

QUESTIONS

1. What are the arguments favoring regulation of financial reporting?

2. What are the arguments against regulation of financial reporting?

3. Why is it difficult to evaluate the regulation question?

4. Why does accounting information have some features of a public good? What are the implications for information production in both unregulated and regulated markets?

5. Why can't optimal regulation be determined? If optimal accounting regulation cannot be determined, how can a regulatory body such as the SEC or FASB make good decisions?

6. A distinction was made in the chapter between two types of regulation: (1) the refinement and standardization of financial statements and (2) expanded disclosure. Why is the distinction important in evaluating the regulation question?

7. Who pays for accounting regulation and who benefits?

8. Can accounting standards and policy making be neutral? In what sense is neutrality really important?

9. Arrow (1963) warns that public participation and a consensual approach to social issues can lead to democratic paralysis—that is, to a failure to act due to an inability to agree on goals or objectives. How did such a situation lead to the demise of the APB (review Chapter 3)? Why is the FASB faring somewhat better?

10. Horngren (1973) argues that accounting policies are a social decision and a matter of public interest. Evaluate this statement.

11. Horngren (1973) believes that accounting standards must be marketed by regulatory bodies. By this he means that affected parties need to be sold on the benefits of standards. How is this concept consistent with the nature of regulation?

12. It was suggested many years ago that a court should be created to resolve disputes in accounting. In what ways does the FASB function as an accounting court? In what ways is it different?

13. What benefit is the conceptual framework project to the FASB if (a) there is no way of determining optimal accounting regulation and (b) regulatory decision making is a political process?

14. What is the relationship between public goods and free riders?

15. What is *Pareto-optimality*? Why would adherence to it minimize accounting standard setting?

16. How do agency theory and the codificational viewpoint differ in assumptions about the behavior of individuals?

17. Why does codification presume a democratic setting?

18. The social goals underlying accounting regulation are information symmetry and comparability. Why are these goals complementary?

19. Would a regular quarterly announcement of earnings-per-share that is "good" be an example of signaling? What about early adoption of a new accounting standard that would reduce income?

20. If accounting were not regulated, we would not be facing the difficult problems that have arisen as a result of Enron and other corporate auditing failures. Do you agree with this statement? Explain.

21. Evaluate Ronen's (2002) financial statement insurance proposal.

22. Under financial statement insurance, why would the relation between the firm and its auditor and investors bear a slight resemblance to the relationship between Saddam Hussein and the weapons inspectors from the United Nations in 2002 and 2003?

23. What is due process in financial accounting standard setting?

24. Why do companies, even those with "bad news," have an incentive to disclose financial reporting information?

25. Does the ability to swiftly—and at no cost—download music files convert this music from a private good to a public good?

CASES, PROBLEMS, AND WRITING ASSIGNMENTS

1. What is the relationship among agency theory, economic consequences, and signaling? Explain in depth.

2. Benston (1982, p. 102), in an analysis of corporate social accounting and reporting (CSAR), says: "The social responsibility of accountants can be expressed by their forbearing from social responsibility accounting." However, in a critique of Benston's analysis, Schreuder and Ramanathan (1984, p. 414) state:

> The comments . . . do not purport to convey the message that there is no value at all in analyzing the potential of CSAR from a shareholder perspective and proceeding from the (implicit) assumption of perfect and complete markets. We do, however, wish to point out that this may not be the most appropriate perspective as (1) CSAR is addressed toward a more inclusive group of stakeholders and (2) one of its main objectives is to include in the accounting system those aspects of corporate behavior that are decidedly not handled well by the market. Therefore, the perspective implied in Benston's analysis is of very limited value at best.

Required:

CSAR assumes there is a legitimate interest or "stake" in the corporation beyond the stockholders' interests and that these other stakeholders' interests are not well served by traditional financial statements. Therefore, it follows that within a broad political economy of accounting, CSAR is an important policy-making issue. Critically evaluate this proposition and indicate your agreement or disagreement and the underlying reasons for your position.

3. Discuss the economic consequences issues that are present in each of the following transaction situations.
   a. SFAS No. 13 allows lease contracts to be set up so that the transaction can usually be set up as an operating lease rather than a capital lease.
   b. When SFAS No. 19 was passed, medium-sized petroleum exploration firms campaigned hard to set it aside. SFAS No. 19 would have allowed successful efforts only, whereas the lobbying firms wanted an unrestricted choice between full costing and successful efforts.
   c. A securities industry group objected to part of APB Opinion No. 10, which would have required that all convertible debt be broken down into debt and equity portions at the time of issue. The debt portion (bonds payable plus premium or minus discount) would be booked at the effective rate without the conversion privilege with the equity portion credited to paid-in capital. The industry group was pleased by APB Opinion No. 14, which did not break out the equity portion of convertible debt except if detachable stock warrants were issued. Why was the securities industry group (which represented investment bankers who floated large loans for industry) unhappy with Opinion No. 10 and pleased with Opinion No. 14?
   d. SFAS No. 87 does not show the full pension obligation or liability in the balance sheet (although a "minimum" liability may be present).
   e. SFAS No. 96 made it much more difficult to recognize deferred tax assets as opposed to deferred tax liability (a more even-handed treatment was used in recognizing deferred tax assets and liabilities in SFAS No. 109, which superseded SFAS No. 96).
   f. The FASB tried to include the cost of stock options as an expense, but they were prevented from doing so by vociferous opposition from the business community, although it now is going to happen under SFAS No. 123R.

4. Although a recent study by Barton and Waymire indicates that there are incentives for higher quality financial information under unregulated financial reporting, why is this finding not an effective one in support of unregulated financial reporting?

CRITICAL THINKING AND ANALYSIS

1. Evaluate the costs and benefits of the accounting standard-setting process (versus an unregulated environment).

2. How might the "capture" of auditors by auditees be mitigated?

Notes

1. *See Francis and Wilson (1988) for an application of agency theory to auditing.*

2. *Watts and Zimmerman (1983).*

3. *Holthausen and Leftwich (1983).*

4. *See Ross (1979) for a summary of this argument.*

5. *See Dye (1990), Holthausen and Verrechia (1988), Leftwich, Watts, and Zimmerman (1981), Verrechia (1990), and Wong (1988).*

6. *Yeo and Ziebart (1995).*

7. *Amir and Ziv (1997a) and Amir and Ziv (1997b).*

8. *Frantz (1997). For a discussion of how stock splits are used, in addition to accruals, to signal managerial optimism, see Louis and Robinson (2005).*

9. *Stigler (1971, pp. 78–100).*

10. *Benston (1973).*

11. *Barton and Waymire (2004).*

12. *See also the comments of Leftwich (2004), the official discussant of the Barton and Waymire paper.*

13. *See, for example, Thornton (2002, p. 38).*

14. *SEC commissioner Stephen Friedman, as quoted in Peat, Marwick, Mitchell & Co. (1981).*

15. *A step toward deregulation is shelf-registration (SEC rule 415). This rule permits the speedier sales of routine offerings of debt and equity securities by large companies. It is not necessary to file a specific prospectus with the SEC for each individual offering of securities. One prospectus can be used for multiple issues within the time period covered by the shelf-registration.*

16. *Hakansson (1977). However, more recent theoretical work such as Wagenhofer (1990) points out that mandated disclosure of proprietary information (such as segmental disclosures) can disadvantage a firm relative to its competitors, in which case mandatory reporting would be extremely costly to a firm. See Chapter 9 for more on this argument.*

17. *One of the most publicized frauds was Equity Funding. See Seidler, Andrews, and Epstein (1977). The S&L failures in the 1980s have undermined public confidence in the financial reporting system. See Merino and Kenney (1994). For a general discussion of auditing and financial reporting failures, see Knapp (1993).*

18. *See Bowers (1974) for a review of the public goods problem.*

19. *Gonedes and Dopuch (1974) and May and Sundem (1976).*

20. *Gaa (1988).*

21. *Ibid. (p. 123).*

22. *Pareto-optimality occurs when it is not possible to make anyone better off without making someone else worse off. A Pareto-optimal economy is considered to be efficient. If it is possible to make someone better off at no cost, then the existing allocation of resources is inefficient and involves a waste of resources owing to suboptimality.*

23. *Arrow (1963).*

24. *Gonedes (1972) argued that it was possible to determine optimal accounting regulation. Later thinking, however, has reversed that conclusion. See Demski (1973) and Gonedes and Dopuch (1974).*

25. *Demsetz (1970).*

26. *Krislov and Musolf (1964, p. 185).*

27. *For examples of this position, see Armstrong (1977) and Kirk (1978).*

28. *Horngren (1973) and Solomons (1978).*

29. *In SEC (1973), accounting standards of the FASB were officially sanctioned as the basis for statutory reports filed with the SEC.*

30. *Watts and Zimmerman (1978).*

31. *Arrow (1963).*

32. *Stigler (1971) and Bernstein (1955). Revsine (1991) sees the "contrived and flexible" reporting standards of accounting as evidence of capture by the regulatees of accounting standard setters.*

33. *The congressional hearings conducted by Senator Lee Metcalf in 1977 and Congressman John E. Moss in 1978 were discussed in Chapter 3. The stuff reports prepared for both hearings were highly critical of financial reporting and accounting regulation. After the hearings, the status quo of accounting regulation was maintained, although the SEC, FASB, and AICPA all responded positively to some of the criticisms made during the hearings.*

34. *Some of the fallout from the Watergate congressional investigations was the discovery of corporate slush funds used to make political contributions. Direct corporate political contributions are of course illegal. It was also discovered that some of these funds were used for bribes in foreign countries. Auditors were held publicly accountable for failing to detect these slush funds in their audits. There were also several well-publicized corporate failures in the 1970s in which the auditors' performance was seriously questioned. To some degree, then, the congressional investigations of the accounting profession reflected a genuine public-interest concern, but they were also part of post-Watergate politics.*

35. *Hussein and Ketz (1980) and Brown (1981).*

36. *However, some questions have arisen relative to the Chairman and Chief Accountant of the SEC. Relative to the Chairman, questions have arisen because of previous consulting work done for the AICPA and Big Five public accounting firms. See Schroeder and Bandler (2002). The Chairman of the SEC resigned in November, 2002. Questions have arisen relative to the chief accountant due to an SEC investigation of his former employer, a Big Five public accounting firm. See Paltrow and Schroeder (2002).*

37. *Watts and Zimmerman (1978). This study was discussed in Chapter 2.*

38. *Two areas in which the AICPA membership balked were the proposals by the SEC for mandatory financial forecasts (proposed rule No. 33-581 issued in 1975) and ASR 177 (also issued in 1975), which would have required auditors to comment on the preferability of a reported change in accounting policy. Because of the resistance by accounting firms to these two proposed requirements, they were subsequently dropped by the SEC. Auditors would have been placed in the position of attesting to information that was, in the case of forecasts, very subjective, and to comment on the preferability of accounting standards when there were no official guidelines for making such a determination (for example, FIFO versus LIFO inventory methods).*

39. *Ronen (2002). Healy and Palepu (2003) note that the current legal environment has effectively reduced the auditing process to a complex "checklist," which insulates the auditor from legal responsibilities for errors in the financial statements. In essence, this checklist is an inferior substitute for a meaningful, professional opinion and lets the auditor "off the hook." Healy and Palepu recommend that auditing firms make a professional judgment regarding the transparency of the financial statements. (This is similar to what is already done by the bond rating agencies.) The stock exchanges would be involved to oversee the process. Forcing the auditors to make a professional judgment of this kind should improve the quality of the information provided. This would undoubtedly increase the cost of stock list and might also increase the cost of audits. If the Healy and Palepu proposal were successful, we believe the benefits would exceed the costs.*

40. *Solomons (1978).*

41. *Zeff (1978, p. 56). See also Blake (1992).*

42. *For example, FASB (1978), Abdel-khalik (1981), and Griffin and Castanias (1987).*

43. *Schreuder and Ramanathan (1984).*

44. *For example, AICPA (1983) and FASB (1983).*

45. *FASB (1986).*

46. *Watts and Zimmerman (1978) and (1990).*

References

Abdel-khalik, A. Rashad (1981). *The Economic Effects on Lessees of FASB Statement No. 13,* Accounting for Leases. FASB.

American Institute of Certified Public Accountants (1983). *Report of the Special Committee on Accounting Standards Overload.* AICPA.

Amir, Eli, and A. Ziv (1997a). "Economic Consequences of Alternative Adoption Rules for New Accounting Standards," *Contemporary Accounting Research* (Fall), pp. 543–568.

——— (1997b). "Recognition, Disclosure or Delay: Timing the Adoption of SFAS No. 106," *Journal of Accounting Research* (Spring), pp. 61–81.

Armstrong, Marshall S. (February 1977). "The Politics of Establishing Accounting Standards," *Journal of Accountancy*, pp. 76–79.

Arrow, Kenneth (1963). *Social Choice and Individual Values.* John Wiley.

Barton, Jan, and G. Waymire (December 2004). "Investor Protection Under Unregulated Financial Reporting," *Journal of Accounting and Economics*, pp. 65–116.

Benston, George J. (March 1973). "Required Disclosure and the Stock Market: An Evaluation of the Securities Act of 1934," *American Economic Review*, pp. 132–155.

——— (1982). "Accounting and Corporate Accountability," *Accounting, Organizations and Society* (Vol. 7, No. 2), pp. 87–105.

Bernstein, Marver H. (1955). *Regulating Business by Independent Commission.* Princeton University Press.

Blake, J. (Autumn 1992). "A Classification System for Economic Consequences Issues in Accounting Regulation," *Accounting and Business Research*, pp. 305–321.

Bowers, Patricia F. (1974). *Private Choice and Public Welfare, the Economics of Public Goods.* The Dryden Press.

Brown, Paul R. (Spring 1981). "A Descriptive Analysis of Select Input Bases of the Financial Accounting Standards Board," *Journal of Accounting Research*, pp. 232–246.

Demsetz, Harold (October 1970). "The Private Production of Public Goods," *Journal of Law and Economics*, pp. 293–306.

Demski, Joel S. (October 1973). "The General Impossibility of Normative Accounting Standards," *Accounting Review*, pp. 718–723.

Dye, Ronald A. (January 1990). "Mandatory Versus Voluntary Disclosures: The Cases of Financial and Real Externalities," *Accounting Review*, pp. 1–24.

Financial Accounting Standards Board (1978). *Economic Consequences of Financial Accounting Standards.* FASB.

——— (1983). *Financial Reporting by Privately Owned Companies: Summary of Responses to FASB Invitation to Comment.* FASB.

——— (1987). "Status Report No. 181," *Financial Accounting Series,* November 3, 1987.

Francis, Jere R., and Earl R. Wilson (October 1988). "Auditor Changes: A Joint Test of Theories Relating to Agency Costs and Auditor Differentiation," *Accounting Review,* pp. 663–682.

Frantz, Pascal (Spring 1997). "Discretionary Accounting Choices: A Debt-Covenants-Based Signalling Approach," *Accounting and Business Research*, pp. 99–110.

Gaa, James C. (1988). "Methodological Foundations of Standard-Setting for Corporate Financial Reporting," *Studies in Accounting Research #28.* American Accounting Association.

Gonedes, Nicholas J. (January 1972). "Efficient Capital Markets and External Accounting," *Accounting Review*, pp. 11–21.

Gonedes, Nicholas J., and Nicholas Dopuch (1974). "Capital Market Equilibrium, Information Production, and Selected Accounting Techniques: Theoretical Framework and Review of Empirical Work," *Studies on Financial Accounting Objectives, 1974* (Supplement to *Journal of Accounting Research*), pp. 48–129.

Griffin, Paul A., and Richard P. Castanias II (1987). *Accounting for the Translation of Foreign Currencies: The Effects of Statement 52 on Equity Analysts.* FASB.

Hakansson, Nils H. (April 1977). "Interim Disclosure and Public Forecasts: An Economic Analysis and Framework for Choice," *Accounting Review*, pp. 396–416.

Healy, Paul, and K. Palepu (July 2003). "How the Quest for Efficiency Corroded the Market," *Harvard Business Review*, pp. 76–85.

Holthausen, Robert W., and Richard W. Leftwich (August 1983). "The Economic Consequences of Accounting Choice: Implications of Costly Contracting and Monitoring," *Journal of Accounting and Economics*, pp. 77–117.

Holthausen, Robert W., and Robert E. Verrechia (Spring 1988). "The Effects of Sequential Information Releases on the Variance of Price Changes in an Intertemporal Multi-Asset Market," *Journal of Accounting Research*, pp. 82–106.

Horngren, Charles T. (October 1973). "The Marketing of Accounting Standards," *Journal of Accountancy*, pp. 61–66.

Hussein, Mohamed E., and J. Edward Ketz (Summer 1980). "Ruling Elites of the FASB: A Study of the Big Eight," *Journal of Accounting, Auditing & Finance*, pp. 354–367.

Knapp, Michael C. (1993). *Contemporary Auditing: Issues and Cases.* West.

Kirk, Donald J. (September 1978). "How to Keep Politics out of Standard Setting: Making Private Sector Rule-Making Work," *Journal of Accountancy*, pp. 92–94.

Krislov, Samuel, and Lloyd D. Musolf (1964). *The Politics of Regulation.* Houghton Mifflin.

Leftwich, Richard (December 2004). "Discussion of: 'Investor Protection Under Unregulated Financial Reporting' (by Jan Barton and Gregory Waymire)," *Journal of Accounting and Economics*, pp. 117–128.

Leftwich, Richard, Ross L. Watts, and Jerold L. Zimmerman (1981). "Voluntary Corporate Disclosure: The Case of Interim Reporting," *Studies on Standardization of Accounting Practices: An Assessment of Alternative Institutional Arrangements, 1981* (Supplement to *Journal of Accounting Research*), pp. 50–88.

Louis, Henock, and Dahlia Robinson (June 2005). "Do Managers Credibly Use Accruals to Signal Private Information? Evidence From the Pricing of Discretionary Accruals Around Stock Splits," *Journal of Accounting and Economics*, pp. 361–380.

May, Robert G., and Gary L. Sundem (October 1976). "Research for Accounting Policy: An Overview," *Accounting Review*, pp. 747–763.

Merino, Barbara D., and Sara York Kenney (1994). "Auditor Liability and Culpability in the Savings and Loan Industry," *Critical Perspectives on Accounting* (Vol. 5), pp. 179–193.

Paltrow, Scott, and M. Schroeder (2002). "SEC Top Accountant Is in Tough Spot," *Wall Street Journal*, (May 22), pp. C1 and C17.

Peat, Marwick, Mitchell & Co. (1981). *Executive Newsletter* (June 3), p. 3.

Revsine, Lawrence (December 1991). "The Selective Financial Misrepresentation Hypothesis," *Accounting Horizons*, pp. 16–27.

Ronen, Joshua (2002). "Policy Reforms in the Aftermath of Accounting Scandals," *Journal of Accounting and Public Policy* (Vol. 21. No. 3), pp. 281–286.

Ross, Steven A. (1979). "Disclosure Regulation in Financial Markets," in *Issues in Financial Regulation*, ed. F. Edwards. McGraw-Hill, pp. 177–202.

Schreuder, Hein, and Kavasseri V. Ramanathan (1984). "Accounting and Corporate Accountability: An Extended Comment," *Accounting, Organizations and Society* (Vol. 9, No. 3/4), pp. 409–415.

Schroeder, Michael, and J. Bandler (2002). "Pitt Faces New Questions on CEO Meetings," *Wall Street Journal* (May 20), pp. C1 and C7.

Securities and Exchange Commission (1973). "Statement of Accounting Policy on the Establishment and Improvement of Accounting Principles and Standards," *Accounting Series Release No. 150*. SEC.

———— (1975). "Notice of Adoption of Amendments to Form 10-Q and Regulation S-X Regarding Interim Reporting," *Accounting Series Release No. 177*. SEC.

Seidler, Lee J., Frederick Andrews, and Marc J. Epstein (1977). *The Equity Funding Papers, Anatomy of a Fraud*. John Wiley & Sons.

Solomons, David (November 1978). "The Politicization of Accounting," *Journal of Accountancy*, pp. 65–72.

Stigler, George J. (Fall 1971). "The Theory of Economic Regulation," *Bell Journal of Economics and Management Science*, pp. 3–21.

———— (1975). *The Citizen and the State: Essays on Regulation*. University of Chicago Press.

Thornton, Emily (2002). "What It Will Take to Police the Street," *Business Week* (Nov. 25), p. 38.

Verrechia, Robert E. (March 1990). "Information Quality and Discretionary Disclosure," *Journal of Accounting and Economics*, pp. 365–380.

Wagenhofer, Alfred (March 1990). "Voluntary Disclosure With a Strategic Opponent," *Journal of Accounting and Economics*, pp. 341–363.

Watts, Ross L., and Jerold L. Zimmerman (January 1978). "Toward a Positive Theory of the Determination of Accounting Standards," *Accounting Review*, pp. 112–134.

———— (October 1983). "Agency Problems, Auditing and the Theory of the Firm: Some Evidence," *Journal of Law and Economics*, pp. 613–634.

———— (January 1990). "Positive Accounting Theory: A Ten Year Perspective," *Accounting Review*, pp. 131–156.

Wong, Jilnaught (April 1988). "Economic Incentives for the Voluntary Disclosure of Current Cost Financial Statements," *Journal of Accounting and Economics*, pp. 151–167.

Yeo, Gillian H. H., and D. Ziebart (Fall 1995). "An Empirical Test of the Signaling Effect of Management's Earnings Forecasts: A Decomposition of the Earnings Surprise and Forecast Surprise Effects," *Journal of Accounting, Auditing & Finance*, pp. 787–802.

Zeff, Stephen A. (December 1978). "The Rise of Economic Consequences," *Journal of Accountancy*, pp. 56–63.

5

Postulates, Principles, and Concepts

Learning Objectives

After reading this chapter, you should be able to:

- Understand the significance of Accounting Research Studies Nos. 1 and 3 and why they failed.
- Be familiar with the basic concepts of postulates and principles that underlie historical costing.
- Grasp the equity theories of accounting, their potential usefulness, and their limitations for analyzing transactions and events.

The need for a theoretical framework in financial accounting has long been felt. The Committee on Accounting Procedure (CAP) was not concerned with the task of deriving an underlying framework, but both the Accounting Principles Board (APB) and the Financial Accounting Standards Board (FASB) have attempted to develop theoretical foundations as a guide to formulating accounting rules. As briefly mentioned in Chapter 3, the APB attempted to derive a system of postulates and principles but was unsuccessful. The FASB instituted the conceptual framework project, a much longer-term endeavor consisting, at the present time, of seven parts.

Despite the fact that Accounting Research Studies (ARSs) 1 and 3 on postulates and principles were not accepted, these studies represent a milestone in the attempt to provide a unified theoretical underpinning for financial accounting rules by the APB. Consequently, it is important to assess why these studies fell short of the goal of obtaining a framework for

APB accounting opinions. Part of the story has already been told: The project advisers, not to mention the profession at large, felt the principles were too much in conflict with existing notions to serve as a frame of reference for the rules that were sure to follow. A closer look at these early studies will help us understand the FASB's conceptual framework and its prospects.

A discussion of postulates and principles would be incomplete without analyzing those concepts that have continued to form an important basis for contemporary historical cost accounting. No matter what form financial statements may take in the future, it is quite likely that many of these ideas will be retained, refined, or modified because they have proved useful in an informal but pragmatic fashion.

Finally, in this chapter we look at another group of concepts that have long played a role in interpreting accounting relationships. These are the equity theories of accounting. They are concerned with the relationship that exists between the firm itself and its ownership interests. Various inferences can be drawn from these relationships, which can have some influence on the standard-setting process.

The two appendices to this chapter are the postulates of ARS 1 and the broad principles of ARS 3. They should be read in conjunction with the discussion of these documents.

Postulates and Principles

It cannot be overstressed that the formation of the APB was a watershed in the development of accounting theory and the role of research. However, Alvin R. Jennings, in his important speech advocating this new approach to the development of accounting principles, did not propose the formation of a new rule-making body. What he did envision was a new research organization within the American Institute of Certified Public Accountants (AICPA) that would issue statements subject to a two-thirds vote of the Council of the AICPA.[1]

The Special Committee on Research Program

The result of Jennings's ideas was the Special Committee on Research Program, which stressed the need for articulating the basic set of postulates underlying accounting. In turn, the principles were to be logically derived from the postulates. The committee thus advocated a deductive approach. Chapter 2 noted that deductive approaches to theory are basically normative in outlook. The committee barely mentioned this fact and its implications in its report:

> The general purpose of the Institute . . . should be to advance the written expression of what constitutes generally accepted accounting principles, for the guidance of its members. . . . This means something more than a survey of existing practice. It means continuing efforts to determine appropriate practice and to narrow the areas of difference and inconsistency in practice. . . . The Institute should take definite steps to lead in the thinking on unsettled and controversial issues.[2]

Although the committee foresaw the need for securing the approval of those who would be subject to the rules of the new APB, it did not anticipate the storm of protest that would erupt in the wake of ARS 3.[3] The committee's conception of postulates and principles was also problematic.

Postulates are generally defined as basic assumptions that cannot be verified. They serve as a basis for inference and a foundation for a theoretical structure that consists of propositions deduced from them.[4] In systems using formal logical techniques, the basic premises are called *axioms* and consist of symbolic notation, and the operations for deducing propositions are mathematically based.[5] The committee's report represented postulates in accounting as few in number and stemming from the economic and political environments as well as from the customs and underlying viewpoints of the business community. The committee thus virtually defined postulates and limited their number for the author of ARS 1. One committee member revealed shortly thereafter that it was not the committee's intention to define postulates.[6]

The APB committee, on the other hand, did not define broad principles, although it did compare them in scope to the definitions and pronouncements that had been issued in four different reports by the American Accounting Association (AAA). These documents and several supplements were published in 1936, 1941, 1948, and 1957. The first two reports contain the word *principles* in their titles, but the word was replaced by *standards* in the 1948 and 1957 reports (the 1948 revision also used *concepts* in its title).[7] These reports contain definitions of basic accounting terms, proposed rules for presentation and measurement of accounting data, and concepts to be applied to published financial reports. The material in these reports thus covers a wide variety of topics, only some of which might be considered pertinent to the topic of principles (the basic definitions and concepts, such as disclosure and uniformity).

These reports did not use the definition of principles contained in Accounting Terminology Bulletin No. 1 of the AICPA: "A general law or rule adopted or professed as a guide to action, a settled ground or basis of conduct or practice. . . ."[8] This definition is quite close to the one used in the philosophy of science, a discipline concerned with scientific method. A principle is closely related to a law. Both are considered statements of a true and generalized nature containing referents to the real world as opposed to purely analytic statements whose truth or falsity is self-contained by their internal logic.[9]

A law contains elements observable by empirical techniques, whereas a principle does not. If a principle could be empirically tested and proven true (or at least not proven false), it would be capable of becoming a law.[10] Principles are general statements that influence the way we view phenomena and the way we think about problems.[11] The "truth" of a law or principle does not mean that it is incapable of replacement by newer systems. However, changes—particularly in the case of laws—should be extremely infrequent.

Accounting Research Study No. 1 (ARS 1)

Given his charge by the Special Committee, Moonitz adopted a frame of reference or outlook that was oriented to the problems dealt with by accountants. He rejected a deductive approach rooted in reasoning alone because it was not broad enough to encompass the experiential and empirical aspects of accounting. Deinzer correctly pointed out, however, that Moonitz did eventually revert to the axiomatic (meaning deductive) method.[12] He did indeed use a deductive type of approach—but without employing symbolic terminology and formal methods—in terms of reasoning to a second level of postulates and some of the principles. However, the postulates themselves are of two decidedly different types. One category (the A and B groups) is made up of general, descriptive postulates that appear to coincide with the committee's charge that postulates should be derived from the economic and political environments and modes of thought and customs from all segments of the community. The second category (the C group) is value judgments. It is this group that may have gone against the committee's charge and definitely labels Moonitz's work as deductive–normative in scope.

The postulates themselves (see Appendix 5-A) are in three groups: the environmental group (A), those stemming from accounting itself (B), and the imperatives (C). Some postulates in the B group appear to stem from the A category, which led to the criticism that no postulates should be reasoned from any others and a similar criticism that postulates were given a rank order. Although these criticisms may have some validity, they could easily be overcome by relabeling. There is no rule that only two levels (postulates and principles) can be used in deductive reasoning. A complex environment, such as that in which accounting operates, can have numerous levels.

A far more telling criticism was that self-evident postulates may not be sufficiently substantive to lead to a unique and meaningful set of accounting principles. This unquestionably appears to be the case with both the A and B groups. If postulates are indeed defined as self-evident generalizations from a particular environment, this raises the question of what their role is in a deductively oriented system in which principles form the basis for more specific rules. Of necessity, it appears that postulates must play a more passive role. The principles and rules should not be in conflict with them, but alone they are not sufficiently important to lead to the desired principles and rules.[13] They are thus necessary, but not sufficient to lead to a viable outcome.

Hence, the key group in Moonitz's set of postulates is the imperatives. These appear to be more like what Mautz has called *concepts* because (a) they are normative in nature and (b) they have developed within the context of accounting practice.[14] The imperatives have the flavor of being objectives that should be attained, which is also a result of their normative aspect.

The key postulate appears to be C-4, stability of the monetary unit. This postulate appears to have two possible outcomes. If purchasing power of the monetary unit is not stable, the postulate implies that some form of inflation accounting should be instituted. If, on the other hand, purchasing power of the monetary unit is relatively stable, two further consequences of the postulate arise—one is that retention of historical cost is justified; the other is that a system of current values is still warranted, despite general stability of the monetary unit, because demand changes can cause considerable price fluctuation for individual products and services. The dual interpretation of C-4 is a definite weakness of this very important postulate. Perhaps Postulate A-1, usefulness of quantitative data, should lead to current values, but this is certainly not self-evident from the Moonitz postulates. At any rate, the profession was generally silent when the postulates appeared. It was undoubtedly awaiting the appearance of the broad principles study.

Accounting Research Study No. 3 (ARS 3)

There are eight broad principles in ARS 3 (see Appendix 5-B). At least three of them (A, B, and D) deal with the problems of changing prices, which was the point of departure for the profession's rather stinging rejection of the study. It is interesting to note that the summary of the eight principles covers some four and one-half pages, two and one-half of which are devoted to Principle D, the asset valuation principle.

Deinzer very appropriately noted that Principle A—which states that revenue is earned by the entire process of operations of the firm rather than at one point only, usually when sale occurs—was not reasoned from any of the 14 postulates.[15] It would appear, then, to belong in the B group of postulates. More importantly, Sprouse and Moonitz apparently needed it to pave the way for their value-oriented principles because it underlies the recognition of changes in replacement cost, which leads to holding gains or losses (Principle B-2).

One of the most pointed criticisms of the asset valuation measures prescribed in Principle D was that they are not *additive*. That is, although current value dollars are being used, different attributes or characteristics are being measured; hence, they cannot theoretically be combined by addition because Sprouse and Moonitz advocated different current-value characteristics for different asset classes. For example, if inventory can easily be sold at a given market price, net realizable value (selling price less known costs of disposal) should be used (D-2). On the other hand, the value of fixed assets, which are not intended for sale, is rooted in terms of the service they can provide over present and future periods. As a result, Sprouse and Moonitz opted for replacement cost as the appropriate characteristic of measurement for this class of assets (D-3). Obviously, the additivity question, where different attributes are being measured, has strong overtones of measurement theory.

Chambers was the principal critic of the lack of additivity of asset values put forth by the broad principles of ARS 3.[16] Chambers strongly advocated the exit-value approach illustrated in Chapter 1, although his position is blurred by his acceptance of replacement cost as a secondary valuation if exit values were unavailable.[17] However, it should be clear that Chambers was attempting to separate conceptual or theoretical issues from measurement problems. Hence, it would almost appear that the additivity issue can be breached only if one's heart is in the right place. The basic theoretical system should be unified in terms of one primary characteristic of assets and liabilities to be measured. However, a less desirable measurement must be employed where the primary measurement system falls short of being able to provide the needed numbers. Nevertheless, the primacy of conceptual issues over measurement problems cannot be ignored. The answer probably lies in determining which current value elements have the most utility for financial statement users, an issue not addressed by Sprouse and Moonitz.

A last criticism to be leveled at ARS 1 and ARS 3 was that a set of postulates should be complete enough to allow no conflicting conclusions to be derived from them. Postulate C-4 says that the monetary unit should be stable. From it, Principle D was derived advocating various current values for different categories of assets. The various choices espoused in Principle D cannot be justified to the exclusion of other possibilities. Hence, the postulate system is not theoretically tight enough to justify it, whether or not one agrees with the resulting principles.

A Perspective on ARS 1 and ARS 3

ARS 1 and ARS 3 failed for a variety of reasons in addition to the most obvious one—the inability of the profession to abandon historical costs. The postulates and principles themselves had several weaknesses. The postulates were not complete and therefore could not exclude other value systems than the one prescribed in the principles. Additionally, at least one principle, Principle A, was not derived from any of the postulates. Finally, the question of whether resulting valuations of various assets should be additive (because they advocated different attributes) became an interesting, and probably moot, point.

Even beyond the questions of logic and adequacy of ARS 1 and ARS 3, a number of issues have since made it clear that the Moonitz–Sprouse efforts could not succeed. It appears that Moonitz and Sprouse were commissioned to find those postulates and principles that would lead to "true income"—in other words, to use a single concept of income that would show it superior to all other challengers. In retrospect, it has become evident that no income measurement can be deemed to have such an advantage over competing concepts.

Aside from Postulate A-1, which states that "quantitative data are helpful in making rational economic decisions," virtually nothing is said in either study about who are the outside users of accounting data and what their particular information needs and abilities might be. It is generally conceded today that users of financial data (with their underlying information needs and abilities to understand and manipulate financial data) cover a broad, relatively heterogeneous spectrum. However, the emphasis on users was not a particularly prominent theoretical accounting issue when ARS 1 and ARS 3 were published (user diversity and its implications are discussed later in Chapter 6). Thus, the postulates and principles approach tended to overlook a theoretical area that has since received a great deal of attention. The rise of the user-needs outlook has produced a new focus on the objectives of published financial statement data. Indeed, as we mentioned, several of the imperative postulates actually began to spill over into the area of financial statement objectives. Formulating the objectives of financial statements and reporting has become an extremely important part of theory formulation.

Finally, we note that the commissioning of ARS 1 and ARS 3 occurred at a time when little formal attention was given to what might be called the politics of rule making. By this we mean that under the FASB there is more opportunity to react to potential accounting rules for those who will be subject to them than was the case with the APB.

Some might say that the postulates and principles studies were a dismal failure. As we view events from the perspective of many decades, we realize that this is not the case. These studies should hold an important place in the history of accounting theory for no other reason than the fact that they were the first attempt in the United States by the practicing arm of the profession to provide a conceptual underpinning for the rule-making function. Furthermore, by examining the difficulties encountered by the APB in drafting a theoretical statement that would meet the approval of those who would be governed by it, the FASB should have learned valuable lessons for its conceptual framework project.

Basic Concepts Underlying Historical Costing

Many accounting concepts have long influenced accounting rules. These concepts have largely evolved from practical operating necessities, including income tax laws, but have also appeared in several theoretical works written mostly in the formative years (1930–1946) of accounting policy-making groups.[18] Perhaps the most outstanding of these was the monograph by Paton and Littleton, *An Introduction to Corporate Accounting Standards*, which approached theory deductively rather than from the point of view of what was being done in practice.[19] This work was not revolutionary, but it did attempt to provide a basic framework that the enterprise could use to assess its accounting practices. The authors hoped that a greater degree of consistency in accounting practice would result from their effort.

Other important works of this period included:

- Canning's attempt to relate asset valuation to future cash flows
- Separate books by Sweeney and MacNeal, which were concerned with accounting for, respectively, the changing value of the monetary unit and the weakness of historical costs
- Sanders, Hatfield, and Moore's monograph on deriving the principles of accounting from practice
- Gilman's book about refining the concept of income
- Littleton's attempt to derive inductively the accounting principles underlying relevant practice[20]

The concepts discussed in this chapter have been called *postulates, axioms, assumptions, doctrines, conventions, constraints, principles,* and *standards.* The word *concepts* is probably an-accurate overall label for these terms. A *concept* is the result of the process of identifying, classifying, and interpreting various phenomena or precepts.[21] It is thus not part of the formal process of theory formulation, but can be used within a theory—as part of the structure of postulates, or in the conclusions deduced from the postulates, or even as the subject of testing in empirical research. Many elements fall into the concept category in accounting, and they are quite rightly considered part of accounting theory. Many have been and will be part of a general theoretical framework for interpreting and presenting financial accounting data as well as individual accounting theories. Indeed, several concepts will be discussed in Chapter 7 in terms of their place in the conceptual framework of the FASB.

Attempts such as ARS 1, ARS 3, and those mentioned in Chapter 2 to set up deductive systems of postulates and principles have failed to achieve a high degree of consensus owing to lack of rigor in reasoning, overlapping definitions, and different value judgments.[22] Bearing this in mind, we have given the following organization to our discussion of concepts strictly for teaching purposes. The concepts are broken down as follows:

- *Postulates* are basic assumptions concerning the business environment.
- *Principles* are general approaches utilized in the recognition and measurement of accounting events. Principles are, in turn, divided into two main types:
    1. *Input-oriented principles* are broad rules that guide the accounting function. Input-oriented principles can be divided into two general classifications: general underlying rules of operation

and constraining principles. As their names imply, the former are general in nature whereas the latter are geared to certain specific types of situations.

2. *Output-oriented principles* involve certain qualities or characteristics that financial statements should possess if the input-oriented principles are appropriately executed.

A schema of these various concepts is shown in Exhibit 5.1.

Exhibit 5.1   Basic Concepts Underlying Historical Costing

Postulates	*Principles*
Going Concern	Input-Oriented Principles
Time Period	• General Underlying Rules of Operation
Accounting Entity	1. Recognition
Monetary Unit	2. Matching
	• Constraining Principles
	1. Conservatism
	2. Disclosure
	3. Materiality
	4. Objectivity (also called verifiability)
	Output-Oriented Principles
	• Applicable to Users
	1. Comparability
	• Applicable to Preparers
	1. Consistency
	2. Uniformity

Postulates

Going Concern or Continuity

The going-concern postulate simply states that unless there is evidence to the contrary, it is assumed that the firm will continue indefinitely. As a result, under ordinary circumstances, reporting liquidation values for assets and equities is in violation of the postulate. However, the continuity assumption is simply too broad to lead to any kind of a choice among valuation systems, including historical cost. Fremgen and Sterling have criticized this postulate extensively.[23] Sterling logically demolishes it because the time period of continuity is presumed to be long enough to conclude the firm's present contractual arrangements. However, by the time these affairs are concluded, they will have been replaced by new arrangements. Hence, the implication is one of indefinite life. However, we know that over the long run, many firms do conclude their activities. Therefore, continuity is more in the nature of a prediction than an underlying assumption. Suffice it to say that, aside from ordinarily excluding liquidation values, going concern has little to add to accounting theory.

Time Period

Business, as well as virtually every form of human and animal activity, operates within fairly rigidly specified periods of time. The time period idea is, nevertheless, somewhat artificial because it creates definite segments out of what is a continuing process. For business entities, the time period is the calendar or business year. As a result, of course, financial reports contain statements of financial condition, earnings, and funds flow over a year's time or a portion thereof. Since the year is a relatively short time in the life of most enterprises, the time period postulate has led to accrual accounting and to the principles of recognition and matching under historical costing. Furthermore, even though the needs of users have required financial reporting for less than full-year intervals, these interim financial statements have their own problems and sets of rules. APB Opinion No. 28 states in general, however, that accounting methods followed in annual financial statements must likewise be followed in interim reports. Hence, interim reports must include estimates of annual amounts.

Accounting Entity

When we view the business entity in the context of accounting as well as in its legal form, it is clear that the entity is separate from its owners, but there are nevertheless two important problems.

First is the problem of defining the entity and accounting for the relationship among its parts. Involved here is the question of whether entities should be considered as one unit as a result of one controlling the other(s). In other words, should accounts be combined or should a noncombinative method of showing the relationship be used? The whole combination issue is made more complex by the presence of foreign operations. Theoretical aspects of these questions are discussed in Chapter 18.

The second issue related to the question of the accounting entity concerns the relationship between the firm and its owners. While the accounting is separate, the point of interface between the firm and the owners exists in the owners' equity accounts. A number of deductive theories purport to describe this relationship and the role of the owners' equity accounts. These ideas influence our interpretation of what constitutes income, the meaning of equities, and other important issues. The equity theories, as they are called, are discussed later in this chapter.

Monetary Unit

In nonbarter economies, money serves as the medium of exchange. As a result, money has also become the principal standard of value and is subject to the measurement process. Thus, financial statements are expressed in terms of the monetary unit of their particular nation or by means of a common monetary unit such as the Euro in the European Union. The assumption, for accounting purposes, that the monetary unit is stable became a mainstay of accounting principles and methods. Hence, the historical cost principle became enshrined as a virtually unchallengeable tenet of accounting.

Severe inflation in the 1970s in the United States and other nations encouraged a fresh examination of valuation theories and new ways of presenting financial information. Current valuation arises in areas such as marketable securities (SFAS No. 115), impaired assets (SFAS No. 121), and derivatives (SFAS No. 133), and SFAS No. 157 will be instituting a fair (current) value measurement system.

Principles

The word *principles* has not been well defined in ARSs of the AICPA. Neither ARS 1 nor ARS 3 precisely defines the word, although the latter contains the phrase "broad accounting principles" in its title. Paul Grady indicated in the preface of ARS 7 that he regarded accounting principles as synonymous with practices.[24] However, some 400 pages later, Grady identifies principles as postulates derived from "experiences and reason" that have proved useful.[25] Deductively, then, it appears that principles are postulates that have been successful in practice, an interpretation that Grady himself would probably tend to reject.

Perhaps the most useful definition of *principles* in official publications comes from APB Statement 4. *Generally accepted accounting principles*, it says, are rooted in "experience, reason, custom, usage, and . . . practical necessity."[26] Furthermore, they "encompass the conventions, rules, and procedures necessary to define accepted accounting practice at a particular time."[27] This still overlaps with Grady's definition, in which principles are identified with acceptable practice, but it distinguishes principles from postulates even though they stem from practical necessity and related experiences.[28] However, a subset of generally accepted accounting principles, *pervasive principles,* is largely synonymous with the way the term is used in APB Statement 4:

> *Pervasive principles* [italics added] are few in number and fundamental in nature . . . pervasive principles specify the general approach accountants take to recognition and measurement of events that affect the financial position and results of operations of enterprises.[29]

Notice that both definitions of *principles* from APB Statement 4 do not include the idea of permanence that is given to the word in the scientific sense. Pervasive principles in accounting overlap with what we refer to here as *input-oriented principles.*

Input-Oriented Principles

Accounting principles are classified here into two broad types: input-oriented principles and output-oriented principles. The distinctions between these groups are at least somewhat clear. *Input-oriented principles* are concerned with general approaches or rules for preparing financial statements and their content, including any necessary supplementary disclosures. *Output-oriented principles* are concerned with the comparability of financial statements of different firms. Although some of these principles apply to preparers of the statements and others to users, there is a close linkage between them.

General Underlying Rules of Operation

The first group of input-oriented principles is the general underlying rules of operation. These are further broken down into those involved with revenue recognition and those involved with expense recognition. These principles illustrate the primary orientation of historical cost accounting toward income measurement rather than asset and liability valuation.

Recognition. Revenue is defined here as the output of the enterprise in terms of its product(s) or service(s). Notice that this definition says nothing about the receipt or inflow of assets as a result of revenue performance because defining revenue in this way can easily lead to problems in terms of when to recognize revenue as being earned. It is generally conceded that revenues arise in conjunction with all of the operations of a firm.[30] For a manufacturing enterprise, these operations would include acquisition of raw materials, production, sale, collection of cash or other consideration from customers, and after-sale services such as product warranties and guarantees.

Recognition concerns the problem of when to enter revenues and expenses in the accounts. The most prevalent revenue recognition point by far is at the point of sale. Other possibilities may, however, arise; for example, revenue may be recognized in accordance with the firm's *critical event*. The *critical event* is the operating function that is the most crucial in terms of the earning process.[31] Revenue recognition points are discussed in Chapter 12. Suffice it to say that the revenue recognition principle is the most pervasive in the canon of historical cost accounting.

The conceptual framework project of the FASB states that revenue recognition occurs in accordance with two criteria: (1) The assets to be received from the performance of the revenue function are realized or realizable, and (2) performance of the revenue function is "substantially accomplished."[32] In the latter case, revenues are referred to as being *earned*, a commonly used term for revenue performance. This conception of revenue recognition has its roots in that fountainhead of the historical cost approach, the Paton and Littleton monograph mentioned previously.[33] The terms *realized* and *realizable* refer to the conversion or ready convertibility of the enterprise's product or service into cash or claims to cash. *Realized* means that the firm's product or service has been converted to cash or claims to cash, while *realizable* has been defined as the ability to convert assets already received or held into known amounts of cash or claims to cash.[34] *Realization* has often been used as a synonym for *recognition*.[35] The conceptual framework project appears to have been instrumental in having the word recognition supplant realization. Attempts to breach revenue recognition rules by recognizing revenue early in order to inflate current income are a considerable problem today. More will be said about this issue in Chapter 12.

Matching. Expenses are defined as costs that expire as a result of generating revenues. Expenses are thus necessary to the production of revenues. If all expenses could be directly identified with either specific revenues or specific time periods, expense measurement would present few problems. Unfortunately, many important expenses cannot be specifically identified with particular revenues, and they also bring benefit to more than one time period.

The process of recognizing cost expiration (expense incurrence) for categories such as depreciation, cost of goods sold, interest, and deferred charges is called *matching*. Matching implies that expenses are being recognized on a fair and equitable basis relative to the recognition of revenues. Matching is thus the second aspect, after recognition, of the primacy of income measurement over asset and liability valuation in our present system, which has been oriented toward historical cost.

Currently, matching is under extensive attack. First, the historical cost approach often tends to substantially understate expense measurements relative to the value of expired-asset services. Second, the "systematic and rational" methods employed under generally accepted accounting principles tend to be extremely arbitrary: A particular problem can be handled in more than one way. This imprecision is known as the "allocation problem" and is discussed in Chapter 9.

Constraining Principles

The second group of input-oriented principles—constraining principles—partially overlaps with the "modifying conventions" mentioned in APB Statement 4. These principles are described in the following fashion: "Certain widely adopted conventions modify the application of the pervasive measurement principles. These modifying conventions . . . have evolved to deal with some of the most difficult and controversial problem areas in financial accounting."[36] The constraining principles either impose limitations on financial statements, as in the case of conservatism, or provide checks on them, as in the case of materiality and disclosure.

Conservatism. Unquestionably, conservatism holds an extremely important place in the ethos of accountants. Indeed, it has even been called the dominant principle of accounting.[37] *Conservatism,* from a preparer's if not a standard setter's orientation, is defined here as the attempt to select "generally accepted" accounting methods that result in any of the following: (a) slower revenue recognition, (b) faster expense recognition, (c) lower asset valuation, (d) higher liability valuation. However, in certain situations some of these criteria can conflict. If so, lower income considerations would take precedence over higher asset valuations in determining whether a method or approach is conservative. For example, in the case of current valuation of assets, one approach—called distributable income—does not include real holding gains in the computation of income. As a result, in an inflationary environment, distributable income often results in higher asset valuations and lower income calculations than would occur under the historical cost alternative. Therefore, the distributable-income approach to current valuation can be more conservative than historical costing even though, generally speaking, historical cost is assumed to be more conservative.

Basu, in a capital markets-oriented context, has interpreted conservatism to mean that "bad news" (the loss of a major customer, for example) relative to reported earnings has a greater impact on security prices than "good news." Basu has found statistical evidence bearing out his point.[38]

Bushman and Piotroski are in agreement with Basu that the more "bad news" beats out "good news" in terms of swiftness of reporting, the more conservative the institutional setting.[39] Bushman and Piotroski's particular contribution lies in their observation that the more fully developed are financial and legal institutions (e.g., courts, Securities and Exchange Commission, Federal Trade Commission), the more conservative will be the accounting rules (e.g., recognizing loss contingencies prior to gain contingencies).[40]

Givoly and Hayn have found evidence of conservative financial reporting over time for 896 firms from 1968 to 1998.[41] Various indirect measures were used, such as the ratio of market value to book value growing over time (indicating a conservative balance sheet) and growth in the ratio of income from continuing operations to total assets. The Givoly and Hayn study should help to put into better perspective some of the recent startling headlines about corporate financial reporting behavior, although earnings management (Chapter 12) remains an extremely important problem.

Watts also sees conservatism as a dominating element of financial accounting.[42] He notes that it stems from both management and standard setters. On the management side, he sees conservatism stemming from contracting arrangements such as debt covenants covering bond issues, attempts to avoid litigation by understating assets, and minimization of taxes.[43] However, relative to standard-setting agencies, he sees the tide going from a conservative orientation (recognizing probable loss contingencies, but not gain contingencies in SFAS No. 5, for example) to more of a future-oriented outlook, helping users predict cash flows (see conceptual framework, Chapter 7). Along the same line, the FASB has backed off an overly dominating place for conservatism since it is not listed in the hierarchical qualities of the conceptual framework, although it is still seen as a "prudent reaction to uncertainty."[44]

As mentioned above, earnings management—which usually arises in regard to either management attempting to meet earnings forecasts or to maximize management compensation arrangements—puts an upward spin on calculating earnings numbers. Watts believes that conservatism is a more important factor than earnings management. We tend to agree with him because we believe that earnings management arises in a more ad hoc short-term context whereas conservatism generally has a longer-run impact, but the relationship between them is certainly open to further examination and research

Disclosure. Moonitz construed disclosure as an imperative postulate (C-5). However, he described it in negative terms: "that which is necessary to make them [accounting reports] not misleading." The fact that it is difficult to quantify the concept of adequate disclosure for users may be the reason for Moonitz's phrasing and for the failure of the Securities and Exchange Commission (SEC) or AICPA sources to define the concept adequately.[45] The FASB has not defined it, although two important FASB Statements, in particular, have dealt with it: SFAS No. 131 on segmental disclosures and SFAS No. 33 on general price-level and current value data. SFAS No. 131 requires segmental disclosures by management's own choice for making operating decisions and assessing performance. One issue that is arising relative to disclosure concerns its *credibility* or believability, which is becoming more important in the light of recent major accounting scandals. Mirroring the conservatism dichotomy mentioned previously that "bad news" affects security prices more than "good news," researchers have found that negative news disclosures are more credible than positive news disclosures.[46]

Disclosure refers to the presentation of relevant financial information both inside and outside the main body of the financial statements themselves, including methods employed in financial statements where more than one choice exists or an unusual or innovative selection of methods arises.[47] The principal outside categories include:

- Supplementary financial statement schedules, such as those pertaining to SFAS No. 131 and SFAS No. 33 (now superseded by SFAS No. 89).
- Disclosure in footnotes of information that cannot be adequately presented in the body of the financial statements themselves.
- Disclosure of material or major post-statement events in the annual report.
- Forecasts of operations for the forthcoming year.
- Management's analysis of operations in the annual report.

Lang and Lundholm have found that disclosure activity frequently increases approximately six months prior to a stock offering.[48] This often results in a stock price increase and a lower cost of capital. If the stock price increase is maintained, it could indicate a lessening of information asymmetry, but if it is not maintained, it may indicate that the stock has been "hyped": The information may be misleading or positive conditions may have been overemphasized.

There are two important reasons for believing that disclosure will become even more important in the future. First, as the business environment grows more complex, expressing important financial and operating information adequately within the confines of the traditional financial statements becomes more difficult. Second, a considerable body of evidence indicates that capital markets are able to absorb and reflect new information within security prices fairly rapidly (see Chapter 8). However, wherever possible, information is preferable within the body of financial statements themselves rather than appearing only in footnote disclosures.

Materiality. *Materiality* refers to the importance of an item (or group of items) to users in terms of its relevance to evaluation or decision making. We can thus view it as the other side of the disclosure coin because what is disclosed should, of course, be material. Unfortunately, materiality levels are determined by auditors on a case-by-case basis and can vary greatly among auditors, among companies, and even by the same auditor over time.[49] Moreover, external users are not informed of the materiality level used by the auditor.

An early and extensive attempt to assess quantitative perceptions of materiality was conducted in Pattillo's study for the Financial Executives Research Foundation (FERF).[50] Pattillo used 684 respondents, including preparers of financial statements (financial executives from Fortune 500 and medium-sized firms), users of accounting information (bankers and financial analysts), auditors, and also academics, to use their own materiality judgments on 28 cases. Pattillo's major findings included the following:

- Although many respondents usually use a range of 5% to 10% of net income as the boundary of materiality, they did not apply a single absolute dollar or percentage relationship to all situations.
- Perceptions of materiality differ between groups, with financial executives having the highest percentage threshold of net income and certified public accountants and financial analysts having the lowest overall percentage.
- Modifying elements, such as the particular characteristics of the firm and the political and economic environment, influence the perception of materiality in particular situations.

In a study using a computer simulation, Turner found that immaterial errors can combine, resulting in a significant impact on financial ratios.[51] This error effect is more marked on profitability ratios such as profit margin on sales and return on assets than on solvency ratios such as the current ratio and debt-to-equity ratio. Among other recent materiality studies has been an attempt to measure it from the user perspective, concentrating on the vantage points of (a) percentage effect on net income, (b) percentage effect on revenues, and (c) percentage effect on total assets.[52] Using "unexpected earnings" divided by the three factors mentioned above, they found that the average investor's materiality threshold is in the range of 0.1% to 0.2% of pretax income, a range significantly below the range of 5% to 10% of net income found by Pattillo and the range used in the auditing literature. These and other empirical studies have helped to shed light on the concept of materiality, although it is not a settled issue.[53]

Despite difficulties, attempts are being made to tighten materiality boundaries. The SEC in Staff Accounting Bulletin (SAB) No. 99 tried to provide materiality guidance for auditors, although it did not provide precise percentage standards of materiality.[54]

Sarbanes-Oxley (SOX) has also become involved with materiality. In discussing SOX, Vorhies notes that using a benchmark of a 5% materiality level as a percentage of income, pretax net income would be "normalized" by adjusting net income from continuing operations for unusual events not expected to recur to arrive at the basic materiality threshold.[55] However, errors and misstatements may still be material even if they fall below 5%. Errors should be aggregated, even though individually small, to see if they breach the 5% barrier.[56] Also, any internal control deficiencies must be evaluated with the 5% materiality threshold in mind. If the accounting estimation process is flawed, the materiality threshold must also be kept in mind. Finally, materiality must also be considered if fraud arises in a context where the firm's financial statements have been misstated.[57]

It is clear that materiality, along with disclosure, will continue to be an important issue in the foreseeable future, not only in the United States, but in other countries as well.[58]

Objectivity. In the past, objectivity has been interpreted in several different ways, but primarily in terms of the quality of evidence underlying transactions that are eventually summarized and organized in the form of financial statements.[59] The concept of quality of evidence was considered apart from those who carry out the measurement function. Now, however, *objectivity* is more commonly thought of in the statistical sense (discussed in Chapter 1) as the degree of consensus among measurers. It is, therefore, an integral part of the measurement process rather than being either a postulate or principle. APB Statement 4 adopts this outlook, although it discusses the concept as a "qualitative objective" of accounting and relabels it as *verifiability*.[60] This newer, statistical sense of verifiability also appears in the Statement of Financial Accounting Concepts No. 2 of the conceptual framework project of the FASB.

Output-Oriented Principles

As mentioned earlier, output-oriented principles express qualities that financial statements should possess when viewed from the standpoint of both preparers and users. Of necessity, then, these concepts overlap somewhat as well as complement each other.

As viewed here, comparability is a concept that applies to users of financial statements, whereas consistency and uniformity focus on preparers of financial information.

Comparability

Comparability has often been described as accounting for like events in a similar manner, but this definition is too simplistic to be operational.[61] It also applies to those who use financial statements. *Comparability*, viewed here from the user's standpoint, refers to the degree of reliability users should find in financial statements when evaluating financial condition or the results of operations on an interfirm basis or predicting income or cash flows.[62]

Obviously, then, comparability is largely dependent on the amount of uniformity attained in recording transactions and preparing financial statements. Despite the secondary role of comparability relative to uniformity, the cost–benefit relationship between them should be kept in mind: Comparability might be improved by more uniformity, but costs may exceed benefits.

Consistency

Consistency refers to a given firm's use of the same accounting methods over consecutive time periods. Consistency is necessary if predictions or evaluations based on a firm's financial statements over more than one time period are to be reliable. Should change occur—because of adoption of a more relevant or objective method—full disclosure must be made to users, and the auditor's opinion must be appropriately qualified.

Consistency is really an aspect of the broader issue of uniformity. Some believe that differing circumstances among firms, particularly when different industries are involved, make it impossible to attain uniformity of accounting techniques on an interfirm basis.[63] Therefore, consistency on an intrafirm basis, with full disclosure when changes occur, would be the most practical goal relative to output-oriented principles.

Uniformity

Uniformity has been and continues to be an important issue in accounting. But it has several subtle aspects that have not always been fully taken into account. Interpretations of uniformity have included the following:

- A uniform set of principles for all firms, with interpretation and application left up to the individual entity
- Similar accounting treatment required in broadly similar situations, regardless of possibly different underlying circumstances (rigid uniformity)
- Accounting treatment that takes into account different economic circumstances in broadly similar transactions (finite uniformity)

The second and third definitions differ from the first because they are concerned with the degree of uniformity that enters into interpretation of transactions. The first definition simply prescribes a broad theoretical framework to serve as a basis for interpretation of transactions. The difference between rigid and finite uniformity is best described by illustration.

SFAS No. 2, which requires immediate expensing of research and development (R&D) costs, is an example of rigid uniformity. Different expectations apply to the broad category of R&D in terms of cash flows that will be received from these costs, but the treatment is uniform even though different patterns of receipt of benefits exist. SFAS No. 13 is an example of finite uniformity. The statement sets down some rather specific criteria for differentiating between capital and operating leases. Hence, different circumstances are taken into account in distinguishing accounting for the two types of leases (we are not concerned here with the question of agreement in terms of the capitalization criteria themselves). Rigid and finite uniformity are extensively discussed in Chapter 9.

Equity Theories

The enterprise interfaces with owners in the owners' equity accounts. Several deductive theories have attempted to depict this relationship and are useful in interpreting nonlegal rights and interests in the owners' equity accounts as well as in determining certain components of income. Previously, these normative theories received considerable attention, but today they play a secondary role to newer, empirical research approaches. The problem with the equity theories is that the relationship between the firm and its owners, while important, does not really provide an adequate base from which to define and interpret all enterprise events. Some writers have stated that to attain consistency, one equity theory must be selected and adhered to, but we do not believe this is necessary. However, these theories, though selectively applied, can still provide useful insights.

Proprietary Theory

The *proprietary theory* assumes that the owners and the firm are virtually identical. This theory, which dates back centuries, is quite descriptive of economies made up largely of the small owner-operated firms that existed prior to the Industrial Revolution. However, Merino's thesis is that the proprietary theory was modified in the late nineteenth century in response to the growth of large oligopolistic firms.[64] At that time, many reformers desired more governmental intervention against absentee owners who were reaping large returns. Proprietary theorists, according to Merino, attempted to bring the absentee owner to center stage when viewing the business enterprise. These absentee ownership claims were legitimized by measuring profit available for distribution to owners rather than the notion that earnings—and capital—belonged to the corporation itself.[65]

Under proprietary theory, the assets belong to the firm's owners, the liabilities are their obligations, and ownership equities accrue to the owners. The balance sheet equation would be

$$\Sigma \text{Assets} - \Sigma \text{Liabilities} = \text{Owners' Equities} \tag{5.1}$$

Expenses include deductions for labor costs, taxes, and interest but not for preferred and common dividends. In other words, income represents the owners' increase in both net assets (assets minus liabilities) and owners' equities arising from operations during the period. The essentials of the proprietary approach largely coincide with the components of income measurement as it is presently construed in historical cost-based systems, although owners certainly do not exercise the control over owners' equity accounts suggested by proprietary theory. Furthermore, the relationship between the firm and its owners has changed markedly since the advent of the giant corporation in technologically advanced societies.

While Merino sees profit available for dividends as a very important idea in the development of the proprietary theory, several writers see wealth—represented by the balance sheet—as being a more important concept than income under the proprietary theory. Consequently, these individuals see either general price-level adjustment or current value approaches as integral to proprietary theory but not entity theory.[66] However, Merino points out that those who tried to revamp proprietary theory at the end of the nineteenth century also wanted accounting elevated to the level of a science that was "fact-oriented," which, in turn, led to a justification of historical costs.[67] We do not believe that either entity or proprietary theory is rich enough in basic assumptions to arrive at a justification for either a historical-cost-based system or departures from it.

Entity Theory

Dissatisfaction with the orientation of the proprietary theory led to development of the entity theory. Its chief architect was William A. Paton, long-time professor at the University of Michigan.[68] Under the *entity theory*, the firm and its owners are separate bodies. The assets belong to the firm itself; both liability and equity holders are investors in those assets with different rights and claims against them. The balance sheet equation would be

$$\Sigma\text{Assets} = \Sigma\text{Equities (including liabilities)} \qquad (5.2)$$

Under orthodox entity theory, there is a dual nature to both the owners' equity accounts and the question of the primary claim to income.[69] Stockholders have rights relative to receiving dividends when declared, voting at the annual corporate meeting, and sharing in net assets after all other claims have been met, if the firm is dissolving. Nevertheless, owners' equity accounts do not represent their interest as owners but simply their claims as equity holders. Similarly, net income does not belong to the owners, although the amount is credited to the claims of equity holders after all other claims have been satisfied. Income does not belong to capital providers until dividends are declared or interest becomes due. In measuring income, both interest and dividends represent distributions of income to providers of capital. Hence, both are treated the same and *neither* is a deduction from income.

If the entity theory were taken to its logical—and unorthodox—conclusion, the owners' equity accounts would belong unequivocally to the firm, despite the presence of stockholder claims. Furthermore, income would belong to the firm itself, and, in turn, interest and dividends would *both* be deductions in calculating it.[70]

The same inconsistency relative to valuation systems and proprietary theory previously discussed is also applicable to the entity theory. Paton and Littleton, in their famed monograph considered to be the classic statement of the historical cost system, take a strong entity theory position. Littleton, in *Structure of Accounting Theory*, held to this same position. Later, Paton, however, moved toward general price-level adjustment, which Devine saw as being totally consistent with the entity orientation.[71] We agree, but would again note that proprietary theory is also considered to be consistent with general price-level adjustment because of its presumed wealth orientation.

Anthony has provided an interesting variant on this more narrow interpretation of the entity theory.[72] The right-hand side of the balance sheet would consist of four main components: liabilities, shareholder equity, equity interest, and entity equity. Shareholder equity would consist of contributed capital, and equity interest would comprise unpaid dividends on both common and preferred stock. Interest cost to the firm would consist of both interest on debt and interest cost on the shareholder equity.[73] Entity equity would be equivalent to retained earnings but would be lower than the latter by the amount of unpaid dividends on both preferred and common stock. The shareholder-equity interest rate suggested by Anthony could either be set equal to the firm's before-tax debt rate or to a specified published rate applicable to all firms set by the United States Treasury Department in accordance with Cost Accounting Standard 414, which was published by the now defunct Cost Accounting Standards Board.

Although the entity theory provides a good description of the relationship between the firm and its shareholders, its dual nature relative to income and owners' equity in the traditional form has probably been responsible for the fact that its precepts have not taken a strong hold in committee reports and releases of various accounting bodies.[74]

Residual Equity Theory

The *residual equity theory* is a variant of both proprietary and entity theory. The theory has been developed by George Staubus, but its roots also lie in the work of William A. Paton.[75] The residual equity holders are that group of equity claimants whose rights are superseded by all other claimants. This group would be the common stockholders, although its members can change if an event such as a reorganization occurs. Common stockholders are, of course, the ultimate risk takers within an enterprise. Their interest in the firm serves as a buffer or protector for all groups with prior claims on the firm, such as preferred stockholders and bond owners.

The underlying assumption of the residual equity theory is that information appropriate for decision-making purposes (predicting cash flows, for example) must be supplied to the residual equity holders. The balance sheet equation under this approach would be

$$\Sigma\text{Assets} - \Sigma\text{Specific Equities (including liabilities and preferred stock)}$$
$$= \text{Residual Equity} \qquad (5.3)$$

Although the assets are still owned by the firm, they are held in a trust type of arrangement and management's objective is maximization of the value of the residual equity. Income accrues to the residual equity holders after all other claims have been met. Interest and preferred dividends (but not common dividends) would be deductions in arriving at income.

In regard to a FASB discussion memorandum concerned with whether the distinction between debt and equity should be maintained, Clark has asserted that the distinction should be kept. She based her position on recent finance literature, which has found that the amount of leverage employed by firms (which distinguishes between debt and equity) affects the risk and return to common stockholders.[76] The higher the leverage, the more risk borne by shareholders and the greater the required return on common shares. Clark has also noted that the finance literature has also found that preferred stockholder claims are viewed as debt, that is, however, subordinate to bonds. Clark, therefore, includes preferred stock as an element of debt in debt/equity ratio calculations, clearly a residual equity position. She also sees modern finance theory as more in line with proprietary theory as opposed to entity theory because the latter does not distinguish sharply between debt and equity.

The development of the residual equity approach has been relatively recent. Nevertheless, it has undoubtedly played a role in the movement toward defining objectives of income measurement with an emphasis on measures that would aid in predicting future cash flows.

Fund Theory

Fund theory, developed by William J. Vatter, backs away from both the entity and proprietary theories because of the inherent weaknesses and inconsistencies of both.[77] A *fund* is simply a group of assets and related obligations devoted to a particular purpose, which may or may not be that of generating income. The balance sheet equation would be

$$\Sigma Assets = \Sigma Restrictions\ on\ Assets \tag{5.4}$$

The restrictions on the assets arise from both liabilities and invested capital. The invested capital must be maintained intact unless specific authority for partial or total liquidation is given. The restriction on assets also includes the specific purposes for their use mandated by law or contract. Fund theory, therefore, is most applicable to the governmental and not-for-profit areas where endowment funds, encumbrances, and special-asset groups often devoted to specific and separate purposes prevail.

Commander Theory

Louis Goldberg was uncomfortable with artificial concepts such as "funds" and "entities."[78] As a result, he proposed the *commander theory*. *Commander* is really a synonym for *management*, and Goldberg was very much concerned with the fact that management needs information so that it can carry out its control and planning functions on behalf of owners. Hence, commander theory might really be viewed as being applicable to managerial accounting rather than financial accounting, but the manager in his or her fiduciary role must apply the commander view to the investor.[79]

Commander theory creates more problems than it solves. The whole issue of agency theory arises, although Goldberg's work precedes the emergence of agency theory by at least 10 years. In addition, the investors' usage of financial statements becomes somewhat unclear. Unfortunately, Goldberg limits the possible scope of shareholder interest to "big picture" numbers and relationships such as dividends and return on investment as opposed to possible interest in slightly lower level operating measures such as income and return on sales.[80]

Outlook on the Equity Theories

We have briefly examined five equity theories. As discussed at the beginning of this section, the equity theories cannot possibly provide a consistent deductive basis for all accounting transactions and events because they take only a very limited view of the enterprise: the relationship between the firm and its owners.[81] Nevertheless, we believe that they can be of some use to standard setters. We wonder if the time is not ripe to combine proprietary and entity theory approaches and show both numbers.[82] In Chapter 12, we suggest that stock option costs that are an expense to shareholders, but not to the firm, should be deducted from entity theory income to arrive at proprietary theory income. This solution might resolve the heated debate that has surrounded the stock option issue.

Summary

Despite APB Statement 4's use of the word *principles* to describe several concepts, the postulates–principles approach had, in essence, died out by 1970. Several factors underlie the failure of the postulates–principles approach and the rise of objectives and standards. The failure of ARS 1 and ARS 3 and the difficulty of building on a postulate base have already been discussed. The demise of the APB was certainly one of the reasons for the end of the postulates and principles orientation to standard setting. It is true that by the late 1960s the APB had abandoned this approach despite the publication in 1965 of Grady's ARS 7. Nevertheless, the APB had become identified with postulates and principles, and its decline signaled the obsolescence of this orientation as a theoretical underpinning for the standard-setting process.

Other, more fundamental factors were also at work. New research and committee reports began taking into account such issues as user needs and diversities, which, in turn, led to a focus on the objectives of financial statements, considerations that were barely mentioned in the postulates and principles literature. As a result, new outlooks and approaches to income formulation and measurement were eventually brought about.

The new outlook began stressing the need for objectives and standards. Several of the concepts that have been loosely labeled as *principles*—disclosure, materiality, and uniformity, for example—will eventually take their place in an objectives-oriented framework. Other concepts, such as going concern and stability of the monetary unit, may diminish in importance.

The equity theories of accounting are normative–deductive theories based on the relationship between the corporation and its owners. Although these theories can provide interesting insights into some problems, their scope is not sufficiently global to permit their extensive use in solving fundamental accounting problems.

Hence, our attention turns next to objectives and standards.[83] We examine important conceptual and institutional pronouncements that occurred after the decline of the postulates and principles approach in Chapter 6.

Appendix 5-A: The Basic Postulates Of Accounting (ARS 1)

Postulates Stemming from the Economic and Political Environment

Postulate A-1. Quantification

Quantitative data are helpful in making rational economic decisions, i.e., in making choices among alternatives so that actions are correctly related to consequences.

Postulate A-2. Exchange

Most of the goods and services that are produced are distributed through exchange, and are not directly consumed by the producers.

Postulate A-3. Entities (including identification of the entity)

Economic activity is carried on through specific units or entities. Any report on the activity must identify clearly the particular unit or entity involved.

Postulate A-4. Time period (including specification of the time period)

Economic activity is carried on during specifiable periods of time. Any report on that activity must identify clearly the period of time involved.

Postulate A-5. Unit of measure
(including identification of the monetary unit)

Money is the common denominator in terms of which goods and services, including labor, natural resources, and capital, are measured. Any report must clearly indicate which money (e.g., dollars, francs, pounds) is being used.

Postulates Stemming from the Field of Accounting Itself

Postulate B-1. Financial statements (Related to A-1)

The results of the accounting process are expressed in a set of fundamentally related financial statements that articulate with each other and rest upon the same underlying data.

Postulate B-2. Market prices (Related to A-2)

Accounting data are based on prices generated by past, present, or future exchanges that have actually taken place or are expected to.

Postulate B-3. Entities (Related to A-3)

The results of the accounting process are expressed in terms of specific units or entities.

Postulate B-4. Tentativeness (Related to A-4)

The results of operations for relatively short periods of time are tentative whenever allocations between past, present, and future periods are required.

The Imperatives

Postulate C-1. Continuity
(including the correlative concept of limited life)

In the absence of evidence to the contrary, the entity should be viewed as remaining in operation indefinitely. In the presence of evidence that the entity has a limited life, it should not be viewed as remaining in operation indefinitely.

Postulate C-2. Objectivity

Changes in assets and liabilities, and the related effects (if any) on revenues, expenses, retained earnings, and the like, should not be given formal recognition in the accounts earlier than the point of time at which they can be measured in objective terms.

Postulate C-3. Consistency

The procedures used in accounting for a given entity should be appropriate for the measurement of its position and its activities and should be followed consistently from period to period.

Postulate C-4. Stable unit

Accounting reports should be based on a stable measuring unit.

Postulate C-5. Disclosure

Accounting reports should disclose that which is necessary to make them not misleading.

SOURCE: Appendix 5-A. The Basic Postulates of Accounting ARS 1 is reprinted by permission of the American Institute of Certified Public Accountants.

APPENDIX 5-B: A Tentative Set of Broad Accounting Principles for Business Enterprises (ARS 3)

The principles summarized here are relevant primarily to formal financial statements made available to third parties as representations by the management of the business enterprise. The "basic postulates of accounting" developed in Accounting Research Study No. 1 are integral parts of this statement of principles.

Broad principles of accounting should not be formulated mainly for the purpose of validating policies (e.g., financial management, taxation, employee compensation) established in other fields, no matter how sound or desirable those policies may be in and of themselves. Accounting draws its real strength from its neutrality as among the demands of competing special interests. Its proper functions derive from the measurement of the resources of specific entities and of changes in these resources. Its principles should be aimed at the achievement of those functions.

The principles developed in this study are as follows:

1. Profit is attributable to the whole process of business activity. Any rule or procedure, therefore, which assigns profit to a portion of the whole process should be continuously re-examined to determine the extent to which it introduces bias into the reporting of the amount of profit assigned to specific periods of time.

2. Changes in resources should be classified among the amounts attributable to
   a. Changes in the dollar (price-level changes) that lead to restatements of capital but not to revenues or expenses.
   b. Changes in replacement costs (above or below the effect of price-level changes) that lead to elements of gain or of loss.
   c. Sale or other transfer, or recognition of net realizable value, all of which lead to revenue or gain.
   d. Other causes, such as accretion or the discovery of previously unknown natural resources.

3. All assets of the enterprise, whether obtained by investments of owners or of creditors, or by other means, should be recorded in the accounts and reported in the financial statements. The existence of an asset is independent of the means by which it was acquired.

4. The problem of measuring (pricing, valuing) an asset is the problem of measuring the future services, and involves at least three steps:
   a. A determination if future services do in fact exist. For example, a building is capable of providing space for manufacturing activity.
   b. An estimate of the quantity of services. For example, a building is estimated to be usable for 20 more years, or for half of its estimated total life.
   c. The choice of a method or basis or formula for pricing (valuing) the quantity of services arrived at under (2) above. In general, the choice of a pricing basis is made from the following three exchange prices:

i. A past exchange price, e.g., acquisition cost or other initial basis. When this basis is used, profit or loss, if any, on the asset being priced will not be recognized until sale or other transfer out of the business entity.

ii. A current exchange price, e.g., replacement cost. When this basis is used, profit or loss on the asset being priced will be recognized in two stages. The first stage will recognize part of the gain or loss in the period or periods from time of acquisition to time of usage or other disposition; the second stage will recognize the remainder of the gain or loss at the time of the sale or other transfer out of the entity, measured by the difference between sale (transfer) price and replacement cost. This method is still a cost method; an asset priced on this basis is being treated as a cost factor awaiting disposition.

iii. A future exchange price, e.g., anticipated selling price. When this basis is used, profit or loss, if any, has already been recognized in the accounts. Any asset priced on this basis is therefore being treated as though it were a receivable, in that sale or other transfer out of the business (including conversion into cash) will result in no gain or loss, except for any interest (discount) arising from the passage of time.

The proper pricing (valuation) of assets and the allocation of profit to accounting periods are dependent in large part upon estimates of the existence of future benefits, regardless of the bases used to price the assets. The need for estimates is unavoidable and cannot be eliminated by the adoption of any formula as to pricing.

i. All assets in the form of money or claims to money should be shown at their discounted present value or the equivalent. The interest rate to be employed in the discounting process is the market (effective) rate at the date the asset was acquired.

The discounting process is not necessary in the case of short-term receivables where the force of interest is small. The carrying-value of receivables should be reduced by allowances for uncollectable elements; estimated collection costs should be recorded in the accounts.

If the claims to money are uncertain as to time or amount of receipt, they should be recorded at their current market value. If the current market value is so uncertain as to be unreliable, these assets should be shown at cost.

ii. Inventories which are readily salable at known prices with readily predictable costs of disposal should be recorded at net realizable value, and the related revenue taken up at the same time. Other inventory items should be recorded at their current (replacement) cost, and the related gain or loss separately reported. Accounting for inventories on either basis will result in recording revenues, gains, or losses before they are validated by sale but they are nevertheless components of the net profit (loss) of the period in which they occur.

Acquisition costs may be used whenever they approximate current (replacement) costs, as would probably be the case when the unit prices of inventory components are reasonably stable and turnover is rapid. In all cases, the basis of measurement actually employed should be "subject to verification by another competent investigator."

iii. All items of plant and equipment in service, or held in stand-by status, should be recorded at cost of acquisition or construction, with appropriate modification for the effect of the changing dollar either in the primary statements or in supplementary statements. In the external reports, plant and equipment should be restated in terms of current replacement costs whenever some significant event occurs, such as a reorganization of the business entity or its merger with another entity or when it becomes a subsidiary of a parent company. Even in the absence of a significant event, the accounts could be restated at periodic intervals, perhaps every five years. The development of satisfactory indexes of construction costs and of machinery and equipment prices would assist materially in making the calculation of replacement costs feasible, practical, and objective.

d. The investment (cost or other basis) in plant and equipment should be amortized over the estimated service life. The basis for adopting a particular method of amortization for a given asset should be its ability to produce an allocation reasonably consistent with the anticipated flow of benefits from the asset.

e. All "intangibles" such as patents, copyrights, research and development, and goodwill should be recorded at cost, with appropriate modification for the effect of the changing dollar either in the primary statements or in supplementary statements. Limited term items should be amortized as expenses over their estimated lives. Unlimited term items should continue to be carried as assets, without amortization.

If the amount of the investment (cost or other basis) in plant and equipment or in the "intangibles" has been increased or decreased as the result of appraisal or the use of index-numbers, depreciation or other amortization should be based on the changed amount.

5. All liabilities of the enterprise should be recorded in the accounts and reported in the financial statements. Those liabilities that call for settlement in cash should be measured by the present (discounted) value of the future payments or the equivalent. The yield (market, effective) rate of interest at date of incurrence of the liability is the pertinent rate to use in the discounting process and in the amortization of "discount" and "premium." "Discount" and "premium" are technical devices for relating the issue price to the principal amount and should therefore be closely associated with principal amount in financial statements.

6. Those liabilities which call for settlement in goods or services (other than cash) should be measured by their agreed selling price. Profit accrues in these cases as the stipulated services are performed or the goods produced or delivered.

7. In a corporation, stockholders' equity should be classified into invested capital and retained earnings (earned surplus). Invested capital should, in turn, be classified according to source, that is, according to the underlying nature of the transactions giving rise to invested capital.

Retained earnings should include the cumulative amount of net profits and net losses, less dividend declarations, and less amounts transferred to invested capital.

In an unincorporated business, the same plan may be followed, but the acceptable alternative is more widely followed of reporting the total interest of each owner or group of owners at the balance sheet date.

8. A statement of the results of operations should reveal the components of profit in sufficient detail to permit comparisons and interpretations to be made. To this end, the data should be classified at least into revenues, expenses, gains, and losses.

a. In general, the revenue of an enterprise during an accounting period represents a measurement of the exchange value of the products (goods and services) of that enterprise during that period. The preceding discussion, under D(2b), is also pertinent here.

b. Broadly speaking, expenses measure the costs of the amount of revenue recognized. They may be directly associated with revenue-producing transactions themselves (e.g., so-called "product costs") or with the accounting period in which the revenues appear (e.g., so-called "period costs").

c. Gains include such items as the results of holding inventories through a price rise, the sale of assets (other than stock-in-trade) at more than book value, and the settlement of liabilities at less than book value. Losses include items such as the result of holding inventories through a price decline, the sale of assets (other than stock-in-trade) at less than book value or their retirement, the settlement of liabilities at more than book value, and the imposition of liabilities through a lawsuit.

SOURCE: Appendix 5-B: A Tentative Set of Broad Accounting Principles for Business Enterprises (ARS 3) is reprinted by permission of the American Institute of Certified Public Accountants.

QUESTIONS

1. Do you think the "broad principles" of ARS 3 are really *principles* as that term is used in science?

2. Assuming all other things equal, it is possible that the lower-of-cost-or-market method can result in any given year in higher income than would be the case under the same inventory costing method without the use of lower-of-cost-or-market. If so, then lower-of-cost-or-market cannot be classified as a conservative method. Do you agree with this statement? Discuss.

3. Why is it that postulates stemming from the economic and political climates as well as the customs and viewpoints of the business community would not serve as a good foundation for deducing a set of accounting principles?

4. Using different studies at different times it still appears to be the case that financial executives have a higher threshold for materiality than either certified public accountants or financial analysts, who, in turn, have a higher materiality threshold than users. Why do you think this ordering exists?

5. Do you think that the so-called equity theories of accounting are really theories in the scientific sense? How would you classify them?

6. Why do you think the equity theories are less important today than they were, say, 50 years ago?

7. Four postulates (going concern, time period, accounting entity, and monetary unit) were discussed as part of the basic concepts underlying historical costing. Can any of the principles discussed under the same general category be deduced or logically derived from these postulates?

8. How does agency theory (Chapters 2 and 4) differ from the equity theories discussed in this chapter?

9. Does the entity theory or the proprietary theory provide a better description of the relationship existing between the large modern corporation and its owners?

10. Why has the entity theory fragmented into two separate conceptions?

11. Of the nine so-called principles shown in Exhibit 5.1, which do you think are the most important in terms of establishing a historical costing system?

12. What is the difference between owners' equity accounts representing shareholders' claims as equity holders and shareholders' interests as owners?

13. Postulates are supposed to be tight enough to prevent conflicting conclusions being deduced from them. Is this the case with ARS 1?

14. Is it fair to categorize ARS 1 and ARS 3 as failures? Why or why not?

15. How do the imperative postulates (group C) differ from the other two categories of postulates?

16. Distinguish among the terms *realized, realizable,* and *realization.*

17. How do conventional retained earnings differ from entity equity under the Anthony conception of the entity theory?

18. What inconsistencies does Merino see in the proprietary theory at the turn of the twentieth century before the advent of entity theory?

19. Why is the earnings-per-share calculation an example of the residual equity of a firm being broader than merely its current common shareholders?

20. Why is the residual equity theory more in line with Clark's assessment of recent research in finance than entity and proprietary theory?

21. Why do you think that security prices are impacted more by "bad news" than "good news"?

22. Why do you think that profitability ratios (e.g., return-on-assets) are more sensitive to the combined effect of immateriality items than would be the case with solvency ratios (debt-to-equity and current ratios)?

23. At present time, the U.S. federal income tax code allows corporations to deduct interest expense but not cash dividends paid to stockholders. Does the tax code tie in with any of the equity theories?

24. Why does it make sense to define materiality from the user's perspective?

25. What similarities are there between materiality and disclosure?

26. Discuss how the concept of conservatism may be changing as viewed by Watts.

CASES, PROBLEMS, AND WRITING ASSIGNMENTS

1. Assume the following for the year 2000 for the Staubus Company:

Revenues		$1,000,000
Operating expenses		
Cost of goods sold	$400,000	
Depreciation	100,000	
Salaries and wages	200,000	
Bond interest (8% Debentures sold at maturity value of $1,000,000)		80,000
Dividends declared on 6% Preferred Stock (par value $500,000)		30,000
Dividends declared of $5 per share on Common Stock (20,000 shares outstanding a par value of $100 per share)		100,000

   a. Determine the income under each of the following equity theories:
- Proprietary theory
- Entity theory (orthodox view)
- Entity theory (unorthodox view)
- Residual equity

   b. Would any of your answers change if the preferred stock is convertible at any time at the ratio of 2 preferred shares for 1 share of common stock?

2. Critique *A Statement of Basic Accounting Postulates and Principles* by the referenced study group at the University of Illinois (it should be on reserve or otherwise made available to you). Your critique should cover, but not be restricted to, the following points:

   a. How do the definitions of postulates, concepts, and principles differ?

   b. Are the examples of postulates, principles, and concepts consistent with their definitions?

   c. Does this set of postulates, principles, and concepts provide a legislative body with a useful framework for deriving operating rules?

3. List and briefly discuss as many areas as you can in which an accepted method or technique is conservative, including why it is conservative.

4. A few years ago both Halliburton Corporation, a large construction company, and its auditor, Arthur Andersen, were chided for allowing Halliburton to book a percentage of cost overruns that Halliburton has attempted to collect from customers after projects are completed but before both agreed settlements with customers and, of course, collection thereof. The practice of trying to collect cost overruns in the construction industry is not uncommon. Until 1998 cost overrun collections were not booked until received. Since that time, Halliburton "began guessing how much of a disputed surcharge would ultimately get paid and crediting itself in advance."

Required:

   a. Is there a case that can be made for allowing Halliburton to book these overruns? What arguments, if any, support Halliburton's accounting methods?

   b. What situations should prevent Halliburton from booking these overruns prior to collection?

CRITICAL THINKING AND ANALYSIS

1. How permanent do you think the postulates and principles underlying historical costing will be?

2. If you could relate materiality, disclosure, and conservatism to types of measurements (nominal, ordinal, interval, and ratio scale), how would you do so?

Notes

1. *Jennings (1958, p. 32).*
2. *Special Committee on Research Program (1958, pp. 62–63).*
3. *See "Comments on 'A Tentative Set of Broad Accounting Principles'" (1963).*

4. *Mautz and Sharaf (1961, p. 37).*

5. *Morgenstern (1963, pp. 23–24). Some examples of axiomatic deductive systems in accounting include Mattessich (1964, pp. 446–465), Ijiri (1975, pp. 71–84), and Carlson and Lamb (1981).*

6. *Mautz (1965).*

7. *AAA (1957).*

8. *AICPA (1953, pp. 9505–9506).*

9. *Caws (1965, p. 85).*

10. *Ibid. (p. 86).*

11. *Harré (1970, p. 206).*

12. *Deinzer (1965, p. 111).*

13. *Vatter (1963, pp. 185–186).*

14. *Mautz (1965, p. 47).*

15. *Deinzer (1965, p. 131).*

16. *Chambers (1964, p. 409).*

17. *For a complete exposition, see Chambers (1966). For additional coverage, see Wright (1967) and Chambers (1970).*

18. *Chatfield (1974, p. 256).*

19. *Paton and Littleton (1940).*

20. *Canning (1929); Sweeney (1936); MacNeal (1939); Sanders, Hatfield, and Moore (1938); Gilman (1939); and Littleton (1953).*

21. *Caws (1965, pp. 24–29).*

22. *For example, Study Group at the University of Illinois (1964). In addition, Anthony has attempted to deductively derive a conceptual framework using premises and concepts: "Premises are descriptive [italics added] statements based on the best available evidence. They are subject to change as new evidence develops. In this framework, concepts are normative statements; they say what financial statement information should be [italics added]. Concepts are deduced from the premises and they must be consistent with the premises and with one another" [Anthony (1983, p. xi)]. While not labeling his system as postulates and principles per se, Anthony is certainly using a deductive–normative approach in terms of developing underlying rules to guide and support the FASB's ongoing operating standards. Anthony states that his premises are "descriptive statements based on the best available evidence," but many surely contain strong normative overtones. For example, Premise 15 (p. xiii) states that "users are primarily interested in the performance of an entity and secondarily in its status." Premise 15-A then states that "between competing accounting practices, the one that provides users with more useful information about performance is preferable to the one that provides more useful information about status" (p. xiii).*

23. *Fremgen (1968) and Sterling (1968).*

24. *Grady (1965, p. ix).*

25. *Ibid. (p. 407).*

26. *AICPA (1970, p. 9084).*

27. *Ibid.*

28. *One reason for the overlap is that APB Statement 4 envisions a three-tiered approach to principles. The bottom level, detailed principles, is made up of the actual operating rules themselves, such as the opinions of the APB (AICPA, 1970, p. 9084).*

29. *Ibid.*

30. *For a classic statement of the idea, see Paton and Littleton (1940, pp. 48–49). Of course, this is also Principle A of ARS 3.*

31. *Myers (1959).*

32. *FASB (1984, p. 28).*

33. *Paton and Littleton (1940, p. 49).*

34. *FASB (1984, p. 28). Devine contends that the concept of realization "is concerned entirely and exclusively with liquidity." Devine (1985a, p. 61).*

35. See AICPA (1970, pp. 9085–9086). For more on the switch from *realization* to *recognition*, see Liang (2001, p. 227).

36. *AICPA (1970, p. 9089).*

37. *Sterling (1967). Skinner (1988) found an important example of conservatism. He estimates that at the end of fiscal 1976–1977 in the United Kingdom fixed asset lives used for depreciation purposes were equal only to about half of the actual period. He attributes the short write-off periods to conservatism as opposed to factors such as inflation and the equalization of book lives and tax lives.*

38. *Basu's (1997) findings were confirmed by Pae, Thornton, and Welker (2005). They also discuss two types of conservatism: (1)* Ex ante conservatism *stems from either GAAP rules (immediate research and development write-offs in SFAS No. 2, for example) or policies that reduce earnings, such as expensing stock option costs that are independent of current business and economic news, and (2)* ex post conservatism, *which is not independent of current economic news such as goodwill write-downs resulting from impairment testing. The separation between these two types of conservatism is not airtight because goodwill write-downs due to impairment result from current events but they are prescribed in SFAS No. 142. For more on these two types of conservatism, see Beaver and Ryan (2004).*

39. *Bushman and Piotroski (2006).*

40. *Lobo and Zhous (2006) discuss several ways in which conservatism has increased after passage of the Sarbanes-Oxley Act. The operating definition of conservatism, given previously, is a working definition of conservatism for purposes of accounting practice, whereas the Basu and Bushman/Piotroski definition is geared more toward research.*

41. *Givoly and Hayn (2000).*

42. *Watts (2003a and 2003b).*

43. *For more on bond covenants and dividend constraints, see Ahmed, Billings, Morton, and Stanford-Harris (2002).*

44. *Financial Accounting Standards Board (1980, para. 95).*

45. *A number of authors have constructed and used disclosure indexes. These indexes provide ordinal measures only because problems of how to weight the components of disclosure indexes cannot be easily solved. The items in the index can only be a relatively small subset of all possible items to be disclosed. Marston and Shrives (1991) provide a good summary of disclosure indexes that have been presented in the literature. They also note (p. 205) that the larger the firm, the greater the likelihood of more disclosure. Of course, managers of larger firms are more likely to understand the importance of disclosure.*

46. *Mercer (2004, p. 186).*

47. *APB Opinion No. 22 (1972).*

48. *Lang and Lundholm (2000).*

49. *Turner (1997).*

50. *Pattillo (1976).*

51. *Turner (1997, p. 126).*

52. *Cho, Hagerman, Nabar, and Patterson (2003).*

53. *Pany and Wheeler (1989) applied a number of rule-of-thumb materiality measures to various industries and found sizable differences within and among industries that vary with the particular measure of materiality employed.*

54. *SEC (1999).*

55. *Vorhies (2005, p. 54).*

56. *Ibid.*

57. *Ibid.*

58. *For a study of materiality in a European context, see Arnold, Bernardi, and Neidermeyer (2001).*

59. *Paton and Littleton (1940, pp. 18–21).*

60. *AICPA (1970, p. 9076). Vatter (1963, p. 190) was an early adherent of the view that objectivity is part of measurement methodology.*

61. *One example is Sprouse (1978, p. 71).*

62. *Revsine (1985) has conceived a formal model of comparability that is consistent with the output approach advocated here. Revsine's model is based on concepts from the information economics literature. His hypothetical application of the model compares the quality of the information signals received by users in terms of (a) historical cost information systems and (b) current cost (value) information systems. He concludes that historical costing will have a* timing difference *problem; that is, different balance sheet valuations will arise because an older asset will almost never have the same valuation as an exactly similar asset (in terms of type and condition) acquired at the balance sheet date. Hence, historical costing is noncomparable across firms. However, current costing systems have a related problem called the* estimation difference*. It arises because actual current valuations for older assets cannot be directly measured and must therefore be indirectly measured. The difference in valuation between the estimated current valuation and the actual current valuation of exactly similar assets would be the estimation difference.*

The timing difference is closely related to representational faithfulness (see Chapter 7), and the estimation difference correlates closely to the principle (concept) of verifiability or objectivity discussed here and in Chapter 1.

63. *For example, see Peloubet (1961, pp. 35–41) and Kemp (1963, pp. 126–132).*

64. *Merino (1993).*

65. *Merino (1993, p. 171) states that proprietary theorists were disingenuous about the centrality of absentee owners because conservatism was also an important tool of these same proprietary theorists, which would have minimized the profit available for dividends to these same absentee owners. Hence, proprietary theorists, while attempting to stress the importance of absentee owners, also attempted to develop accounting rules that would focus on curbing their greed by minimizing income.*

66. *For example, Lorig (1964, p. 572).*

67. *Merino (1993, p. 174).*

68. *Paton (1922, pp. 50–84).*

69. *The duality between the firm itself and its owners can lead to some strange interpretations. Husband (1938) has pointed out that a stock dividend under the conventional entity theory approach would be income to the shareholder because a transfer is made from the* firm's *account (retained earnings) to the* owners' *account (capital stock). To get around this problem, Husband viewed the corporation as an association of individuals with the affairs of the corporation largely being carried out by management. This association view—which has overtones of proprietary theory—is contrasted with the older entity view, which sees the firm as an artificial person separate and apart from its owners. We do not believe that stock dividends can be interpreted as being income to shareholders under any equity theory.*

70. *Li (1960).*

71. *Devine (1985b, p. 91).*

72. *See Anthony (1983, pp. 92–98).*

73. *An interesting sidelight to Anthony's interest on equity capital proposal is that Merino (1993, pp. 176–177) noted that proprietary theorists at the end of the nineteenth century were afraid that if interest were capitalized on owners' equities, amounts of owners' equities in excess of the capitalized interest might be claimed by labor, consumers, and government.*

74. *AAA (1957, p. 5) discusses enterprise net income in which interest, taxes, and dividends are excluded from the determination of net income; hence, a broad entity theory approach is advocated. Enterprise net income, however, is contrasted with income to shareholders, which coincides with proprietary theory.*

75. *See Staubus (1961, pp. 17–27) for an overview, and Paton (1922, pp. 84–89).*

76. *Clark (1993, p. 121).*

77. *Vatter (1947).*

78. *Goldberg (1965, p. 149) believes that totally depersonalizing the firm is much too restrictive because enterprise functions and endeavors are carried out by people. He also states that criteria for determining what funds should be established are not clearly set out by Vatter.*

79. *Ibid. (p. 169).*

80. *Ibid. (p. 173).*

81. *Rosenfield (2005) rejects both the entity and proprietary theories in favor of putting the "focus of attention" on the reporting entity itself. He appears to arrive at his own modification of the entity theory.*

82. *A European view of entity and proprietary theories sees a renewal of interest in these theories. See Zambon and Zan (2000).*

83. *Paton and Littleton noted that the word* standards *has less of a flavor of permanence than does the word* principles. *Paton and Littleton (1940, p. 4).*

References

Accounting Principles Board (1972). Opinion No. 22, *Disclosure of Accounting Policies.* Accounting Principles Board.

Ahmed, Anwer, B.K. Billings, R.M. Morton, and M. Stanford-Harris (October 2002). "The Role of Accounting Conservatism in Mitigating Bondholder-Shareholder Conflicts Over Dividend Policy and in Reducing Debt Costs," *Accounting Review,* pp. 867–890.

American Accounting Association (1957). *Accounting and Reporting Standards for Corporate Financial Statements and Preceding Statements and Supplements.* American Accounting Association.

American Institute of Certified Public Accountants (1953). *Accounting Terminology Bulletin* No. 1. AICPA, pp. 9503–9517.

American Institute of Certified Public Accountants (April 1963). "Comments on a Tentative Set of Broad Accounting Principles," *Journal of Accountancy,* pp. 36–48.

——— (1970). APB Statement No. 4, *Basic Concepts and Accounting Principles Underlying Financial Statements of Business Enterprises.* AICPA, pp. 9057–9106.

Anthony, Robert N. (1983). *Tell It Like It Was.* Richard D. Irwin.

Arnold, Donald, R. A. Bernardi, and P. E. Neidermeyer (2001). "The Association Between European Materiality Estimates and Client Integrity, National Cultures, and Litigation," *International Journal of Accounting* (Vol. 36, No. 4), pp. 459–483.

Basu, Sudipta (December 1997). "The Conservatism Principle and the Asymmetric Timeliness of Earnings," *Journal of Accounting and Economics,* pp. 3–37.

Beaver, William, and S. G. Ryan (2004). Working Paper, "Conditional and Unconditional Conservatism: Concepts and Modeling." New York University: Stern Graduate School of Business.

Bushman, Robert, and J. Piotroski (October 2006). "Financial Reporting Incentives for Conservative Accounting: The Influence of Legal and Political Institutions," *Journal of Accounting and Economics,* pp. 107–148.

Canning, John B. (1929). *The Economics of Accountancy.* Ronald Press.

Carlson, Marvin L., and James W. Lamb (July 1981). "Constructing a Theory of Accounting—An Axiomatic Approach," *Accounting Review*, pp. 554–573.

Caws, Peter (1965). *The Philosophy of Science*. D. Van Nostrand.

Chambers, Raymond J. (1964). "The Moonitz and Sprouse Studies on Postulates and Principles," in *Accounting, Finance and Management*. Butterworth, pp. 396–414.

——— (1966). *Accounting, Evaluation and Economic Behavior*. Prentice Hall.

——— (September 1970). "Second Thoughts on Continuously Contemporary Accounting," *Abacus*, pp. 39–55.

Chatfield, Michael (1974). *A History of Accounting Thought*. The Dryden Press.

Cho, Seong-Yeon, R. L. Hagerman, S. Nabar, and E. R. Patterson (2003). "Measuring Stockholder Materiality," *Accounting Horizons* (Supplement), pp. 63–76.

Clark, Myrtle W. (September 1993). "Entity Theory, Modern Capital Structure Theory, and the Distinction Between Debt and Equity," *Accounting Horizons*, pp. 14–31.

Deinzer, Harvey T. (1965). *Development of Accounting Thought*. Holt, Rinehart and Winston.

Devine, Carl T. (1985a). "Recognition Requirements—Income Earned and Realized," in *Essays in Accounting Theory*, Vol. II, Studies in Accounting Research #22, ed. Stephen Zeff. American Accounting Association, pp. 57–67.

——— (1985b). "Comments on Paton's Entity Theory as Organization Theory," in *Essays in Accounting Theory*, Vol. IV, Studies in Accounting Research #22, ed. Stephen Zeff. American Accounting Association, pp. 83–99.

Financial Accounting Standards Board (1980). Statement of Financial Accounting Concepts No. 2, *Qualitative Characteristics of Accounting Information*. FASB.

——— (1984). Statement of Financial Accounting Concepts No. 5, *Recognition and Measurement in Financial Statements of Business Enterprises*. FASB.

Fremgen, James (October 1968). "The Going Concern Assumption: A Critical Appraisal," *Accounting Review*, pp. 49–56.

Gilman, Stephen (1939). *Accounting Concepts of Profit*. Ronald Press.

Givoly, Dan, and C. Hayn (2000). "The Changing Time-Series Properties of Earnings, Cash Flows and Accruals: Has Financial Reporting Become More Conservative?" *Journal of Accounting and Economics*, (Vol. 29, No. 3), pp. 287–320.

Goldberg, Louis (1965). *An Inquiry Into the Nature of Accounting*. American Accounting Association.

Grady, Paul (1965). Accounting Research Study No. 7, *Inventory of Generally Accepted Accounting Principles*. AICPA.

Harré, Rom (1970). *The Principles of Scientific Thinking*. University of Chicago Press.

Husband, George R. (September 1938). "The Corporate-Entity Fiction and Accounting Theory," *Accounting Review*, pp. 241–253.

Ijiri, Yuji (1975). Studies in Accounting Research #10, *Theory of Accounting Measurement*. American Accounting Association.

Jennings, Alvin R. (January 1958). "Present-Day Challenges in Financial Reporting," *Journal of Accountancy*, pp. 28–34.

Kemp, Patrick (January 1963). "Controversies on the Construction of Financial Statements," *Accounting Review*, pp. 126–132.

Lang, Mark H., and Russell Lundholm (2000). "Voluntary Disclosures and Equity Offerings: Reducing Information Asymmetry or Hyping the Stock?," *Contemporary Accounting Research* (Vol. 17, No. 4), pp. 623–662.

Li, David H. (October 1960). "The Nature and Treatment of Dividends Under the Entity Concept," *Accounting Review*, pp. 674–679.

Liang, Pierre J. (September 2001). "Recognition: An Information Content Perspective," *Accounting Horizons*, pp. 223–242.

Littleton, A. C. (1953). *Structure of Accounting Theory*. American Accounting Association.

Lobo, Gerald, and J. Zhous (March 2006). "Did Conservatism in Financial Reporting Increase After the Sarbanes-Oxley Act? Initial Evidence," *Accounting Horizons*, pp. 57–73.

Lorig, Arthur N. (July 1964). "Some Basic Concepts of Accounting and Their Implications," *Accounting Review*, pp. 563–573.

MacNeal, Kenneth (1939; reissued 1970). *Truth in Accounting*. Scholars.

Marston, Claire L., and Philip J. Shrives (September 1991). "The Use of Disclosure Indices in Accounting Research: A Review Article," *British Accounting Review*, pp. 195–210.

Mattessich, Richard (1964). *Accounting and Analytical Methods*. Richard D. Irwin.

Mautz, Robert K. (January 1965). "The Place of Postulates in Accounting," *Journal of Accountancy*, pp. 46–49.

Mautz, Robert K., and Hussein A. Sharaf (1961). *The Philosophy of Auditing*. American Accounting Association.

Mercer, Molly (September 2004). "How Do Investors Assess the Credibility of Management Disclosures?" *Accounting Horizons*, pp. 185–196.

Merino, Barbara D. (February/April 1993). "An Analysis of the Development of Accounting Knowledge: A Pragmatic Approach," *Accounting, Organizations and Society*, pp. 163–185.

Moonitz, Maurice (1961). Accounting Research Study #1, *The Basic Postulates of Accounting*. American Institute of Certified Public Accountants.

Morgenstern, Oscar (1963). "Limits to the Use of Mathematics in Economics," in *Mathematics and the Social Sciences*, ed. J. C. Charlesworth. American Academy of Political and Social Science, pp. 12–39.

Myers, John H. (October 1959). "The Critical Event and Recognition of Net Profit," *Accounting Review*, pp. 528–532.

Pae, Jinhan, D. B. Thornton, and M. Welker (Fall 2005). "The Link Between Earnings Conservatism and the Price-to-Book Ratio," *Contemporary Accounting Research*, pp. 693–717.

Pany, Kurt, and Stephen Wheeler (December 1989). "Materiality: An Inter-Industry Comparison of the Magnitudes and Stabilities of Various Quantitative Measures," *Accounting Horizons*, pp. 71–78.

Paton, William A. (1922; reissued 1962). *Accounting Theory*. Accounting Studies Press.

Paton, William A., and A. C. Littleton (1940). *An Introduction to Corporate Accounting Standards*. American Accounting Association.

Pattillo, James W. (1976). *The Concept of Materiality in Financial Reporting*. Financial Executives Research Foundation.

Peloubet, Maurice (April 1961). "Is Further Uniformity Desirable or Possible?," *Journal of Accountancy*, pp. 35–41.

Revsine, Lawrence (Spring 1985). "Comparability: An Analytic Examination," *Journal of Accounting and Public Policy*, pp. 1–12.

Rosenfield, Paul (February 2005). "The Focus of Attention in Financial Reporting," *Abacus*, pp. 1–20.

Sanders, Thomas H., Henry Rand Hatfield, and Underhill Moore (1938). *A Statement of Accounting Principles*. American Accounting Association.

Securities and Exchange Commission (1999). SEC Staff Accounting Bulletin No. 99, *Materiality*. Government Printing Office.

Skinner, R. C. (Spring 1988). "The Role of Conservatism in Determining the Accounting Lives of Fixed Assets," *International Journal of Accounting*, pp. 1–18.

Special Committee on Research Program (December 1958). "Report to Council of the Special Committee on Research Program," *Journal of Accountancy*, pp. 62–68.

Sprouse, Robert T. (January 1978). "The Importance of Earnings in the Conceptual Framework," *Journal of Accountancy*, pp. 64–71.

Sprouse, Robert T., and Maurice Moonitz (1962). Accounting Research Study No. 3, *A Tentative Set of Broad Accounting Principles for Business Enterprises.* AICPA.

Staubus, George (1961). *Accounting to Investors*. University of California Press.

Sterling, Robert R. (December 1967). "Conservatism: The Fundamental Principle of Valuation in Accounting," *Abacus*, pp. 109–132.

——— (July 1968). "The Going Concern: An Examination," *Accounting Review*, pp. 481–502.

Study Group at the University of Illinois (1964). *A Statement of Basic Postulates and Principles*. Center for International Education and Research in Accounting, University of Illinois.

Sweeney, Henry W. (1936). *Stabilized Accounting*. Holt, Rinehart & Winston.

Turner, Jerry L. (Spring 1997). "The Impact of Materiality Decisions on Financial Ratios: A Computer Simulation," *Journal of Accounting, Auditing & Finance*, pp. 125–147.

Vatter, William J. (1947). *The Fund Theory of Accounting and Its Implications for Financial Reports*. University of Chicago Press.

——— (Autumn 1963). "Postulates and Principles," *Journal of Accounting Research*, pp. 179–197.

Vorhies, James B. (May 2005). "The New Importance of Materiality," *Journal of Accountancy*, pp. 53–59.

Watts, Ross (2003a). "Conservatism in Accounting Part I: Explanations and Implications," *Accounting Horizons* (September), pp. 207–221.

——— (2003b). "Conservatism in Accounting Part II: Evidence and Research Opportunities," *Accounting Horizons* (December), pp. 287–301.

Wright, F. K. (August 1967). "Capacity for Adaptation and the Asset Measurement Problem," *Abacus*, pp. 74–79.

Zambon, Stefano, and L. Zan (2000). "Accounting Relativism: The Unstable Relationship Between Income Measurement and Theories of the Firm," *Accounting, Organizations and Society* (Vol. 25, No. 89), pp. 799–822.

6

The Search for Objectives

Learning Objectives

After reading this chapter, you should be able to:

- Understand the rise in importance of user needs and objectives after Accounting Research Studies 1 and 3.
- Appreciate the significance of the reports and documents covered here that chronologically came between Accounting Research Studies 1 and 3 and the conceptual framework.
- Comprehend the basic objectives of financial reporting.
- Understand the user heterogeneity issue.

The postulates and principles approach largely ignored the question of user objectives. However, user objectives assumed a more prominent role in the late 1960s in both research and important theoretically oriented monographs and pronouncements sponsored by such organizations as the American Accounting Association (AAA), American Institute of Certified Public Accountants (AICPA), Accounting Principles Board (APB), and the Financial Accounting Standards Board (FASB). In fact, user needs and objectives became an important connecting link among these documents, many of which were attempting to forge a solid theoretical underpinning for financial accounting standards. Therefore, we will examine chronologically the important committee reports and documents that gave rise to objectives and standards in place of the postulates and principles approach. Our discussion and analysis include the following works:

Title	Published by	Year
A Statement of Basic Accounting Theory (ASOBAT)	AAA	1966
Basic Concepts and Accounting Principles Underlying Financial Statements of Business Enterprises (APB Statement 4)	APB	1970
Objectives of Financial Statements (Trueblood Committee Report)	AICPA	1973
Statement of Accounting Theory and Theory Acceptance (SATTA)	AAA	1977

A general criticism that can be, and has been, leveled at these works is that they have not broken any new ground. Although largely true, this is not the appropriate issue. New research findings and totally new deductive proposals generally do not come from committee reports and similar documents. Instead, the reports evaluate current positions in either practice or research. Therefore, the important question is what positions have been adopted or what is the general outlook of the work. From this standpoint, these reports are highly significant. Major financial accounting change is an evolutionary process that will continue to unfold indefinitely. The reports covered here have played and could continue to play an important evolutionary role in financial accounting theory.

We conclude by discussing two topics that received considerable attention in the reports discussed in this chapter: (1) user objectives and (2) user diversity.

ASOBAT

A Statement of Basic Accounting Theory (ASOBAT) represented an important change in the work of the AAA. It made a relatively sharp break from the four previous statements and numerous supplements published between 1936 and 1964. The latter were both descriptive and normative in nature, stating general rules or approaches to recording transactions and to presenting financial statements. However, the Executive Committee of the AAA in 1964 diverged from the previous approach by giving the committee a charge of developing "an integrated statement of basic accounting theory which will serve as a guide to educators, practitioners, and others interested in accounting. . . . The committee may want to consider . . . the role, nature, and limitations of accounting."[1]

Development of the User Approach

The committee's definition of accounting represented a fundamental departure from the past. ASOBAT defined accounting as "the process of identifying, measuring and communicating economic information to *permit informed judgments and decisions by users of the information* [italics added]."[2]

Perhaps the most widely disseminated previous definition was developed in 1941 and was used in *Accounting Terminology Bulletin No. 1* of 1953, which stated: "Accounting is the art of recording, classifying, and summarizing in a significant manner and in terms of money, transactions, and events which are in part at least of a financial character, and interpreting the results thereof."[3]

The emphasis is on the work and skill of the accountant, with virtually no mention of the user. In further elaborating on the definition and work of the accountant, the *Terminology Bulletin* stated:

It is more important to emphasize the creative skill and ability with which the accountant applies his knowledge to a given problem. . . . The complexities of modern business have brought to management some problems, which only accounting can solve, and on which accounting throws necessary and helpful light.[4]

Hence, the accountant is the "wise man" who alone is responsible for bringing some semblance of order out of the chaotic affairs of business, and it is up to users to accommodate themselves to this highly skilled practitioner. From the sociological viewpoint, the definition and discussion in the bulletin strongly appear to be fortifying the perception of the accountant as a learned professional whose presentation must be accepted by those who do not have his qualifications and credentials. This view, however, has undergone considerable change in recent years as accountants (and external auditors as well) have been seen as members of the management team. Thanks to recent scandals, the image of internal accountants and outside auditors has become somewhat tarnished. It will be up to the profession to restore a more positive view, and we are optimistic that this can occur, but it will require real work, not just a public relations campaign.

Emphasis on users and their needs first appears in the literature in the 1950s, an amazingly recent time in light of the long history of accounting.[5]

Orientation to Theory

The committee defined *theory* as "a cohesive set of hypothetical, conceptual and pragmatic principles forming a general frame of reference for a field of study."[6] In applying the definition, it sought to carry out the following tasks:

1. To identify the field of accounting so that useful generalizations about it could be made and a theory developed.

2. To establish standards by which accounting information might be judged.

3. To point out possible improvements in accounting practice.

4. To present a useful framework for accounting researchers seeking to extend the uses of accounting and the scope of accounting subject matter as needs of society expand.[7]

Notice that ASOBAT's definition of theory is a subset of the definition presented in Chapter 1. Our definition is broader because it not only encompasses the ideas expressed above but also accommodates valuation systems as well as empirical work in financial accounting.

The ASOBAT definition specifically focused on setting up a framework for evaluating systematic approaches to recording transactions and presenting financial statements geared to users. The concern—with the conceptual apparatus for evaluating specific accounting models and rules—is, therefore, with a *metatheory* of accounting, the topmost part of the theoretical structure for the purposes and goals of accounting information. A metatheory would also be concerned with determining certain restrictions on published accounting information as well as with delineating criteria or guidelines for selecting among alternatives.

Objectives of Accounting

Since accounting is concerned with user needs, a set of objectives relating to user needs stands at the apex of the metatheory. Below these objectives would be a set of definitions, qualitative characteristics, and supporting guidelines that would facilitate the implementation of the objectives. Despite the importance of objectives, however, ASOBAT covered them rather briefly. Therefore, it appears that ASOBAT assumed that the evaluative framework of standards and guidelines could be largely independent of the objectives themselves.

Despite the brevity given to objectives by ASOBAT, we should discuss them briefly. The four objectives are:

1. To make decisions concerning the use of limited resources (including the identification of crucial decision areas) and to determine objectives and goals.

2. To direct and control an organization's human and material resources effectively.

3. To maintain and report on the custodianship of resources.

4. To facilitate social functions and controls.[8]

Making Decisions Concerning Limited Resources

Decision making involves an evaluation of what is expected to happen in the future. These assessments can be done in an informal manner or can involve extremely complex calculations. The discounted cash flow model used in capital budgeting analysis as a means of selecting among competing capital projects is an example of the complex approach. Payback and nondiscounted cash flow methods are simpler—and, presumably, less effective—tools for appraising the likely future. Whether extremely crude or highly complex and refined, the methods used for assessing what will happen in the future are called *decision models*. The capacity to provide information that is useful in the decision-making process is called *predictive ability*.[9] In the user-oriented approach, the most important objective of accounting is to provide information useful for making decisions.

If all decision makers required the same information, the accounting theory problem would be less difficult. Unfortunately, as ASOBAT recognized, users of accounting reports come from several different groups—creditors, investors, customers and suppliers, governmental agencies, and employees—with widely diverging backgrounds and abilities. Whether user diversity leads to heterogeneous information needs in the different user groups has become absolutely crucial to the future development of accounting (a question that had not fully emerged when ASOBAT was written).

Predictive ability is discussed in ASOBAT in terms of gauging future earnings, financial position, and debt-paying ability. It made an important, though brief, point that accounting reports do not make predictions; rather, users must make predictions, employing inputs from accounting reports as data in their decision models.

Directing and Controlling Resources

This objective is directed toward managerial uses of accounting data. ASOBAT saw managerial needs as different from those of external users but subject to the same four standards of reporting (to be discussed shortly), although the standards themselves may be applied differently. Managerial needs and uses of accounting data are beyond the scope of this text, so we will not be concerned with this objective. However, we note that some individuals do not perceive any differences between internal (managerial) and external (financial) uses of accounting data.[10]

Maintaining Custodianship of Resources

The third objective is commonly called *stewardship*. A proper accounting for the use by one party (management) of funds that have been entrusted to it by another party (investors) is a relationship extending, in one guise or another, back to the Middle Ages. In modern times, this objective has broadened under conditions of absentee ownership and easy acquisition and disposition of ownership shares through the medium of securities exchanges.[11] The stewardship association has led to the agency theory view of the firm discussed in Chapters 2 and 4. In light of the Enron, WorldCom, and Tyco debacles, this objective needs to be given more attention.

Facilitating Social Functions and Controls

The last objective appears to be an extension of the stewardship function to society as a whole. Thus, accounting is concerned with such areas as taxation, fraud prevention, governmental regulation, and collection of statistics for purposes of measuring economic activity. An issue not addressed by ASOBAT concerns who should bear the cost of producing this additional data.

Although objectives stand at the summit of a metatheory, it is clear that they were not the main concern of ASOBAT. Subsequent reports, however, began to address this topic.

Standards for Accounting Information

Four standards for evaluating accounting—relevance, verifiability, freedom from bias, and quantifiability—are at the heart of ASOBAT. These standards, the subsequent guidelines for communicating accounting information, and the objectives could be viewed as part of a metatheory of accounting. Like other parts of ASOBAT, the standards appear to be aimed at evaluating published financial statement information. However, a policy-making body to assess proposed rules could also use them.

Relevance

Relevance pertains to usefulness in making the decision at hand. It arises directly from the four objectives for various types of information; hence, it is the primary standard. Since there are different user groups with different backgrounds making decisions in different contexts, relevance can be thought of as the major issue of accounting. Further defining relevance, however, was beyond the scope of ASOBAT, save for a few simple and obvious examples.

Verifiability

Verifiability is synonymous with objectivity as it is defined in Chapter 1. It is thus an aspect of measurement. Chapter 1 stated that measurement has to be considered as an important aspect of accounting theory even though some believe they involve different domains. The selection of valuation systems in their totality, as well as individual rules for subsets of the systems, should be primarily based on questions of relevance. However, aspects of measurement must also be considered because valuation systems and methods that have a low consensus (in terms of agreement among measurers) might have to be bypassed in favor of approaches that are less desirable from the standpoint of usefulness.

Hence, the selection of methods should not be based on relevance alone without considering verifiability, nor should verifiability take precedence over relevance. Therefore, standards of measurement are a necessary part of the metatheoretical framework. A last point to reiterate here is that *verifiability* appears to have supplanted *objectivity* as the appropriate term for describing the degree of statistical consensus among measurers.

Freedom From Bias

This standard is necessary because of the problem of user heterogeneity as well as the potentially adversarial relationship between management (which, of course, is responsible for statement preparation) and external users. Biases, of course, may be subtle or flagrant and may be extremely difficult to resolve equitably. Suppose, for example, that in the interests of relevance and disclosure, a firm were required to quantify in financial statements or the notes thereto amounts of expected judgments against it in legal cases. An enterprise's own best interests—minimizing legal damages—would conflict with standards of relevance and disclosure because the court's judgment could be influenced by the firm's supposed admission of guilt in financial statements.

Freedom from bias is complementary to the qualitative characteristic of neutrality in the conceptual framework (discussed in Chapter 7). Neutrality refers to the orientation of standard-setting agencies, whereas freedom from bias is concerned with the preparation of financial statements.

Quantifiability

Quantifiability appears to be very closely related to measurement theory. However, while measurement and quantification are both important to the metatheoretical structure,

ASOBAT appears, if anything, to have gone too far in emphasizing quantifiability: "It can be said that the primary, if not the total concern of accountants, is with quantification and quantified data."[12] The recent push toward disclosure, emanating largely from the efficient-markets hypothesis literature, goes beyond mere quantification. One minor problem with a standard that refers largely to the general area of measurement is that since verifiability is an aspect of measurement theory, verifiability appears to be a subset of quantifiability.

An important point is brought up by ASOBAT in its questioning of why accounting should be restricted to single numbers in financial statements. ASOBAT suggests using ranges and also multiple valuation bases in "side-by-side" columnar arrangements. These possibilities are seen both as responses to the increased data and information needs of users and as possible solutions to the problem posed by heterogeneous user groups. In addition, they might be a means for resolving the overriding problem of choice among accounting methods faced by a rule-making body. Providing more information, known as *data expansion*, could lead, however, to *information overload* on the part of users.[13] Any attempt to circumvent the problem of choice among valuation systems or methods by simply providing more data is subject to the information-processing constraints of users, a point not discussed in ASOBAT.

Guidelines for Communicating Accounting Information

In addition to the four standards, ASOBAT presents five guidelines for the communication of accounting information:

1. Appropriateness to expected use.
2. Disclosure of significant relationships.
3. Inclusion of environmental information.
4. Uniformity of practice within and among entities.
5. Consistency of practices through time.[14]

The report itself notes that there is overlap between standards and guidelines, although it concedes the latter are less fundamental.

Appropriateness to Expected Use

The first guideline basically reiterates the relevance standard for user needs, although it also mentions timeliness of presentation. The use of information by management is also discussed here.

Disclosure of Significant Relationships

Despite its title, this guideline deals with only one aspect of the broad problem of disclosure discussed in Chapter 5. Its concern is with the problem of aggregation of data in which important information may be buried or hidden in the summarizing figures in financial reports. Statement of Financial Accounting Standards (SFAS) No. 131 on segmental disclosure is one statement that has dealt with this problem.

Inclusion of Environmental Information

As used here, *environmental information* refers to the very broad category of conditions under which data were collected and the preparer's assumptions relative to the uses of the information, particularly if the information is intended for specific rather than general purposes. More detail may well be appropriate where information will be applied to specific uses intended.

Uniformity of Practices Within and Among
Entities and Consistency of Practices Through Time

The last two guidelines refer directly to uniformity and consistency as discussed in Chapter 5. ASOBAT desired the type of uniformity that appears to correspond to finite uniformity as that term was previously defined. Finite uniformity cannot be achieved merely by setting it up as a guideline or even a standard. There must be sufficient detail in the theoretical structure; a topic to be further probed in Chapter 9.

Concluding Remarks on ASOBAT

ASOBAT can be criticized on numerous grounds. Certainly its guidelines were far too brief to cover the topics adequately. The metatheoretical structure could have been extended and used more appropriate terminology. However, these are carping criticisms. ASOBAT has had an important and beneficial influence on succeeding documents and reports, as will become evident in the remainder of this chapter and the next chapter.

APB Statement 4

APB Statement 4, *Basic Concepts and Accounting Principles Underlying Financial Statements of Business Enterprises*, appeared when the postulates and principles approach had run its course and objectives and standards were emerging. The statement was published in October 1970, exactly a half year prior to the formation of the Wheat and Trueblood committees. At that time, the APB was under heavy fire for Opinions 16 and 17 on business combinations and goodwill in addition to broader criticisms, such as inadequacy of research, lack of independence of its members, and lack of sufficient exposure of its work prior to final publication.

The purpose of APB Statement 4 was to state fundamental concepts of financial reporting to serve as a foundation for the opinions of the APB. This charge from the Special Committee on Opinions of the APB in May 1965 came at a time when it certainly seemed that the APB would continue indefinitely despite problems that had already begun to surface. Moonitz felt that the statement should have been issued as an *opinion* rather than as a *statement*—since departures from "generally accepted accounting principles" made in a statement need not be disclosed.[15] Should, however, a theoretical structure—the intended charge to the drafters of the statement—be forced by fiat? Acceptance of a metatheory cannot be easily mandated, as we will see later in this chapter.

Orientation to Definitions

Definition of Accounting

APB Statement 4 started by defining accounting along the newer, user-oriented track that ASO-BAT took: "Accounting is a service activity. Its function is to provide quantitative information, primarily financial in nature, about economic entities that is *intended to be useful in making economic decisions* [italics added]."[16]

The statement also adopted ASOBAT's very strong emphasis on the diversity of users. Users of financial information are classified into two groups: those with direct interests in the enterprise and those with indirect interests. APB Statement 4 went further than ASOBAT—which had been silent on this issue—by stating that users of financial statements should be knowledgeable and should understand the characteristics and limitations of financial statements. Finally, and in agreement with ASOBAT, it viewed financial statements as being general purpose in nature as opposed to being oriented toward a limited group of users.

Other Definitions

Despite its promising start, APB Statement 4 often reverted to useless definitions. It defined assets, liabilities, owners' equity, revenues, and expenses as the "basic elements of financial accounting." All these definitions (save owners' equity, which is a residual) state that they are "recognized and measured in conformity with generally accepted accounting principles."[17] However, the statement is later made that "generally accepted accounting principles incorporate the consensus at a particular time as to which economic resources and obligations should be recorded as assets and liabilities. . . ."[18] Hence, basic accounting terminology was once again defined by whatever was being done in practice. Furthermore, since the document was a statement rather than an opinion and thus carried less enforcement status, the decision not to take a stronger prescriptive position in terms of basic definitions was doubly disappointing.

Other Aspects of APB Statement 4

Despite the shortcomings, there are many good aspects of this document. For example, the fact that accounting is a measurement discipline is noted in paragraph 67. The section on objectives parallels the work of ASOBAT. The standards and guidelines of that report have been combined and largely overlap with the "qualitative objectives" of APB Statement 4.

The qualitative objectives consist of relevance, understandability, verifiability, neutrality, timeliness, comparability, and completeness. These would appear as "qualitative characteristics" in the conceptual framework. There is no hierarchical ranking of these qualities in APB Statement 4. Timeliness, received scant mention in ASOBAT. APB Statement 4 concurs with ASOBAT on possible conflict among objectives (such as relevance and reliability) and that the conflict is a very knotty problem that should be resolved in the metatheoretical framework. While APB Statement 4 agrees with ASOBAT on the need for finite uniformity, it acknowledges the difficulty of accomplishing this goal. Finally, APB Statement 4, independent of ASOBAT, concentrated on developing the user-oriented approach (work in this area may actually have started prior to ASOBAT's undertaking).

Other aspects of APB Statement 4 are less innovative. The "basic features" of financial accounting are largely a rehash of some of the postulates from ARS 1, *The Basic Postulates of Accounting*. The pervasive principles and modifying conventions in the section on generally accepted accounting principles consist of those concepts that constitute the heart of the presently ill-defined system of historical costing. The remaining sections of the report, which include statements of the principles of selection and measurement and financial statement presentation, likewise present virtually no theoretical innovation.

Concluding Remarks on APB Statement 4

Large parts of APB Statement 4 are restatements of the conventional wisdom of the time, whereas other parts recognize that important evolutionary changes had begun to occur.[19] The conventional wisdom is stated relatively concisely and completely. In fact, public accounting firms in papers outlining their positions on various proposals often quoted the document. However, the many parts of the document do not tie together as a whole. For example, it is extremely questionable whether the objectives, which largely stem from ASOBAT, can be implemented by means of the various principles derived from the existing body of accounting. This problem is further compounded by the loosely—if not circularly—worded set of definitions. Hence, the document is, to a large extent, justly accused of trying to be all things to all people. Nevertheless, considering its positive aspects as well as the fact that the APB was under heavy fire during the document's drafting, it has served a useful purpose.

The Trueblood Committee Report

The AICPA formed the Trueblood Committee in April 1971, at a time when the APB was under heavy criticism but also at a point when some degree of quiet progress was being made in terms of reformulating the structure of accounting theory. The committee was charged with using APB Statement 4 as a vehicle for refining the objectives of financial statements as a part of a metatheoretical structure.

The committee enumerated a total of 12 objectives of financial accounting:

1. *The basic objective of financial statements is to provide information useful for making economic decisions.*

2. *An objective of financial statements is to serve primarily those users who have limited authority, ability, or resources to obtain information and who rely on financial statements as their principal source of information about an enterprise's economic activities.*

3. *An objective of financial statements is to provide information useful to investors and creditors for predicting, comparing, and evaluating potential cash flows to them in terms of amount, timing, and related uncertainty.*

4. *An objective of financial statements is to provide users with information for predicting, comparing, and evaluating enterprise earning power.*

5. *An objective of financial statements is to supply information useful in judging management's ability to utilize enterprise resources effectively in achieving the primary enterprise goal.*

6. *An objective of financial statements is to provide factual and interpretive information about transactions and other events, which is useful for predicting, comparing, and evaluating enterprise earning power. Basic underlying assumptions with respect to matters subject to interpretation, evaluation, prediction, or estimation should be disclosed.*

7. *An objective is to provide a statement of financial position useful for predicting, comparing, and evaluating enterprise earning power. This statement should provide information concerning enterprise transactions and other events that are part of incomplete earning cycles. Current values should also be reported when they differ significantly from historical costs. Assets and liabilities should be grouped or segregated by the relative uncertainty of the amount and timing of prospective realization or liquidation.*

8. *An objective is to provide a statement of periodic earnings useful for predicting, comparing, and evaluating enterprise earning power. The net result of completed earnings cycles and enterprise activities resulting in recognizable progress toward completion of incomplete cycles should be reported. Changes in the values reflected in successive statements of financial position should be reported, but separately, since they differ in terms of their certainty of realization.*

9. *Another objective is to provide a statement of financial activities useful for predicting, comparing, and evaluating enterprise earning power. This statement should report mainly on factual aspects of enterprise transactions having or expected to have significant cash consequences. This statement should report data that require minimal judgment and interpretation by the preparer.*

10. *An objective of financial statements is to provide information useful for the predictive process. Financial forecasts should be provided when they will enhance the reliability of users' predictions.*

11. *An objective of financial statements for governmental and not-for-profit organizations is to provide information useful for evaluating the effectiveness of the management of resources in achieving the organization's goals. Performance measures should be quantified in terms of identified goals.*

12. *An objective of financial statements is to report on those activities of the enterprise that affect society which can be determined and described or measured and which are important to the role of the enterprise in its social environment.*[20]

SOURCE: *The Trueblood Committee Report,* 1973, reproduced with permission of the American Institute of Certified Public Accountants.

The committee did not indicate a structural order for these objectives, but a study by Sorter and Gans and another by Anton arranged them in a hierarchical framework.[21] Sorter and Gans, it should be noted, were the research director and the administrative director, respectively, of the staff for the study group. Exhibit 6.1 (see p. 164) shows the arrangement of Sorter and Gans. The Anton structuring agreed with Sorter and Gans on most major points.

Objectives of Financial Statements

Objective 1

The topmost objective agrees with the emphasis on the user of both ASOBAT and APB Statement 4. Objective 1 overlaps with the standard of relevance and the guideline of appropriateness to expected use of ASOBAT and the general objectives of APB Statement 4. This objective is not an operational one; rather, it is a very broad statement of a goal or direction for the standard-setting process.

Objective 2

The second objective describes the primary users being served by financial statements. By zeroing in on users with "limited authority, ability, or resources," the Trueblood Committee diverged from its two predecessors. In terms of ability, ASOBAT had nothing to say. To the extent the matter was discussed in APB Statement 4, users were expected to be knowledgeable about financial statements and information. Opting to serve users with limitations may seem an unusual choice in light of the efficient-markets hypothesis, which had just become well known at the time of the Trueblood Report. This body of research states that even naive investors are not penalized in an efficient market. However, Sorter and Gans made a curious disclaimer on this point:

> This objective may be the most misunderstood of all objectives. Although it may be interpreted to mean that financial statements should serve those with "limited ability," that was not the study group's intention. . . . Financial statements should not serve special or narrow needs of specific users but rather should serve the general needs of all users. Among the implications of this objective are: 1) that financial statements . . . should provide full disclosure; and 2) that all information should be presented as *simply* [italics added] as the subject matter allows.[22]

"Limited ability," then, may simply be code for full disclosure and broad, general-purpose financial statements. Furthermore, the discussion of the primary user group in the Trueblood Report reveals an extremely important value judgment: While user groups may differ, their economic decisions are essentially similar. This, in turn, leads deductively to the idea that the various user groups have similar information needs, hence the justification for general-purpose financial statements with disclosure, as noted in the previous Sorter and Gans quotation.

Objective 3

The third objective is on the importance of cash flows. The users mentioned for whom this information is necessary are lenders and investors. Although lenders and investors may well be the most important user groups, it is not totally clear why it was necessary to single them out in light of the committee's value judgment that user decisions and information needs are largely homogeneous. Since the cash flows discussed are future (potential) in nature, they must be predicted, which requires high quality operating and financial information.

Objective 4

Earning power (income-generating potential), important in its own right, is seen as one of the extremely useful measures for helping to predict, compare, and evaluate cash flow potential. Over the long run, cash flow and earnings have a high correlation. However, in the short run, earnings may actually be a better predictor of cash-generating potential than cash flows themselves because much of the latter may be either nonoperational or plowed back into the enterprise for the purpose of breeding future cash flows and earnings.

Objective 5

The word *accountability* was used both in the Trueblood Report itself and by Sorter and Gans (Exhibit 6.1) to summarize the fifth objective. It extends beyond the ancient concept of stewardship (which is limited to the functions of safekeeping of assets and ensuring that they are used in accordance with investors' purposes).[23] Here, accountability also includes the ideas of effectively and efficiently utilizing assets to carry out the enterprise objective of maximizing future cash flows consistent with a given level of risk. As such, accountability and the word *evaluating* used in Objectives 3 and 4 appear to overlap significantly.

Objective 6

The key words in the sixth objective are *factual* and *interpretive*. The difference between these two qualities is connected to the concept of the various enterprise cycles. Cycles can be either broad or narrow. The acquisition, usage, and disposition of a fixed asset would be an example of a broad cycle. The broadest of all cycles would comprise the beginning and end of the enterprise itself. A fairly narrow cycle would be cash to inventory to accounts receivable to cash. From the standpoint of cycles, the broader the cycle is, the more interpretive and the less factual the accounting information is likely to be. For a broad cycle such as acquisition, usage, and disposition of fixed assets, current values of fixed assets may be indicative of progress toward completion of the cycle, although these values may be subject to a great deal of uncertainty.

Generally speaking, the cash flow statement probably provides more factual and less interpretive information than the income statement, which, in turn, has more factual and less interpretive information than the balance sheet. In drawing the distinction between factual and interpretive information, Objective 6 provides the rationale for presenting different types and qualities of information to users.

Objectives 7, 8, and 9

Objectives 7, 8, and 9 call for a balance sheet, an earnings (income) statement, and a funds flow type of statement that will be useful for prediction, comparison, and evaluation of enterprise earning power—without prescribing the format of these statements.

In the statement of financial position (balance sheet), current values are indicative of the present value of future cash flows as determined by the market. Hence, these values are

Exhibit 6.1   Hierarchy of Objectives

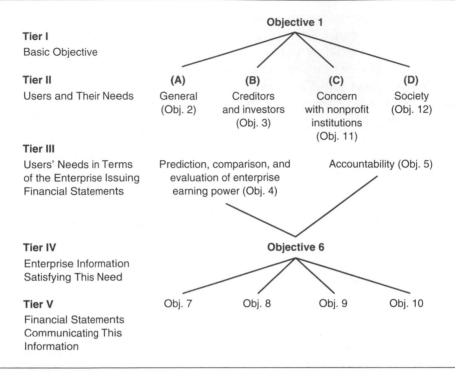

SOURCE: From Sorter, G. H., and Gans, M. S., "Opportunities and Implications of the Report on the Objectives of Financial Statements," *Studies on Financial Accounting Objectives*, 1974 (Supplement to *Journal of Accounting Research*), p. 4. Reprinted with the permission of Blackwell Publishing.

useful for predicting, comparing, and evaluating enterprise earning power.[24] Except for cash and, to a slightly lesser extent, accounts and notes receivable, the great majority of assets held represent the results of incomplete cycles. Hence, current valuation, as opposed to historical cost, is a means of presenting interpretive information where incomplete cycles exist. This does not necessarily mean, however, that all historical cost information is factual.

Earnings statements could largely be restricted to a completed earnings cycle basis by eliminating from them expense measurements pertaining to long-lived assets consumed during the period. However, statements of this type would not be as useful as a more complete model in terms of predicting, comparing, and evaluating enterprise earning power. This objective might be further abetted by using current value measurements of expired assets rather than historical cost approaches. The committee itself was divided on the question of whether the earnings figure should include valuation changes relative to unexpired assets. The report appears to call for a multistep income statement where separate amounts are shown for earnings components having different degrees of certainty relative to the factual basis (completion of cycle) of the figures involved.

The statement of financial activities would supplement the other two statements because there would be much less uncertainty about the information presented. The statement could concentrate on highly probable effects on changes in cash (such as revenues and purchases) rather than "narrower"—but even more highly probable—figures such as cash receipts and cash disbursements. The statement would also show acquisitions and dispositions of fixed assets, changes in long-term debt, and contributions and distributions of capital. In addition, information not shown elsewhere, such as purchase commitments and sales backlog differentials, could also be shown here. All these components would be factual in nature, even though some of them (fixed-asset acquisitions, for example) pertain to incomplete cycles.

Objective 10

Financial forecasts are, of course, subjective in nature. As a result, excessive optimism or pessimism may unduly influence them. Furthermore, public accounting firms do not show any great enthusiasm for auditing forecasts. At the present time, the SEC encourages—but by no means requires—firms to make them.[25] Their potential usefulness for predicting, comparing, and evaluating enterprise earning power should be readily apparent.

Objectives 11 and 12

Accounting for governmental and not-for-profit organizations is an important area: the costs to society that are not borne by business. In addition, there are many activities carried on by business that are not reported on financial statements—those affecting the environment—which would be of considerable interest to users. However, both of these objectives are beyond the general scope of this text, so they will not be discussed here.

Concluding Remarks on the Trueblood Committee Report

The Trueblood Report also contains a short chapter on "qualitative characteristics of reporting" based largely on the standards and guidelines of ASOBAT and the qualitative objectives of APB Statement 4. In addition, there is a brief but useful chapter on the various valuation systems of accounting. The report expresses the belief that different valuation bases are appropriate for different assets and liabilities, a view that ignores the additivity argument.

But it is on its definition of the objectives of financial statements that the report must be evaluated. Critics have pointed out that the objectives are obvious and do not specify operational objectives that could be put into practice.[26] The criticism is true but largely irrelevant. These objectives represented an important step taken toward establishing a meaningful conceptual framework of objectives.

Finally, it is important to reiterate that the Trueblood Report emphasizes the importance of cash flows to users and the relation of earning-power measurements to the generation of future cash flows. The earning-power orientation to income is grounded in the notion that economic income is the change in the present value of future cash flows discounted at an appropriate rate.

SATTA

The Executive Committee of the AAA commissioned SATTA, *A Statement on Accounting Theory and Theory Acceptance*, in 1973. Its overall purpose, similar to that of ASOBAT a decade earlier, was to provide a survey of the current financial accounting literature and a statement of where the profession stood relative to accounting theory. The report accomplished its objectives admirably. However, the results were not necessarily pleasing to accounting theorists and policy makers.

To comprehend SATTA more fully, it is necessary to understand its relationship to ASO-BAT. Both documents, of course, are products of AAA committees having similarly broad guidelines. ASOBAT attempted to develop metatheoretical guidelines for the evaluation of accounting information and valuation systems. SATTA, on the other hand, took into account the many valuation systems of accounting as well as other theoretical considerations and enumerated the reasons why it was impossible to develop criteria that would enable the profession to unequivocally accept a single valuation system for accounting. In effect, then, SATTA is a very cautionary document in terms of the possibility for adopting any one valuation theory.

Theory Approaches in Accounting

Classical Approaches

SATTA concisely and efficiently traced and categorized the various valuation systems presented in the literature. Older systems were classified as "classical approaches to theory development."[27] Most of the listings in this group were characterized as primarily normative and deductive and as indifferent to the decision needs of users, even though the developers of the models rationalized that their models were superior for user needs to competing alternatives. In some cases, classical writers used what SATTA called an inductive approach, but "inductive" in a rather special sense—a gleaning from the accounting literature itself as well as from some observations of practice—instead of the usual sense of a systematic review and analysis of practice, or another designated population.

Decision-Usefulness Approach

Among the contemporary approaches to accounting theory is the large body of research that has concentrated on users of accounting reports, their decisions, information needs, and information-processing abilities. The decision-usefulness approach has been further dichotomized into *decision models* and *decision makers*.

Decision-Model Orientation. The metatheoretical frameworks (or parts thereof) developed in ASOBAT and the Trueblood Report reflect the decision-model orientation. The systems that fall into this category all share the following characteristics:

- They are normative and deductive since the theoretical system must meet, as closely as possible, criteria of a metatheoretical framework.
- Some form of relevance for particular decisions by a particular user group or groups is stressed.
- The relevance criterion is instrumental in measuring the selected attributes of assets, liabilities, and income transactions.

Decision-model approaches often stem from formal investment decision models, such as discounted cash flow.[28] Since decision-model approaches are deemed appropriate for communicating extremely relevant information for decision making, a rather unpleasant problem arises if users do not understand or prefer these systems. At least one individual has taken the position that users must be educated to understand the method, an argument consistent with the normative framework of the approach.[29] However, the task of normatively selecting a model and forcing it on users, particularly if they neither prefer nor understand it, is indeed extremely formidable.

Decision-Maker Orientation. The main point about the decision-maker orientation is that it is descriptive rather than normative because it attempts to find out what information is actually used or desired. The assumption is that the information that is desired should be supplied.[30] Hence, in addition to being descriptive, research that falls into the decision-maker category is also inductive (empirical). Much of the behavioral research mentioned in Chapter 2 falls into the decision-maker category.

Although many important "bits" of information have come from the rather extensive research conducted with this approach, questions of relevance versus reliability remain paramount. Nevertheless, since the decision-model approach is normative, it has produced advocacy for particular valuation systems and income measurement systems.

Information Economics Approach

Information economics as applied to accounting theory does not deal directly with alternative valuation systems. Instead, it is concerned with the issue of costs and benefits arising from information production and usage. Hence, accounting information is viewed as an economic good, an outlook that had not previously been considered in theory formulation.

Deficiencies of Present Approaches to Theory

The overriding message of SATTA relates to why we cannot achieve theory closure—acceptance of a particular valuation system—at this time. Our analysis of this aspect of SATTA will cover the most important issues raised from the standpoint of accounting theory.

Perhaps the principal problem brought up by SATTA is the diversity of users in terms of their decisions and their differing information needs. Both ASOBAT and APB Statement 4 recognized the fact that many user groups require information for decision-making purposes. One of ASOBAT's reactions to this problem was to call for multiple measures. However, there are perceived limits to the ability of users to absorb and process additional information, so data expansion is not a cure-all.[31] The Trueblood Report, on the other hand, establishes rather early the premise that although there are different user groups, they make similar decisions and have similar information needs. Like ASOBAT, the Trueblood Report is concerned with providing a part of the metatheoretical framework for evaluating theoretical systems and methods from a normative viewpoint. The Trueblood Report is, thus, also closely related to the decision-model school.

SATTA was much more pessimistic than the Trueblood Report about decisions and information preferences both among and within user groups. Venn diagrams illustrate the differences between user homogeneity and user heterogeneity in information needs (see Exhibit 6.2). The circles represent user groups and their information needs. There is a large degree of overlap in the high user homogeneity part of the diagram and much less in the other part.

Heterogeneity of information preferences and needs compounds an already difficult situation. Corporate financial reports and disclosures are a free good. Users do not pay the preparer for the information received, and the information is available to virtually anyone who really desires it. Accounting information is, therefore, a public good rather than a private good. If it were a private good, the information required would be amenable to a market type of solution: It would be determined by supply and demand.

Given user heterogeneity and the public-good character of financial information, the formulation of accounting standards and prescribed methods necessarily reaches an impasse. Providing one set of accounting information rather than another means that one set of users is being favored to the detriment of other user groups. Moreover, different sets of accounting information lead to different security prices, which again means that some individuals are being favored at the expense of others. Furthermore, if a value judgment is adopted that states

Exhibit 6.2   Degrees of User Homogeneity of Information Needs

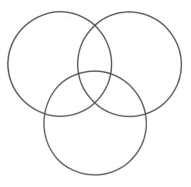
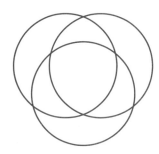

Low User Homogeneity   **High User Homogeneity**

that a policy-setting organization should not take actions that make one group better off at the expense of another, then accounting policy formulation becomes totally straitjacketed. Hence, SATTA presented a very bleak prospect for theory closure.

SATTA attempted to describe the status of financial accounting theory as of the late 1970s. We do not wish to quarrel with SATTA's conclusion; nevertheless, a few remarks are in order. The assumption that user information needs are heterogeneous is far from proved. The assertions of both homogeneity and heterogeneity proponents are totally a priori in nature.[32] Empirical research is desperately needed to shed some light on this extremely important question. Herbert Miller has stated the case very well:

> Certainly I am in favor of on-going research to discover the needs of statement users. But I would not be surprised if users were to indicate that they expect accounting information questions to be resolved by the experts who know something about the merits and helpfulness of accounting measurements. So I believe it is reasonable to expect users to look to the accountant for guidance. This line of reasoning has led me to believe there is a risk that accountants may have been giving too much weight to the lack of (and the desire for) knowledge about users' needs.[33]

Strict adherence to Pareto-optimality is also open to question. In a situation of any social complexity, it will be virtually impossible for any policy-making organization to conform to the very rigid criteria of Pareto-optimality. Pareto himself, a well-known Italian economist, did not see his optimality approach as the sole decision rule.[34] Perhaps what is needed are judiciously applied constraints by policy-setting organizations to control their actions to attain the greatest good for the greatest number of individuals. Unquestionably, even this easing of the Paretian reins still leaves organizations such as FASB with a herculean task.

Concluding Remarks on SATTA

SATTA was a remarkable synthesis of the theoretical financial accounting literature. The jury is still out on the question of heterogeneity of information needs and the application of Pareto-optimality, but it is difficult to argue with SATTA's conclusion. We cannot expect accounting theorists to develop a theoretical framework that will be universally satisfactory. In turn, we can expect the statements and pronouncements of a rule-making group, such as the FASB, which are propounded in an incomplete market setting, to be met with less than full enthusiasm. Hence, a paradoxical situation arose. An important document authored by a distinguished group of academicians took a very pessimistic view of the role and possibilities of accounting theory formulation at exactly the same time that a conceptual framework—a theoretical document—was begun by a rule-making body.

User Objectives and User Diversity

The search for user objectives has been clouded by the user diversity problem discussed in the SATTA report. In this section, we will briefly discuss the major and minor objectives of corporate reporting and then relate the user diversity problem to the objectives.

User Objectives

The user objectives stated in such documents as the Trueblood Report and the conceptual framework are quite broad and general. Further specificity may be necessary if policy making is to be appropriately executed. Unfortunately, only a very limited amount of accounting research has focused on this issue. Nevertheless, there appear to be two major areas in which broad information is applicable to many user groups. The first of these is referred to as the *predictive ability* objective. The second is an extension of stewardship called *accountability*. Both objectives can be divided into numerous subcategories. Our discussion, however, is restricted to the principal aspects of each objective.

Predictive Ability

The usefulness of accounting data as an aid to predict future variables within the context of a capital market that is largely "efficient" (new information is rapidly reflected in security prices) has become extremely important in accounting research and will be examined in Chapter 8. Even though market efficiency validates the predictive ability objective, the FASB's task is still one of selecting among competing accounting alternatives within a context where benefits of accounting standards should exceed their costs.

Numerous early studies attempted to use accounting data to predict future variables. One group of studies has attempted to predict future income on the basis of present and past income numbers.[35] One of the purposes of these studies was to obtain evidence concerning whether historical cost income, general price-level-adjusted income, or current value income is a better predictor of itself. These studies indicate that historical cost appears to be at least as good a predictor of itself as the other two methods.

However, Revsine has pointed out that income itself is an "artifact."[36] An artifact, in this sense, refers to a number, the determination of which is based on prescribed rules rather than representational faithfulness to the attribute being measured. Furthermore, because there is sufficient latitude in selecting alternative methods (combined with the potential desire of management to smooth or manage income), it is not surprising that historical income appears to be a better predictor of itself than other income measurement methods that intuitively appear to contain numbers more economically relevant. Revsine also suggests that since income is an "artificial construct," its predictive importance lies in the ability to anticipate a real event, such as future cash flows.[37] Finally, since the real event may itself be quite volatile, the predictor should be similarly volatile, whereas the research discussed before was really examining the issue of income smoothing.[38]

Many other early studies focused on the predictive ability of two other sets of accounting-generated numbers: quarterly earnings announcements as predictors of annual earnings and financial ratios as predictors of bankruptcy.[39] In both cases, the accounting data—as might be expected—have been highly useful in the predictive process. One cautionary note, however, is that these studies have employed particular models as part of the predictive ability process. Only insofar as users avail themselves of at least roughly similar methods can predictive ability tests be relied upon.[40] The alternative, of course, involves attempting to educate users about what are presumed to be the best predictive models—a task, as noted previously, that could be quite difficult. Another point to keep in mind is that valuation and income methods presumed to be best for one objective, such as predictive ability, may conflict with other objectives, as will be discussed in Chapter 7.

Among many types of predictive studies are relationships between cash flows and security prices and accrued earnings and security prices.[41] Research has also found that assets and liabilities of the enterprise are priced by the market.[42] Even unrecorded assets and liabilities (unrecognized pension assets and liabilities) are priced by the market.[43]

Accountability

We use the word *accountability* to mean a broader concept than the narrower one of stewardship, which is mainly concerned with the safeguarding of assets. This meaning follows Ijiri's usage—the responsibility of management to report on achieving goals for the effective and efficient utilization of enterprise resources.[44] Measurements based on the accountability objective would include earnings per share and return on investment and its components (capital turnover and profit margin). The question of which valuation system provides the best input for these and other accountability-oriented measurements is important. Ijiri, for example, makes a strong case for historical costs (including the possibility of general price-level adjustments).[45]

Predictive ability and accountability are separate objectives. One is concerned with data that will be useful in terms of assessing future prospects, whereas the other is concerned with evaluating enterprise performance. Between these two objectives, there is, of course, a linkage of a feed-forward nature. How well a firm is presently doing can certainly be an important input for predictive purposes.[46] However, as previously stated, we believe that there are conflicts between predictive ability and accountability. Thus, it is possible that the same information set may not be compatible for both objectives. It is hoped, though, that this problem—if indeed there is one—can eventually be resolved.

Accountability has received some attention as a possible substitute for the predictive-ability objective. Ijiri has called for a conceptual framework geared to accountability.[47] Objectivity and verifiability would be important components of this framework. Williams and Pallot stress the need for fairness.[48] Williams stresses that accountability is concerned with equity among competing groups and claims to distribution of income and wealth, both of which are concerned with fairness. However, decision usefulness (predictive ability) is not grounded in these same concerns. Pallot points out that there are two concepts of fairness: (1) an individualistic approach that is concerned with rights, contracts, and individual efforts and contributions and (2) a communitarian approach based more on equality and need. Both concepts must be considered in a conceptual-framework-type document. However, the question of objectives is of paramount concern to standard setters.

Secondary Objectives

We see two other possible user objectives for which accounting information can be extremely useful. They are narrower than the concepts of predictive ability and accountability. One is a measure of *capital maintenance*, which gives information about the amount of dividends that can be paid during a period without returning capital to the stockholders. Another possible objective would be that of *adaptability*. This objective is concerned with measuring total liquidity available to the firm. By definition, this is determined by measuring the exit value of the firm's assets minus its liabilities. The exit-value approach is illustrated in Appendix 1-A. An income statement under the exit-value approach measures the change in liquidity occurring during the period as a result of operations.[49] Chambers and Sterling have been the principal proponents of this system and also of this objective.[50]

A measure of total liquidity available to a firm certainly has some relevance, but we consider adaptability far less important than predictive ability and accountability. Firms that are successful going concerns will probably draw upon only a very small portion of the total available liquidity during relatively short time periods. Adaptability measures would probably be most important to the owners of small, closely held firms and possibly short-term creditors. Consequently, the adaptive approach appears to be more closely linked to proprietary theory than to entity theory (see Chapter 5). Exit-value approaches appear to have limited usefulness for predictive ability and accountability purposes. Indeed, Chambers stoutly denies that accounting figures can have any relevance for predictive purposes.[51] We have discussed these four objectives in fairly broad terms. More detailed examination of issues, such as attributes to be measured and valuation systems to be employed, must also be considered in a conceptual-framework-type document. However, the question of objectives is a dominant concern for standard setters. Closely linked to the issue of objectives of financial reporting is the question of user diversity.

User Diversity

Unquestionably, there are a large and diverse number of users of published financial statements.[52] What is not clear, however, is whether their information needs for the various types of objectives can be satisfied by general-purpose statements. The list of possible user groups is indeed lengthy. It would include:

- Shareholders
- Creditors
- Financial analysts and advisers
- Employees
- Labor unions
- Customers
- Suppliers
- Industry trade associations
- Governmental agencies
- Public-interest groups
- Researchers and standard setters
- Auditors
- Management
- Communities touched by the firms operations

Furthermore, even within these groups there is extensive diversity. Shareholders include those whose portfolios are diversified versus those whose are not, those using professional financial advisers and those who do not, those knowledgeable about financial statements versus those who are uninformed, and actual versus potential owners of securities. Creditors can be segregated into short-term and long-term types. Public-interest groups would include, among others, consumer and environmental groups. Researchers and standard setters include academic accountants, members of the SEC and FASB, and economists. Governmental agencies (such as the Internal Revenue Service, Interstate Commerce Commission, and Federal Trade Commission), unlike the other groups, are often able to acquire by mandate the information they desire.

Some of the information needs of different user groups may be complementary. For example, short-term creditors may be concerned with liquidity measurements, such as the current or quick ratios, whereas long-term creditors may have greater interest in the composition of capital structures. Serious problems do not appear to exist where there are complementary needs. Perhaps the most serious conflict lies between actual and potential security holders. The former would probably desire information that would maximize security prices, whereas the latter would prefer information that would minimize security prices (this would change if potential security owners acquire shares).

One interesting example of specific user needs is provided by the CFA (Chartered Financial Analysts) Institute in a business reporting model for equity investors.[53] Their model stresses current values (now more frequently called *fair values*) for all assets and liabilities for the purpose of helping to predict future cash flows. The CFA Institute shows a clear preference for relevance over reliability. If links to provide enough information for accountability purposes can be provided and tradeoffs between relevance and reliability can be reasonably accommodated, such a system should find a very wide acceptance among different user groups.

In the discussion of SATTA, it was noted that several writers invoked Pareto-optimality as an underlying assumption that would render a set of objectives of financial statements impossible to attain in the presence of heterogeneous user groups and needs. We believe that the seriousness of this problem has been overstated. The discussion in SATTA on user heterogeneity centers largely on the question of what valuation system to employ (e.g., discounted cash flows, replacement cost, exit value, or general price-level adjustment).

Several efforts have been made, with some success, to get around the perceived user heterogeneity problem.[54] Ogan and Ziebart see different information needs for five different groups: owners, government employees, creditors, customers, and general society.[55] Their concern, however, is really with additional disclosure, a viewpoint that we are in agreement with and which is further discussed in Chapter 9. Ogan and Ziebart make two additional points that are quite important: (1) There may be considerable overlap among these groups, and (2) the specialized information that is needed by these various groups may already have been produced, and information technology makes dissemination of the information relatively inexpensive.[56]

A major effort to examine user needs was made by an important AICPA committee.[57] The committee clearly saw a diversity of user needs: "For example, contrast the information needs of a bank credit officer who is evaluating an excellent credit risk and a bank trust department evaluating the same company's stock."[58]

The diversity of information needs discussed in the report is clearly complementary for the different user populations rather than at odds with each other. The committee report even develops a financial reporting approach in line with expanded information needs of investors and creditors. The main problem standing in the way of newer information approaches is the perceived competitive disadvantage of making public matters that management would prefer to keep secret.

Little, if any, empirical research has been done on different user group needs.[59] However, an interesting study was done by Plummer and Tse.[60] Their findings showed that as firm earnings declined and bond ratings were lowered, this information became more important for bondholders and less important for shareholders (many of whom may have decided to sell the stock). With the firm doing well, the opposite situation prevailed: Financial performance became more important to stockholders. Notice that this is *not* a situation of user heterogeneity. Rather it is saying that different groups may value the same information differently depending on the circumstances. This should not be a surprise. We believe that the valuation orientation differences discussed in SATTA overstate the problem.

As discussed in Chapter 4, real differences exist among auditors, management, and all other groups. Auditors desire to maximize their revenues, minimize their risks, and to promote consulting services to their clients. Managers generally want higher income to increase stock prices in order to be evaluated well by shareholders and also increase their own income through bonus arrangements or to increase stock option spreads (Chapter 12). These desires by management result in the problem of earnings management (also Chapter 12).

We believe that differences among the other user groups are relatively small, with the possible exception of financial analysts and advisers, who may be under orders to "push" certain securities. We do not consider the desires of auditors, management, and possibly financial analysts and advisers to fall under the umbrella of unbiased and neutral financial statements. On the contrary, the duty of standard setters is to fend off the special interests of these groups. Whether a conceptual framework can enhance the task of improving financial standards and financial reporting is the subject of the next chapter.

Summary

The most common thread running through the various documents, reports, and monographs discussed in this chapter is that the field reached the conclusion that financial statements should be relevant to users for decision-making purposes. As a result, the standard-setting bodies turned away from the postulates and principles orientation and toward an objectives and standards orientation.

ASOBAT was the first document based on the new orientation toward user relevance. However, it provided little further detail or explication of user relevance. APB Statement 4 continued the emphasis on user relevance, although it is a curious mixture of the old and new approaches owing to the fact that the document appeared at a time of transition. It was clear that the APB would be replaced, but the nature of its successor was not apparent.

The first statement to address the issue of user objectives extensively was the Trueblood Report. Although it mentions predictive ability and accountability, the discussion is still not at an operational level. However, a preliminary statement of this type can do nothing more than point the way for future efforts.

SATTA was to the 1970s what ASOBAT was to the 1960s. Both are the product of AAA committees that were attempting to summarize the "state of the art" concerning accounting theory. SATTA expressed the opinion that choice among accounting theories (valuation systems) could not be made at that time owing to the diversity of users and their presumably different objectives and information needs.

The crucial issues discussed in this chapter concern what the objectives of financial statements are, or at least are perceived to be, and what are the information needs of the heterogeneous users of financial statements. The consensus seems to be that the major objectives are predictive ability and accountability. Accountability is an extension of the traditional stewardship objective to the effective and efficient usage of enterprise resources by management. Minor objectives appear to be capital maintenance measurement and adaptability. Adaptability is best determined by exit valuation of assets, which gives a result that has little if any utility for predictive ability or accountability purposes. Among (and within) all of these objectives, there is some potential conflict. Despite the heterogeneity of groups of users as well as within groups, we believe a strong information overlap may exist. It has not been proved that the groups have strongly differentiated information needs, save for auditors, management, and possibly financial analysts and advisers, but these are, in effect, special interest groups.

QUESTIONS

1. How do objectives differ from postulates?

2. Do you think that the cash flow statement is more "factual" and less "interpretative" than the income statement and balance sheet?

3. Do you think that the standards mentioned in ASOBAT are really standards? Why or why not?

4. Why is the problem of heterogeneous users so critical in the development of accounting theory?

5. APB Statement 4 defines assets in the following terms: "Assets are economic resources of an enterprise that are recognized and measured in conformity with generally accepted accounting principles. Assets also include certain deferred charges that are not resources but that are recognized and measured in conformity with generally accepted accounting principles." Do you think this is a useful definition? Why or why not?

6. How do the research orientations of accounting in Chapter 2 compare with SATTA's organization of research?

7. The statement of Herbert Miller (footnote 33) is closest to which theoretical approach delineated in SATTA?

8. How has the definition of *accounting* been modified in recent years?

9. What potential conflicts are present in terms of different user needs?

10. Why has Ijiri advocated the need for a conceptual framework to implement accountability?

11. The Trueblood Committee Report advocated the use of financial forecasts. Why do you think that adoption of this suggestion has been very unenthusiastically received by preparers and auditors?

12. Under an accountability orientation, Ijiri makes a strong case for the use of historical costing including the possibility of general price-level adjustments. Why do you think he has made this choice?

13. The viewpoint has been expressed that financial statement preparers are also the largest class of users of financial statements. Hence, the preparer has a "unique ability" to recognize user needs that the FASB does not really appreciate. Critique this viewpoint.

14. Why would "fairness" in financial reporting be difficult to implement?

15. What is the relationship between "stewardship" and "accountability"? Discuss.

16. Do you think that the income tax return mandated by the federal government is an example of user heterogeneity? Why or why not?

17. If a division manager of a firm were fired due to poor operating results, would this be an example of stewardship? Why or why not?

❖

CASES, PROBLEMS, AND WRITING ASSIGNMENTS

1. A crucial question brought up in this chapter concerns the issue of whether the admittedly heterogeneous users of financial statements have highly diverse information needs in terms of their underlying objectives. State as carefully as you can (a) why the user groups have largely diverse information needs and (b) why the user groups may have relatively similar information needs. Do you think user diversity or different user objectives present the greater problem for accounting standard setters?

2. Using the different valuation methods discussed in Appendix 1-A, what possible different user preferences do you see among the various user groups?

CRITICAL THINKING AND ANALYSIS

1. Do you see an evolutionary process involving the documents and reports presented in this chapter? Explain.

2. If different user groups do have different objectives, how might the situation be handled?

Notes

1. *AAA (1966, p. v).*
2. *Ibid. (p. 1).*
3. *AICPA (1953, para. 9).*
4. *Ibid. (paras. 11 and 13).*
5. *AAA (1977b, p. 10).*
6. *AAA (1966, p. 1).*
7. *Ibid.*
8. *Ibid. (p. 4).*
9. *An important early article is Beaver, Kennelly, and Voss (1968).*
10. *Borst (1981), for example.*
11. *See Ijiri (1975) for more on the background and extension of stewardship to accountability.*
12. *AAA (1966, p. 12).*
13. *Within a given time frame in a "complex environment," such as that provided by financial information, an individual reaches a point at which additional information cannot be processed or absorbed. See Revsine (1970b) and Henry Miller (1972). However, disclosure (providing additional information) is seen as important to resolving reporting problems because the market uses a broad informational set. See, for example, AAA (1977a, pp. 20–21). Additional research is needed in terms of both individual abilities to process accounting information and the "black box" effect when going from individuals to the aggregated level of the market.*
14. *AAA (1966, p. 7).*
15. *Moonitz (1971).*
16. *AICPA (1970, para. 9).*
17. *Ibid. (paras. 132 and 134). One member of the APB insisted that the definitions be stated as being in accordance with generally accepted accounting principles (Rosenfield, Paul , personal communication).*
18. *Ibid. (para. 137).*
19. *Critiques of APB Statement 4 recognized the dual nature of the document. See Ijiri (1971), Schattke (1972), and Staubus (1972).*
20. *AICPA (1973).*
21. *Sorter and Gans (1974, p. 4) and Anton (1976, pp. 4 and 5).*
22. *Sorter and Gans (1974, p. 6).*
23. *Accountability is used in a similar manner, extending well beyond the bounds of stewardship, by Ijiri (1975, pp. ix and x and 32–35).*
24. *Revsine (1970a) shows that current value income using replacement costs is an indirect measurement of "economic income" (the discounted cash flow approach illustrated in Chapter 1) under conditions of perfect competition. However, replacement cost income is a "mere approximation" of economic income under real-world conditions of imperfect competition. For additional coverage, see Barton (1974).*
25. *Rule 175 of the SEC issued in 1979 provides "safe harbors" from liability provisions of the federal securities laws where forecasts are made.*
26. *Miller (1974, p. 18).*
27. *Older approaches covered the years from 1922 to 1962—with the single exception of a work by Ijiri (1975), which was a defense of historical cost accounting based on the importance of accountability. Many of the items listed, however, were current valuation methods.*
28. *A good example would be AAA (1969), which used a present value model of gains or losses on long-term debt and equity investments to evaluate elements used in financial reports. We should also note that Peasnall has*

observed that the distinction between the classical and the decision-model approaches is largely artificial because both are normative and deductive. See Peasnall (1978), p. 222.

29. *Sterling (1967, p. 106).*

30. *Unfortunately, the problem of determining user information preferences appears to be extremely difficult. Abdel-khalik (1971) developed a stochastic model for measuring preference ordering of users, but the model has never been implemented.*

31. *See footnote 13.*

32. *Beaver and Demski (1974) lean toward user heterogeneity on an a priori basis. Dopuch and Sunder (1980) see potential heterogeneity among three groups: management, auditors, and users. In turn, the user group is itself heterogeneous. They see the heterogeneity among the three groups at three different levels: desired information in financial statements, desired accounting principles, and desired objectives. As a result, they regard attempting to arrive at objectives as a futile exercise, and the FASB's task, therefore, as one of knowing how to mediate among competing interests.*

33. *Miller (1974, pp. 19–20).*

34. *There are two important points that should be borne in mind relative to Pareto-optimality. First, the status quo should not be treated as a unique Pareto-optimum situation. There are many possible Pareto-optimum situations in which change in social rules cannot be made without adversely affecting some parties. Second, Pareto himself did not see his optimality approach as the sole decision rule. Ethics and cost-benefit analysis, for example, could also be used for judging social change. For further coverage, see Samuels (1974, pp. 200–206).*

35. *Simmons and Gray (1969) and Frank (1969).*

36. *Revsine (1971, pp. 480–481).*

37. *Ibid. (p. 487).*

38. *Barnea, Ronen, and Sadan (1975) suggest the segregation of recurring income components from the transitory elements in order to facilitate the prediction of cash flows by users. Excluded from recurring income would be extraordinary (nonrecurring and nonoperating) items designated in APB Opinion No. 30, as well as nonrecurring operating factors.*

39. *For predictive aspects of quarterly data, see Coates (1972), Brown and Kennelly (1972), and Foster (1977). For financial ratios as predictors, see Beaver (1966) and Elam (1975). For a critical look at the predictive ability objective, see Greenball (1971).*

40. *The seminal article on predictive ability and its limitations is Beaver, Kennelly, and Voss (1968).*

41. *Beaver (1998, pp. 89-115).*

42. *Ibid. (pp. 114–115).*

43. *Ibid.*

44. *Ijiri (1975, pp. ix–x).*

45. *Ibid. (pp. 85–90). Ijiri also sees historical costs being important for decision-making purposes, which involves prediction.*

46. *Devine (1985) sees a rather close link between the predictive and accountability functions and hence identical underlying information needs for both functions.*

47. *Ijiri (1983).*

48. *Williams (1987) and Pallot (1991).*

49. *It is quite unlikely that an exit-value income statement would be particularly useful for either predictive ability or accountability purposes. The sizable declines in exit values for many fixed assets in the early years of usage occur because of market imperfections. These lowered exit values result in excessive depreciation charges, which make the exit-value income statement unrepresentative. SFAS No. 157 (Chapter 14) on fair value measurement uses a modified version of the exit-value approach.*

50. *Chambers (1967) and Sterling (1981, p. 119), for example.*

51. *Chambers (1968, p. 246).*

52. *A good short summary of users and their needs is provided in Stamp (1980, pp. 39–51). For a succinct statement on general-purpose statements versus specialized-purpose information, see Mattessich (1998).*

53. *CFA Centre for Financial Market Integrity (2005).*

54. *Stamp (1980), for example, was quite aware of different user needs. He saw these needs giving rise to different valuation system preferences such as historical cost, replacement cost, and exit valuation. His desire was to have expert accountants concerned with the public interest (and sitting on a standard-setting board) use objectives such as comparability, relevance, verifiability, and full disclosure as bases for developing standards. The process of developing standards would employ research, feedback from constituencies, and the eventual development of consensus. Stamp's approach would rely much less on definitions and more on a legal or jurisprudential approach than is the case with the FASB. He also saw that information technology might make it possible to satisfy different user needs in a relatively cost-effective manner. See Mumford (1993) for further coverage.*

55. *Ogan and Ziebart (1991).*

56. *Ibid.*

57. *AICPA (1994).*

58. *Ibid. (p. 19).*

59. *For a theoretical discussion involving commonality of user needs, see Aitken (1990).*

60. *Plummer and Tse (1999).*

References

Abdel-khalik, A. Rashad (July 1971). "User Preference Ordering Value: A Model," *Accounting Review*, pp. 437–471.

Aitken, Michael J. (1990). "A General Theory of Financial Reporting: Is it Possible?" *International Journal of Accounting* (Vol. 25, No. 4), pp. 221–233.

American Accounting Association (1966). *A Statement of Basic Accounting Theory.* American Accounting Association.

——— (1969). "An Evaluation of External Reporting Practices: A Report of the 1966–68 Committee on External Reporting," *Accounting Review Supplement.* American Accounting Association. pp. 79–123.

——— (1977a). *Responses to the Financial Accounting Standards Board's* Tentative Conclusions on Objectives of Financial Statements of Business Enterprises *and* Conceptual Framework for Financial Accounting and Reporting: Elements of Financial Statements and Their Measurement. American Accounting Association.

——— (1977b). *Statement on Accounting Theory and Theory Acceptance.* American Accounting Association.

American Institute of Certified Public Accountants (1953). *Accounting Terminology Bulletin No. 1.* AICPA.

——— (1970). "Basic Concepts and Accounting Principles Underlying Financial Statements of Business Enterprises," *APB Statement No. 4.* American Institute of Certified Public Accountants. pp. 9057–9106.

——— (1973). *Objectives of Financial Statements.* American Institute of Certified Public Accountants.

——— (1994). *Improving Business Reporting—A Customer Focus.* American Institute of Certified Public Accountants.

Anton, Hector (January 1976). "Objectives of Financial Accounting: Review and Analysis," *Journal of Accountancy*, pp. 40–51.

Barnea, Amir, Joshua Ronen, and Simcha Sadan (January 1975). "The Implementation of Accounting Objectives: An Application to Extraordinary Items," *Accounting Review*, pp. 58–68.

Barton, A. D. (October 1974). "Expectations and Achievements in Income Theory," *Accounting Review*, pp. 664–681.

Beaver, William H. (1966). "Financial Ratios as Predictors of Failure," *Empirical Research in Accounting: Selected Studies, 1966* (Supplement to *Journal of Accounting Research*), pp. 71–111.

——— (1998). *Financial Reporting: An Accounting Revolution*, 3rd ed. Prentice Hall.

Beaver, William H., and Joel S. Demski (1974). "The Nature of Financial Accounting Objectives: A Summary and Synthesis," *Studies on Financial Accounting Objectives, 1974* (Supplement to *Journal of Accounting Research*), pp. 170–185.

Beaver, William H., John W. Kennelly, and William M. Voss (October 1968). "Predictive Ability as a Criterion for the Evaluation of Accounting Data," *Accounting Review*, pp. 675–683.

Borst, Duane (July 1981). "Accounting vs. Reality: How Wide Is the 'GAAP'?" *Financial Executive*, pp. 12–15.

Brown, Philip, and John W. Kennelly (July 1972). "The Information Content of Quarterly Earnings—An Extension and Some Further Evidence," *Journal of Business*, pp. 403–415.

CFA Centre for Financial Integrity (2005). *A Comprehensive Business Reporting Model: Financial Reporting for Investors*. CFA.

Chambers, Raymond J. (October 1967). "Continuously Contemporary Accounting—Additivity and Action," *Accounting Review*, pp. 751–757.

——— (April 1968). "Measures and Values: A Reply to Professor Staubus," *Accounting Review*, pp. 239–247.

Coates, Robert (1972). "The Predictive Content of Interim Reports: A Time Series Analysis," *Empirical Research in Accounting: Selected Studies, 1973* (Supplement to *Journal of Accounting Research*), pp. 132–144.

Devine, Carl T. (1985). "Comments on Prediction, Evaluation and Decision Making," *Essays in Accounting Theory*, Vol. IV, *Studies in Accounting Research* No. 22. American Accounting Association, pp. 69–81.

Dopuch, Nicholas, and Shyam Sunder (January 1980). "FASB's Statements on Objectives and Elements of Financial Accounting: A Review," *Accounting Review*, pp. 1–21.

Elam, Rick (January 1975). "The Effect of Lease Data on the Predictive Ability of Financial Ratios," *Accounting Review*, pp. 25–43.

Foster, George (January 1977). "Quarterly Accounting Data: Time-Series Properties and Predictive-Ability Results," *Accounting Review*, pp. 1–21.

Frank, Werner (Spring 1969). "A Study of the Predictive Significance of Two Income Statements," *Journal of Accounting Research*, pp. 123–136.

Greenball, Melvin N. (June 1971). "The Predictive-Ability Criterion: Its Relevance in Evaluating Accounting Data," *Abacus*, pp. 1–7.

Ijiri, Yuji (November 1971). "Critique of the APB Fundamentals Statement," *Journal of Accountancy*, pp. 43–50.

——— (1975). "Theory of Accounting Measurement," *Studies in Accounting Research* No. 10. American Accounting Association.

——— (Summer 1983). "On the Accountability-Based Conceptual Framework of Accounting," *Journal of Accounting and Public Policy*, pp. 75–81.

Mattessich, Richard (March 1998). "In Search of a Framework for Deprival Value and Other Purpose-Oriented Valuation Methods," *Abacus*, pp. 4–7.

Miller, Henry (January 1972). "Environmental Complexity and Financial Reports," *Accounting Review*, pp. 31–37.

Miller, Herbert E. (1974). "Discussion of Opportunities and Implications of the Report on Objectives of Financial Statements," *Studies on Financial Accounting Objectives, 1974* (Supplement to *Journal of Accounting Research*), pp. 18–20.

Moonitz, Maurice (May 1971). "The Accounting Principles Board Revisited," *New York Certified Public Accountant*, pp. 341–345.

Mumford, M. J. (1993). "Users, Characteristics and Standards," in *Philosophical Perspectives on Accounting: Essays in Honour of Edward Stamp,* eds. M. J. Mumford and K. V. Peasnall. Routledge, pp. 7–29.

Ogan, Pekin, and David A. Ziebart (Summer 1991). "Corporate Reporting and the Accounting Profession: An Interpretive Paradigm," *Journal of Accounting, Auditing & Finance*, pp. 387–406.

Pallot, June (1991). "The Legitimate Concern With Fairness: A Comment," *Accounting, Organizations and Society* (Vol. 16, No. 2), pp. 201–208.

Peasnall, K. V. (1978). "Statement of Accounting Theory and Theory Acceptance: A Review Article," *Accounting and Business Research*, pp. 217–225.

Plummer, C. Elizabeth, and S. Y. Tse (1999). "The Effect of Limited Liability on the Informativeness of Earnings: Evidence From the Stock and Bond Markets," *Contemporary Accounting Research* (Vol. 16, No. 3), pp. 541–574.

Revsine, Lawrence (1970a). "On the Correspondence Between Replacement Cost Income and Economic Income," *Accounting Review* (July), pp. 513–523.

——— (1970b). "Data Expansion and Conceptual Structure," *Accounting Review* (October), pp. 704–711.

——— (July 1971). "Predictive Ability, Market Prices, and Operating Flows," *Accounting Review*, pp. 480–489.

Samuels, Warren (1974). *Pareto on Policy*. Elsevier.

Schattke, R. W. (April 1972). "An Analysis of APB Statement No. 4," *Accounting Review*, pp. 233–244.

Simmons, John K., and Jack Gray (October 1969). "An Investigation of the Effect of Differing Accounting Frameworks on the Prediction of Net Income," *Accounting Review*, pp. 757–776.

Sorter, George H., and Martin S. Gans (1974). "Opportunities and Implications of the Report on the Objectives of Financial Statements," *Studies on Financial Accounting Objectives, 1974* (Supplement to *Journal of Accounting Research*), pp. 1–12.

Stamp, Edward (1980). *Corporate Reporting: Its Future Evolution*. Canadian Institute of Chartered Accountants.

Staubus, George (February 1972). "An Analysis of APB Statement No. 4," *Journal of Accountancy*, pp. 36–43.

Sterling, Robert R. (Spring 1967). "A Statement of Basic Accounting Theory: A Review Article," *Journal of Accounting Research*, pp. 94–112.

——— (December 1981). "Costs (Historical Versus Current) Versus Exit Values," *Abacus*, pp. 93–129.

Williams, Paul F. (1987). "The Legitimate Concern With Fairness," *Accounting, Organizations and Society* (Vol. 12, No. 2), pp. 169–189.

7

The FASB's Conceptual Framework

Learning Objectives

After reading this chapter, you should be able to:

- Recognize the linkage between the conceptual framework and the documents discussed in Chapter 6.
- Understand the components of the conceptual framework.
- Comprehend the trade-off problems that standard setters face.
- Appreciate the conflict between representational faithfulness and economic consequences.
- Assess empirical research on the conceptual framework.
- View the conceptual framework from the codificational standpoint and the jurisprudential view.

In Chapter 6, we examined a number of committee reports and documents emanating from the American Institute of Certified Public Accountants (AICPA), Accounting Principles Board (APB), and the American Accounting Association (AAA). The chronology of these documents is extremely important. The first one (ASOBAT, *A Statement of Basic Accounting Theory*) appeared shortly after ARSs 1 and 3 (the Moonitz and Sprouse and Moonitz postulates and principles studies) and the last one (SATTA, *Statement of Accounting Theory and Theory Acceptance*) just prior to publication of the first part of the conceptual framework. Since the documents studied in Chapter 6 appeared just prior to the FASB's conceptual framework project, they played an important role in the development of the conceptual framework.

There are two important points to keep in mind as we examine the contents of the conceptual framework. First, the project can be viewed as an evolutionary document with important parts drawing heavily upon the works discussed in Chapter 6. Second, while much criticism can (and will) be directed toward the conceptual framework, the document can be improved so that it may yet provide a sound underpinning for future accounting standards.

The conceptual framework consists of seven different statements. The seventh came out in 2000, 15 years after No. 6. Each of these seven parts is referred to as a statement of financial accounting concepts (SFAC), and our discussion of these parts will proceed chronologically. The seven SFACs and the year of publication by the FASB are:

Statements of Financial Accounting Concepts:

No. 1, *OBJECTIVES OF FINANCIAL REPORTING BY BUSINESS ENTERPRISES* (SFAC No. 1)	1978
No. 2, *QUALITATIVE CHARACTERISTICS OF ACCOUNTING INFORMATION* (SFAC No. 2)	1980
No. 3, *ELEMENTS OF FINANCIAL STATEMENTS OF BUSINESS ENTERPRISES* (SFAC No. 3)	1980
No. 4, *OBJECTIVES OF FINANCIAL REPORTING BY NONBUSINESS ORGANIZATIONS* (SFAC No. 4)	1980
No. 5, *RECOGNITION AND MEASUREMENT IN FINANCIAL STATEMENTS OF BUSINESS ENTERPRISES* (SFAC No. 5)	1984
No. 6, *ELEMENTS OF FINANCIAL STATEMENTS; A REPLACEMENT OF FASB CONCEPTS STATEMENT NO. 3 ALSO INCORPORATING AN AMENDMENT OF FASB CONCEPTS STATEMENT NO. 2* (SFAC NO. 6)	1985
No. 7, *USING CASH FLOW INFORMATION AND PRESENT VALUE IN ACCOUNTING MEASUREMENTS* (SFAC No. 7)	2000

We will give an overview of each of the SFACs and will also discuss several different problem areas. These include problems between two of the objectives and the question of whether representational faithfulness or economic consequences (Chapter 4) should dominate in the standard-setting process. We close by examining some philosophical orientations to a conceptual framework and mention empirical research pertaining to the conceptual framework. Before proceeding to the conceptual framework itself, we commence by mentioning the discussion memorandum that preceded.[1]

The FASB's Conceptual Framework

The conceptual framework is supposed to embody "a coherent system of interrelated objectives and fundamentals that can lead to consistent standards and that prescribes the nature, function, and limits of financial accounting and financial statements."[2] The conceptual framework is an attempt to provide a metatheoretical structure for financial accounting. The project includes seven statements of financial accounting concepts, kicked off by an important discussion memorandum.

Discussion Memorandum

A discussion memorandum is, of course, not the end product of the FASB's deliberations. However, the discussion memorandum for the conceptual framework was a massive study, perhaps the most extensive ever published by the FASB. In addition, it was widely disseminated and publicized. The discussion memorandum was accompanied by another document pertaining to tentative conclusions of the Trueblood Report on objectives.[3] This latter report accepted the Trueblood Report's user orientation and emphasis on cash flows but added little more of substance.

The discussion memorandum brought up two new basic issues: (1) three views of financial accounting and financial statements (discussed in Chapter 11) and (2) an outline of the various approaches to capital maintenance. The former might be termed orientations to the financial statements. In both cases, in order to elicit responses from the profession, the memorandum attempted to show the various alternatives and possibilities open for adoption. In addition, it presented various definitions for such basic terms as *assets, liabilities, revenues, expenses, gains,* and *losses*—along with a discussion of qualitative characteristics of financial statements (these will be considered in our discussion of SFAC No. 2).

The most important new issue brought up in the document was capital maintenance. Chapter 2 noted that this concept is concerned with how earnings are measured in terms of maintaining intact the firm's capital (assets minus liabilities) existing at the beginning of the period. This is an important problem that should be given a very prominent place in the normative objectives of a metatheoretical structure. It was not considered extensively, if at all, in any of the other documents considered in Chapter 6.

Statements of Financial Accounting Concepts

The SFACs constitute the finished portion of the conceptual framework project. These statements are analogous to APB Statement 4 in one respect: Like that document, these statements do not establish generally accepted accounting principles (GAAP) and are not intended to invoke Rule 203 of the Rules of Conduct of the AICPA (which prohibits departures from GAAP). This weakness may be disappointing, but it nonetheless provides some important benefits. First of all, the possibility of a crisis arising from a failure to comply with the statements is avoided. Second, the process of arriving at a workable and utilitarian metatheoretical-type structure must be acknowledged as a slow, evolutionary process. Trial and error should certainly be expected, and the tentative nature of the statements may make it easier to change components as the need arises. Unfortunately, the possibility also exists that these statements will have only a purely cosmetic effect. However, the appearance of SFAC No. 7, after a 15-year gap, is a welcome sign.

Statement No. 1

SFAC No. 1 is concerned with the objectives of business financial reporting. Its overall purpose is to provide information that is useful for making business and economic decisions (para. 9). The statement is a direct descendant of the Trueblood Report and is generally a boiled-down version of that report, with some necessary value judgments as well as some redundant statements scattered throughout. SFAC No. 1 continues the user orientation of the documents reviewed in Chapter 6.

Although it acknowledges the heterogeneity of external user groups, it states that a common core characteristic of all outside users is their interest in the prediction of the amounts, timing, and uncertainties of future cash flows. Hence, SFAC No. 1 maintains that financial statements must be general purpose in nature rather than geared toward specific needs of a particular user group, although investors, creditors, and their advisers are singled out among external users.[4]

While it is difficult to tell what changes might have occurred, if any, a broader user focus embracing customers, employees, and the general public might have given the Board a broader outlook. The report also takes the position that users of financial statements must be assumed to be knowledgeable about financial information and reporting, an apparent departure from the Trueblood Report's statement assuming "limited ability" of users. (We have already noted the potential qualification of the literal meaning of that phrase in Chapter 6.) As in the Trueblood Report, users are assumed to have limited authority.

The statement also notes the importance of stewardship in terms of assessing how well management has discharged its duties and obligations to owners and other interested groups. The notion of stewardship goes beyond the narrow interpretation of proper custodianship of the firm's resources and moves toward accountability, a preferable term.

Several important value judgments are made throughout the report:

- Information is not costless to provide, so benefits of usage should exceed costs of production.
- Accounting reports are by no means the only source of information about enterprises.
- Accrual accounting is extremely useful in assessing and predicting earning power and cash flows of an enterprise.
- The information provided should be helpful, but users make their own predictions and assessments.

Finally, the document does not specify what statements should be used, much less what their format should be. It does mention, however, that financial reporting should provide information relative to the firm's economic resources, obligations, and owners' equity (para. 41). Also, how firm performance is provided by measurements of earnings and its components (para. 43) as well as how cash is acquired and disbursed (para. 49) are discussed. Hence, SFAC No. 1 is an extremely cautious invocation of the Trueblood Committee objectives and it maintains a high degree of generality.

Statement No. 2

SFAC No. 2 deals with qualitative characteristics of accounting information. The term *qualitative characteristics* was used in APB Statement 4, but the concepts discussed here proceed directly from ASOBAT. Exhibit 7.1, which comes from SFAC No. 2, best illustrates the document.

Decision makers stand at the apex of the diagram, a position indicative of the orientation of the financial accounting function to serve the decision needs of users. With regard to users, SFAC No. 1 previously established that financial statements should be aimed at a common core of similar information needs. Users are also presumed to be knowledgeable about financial statements and information; hence, understandability is recognized in Exhibit 7.1 as a "user-specific quality." However, even if users are assumed to be knowledgeable, information itself can have different degrees of comprehensibility. The quality of understandability is a characteristic influenced by both users and preparers of accounting information. Listed above understandability is the pervasive constraint that benefits of financial information must exceed its costs. The importance of this idea is shown by its place on the diagram. The specific qualitative characteristics of accounting that SFAC No. 2 has centered on come under the general heading of "decision usefulness," which simply continues the emphasis on decision makers and their needs. Before discussing the two principal qualities of relevance and reliability, the pervasive constraint of requiring benefits to be greater than costs needs to be further discussed.

Benefits Greater Than Costs

The pervasive constraint that benefits be greater than costs stems from information economics. Although it is a very necessary component of a conceptual framework, it is perhaps the most difficult part of the conceptual framework to apply in practice. It is virtually impossible to get a solid, quantifiable handle on the various costs and benefits. Moreover, there is an important question in terms of how far the net should be cast over the numerous costs of information that could be considered.

The benefits of accounting information are represented primarily by the utility of the information for the various user groups—centering on investors and creditors—in the decision-making process. Thus, the benefits pertain to how useful the accounting information is relative to predictive and accountability objectives.

The direct costs of information pertain to gathering, preparing, and disseminating information. A good example was provided by SFAS No. 33, *Financial Reporting and Changing Prices,* which required certain additional disclosures in the form of general price-level adjusted information and current value (replacement cost) information. To produce this information, firms generally had to obtain consumer price indexes and appropriate specific price indexes, if direct measurements could not be made. Numerous calculations were required along the lines illustrated in Appendix 1-A. The state of information technology now existing makes the cost of information production relatively low but not necessarily nontrivial. Pension and other postretirement calculations are extremely complex, for example.

There are two indirect costs of information that immediately come to mind. Published information may create a competitive disadvantage. SFAS No. 131 on segmental reporting,

Exhibit 7.1   A Hierarchy of Accounting Qualities

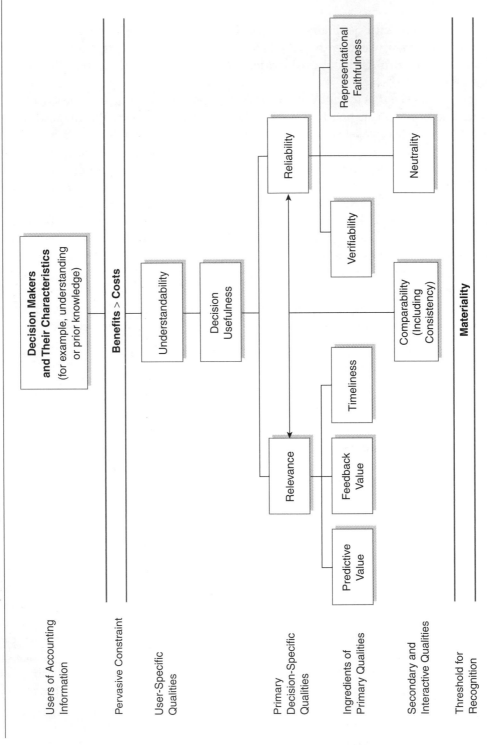

SOURCE: FASB Concepts Statement No. 2, *Qualitative Characteristics of Accounting Information*, page 15. Used with permission by FASB.

for example, requires disclosures pertaining to the profitability of product lines, territories, and major customers for many firms. This information can obviously be quite useful for competitors, although the traffic is likely to flow in both directions on this issue. A more graphic example of this problem pertains to SFAS No. 5 on loss contingencies. If an enterprise is having legal problems with a customer and a loss is both "probable" and the amount of the loss can be "reasonably estimated," then the firm is required to make the appropriate entries. However, booking the loss in this fashion is a virtual admission of guilt that could, in effect, be a self-fulfilling prophecy.

Another indirect cost pertains to the understandability of information that is listed as a separate qualitative characteristic. Most evidence indicates that the additional disclosures of SFAS No. 33 were not well understood by users. Since the information was relatively costly to produce, the pervasive constraint was not met because the benefits were negated owing to the lack of understandability. Another problem that arises here concerns information overload: the ability of individuals and the market to absorb and use information. Notice that the pervasive constraint goes beyond the firm itself when understandability is factored into the pervasive constraint equation.

The benefits and the costs of information, both direct and indirect, involve economic consequences, which were discussed in Chapter 4. Many other economic consequences of accounting information arise that are extremely difficult to evaluate. Some are quite legitimate and desirable. For example, the intention of SFAS No. 106, *Employers' Accounting for Postretirement Benefits Other Than Pensions,* is to book postretirement health care costs of employees as they accrue rather than handling these costs on a cash basis, as was done prior to the standard. We can certainly make a good case that this is useful information for predictive or accountability purposes for all user groups. However, a valuation problem arises: Should we value the expense and liability at currently existing costs or attempt to estimate what the costs will be when they are actually incurred (discounting to present value is appropriate in both cases)? If we use future costs, which will most likely be considerably higher than present costs, several consequences are possible:

1. Management bonuses might be adversely affected if they are based on reported income.

2. The evaluation of management's accountability might be downgraded owing to lower reported income.

3. Dividends to shareholders might be adversely affected due to lower income negatively impacting upon debt-equity ratios.

4. Bondholders could be better protected as a result of (1) and (3).

5. Because of (1), (2), and (3), postretirement benefits might be reduced, which would adversely affect employees.

As can be seen from these relatively simple examples, the economic consequence issues arising from the pervasive constraint can cause huge problems for standard setters. The discussion of the pervasive constraint in paragraphs 133–144 of SFAC No. 2 provides little help in resolving the issue. An attempt has been made to concentrate on the representational faithfulness characteristic rather than economic consequences, but this has been a very qualified success at best. The relationship between representational faithfulness and economic conse-quences in the shaping of accounting standards will be discussed shortly.

Relevance

Relevance is a quality carried forward from ASOBAT and is rather awkwardly expressed in SFAC No. 2 as being "capable of making a difference in a decision by helping users to form predictions about the outcomes of past, present, and future events or to confirm or correct expectations."[5] Relevance has two main aspects—predictive value and feedback value—and one minor one—timeliness.

Predictive Value. Predictive value, as in previous documents, refers to usefulness of inputs for predictions, such as cash flows or earning power, rather than being an actual prediction itself.

Feedback Value. Feedback value concerns "confirming or correcting their [decision makers] earlier expectations."[6] It thus refers to assessing where the firm presently stands and overlaps with how well management has carried out its functions. When viewed broadly, feedback value is closely related to accountability. Information providing this quality must also influence or affect predictive value. Hence, there appears to be a dual meaning to the term *feedback value* that is somewhat confusing. This confusion does not, however, negate the linkage between feedback value and predictive value, which will be expanded upon very shortly.

Timeliness. Timeliness is really a constraint on both of the other aspects of relevance. To be relevant, information must be timely, which means that it must be "available to decision makers before it loses its capacity to influence decisions."[7] There is a conflict between timeli-ness and the other aspects of relevance because information can be more complete and accu-rate if the time constraint is relaxed. Hence, a trade-off is often present between timeliness and other components of relevance.

Possible Inconsistency Between Predictive Value and Feedback Value. Predictive value and feedback value, which are qualitative characteristics, derive from the objectives of providing information useful for predicting cash flows and accountability. In going from the Trueblood Report to SFAC No. 1 and then SFAC No. 2, slightly more detail and specificity were added in each succeeding document. Throughout these three documents, the importance of decision making by outside users is stressed.[8] Obviously, predictive ability is very closely related to decision making. However, SFAC No. 2 notes that stewardship (feedback) is also involved with decision making:

> The (stewardship) measurement confirms expectations or shows how far actual achievements diverged from them. The confirmation or divergence becomes the basis for a decision—which will often be a decision to leave things alone. To say that stewardship reporting is an aspect of account-ing's decision-making role is simply to say that its purpose is to guide actions that may need to be taken in relation to the steward on ... the action that is being monitored.[9]

Hence, feedback value really involves two user objectives: (1) assessing how well manage-ment has done, which is stated as confirming or disconfirming expectations relative to its accountability, and (2) decision making. Predictive value may utilize, to some extent, how well management has performed during the current period.[10] However, conflicts between predictive value and feedback value may arise.

One case in which this has occurred is in defined benefit pension accounting.[11] SFAS No. 87 made a sharp departure from its predecessor, APB Opinion No. 8. Periodic pension cost measurement is determined by multiplying factors based on service of covered employees earned to date (years of service) and annual salary. The latter is the point of contention. Most pension plans base the annual salary on either the employee's final salary just prior to retirement or on an average of annual salaries over the employee's last few years of service prior to retirement.

In APB Opinion No. 8, pension cost was based on currently existing salaries. SFAS No. 87, however, changed the cost factor to an estimate of final salary or final average salary, whichever was in force in the firm's pension contract, and which will be used to determine actual pension payments.[12] Future salaries are, of course, dependent upon future events such as general and specific inflation, employee advancement, and improved quality of employee services (with or without promotion). Future management and not current management will determine the actual decision relative to promotion and amount of future salaries. Present management is thus being asked to determine a present expense by estimating what future salaries will be, a factor that is clearly beyond current management's control. Furthermore, employee advancement and improved quality of employee services are totally executory in nature: Neither party, employees or employer, has performed his part of the contract by either performing the required future services or paying for them.[13]

The FASB justified its choice of the future salary orientation of the pension cost measurement in SFAS No. 87 on the grounds that prediction of future cash flows is the paramount objective of financial reporting.[14] However, from the standpoint of accountability, the future salary orientation simply will not do. How can present management estimate—and be held accountable for—expenses that are based on future costs, which current management (a) will not actually determine and (b) cannot therefrom receive the benefits? In addition to the accountability problem, there are also verifiability problems relative to estimating future salaries as well as a very obvious agency theory problem, particularly if management bonuses are based on current income.

In summary, pension accounting provides an example in which measurements that may be useful for predictions of cash flows are definitely suboptimal relative to accountability purposes. If pension cost measurements were based on currently existing salaries (as they were in APB Opinion No. 8 and SFAS No. 35), the measurement would be useful for both accountability and predictive purposes (although not as useful for prediction of cash flows as the SFAS No. 87 requirements).[15] The example of defined benefit pension accounting is a very good one for illustrating the importance of objectives of financial reporting and the potential conflicts that can be present.[16] However, we believe that most conflicts between predictive value and feedback value can be reasonably, if not optimally, solved.

Reliability

Reliability is composed of three parts: verifiability, representational faithfulness, and neutrality.

Verifiability. Verifiability in SFAC No. 2 refers, as in previous documents, to the degree of consensus among measurers. It is thus concerned with measurement theory. Unlike aspects of relevance, there is a quantifiable element to verifiability. However, it is unquestionably difficult to measure, so SFAC No. 2 stops short of specifying how high the degree of verifiability should be.

Representational Faithfulness. Representational faithfulness, likewise, pertains to measurement theory. It refers to the idea that the measurement itself should correspond with the phenomenon it is attempting to measure. A simple example from baseball might clarify the concept. If one wanted to determine who the "fastest pitcher" is, a radar gun, which provides highly accurate measurements, can calculate the speed of the pitch in miles-per-hour, which would be representationally faithful. An indirect measurement such as average number of strikeouts per inning would not necessarily be representationally faithful because speed alone is not the only component of the strikeout matrix; an effective slow-ball pitcher may have a high strikeout-per-inning ratio.

In accounting, valuation of all fixed assets might be calculated by employing straight-line depreciation for 20 years with no salvage value. There would be an extremely high degree of verifiability. However, if this characteristic is supposed to be indicative of the proportion of historical cost that still has economic utility, the resulting values would, in most cases, not be representative of the attribute of unamortized cost. Individually determined depreciation schedules might represent a better calculation of the attribute of unamortized cost as previously defined. Similarly, if replacement cost were selected as the property to be measured, actual market values, if available, would accomplish representational faithfulness, whereas the amount the firm could sell the asset for would not.

It is clear that there can easily be a conflict between verifiability and representational faithfulness, and the need to make a trade-off between these two characteristics of reliability may well arise. Sterling appears to minimize the possibility of a trade-off between representational faithfulness and verifiability. Relevant phenomena pertaining to a decision must be faithfully represented; an unfaithful representation of a relevant characteristic would not be useful for decision-making purposes.[17] Nevertheless, we are still left with the problem of dealing with relevant characteristics (of assets or liabilities) that cannot be easily measured. Whether criteria can ever be developed to guide implementation of the many potential trade-offs is a very speculative question.

Neutrality. Neutrality refers to the belief that the policy-setting process should be primarily concerned with relevance and reliability rather than the effect a standard or rule might have on a specific user group or the enterprise itself. In other words, neutrality is concerned with financial statements "telling it like it is" rather than the way a particular interest group, such as management or stockholders, might like it to be. Neutrality is the only qualitative characteristic that pertains wholly to the attitude of Board members as opposed to being more directly concerned with specific aspects of the information itself. The purpose of neutrality, as seen by Wyatt and Brown, was a conscious attempt to ward off interference by groups having an important interest in financial statements and the accounting standards underlying them.[18] As we shall soon see, the role of neutrality has generated a great deal of controversy.

Representational Faithfulness Versus Economic Consequences

One of the central issues regarding the conceptual framework is whether representational faithfulness or economic consequences should underlie the promulgation of accounting standards. Representational faithfulness is part of the conceptual framework, whereas economic consequences is not. Several articles have examined this important issue.

Sole Emphasis Upon Representational Faithfulness. Ruland clearly favors exclusive emphasis on representational faithfulness as an obligation of the FASB in drafting standards.[19] He sees representational faithfulness as sufficient justification for accounting standards. If economic consequences were to be the criterion for standard setting, outcomes of accounting policy making would have to be carefully determined but could by no means be certain.[20]

The Complementary Roles of Representational Faithfulness and Economic Consequences. Ingram and Rayburn have taken a dualistic position relative to the roles of representational faithfulness and economic consequences in the standard-setting process.[21] Unfortunately, difficulties are inherent in achieving representational faithfulness. For example, the definition of assets in SFAC No. 6 is not complete enough to enable us to determine a unique amount for the cost of an oil producer's petroleum field holdings. Under the full cost approach, a country or even a continent could be considered a cost center. The components of the definition in SFAC No. 6 are, thus, necessary, but not sufficient, to fully define assets.[22] Even moving to current valuation would not eliminate the problem of levels of aggregation in achieving representational faithfulness (an oil well as opposed to an oil field with many wells or even wider aggregational units, such as countries or continents). Hence, in Ingram and Rayburn's view, faithfulness of representation is often a matter of employing measurement rules (or calculation rules, as Sterling would have it) rather than "mapping reality"—that is, determining a "true" figure from the representational faithfulness standpoint. Because it cannot employ an easily ascertainable means to objective truth, the standard-setting process necessarily entails a consideration of economic consequences: how users, preparers, and other parties are affected by prospective accounting standards. Ingram and Rayburn conclude that representational faithfulness and economic consequences are not either/or alternatives in the standard-setting process; rather, they are complementary to each other.[23]

The Preeminence of the Economic Consequences View. Daley and Tranter's position relative to faithful representations and economic consequences is at the opposite pole from Ruland's.[24] They see economic consequences embodied in the conceptual framework—like the camel gaining access to the tent by slipping its nose under the flap—despite the FASB's attempt to give representational faithfulness primacy in setting accounting standards. The underlying reason for Daley and Tranter's conclusion is that the FASB cannot be neutral in assessing the relevance and reliability of accounting information given the pervasive constraint of the benefits/costs trade-off.

Daley and Tranter view the benefits/costs trade-off as covering a broad gamut of economic consequence issues. For example, they state that:

This process of weighing costs and benefits on differing sectors of our society is not neutral. It cannot be. In the case of marketable equities securities *the decision was clearly that the interests of the insurance industry outweighed the general benefits to financial statement users* [italics added] of moving to flow-through accounting, even though this method has much support in the conceptual framework.[25]

However, Ruland interprets the benefits/costs trade-off as a materiality threshold for assessing the usefulness of an accounting standard: Benefits to users should be greater than the costs of preparation.[26] Moreover, the discussion of the pervasive constraint of benefits/costs in SFAC No. 2 focuses mainly on such issues as the fact that the preparer initially bears the cost of collecting, processing, and disseminating information to users and makes only limited mention of distributional effects on different user groups (for example, the benefit of off-balance-sheet financing for investors as opposed to creditors).[27]

In one sense, Daley and Tranter are certainly correct. The benefits/costs trade-off unquestionably involves economic consequences involving the costs of preparing information relative to the benefits to users. Clearly, this aspect of standard setting by its very nature is an inherent part of the process and should thus be viewed as a special type of economic consequence. In other words, standard setters directly affect the cost of information preparation as a result of the standards that they generate. Beyond this point, however, the role neutrality plays is appropriate because it focuses concern on relevance and reliability (given the benefits/costs constraint, with costs being restricted to cost of preparation) rather than on other types of economic consequences. While the role assigned to neutrality is conceptually appropriate, attaining representational faithfulness has proved to be an extremely difficult task for the FASB.

Daley and Tranter do not believe that neutrality can be a component of reliability because the pervasive constraint (benefits of standards exceeding their cost) above reliability necessarily entails economic consequences.[28] We believe that rather than being inconsistent, the problem is one of maintaining a difficult balancing act. The FASB's primary objective is providing useful information for external users subject to the benefits/costs constraint. Information can both be useful for decision making and also involve economic consequences. Neutrality means being concerned primarily with decision usefulness rather than distributive effects.

In reality, the FASB has been concerned with economic consequences beyond the benefits/costs constraint, having commissioned several economic consequences studies. Furthermore, the FASB has not been immune to influence from the political process resulting from economic consequences.[29] From a theoretical perspective, taking cognizance of economic consequences by means of research studies can be valuable provided it is understood that relevance and reliability are the primary characteristics with which standard setters should be concerned.[30]

Conservatism

Conservatism is not shown in Exhibit 7.1, but, curiously enough, it is discussed in SFAC No. 2, where it is called a *convention*. SFAC No. 2 is not in favor of deliberate understatements or overstatements of assets or income. Deliberate understatement conflicts with representational faithfulness, neutrality, and both of the main aspects of relevance. Conservatism is associated with the need for "prudent reporting" by which readers are to be informed where uncertainties and risks lie. Thus, conservatism really appears to pertain to disclosure, an extremely important concept that is not discussed in SFAC No. 2. Conservatism is extensively discussed in Chapter 5.

Comparability and Consistency

These qualities are defined essentially the same way that they were defined in Chapter 5. We view these characteristics as being output oriented. Hence, comparability and consistency should be the result of a viable conceptual framework rather than part of the theoretical structure itself. More will be said about comparability in Chapter 9.

Materiality

Materiality is also discussed in much the same fashion as in Chapter 5. The question that must be raised relative to materiality is whether an item is large enough to influence users' decisions. Materiality is recognized as being a quantitative characteristic, and some progress is being made in the area as was discussed in Chapter 5. Materiality is also a relative concept rather than an absolute one, an aspect that most research in this area has stressed.

Statement No. 3

SFAC No. 3 defines 10 elements of financial statements. It is obviously a resolution of the definitions presented in the discussion memorandum for the conceptual framework project. Since these definitions were amended in SFAC No. 6, they will be presented in the discussion of that document.

Several observations are worth making, particularly about what SFAC No. 3 does not include. First of all, it barely mentions the three views of financial accounting (revenue-expense, asset-liability, and nonarticulated) as put forth in the discussion memorandum. It also does not specify the type of capital maintenance concept to employ. Likewise, it does not address matters of recognition (realization) and measurement as well as "display" in financial statements. Thus, the definitions in the statement seem to be a "first screen" in determining the content of financial statements. It is clear that much work remained to be done in prescribing the properties of these various elements, not to mention their arrangement in financial statements.

SFAC No. 3 also reveals a reversal of terminology.[31] Throughout the discussion memorandum and SFAC No. 1, the word *earnings* had supplanted the more commonly used *income*. However, in SFAC No. 2, *earnings* had disappeared and *income* was used in paragraphs 90 and 94. Finally, SFAC No. 3 made the reversal official by designating *income* as the term to indicate the comprehensive or total change in net assets occurring during the period as a result of operations. *Earnings* was reserved as a possible component of income, to be specified at a later date (see the discussion of SFAC No. 5).

Statement No. 4

SFAC No. 4 is concerned with objectives of nonbusiness financial reporting. Nonbusiness organizations are characterized by

1. receipts of significant amounts of resources from providers who do not expect to receive either repayment or economic benefits proportionate to resources provided;

2. operating purposes that are primarily other than to provide goods or services at a profit . . . ;

3. absence of defined ownership interests that can be sold, transferred, or redeemed, or that convey entitlement to a share of residual distribution of resources in the event of liquidation of the organization.[32]

SFAC No. 4 also notes that nonbusiness organizations do not have a single indicator of the entity's performance comparable to income measurement in the profit sector.[33] Since the emphasis in this text is on the profit sector, SFAC No. 4 is outside the scope of our interest.

Statement No. 5

The long-awaited SFAC No. 5 finally appeared in December 1984, exactly four years after SFAC No. 4. Since this statement was to deal with the difficult issues of recognition and measurement, it was clear that it would be the linchpin for the success or failure of the entire project. The statement let the cat out of the bag immediately in paragraph 2, which made it quite clear that there would be no extensive attempt to come to grips with the issues of recognition and measurement:

> The recognition criteria and guidance in this Statement are generally consistent with current practice and do not imply radical change. Nor do they foreclose the possibility of future change in practice. The Board intends future change to occur in the gradual, evolutionary way that has characterized past change.[34]

The statement's reliance on the evolutionary process made Solomons angry; he termed it a "cop-out."[35] He was also disappointed with the Board's failure to deal with executory contracts in terms of either their possible inclusion within the body of the statement, their disclosure in footnotes, or getting no mention at all.[36]

Scope of the Statement

SFAC No. 5 makes clear that the concepts discussed apply strictly to financial statements and not other means of disclosure. Indeed, it is almost vehement on the subject:

> Disclosure by other means is *not* [italics added] recognition. Disclosure of information about the items in financial statements and their measures that may be provided by notes or parenthetically on the face of financial statements, by supplementary information, or by other means of financial reporting is not a substitute for recognition in financial statements for items that meet recognition criteria.[37]

Although it doesn't say so explicitly, SFAC No. 5 appears to deny one of the main tenets of the efficient-markets hypothesis (Chapter 8)—that disclosure outside of the body of the financial statements is as effective as disclosure within the statements themselves. However, numerous criticisms of the efficient-markets hypothesis have arisen, which may well justify the FASB's opinion. The various formats for presenting financial information are well illustrated in SFAC No. 5 (Exhibit 7.2).

Exhibit 7.2 Delineation of Formats for Presenting Financial Information

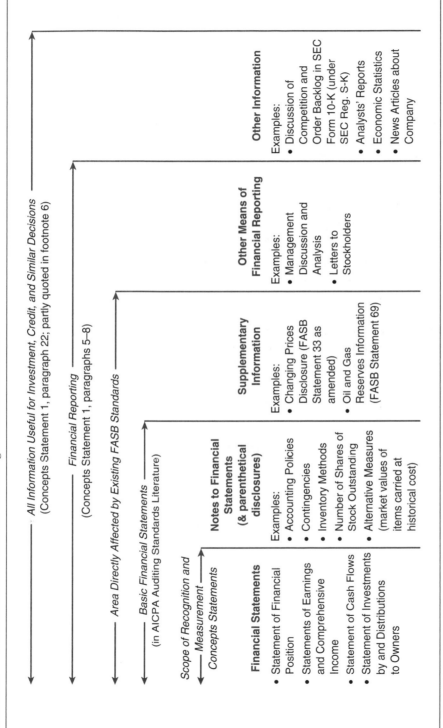

SOURCE: FASB Concepts Statement No. 5, *Recognition and Measurement in Financial Statements of Business Enterprises*, pages 5, 13, and 16. Used with permission of FASB.

Earnings and Comprehensive Income

One of the principal concerns of SFAC No. 5 was the format and presentation of changes in owners' equity that do not arise from transactions with owners. This has been referred to as the matter of "display." Earnings would replace net income and would differ from the latter by excluding the cumulative effect on prior years of a change in accounting principle, such as a switch from straight-line depreciation to sum-of-the-years'-digits, for example. Earnings would thus be a better indicator of current operating performance than net income. A hypothetical comparison between the two is shown in Exhibit 7.3.

Accompanying the statement of earnings would be a statement of comprehensive income. The latter is now conceived as a statement that covers all changes in owners' equity during the period except for transactions with owners. The previously mentioned cumulative effect of a change in accounting principle would appear here. Also appearing here would be such items as the income effect of losses or gains (to the extent recognized) of marketable securities that are not classified as current assets as well as foreign currency translation adjustments. Finally, the only two items that are now classified as prior period adjustments (Chapter 12) would enter into a comprehensive income statement. A quick comparison of earnings and comprehensive income is shown in Exhibit 7.4 (see p. 200).

The recasting of performance into earnings and comprehensive income in SFAC No. 5 arose as a result of the inability to come to grips with the measurement problem. Using earnings was, more or less, an attempt to maintain the status quo of income, and the possibility was open in the future to include unrealized holding gains in comprehensive income.[38] More will be said about comprehensive income in Chapter 12.

Recognition Criteria

Recognition criteria refers to when an asset, liability, expense, revenue, gain, or loss should be recorded in the accounts. The fundamental recognition criteria from earlier parts of the conceptual framework are

- Definitions. The item meets the definition of an element of financial statements.
- Measurability. It has a relevant attribute measurable with sufficient reliability.
- Relevance. The information about it is capable of making a difference in user decisions.
- Reliability. The information is representationally faithful, verifiable, and neutral.

In applying recognition criteria to revenue and gain situations, recognition requires that the asset to be received has been realized or is realizable and that the revenue should be earned, as discussed in Chapter 5. Likewise, recognition criteria for expenses and losses arise as the asset is used up or when no further benefits are expected (para. 85). Recognition methods for expenses include matching with revenues, write-off during the period when cash is expended or liabilities incurred for very short-lived expense items, or other systematic and rational procedures (para. 86).

Although resorting to previous statements logically closed the circle, SFAC No. 5 needed to do much more work on recognition criteria than its two-page coverage. To take one

Exhibit 7.3   Earnings Versus Net Income

	Present Net Income		Proposed Earnings	
Revenues		$100		$100
Expenses		−80		−80
Gain from unusual source		3		3
Income from continuing operations		23		23
Loss on discontinued operations				
Income from operating discontinued segment	10		10	
Loss on disposal of discontinued segment	−12	−2	−12	−2
Income before extraordinary items and effect of a change in accounting principle		21		21
Extraordinary loss	−6			−6
Cumulative effect on prior years of a change in accounting principle	−2	−8		
Present earnings or proposed net income		13		15

SOURCE: SFAC No. 5, p. 13.

Exhibit 7.4   Earnings and Comprehensive Income

+	Revenues	$100		+	Earnings	$15
–	Expenses	80		–	Cumulative accounting adjustments	2
+	Gains	3		+	Other nonowner changes in equity	1
–	Losses	8				
=	Earnings	$ 15		=	Comprehensive income	$14

SOURCE: SFAC No. 5, p. 16.

example, the definitions of elements from SFAC No. 3 and SFAC No. 6 are clearly superior to previous definitions. They are necessary in and of themselves, but not sufficient. Solomons notes that the definition of a liability is difficult to apply to pensions:

> Quite apart from the measurement problems resulting from uncertainties, what is an employer's present obligation to the participants in a pension plan? Is it the (discounted) amount of all future payments to all eligible employees, past and present? Or is it the amount that would be payable if the plan is discontinued at the balance sheet date? Or is it the amount of benefits vested at the balance sheet date? Or is it only the amounts currently due and payable to those who have already retired at the balance sheet date?[39]

Similar examples of the incompleteness of definitions are the liability definition as applied to deferred taxes and the asset definition regarding the level of aggregation (full costing or successful efforts) in accounting for oil and gas exploration costs. Suffice it to say that much greater detail was necessary to successfully implement recognition criteria. Tying recognition criteria to SFAC Nos. 2 and 3 barely began the job.

Measurement Attributes

The five measurement attributes that had been extensively discussed in the discussion memorandum of 1976 were dusted off and brought forward in SFAC No. 5:

1. Historical cost

2. Current cost (replacement cost)

3. Current market value (exit value)

4. Net realizable value (selling cost less any costs to complete or dispose)

5. Present (discounted) value of future cash flows

However, as noted previously, the statement backed away from considering possible criteria for change, which suggests a continued use of present measurement attributes and reliance on an evolutionary approach.

SFAC No. 5 must be considered a distinct letdown, if not an outright failure. Sterling has made an extremely trenchant point relative to it: By dealing with recognition before measurement, the FASB put the cart before the horse. The issue of when to recognize an element cannot be discussed until we know the measurement characteristics that are to be recognized.[40] This is the shortcoming of SFAC No. 5.

In addition, Miller's analysis of the conceptual framework project and, in particular, SFAC No. 5 is also of great interest.[41] Miller was a faculty fellow at the FASB in 1982–1983 where he was involved with the conceptual framework project. He believes that the first three SFACs would have led to "radical changes" in accounting practice and, therefore, SFAC No. 5 acted as a "counterreformation" to real progress. The linchpin of what Miller calls the "reformation" is the user orientation of SFAC No. 1 as opposed to the CAP's and APB's emphasis on the needs of auditors. In addition, the move toward the asset–liability viewpoint in the first three documents, as reflected in the definition of assets and liabilities, was a shift toward current valuation and away from matching. The counterreformation, led by the preparer constituency (in particular, members of Financial Executives International) and supported by three members of the FASB, appeared when SFAC No. 5 was being drafted.[42] SFAC No. 5, particularly paragraph 2's statements to the effect that change should occur in a gradual and evolutionary manner, effectively stymied reform, at least for the time being.

Statement No. 6

SFAC No. 6 is a replacement (not a revision) of SFAC No. 3. However, its definitions are virtually identical to those in SFAC No. 3 except that they are extended to nonbusiness organizations. Likewise, the qualitative characteristics of accounting information of SFAC No. 2 are extended to nonbusiness organizations. Clearly, then, SFAC No. 6 added nothing further to the conceptual framework from the perspective of business enterprises.

Perhaps, however, there was a hidden agenda behind the apparent conclusion of the conceptual framework with a virtual repetition of an earlier segment of the framework. Terminating with SFAC No. 5 would have meant that the project would end on a low—if not a sour—note. Possibly for this reason the project was concluded by reprising SFAC No. 3 (with the previously mentioned extensions to nonbusiness organizations).[43] In any event, the definitions of the 10 elements of financial statements presented in SFAC No. 6 (with very slight modification from SFAC No. 3) are as follows:

1. Assets are probable future economic benefits obtained or controlled by a particular entity as a result of past transactions or events.

2. Liabilities are probable future sacrifices of economic benefits arising from present obligations of a particular entity to transfer assets or provide services to other entities in the future as a result of past transactions or events.

3. Equity or net assets is the residual interest in the assets of an entity that remains after deducting its liabilities. In a business enterprise, the equity is the ownership interest. In a not-for-profit organization, which has no ownership interest in the same sense as a business enterprise, net assets is divided into three classes based on the presence or absence of donor-imposed restrictions—permanently restricted, temporarily restricted, and unrestricted net assets.

4. Investments by owners are increases in equity of a particular business enterprise resulting from transfers to it from other entities of something valuable to obtain or increase ownership interests

(or equity) in it. Owners most commonly receive assets as investments, but that which is received may also include services or satisfaction or conversion of liabilities of the enterprise.

5. Distributions to owners are decreases in equity of a particular business enterprise resulting from transferring assets, rendering services, or incurring liabilities by the enterprise to owners. Distributions to owners decrease ownership interest (or equity) in an enterprise.

6. Comprehensive income is the change in equity of a business enterprise during a period from transactions and other events and circumstances from nonowner sources. It includes all changes in equity during a period except those resulting from investments by owners and distributions to owners.

7. Revenues are inflows or other enhancements of assets of an entity or settlements of its liabilities (or a combination of both) from delivering or producing goods, rendering services, or other activities that constitute the entity's ongoing major or central operations.

8. Expenses are outflows or other depletions of assets or incurrences of liabilities (or a combination of both) from delivering or producing goods, rendering services, or carrying out other activities that constitute the entity's ongoing major or central operations.

9. Gains are increases in equity (net assets) from peripheral or incidental transactions of an entity and from all other transactions and other events and circumstances affecting the entity except those that result from revenues or investments by owners.

10. Losses are decreases in equity (net assets) from peripheral or incidental transactions of an entity and from all other transactions and other events and circumstances affecting the entity except those that result from expenses or distributions to owners.[44]

SOURCE: FASB Concepts Statement No. 6, *Elements of Financial Statements*, pages ix and x. Used with permission of FASB.

These definitions are a marked improvement over their immediate predecessor, the circular and redundant definitions of APB Statement 4.[45] Dopuch and Sunder have criticized these definitions on the grounds that the various criteria for each of the categories are necessary but not sufficient to determine whether a general type of accounting event falls into a particular definitional category.[46] For example, deferred tax credits could be interpreted as liabilities from the individual asset perspective because repayment of benefits generally does occur; but when deferred tax credits are viewed from the aggregate perspective, repayment is far less likely. However, Brown, Collins, and Thornton point out that it would be impossible to completely specify all characteristics of elements such as assets and liabilities.[47] They also point out that when enumerating definitions or prescribing standards, it is impossible to be absolutely complete or sufficient. The more complete and sufficient definitions and standards are, the more lengthy and cumbersome they would become. However, the lack of completeness must be supplemented by the professional judgment capabilities of the accountant and auditor.[48]

Samuelson has criticized the conceptual framework definition of assets.[49] He believes that the FASB definition, which emphasizes future economic benefits (future cash inflows), is grounded in future revenues and costs. Consequently, he believes that the matching concept— matching costs against revenues—is the primary focus of this definition. Matching is a historical cost notion. Therefore, we do not agree with Samuelson's interpretation of the FASB's asset definition being matching oriented.

Samuelson believes that the asset definition should concentrate on property rights that are concerned with wealth, which provides a solid balance sheet orientation. One of the key points about the property rights approach lies in exchangeability of the asset. Samuelson's viewpoint would result in certain deferred charges being expensed immediately even though their incurrence may bring about future economic benefits. Some costs that fall into this category include training costs, relocation costs, plant rearrangement costs, and prior service costs when pension plans are either adopted or amended.[50]

Another contentious point of these definitions concerns how broadly the term "past transactions" can be interpreted under the asset and liability definitions. As previously mentioned in the discussion of SFAC No. 2, in pension accounting (SFAS No. 87) and other postretirement benefits (SFAS No. 106) future costs have been combined with service to date in determining these costs. The problem involves a conflict among objectives, but the meaning and interpretation of "past transactions" still requires resolution. In summary, these definitions are an improvement over their predecessors, but further refinement may yet take place.

Finally, SFAC No. 6 (paras. 150–151 and 169) mentions a small and limited number of transactions involving owners' equity that are nonreciprocal in nature. These include receipts of cash by the firm with (presumably) no strings attached or with no presumed necessity to transfer assets in the future. Nonreciprocity is extremely rare and should not be used as a basis for transaction avoidance.

Statement No. 7

Two important points should be immediately made about SFAC No. 7. First, in light of the importance of the Trueblood Committee Report with its emphasis on the importance of cash flows, it is surprising that it took this long (15 years after SFAC No. 6) for this statement to appear, although work had begun on the project in 1988. Second, this statement concerns specific measurement issues rather than broader conceptual-type issues, hence it might be viewed as a subset of SFAC No. 5. SFAC No. 7 applies to situations in which present market-determined amounts such as cash received or paid and current cost or market value are not available at the point of recognition. Instead estimated future cash flows must be used for asset or liability measurement.

In SFAC No. 7, the Board recognized that present valuation methods were inconsistently applied in various standards. To take two examples, in APB Opinion No. 16 on business combinations, assets that are acquired by incurring liabilities are to be booked at present value without specifying how to determine the rate, whereas in the case of leases, the lessee uses its own incremental borrowing rate unless the lessor's implicit interest rate can be determined and it is lower than the lessee's incremental rate. SFAC No. 7 applies only to initial recognition and not subsequent revaluations, which it terms "fresh-start measurements."[51] The SFAC is divided into two parts: asset measurement and liability measurement.

Present Value Asset Measurement

The most important point about asset measurement is that present value measurements are intended to simulate fair value rather than the particular present value of the asset to the firm itself. For example, the asset might have a higher value to the firm because it holds special manufacturing processes or other preferences that increase the value of the asset to the particular enterprise.[52] Thus any value accruing to the particular firm because the simulated fair value is less than the present value of the asset to the firm is to be realized in the form of cost savings during usage rather than in higher initial valuation. Hence if the firm did not know the specific market value of a particular asset, it would strive for that discount rate, which would lead as closely as possible to estimated fair value. Discount rates should also include risk and uncertainty, which would reflect the assessment by the market of the asset's value.[53] It is important to note that the FASB's preference for fair value rather than specific firm valuation emphasizes the severability of the asset.

One specific measurement technique should be mentioned. If a particular asset has several possible cash flows within specific years, the expected cash flows should be determined (the probability weighted average of the possible individual cash flows) rather than using the single most likely cash flow (the mode).

Present Value Liability Measurement

The key point about liability measurement is that the discount rate must be tied to the credit standing of the firm. The carrying value of the original liability is tied to the firm's credit standing. Notice that this means that if the firm's credit standing deteriorates, the valuation of the liability decreases (because a poorer credit standing means that the applicable discount rate would rise). Hence any firm acquiring the liability from the original creditor would pay less to acquire the liability owing to the debtor's worsening credit standing.

Asset and liability measurements under SFAC No. 7 are not inconsistent. An asset can be viewed and therefore valued separately from the firm owning it, but a liability cannot be separately viewed. In other words, a liability must ultimately be resolved by the debtor. An asset's value to others is separate from its current owner.

Subsequent Revaluations

Although SFAC No. 7 does not address "fresh-start" measurements occurring after initial acquisition, it does state preferences. If estimated cash flows of an asset or liability change, the original discount rate would be applied to the revised cash flows.[54] The FASB refers to this method as the "catch-up approach."

The Conceptual Framework as a Codificational Document

Now that we have outlined the conceptual framework, it will be instructive to consider what kind of document it is. The postulates and principles approach of ARSs 1 and 3 has been called an example of foundational standard setting because it attempts to provide a logical foundation for deductively deriving "correct," or at least appropriate, accounting standards.[55]

On the other hand, the conceptual framework has been likened to a constitution in the sense that alternatives to it could be viewed as either within the law or outside of it.[56] The constitutional approach clearly does not provide as strong a logical structure as does the foundational approach. The conceptual framework, however, is not a legally binding instrument, nor does it contain arbitrary elements as a constitution may (such as the number of senators from each state). In Solomons's view, a conceptual framework does not have room for arbitrariness, and so his enthusiasm for the constitutional metaphor diminished.

We have already seen in Chapter 4 that standard setting by an organization such as the FASB has been justified on codificational grounds. Codification is a justification of the standard-setting process itself rather than of the individual standards that result from that process. The codificational approach is seen as rational and as one requiring presumably good reasons for the choice of accounting standards, although these may not necessarily be the "best" possible standards. Also, it should be understood that codification refers to the process and not to the individual members (of the FASB) who are responsible for carrying out that process. It should also be remembered that choosing standards by a rational process implies that standards can be changed and improved.

Within the codificational view of standard setting, a conceptual framework makes good sense because it can support and promote the rational nature of that process. Gaa sees the conceptual framework as embodying aspects of both a constitution and a theory.[57] The constitutional view of Gaa differs from Solomons's more legalistic and empowering view. For Gaa, the distributional question concerning who financial information is intended to benefit is involved. As we have seen, SFAC No. 1 resolved the user-heterogeneity problem through the objective of providing information that is useful to present and potential investors and creditors and other external users who have a reasonable understanding of business and economic activities.

The conceptual framework also, in Gaa's view, has theoretical aspects because it does provide criteria for choice when evaluating accounting alternatives. These include factors such as relevance, reliability, and the benefits/costs constraint discussed in SFAC No. 2, as well as the definitions provided in SFAC No. 6. These criteria for choice can help or guide the FASB, but they cannot guarantee the best outcome despite the constitutional guideline for information that is useful for actual and prospective investors, creditors, and other outside users. According to the codificational view, not only can standards be improved upon, but the conceptual framework itself is also subject to correction and refinement.

The Jurisprudential View

Somewhat similar to the codificational view is the jurisprudential view of the FASB advocated by Archer.[58] The jurisprudential view is concerned with the process of legitimization and acceptance of the conceptual framework as opposed to the actual "theory" embodied in the document. Archer raises some very trenchant points relative to how the conceptual framework was developed. He questions whether a solid theoretical document can be developed on the one hand while the other hand resorts to an arrangement utilizing consensus among the various affected groups (preparers, users, and auditors) by means of a system of discussion memoranda and exposure drafts.[59] Archer also criticizes the FASB from the standpoint of confusing means and ends in the development of the conceptual framework with a strong desire to maintain the status quo.[60] Certainly SFAC No. 5's adherence to historical costing can be seen as an attempt to preserve the old order. Archer would attempt, as part of his jurisprudential approach, the use of benefits/costs analysis for assessing the social desirability of the various alternatives.[61] This approach, of course, would be fraught with its own difficulties.

Archer, as opposed to Dopuch and Sunder, is not unalterably opposed to a conceptual framework. Dopuch and Sunder as well as Hines basically see a conceptual framework as a self-justifying type of document that serves as a source for deflecting the attacks of interested parties.[62] Archer, in fact, favors the use of a conceptual framework but hoped that it would be more systematic and philosophic (jurisprudential) in its drafting. Archer also appears to subscribe to the position of Ingram and Rayburn, discussed previously, that a conceptual framework cannot ignore the consideration of taking into account economic consequences.[63]

Power, another constructive critic of the conceptual framework, sees the document as one capable of providing help to standard setters but not providing final and conclusive answers (as would also be true of Archer): "A conceptual framework is not an ultimate foundation in any classical sense but a point of reference in the network of accounting standards and practices that serves to 'organize' thinking about them."[64]

Power would use a combination of essentially deductive and inductive reasoning to determine accounting standards with a conceptual framework playing a partial—but not total—role in the determination of accounting standards.[65] The deductive aspect of Power's approach would be a conceptual framework, but it would be used in conjunction with "accepted accounting practice," which would be the inductive aspect of the standard-setting process.

Both Archer and Power provide useful critiques for the construction of a conceptual framework. However, we have a conceptual framework, and the issue is how it can be improved so that it will perform a more useful role in the standard-setting process. Not surprisingly, perhaps, an evolutionary—but hopefully not glacial—approach is certainly possible. The evolutionary approach is certainly not inconsistent with both Archer and Power, and it embodies the codificational approach discussed by Gaa. In particular, the evolutionary approach to the conceptual framework could possess both deductive and inductive aspects similar to Power's suggestions. For example, it would be possible to update SFAC No. 5 in terms of more vigorously advocating current costs where verifiability is not a major problem, such as with "mark-to-market," which is already occurring with many debt and equity securities as discussed in SFAS No. 115 (see Chapter 11). This would be an example of the deductive approach going forward from the conceptual framework to individual accounting standards.

The inductive approach would work backward from standards to the conceptual framework. A possible example would be the case of pensions in SFAS No. 87 discussed earlier in the chapter. That analysis suggested a strong emphasis on prediction of future cash flows, which would conflict with the accountability objective. Therefore, concentrating on accountability where conflicts arise might give accounting standards more flexibility since accountability-oriented numbers are useful for decision making. Certainly, the pension analysis helps us to understand the conflict between the predictive and accountability objectives. At any rate, we believe that the FASB and International Accounting Standards Board (IASB) convergence project involving conceptual frameworks might take into account these considerations (the IASB conceptual framework will be discussed in Chapter 10).

Empirical Research on the Conceptual Framework

There has been a limited amount of empirical work on the conceptual framework. In an experiment involving 28 former members of the FASB and APB who attempted to use the qualitative characteristics of SFAC No. 2, only verifiability and costs (as in benefits outweighing costs) were found to be operational in terms of having some degree of common meaning to the standard setters.[66] Although these results are not encouraging, the researchers noted that the understanding of the concepts prior to the publication of SFAC No. 2 could have been considerably lower. In addition, subjects answered questions independently and not in the "give-and-take" atmosphere of the actual standard-setting process.

Hudack and McAllister did a content analysis examination of the first 117 SFASs.[67] They found that the Board emphasized, more or less evenly, both relevance and reliability from SFAC No. 2. However, in standards emphasizing disclosure (footnotes or separate schedules) rather than recognition (numbers appearing in the body of the statements), a stronger emphasis was placed on relevance rather than reliability.

Another study was concerned with the importance of the qualitative characteristics of SFAC No. 2 to three groups: preparers, auditors, and users.[68] The sample selected was 600 CPAs in Pennsylvania who were identified based on the majority of their work experience as preparers, auditors, or users (55% of respondents were identified as auditors with the remainder splitting evenly between the other two categories). Users and preparers gave more weight to relevance than did auditors. Results were not significantly different among the three groups within the reliability category, although auditors gave more importance to neutrality than did the other two groups. Reliability was more important for auditors than was relevance. Materiality, as a pervasive constraint, ranked approximately even with relevance and reliability within each of the three groups.

Assessing the Conceptual Framework

Many opinions have been expressed about the conceptual framework, with most being negative.[69] Certainly there are some fine things in the SFACs, including the qualitative characteristics (SFAC No. 2), the definitions of the elements (SFAC No. 6), and the refining of present value measurements (SFAC No. 7). It is somewhat difficult to take this project seriously, despite all the time, money, and effort spent on it when in the preface to each of the standards the Board declares that that SFACs do not "(a) require a change in existing generally accepted accounting principles; (b) amend, modify, or interpret statements of Financial Accounting Standards . . . or

(c) justify either changing existing generally accepted accounting and reporting practices . . ." Certainly one might hope that deferred tax assets and liabilities (SFAS No. 109) will be discounted, but this disclaimer tells us not to hold our breath. On the other hand, one might hope that the FASB is merely cutting itself some slack and that good things will eventually happen.

However, one good sign relative to the possible use of the conceptual framework is arising in the area of leases (see Chapter 17). Another positive note is that beginning with SFAS No. 141, summaries of each major standard have a short section entitled, "How the Conclusion in the Statement Relates to the Conceptual Framework."

Opinion is virtually unanimous that SFAC No. 5 on recognition and measurement is the low point of the conceptual framework. However, in areas such as marketable securities (SFAS No. 115), derivatives (SFAS No. 133), and impaired assets (SFAS No. 121), the FASB has instituted some aspects of fair (current) value. A huge test will be how well SFAS No. 157 on fair value measurement will be implemented and accepted.

Summary

The seven SFACs that comprise the conceptual framework were completed between 1978 and 2000. The document is an evolutionary one because the objectives were rooted in the Trueblood Report and the qualitative characteristics that stemmed from ASOBAT via APB Statement 4. The definitions of SFAC No. 6, while not perfect, are a distinct improvement over the circular and illogical definitions of APB Statement 4. The Achilles' heel of the document is SFAC No. 5, which then reaffirmed historical cost as the basic measurement system.

Perhaps the key document in the series is SFAC No. 2. The principal qualitative characteristics are relevance and reliability. Numerous trade-offs exist both within the two components (such as predictive value versus feedback value and representational faithfulness versus verifiability) as well as between relevance and reliability. However, an important theoretical issue that is still being debated today is whether representational faithfulness can be attained (subject to the other qualitative characteristics) or whether economic consequences of standards should be the dominant consideration. This also involves whether the FASB itself can retain its neutrality, particularly in light of the pervasive constraint that benefits of standards should exceed their costs. The task of maintaining neutrality should be easier given that the FASB is now being financed by the Securities and Exchange Commission (SEC) rather than by corporate preparers, as discussed in Chapter 3.

The conceptual framework is far from a perfect document, as many of its critics have certainly noted. Drafting a document that all parties resoundingly approve of has about as much possibility of occurring as the likelihood of attaining a just and lasting peace in the Middle East. Fortunately, that is not the issue. When viewed from the evolutionary standpoint, the document is definitely capable of being improved. This evolutionary improvement is consistent with the codificational viewpoint of the conceptual framework. Despite all of the criticism of the conceptual framework, it still has a very important role to play in helping financial accounting standards bring about more consistency and comparability in financial reporting.

QUESTIONS

1. Of what importance in a conceptual framework or metatheory are definitions of such basic terms as assets, liabilities, revenues, and expenses?

2. What is the relationship between the economic consequences of accounting standards and the quality of neutrality presented in SFAC No. 2?

3. Why must objectives be at the topmost level of a conceptual framework of accounting?

4. How does the freedom from bias mentioned in ASOBAT compare to the quality of neutrality mentioned in SFAC No. 2?

5. How does earnings as discussed in SFAC No. 5 differ from net income?

6. What is comprehensive income?

7. Is neutrality consistent with the external user primary orientation of SFAC No. 1 and the pervasive constraint (benefits outweighing costs) of SFAC No. 2?

8. SFAC No. 6 is largely a repetition of SFAC No. 3. Discuss two possible reasons why this repetition occurred.

9. Very carefully explain why conflicts can exist between prediction of cash flows and accountability. Can these conflicts be resolved?

10. How does feedback value relate to predictive ability and accountability?

11. Is there a similarity between the codificational approach (Gaa) to standard setting and the jurisprudential approach?

12. Verifiability is part of reliability in SFAC No. 2. How does verifiability differ from the older concept of objectivity, and which do you think is more restrictive?

13. Conservatism is discussed in paragraphs 91–97 of SFAC No. 2. Why is its role in SFAC No. 2 rather ambiguous?

14. A study (discussed in the chapter) found a heavier emphasis placed on relevance rather than reliability in disclosure standards by the FASB. Why do you think this is the case?

15. Samuelson would use a property rights definition of assets (discussed in the chapter). Do you think that SFAS No. 2 requiring immediate expensing of research and development costs is an example of Samuelson's property rights approach? Discuss.

16. Would changing the asset definition in the conceptual framework to one concerned with property rights have any other ramifications? Discuss.

17. Is capital maintenance oriented toward proprietary theory or entity theory?

18. Do you see any inconsistency in SFAC No. 1, which sees financial statements as general purpose but geared primarily toward investors and creditors?

19. Do you see any inconsistency between the present value of assets and liabilities in SFAC No. 7 since the latter is based on a firm-specific discount rate and the former does not use a firm-specific rate? Discuss.

CASES, PROBLEMS, AND WRITING ASSIGNMENTS

1. Discuss as many of the potential trade-offs among the qualities mentioned in SFAC No. 2 as you can and give either a general or a concrete example of each one.

2. Analyze three accounting standards promulgated by the FASB and show how economic consequences (rather than representational faithfulness) influenced the shaping of the standard (your professor may suggest particular standards for this case).

3. One of the principal problems of SFAC No. 2 is whether representational faithfulness should predominate over economic consequences or the reverse relative to drafting accounting standards. State the case as carefully as you can for each of the two possibilities.

4. Part 1. Tucker Company has an asset in the form of a cash flow that it expects to collect in three years. However, the amount of the cash flow is not certain. These are the probabilities underlying the cash flow.

Amount	Probability
$3,000	.30
4,000	.30
5,200	.40

The discount rate is 10%.

Required:

a. How should the asset be valued according to SFAC No. 7?
b. What other valuation is possible?
c. Which valuation do you prefer?

Part 2. Donahoe Company has a liability of $10,000, which is due in three years. The discount rate applicable to the liability is 10%. Assume that the firm's credit standing is adversely affected by an untoward economic event. As a result, the discount rate applicable to the liability goes up to 12%.

Required:

   a. How does the value of the liability change?

   b. If the firm's financial condition worsens, does it make sense for the value of the liabilities to decline? Explain.

5. In examining recognition and measurement, Sterling believes that measurement should precede recognition whereas Archer believes that it is "logical" for recognition to precede measurement. What is your position?

CRITICAL THINKING AND ANALYSIS

1. Are the benefits of a conceptual framework greater than the costs?

Notes

1. *FASB (1976a).*
2. *FASB (1976b, p. 2).*
3. *See FASB (1976a) and FASB (1976c).*
4. *FASB (1978, para. 30).*
5. *FASB (1980a, para. 47).*
6. *Ibid. (para. 51).*
7. *Ibid. (para. 56).*
8. *Ibid. (para. 30, for example).*
9. *Ibid. (para. 29).*
10. *FASB (1980a, para. 51) states that most information is useful for both predictive and accountability objectives.*
11. *See Wolk and Vaughan (1993) for further detail relative to the split between predictive and accountability objectives in pension accounting.*
12. *For a simple example of basing pension costs on current or future salaries, see Appendix 16-A in this text.*
13. *The role of future events in accounting is now being examined. See Beaver (1991) for a discussion of some of the problems. An important question is whether the future event orientation of SFAS No. 87 is consistent with the "past transactions or events" part of the liability definition in SFAC No. 6.*
14. *The primacy of predicting future cash flows is discussed in FASB (1978, paras. 25 and 30).*
15. *Ijiri (1975) sees accountability as the most important function of financial reporting and has even brought up the idea of a conceptual framework based on accountability (Ijiri, 1983).*
16. *Another area in which the split between predictive ability and accountability arises is in other postretirement benefits, the subject matter of SFAS No. 106. See Chapter16.*
17. *Sterling (1985, pp. 30 and 31), but see p. 29 on the inability to obtain absolute precision. Within the broad context of relevance versus reliability, the Financial Accounting Standards Advisory Council (FASAC) has discussed this trade-off dispute concerning the general balance sheet movement toward fair values. FASAC members have brought up the issue of the greater reliability of historical costs, particularly in light of auditing concerns. See FASAC (2004).*

18. *Wyatt (1990) and Brown (1990). At the time of these publications, Wyatt was a former Board member and Brown was a current member of the FASB.*

19. *Ruland (1984).*

20. *Ruland (1989, p. 233).*

21. *Ingram and Rayburn (1989).*

22. *For more coverage, see the critique of Dopuch and Sunder (1980, p. 7). The FASB attempted to limit diversity in asset values in SFAS No. 19,* Financial Accounting and Reporting by Oil and Gas Producing Companies, *by allowing only successful efforts, but it was forced to suspend SFAS No. 19 as a result of political pressure.*

23. *While Ingram and Rayburn (1989, p. 65) maintain the balanced view, they state that "good economic consequences . . . are difficult to achieve" while "representational faithfulness . . . is impossible to achieve."*

24. *Daley and Tranter (1990).*

25. *Ibid. (p. 19).*

26. *Ruland (1989, p. 72).*

27. *Paragraph 137 of SFAC No. 2 mentions factors under the costs of providing information such as loss of competitive advantages and dangers of litigation, which could support the broader Daley and Tranter view of economic consequences, but the main discussion concerns the narrower interpretation of what might be termed the direct costs of preparation. See FASB (1980a, pp. 54–58).*

28. *Daley and Tranter (1990, p. 17).*

29. *Ibid. (pp. 18–21).*

30. *Solomons (1991a and 1991b) and Tinker (1991) debated the issue of neutrality versus the accountant's role in distributive issues (economic consequences). Bell (1993), like Solomons, is a strong proponent of the primacy of representational faithfulness over economic consequences. He believes that the qualitative characteristics of costs, benefits, and neutrality were concerned with allocative efficiency only (maximizing the utility stemming from the investment of scarce resources). However, because the FASB needed consensus among the various affected parties, allocative efficiency was broadened into a notion of distributional equity. Stated slightly differently, the FASB should be concerned with direct economic consequences only, but the need for consensus has led to a concern with indirect economic consequences as well as direct ones.*

31. *FASB (1980b, footnote 1, page 1)*

32. *FASB (1980c, p. x).*

33. *Ibid. (p. xi).*

34. *FASB (1984, para. 2).*

35. *Solomons (1986, p. 122).*

36. *Ibid. (p. 116).*

37. *FASB (1985, para. 9).*

38. *Kirk (1989, p. 102). Newberry (2003, pp. 327–328) attacks the conceptual framework for inconsistencies in the measurement of income (called "earnings" in SFAC No. 5) (a) if it is to be a measure of wealth enhancement to owners, exit valuations in asset values and depreciation is implied and (b) if it is to be a measure of performance, replacement values of assets and depreciation should be employed.*

39. *Solomons (1986, p. 121).*

40. *Sterling (1985, pp. 43–47).*

41. *Miller (1990).*

42. *Ibid. (p. 28).*

43. *Miller (1990, p. 29) views SFAC No. 6 in different terms. He sees it as upholding the progress made in SFAC Nos. 1–3 and thus a bulwark against the advocates of the counterreformation represented by SFAC No. 5. Perhaps SFAS No. 157 on fair value measurement upholds Miller's opinion.*

44. *FASB (1985, pp. ix–x).*

45. *Schipper (2002, p. 6) has noted an inconsistency between the definition of revenues in SFAC No. 6, which is grounded in changes in assets and liabilities, indicating the preeminence of the balance sheet, and the revenue recognition criteria in SFAC No. 5, based on "substantially accomplishing" the revenue task, which is based on income statement primacy.*

46. *Dopuch and Sunder (1980, pp. 3–5).*

47. *Brown, Collins, and Thornton (1993).*

48. *For an excellent discussion of professional judgment, see Mason (1993).*

49. *Samuelson (1996).*

50. *Somewhat similar criticisms are made by Schuetze (1993) and Chambers (1996), although the latter is primarily concerned with valuation issues.*

51. *FASB (2000, para. 15).*

52. *Ibid. (para. 32).*

53. *Ibid. (para. 67).*

54. *Ibid. (para. 97).*

55. *Gaa (1988, pp. 103–105).*

56. *Solomons (1986, p. 114).*

57. *Gaa (1988, pp. 146–161).*

58. *Archer (1993).*

59. *Ibid. (p. 73).*

60. *Ibid. (p. 80).*

61. *Ibid. (pp. 104–107).*

62. *Dopuch and Sunder (1980) and Hines (1989). For a similar criticism, see Christensen and Demski (2003, p. 429).*

63. *Archer (1997, p. 236).*

64. *Power (1993, p. 53).*

65. *Ibid. (pp. 55–56).*

66. *Joyce, Libby, and Sunder (1982).*

67. *Hudack and McAllister (1994).*

68. *Kennedy, Ugras, Leauby, and Tavana (1995).*

69. *For a wide range of opinions, see Zeff (1999, pp. 119–125).*

References

Archer, Simon (1993). "On the Methodology of Constructing a Conceptual Framework for Financial Accounting," in *Philosophical Perspectives on Accounting: Essays in Honour of Edward Stamp*, eds. M. J. Mumford and K. V. Peasnall. Routledge, pp. 62–122.

———— (Summer 1997). "The ASB's Exposure Draft Statement of Principles: A Comment," *Accounting and Business Research*, pp. 229–241.

Beaver, William H. (December 1991). "Problems and Paradoxes in Reporting Future Events," *Accounting Horizons*, pp. 122–134.

Bell, Philip W. (February 1993). "Establishing Guidelines for Financial Reporting," *Accounting Enquiries*, pp. 262–306.

Brown, Grant A., Roger Collins, and Daniel B. Thornton (1993). "Professional Judgment and Accounting Standards," *Accounting, Organizations and Society* (Vol. 18, No. 2), pp. 275–289.

Brown, Victor H. (September 1990). "Accounting Standards: Their Economic and Social Consequences," *Accounting Horizons*, pp. 89–97.

Chambers, R. J. (September 1996). "Ends, Ways, Means, and Conceptual Frameworks," *Abacus*, pp. 119–132.

Christensen, John A., and J. Demski (2003). *Accounting Theory*. McGraw-Hill Irwin.

Daley, Lane A., and Terry Tranter (March 1990). "Limitations on the Value of the Conceptual Framework in Evaluating Extant Accounting Standards," *Accounting Horizons*, pp. 15–24.

Dopuch, Nicholas, and Shyam Sunder (January 1980). "FASB's Statements on Objectives and Elements of Financial Accounting: A Review," *Accounting Review*, pp. 1–21.

Financial Accounting Standards Advisory Council (September 2004). "The FASB's Conceptual Framework: Relevance and Reliability," *FASAC, Attachment E*, pp. 1–11.

Financial Accounting Standards Board (1976a). FASB Discussion Memorandum, *Conceptual Framework for Financial Accounting and Reporting: Elements of Financial Statements and Their Measurement*. FASB.

——— (1976b). *Scope and Implications of the Conceptual Framework Project*. FASB.

——— (1976c). *Tentative Conclusions on Objectives of Financial Statements of Business Enterprises*. FASB.

——— (1978). Statement of Financial Accounting Concepts No. 1, *Objectives of Financial Reporting by Business Enterprises*. FASB.

——— (1980a). Statement of Financial Accounting Concepts No. 2, *Qualitative Characteristics of Accounting Information*. FASB.

——— (1980b). Statement of Financial Accounting Concepts No. 3, *Elements of Financial Statements of Business Enterprises*. FASB.

——— (1980c). Statement of Financial Accounting Concepts No. 4, *Objectives of Financial Reporting by Nonbusiness Organizations*. FASB.

——— (1984). Statement of Financial Accounting Concepts No. 5, *Recognition and Measurement in Financial Statements of Business Enterprises*. FASB.

——— (1985). Statement of Financial Accounting Concepts No. 6, *Elements of Financial Statements: A Replacement of FASB Concepts Statement No. 3 (incorporating an amendment of FASB Concepts Statement No. 2)*. FASB.

——— (2000). Statement of Financial Accounting Concepts No. 7, *Using Cash Flow Information and Present Value in Accounting Measurements*. FASB.

Gaa, James C. (1988). "Methodological Foundations of Standard-Setting for Corporate Financial Reporting," *Studies in Accounting Research No. 28*. American Accounting Association.

Hines, Ruth D. (1989). "Financial Accounting Knowledge, Conceptual Framework Projects and the Social Construction of the Accounting Profession," *Accounting, Auditing & Accountability Journal* (Vol. 2, No. 2), pp. 72–92.

Hudack, Lawrence, and J. P. McAllister (September 1994). "An Investigation of the FASB's Application of Its Decision Usefulness Criteria," *Accounting Horizons*, pp. 1–18.

Ijiri, Yuji (1975). "Theory of Accounting Measurement," *Studies in Accounting Research No. 10*. American Accounting Association.

——— (Summer 1983). "On the Accountability Based Conceptual Framework of Accounting," *Journal of Accounting and Public Policy*, pp. 75–81.

Ingram, Robert W., and Frank P. Rayburn (Spring 1989). "Representational Faithfulness and Economic Consequences: Their Roles in Accounting Policy," *Journal of Accounting and Public Policy*, pp. 57–68.

Joyce, Edward, Robert Libby, and Shyam Sunder (Autumn 1982). "Using the FASB's Qualitative Characteristics in Accounting Policy Choices," *Journal of Accounting Research* (Pt. II), pp. 654–675.

Kennedy, Dennis, Y. J. Ugras, B. A. Leauby, and Madjid Tavana (February 1995). "An Investigation of the Relative Importance Attached to the Qualitative Characteristics in the SFAC 2 Hierarchy," *Accounting Enquiries*, pp. 249–288.

Kirk, Donald J. (Fall 1989). "Reflections on a 'Reconceptualization of Accounting': A Commentary on Parts I–IV of Homer Kripke's Paper, 'Reflections on the FASB's Conceptual Framework for Accounting and on Auditing,'" *Journal of Accounting, Auditing & Finance*, pp. 83–105.

Mason, Alister K. (1993). "Professional Judgment and Professional Standards," in *Philosophical Perspectives on Accounting: Essays in Honour of Edward Stamp*, eds. M. J. Mumford and K. V. Peasnall Routledge, pp. 30–43.

Miller, Paul B. W. (June 1990). "The Conceptual Framework as Reformation and Counter-Reformation," *Accounting Horizons*, pp. 23–32.

Newberry, Susan (October 2003). "Reporting Comprehensive Income and Its Components," *Abacus*, pp. 325–339.

Power, Michael K. (1993). "On the Idea of a Conceptual Framework for Financial Reporting," in *Philosophical Perspectives on Accounting: Essays in Honour of Edward Stamp*, eds. M. J. Mumford and K. V. Peasnall. Routledge, pp. 44–61.

Ruland, Robert G. (Autumn 1984). "Duty, Obligation, and Responsibility in Accounting Policy Making," *Journal of Accounting and Public Policy*, pp. 223–237.

——— (Spring 1989). "The Pragmatic and Ethical Distinction Between Two Approaches to Accounting Policy Making," *Journal of Accounting and Public Policy*, pp. 69–80.

Samuelson, Richard (September 1996). "The Concept of Assets in Accounting Theory," *Accounting Horizons*, pp. 147–157.

Schipper, Katherine (2002). "Implications of Accounting Research for Financial Reporting and Standard Setting," speech given at the *Emanuel Saxe Lecture of Baruch College*, pp. 1–19.

Schuetze, Walter (September 1993). "What is an Asset?" *Accounting Horizons*, pp. 66–70.

Solomons, David (June 1986). "The FASB's Conceptual Framework: An Evaluation," *Journal of Accountancy*, pp. 114–124.

——— (1991a). "Accounting and Social Change: A Neutralist View," *Accounting, Organizations and Society* (Vol. 16, No. 2), pp. 287–295.

——— (1991b). "A Rejoinder," *Accounting, Organizations and Society* (Vol. 16, No. 2), pp. 311–312.

Sterling, Robert R. (1985). *An Essay on Recognition*. University of Sydney, Accounting Research Centre.

Tinker, Tony (1991). "The Accountant as Partisan," *Accounting, Organizations and Society* (Vol. 16, No. 2), pp. 297–310.

Wolk, Harry I., and Terri M. Vaughan (February 1993). "A Conceptual Framework Analysis of Pension and Other Postretirement Benefit Accounting," *Accounting Enquiries*, pp. 228–261.

Wyatt, Arthur (September 1990). "Accounting Standards: Conceptual or Political?" *Accounting Horizons*, pp. 83–88.

Zeff, Stephen A. (1999). "The Evolution of the Conceptual Framework for Business Enterprises in the United States," *Accounting Historians Journal* (Vol. 26, Part 2), pp. 89–131.

8

Usefulness of Accounting Information to Investors and Creditors

---

Learning Objectives

After reading this chapter, you should be able to:

- Understand the link between accounting information, dividends, and stock prices.
- Understand the basics of residual income models, their strengths and weaknesses, and how they are used for valuation and performance assessment.
- Understand the basics of the efficient-markets hypothesis, its implications for accounting information, and why it has come under attack.
- Understand the basics of event studies and cross-sectional valuation studies.
- Be familiar with the general findings of market-based accounting research regarding the usefulness of accounting information for investors.
- Understand that accounting information is useful to creditors in evaluating default risk and predicting bankruptcy.
- Understand the role of accounting information for use in forecasting earnings.

The Financial Accounting Standards Board (FASB) recognizes the existence of a diverse and pluralistic user group (see Chapter 7). However, in practice, the FASB has focused on what it calls *primary user groups* (investors and creditors) who are assumed to be mainly interested in the amounts, timing, and uncertainties of future cash flows[1]. The rationale for the investor–creditor focus is that other users (e.g., governments, utility rate-setting bodies) have a commonality of interest with investors and creditors or the means of getting alternative information. The FASB's cost–benefit calculus is similarly restricted to benefits for investors and creditors, and cost considerations are confined only to producers.

The purpose of this chapter is to examine theoretical and empirical evidence for the usefulness of financial accounting data to users. While we are largely focused on the FASB's primary user group—investors and creditors—we wish to note that in its broadest sense, this group is quite large. Investors include both individual and institutional shareholders, holders of interest-bearing debt (bondholders, financial institutions, etc.), and the firm's board of directors, who act on behalf of shareholders.[2] Although they are not strictly investors per se, equity analysts make extensive use of financial statements and are an integral part of the investing process.

Creditors are mainly considered suppliers of materials and services (accounts payable). They need financial information about their customers to determine the terms of credit. However, in a broader sense, creditors may also include taxing authorities (taxes payable) and other individuals or entities that have claims on the firm ahead of shareholders.[3]

Existing and potential shareholders need information to estimate the value of the firm's shares and make wealth-enhancing capital-allocation decisions, which are also beneficial to the economy. The board of directors has the responsibility for creating and implementing strategies and policies that create wealth and ensure that management acts in the interests of the shareholders.[4] In this role, the board needs to be able to evaluate and reward management's efforts, abilities, and decisions, particularly management's capital-allocation decisions.[5]

Getting paid is certainly a major concern of the holders of interest-bearing debt, but their concern goes beyond that. While loans from commercial banks typically have maturities of a few years, corporate bonds have much longer maturities.[6] The bonds may be sold before they mature, and changes in the value of the firm affect the market value of those bonds. Bondholders must be concerned with the value of the entire firm.

Our point is that many individuals and entities have a vested interest in understanding the financial well-being of a firm. When it works well, we end up with correct securities pricing and the efficient allocation of capital in the economy (allocational efficiency). Everyone is better off—better homes, healthier children, and money for violin lessons, baseball bats, and college tuition.

We begin this chapter by examining models of equity valuation and the role of accounting information in these models. Next, we examine the role of residual income models for motivating and assessing managerial performance and valuing the firm. We then provide a background on risk and return and the efficient-markets hypothesis (EMH). Using accounting-related capital markets research, we discuss the usefulness of accounting information for the primary user groups. In that context, we show why the efficient-markets hypothesis is being challenged. We then discuss the role of accounting data for creditors and discuss the importance of earnings for forecasting. We conclude with a brief discussion of empirical research and standard setting.

Earnings, Dividends, and Stock Prices

One of the major uses of accounting data relates to valuation. In this section, we examine a model relating earnings, dividends, and stock prices. While we briefly discuss cash flows, we defer a detailed discussion of this topic to Chapter 13.

Earnings and Dividends

Lintner detailed the results of a series of interviews with corporate managers regarding the determinants of their dividend policies.[7] Managers indicated that major changes in "permanent" earnings were the most important determinants of the companies' dividend decisions. After giving serious consideration to both an established target payout ratio and the existing payout ratio, managers adjusted dividends to reflect the change in "permanent" earnings. Since managers perceived that shareholders valued a *smooth* dividend stream, the managers made adjustments to dividend payout rates gradually. Furthermore, most managers avoided making changes to dividends that had a significant probability of being reversed in the near future. Given the seriousness and forward-looking nature of the dividend policy decision, investors regard cash dividends as credible signals of future performance. We say that a change in the cash dividend has *information content*.

Cash dividends are the cash flows that investors receive from a dividend-paying stock. As such, the stock price (P_0) may be modeled as the present value of the future expected dividends, or

$$P_0 = \sum_{t=1}^{\infty} \frac{D_t}{(1+r)^t} \qquad (8.1)$$

where

D_t = the dividend expected at time t, and

r = the rate of return expected by the shareholders.

If the cash dividends are expected to grow at a constant rate (g), the present value of the future expected dividends may be expressed as the present value of a growing perpetuity.[8]

$$P_0 = \frac{D_1}{(r-g)} \qquad (8.2)$$

For a firm in equilibrium, a future expected dividend can be expressed in terms of a constant dividend payout ratio (PO) and earnings per share at time t (EPS$_t$), or D_t = (PO)(EPS$_t$). This allows us to rewrite Equation 8.1 as

$$P_0 = PO \sum_{t=1}^{\infty} \frac{EPS_t}{(1+r)^t} \tag{8.3}$$

and Equation 8.2 as:

$$P_0 = PO \left(\frac{EPS_1}{r-g} \right) \tag{8.4}$$

In these forms, we say that the stock price is equal to present value (capitalized value) of future expected earnings, adjusted by the dividend payout ratio. While we started with the dividend discount model, we now have the earnings model of stock valuation. Given its relation to cash dividends, it is no surprise that future earnings have a major effect on the share price.

Predicting Dividends From Current Earnings

Beaver uses the dividend valuation model to formulate the role of accounting earnings in determining firm value.[9] Security prices are modeled as a function of expected future dividends (Equation 8.1). Furthermore, future dividends themselves are a function of future earnings (Equation 8.3). Moreover, current accounting income is useful in predicting future earnings. As such, current income has value in predicting future dividends via its value to predict future earnings. This *predictive* value is one of the major arguments for the relevance of accounting information (see the discussion of SFAC No. 2 in Chapter 7).

Connecting the Dots: From Earnings to Stock Prices

Work in financial economics regarding the theoretical value of the firm traces back to Miller and Modigliani's seminal work in which they argue that dividend policy is irrelevant to firm valuation.[10] Ignoring the complicating effect of taxes, they show that the value of the firm is equal to the present value of future expected net cash flows. These net cash flows per period are defined as operating cash flow minus cash investment in assets. (This is the same definition as that used for capital budgeting analysis.)

Miller and Modigliani's net cash flow model was originally a certainty-equivalent model but has been extended to a more general model reflecting the uncertainty of future operating cash flows.[11] The attractiveness of the cash flow valuation model for accounting is that it maps directly onto the accounting system; cash flows are explicitly measured in accounting systems. In contrast, dividends are a matter of corporate policy and are not a direct function of accounting systems. We make further tie-ins between cash flows and decision making in Chapter 13.

Interestingly, the FASB has implicitly adopted the cash flow valuation model. In SFAC No. 1, *Objectives of Financial Reporting by Business Enterprises*, the role of financial reporting is characterized as aiding investors, creditors, and others in assessing the amounts, timing, and uncertainty of the enterprise's prospective *net cash flows*. Further, the FASB has asserted that accrual accounting systems, and accrual income numbers in particular, are more useful for this purpose than are simpler cash-based systems: "Accrual accounting generally provides a better indication of an enterprise's present and continuing ability to generate favorable cash flows than information limited to the financial effects of cash receipts and payments."[12]

Beaver agrees with this assertion, arguing that "an accrual can be viewed as a form of forecast about the future . . ."[13] There is empirical evidence that future cash flows are better forecast with accrual data than with cash flow data.[14] In addition, in stock market studies, security prices are more highly correlated with accrual income than with either cash flows or working capital flows.[15] Numerous studies have documented that *changes* in reported accounting earnings affect the value of the firm and its stock. This is not surprising if investors view such changes as permanent or persisting into the future. As such, expectations of *future* cash flows should also be affected; hence, the explanation for changes in stock prices as a function of the expected persistency of earnings changes.[16]

The implication of this literature is that accrual accounting systems ultimately incorporate the attribute that determines firm valuation—net cash flow data. However, the value of the information in financial reporting does not lie in its role as a historical record but rather in its use in helping investors to forecast future expected net cash flows and dividends. (This information is also useful for feedback purposes. See Chapter 7.)

Residual Income Models

Capital is necessary to generate income. *Residual income* is a general term for income in excess of a charge for the capital that is employed to generate that income.[17] The residual income concept may be applied to the enterprise as a whole or to the firm's common equity. When applied to the enterprise's operating income and invested capital, residual income is often called economic profit or Economic Value Added (EVA).[18] When applied to the firm's net income and common equity, residual income is often called residual income or abnormal earnings.[19]

Economic Profit

It is well established that the value of a firm is equal to the present value of the future expected net cash flows.[20] Net cash flows are the periodic cash flows that are available to all investor claims (interest-bearing debt, preferred stock, and common stock). They are much less subject to manipulation than earnings.

One shortcoming of net cash flows is that they do not provide investors with a metric for gauging periodic performance. For example, even a highly profitable, well-managed firm can have negative net cash flows in a given period if the firm makes large investments in that period. If the investments have a positive net present value, negative net cash flows in one period is hardly a cause for concern.[21] Economic profit attempts to bridge the gap, providing not only a means to value the firm but also a means to assess its periodic performance.

Economic profit starts with the amount of capital that is invested at the beginning of the period. This investment has a cost. When expressed as a rate, this cost is known as the *weighted average cost of capital (WACC)*. (We can think of the WACC as the required rate of return to all investor claims, commensurate with the risk of the net cash flows.) The WACC and the amount of capital invested determine the periodic after-tax operating income that investors expect the firm to generate. This is the dollar cost of invested capital, the charge for capital employed, or simply the capital charge. The realized after-tax operating income is compared to the amount that is expected. If the after-tax operating income exceeds the income expected, the firm has generated an amount of income above and beyond the call of duty. This excess income is called economic profit.

More formally,

$$\text{Economic profit} = \text{NOPAT} - \text{capital charge} \qquad (8.5)$$

where NOPAT is net operating profit, less taxes paid.[22] Expressing the capital charge as a function of the WACC and invested capital at the beginning of the period, we have:

$$\text{Economic profit} = \text{NOPAT} - (\text{WACC})(\text{invested capital}) \qquad (8.6)$$

Equation 8.6 indicates that if the firm's NOPAT exceeds the capital charge, it earns an economic profit and creates wealth.[23] To increase economic profit, the firm can increase NOPAT by increasing sales or decreasing costs, decrease invested capital, or lower the firm's cost of capital (WACC).

Exhibit 8.1 presents a statement of invested capital for ABC Company. We constructed the statement from ABC's balance sheet, shown in Chapter 13, Exhibit 13.7. Note that the statement of invested capital is simply a rearrangement of the firm's balance sheet, putting net operating assets on the "left hand side," and all investor claims on the "right hand side."

Exhibit 8.1   Statement of Invested Capital for ABC Company

Statement of Invested Capital	2004	2005	2006	2007
Cash and equivalents	$300	$244	$323	$339
Accounts receivable	930	915	1,035	1,018
Inventories	1,010	1,037	970	1,154
Accounts payable	$(850)	$(854)	$(841)	$(883)
Net operating working capital	$1,390	$1,342	$1,487	$1,628
Property, plant and equipment	2,500	2,562	2,651	2,783
Invested capital (assets)	$3,890	$3,904	$4,138	$4,411
Notes payable	73	58	60	67
Long-term debt	657	524	539	606
Total interest bearing debt	730	582	599	673
Common stock	860	830	860	860
Retained earnings	2,300	2,492	2,679	2,878
Total common equity	3,160	3,322	3,539	3,738
Invested capital (equities)	$3,890	$3,904	$4,138	$4,411

Exhibit 8.2 presents a statement of economic profit for ABC Company. This statement uses invested capital from Exhibit 8.1 and operating income from ABC's income statement presented in Exhibit 13.7 in Chapter 13. Notice that economic profit is positive for all three years. However, economic profit declined in 2006 due to an increase in invested capital in 2005 and lower net operating profit after tax (NOPAT) for 2006.

Conceptually, economic profit has valuable characteristics from a performance evaluation perspective. Managers can increase economic profit, and their bonuses, by increasing NOPAT. Thus, managers have an incentive to control costs and increase sales. Furthermore, managers can increase economic profit by reducing the amount of invested capital.

In contrast, net income is a performance metric that ignores the amount of capital employed. If the firm rewards its managers based on net income, and if additional invested capital generates some additional net income, managers have an incentive to invest, even if the incremental investment does not earn its cost of capital.

The economic profit approach has the added benefit that it can also be used to value the enterprise. The value obtained is equal to the present value of the net cash flows.[24] Using the economic profit approach, the value of the firm at time 0 is equal to the invested capital in place at time 0, plus the present value of future expected economic profit, or:

$$V_0(\text{firm}) = \text{Invested capital}_0 + \sum_{t=1}^{\infty} \frac{\text{NOPAT} - (\text{WACC})(\text{invested capital})_t}{(1 + WACC)^t} \qquad (8.7)$$

In an attempt to improve economic profit as a performance metric, some users make adjustments to the way invested capital and NOPAT are calculated. The best-known application of economic profit is EVA, a proprietary form of economic profit developed by Stern Stewart & Co. Stewart (2003) notes:

> Stated in brief ... EVA begins with ... residual income [economic profit] ... and then proposes a series of additional adjustments to GAAP accounting that are designed to produce a reliable measure of a company's annual, sustainable *cash* [italics added]-generating capacity.[25]

Exhibit 8.2   Statement of Economic Profit for ABC Company

Statement of Economic Profit	2004	2005	2006	2007
Invested capital	$3,890.0	$3,904.0	$4,138.0	$4,411.0
Operating income		578.0	555.0	587.0
Taxes on operating income (40%)		(231.2)	(222.0)	(234.8)
Net operating profit after tax		346.8	333.0	352.2
Capital charage on invested capital (8%)		(311.2)	(312.3)	(331.0)
Economic profit		$35.6	$20.7	$21.2

Young notes that the most common accounting adjustments relate to nonrecurring gains and losses, research and development, deferred taxes, provisions for warranties and bad debts, LIFO reserves, goodwill, depreciation, and operating losses.[26]

Residual Income and the Dividend Discount Model

Economic profit and EVA focus on the valuation and performance measurement of the operations of the enterprise as a whole. Residual income—sometimes called *abnormal earnings*—is focused on net income and the firm's common equity. It is defined as:

$$\text{Residual income} = \text{actual earnings} - \text{required earnings} \qquad (8.8)$$

where required earnings are the amount of earnings that compensates shareholders for the equity capital invested and the risk they bear. Required earnings may be written as the beginning-of-period book equity, multiplied by the cost of equity (r):

$$\text{Residual income} = \text{earnings} - r(\text{book equity}) \qquad (8.9)$$

Note the similarity between Equation 8.9 and Equation 8.6. Ohlson and, also, Feltham and Ohlson use a residual income framework to predict and explain stock prices.[27] The model starts with the dividend discount model (Equation 8.1). Next, it specifies that all profit and loss elements go through income. This specification, known as *clean surplus accounting*, relates the current book equity to previous book equity, earnings, and dividends:

$$\text{Book equity}_t = \text{book equity}_{t-1} + \text{earnings}_t - \text{dividends}_t \qquad (8.10)$$

The FASB comprehensive orientation of SFAS No. 130 (Chapter 11) ties in well with the clean surplus approach. Rearranging Equation 8.10 allows dividends to be expressed in terms of book values and earnings:

$$\text{Dividends}_t = \text{earnings}_t - (\text{book equity}_t - \text{book equity}_{t-1}) \qquad (8.11)$$

By using Equations 8.1 and 8.11, it can be shown that the price of the firm's stock is equal to:

$$P_0 = \text{Book equity}_0 + \sum_{t=1}^{\infty} \frac{[\text{earnings}_t - r(\text{book equity}_{t-1})]}{(1+r)^t} \qquad (8.12)$$

where r is the cost of equity and the numerator of the second expression is residual income or abnormal earnings. Note the similarity between Equation 8.12 and Equation 8.7.

We started with Equations 8.1 (dividend discount model) and 8.11 and rearranged them to obtain Equation 8.12. As such, Equation 8.12 is simply a restatement of the dividend discount model in terms of future expected earnings, the cost of equity, and current and future expected book equity. By itself, this model offers little additional utility over the dividend discount model per se. However, the utility of the Equation 8.12 can be increased if the user can incorporate additional information regarding forecasts of future abnormal earnings.[28]

Dechow, Hutton, and Sloan perform an empirical assessment of the residual income model. They find that "residual income follows a mean reverting process . . . associated with firm characteristics suggested by accounting and economic analysis."[29] The rate of mean reversion decreases with the quality of earnings and increases with the dividend payout ratio. It is also correlated across firms in the same industry. They also find that "incorporating information in analysts' forecasts of earnings into the information dynamics increases forecast accuracy."[30] Hence, the residual income model allows the user to incorporate non-accounting information into the model to improve its forecast accuracy.

Note that the higher are the abnormal earnings, the higher is the value of the firm's common equity. Beaver discusses several sources that give rise to abnormal earnings.[31] First, firms do not carry on the balance sheet, the positive excess present value above the cost of the project (positive net present value). Second, many matching and recognition procedures under historical costing tend to be conservative in nature (e.g., accelerated depreciation methods and LIFO costing for inventories and cost of goods sold, immediate write-off of research and development, and possible undervaluation of other intangibles).

Qiang demonstrates that abnormal earnings increase with industry concentration, industry-level barriers to entry, and industry conservative accounting factors. The author also finds that differences in firm abnormal earnings increase with "market share, firm size, firm-level barriers to entry, and firm conservative accounting factors."[32]

Residual Income and Performance Measurement: The Good and Bad

In this section, we examine the pros and cons of residual income models used for performance measurement.[33] While our focus is broader than EVA per se, much of the research on residual income has been done in the context of evaluating EVA.

Residual Income: The Good

Residual income is an accounting measure, which in its basic form uses financial data that follow a defined set of rules. Unlike the stock price, it can be used as a company and intracompany performance measurement tool.

It recognizes that *all* capital—debt as well as equity—has a cost; capital is not a free good. Making capital an explicit part of the model raises the awareness of using excess capital to generate income. Stewart notes:

> If a firm cannot give its shareholders at least the return that they could earn by investing on their own, it will lose value. Thus in an economist's view, a company does not begin to earn a profit until it can cover the opportunity cost of equity capital.[34]

Although not explicitly designated as an application of residual income, Berkshire Hathaway and CEO Warren Buffett explicitly recognize the cost of capital in communications with corporate shareholders and also with its subsidiary managers.

When capital invested in an operation is significant, we also both charge managers a high rate for incremental capital they employ and credit them at an equally high rate for capital they release. . . . The consequence of this two-way arrangement is that it pays [managers]—and pays [them] well—to send to Omaha any cash he can't advantageously use in his business.[35]

As a proprietary form of residual income, EVA goes one step further and attempts to address some of the issues related to pensions, mixing financing and operations, reserves, research and development, energy exploration, divestitures and restructuring transactions, investment, depreciation, and stock options.[36]

Rogerson demonstrates that residual income is an income-based compensation system that provides an incentive for the management to allocate capital efficiently over time. (See Berkshire Hathaway discussion above.) The corporate form of organization exhibits the separation of ownership from control. Managers are typically better informed about investment opportunities than shareholders are. This separation of ownership from control and the lack of a capital charge would make it difficult to design an income-based compensation system that creates an incentive for managers to choose the correct level of investment. Calculating income, net of a charge for the capital employed, creates an incentive for efficient allocation of capital, mitigating the incentive for managers to game the system by maximizing current income at the expense of future income.[37]

Residual income models might be of direct help to investors. For example, Feltham et al. provide evidence that EVA has more explanatory power than reported earnings or cash flow from operations.[38]

Residual Income: The Bad

There are a number of weaknesses associated with the various forms of residual income. For any given year, the determination of the residual income itself is dependent on an accurate estimate of the cost of capital, no simple task. For valuation purposes, forecasts are crucial.[39]

All forms of residual income are consistent with discounted net cash flows for *any* book value and *any* method of depreciation.[40] While this might appear advantageous, changing depreciation schedules has a direct impact on residual income (or economic profit) for individual periods. Hence, lengthening the depreciable life of fixed assets decreases the per-period depreciation expense, increases NOPAT, and increases the residual income. In some cases, it may not be possible to determine whether the residual income calculated is actually owing to management's efforts or lack thereof.

Residual income is an accounting measure and, as stated in the depreciation example above, can be manipulated for any one period. Furthermore, if improperly applied, residual income could bias management against long-term investments. Unlike the stock price, which is forward looking, residual income focuses on *historical* performance.

In spite of the name given to some forms of residual income, residual income is *not* economic income. A firm's *economic income* is equal to net cash flows plus a change in present value or market value of the firm.

For EVA, the additional effort to make additional adjustments to GAAP may not be justified. Chen and Dodd investigate EVA as a tool for investors to find profitable investment opportunities. They find that while EVA does provide information in addition to traditional accounting measures, it should not replace them. Furthermore, they find that there is no significant difference between EVA and residual income in terms of explaining stock returns.[41]

Dodd and Johns express concerns that the overemphasis on EVA might lead companies to exclude other important measures:

It appears that when companies adopt EVA, a subtle movement away from customer-related measures may occur. If these early observations represent the beginning of a trend within EVA adopters, we see this as one laden with risk over the longer-term. The idea that a company can use a single financial measure to manage its operations does not make sense in today's environment.[42]

The evidence for the ability of residual income to explain shareholder returns is mixed. For example, in contrast to Feltham et al., Copeland and Dolgoff find that EVA does not provide much explanatory power as it relates to total shareholder returns:

It may surprise you to learn that EVA (also called economic profit) and commonly used performance measures such as earnings per share and the growth in earnings per share have at most a weak correlation (at least at the level of the individual company) with the total return to shareholders.[43]

If any adjustments are made to GAAP, EVA—and presumably other forms of residual income—may not be applied consistently or be sufficiently transparent to outside investors. Using survey data from 29 respondents (40% response rate), Weaver notes:

Although a consistent philosophy has been applied, none of the companies measure EVA the same way. . . . Due to the measurement differences, Economic Value Added is a limited tool that cannot be used for competitive analysis. In practice, there is no one consistent definition of EVA and numerous fundamental differences exist with respect to NOPAT [net operating profit after tax], IC [invested capital] and COC [cost of capital] Further, some data may not be publicly reported, and more fundamentally, managers will behave differently when their performance is measured differently.[44]

Do firms that adopt EVA do so because of poor stock performance? Does the adoption of EVA lead to improved stock performance? Ferguson et al. examine these questions using an event study methodology. They find:

Firms that adopt EVA appear to have above average profitability relative to their peers both *before and after* [italics added] the adoption of EVA; further, there is some evidence that EVA adopters experience increased profitability relative to their peers following adoption.[45]

This suggests that EVA adopters were already good managers, already working to improve performance.

Do firms that have implemented an EVA-driven compensation system outperform the market? Is EVA a valid forecaster of stock performance? Griffith examines these questions using an event study methodology, estimating abnormal returns of EVA adopters for various holding periods starting from a firm's adoption to up to five years after its adoption of EVA. His findings are not encouraging: Before they adopted EVA as a measure of firm performance, the firms . . . underperformed both their peers and the market. After implementation of the EVA compensation system, the companies continued to underperform significantly.[46]

Are We Asking Too Much?

We think there is value in the various forms of residual income models for purposes of valuation when the user can incorporate additional information regarding forecasts of future economic profit or abnormal earnings. We also think that these models have value for performance assessment and motivating managers to control costs and avoid overinvestment. However, residual income models are no panacea for a firm or industry plagued by unsolvable problems.[47] Alternatively, if value-minded managers in good companies or industries adopt EVA, will the market be able to detect a difference?

For compensation purposes, Dutta and Reichelstein conclude that historical accounting measures, and even cash flows, are too backward looking *by themselves* and must be combined with forward-looking measures. They conclude:

> An optimal performance measure must rely on *both* accounting variables *and* [italics added] stock price. The familiar performance [metric] . . . of Economic Value Added (residual income) [is] useful for calibrating stock price and accounting income to the relevant history, in particular to the firm's dividend policy.[48]

Finally, we note that if the value of the firm is determined as modeled by a residual income model (Equation 8.7 or 8.12), the total return to shareholders in any given year is dependent on revisions to *all* current and *future* residual income. Why should we necessarily expect a strong relationship between the current year's residual income and the total returns to shareholders?

Clearly, the jury is still out on the utility of various forms of residual income, whether for purposes of valuation or performance assessment. We think that residual income models hold promise for both security valuation and performance assessment. Still, there is much to be done in terms of theoretical development, application, and empirical validation.

Background on Risk and Return

The usefulness of accounting information to investors has been empirically investigated through tests of association between publicly released accounting data and changes in security prices. If there is a significant association, then there is evidence that accounting information is useful with respect to firm valuation. These studies also constitute tests of the EMH.

Efficient-Markets Hypothesis (EMH)

Market efficiency refers to the speed with which securities in the capital markets respond to new information. The (EMH) states that capital markets fully and instantaneously reflect new information in security prices.[49] If the hypothesis is correct, the value of new information is fully and completely demonstrated via the security's price response. When this occurs, the item of information is said to have *information content*.

There are three forms of the EMH. The *weak* form says that security prices reflect information contained in historical (past) prices. The *semistrong* form says that security prices reflect all publicly available information. Finally, the *strong* form says that security prices reflect all information, both public and private. Most testing has been of the semistrong form. Much of the information tested has been of an accounting nature—for example, financial statement data and earnings announcements. In our discussion, we concern ourselves only with publicly available information.

Rationale and Implications of the EMH

The rationale for the EMH is simple. There are thousands of self-interested investors and analysts trying to maximize their wealth by trading securities. These individuals are motivated to uncover any information that might give them a financial edge. Given that publicly available information is available to everyone at about the same time, it makes sense that wealth-maximizing individuals quickly analyze that information and trade accordingly.[50] Given that news arrives in a random fashion, we would expect that security price changes will be random as well.

The implications for efficient markets are profound. If markets are efficient, it is useless to analyze past financial statements or read historical articles about companies. Furthermore, it is not possible to "beat the market" on a risk-adjusted basis. There is evidence to support this view. Malkiel notes that even professional mutual fund managers have difficulty beating the market after fees.

> During the year ended December 31, 2003, close to three quarters of the mutual funds holding large capitalization stocks were outperformed by the (large capitalization) Standard and Poor's 500 stock index. Results are similar for other one-year period[s]. When returns are measured over periods of 10 years or longer, over 80% of active managers are outperformed by the index. . . . We see that the typical actively managed fund underperforms the index fund by over 200 basis points.[51]

Anomalies

For some time, it was largely accepted that the market was indeed efficient. Then, De Bondt and Thaler presented convincing evidence that markets often overreact or underreact. In addition, the mispricing does not appear to correct rapidly:

> Consistent with the predictions of the overreacting hypothesis, portfolios of prior "losers" are found to outperform prior "winners." Thirty-six months after portfolio formation, the losing stocks have earned about 25% more than the winners, even though the latter are significantly more risky.[52]

The debate continues to rage. In fact, it has created a new field of "behavioral finance." The "technology bubble" of the late 1990s helped to fuel the fire. Consider the case of the Nasdaq Composite Index, a commonly known indicator of technology stocks. On March 10, 2000, the Index reached a level of 5049, only to fall 3935 points (78%) to 1114 by October 9, 2002. Which date reflected the correct pricing of the stocks in the Nasdaq Composite Index: March 10, 2000, or October 9, 2002? As we write this chapter in mid 2007, the index still has recovered approximately half of its loss.[53]

Amazon.com Inc. typified the late 1990s bubble. On December 31, 1999, its stock price, adjusted for splits, was $76.12, while it reported an operating loss of almost $606 million. Exhibit 8.3 reveals why some, to their chagrin, questioned the link between Amazon's earnings and its stock price in the late 1990s. It would almost appear that the earnings were anticipating the stock price, instead of the other way around.

The bubble had devastating effects for managers who analyzed companies "the old-fashioned way." Consider the demise of Tiger Management.

> The sudden farewell of Tiger Management, the giant hedge fund, is being heralded in some quarters as a death knell for long-term value investing. . . . In announcing that he would liquidate and give back his investors' money, Julian Robertson Jr. . . . admitted that he is out of step with a world in which Palm, the maker of the hand-held Palm Pilot, is valued at more than GM and in which Priceline.com (which sells airline tickets but has neither earnings nor planes) was valued at more than US Airways and most of the other publicly traded airlines combined. . . . "There is no point in subjecting our investors to risk in a market which I frankly do not understand . . ."[54]

Portfolio Diversification

The theoretical foundation of capital market or security price research comes from portfolio theory, which is a theory of rational investment choice and utility maximization. As long as security returns are imperfectly correlated (correlation is less than 1.0), the risk of

Exhibit 8.3   Amazon.com Inc.: Income From Operations and Stock Price

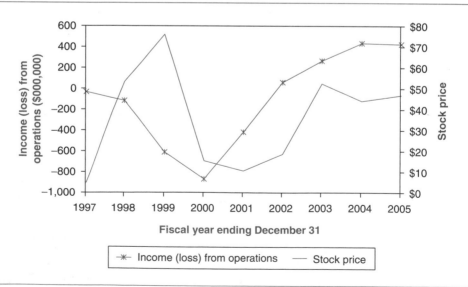

SOURCE: Mergent Online (www.mergentonline.com) and Yahoo! Finance (http://finance.yahoo.com). Accessed February 2, 2007.

a portfolio as measured by its standard deviation of return is reduced by adding additional securities. See Exhibit 8.4.

The risk that can be eliminated in this manner is called *unsystematic (diversifiable, unique) risk.* The remaining portfolio risk is called *systematic (undiversifiable, market) risk.* Systematic risk is also known as the *relevant risk,* as this risk is not affected by diversification; investors have no other choice than to bear it.

Capital Asset Pricing Model (CAPM)

The relationship between risk and return is embodied in a theory known as the *capital asset pricing model (CAPM).* The relationship between risk and return for diversified portfolios is modeled by the *Capital Market Line (CML).* For individual assets, the relationship is modeled by the *Security Market Line (SML).*

Capital Market Line (CML)

The standard deviation of a portfolio declines as more assets are added to the portfolio. When all tradable and nontradable assets (stocks, bonds, real estate, etc.) have been added to a portfolio, we have the *market portfolio.* The theoretical choice of portfolios is graphically presented in Exhibit 8.5 (see page 234) for two risky assets. The points on the curved line, the *feasible set,* reflect portfolios formed by combining different proportions of two risky assets. Each portfolio has its own unique expected return and standard deviation.[55]

The straight line is called the Capital Market Line (CML). The CML intersects the Y-axis at the risk-free rate of interest, typically considered to be a 90-day Treasury bill. At this point, the

Exhibit 8.4   The Effect of the Number of Securities on Portfolio Risk

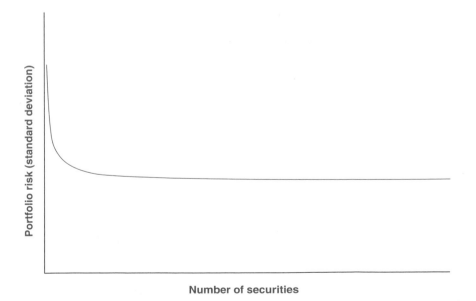

Portfolio risk (standard deviation)

Number of securities

standard deviation is equal to zero. The CML is tangent to the feasible set at point M. (If portfolio M contained all risky assets, it would be the market portfolio.) The points on the CML reflect various proportions of an investor's wealth invested in M and the risk-free asset. When drawn through M, the CML provides the highest risk premium—the expected return above and beyond the risk-free rate—per unit of standard deviation of return (risk). Since investors are risk averse, the expected portfolio return increases as risk (standard deviation of return) increases. The capital market line is linear only under restrictive conditions, but whether linear or curvilinear, a direct relationship exists between the level of risk and expected returns.

Security Market Line (SML)

Theoretically, with the formation of the market portfolio, the unsystematic risk of individual securities has been eliminated, and only systematic risk matters. Hence, the relevant risk for an individual security is systematic risk, which is the risk of the security relative to the market portfolio.[56] The systematic risk for an individual security is measured by beta (β), which measures the volatility of a security's returns relative to the market portfolio.[57] By definition, the beta of the market is equal to 1.0. A security with a beta of 2.0 is twice as risky as the market, whereas a security with a beta of 0.5 is half as risky as the market.

According to the CAPM, the relationship between the expected return on individual securities and beta is embodied in an equation known as the Security Market Line (SML):

$$R_j = R_f + \beta_j [R_m - R_f] \qquad (8.13)$$

where

R_j = the expected return on security j,

R_f = the risk-free rate of return (typically the return on Treasury bills),

R_m = the expected return on the market portfolio, and

β_j = the beta coefficient for security j.

Beta is estimated by performing a regression of the returns of security j on those of the market. Beta is the slope of this regression. Statistically, beta is defined as

$$\beta_j = \rho_{jm} \sigma_j \sigma_m / \sigma_m^2 \qquad (8.14)$$

where

ρ_{jm} = the correlation coefficient between security j and m,

σ_j = the standard deviation of the returns on security j,

σ_m = the standard deviation of the returns on the market portfolio,

σ_m^2 = the variance of the returns of the market portfolio, and

$\rho_{jm} \sigma_j \sigma_m$ = the covariance of the returns of security j with those of market portfolio.

In practice, the relation between risk and return is not exactly the way the CAPM specifies. Nevertheless, the model has received support among academics and practitioners.[58]

Introduction to Capital Markets Research in Accounting

Capital markets research in accounting examines the relationship between the security prices and the information contained in the firm's financial statements and associated documentation. Aside from its importance as an academic exercise, this body of research is of utmost importance to investors, managers, and standard setters. Why? At a high level, the ability of markets to efficiently allocate resources (allocational efficiency) is crucially dependent on accounting information for analysis, valuation, and performance measurement. However, investors need to know if analysis of accounting data is a value-enhancing activity. Furthermore, standard setters need to know if the existing standards are fulfilling their intended purpose to improve the informational and allocational efficiency of markets. If not, it might be time for a new standard. Ultimately, everyone has a stake in the process.

In the sections that follow, we examine some of the capital markets research in accounting. Our intent is not to present a comprehensive review or critique but to provide a status report and outlook.

The Market Model

Many empirical studies in accounting use the empirical form of the CAPM known as the *market model*:

$$R_j = \alpha + \beta_{jt} R_{mt} + \varepsilon_t \tag{8.15}$$

where

t is a time subscript,

R_j, β_j, and R_m are the same as in Equation 8.13,

$\alpha =$ the intercept term, and

$\varepsilon =$ a random error term.

The model states that the returns for security j are a function of the return on the market. (As a rearrangement of the Security Market Line, the intercept, α, is equal to $R_f[1 - \beta_j]$). The portion of the return not explained by the market is reflected in ε, the error term.

Event Studies

An empirical research method used in accounting and finance studies to detect the market's reaction to some event is the *event study*.[59] The announcement of an unexpected event (e.g., merger or acquisition) should have an impact on the stock price. An event study divides the period related to the event into three "windows": an estimation window, the event window, and the post-event window. The "normal" relationship between a security's returns and those of the market are estimated during the estimation window. This allows the researcher to estimate the parameters (α and β) of Equation 8.15 using linear regression. This is shown graphically in Exhibit 8.6. (see page 237).

After the parameters of Equation 8.15 have been estimated, the equation is used to estimate the returns at the time of and subsequent to the event. The difference between the actual return and the return expected using Equation 8.15 is called an *abnormal return (AR)*. The sum of the ARs is known as the *cumulative abnormal return (CAR)*. In the absence of an event, the ARs should randomly fluctuate around zero, and the CARs should show no upward or downward trend.

If an unexpected event has occurred, the AR and the CAR should depart significantly from zero on the date of the event. However, if the market fully and immediately reflects the new information in the stock price, the subsequent ARs should again randomly fluctuate around zero, and the CARs should show no trend. See Exhibit 8.7, page 238.

In contrast, if the market does not fully, immediately, and accurately reflect the news contained in the event, we might observe an upward or downward bias in ARs and the tendency of the CARs to drift up or down. Exhibit 8.8 (see page 239) shows a graph of the ARs and CARs in which the market has not fully adjusted to good news at the time of the event.

Before reviewing the empirical findings, we need to make a few observations regarding the difficulties of doing this type of research.[60] The study of price movements and the pricing

Exhibit 8.5   Capital Market Line

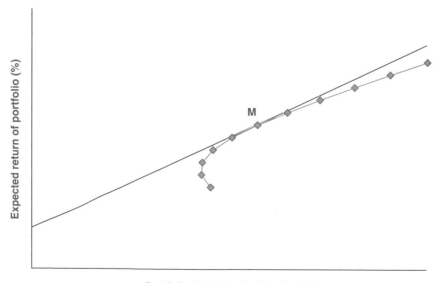

Portfolio risk (standard deviation)

mechanism in any market is an imposing task. Determining cause and effect between information and security prices is especially difficult because new information is continuously arriving. Since the set of information affecting security prices is large, it is difficult to isolate the effects of one piece of information. Furthermore, we are examining only a relatively small group of investors—those at the margin who influence stock prices. This difficulty means that the tests are going to be somewhat crude rather than precise.[61] The research should be examined with this in mind. Failure to find evidence of information content should thus be interpreted cautiously, for the methodology is not always capable of detecting information content. For this reason, the stronger evidence from efficient-markets research exists when there is information content rather than where there is none.

Another weakness of capital market research is that it is a joint test of both market efficiency and the model used to estimate the abnormal returns. The absence of price responses is usually interpreted to mean that the information tested has no information content. This interpretation is correct only if the market is efficient *and* if the model used is correct. But what if the market is inefficient or if the model used is incorrect? In either case, there is no way of determining what the absence of a price response means. This is another reason why the research findings are much stronger when there is evidence of information content.

A final point is that market-based research necessarily considers only the *aggregate* effect of individual investor decision making. That is, the role of accounting information vis-à-vis an individual investor's decision making is implicitly modeled as a black box: An "event," occurs, and the effect of this event is then inferred from whether there was an aggregate (market) reaction.

Overview of Capital Markets Research in Accounting

Kothari provides an excellent review of the literature on capital market research in accounting.[62] The main areas of interest for capital markets research in accounting deal with fundamental analysis and valuation, tests of market efficiency relating to accounting information, and the value relevance of financial reporting. We focus on the first two areas.

In an efficient market, the value of the firm is equal to the present value of the future expected net cash flows. From a valuation perspective, the firm's financial statements are useful to the extent that they are helpful in forecasting future cash flows. Fundamental analysis deals with using economic information, including the information contained in the firm's financial statements, to forecast future cash flows and estimate the firm's intrinsic value (inherent economic value).

Given that security prices serve as a mechanism to allocate resources, the informational efficiency of financial markets is of utmost importance. Short-term event studies have long been the staple for analyzing the degree to which markets are efficient. Long-horizon event studies and cross-sectional tests have increased the number of research opportunities.[63] *Association studies* test for correlation between some accounting performance measure and stock returns. In general, the point of these tests is to determine if and how rapidly accounting information is reflected in security prices. As we have mentioned previously, it is sometimes difficult to attribute a market reaction to a piece of accounting information as market participants may have access to other, timelier sources of information. For example, some of the information contained in annual reports is revealed long before the report is published.

Early studies provided evidence that there is information content in earnings announcements, but the market's reaction may not be fully and immediately reflected in security prices. Furthermore, accounting information is not necessarily the timeliest source of data affecting security prices.

Later research focused on methodological research, alternative performance measures, valuation and fundamental analysis, and tests of market efficiency. There is evidence that accounting information is not always immediately and fully reflected in security prices. From both an academic and investor perspective, the research in the area of fundamental analysis is particularly intriguing owing to the economic implications of "mounting evidence that suggests capital markets might be informationally inefficient and the prices might take years before they fully reflect available information."[64] However, Kothari notes that additional work must be done to improve research design and develop refutable theories of market inefficiency.

The null hypothesis for much of the capital markets research in accounting has been that the market fully and instantaneously adjusts to new information; the market price is equal to the security's intrinsic value. This "umpire view" of the market is an extreme view and may not hold up. Lee provides an intriguing and practical alternative:

A naive view of market efficiency, in which price is assumed to equal fundamental value, is an inadequate conceptual starting point for future market-related research. . . . It is an over simplification that fails to capture the richness of market pricing dynamics and the process of price discovery. Prices do not adjust to fundamental value instantly by fiat. Price convergence toward fundamental value is better characterized as a process, which is accomplished through the interplay between noise traders and information arbitrageurs. This process requires time and effort, and is only achieved at substantial cost to society.[65]

Furthermore, Lee suggests that we have been asking the wrong questions:

We need to unshackle ourselves from the notion that price is equal to value. That is, we should begin thinking about fundamental value and the current market price as two distinct measures. . . . Rather than assuming market efficiency, we should study how, when, and why price becomes efficient (and why at other times it fails to do so). Rather than ignoring the current market price, we should seek to improve it.[66]

The Value of Accounting Information: Evidence From Return Data

Information Contents of Earnings Announcements

The strongest evidence from capital market research concerns the information content of annual accounting earnings numbers. The seminal study, published in 1968, showed that the direction of change in reported accounting earnings (from the prior year) was positively correlated with security price movements.[67] The study also found that the price movements anticipated the earnings results and that there was virtually no abnormal price movement one month after the earnings were announced. This is consistent with the semistrong form of the efficient-markets hypothesis. A later study showed that the *magnitude* as well as *direction* of unexpected earnings are associated with changes in security prices.[68] Quarterly earnings announcements have also shown the same general results.[69]

These results are not surprising. We would expect accounting income to be part of the information used by investors in assessing risk and return. Capital market research has confirmed an almost self-evident proposition. The findings are important, though, in formally linking accounting information with investment decisions and hence with usefulness to investors.

Market Reaction to Alternative Accounting Policies

A more complex type of securities-price research has examined the effect of alternative accounting policies on security prices. The initial purpose of these tests was to investigate the so-called naive-investor hypothesis. Research has found that security prices respond to accounting income numbers. Alternative accounting policies—for example, flexibility in the choice of depreciation and inventory methods—can affect net income. Although these methods affect reported earnings, there is no apparent impact on company cash flows. These types of accounting alternatives simply represent different patterns of expense recognition or cost allocations.

The question of interest to researchers is whether alternative accounting policies have a systematic effect on security prices. If security prices do respond to income levels that differ solely because of alternative accounting methods, with no cash flow consequences, then there is support for the naive-investor hypothesis. On the other hand, if security prices do not respond to such artificial book-income differences, then there is evidence that investors in the market are sophisticated and able to see through such superficial bookkeeping differences.

Exhibit 8.6   Estimation of Equation 8.15

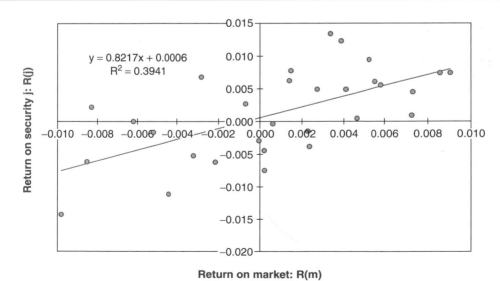

Return on market: R(m)

Virtually all the initial research was interpreted as rejecting the naive-investor hypothesis. However, some research findings have challenged some of the earlier conclusions and reopened what was once considered a closed issue in accounting research.[70]

Alternatives With No Known Cash Flow Consequences

Several studies have compared companies using different accounting methods. One of the earliest studies compared companies using accelerated versus straight-line depreciation methods.[71] The two groups of companies had different accounting income numbers because they used alternative depreciation methods; thus there were differences in income between the two groups of companies owing to the use of alternative depreciation accounting methods. There were also differences in price–earnings multiples between the two groups. Companies using accelerated methods had lower earnings but higher price–earnings multiples than companies using straight-line. However, when earnings of companies using accelerated methods were adjusted to a straight-line depreciation basis, the price–earnings multiple between the two groups of companies was not significantly different.

The assessments of the companies in the market did not appear to be affected by arbitrary and alternative accounting income numbers. This finding is often expressed as the market not being "fooled" by arbitrary accounting differences. Other similar research has supported this conclusion. Additional areas tested include purchase versus pooling accounting, expensing versus capitalizing research and development costs, and recognition versus deferral of unrealized holding gains on marketable securities.[72]

A related area of investigation concerns security price responses to a reported change in accounting policy by a company. Changes in depreciation policy have been researched, and there is no evidence that the change per se affects security prices.[73] Another area tested has been a change from the deferral to flow-through method of accounting for the investment

Exhibit 8.7   Graph Showing Full and Immediate Adjustment to an Event

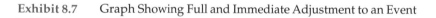

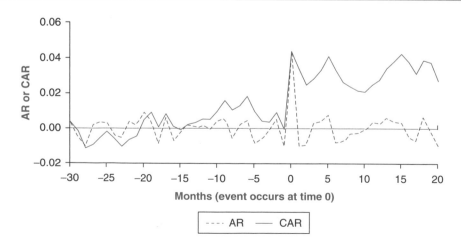

Exhibit 8.8   Graph Showing Incomplete Adjustment to an Event

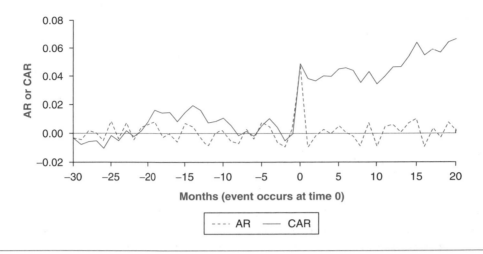

credit.[74] Again, no price effects were found. Although changes in accounting policies may cause the income number to change (solely because of the policy change), these research studies have not found that security prices respond to the changes. Higher accounting income achieved solely from a change in accounting policy with no apparent real changes in underlying cash flows does not appear to fool the market.

Evidence from the type of research discussed in the preceding paragraphs supports the claim that there is no information content in accounting policy changes, at least where there are no apparent underlying changes in cash flows. This finding has also been interpreted as a rejection of the naive-investor hypothesis. Investors appear to adjust accounting income to compensate for artificial bookkeeping differences with no real substance. That is, investors do not appear to respond mechanistically and naively to changes in reported accounting income numbers. Thus, early research appeared to be in line with the semistrong form of the EMH.

An Alternative With Cash Flow Consequences: The LIFO Choice

One type of change in accounting policy that does produce a security price response is a change from FIFO to LIFO inventory accounting. Changes to LIFO have been associated with a positive security price movement, even though LIFO lowers accounting income in a period of rising inventory prices.[75] Given the apparent sophistication of investors in other areas of accounting policy differences, what can be the logical explanation for these price responses? The suggested reason for the price response is that LIFO must be adopted for financial statement purposes if the tax benefit is desired. In a period of rising prices, tax expense will be lower for companies that use LIFO, in which case there are real cash flow consequences owing to the change in accounting policy. Even though book income is lowered by the use of LIFO, cash flows are higher because the taxable income is lower. Positive security price responses are therefore consistent with an increase in the value of the firm due to tax savings.

Later studies, however, contradicted these findings concerning the effect of the changes.[76] These studies either found no evidence of price response or found evidence of a negative price response. The more recent studies suggest that the earlier research may have failed to isolate the real effect of the LIFO change because of a *self-selection bias*. (Companies selected because of a LIFO change could have also been experiencing other positive events, which may have been the actual cause of the positive price response.) Since LIFO lowers accounting book income, a negative price response could be interpreted as a mechanistic response to a lower accounting number by naive investors, who did not consider the positive cash flow consequences of lower taxes.

More recent studies find support for a positive security price movement when LIFO was adopted. Pincus and Wasley examined LIFO adoptions from 1978 to 1987 and found evidence for the possibility that LIFO is a "good news" signaling event that could account for the positive security price movement presumably resulting from its adoption.[77] On the other hand, Kang brings up the possibility of potentially high adoption costs relative to LIFO, such as accounting system changes and a higher probability of violating debt contract provisions (e.g., lower current asset ratios and higher debt-to-equity ratios) and renegotiation of management contracts involving bonus arrangements.[78] These factors might account for some of the negative price reactions since they might offset the future tax savings.

As discussed at the beginning of this section, security price research is extremely difficult to conduct. The LIFO choice issue amply illustrates this point. The early LIFO research rejected the naive-investor hypothesis. Later research on the LIFO question reopened what was once thought to be a closed issue with respect to market efficiency. However, more recent research shows how complex the issue of LIFO adoption may be. The more recent research on LIFO adoption has begun focusing on indirect cash flow consequences, which we examine next.

Alternatives With Indirect Cash Consequences

Security price research has been probing a more subtle issue referred to as indirect consequences. An *indirect consequence* occurs when an accounting policy change affects the value of the firm through an indirect effect on owners rather than a direct effect on company cash flows. One such study was motivated by an attempt to explain why securities prices of certain oil and gas companies responded negatively to a mandatory change in accounting policy.[79] The required change from full costing to successful efforts was regarded as simply a change in how exploration costs are allocated to the income statement. Therefore, it was expected that no security price response would be evident since there was no direct cash flow consequence to the companies.

However, security price responses were found to exist. Since previous research had predominantly rejected the naive-investor hypothesis, a search was made for the existence of some indirect cash flow consequences to explain the price response. The study posited that a change to successful efforts accounting for oil and gas exploration costs lowered firms' ability to pay dividends in the short term because of restrictive debt covenants. Therefore, even though the change in accounting policy appeared to affect only book income on the surface, there were indirect cash flow consequences to investors, which might explain the negative price response. This explanation derives from agency theory. When accounting numbers are used to monitor agency contracts, there can be indirect consequences from changes in accounting policies. In the case of debt covenants restricting dividend payments, accounting numbers are used to protect the security of bondholders at the expense of stockholders. If an accounting policy change lowers accounting income (as could occur in a mandatory change to successful efforts), present or future cash dividends could be reduced, causing a negative price response.[80]

A similar type of study found negative security price responses for firms using purchase accounting when pooling was restricted by the Accounting Principles Board (APB) in favor of purchase accounting for combinations.[81] Differences between purchase and pooling accounting appear on the surface to affect only book income, with no real cash effects. However, the reduced use of pooling accounting could affect dividend distribution because of debt covenants. Income would normally be lower under purchase accounting than pooling, and the same effect of dividend restrictions as argued in the oil and gas study were also argued in the purchase/pooling study.

Another study along these lines examined the requirement to capitalize leases that had previously been reported as operating leases.[82] Although there was some evidence of negative price responses for certain companies, the price response could have been caused by the constraints imposed by the existence of debt covenants.

Anomalies

Over longer periods of time, financial markets appear to be informationally efficient. How rapidly and completely they respond to new information is an open question. While it is difficult to prove with certainty, there is convincing evidence that markets may not be as efficient as postulated in the semistrong form of the efficient-markets hypothesis.

Lags in Processing Fundamental Data

In a very extensive study, Ou and Penman examined the utility of fundamental analysis. *Fundamental analysis* assumes that securities markets are inefficient and that underpriced shares can be found by means of financial statement analysis. This view is directly opposed to the efficient-markets view that prices of securities fully and rapidly reflect all publicly available information (the semistrong form of the hypothesis).

Ou and Penman used traditional accounting measures such as return on total assets, gross margin ratio, and percentage change in current assets in a multivariate model to predict whether the following year's income would increase or decrease. Using data for the period between 1965 and 1977, the model included almost 20 accounting measures and reflected approximately 23,000 observations.[83] Ou and Penman were able to describe the following year's earnings changes correctly almost 80% of the time.[84] The key point concerns whether their predictors were capturing information that was already reflected in security prices (indicating an efficient market) or were predicting future earnings based on analysis of the accounting measures previously mentioned. The latter situation would result in abnormal security returns if investment were based on their predictions.

Ou and Penman's analysis did indeed produce abnormal returns.[85] They also believed that the excess security returns were not attributable to excess risk factors.[86] Ou and Penman's research thus suggests that markets are not as efficient as efficient-markets advocates would like to believe; fundamental analysis is still important for investment purposes. This study also suggests that "better" accounting standards might improve the predictive ability of accounting information.

Low Correlation Between Earnings and Stock Returns

Lev concentrated on an issue that is complementary to the factors in the Ou and Penman study. Specifically, his point is that both over time and within years (cross-sectional studies), the correlation between earnings numbers and stock returns has been exceedingly low.[87] In other words, earnings have very little explanatory power (as measured by R^2, the coefficient of correlation) relative to changes in stock prices. Lev believes that one of the principal reasons for this situation lies with the low quality of reported income numbers:

> Research on the quality of earnings shifts the focus to an explicit consideration of accounting issues by calling for a systematic examination of the extent to which the specific principles underlying accounting measurements and valuations, as well as managerial manipulations, detract from the usefulness of earnings and other financial variables. Such research has the potential both to further our understanding of the role of financial information in asset valuation and to contribute meaningfully to accounting policymaking.[88]

Lev and the Ou and Penman papers are complementary. Lev finds a low explanatory relationship between earnings and stock returns while Ou and Penman see a predictive role for accounting data in an imperfectly efficient market. Lev focuses directly on the issue of improving accounting measurements while the Ou and Penman's work seems to imply this point.[89]

Post-Earnings-Announcement Drift

Further questions concerning market efficiency have arisen over the phenomenon known as *post-earnings-announcement drift.* While markets do react significantly at the time of the earnings announcement, it takes up to 60 days for the full effect of earnings announcements to be impounded in security prices.[90] This effect appears to be more pronounced for smaller firms.[91] It also appears that earnings surprises have a more persistent effect when the earnings surprise is due to higher revenue surprises than to lower expense surprises.[92]

This anomaly has not escaped the notice of professional investors. Transient institutions—those actively trading to maximize short-term profits—appear to be able to exploit post-earnings-announcement drift. Ke and Ramalingegowda find that these institutions are able to earn a three-month mean abnormal return of 5.1% (or 22% annually) net of transactions costs from their arbitrage trades.[93]

At least part of the blame for post-earnings-announcement drift has been laid at the feet of financial analysts. Abarbanell and Bushee concluded that financial analysts underreact to very fundamental signals stemming from securities, which in turn lead to forecast errors and incomplete security price adjustments.[94] Sloan found evidence that shareholders do not distinguish well between cash flow portions of earnings and the accrual segment thereof.[95]

The cash flow portion persists longer into the future and is less subject to manipulation than the accrual part of earnings. Another possibility is that in some cases, transaction costs are too high relative to the potential gain that can be earned from the mispricing of the securities. Although securities markets may be "efficient," they may not be as efficient as once believed. This suggests that it is even more important to attempt to improve the quality of accounting standards.[96]

Finally, Mikhail, Walther, and Willis examine if analyst experience is related to post-earnings-announcement drift. Experience matters. Financial markets are more efficient in the presence of experienced financial analysts, and the effect is not trivial:

> The results . . . indicate the average magnitude of the post-earnings-announcement drift is reduced by approximately 18 percent . . . when the experience level of the analysts following the firm increases from the lowest decile to the highest decile.[97]

Mispricing Related to Accruals

Richardson et al. focus on the reliability of accounting numbers. They develop a comprehensive definition and categorization of accruals, decomposing accruals into broad balance sheet categories. They use their "knowledge of the measurement issues underlying each accrual category to make qualitative assessments concerning the relative reliability of each category."[98] They then analyze the persistence of the cash flow and accrual components of earnings. Finally, they analyze the abnormal returns for the firms' common stock to determine if the market impounds the information contained in various accruals as it relates to earnings persistence. If the information contained in accrual reliability is impounded in stock prices, accruals and future abnormal stock returns should be independent of each other.

Interestingly, they find that the less reliable the accruals, the lower the earnings persistence. More importantly, and somewhat unsettling, they find that the market does not fully price the less reliable accruals: "Overall, the results are consistent with the naive investor hypothesis. Future stock returns are negatively related to accruals, and the negative relation is stronger for less reliable accruals."[99]

Furthermore, their findings underscore the importance of distinguishing between earnings and free cash flow:

> The standard textbook definition of free cash flow adjusts earnings by adding back depreciation and amortization and subtracting changes in working capital and capital expenditures. . . . The accruals that we find to be the least reliable correspond closely to the adjustments that are made to earnings in arriving at free cash flow. Free cash flow represents a combination of actual cash flows plus the relatively reliable financing accruals.[100]

Liu and Qi provide evidence that the potential mispricing of accruals is substantial. They form companies into portfolios based on total accruals and the "probability of information"–based trading (PIN). A hedge strategy formed by investing in the lowest accrual decile and selling short the highest accrual decile, and confined to high PIN stocks, yielded an annualized abnormal return of almost 19%.[101]

Chan et al. examine three explanations of why accruals predict stock returns: manipulation, changing prospects, and overoptimistic expectations. The bulk of the evidence alludes to managers' manipulation of earnings:

> A large increase in accruals marks a sharp turning point in the fortunes of a company. . . . In the year in which accruals are high . . . earnings show no weakness but continue to grow rapidly. These patterns suggest that firms with high accruals already face symptoms of a cooling in their growth, but they use creative accounting to delay reporting the bad news.[102]

The Incomplete Revelation Hypothesis

Questions concerning market efficiency (or the lack thereof) have coalesced into a new hypothesis, the *incomplete revelation hypothesis* (IRH). Bloomfield sees two principal reasons for the IRH.[103] First, some accounting numbers or relationships are more difficult or costly to uncover and their effects may not be fully revealed in security prices. For example, historically, information about stock option "expense" was revealed in footnote information only as opposed to being in the body of the income statement.[104] Hence, the information and its import may be more difficult to extract in footnote form, and it might take longer for this information to fully impact security prices. This is diametrically opposed to the efficient-markets hypothesis that disclosure—in whatever form—is all that is needed to fully impact security prices.

The second factor of the IRH is the presence of "noise traders" in the market. *Noise traders* are individuals who do not necessarily respond in a completely rational way to new information. They may be rebalancing their portfolios, responding to liquidity shocks, or even acting upon whims.[105] Thus, from the perspective of information effects on security prices, we have a group of individuals who are responding to a different set of criteria. This "distraction" impedes the market from responding in a fully efficient manner. Finally, notice that the IRH is not only fully consistent with post-earnings-announcement drift. However, it may help to explain that particular phenomenon.

Accounting Information and Risk Assessment

Capital market research has also investigated the usefulness of accounting numbers for assessing the risk of securities and portfolios. These studies have found high correlations between the variability of accounting earnings and beta, the market-risk measure.[106] The high correlations imply that accounting data may be useful for assessing risk, or at least confirming it.

Other research has tried to determine if alternative accounting policies have any effect on risk. The purpose of this type of research is to identify how alternative accounting policies or disclosures may affect the usefulness of accounting numbers for assessing risk. For example, one study tried to determine if unfunded pension benefits (reported in footnotes) affected beta.[107] There was no significant impact. From this evidence, it might be concluded that pension information is not useful for risk assessments. However, other studies found that supplemental segment (line of business) disclosures resulted in a revision of systematic risk, which suggests that such information is useful for risk assessments.[108]

Other studies have tested the association of financial ratios with beta.[109] Some of the ratios and computations tested include dividend payout ratio, leverage, growth rates, asset size, liquidity, and pretax interest coverage, as well as earnings and earnings variability. In general, these tests indicate a strong association between the accounting-based ratios and beta.

Summary of Capital Market Research

We draw the following conclusions from the empirical evidence provided by capital market research:

- Accounting earnings appear to have information content and to affect security prices.
- Alternative accounting policies with no apparent direct or indirect cash flow consequences to the firm do not seem to affect security prices.
- Alternative accounting policies that have direct or indirect cash flow consequences to the firm (or its owners) do affect security prices.
- There is evidence that security markets do not react fully and instantaneously to certain types of accounting data in certain situations (e.g., high accruals, small stocks, low analyst coverage).
- There are incentives to choose certain accounting policies, where choice exists, owing to indirect cash consequences.
- Accounting-based risk measures correlate with market risk measures, suggesting that accounting numbers are useful for risk assessment.

Capital market research continues to be useful in empirically evaluating economic consequences of accounting policies vis-à-vis security prices and the usefulness of accounting numbers for risk-and-return assessments. Perhaps more than anything else, though, the impact of capital market research is that it brought a different perspective to accounting theory and policy at a time when the emphasis was primarily on deductively based theory.

Evidence From Survey Data

Another way of determining the usefulness of accounting information is to directly ask investors how (if at all) they use annual reports. Surveys of investors have been undertaken in several countries and generally have shown a rather low readership of accounting information.[110] Approximately one-half of the investors surveyed indicated they read financial statements. Institutional investors have shown a much higher level of readership.[111] These surveys, particularly of individual investors, should be interpreted cautiously, however. Individual investors may rely on investment analysts to process accounting information. It would be simplistic to assume accounting information has no usefulness to investors merely because many individual stockholders do not read annual reports in detail.

Another type of survey research has asked investors to weigh the importance of different types of investment information, including accounting information. Several studies of this type have been reported.[112] Accounting information ranks fairly high in importance in these surveys, though not at the top. This status seems to be attributable to the historical nature of accounting information and the reporting-lag effect. More timely accounting information from company press releases, and nonaccounting information such as general economic conditions and company announcements on products and markets, rank ahead of annual reports in perceived importance.

The Value of Accounting Information: Evidence From Direct Valuation

The research discussed in the previous section primarily examined the relationship between accounting data and unexpected changes in stock prices, measured as *abnormal returns*. Another approach has been to examine the association between accounting data reported in annual financial statements and the *levels* of stock prices (i.e., firm valuation, measured as market capitalization).[113] Conceptually, this approach, which is referred to as *cross-sectional valuation*, attempts to empirically estimate the theoretical model of equity valuation described at the beginning of this chapter. This approach has been used to investigate how (if at all) specific components of the financial statements are "priced" in the sense of being associated with the market valuation of the firm. If an item is priced as an asset/revenue, it should normally have a positive relation to market value, whereas if the item is priced as a liability/expense it should normally have a negative relation with market value. A number of authors have expressed enthusiasm for this methodology as a framework for evaluating the merits of alternative accounting methods/valuations.[114]

Evidence From Pensions

Several studies have used this framework to determine that a firm's pension plan assets and liabilities (as reported off balance sheet in footnote disclosures) are consistent with their being viewed as *on*-balance-sheet assets and liabilities, respectively.[115] Another study determined that components of pension expense (per SFAS No. 87) are not weighted equally in terms of their association with market valuation.[116] Of particular interest is that the transitional asset amortization component of pension expense was implicitly valued at zero, which is consistent with the fact that there are no cash flows associated with the item.

Franzoni and Marín present evidence that the market significantly overvalues firms with severely underfunded defined benefit pension plans. Furthermore, the effects of the overvaluation persist for a long time.

> In particular, we show that the portfolio with the most underfunded firms earns low raw returns relative to portfolios of firms with healthier pension plans. This phenomenon persists for at least 5 years after the emergence of the large underfunding. Also, the risk-adjusted returns of this portfolio are significantly negative. The magnitude of the discount in returns is around 10% annually.[117]

While investors may recognize the severe underfunding, it is possible that they may not be adequately factoring in the *implications* of that underfunding, such as difficulty in refinancing at favorable terms or refinancing at all. Companies can postpone the recognition of the pension liability of its earnings, and the underfunding eventually impacts the firm's future earnings. Franzoni and Marín also find that a severely underfunded pension is associated with higher leverage, which also constrains the ability of the firm to undertake value-enhancing investments.

One may debate whether poor operating performance and suboptimal investment decisions leads to severe underfunding, or whether poor management of the pension fund in the form of severe underfunding eventually leads to poor operating performance and suboptimal investment decisions. In any case, it appears that investors do not fully recognize that the severe underfunding has negative valuation effects. Why this happens is yet to be resolved.

Evidence From Research and Development

Another study examined the association of research and development (R&D) expenditures with firm value. The major finding was that, on average, each dollar of R&D was associated with a five-dollar increase in market value.[118] This result provides evidence that the market is implicitly capitalizing R&D outlays even though SFAS No. 2 prohibits explicit capitalization. In other words, the market interprets R&D as an asset (investment) rather than an expense, contrary to the accounting treatment required by SFAS No. 2.[119]

Evidence From Financial Services

The financial services industry is another area in which cross-sectional valuation models have been used. Studies have examined supplemental disclosures of nonperforming loans (default risk) and interest rate risk in banks and thrifts.[120] Nonperforming loans are negatively associated with firm value, though this effect is greater for banks than for thrifts. Interest rate risk was negatively associated with firm value only for banks. Another study reported that banks' supplemental disclosure of the fair market value of investment securities is associated with market value over and above that explained by historical costs *alone.* This finding gives credence to the SEC's and FASB's recent push for mark-to-market accounting and eventually to fair value measurement in SFAS No. 157.[121]

Accounting Data and Creditors

Theories underlying the usefulness of accounting information to creditors are not as well developed as is the role of accounting numbers vis-à-vis stock prices. Part of the problem is that interest-bearing debt securities trade infrequently. It is, however, generally agreed that the price of interest-bearing debt is based on the *default risk premium*, which is defined as the premium in excess of the risk-free interest rate on otherwise identical debt (for example, U.S. Treasury obligations). Thus, firm-specific information, including accounting data, aids creditors in assessing default risk.

Several distinct lines of research have emerged: (a) the usefulness of accounting data in predicting corporate bankruptcy (which encompasses loan default); (b) the association of accounting data with bond ratings wherein such ratings are presumed to proxy for default risk; (c) the association of accounting data with estimates of interest-rate risk premiums on debt; and (d) experimental studies of the role of accounting data in lending decisions. We will present a brief overview of the research findings for the first two.

Evidence From Bankruptcies

Accounting-based ratios have been very useful in discriminating between firms that subsequently went bankrupt and those that did not.[122] Bankrupt companies tend to have financial ratios prior to bankruptcy that differ from nonbankrupt companies. Predictability up to five years prior to bankruptcy has been demonstrated. These findings do not mean that companies with "bad" ratios will necessarily go bankrupt in the future, but rather that bankruptcy is more probable.

Evidence From Credit Ratings

Accounting data are also associated with both bond ratings and default risk premiums.[123] Among the important ratios are profitability, earnings variability, and leverage. Research has also been used to evaluate which of alternative sets of accounting data are more highly associated with bankruptcy prediction, bond ratings, and risk premiums. Among the issues examined have been historical cost versus price-level adjusted income, the effect of lease capitalization versus noncapitalization, and recognition of pension liabilities versus footnote-only disclosure.[124]

Experimental (laboratory) studies have also tested the usefulness of accounting data for creditors. Accounting data in the context of a loan-related decision (for example, loan amount, bankruptcy prediction, and interest rates) are provided to subjects to determine how, if at all, it affects their hypothetical decisions.[125] In these experiments, the accounting data are manipulated to see if the judgments are sensitive to whatever manipulations take place. For example, changes are made to the magnitudes of accounting ratios or financial statements prepared under alternative policies (for example, lease capitalization versus noncapitalization). Generally, these studies support the sensitivity of loan-related decision making to key accounting data and, in this sense, complement the findings based on economic field data.

Importance of Earnings Forecasting

Copeland and Dolgoff examine the relationship between the annual total return to shareholders and several commonly used performance measures (sales, earnings per share, growth in earnings per share, forecasts of earnings, etc.) They used data about analyst expectations as a proxy for investor expectations. The highest correlation (47%) was between the "annual return to shareholders and changes during the year in *expectations* [italics added] about the same year's earnings, the following year's earnings, and earnings three to five years out."[126] This highlights the importance of business performance, measured by accounting data, relative to market expectations. The researchers also note that that the importance of expectations is "consistent with a discounted cash flow view of the world . . ."

As we noted previously, the residual income model provides a central role for future earnings forecasts in determining the intrinsic value of a stock.[127] Accurate estimates might lead to abnormal stock returns. Indeed, there is evidence that better earnings forecasts make for wealthier investors. Loh and Mian examine the usefulness of accurate earnings forecasts from security analysts. Each firm-year, they sort analysts based on the accuracy of their forecasts of annual earnings. If analysts with the best earnings forecasts provide the best returns, there is support for fundamental analysis of accounting data. Loh and Mian note: "If the analysts with the most profitable recommendations also exhibit superior forecasting skills, it would suggest that their stock-picking ability is real, and that it is founded on economic rationale."[128]

They find that the "recommendations of superior earnings forecasters significantly outperform the recommendations of inferior forecasters."[129] This is consistent with the value of fundamental accounting analysis.[130] It also raises questions about the informational efficiency of financial markets.

While the value of the firm is equal to the present value of the expected future cash flows, earnings appear to play an important role in predicting those cash flows. Dechow, Kothari, and Watts develop a model of operating cash flows and the accounting process by which operating cash flows are converted into accounting earnings. The model explains why "current earnings by itself is a better forecast of future operating cash flows than current operating cash flows by itself."[131] In addition, this prediction was borne out empirically using a sample of 1,337 firms. Furthermore, the forecast ability is a positive function of the firm's expected operating cash cycle.

> Over the years, the relationship between earnings and stock prices has diminished. However, the ability of earnings to forecast future cash flows has not. Kim and Kross examine the ability of earnings to forecast one-year ahead operating cash flows by examining three decades of data (1972–2001). Their findings are positive: "We found an increasing relationship over time between earnings and one-year ahead operating cash flows. . . . Further, we found that the accuracy of cash flow predictions based on current earnings also increased over time."[132]

They hypothesize that changing accounting conservatism might play a role. In any case, we note that the value of a stock is dependent on much more than a one-year cash flow forecast. Clearly, more work needs to be done.

Gulliver provides an analyst's perspective on financial analysis, forecasting, and stock underperformance. He identifies five causes of stock price underperformance: aggressive accounting, financial deterioration, change in the industry or competitive situation, bad acquisitions, and overvaluation. The bad news: Analyzing financial statements can be difficult. The information is contained on three separate statements and in many footnotes. Numerous assumptions are involved, and financial rules are complex and sometimes ambiguous. Finally, in some cases, the financial rules are used to conceal the truth. The good news: There are numerous cases in which "analysts and managers could have identified problem stocks in advance of market reaction by digging deeper into the data with an eye on earnings quality, operating efficiency, cash flow quality, and balance sheet quality."[133]

Empirical Research and Standard Setting

In the early 1970s, some argued that capital market research could be used as a basis for choosing the best accounting policies and evaluating the economic consequences of alternative accounting policies on security prices.[134] Accounting policies that most affected security prices were thought to be most useful. In other words, such policies would have had the most information content. The argument had intuitive appeal, particularly since deductively based research had proved unable to resolve the normative accounting theory debate about the most desirable form of accounting. However, the early advocates of security price research now recognize the limitations of this research for such a use.[135] Reasons for these limitations are the public-good nature of accounting information, the existence of free riders, and the resultant market failure in terms of optimal resource allocation. The potential impact of empirical research on the standard-setting issue recently arose again.

Opinions are mixed on whether empirical research can aid standard setting. Holthausen and Watts have taken the negative position.[136] The main obstacle to them involves the problem of different user groups with different needs, a problem discussed in Chapter 6. For example, creditors might be most interested in predicting debt default. Many standards involve contractual issues, litigation, tax issues, and conservatism (booking loss contingencies and not gain contingencies, for example). Hence, they see empirical studies examining different alternatives and their effect on valuation and cash flow predictions as not providing useful information for standard setters. Holthausen and Watts also believe that before empirical research can be used as inputs for standard-setting purposes, a theory of accounting and standard setting must be set. What the role of such a theory might be is not made explicit. We would also question whether a theory of this type could ever be developed.

Barth, Beaver, and Landsman take the opposite tack.[137] They believe that multiple user groups and diverse uses of accounting information do not prevent empirical research from being useful for standard setters. For example, they cite a study showing that accumulated and projected benefit obligations in pension accounting (Chapter 16) measures the pension liability implicit in security prices more reliably than just the vested benefit obligation (the two former measures give a fuller picture of the pension liability than the latter).

Hence, the difference between the groups involves an empirical issue, which is presently unresolved: the multiple-user-group problem. We lean toward the potential usefulness of empirical research in areas such as valuation and prediction of cash flows as having potential usefulness for standard-setting groups. On the question of diverse user groups with somewhat different purposes, we believe that a complementarity rather than conflict among users results. Indeed, if extreme conflict among user groups and uses existed, we doubt that empirical research would be useful for any purpose.

Summary

This chapter has surveyed the research literature on the usefulness of accounting information to what the FASB calls the *primary* user group of investors and creditors. The picture that emerges is that accounting data are important to investors for valuing securities, assessing the performance of managers, and making loan-related decisions by creditors. There should, however, be no illusions about the relative importance of financial reporting for these external users. For example, unexpected accounting earnings explain only a small percentage (around 5%) of the firm's revaluation vis-à-vis security prices. Although some of this is owing to econometric problems in the research, it is more or less consistent with investor surveys that show accounting information ranking lower in importance than more timely information about the economy, the relevant industry, and the firm itself.

Market efficiency has increasingly come under challenge. There is evidence that it is possible to earn abnormal returns through diligent analysis. In some cases, the information from earnings announcements is not totally or rapidly absorbed into security prices.

Further, although the evidence supports the usefulness of accounting information to this primary user group, we do not really know just how valuable it is. The good news for accountants, analysts, and investors is the systematic evidence that financial reporting and analysis is useful. The bad news is that we still know very little about how useful it is, and we are unable to infer much about the social benefits of the current investment in accounting information production. Nevertheless, we believe that efforts to improve the quality of earnings and other accounting numbers are valid and meaningful.

QUESTIONS

1. How is accounting data useful to investors? To creditors?

2. In what ways do you think information useful for investors (in assessing future cash flows) differs from that useful for creditors (in assessing default risk)?

3. Besides the primary investor–creditor group, what other user groups could claim to be stakeholders in the firm? How might their information needs be the same as the primary investor–creditor group? How might their information needs differ?

4. Who are creditors?

5. Why do we sometimes say that the dividend discount model is actually an earnings model? How do Lintner's findings relate dividends and earnings?

6. What is residual income? Abnormal earnings? Economic profit? EVA?

7. How does EVA differ from economic profit?

8. What are some advantages and disadvantages of using residual income (including economic profit and EVA) for performance measurement?

9. Comment on the following statement: The residual income model is no different from the dividend discount model. Therefore, it has no value to investors and analysts.

10. Comment on the following: Maximizing residual income is the same as maximizing earnings. Managers should be rewarded for maximizing either one.

11. Why do managers of Berkshire Hathaway have an incentive to send cash to Omaha?

12. Should firms capitalize research and development expenditures? Why or why not?

13. What is clean surplus accounting? What is its role in linking dividends and abnormal earnings?

14. What is the efficient-markets hypothesis?

15. Why does the concept of market efficiency (with respect to information) have no necessary relation to the quality of accounting information? Why is this distinction important with respect to accounting policy making?

16. Why is the efficient-markets hypothesis being challenged?

17. What is meant by "information content," and how does capital market research determine the information content of accounting numbers?

18. What is the advantage of being well diversified? Is there a downside? Why or why not?

19. If investors are well diversified (e.g., own several hundred stocks), will they have a greater or lesser need for accounting information? What does this say about diversification?

20. What are some limitations of capital market research?

21. What is an event study?

22. What are abnormal returns (AR) and cumulative abnormal returns (CARs)? What do they have to do with research in accounting? What do they have to do with accounting standards?

23. Explain Lee's (2001) view of market efficiency.

24. Lee (2001) rejects the "naive view" of market efficiency. Explain. If Lee is correct, what are the implications for capital markets research in accounting?

25. For event studies, the post-event window is typically short (days or months). What are some issues associated with examining longer event windows (e.g., years)?

26. What do we mean when we say that capital market research involves a joint test of both market efficiency and the model used to estimate abnormal returns?

27. Describe the general findings from capital market research concerning the information content of accounting numbers and the effects of alternative accounting policies.

28. Why is the choice between the FIFO–LIFO inventory methods an interesting issue in capital market research?

29. As an investor, how would you react to a company changing its inventory accounting from FIFO to LIFO? Why?

30. Over the years, the research findings regarding changing from FIFO to LIFO have varied. Why do you suppose this is the case?

31. Why may accounting policies with no direct cash flow consequences indirectly affect investors or creditors?

32. Why is it argued that capital market research cannot determine the optimality of accounting policies even for the limited investor–creditor group?

33. How do market-level and individual decision-maker analyses complement one another in studying the usefulness of accounting information to investors and creditors?

34. Lev talks about the low correlation between earnings and stock returns. Ou and Penman discuss the possibility of making abnormal returns based on published financial data. Are these papers in conflict with each other or complementary to each other? Why?

35. What is post-earnings-announcement drift?

36. Why does post-earnings-announcement drift challenge the efficient-markets hypothesis?

37. Why does post-earnings-announcement drift appear to be more pronounced with smaller firms? What could be done from a company perspective to rectify this situation? What could be done from a standard setting perspective to mitigate the effects of post-earnings-announcement drift?

38. What is the incomplete revelation hypothesis?

39. Suppose an accounting event occurs and there is no market reaction. What should we conclude?

40. Give some examples in which accounting information is not the most timely source of information affecting security prices.

41. Instead of employing capital markets research techniques (e.g., event studies) why don't we just ask investors how they would react to a hypothetical event? Why don't we ask managers why they make specific accounting changes?

42. Why is it important to improve the quality of accounting standards?

43. What do pensions have to do with a company's operating performance? What do pensions have to do with the firm's financing and investment decisions?

44. There is evidence that investors do not fully recognize the valuation effects of severe pension underfunding. (See, for example, Franzoni and Marín [2006]). Why do you suppose this is the case? What changes could be made to mitigate this problem?

45. Why are accounting ratios valuable for predicting bankruptcy? What cautions do we need in evaluating accounting ratios?

46. Accounting earnings are useful in predicting one-year-ahead cash flows. Is this sufficient? Why or why not?

47. Why do high levels of accruals appear to be mispriced?

CASES, PROBLEMS, AND WRITING ASSIGNMENTS

1. The usefulness of accounting data to investors and creditors for *predictive* purposes is necessarily forward looking. However, under generally accepted accounting principles, financial statements are constructed primarily as an historical record.

Required:

a. What limitation does this impose on the usefulness of financial statements for predictive purposes, and how is this limitation evident from the research reviewed in the chapter?

b. Provide examples of important forward-looking events that either are not reported in financial statements or are not reported in a timely manner.

c. Why may the feedback value of audited financial statements make them very important to investors and creditors even though predictive value is not necessarily high?

2. A retail company begins operations late in 2000 by purchasing $600,000 of merchandise. There are no sales in 2000. During 2001, additional merchandise of $3,000,000 is purchased. Operating expenses (excluding management bonuses) are $400,000, and sales are $6,000,000. The management compensation agreement provides for incentive bonuses totaling 1% of after-tax income (before the bonuses). Taxes are 25%, and accounting and taxable income will be the same.

The company is undecided about the selection of the LIFO or FIFO inventory methods. For the year ended 2001, ending inventory would be $700,000 and $1,000,000, respectively, under LIFO and FIFO.

Required:

a. How are accounting numbers used to monitor this agency contract between owners and managers?
b. Evaluate management incentives to choose LIFO versus FIFO.
c. Assuming an efficient capital market, what effect should the alternative policies have on security prices and shareholder wealth?
d. Why is the management compensation agreement potentially counterproductive as an agency-monitoring mechanism?
e. Devise an alternative bonus system to avoid the problem in the existing plan.

CRITICAL THINKING AND ANALYSIS

1. How do you think the efficient-markets hypothesis should impact upon the drafting of accounting standards? Bear in mind that many questions have been raised about the efficient-markets hypothesis itself.

Notes

1. *FASB (1978, paras. 24–30).*

2. *Management might be considered another user group. Sometimes this user group has a "dark side." If their compensation depends on net income, managers might attempt to manipulate the financial statements to serve their own purpose. See Graham, Harvey, and Rajgopal (2006). We will return to this problem later. Earnings management is discussed in Chapter 12.*

3. *While not considered a primary user group, employees certainly have a major interest in the financial well-being of the firm. This even extends to potential employees. Would you want to accept a job with a firm in financial distress?*

4. *We ignore any conflicts of interest between shareholders and debt holders that might occur in the presence of financial distress. Hence, actions that maximize the value of the firm benefit all investors.*

5. *Capital allocation (investment) decisions are long-term decisions and are not easily reversed. In his 1987 letter to shareholders, Warren Buffett notes: "After ten years on the job, a CEO whose company annually retains earnings equal to 10% of net worth will have been responsible for the deployment of more than 60% of all the capital at work in the business."*

6. *The typical maturity for corporate bonds is in the 10–30 year range. However, the maturities sometimes extend well beyond that. In July 1993, Walt Disney sold $300 million of 100-year bonds. Coca-Cola Co. followed by selling $150 million of 100-year bonds. In November 1995, BellSouth sold 100-year bonds.*

7. *Lintner (1956).*

8. *This model is often called the "Gordon Model" after Myron Gordon, who popularized its use. See Gordon (1962).*

9. *Beaver (1998, Chapter 4).*

10. *Miller and Modigliani (1961); see also Fama and Miller (1972).*

11. *Miller and Rock (1985).*

12. *See the preface to FASB (1978).*

13. *Beaver (1998, p. 81).*

14. *See Bowen, Burgstahler, and Daley (1986) and Greenberg, Johnson, and Ramesh (1986), for example.*

15. *Rayburn (1986), Bernard and Stober (1989), Livnat and Zarowin (1990), and Neill, Schaefer, Bahnson, and Bradbury (1991).*

16. *Beaver (1998, pp. 48–49) referred to this effect as permanent earnings. See also Lintner (1956). Studies investigating cross-sectional differences in the earnings-price relationship (i.e., earnings response coefficients) have used the term "persistence of earnings changes" (e.g. Collins and Kothari [1989], Easton and Zmijewski [1989], Kormendi and Lipe [1987]).*

17. *Feltham et al. (2004, p. 84) note that the term "residual income" was "coined by General Electric to gauge the performance of its decentralized divisions."*

18. *EVA® is registered trademark of Stern Stewart & Co. and may be considered a proprietary form of economic profit. Henceforth, we drop the symbol for the registered trademark and simply use EVA.*

19. *This is the most common usage of the term "residual income" we have encountered. See, for example, Dechow, Hutton, and Sloan (1999). However, we have also seen applications to operating income and invested capital called residual income.*

20. *Net cash flows are equal to the cash generated by the firm, less the amount reinvested in net operating working capital, property, plant, and equipment, etc. In the context of a firm, net cash flows are often called free cash flows. See Chapter 13 for a detailed discussion of free cash flows.*

21. *However, see our discussion of WorldCom in Chapter 13 for a different situation.*

22. *The provision for taxes listed on the income statement is based on taxable income and not on net operating profits only.*

23. *See Koller, Goedhart, and Wessels (2005) for an excellent presentation of using economic profit to value a firm. The concept of economic profit is not new. Koller, Goedhert, and Wessels (p. 63) trace the concept back to economist Alfred Marshall, who discussed it in his famed textbook,* Principles of Economics, *published in 1890.*

24. *See Koller, Goedhart, and Wessels (2005, p. 713).*

25. *See Stewart (2003, p. 65).*

26. *Young (1999).*

27. *Ohlson (1995) and Feltham and Ohlson (1995).*

28. *For example, if an analyst knew that abnormal earnings were extremely high or extremely low, and were mean reverting, he or she could use this information to create better forecasts of residual income. See discussion of Dechow, Hutton, and Sloan (1999).*

29. *Ibid. (p. 2).*

30. *Ibid.*

31. *Beaver (1998, pp. 78–80).*

32. *See Qiang (2005, p. 86).*

33. *For an overview of using residual income as a performance measure, see Chapter 12 of Brealey, Myers, and Allen (2006).*

34. *See Stewart (2003, p. 66–67).*

35. *Buffett (1994). Contrast Buffett's two-way application of a bonus system to the one-way application of stock options; a manager cannot lose with stock options.*

36. *See Stewart (2003). For a different opinion, see Benston (2003).*

37. *Rogerson (1997).*

38. *See Feltham et al. (2004). However, note that even in the best of circumstances, the R2s for this study are under 11%.*

39. *For prediction problems relative to estimating residual income, see Myers (1999).*

40. *Pfeiffer (2004).*

41. *Chen and Dodd (1997). Dodd and Chen (1996) find that EVA accounts for about 20% of the variation in stock returns as compared to the return on assets, which explains over 24%.*

42. *Dodd and Johns (1999.*

43. *Copeland and Dolgoff (2006, p. 82). This finding is also supported by Koller, Goodhart, and Wessels (2005, pp. 76–78). Tsuji (2006) reports similar findings for Japanese firms. See also Chen and Dodd (1997) and Dodd and Chen (1996).*

44. *Weaver (2001, p. 51).*

45. *Ferguson et al. (2005).*

46. *Griffith (2004, p. 28).*

47. *In his 1989 letter to shareholders, Warren Buffett expresses it this way: "Good jockeys will do well on good horses, but not on broken-down nags."*

48. *Dutta and Reichelstein (2005, p.1091).*

49. *See Fama (1970). We note that to impact the security price, the information must be different from that which was expected.*

50. *We might also add that the analysis must be correct. In efficient markets, the market's rapid reaction to new information might be compared to that of a baseball umpire calling balls and strikes.*

51. *Malkiel (2005, p. 3).*

52. *De Bondt and Thaler (1985, p. 804).*

53. *Penman (2003) provides an insightful and highly readable perspective on the relationship between the quality of financial reporting during the 1990s and the 1990s stock market bubble. He argues that properly applied, GAAP are a "secure anchor" during bubbles, dampening speculation. Unfortunately, this only works if managers, investors, and analysts have the interest and willingness to use them properly.*

54. *Lowenstein (2000, p. A 48).*

55. *Theoretically, there is an infinite number of ways that two assets may be combined to form a portfolio. When we consider the thousands of assets that exist (stocks, bonds, real estate, etc.), the number of portfolios that can be formed in practice is mind boggling. In practice, it is impossible to construct the market portfolio. For expediency, a crude proxy, such as the S&P 500 Index, is used instead.*

56. *Of course, investors are not forced to diversify to eliminate unsystematic risk. However, it is an unnecessary risk to bear.*

57. *Ryan (1997) provides a broad-ranging discussion on improving measures of risk provided by accounting numbers. See also Schrand and Elliott (1998) for a summary of the 1997 AAA/FASB conference involving risk and financial reporting.*

58. *Black's (1993) findings provide empirical support. The model also enjoys broad support among managers. See Graham and Harvey (2001). Still, the CAPM has its shortcomings. See Fama and French (1992).*

59. *For an excellent discussion of event studies, see MacKinlay (1997).*

60. *For critiques of this research methodology, see Roll (1977), Foster (1980), and Ball (1992).*

61. *Beaver (1981) and Vickrey (1994) use information economics to analyze market efficiency, including factors such as all market actors not receiving the information or processing information incorrectly. Lundholm (1991) used similar assumptions in a laboratory study (behavioral research) to assess how different features affect a market's "efficiency." Ketz and Wyatt (1983) anticipated much of this work in their characterization of markets being "partially efficient." Ketz and Wyatt essentially take an accountability standpoint because they see investment decisions as only one use of accounting information. Among other users, they mention employees, customers, and regulatory authorities.*

62. *Kothari (2001).*

63. *Short-term event studies typically examine the market's reaction within a narrow window-days or weeks-surrounding an event. Long-horizon event studies follow the effects for much longer periods of time, perhaps years. See the above discussion regarding the difficulties involved in performing such studies.*

64. *Kothari (2001, p. 208).*

65. *Lee (2001, pp. 234–35).*

66. *Ibid. (p. 251).*

67. *Ball and Brown (1968).*

68. *Beaver, Clarke, and Wright (1979).*

69. *Brown and Kennelly (1972), Foster (1977a), and Cornell and Landsman (1989). For some literature reviews of stock market research, see Brown (1989) and Bernard (1989).*

70. *Hand (1990) believes that some stock prices may occasionally be determined by naive investors who are unduly influenced by bottom-line results. This would be more likely for small firms having a high proportion of stock owned by individual investors. Tinic (1990) urges caution in accepting Hand's results. From the conceptual standpoint, Tinic (p. 785) believes that knowledgeable investors would capitalize on the errors of the naive investors and eventually eliminate the valuation error. A more recent study by Ball and Kothari (1991) provides counter-evidence to Hand's results.*

71. *Beaver and Dukes (1972).*

72. *Hong, Kaplan, and Mandelker (1978), Dukes (1976), and Foster (1977b).*

73. *Archibald (1972) and Comiskey (1971).*

74. *Cassidy (1976).*

75. *Ball (1972), Sunder (1973, 1975), and Biddle and Lindahl (1982). For reviews of LIFO studies, see Lindahl, Emby, and Ashton (1988) and Jennings, Mest, and Thompson (1992).*

76. *Brown (1980), Ricks (1982), Biddle and Ricks (1988), and Stevenson (1987).*

77. *Pincus and Wasley (1996).*

78. *Kang (1993).*

79. *Collins, Rozeff, and Dhaliwal (1981). See also Lys (1984).*

80. *We wonder if the negative price response was due to investor concerns that cash dividends would be reduced or deferred, or to concerns that management now had more cash for overinvestment. The latter concern might be mitigated if management compensation were based on residual income.*

81. *Leftwich (1981).*

82. *Pfeiffer (1980).*

83. *Ou and Penman (1989, pp. 303–307). However, Greig's (1992) study disputes their findings.*

84. *Ibid. (p. 306).*

85. *Ibid. (pp. 309–313). For related studies, see also Ball (1992) and Bernard and Thomas (1990).*

86. *Ibid. (pp. 316–320).*

87. *Lev (1989). Collins et al. (1994) see the low correlation between returns and earnings resulting from "timeliness" factors, which include historical costing and transaction-based accounting, along with conservatism,*

as factors that slow the capture of value-relevant events. This "lack of timeliness results in a positive association between current earnings and past returns" (p. 290).

88. *Lev (1989, p. 178).*

89. *Wyatt (1983) stresses the importance of improving accounting measurements (the quality of earnings issue) given a securities market that is efficient.*

90. *Bernard and Thomas (1989).*

91. *Ibid. In a study of 206 firms on the London Stock Exchange, Hew et al. (1996) found evidence for post-earnings-announcement drift in the lower quartile in terms of firm size.*

92. *Jegadeesh and Livnat (2006).*

93. *Ke and Ramalingegowda (2005).*

94. *Abarbanell and Bushee (1997 and 1998).*

95. *Sloan (1996).*

96. *Wyatt (1983) stresses this same point.*

97. *Mikhail, Walther, and Willis (2003, p. 530).*

98. *Richardson et al. (2005, p. 446).*

99. *Ibid. (p. 478). Francis et al. (2005) also examine the pricing of accruals quality. They find that poorer accruals quality is associated with larger costs of debt and equity. Accruals quality effects are greater when driven by the firm's business model and operating environment (innate) than when driven by management interventions (discretionary).*

100. *Francis et al. (2005, pp. 483–484). Hirshleifer et al. (2004) note that if cumulative net operating income exceeds cumulative free cash flow, subsequent earnings are weak. We discuss free cash flow in detail in Chapter 13.*

101. *Liu and Qi (2006, p. 66).*

102. *Chan et al. (2006, pp. 1076–1077).*

103. *Bloomfield (2002).*

104. *FASB (2004). (Under SFAS 123R, issued in 2004, stock options costs are expensed.)*

105. *Ibid. (p. 234).*

106. *Beaver, Kettler, and Scholes (1970), Bildersee (1975), Thompson (1976), Eskew (1979), and Elgers (1980). For a review of the methodological problems in this type of research, see Elgers and Murray (1982).*

107. *Stone (1981).*

108. *See Mohr (1983) for a comprehensive review.*

109. *For example, Beaver, Kettler, and Scholes (1970), Bildersee (1975), and Thompson (1976).*

110. *Epstein (1975) and Lee and Tweedie (1975).*

111. *Anderson (1981).*

112. *See Hines (1982) for a summary of the major investment surveys.*

113. *For theoretical descriptions of these models, see Atiase and Tse (1986), Landsman and Magliolo (1988), and Ohlson (1990, 1991).*

114. *Lev and Ohlson (1982), Landsman and Magliolo (1988), and Bernard (1989).*

115. *Daley (1984), Landsman (1986), Barth (1991), and Landsman and Ohlson (1990).*

116. *Barth, Beaver, and Landsman (1992).*

117. *Franzoni and Marín (2006, p. 953).*

118. *Sougiannis (1994).*

119. *This is consistent with the adjustments made to compute EVA. See Young (1999).*

120. *Barth, Beaver, and Stinson (1991) and Beaver et al. (1989).*

121. *Barth (1994).*

122. *Altman (1971), Beaver (1967), and Ohlson (1980). See Jones (1987) for a review of bankruptcy studies.*

123. *Cook and Hendershott (1978), Fisher (1959), Horrigan (1966), and Kaplan and Urwitz (1979). See Reiter (1990) for a literature review.*

124. *Baran, Lakonishok, and Ofer (1980), Elam (1975), and Reiter (1985).*

125. *Libby (1975), Wright (1977), and Wilkins and Zimmer (1983).*

126. *Copeland and Dolgoff (2006, p. 89).*

127. *See Ohlson (1995).*

128. *See Loh and Mian (2006, p. 457).*

129. *Ibid. (p. 482).*

130. *Interestingly, the usefulness of quarterly earnings announcements does not appear to be eliminated by earnings forecasts contained in security analysts reports. Francis, Schipper, and Vincent (2002, p. 316) provide evidence that "the aggregate information in analyst reports does not pre-empt or substitute for the information in earnings announcements . . ."*

131. *Dechow, Kothari, and Watts (1998, p. 163).*

132. *Kim and Kross (2005, p. 778).*

133. *See Gulliver (2005, p. 29). Examples included channel stuffing (Safeskin Corporation), use of third-party sources (Biovail Corporation), booking revenues (MicroStrategy Inc.), understating expenses (WorldCom Corp. and Rainbow Technologies), competitive problems (Lexar Media), imprudent and excessive lending to customers (Lucent Technologies), and employee stock options creating misleading levels of cash flow from operating activities (Corporate Executive Board).*

134. *Gonedes (1972), and Beaver and Dukes (1972).*

135. *Gonedes and Dopuch (1974) argue that the free-rider problem makes it impossible to use capital market research to identify optimal accounting policies. The reason is that production costs cannot be internalized on users because accounting information has characteristics of a public good. See the discussion in Chapter 4. So, even though mandatory information may have information content, there is no way of determining if users would really demand the information in a free-market situation. For an overview of recent capital market research, see Beaver (2002).*

136. *Holthausen and Watts (2001).*

137. *Barth, Beaver, and Landsman (2001).*

References

Abarbanell, Jeffery S., and B. J. Bushee (Spring 1997). "Fundamental Analysis, Future Earnings, and Stock Prices," *Journal of Accounting Research*, pp. 1–24.

——— (January 1998). "Abnormal Returns to a Fundamental Analysis Strategy," *Accounting Review*, pp. 19–45.

Altman, Edward I. (1971). *Corporate Bankruptcy in America*. Heath.

Anderson, Ray (Autumn 1981). "The Usefulness of Accounting and Other Information Disclosures in Corporate Annual Reports to Institutional Investors in Australia," *Accounting and Business Research*, pp. 259–265.

Archibald, T. Ross (January 1972). "Stock Market Reaction to Depreciation Switch-Back," *Accounting Review*, pp. 22–30.

Atiase, Rowland K., and Senyo Tse (1986). "Stock Valuation Models and Accounting Information: A Review and Synthesis," *Journal of Accounting Literature*, pp. 1–33.

Ball, Ray (1972). "Changes in Accounting Techniques and Stock Prices," *Empirical Research in Accounting: Selected Studies, 1972* (Supplement to *Journal of Accounting Research*), pp. 1–38.

———— (June/September 1992). "The Earnings-Price Anomaly," *Journal of Accounting and Economics*, pp. 319–345.

Ball, Ray, and Philip Brown (Autumn 1968). "An Empirical Evaluation of Accounting Income Numbers," *Journal of Accounting Research*, pp. 159–177.

Ball, Ray, and S. P. Kothari (October 1991). "Security Returns Around Earnings Announcements," *Accounting Review*, pp. 718–738.

Baran, A., J. Lakonishok, and A. Ofer (January 1980). "The Information Content of Adjusted Accounting Earnings: Some Empirical Evidence," *Accounting Review*, pp. 22–35.

Barth, Mary E. (July 1991). "Relative Measurement Errors Among Alternative Pension Asset and Liability Measures," *Accounting Review*, pp. 433–463.

———— (January 1994). "Fair Value Accounting: Evidence From Investment Securities and the Market Valuation of Banks," *Accounting Review*, pp. 1–25.

Barth, Mary E., William H. Beaver, and Wayne R. Landsman (March 1992). "The Market Valuation Implications of Net Periodic Pension Expense," *Journal of Accounting and Economics* , pp. 27–62.

Barth, Mary E., William H. Beaver, and Wayne R. Landsman (2001). "The Relevance of Value Relevance Research," *Journal of Accounting and Economics* (Vol. 31), pp. 77–104.

Barth, Mary E., William H. Beaver, and Christopher H. Stinson (January 1991). "Supplemental Data and the Structure of Thrift Share Prices," *Accounting Review*, pp. 56–66.

Beaver, William H. (1967). "Financial Ratios as Predictors of Failure," *Empirical Research in Accounting: Selected Studies, 1967* (Supplement to *Journal of Accounting Research*), pp. 71–111.

———— (January 1981). "Market Efficiency," *Accounting Review*, pp. 23–37.

———— (1998). *Financial Reporting: An Accounting Revolution,* 3rd ed. Prentice Hall.

———— (April 2002). "Perspectives on Recent Capital Market Research," *Accounting Review,* pp. 453–474.

Beaver, William H., Roger Clarke, and William F. Wright (Autumn 1979). "The Association Between Unsystematic Security Returns and the Magnitude of Earnings Forecast Errors," *Journal of Accounting Research*, pp. 316–340.

Beaver, William H., and Roland E. Dukes (April 1972). "Interperiod Tax Allocation, Earnings Expectations, and the Behavior of Security Prices," *Accounting Review*, pp. 320–332.

Beaver, William H., Carol E. Eger, Stephen G. Ryan, and Mark A. Wolfson (Autumn 1989). "Financial Reporting, Supplemental Disclosures, and the Structure of Bank Prices," *Journal of Accounting Research*, pp. 157–178.

Beaver, William H., Paul Kettler, and Myron Scholes (October 1970). "The Association Between Market-Determined and Accounting-Determined Risk Measures," *Accounting Review*, pp. 654–682.

Benston, George J. (Spring 2003). "Accounting Doesn't Need Much Fixing (Just Some Reinterpreting)," *Journal of Applied Corporate Finance*, pp. 83–96.

Bernard, Victor L. (1989). "Capital Markets Research in Accounting During the 1980s: A Critical Review," in *The State of Accounting Research as We Enter the 1990s: Illinois Ph.D. Jubilee 1939–1989*, ed. Thomas J. Frecka. University of Illinois.

Bernard, Victor L., and Thomas L. Stober (October 1989). "The Nature and Amount of Information in Cash Flows and Accruals," *Accounting Review*, pp. 624–652.

Bernard, Victor L., and J. Thomas (1989). "Post-Earnings-Announcement Drift: Delayed Price Reaction or Risk Premium?" *Current Studies on the Information Content of Accounting Earnings* (Supplement to *Journal of Accounting Research*), pp. 1–36.

Bernard, Victor L., and J. Thomas (December 1990). "Evidence That Stock Prices Do Not Fully Reflect the Implications of Current Earnings for Future Earnings," *Journal of Accounting and Economics*, pp. 305–340.

Biddle, Gary C., and Frederick W. Lindahl (Autumn 1982). "Stock Price Reactions to LIFO Adoptions: The Association Between Excess Returns and LIFO Tax Savings," *Journal of Accounting Research* (Part 2), pp. 551–588.

Biddle, Gary C., and William D. Ricks (Spring 1988). "Analyst Forecast Errors and Stock Price Behavior Near the Earnings Announcement Dates of LIFO Adopters," *Journal of Accounting Research*, pp. 169–194.

Bildersee, John S. (January 1975). "Market-Determined and Alternative Measures of Risk," *Accounting Review*, pp. 81–98.

Black, Fischer (Fall 1993). "Beta and Return," *Journal of Portfolio Management*, pp. 8–18.

Bloomfield, Robert J. (September 2002). "The 'Incomplete Revelation Hypothesis' and Financial Reporting," *Accounting Horizons*, pp. 233–243.

Bowen, Robert M., David Burgstahler, and Lane A. Daley (October 1986). "Evidence on the Relationships Between Various Earnings Measures of Cash Flow," *Accounting Review*, pp. 713–725.

Brealey, Richard A., Stewart C. Myers, and Franklin Allen (2006), *Principles of Corporate Finance,* 8th ed. McGraw-Hill Irwin.

Brown, Philip (1989). "Ball and Brown [1968]," *Current Studies on the Information Content of Accounting Earnings, 1989* (Supplement to *Journal of Accounting Research*), pp. 202–217.

Brown, Philip, and John W. Kennelly (July 1972). "The Information Content of Quarterly Earnings," *Journal of Business*, pp. 403–421.

Brown, Robert Moren (Spring 1980). "Short-Range Market Reactions to Changes to LIFO Accounting Using Preliminary Earnings Announcements," *Journal of Accounting Research*, pp. 38–62.

Buffett, Warren E. (1987). "Letter to Shareholders," *Berkshire Hathaway Inc. Annual Report to Shareholders* (1987). Available from www.berkshirehathaway.com; accessed June 15, 2006.

——— (1989). "Letter to Shareholders," *Berkshire Hathaway Inc. Annual Report to Shareholders* (1989). Available from www.berkshirehathaway.com; accessed June 15, 2006.

——— (1994). "Letter to Shareholders," *Berkshire Hathaway Inc. Annual Report to Shareholders* (1994). Available from www.berkshirehathaway.com; accessed June 15, 2006.

Cassidy, D. (Autumn 1976). "Investor Evaluation of Accounting Information: Some Additional Evidence," *Journal of Accounting Research*, pp. 212–229.

Chan, Konan, Louis K. C. Chan, Narasimhan Jegadeesh, and Josef Lakonishok (2006). "Earnings Quality and Stock Returns," *Journal of Business* (Vol. 79, No. 3), pp. 1041–1082.

Chen, Shimin, and James L. Dodd (1997) "Economic Value Added®: An Empirical Examination of a New Corporate Performance Measure," *Journal of Managerial Issues,* (Vol. 9).

Collins, Daniel W., and S. P. Kothari (July 1989). "An Analysis of Intertemporal and Cross-sectional Determinants of Earnings Response Coefficients," *Journal of Accounting and Economics*, pp. 143–181.

Collins, Daniel W., S. P. Kothari, Jay Shanken, and Richard Sloan (November 1994). "Lack of Timeliness and Noise as Explanations for the Low Contemporaneous Return-Earnings Association," *Journal of Accounting and Economics*, pp. 289–324.

Collins, Daniel W., Michael S. Rozeff, and Dan S. Dhaliwal (March 1981). "The Economic Determinants of the Market Reaction to Proposed Mandatory Accounting Changes in the Oil and Gas Industry," *Journal of Accounting and Economics*, pp. 37–71.

Comiskey, Eugene (April 1971). "Market Response to Changes in Depreciation Accounting," *Accounting Review*, pp. 271–285.

Cook, T. Q., and P. H. Hendershott (September 1978). "The Impact of Taxes, Risk and Relative Security Supplies on Interest Rate Differentials," *Journal of Finance*, pp. 1173–1186.

Copeland, Tom, and Aaron Dolgoff (Spring 2006). "Expectations-Based Management," *Journal of Applied Corporate Finance*, pp. 82–97.

Cornell, Bradford, and Wayne R. Landsman (October 1989). "Security Price Response to Quarterly Earnings Announcements and Analysts' Forecast Revisions," *Accounting Review*, pp. 680–692.

Daley, Lane (April 1984). "The Valuation of Reported Pension Measures for Firms Sponsoring Defined Benefit Pension Plans," *Accounting Review*, pp. 177–198.

Davidson, R., and D. Neu (Spring 1993). "A Note on the Association Between Audit Firm Size and Audit Quality," *Contemporary Accounting Research*, pp. 479–488.

De Bondt, Werner F., and Richard Thaler (July 1985). "Does the Stock Market Overreact?" *Journal of Finance*, pp. 793–805.

Dechow, Patricia M., S. P. Kothari, and Ross L. Watts (1998). "The Relation Between Earnings and Cash Flows," *Journal of Accounting and Economics* (Vol. 25), pp. 133–168.

Dechow, Patricia M., Amy P. Hutton, and Richard G. Sloan (January 1999). "An Empirical Assessment of the Residual Income Valuation Model," *Journal of Accounting and Economics*, pp. 1–34.

Dodd, James L., and Jason Johns (April–June 1999). "EVA Reconsidered," *Business and Economic Review*, 13–18.

Dodd, James L., and Shimin Chen (July–September 1996), "EVA: A New Panacea?," *Business and Economics Review*, pp. 26-28.

Dukes, Roland (1976). "An Empirical Investigation of the Effects of Expensing Research and Development Costs on Security Prices," in *Proceedings on Topical Research in Accounting*, eds. Michael Schiff and George Sorter. Ross Institute of Accounting Research, New York University.

Dutta, Junil, and Stefan Reichelstein (October 2005). "Stock Price, Earnings, and Book Value in Managerial Performance Measures," *Accounting Review*, pp. 1069–1100.

Easton, Peter D., and Mark E. Zmijewski (July 1989). "Cross-Sectional Variation in the Stock Market Response to Accounting Earnings Announcements," *Journal of Accounting and Economics*, pp. 117–141.

Elam, Rick (January 1975). "The Effect of Lease Data on the Predictive Ability of Financial Ratios," *Accounting Review*, pp. 25–43.

Elgers, Pieter T. (July 1980). "Accounting-Based Risk Measures: A Re-Examination," *Accounting Review*, pp. 389–408.

Elgers, Pieter T., and Dennis Murray (April 1982). "The Impact of the Choice of Market Index on the Empirical Evaluation of Accounting Risk Measures," *Accounting Review*, pp. 358–375.

Epstein, Marc (1975). *The Usefulness of Annual Reports to Corporate Stockholders.* California State University, Los Angeles—Bureau of Business and Economic Research.

Eskew, Robert K. (January 1979). "The Forecasting Ability of Accounting Risk Measures: Some Additional Evidence," *Accounting Review*, pp. 107–118.

Fama, Eugene F. (1970). "Efficient Capital Markets: A Review of Theory and Empirical Work," *Journal of Finance* (May 1970), pp. 383–417.

Fama, Eugene F., and Merton H. Miller (1972). *The Theory of Finance.* Dryden Press.

Fama, Eugene F., and Kenneth R. French (June 1992). "The Cross-Section of Expected Stock Returns," *Journal of Finance*, pp. 427–465.

Feltham, Glenn D., Grant E. Isaac, Chima Mbagwu, and Ganesh Vaidyanathan (Winter 2004). "Perhaps EVA Does Beat Earnings—Revisiting Previous Evidence," *Journal of Applied Corporate Finance*, pp. 83–88.

Feltham, Gerald, and J. Ohlson (Spring 1995). "Valuation and Clean Surplus Accounting," *Contemporary Accounting Research*, pp. 689–732.

Ferguson, Robert, Joel Rentzler, and Susana Yu (Fall/Winter 2005). "Economic Value Added (EVA) Improve Stock Performance Profitability?," *Journal of Applied Finance*, pp. 101–113.

Financial Accounting Standards Board (1978). Statement of Financial Accounting Concepts No. 1, *Objectives of Financial Reporting by Business Enterprises.* FASB.

——— (2004). Statement of Financial Accounting Standards 123R, *Share-Based Payment*. (FASB).

Fisher, L. (June 1959). "Determinants of Risk Premiums on Corporate Bonds," *Journal of Political Economy*, pp. 217–237.

Foster, George (1977a). "Quarterly Earnings Data: Time Series Properties and Predictive Ability Results," *Accounting Review* (January), pp. 1–21.

——— (1977b). "Valuation Parameters of Property-Liability Companies," *Journal of Finance* (June), pp. 823–836.

——— (March 1980). "Accounting Policy Decisions and Capital Market Research," *Journal of Accounting and Economics*, pp. 26–62.

Francis, Jennifer, Katherine Schipper, and Linda Vincent (August 2002). "Earnings Announcements and Competing Information," *Journal of Accounting and Economics*, pp. 313–342.

Francis, Jennifer, Ryan LaFond, Per Olsson, and Katherine Schipper (June 2005). "The Market Pricing of Accruals Quality," *Journal of Accounting and Economics*, pp. 295–327.

Franzoni, Francesco, and José M. Marín (April 2006). "Pension Plan Funding and Stock Market Efficiency," *Journal of Finance*, pp.921–956.

Gonedes, Nicholas J. (January 1972). "Efficient Capital Markets and External Accounting," *Accounting Review*, pp. 11–21.

Gonedes, Nicholas J., and Nicholas Dopuch (1974). "Capital Market Equilibrium, Information Production, and Selected Accounting Techniques: Theoretical Framework and Review of Empirical Work," *Studies on Financial Accounting Objectives, 1974* (Supplement to *Journal of Accounting Research*), pp. 48–129.

Gordon, Myron J. (1962). *The Investment, Financing and Valuation of the Corporation*. Richard D. Irwin.

Graham, John R., and Campbell R. Harvey (May/June 2001). "The Theory and Practice of Corporate Finance: Evidence From the Field, *Journal of Financial Economics*, pp. 187–243.

Graham, John R., Campbell R. Harvey, and Shiva Rajgopal (November/December 2006). "Value Destruction and Financial Reporting Decisions, *Financial Analysts Journal*, pp. 27–39.

Greenberg, Robert R., Glen L. Johnson, and K. Ramesh (Fall 1986). "Earnings Versus Cash Flow as a Predictor of Future Cash Flow Measures," *Journal of Accounting, Auditing & Finance*, pp. 266–277.

Greig, Anthony C. (June/September 1992). "Fundamental Analysis and Subsequent Stock Returns," *Journal of Accounting and Economics*, pp. 413–442.

Griffith, John (Fall/Winter 2004). "The True Value of EVA®," *Journal of Applied Finance*, , pp. 25–29.

Gulliver, Bruce A. (June 2005). "An Analyst's Perspective on Financial Reporting," *CFA Institute Conference Proceedings*, pp. 29–41.

Hand, John R. M. (October 1990). "A Test of the Extended Functional Fixation Hypothesis," *Accounting Review*, pp. 740–763.

Hew, Denis, L. Skerrat, N. Strong, and M. Walker (Autumn 1996). "Post-Earnings-Announcement Drift: Some Preliminary Evidence for the UK," *Accounting and Business Research*, pp. 283–293.

Hines, R. D. (Autumn 1982). "The Usefulness of Annual Reports: The Anomaly Between the Efficient Markets Hypothesis and Shareholder Surveys," *Accounting and Business Research*, pp. 296–309.

Hirshleifer, David A., Kewei Hou, Siew Hong Teoh, and Yinglei Zhang (December 2004). "Do Investors Overvalue Firms With Bloated Balance Sheets?" *Journal of Accounting and Economics*, pp. 297–331.

Holthausen, Robert W., and Ross L. Watts (2001). "The Relevance of the Value-Relevance Literature for Financial Accounting Standard Setting," *Journal of Accounting and Economics* (Vol. 31), pp. 3–75.

Hong, Hai, Robert S. Kaplan, and Gershon Mandelker (January 1978). "Pooling vs. Purchase: The Effects of Accounting for Mergers on Stock Prices," *Accounting Review*, pp. 31–47.

Horrigan, J. O. (1966). "The Determination of Long-Term Credit Standing With Financial Ratios," *Empirical Research in Accounting: Selected Studies, 1966* (Supplement to *Journal of Accounting Research*), pp. 44–62.

Jegadeesh, Narasimhan, and Joshua Livnat (March/April 2006). "Post-Earnings-Announcement Drift: The Role of Revenue Surprises," *Financial Analysts Journal*, pp. 22–34.

Jennings, Ross, David P. Mest, and Robert B. Thompson, II (April 1992). "Investor Reaction to Disclosures of 1974–75 LIFO Adoption Decisions," *Accounting Review*, pp. 337–354.

Jones, Frederick L. (1987). "Current Techniques in Bankruptcy Prediction," *Journal of Accounting Literature*, pp. 131–164.

Kang, S-H (Spring 1993). "The Stock Price Effects of LIFO Benefits: A Conceptual Framework," *Journal of Accounting Research*, pp. 50–61.

Kaplan, R. S., and G. Urwitz (April 1979). "Statistical Models of Bond Ratings: A Methodological Inquiry," *Journal of Business*, pp. 231–261.

Ke, Bin, and Santhosh Ramalingegowda (February 2005). "Do Institutional Investors Exploit the Post-Earnings Announcement Drift?," *Journal of Accounting and Economics*, pp. 25–53.

Ketz, J. Edward, and Arthur Wyatt (Fall 1983). "The FASB in a World With Partially Efficient Markets," *Journal of Accounting, Auditing & Finance*, pp. 29–43.

Kim, Myungsun, and William Kross (December 2005). "The Ability of Earnings to Predict Future Operating Cash Flows Has Been Increasing—Not Decreasing," *Journal of Accounting Research*, pp. 753–780.

Koller, Tim, Marc Goedhart, and David Wessels (2005). *Valuation: Measuring and Managing the Value of Companies,* 4th ed. John Wiley & Sons.

Kormendi, R., and R. Lipe (July 1987). "Earnings Innovations, Earnings Persistence and Stock Returns," *Journal of Business*, pp. 323–345.

Kothari, S. P. (2001). "Capital Markets Research in Accounting," *Journal of Accounting and Economics* (Vol. 31), pp. 105–231.

Landsman, Wayne R.(October 1986). "An Empirical Investigation of Pension Fund Property Rights," *Accounting Review*, pp. 662–691.

Landsman, Wayne R., and Joseph Magliolo (October 1988). "Cross-Sectional Capital Market Research and Model Specification," *Accounting Review*, pp. 586–604.

Landsman, Wayne R., and James A. Ohlson (Fall 1990). "Evaluation of Market Efficiency for Supplementary Accounting Disclosures: The Case of Pension Assets and Liabilities," *Contemporary Accounting Research*, pp. 185–198.

Lee, Charles M.C. (2001). "Market Efficiency and Accounting Research: A Discussion of 'Capital Market Research in Accounting' by S. P. Kothari," *Journal of Accounting and Economics* (Vol. 31), pp. 233–253.

Lee, T. A., and D. P. Tweedie (Autumn 1975). "Accounting Information: An Investigation of Private Shareholder Usage," *Accounting and Business Research*, pp. 280–291.

Leftwich, Richard W. (March 1981). "Evidence on the Impact of Mandatory Changes in Accounting Principles on Corporate Loan Agreements," *Journal of Accounting and Economics*, pp. 3–36.

Lev, Baruch (1989). "On the Usefulness of Earnings and Earnings Research: Lessons and Directions From Two Decades of Empirical Research," *Current Studies on the Information Content of Accounting Earnings, 1989* (Supplement to *Journal of Accounting Research*), pp. 153–192.

Lev, Baruch, and James A. Ohlson (1982). "Market-Based Empirical Research in Accounting: A Review, Interpretation, and Extension," *Studies on Current Research Methodologies in Accounting: A Critical Evaluation, 1982* (Supplement to *Journal of Accounting Research*), pp. 249–232.

Libby, Robert (Spring 1975). "Accounting Ratios and the Prediction of Failure: Some Behavioral Evidence," *Journal of Accounting Research*, pp. 150–161.

Lindahl, Frederick W., Craig Emby, and Robert H. Ashton (1988). "Empirical Research on LIFO: A Review and Analysis," *Journal of Accounting Literature*, pp. 310–333.

Lintner, John (May 1956). "Distribution of Incomes of Corporations Among Dividends, Retained Earnings, and Taxes," *American Economic Review*, pp. 97–113.

Liu, Qiao, and Rong Qi (July/August 2006). "Do We Accept Accrual Profits at Our Peril?," *Financial Analysts Journal*, pp. 62–75.

Livnat, Joshua, and Paul Zarowin (May 1990). "The Incremental Information Content of Cash-Flow Components," *Journal of Accounting and Economics*, pp. 25–46.

Loh, Roger K., and G. Mujtaba Mian (May 2006). "Do Accurate Earnings Forecasts Facilitate Superior Investment Recommendations?," *Journal of Financial Economics*, pp. 455–483.

Lowenstein, Roger (2000). "Manager's Journal: The Tiger Fund Is Gone; Who's Next?," *Wall Street Journal* (April 3), p. A.48.

Lundholm, Russell (July 1991). "What Affects the Efficiency of a Market? Some Answers From the Laboratory," *Accounting Review*, pp. 486–515.

Lys, Tom (April 1984). "Mandated Accounting Changes and Accounting Debt Covenants: The Case of Oil and Gas Accounting," *Journal of Accounting and Economics*, pp. 39–66.

MacKinlay, A. Craig (March 1997). "Event Studies in Economics and Finance," *Journal of Economic Literature*, pp. 13–39.

Malkiel, Burton G. (February 2005). "Reflections on the Efficient Market Hypothesis: 30 Years Later," *Financial Review*, pp. 1–9

Mikhail, Michael B., Beverly R. Walther, and Richard H Willis (Fall 2003). "Security Analyst Experience and Post-Earnings-Announcement Drift," *Journal of Accounting, Auditing & Finance*, pp. 529–550.

Miller, Merton H., and Franco Modigliani (October 1961). "Dividend Policy, Growth and the Valuation of Shares," *Journal of Business*, pp. 411–433.

Miller, Merton H., and Kevin Rock (September 1985). "Dividend Policy Under Asymmetric Information," *Journal of Finance*, pp. 1031–1051.

Mohr, Rosanne M. (1983). "The Segmental Reporting Issue: A Review of the Empirical Research," *Journal of Accounting Literature*, pp. 39–71.

Myers, James N. (January 1999). "Implementing Residual Income Valuation With Linear Information Dynamics," *Accounting Review*, pp. 1–28.

Neill, John D., Thomas F. Schaefer, Paul R. Bahnson, and Michael E. Bradbury (1991). "The Usefulness of Cash Flow Data: A Review and Synthesis," *Journal of Accounting Literature* (Vol. 10), pp. 117–149.

Ohlson, James A. (Spring 1980). "Financial Ratios and the Probabilistic Prediction of Bankruptcy," *Journal of Accounting Research*, pp. 109–131.

——— (Spring 1990). "A Synthesis of Security Valuation Theory and the Role of Dividends, Cash Flows, and Earnings," *Contemporary Accounting Research*, (No. 2-II), pp. 648–676.

——— (Fall 1991). "The Theory of Value and Earnings, and an Introduction to the Ball–Brown Analysis," *Contemporary Accounting Research*, pp. 1–19.

——— (Spring 1995). "Book Values and Dividends in Security Valuation," *Contemporary Accounting Research*, pp. 661–688.

Ou, Jane, and Stephen Penman (Autumn 1989). "Financial Statement Analysis and the Prediction of Stock Returns," *Journal of Accounting and Economics*, pp. 295–329.

Penman, Stephen H. (2003). "The Quality of Financial Statements: Perspectives From the Recent Stock Market Bubble," *Accounting Horizons Supplement*, pp. 77–96.

Pfeiffer, G. (1980). "The Economic Effects of Accounting Policy Regulation: Evidence on the Lease Accounting Issue" (PhD diss., Cornell University).

Pfeiffer, Thomas (September/October 2004). "Net Present Value-Consistent Investment Criteria Based on Accruals: A Generalisation of the Residual Income-Identity." *Journal of Business Finance & Accounting,* pp. 905–926.

Pincus, Morton, and C. E. Wasley (Fall 1996). "Stock Price Behavior Associated with Post-1974–75 LIFO Adoptions Announced at Alternative Disclosure Times," *Journal of Accounting, Auditing & Finance,* pp. 535–564.

Qiang, Cheng (January 2005). "What Determines Residual Income?," *Accounting Review,* pp. 58–112.

Rayburn, Judy (1986). "The Association of Operating Cash Flow and Accruals With Security Returns," *Studies on Alternative Measures of Accounting Income, 1986* (Supplement to *Journal of Accounting Research*), pp. 112–133.

Reiter, Sara Ann (1985). "The Effect of Defined Benefit Pension Plan Disclosures on Bond Risk Premiums and Bond Ratings" (PhD diss., University of Missouri).

———— (Spring 1990). "The Use of Bond Market Data in Accounting Research," *Journal of Accounting Research,* pp. 183–227.

Richardson, Scott A., Richard G. Sloan, Mark T. Soliman, and Irem Tuna (September 2005). "Accrual Reliability, Earnings Persistence and Stock Prices," *Journal of Accounting and Economics,* pp. 437–485.

Ricks, William E. (Autumn 1982). "The Market's Response to the 1974 LIFO Adoptions," *Journal of Accounting Research,* pp. 367–387.

Rogerson, William P. (1997). "Intertemporal Cost Allocation and Managerial Investment Incentives: A Theory Explaining the Use of Economic Value Added as a Performance Measure," *Journal of Political Economy* (Vol. 105, No. 4), pp. 770–795.

Roll, Richard (March 1977). "A Critique of the Asset Pricing Theory's Tests, Part 1: On Past and Potential Testability of the Theory," *Journal of Financial Economics,* pp. 129–176.

Ryan, Stephen (June 1997). "A Survey of Research Relating Accounting Numbers to Systematic Equity Risk With Implications for Risk Disclosure Policy," *Accounting Horizons,* pp. 82–95.

Schrand, Catherine M., and J. Elliott (September 1998). "Risk and Financial Reporting: A Summary of the Discussion at the 1997 AAA/FASB Conference," *Accounting Horizons,* pp. 271–282.

Sloan, Richard (July 1996). "Do Stock Prices Fully Reflect Information in Accruals and Cash Flows About Future Earnings?," *Accounting Review,* pp. 289–316.

Sougiannis, Theodore (January 1994). "The Accounting-Based Valuation of Corporate R&D," *Accounting Review,* pp. 44–68.

Stevenson, Frank L. (Autumn 1987). "New Evidence on LIFO Adoptions: The Effects of More Precise Event Dates," *Journal of Accounting Research,* pp. 306–316.

Stewart III, G. Bennett (Spring 2003). "How to Fix Accounting—Measure Economic Profit," *Journal of Applied Corporate Finance,* pp. 63–82.

Stone, Mary S. (1981). "An Examination of the Effect of Disclosures Concerning Unfunded Pension Benefits on Market Risk Measures" (PhD diss., University of Illinois).

Sunder, Shyam (1973). "Relationship Between Accounting Changes and Stock Prices: Problems of Measurement and Some Empirical Evidence," *Empirical Research in Accounting: Selected Studies, 1973* (Supplement to *Journal of Accounting Research*), pp. 1–45.

———— (April 1975). "Stock Price and Risk Related to Accounting Changes in Inventory Valuation," *Accounting Review,* pp. 305–316.

Thompson, Donald J. (April 1976). "Sources of Systematic Risk in Common Stock," *Journal of Business*, pp. 173–188.

Tinic, Seha M. (October 1990). "A Perspective on the Stock Market's Fixation on Accounting Numbers," *Accounting Review*, pp. 781–796.

Tsuji, Chikashi (October 2006). "Does EVA Beat Earnings and Cash Flow in Japan?," *Applied Financial Economics*, pp. 1199–1216.

Vickrey, Don (1994). "An Internationally Relevant Alternative Price-Oriented Concept of Market Efficiency," *International Journal of Accounting* (Vol. 29, No. 3), pp. 206–219.

Weaver, Samuel C. (2001). "Measuring Economic Value Added: A Survey of the Practices of EVA® Proponents," *Journal of Applied Finance* (Vol. 11, No. 1), pp. 50–60.

Wilkins, Trevor, and Ian Zimmer (October 1983). "The Effect of Leasing and Different Methods of Accounting for Leases on Credit Evaluations," *Accounting Review*, pp. 749–764.

Wright, William F. (July 1977). "Financial Information Processing Models: An Empirical Study," *Accounting Review*, pp. 676–689.

Wyatt, Arthur (February 1983). "Efficient Market Theory: Its Impact on Accounting," *Journal of Accountancy*, pp. 56–65.

Young, S. David (Winter 1999). "Some Reflections on Accounting Adjustments and Economic Value Added," *Journal of Financial Statement Analysis*, pp. 7–19.

9

Uniformity
and Disclosure

Some Policy-Making Directions

Learning Objectives

After reading this chapter, you should be able to:

- Appreciate why different alternatives exist in accounting.
- Understand what relevant circumstances are.
- Understand the nature of finite and rigid uniformity and flexibility.
- Analyze whether standards are utilizing finite uniformity, rigid uniformity, or flexibility.
- Grasp the importance of allocations and understand why they are arbitrary.
- Understand the growing role of disclosure.
- Distinguish between selective and differential disclosure.
- Grasp the significance of how management earnings forecasts, management's discussion and analysis, segmental disclosures, and quarterly reporting provide important information to users.

We have seen in Chapter 7 that the Financial Accounting Standards Board (FASB) has developed a metatheoretical structure of accounting. Uniformity and disclosure and their potential place in such a structure are the subject of this chapter.

A conceptual framework is a normative structure because both the objectives and standards are the result of choice. If a conceptual framework is in place, it should provide guidance for standard setting. A quasi-deductive relationship thus exists between a metatheoretical structure and rule making. Although theoretical work should obviously be allowed to influence a conceptual framework as it emerges, as well as the rule-making process itself, theory and policy making lie in separate domains. However, Ijiri has pointed out that theory and policy appear to be more intertwined in accounting than in other fields.[1] We have already seen that attempting to combine these functions led to the demise of the Accounting Principles Board (APB). The FASB has been and will continue to be under pressure from outside bodies and groups over its part in both the conceptual framework and standard-setting activities. Clearly, the issues and concepts that derive from a metatheoretical structure must be as clear and complete as possible to minimize discrepancies between the structure and subsequent policy making. In other words, conceptual clarity and completeness are necessary if the resulting standards are to be consistent with the metatheoretical structure. While the FASB's conceptual framework has been criticized in Chapter 7, it at least provides a theoretical structure for assessing potential standards as they move toward fruition despite the political maneuverings by affected groups.[2] Of course, the situation is now one of attaining convergence with the International Accounting Standards Board's framework.

In this chapter, we examine two extremely important conceptual issues that must play an important role in determining the structure and components of a metatheoretical framework: uniformity and disclosure. A conceptual framework in a discipline such as accounting should always be an evolving instrument, changing in response to new needs and new research findings.[3]

We begin by examining the reasons underlying the choice among accounting methods. Next we undertake an analysis of uniformity. It is a topic discussed extensively in the accounting literature and statements and pronouncements of policy-making organizations, but it has not been precisely formulated. The type of uniformity desired should influence the structure of the metatheoretical framework. Information economics (benefits/costs considerations) obviously play a key role in this determination.

An appropriate starting point for understanding uniformity comes, we believe, from an analysis of event types. *Events* are economic occurrences that require accounting entries. They can be classified as simple or complex. Complex events where "effect of circumstances" exists are broadly similar and might justify different accounting treatments than simple events. Effect of circumstances, or relevant circumstances, are thus economically significant variables that should be identified and categorized.

After defining relevant circumstances, we are in a better position to analyze the uniformity question. In our opinion, there are two concepts of uniformity that have been evolving in the accounting literature—finite and rigid.

The uniformity section concludes with an analysis of how certain accounting standards are inconsistent with each other from the standpoint of uniformity. The term *flexibility* is also introduced in this part of the chapter. We also examine the nature of accounting allocations and why they are useful.

Finally, we examine the concept of disclosure, including the early distinction between protective and informative disclosure. We also look at the forms of disclosure, including management's discussion and analysis in the annual report, segmental disclosure, quarterly reporting, and management earnings forecasts. Disclosure, we believe, will continue to grow in importance in the foreseeable future.

There is a complementary relationship between uniformity and disclosure. As circumstances and transactions become more complex, it becomes more difficult to reflect important conditions and relationships within the body of the financial statements, hence the importance of disclosure. Furthermore, in an era when many firms are trying to obtain important information from the financial statements, adequate disclosure must be improved and extended.

What Underlies the Choice Among Accounting Methods?

The subject matter of this chapter is concerned with the attempt to limit or restrict choices among accounting methods that can exist in the same transaction or event situation. Some simple examples of these choices include (a) LIFO versus FIFO, (b) straight-line versus accelerated depreciation methods, and (c) purchase versus pooling of interests (pooling for new acquisitions is no longer allowed under Statement of Financial Accounting Standards [SFAS] No. 141).

Thus an interesting question arises in terms of what causes a firm to choose one accounting method over another when a free choice can be made. Fields, Lys, and Vincent (hereinafter FLV) see three possible reasons underlying management choice.[4] The first involves minimizing agency costs, the second concerns signaling information that management wants to send to outside parties, and the third involves externalities.

As an example of agency cost minimization, FLV mention the use of operating leases over capital leases (and the need to structure the lease contract in this fashion). As a result, debt would be kept off of the balance sheet with both a better debt–equity ratio and a better debt covenant situation. Another FLV example involves pooling over purchase accounting, which would result in higher reported income.

A weak firm might choose to structure a lease as an *operating* lease. Hence the choice could be made not in terms of the selected accounting method portraying the economic reality of the situation more accurately, but rather in terms of the perceived economic consequences affecting the agency situation underlying the choice. Thus, if an asset is leased for 15 years, the lessee might assume the asset has an estimated life of 21 years, rather than 20 years, making it an operating lease. As a result, the estimated period of the lease slips under 75% of its expected useful life. Seventy-five percent is the breakpoint between capital and operating leases, assuming no other lease capitalization criteria apply. Thus, the capital versus expense choice can be based on an extremely thin reed (see later in this chapter and in Chapter 17 for further discussion of leases).

Regarding the second reason for choosing a given accounting method, signaling, management might select accounting methods that give shareholders and potential shareholders information about future cash flows. Of course as FLV admit, the signaling incentive cannot easily be separated from management attempts to increase management salaries and bonuses.

The third reason underlying choice among accounting methods involves attempts to "influence" outside parties. Simple examples might include a choice of LIFO over FIFO to minimize income taxes and choice of accelerated depreciation over straight-line depreciation to minimize income to make a firm's dominating market position look less dominating.

FLV's examples involve accounting choices where the economics of the particular situation are not the main consideration. Our aim in this chapter is to make the selection among accounting methods more closely attuned to the economics of the specific transaction. We next turn to an examination of uniformity in financial accounting.

Uniformity

In the accounting literature, the concept of uniformity appears to overlap with comparability. For example, Sprouse has stated:

> Finally, because comparing alternative investment and lending opportunities is an essential part of most investor and creditor decisions, the quest for comparability is central. The term comparability is used here to mean accounting for similar transactions similarly and for different circumstances differently. A conceptual framework should foster consistent treatment of like things, provide the means for identifying unlike things, and leave open for judgment the estimates inherent in the accounting process.[5]

Sprouse sees comparability as both a process (accounting for circumstances in accordance with similarities or differences) and an end result of this process (comparing alternatives to make a decision). We view *comparability* here only in the latter context, while *uniformity* is seen as the concept that influences comparability.[6] Because comparability is linked to uniformity, the degree of comparability that users can rely on is directly dependent on the level of uniformity present in financial statements.

The relationship between uniformity and comparability espoused here is quite close to the position taken in SFAC No. 2. Comparability is not an inherent quality of accounting numbers in the sense that relevance and reliability are, but instead deals with the relationship between accounting numbers: "The purpose of comparison is to explain similarities and differences."[7] However, SFAC No. 2 also states, "Comparability should not be confused with identity, and sometimes more can be learned from differences than from similarities if the differences can be explained."[8]

Although uniformity and comparability are usually discussed in terms of the need to account for similar events in a similar manner, no extensive formal attempt has been made to specify the dividing line between similarity and difference. Consequently, a fruitful starting point for examining the uniformity issue is analyzing events.

The Nature and Complexity of Events

Transactions are economic or financial events that are recorded in the firm's accounts. An *event* has been defined in SFAC No. 6 as "a happening of consequence to an entity."[9] Transactions occur between entities, between a firm and its employees, and between a firm and investors or lenders. *Transactions* are thus events external to an enterprise. Events that are internal to the firm also require entries in the firm's accounts. Examples would include recognition of depreciation and completion of work-in-process inventories. It is up to the rules of accounting to specify the necessary criteria for event recognition. Rules of recognition are concerned, for example, with the question of when to recognize revenues as being earned.

Another aspect of events that particularly concerns us here is their degree of simplicity or complexity. In a complicated and involved business environment, events are often accompanied by a complex set of restrictions, contingencies, and conditions. For example, in the case of long-term leases, some of the complicating factors would be:

- A clause in the lease providing for cancellation by either party
- The proportion of the asset's life the lease period is expected to cover
- The possible existence of favorable renewal privileges (either for purchase or rental) at the end of the original lease period

Some other examples of event complexity would involve situations such as the following:

- Acquisition of common stock for control purposes where the percentage of stock owned may vary
- Differing expected usage or benefit patterns of depreciable fixed assets and intangibles
- Long-term construction contracts in which payment by the buyer becomes uncertain

Before we examine the nature of complex events further, we should mention that there are many events that do not have any significant economic variables that lead to essentially different recording. We denote these as *simple events*. For example, payment for services acquired on an account with no discount involved would be a simple event. Some complex events may also be handled with dispatch. Whether the buyer or vendor will pay the freight for acquired inventories is the key issue in recording this event, but under either circumstance it is easily handled. If the buyer pays, the situation comes under the "cost rule," which charges all costs necessary for acquisition and installation to the asset rather than directly to expense. If the seller pays, transportation costs are charged to a freight-out type of account. These situations are similar enough to result in a highly uniform recording of events. Complex events, however, can be considerably more involved than the freight situation and may be much more difficult to resolve. The literature uses the term *effect of circumstances* to describe these situations, but we prefer the less cumbersome *relevant circumstances*.

Relevant Circumstances

With regard to the complex events discussed above, we can say that, while the variables mentioned represent potential economic differences between relatively similar events, there are some subtle differences as well. In the case of leases, all the elements considered would be stipulated in the contract; hence, they would be known at the inception of the lease (except for the expected life of the asset). Similarly, the percentage of common stock owned is a condition that would be known at the time of the transaction. On the other hand, expected usage or benefit patterns of depreciable assets pertain to future events.

The Terminology of Relevance

Relevant circumstances are economically significant circumstances that can affect broadly similar events. These economically significant circumstances are general conditions or factors associated with complex events that are expected to influence the incidence or timing of cash flows. As the preceding examples suggest, relevant circumstances are of two general types.[10] Those conditions known at the time of the event will be referred to as *present magnitudes*. Factors that can be known only at a later date shall be called *future contingencies*. Relevant circumstances pertain directly to the event being accounted for and influence the accounting method selected to represent that event.

The percentage of stock owned in another firm would be an example of a present magnitude. The usage or benefit pattern of a fixed asset would be a future contingency. Although there may be a desired pattern of usage of the fixed asset, future events could well change this pattern.

A case can certainly be made that one of the principal tasks of a rule-making body should be identifying appropriate relevant circumstances and setting up criteria for how they should govern the recording of events or the format of financial statements. Rule-making bodies have done this in a rather unsystematic fashion in such areas as lease capitalization (SFAS No. 13) and choice among full consolidation, equity, and fair-market value methods where common stock investments in other firms exist (ARB 51, APB Opinion No. 18, SFAS No. 94, and SFAS No. 115). Identifying relevant circumstances, not to mention setting criteria to govern choice among accounting methods or format of financial statements, is a formidable task. Whether a conceptual framework can be useful is an important question that will be addressed later in this chapter.

The Role of Management in Relevant Circumstances

Given that relevant circumstances are an extremely important aspect of the uniformity issue, the question arises as to whether management should have the choice of determining them. Weldon Powell, the former managing partner of a then Big Eight firm, regarded managerial influence as an important consideration in terms of allowing different methods.[11] For example, assume two firms acquired the same type of fixed asset. One intended to use the asset intensively in the early years whereas the other anticipated relatively even usage throughout its life. From Powell's viewpoint, the first firm would be justified in using an accelerated depreciation method and the second could select straight-line depreciation.

These choices might be valid, but the problem is that selection of accounting methods might be guided by motives different from those dictated by the presumed relevant circumstances. These ulterior motives would include the following:

- Maximizing short-run reported income if managerial compensation is based on it
- Minimizing short-run reported income if there is fear of governmental intervention on antitrust grounds
- Smoothing income (minimizing deviations in income from year to year) if it is believed that stockholders perceive the firm has a lower amount of risk than would be the case if greater fluctuations of earnings were present[12]

Because management is potentially capable of distorting income measurement, Cadenhead favors limiting relevant circumstances to elements beyond managerial control, elements he refers to as *environmental conditions*.[13] Environmental conditions differ between firms and lead to either excessive measurement costs or a low degree of verifiability relative to the preferred accounting method.[14] If environmental conditions possess either of these two qualities, they are designated *circumstantial variables* by Cadenhead. For example, if the valuation of inventories was to be based on the specific identification method, the cost of record keeping would be exorbitant for retail firms having extensive inventories with a low unit value. Also, if the net realizable value of inventories was required, costs of completion and disposal might be extremely difficult to estimate in some industries, leading to a low degree of verifiability. Only in cases involving circumstantial variables would Cadenhead allow departure from rigidly prescribed accounting methods.

Despite the importance of relevant circumstances in allowing different accounting treatments in generally similar transactions, little research has been done on the topic. Nevertheless, two concepts of uniformity have evolved in both the accounting literature and the standards propounded by rule-making bodies without a sharp underlying definition and explication of relevant circumstances (or some similar term).

Finite and Rigid Uniformity

Finite uniformity attempts to equate prescribed accounting methods with the relevant circumstances in generally similar situations. The word *finite* was selected in accordance with the *Random House Dictionary* definition of "having bounds or limits; not too great or too small to be measurable." SFAS No. 13 on long-term leases provides a good example of finite uniformity. If a lessee has a long-term lease for 75% or more of the estimated economic life of an asset, capitalization is required. However, if the lease period is for less than 75% of the estimated economic life of the asset, the lease is not capitalized.[15] This lease provision is one of four set down in the standard, any of which is sufficient to require capitalization on the grounds that the lease contract "transfers substantially all of the benefits and risks incident to the ownership of the property" to the lessee, including lower annual rental costs for the property due to the long-term nature of the lease.

An obvious difficulty with the 75% lease period provision is the fact that it attempts to draw an exact boundary where a continuum exists. Would 70% or even 60% have been a better break point between capital and operating leases? The point is very debatable and can never be totally resolved. Furthermore, as previously discussed, the door is open to manipulation if management wants noncapitalization. All it has to do is extend, within reasonable bounds, the estimated economic life of the asset or shorten the lease period to just under 75% of the estimated economic life.[16]

The Need for an Alternative to Finite Uniformity

Since establishing appropriate criteria for relevant circumstances is difficult and often somewhat arbitrary, an alternative type of uniformity has been implicitly formulated. *Rigid uniformity* means prescribing one method for generally similar transactions even though relevant circumstances may be present. For example, SFAS No. 2 requires that research and development costs must be expensed even though future benefits may be present. SFAS No. 109 requires that income tax allocation must be used even if there is no anticipated reversal of deferred tax liabilities during the foreseeable future.

SFAC No. 2 (conceptual framework) appears to accept implicitly the idea of finite uniformity, as the following example reveals:

> For example, to find whether a man is overweight, one compares his weight with that of other men— not women—of the same height. . . . Clearly, valid comparison is possible only if the measurements used—quantities or ratios—reliably represent the characteristic that is the subject of comparison.[17]

But it also implicitly mentions rigid uniformity in the context of improving comparability (by using the same accounting method) in situations in which representational faithfulness is not the goal. However, "improving" comparability may, in reality, be counterproductive:

> Improving comparability may destroy or weaken relevance or reliability if, to secure comparability between two measures, one of them has to be obtained by a method yielding less relevant or reliable information. Historically, extreme examples . . . have been provided . . . in which the use of standardized charts of accounts has been made mandatory in the interest of interfirm comparability but at the expense of relevance and often reliability as well. That kind of uniformity may even adversely affect comparability of information if it conceals real differences between enterprises.[18]

Finite and Rigid Uniformity Relative to Representational Faithfulness and Verifiability

Finite uniformity should be more representationally faithful than rigid uniformity. If a fixed asset were to be intensively utilized in its early years, a more faithful representation of unamortized cost and depreciation expense would be provided by an accelerated method of depreciation rather than straight-line depreciation (depreciation accounting is presently a matter of flexibility since free choice is allowed relative to acceptable methods). In the case of research and development (R&D) costs under SFAS No. 2, rigid uniformity is applied. Greater representational faithfulness would result if R&D costs were accounted for similarly to successful efforts in oil and gas accounting, an example of finite uniformity. Successful R&D costs would be capitalized whereas unsuccessful efforts would be expensed when it became clear that future benefits were no longer expected. The finite uniformity approach would be more relevant but less verifiable than the immediate write-off required by SFAS No. 2.

The approach to representational faithfulness under finite uniformity is that there are degrees of representational faithfulness. In contrast, Sterling sees representational faithfulness in a binary context: Either a measurement of a characteristic of an asset is representationally faithful or it is not.[19] Hence, for decision usefulness, Sterling believes that representational faithfulness is a prime characteristic of usefulness that cannot be "traded off" with verifiability, even though some measurements of relevant qualities might "lack precision." Not surprisingly, Sterling totally rejects historical costs as a viable valuation approach in favor of current values (he prefers exit values). We believe that both of these orientations are internally consistent (historical costs using a mix of finite and rigid uniformity under a policy approach to be discussed shortly versus a system embracing only current values). Of course, as we move toward the era of fair value measurement, as represented by SFAS No. 157, it is difficult to say how uniformity concepts will be affected. Uniformity may well be an issue relative to different measurement methods being used to determine fair value. Certainly, relevance, reliability, and comparability will still be important theoretical concepts. Let us next examine finite and rigid uniformity in practice and examine whether a policy for their use in practice can be developed.

The Present Status of Uniformity

Finite uniformity and rigid uniformity are, to a certain extent, ideals. At present, a mixed system exists in which some standards attempt to take into account relevant circumstances whereas others are clearly examples of rigid uniformity. However, we must make clear several qualifications before giving some examples.

First, the fact that a standard is an example of finite uniformity should not necessarily be construed to mean that the standard cannot be improved or even that the factor selected as the relevant circumstance is appropriate. Second, where rigid uniformity is in effect, the underlying reasons may be attributable to one or more of the following factors: (a) a desire for conservatism, (b) an inability of the standard-setting organization to determine meaningful relevant circumstances, (c) an attempt to increase verifiability of the measurement, (d) recognition of the fact that an allocation is involved, and (e) the perception that, given adequate disclosure and an efficient securities market, the costs of implementing relevant circumstances exceed the resulting benefits. Third, another approach to the uniformity problem, usually called *flexibility*, has formed many accounting rules.

Flexibility applies to situations in which there are no discernible relevant circumstances but more than one possible accounting method exists, any of which may be selected at the firm's discretion.[20] The investment tax credit (now defunct) was a good example of flexibility. Holding aside the carry-forward problem, which was relatively rare, no relevant circumstance appeared to be present (unless the firm expected to hold the asset for a relatively short period, in which case the government would have recaptured some or all of the investment tax credit benefits). However, APB Opinion No. 4 allowed enterprises to take all benefits immediately in the year of acquisition or spread them over the useful life of the asset. Either alternative was acceptable.

We will give some examples of rigid uniformity, finite uniformity, and flexibility. These examples are intended to be illustrative only and do not cover the entire range of policies comprising generally accepted accounting principles. We will highlight relevant circumstances and allowable alternatives; intermediate or advanced accounting texts should be consulted for in-depth discussion of the various methods and other details.

Rigid Uniformity

There are numerous examples of rigid uniformity in official pronouncements of standard-setting bodies. Comprehensive income tax allocation is required by SFAS No. 109 whether or not deferred tax liabilities are realistically expected to reverse. In the case of research and development costs, despite the presumed presence of future benefits arising from an important proportion of these costs, SFAS No. 2 requires they be immediately expensed.

Finite Uniformity

Examples of finite uniformity include long-term leases and ownership of common stock of another firm for control purposes. In the former case, any one of four conditions is sufficient to warrant capitalization, whereas the absence of all four results in an operating lease. In the second situation, ownership of various percentage ranges of common stock results in either full consolidation, equity, or fair market value method. However, the FASB recognized the fuzziness of stock ownership as a criterion for degree of control when it noted in Interpretation No. 35 that the 20% demarcation point between cost then in effect and equity methods is to be construed as a guideline rather than an inviolable rule.

These two illustrations of finite uniformity involve situations of present magnitudes. The question of reversal of deferred tax liabilities is a case of finite uniformity where future contingencies are involved. Reversal was a relevant circumstance in the United Kingdom where partial tax allocation was used until recently. Allocation had to be used if reversal (repayment of tax benefits) was expected to occur. In the United States, we must allocate. Hence, rigid uniformity must be used in the United States.

Another case of finite uniformity involving a future contingency concerns loss contingencies. SFAS No. 5 sets up two conditions under which a contingent loss must be charged against income of the current year: (a) the likely occurrence of an adverse future event, such as an expropriation of assets by a foreign government, and (b) the ability to make a reasonable estimate of the amount of the loss. If either or both of these conditions are not met, disclosure of the loss contingency (presumably in the footnotes) should be made if there is at least a "reasonable possibility" of a loss occurring. SFAS No. 5 can also be interpreted as an example of conservatism because gain contingencies are not mentioned except for the statement that ARB

No. 50 is still in effect relative to them. ARB No. 50 states that gain contingencies are not reflected in income prior to realization. However, adequate disclosure is to be made, though care must be exercised "to avoid misleading implications as to the likelihood of realization."[21]

Flexibility

Flexibility is very prevalent in generally accepted accounting principles.[22] In addition to the investment tax credit, depreciation accounting provides a special example of flexibility. The estimated usage pattern of the asset provides a potential relevant circumstance.[23] However, choice among the many acceptable methods—such as straight-line, accelerated methods, and the annuity method—is again at management's discretion and need not be related to the estimated pattern of usage.

Another example of flexibility is provided by treasury stock that is acquired for later reissuance. Among the reasons for acquisition are (a) issuance to employees under stock option plans, (b) acquiring stock of another corporation in a business combination, and (c) supporting the market value of the stock. The cash flow consequences of these different reasons are simply not clear. It is thus very doubtful that they could be considered as future contingencies. Nevertheless, there are two methods for handling treasury stock acquisitions: the par value and the cost methods. Once again, either method can be used at the firm's option. Inventory and cost of goods sold accounting would have been an example of flexibility, were it not for the tax implications.

Overview of Practice

The present situation in financial accounting can, perhaps, be best understood by means of Exhibit 9.1, which shows a two-by-two matrix with one illustration in each cell. Column I represents situations in which relevant circumstances are present. Column II represents situations in which relevant circumstances are not present. Row A depicts transactions in which a policy-setting body has treated the situation as if it were finite. Similarly, Row B represents transactions in which a policy-setting body has treated the situation as one of rigid uniformity.

The cells where policy matches the complexity of the situation are IA and IIB. In IA, a relevant circumstance is present and the policy-making body has given it recognition. In IIB, no relevant circumstance is present and the rule-making organization has attempted to treat the situation with rigid uniformity.

The cells where suboptimization is present are IIA and IB. In IIA, no relevant circumstances are present, but the policy-setting group has set up criteria as if relevant circumstances existed. The result is two different methods of treatment that do not appear to have any real basis in fact. In IB, relevant circumstances are present but the policy-making group has not been able to implement them, resulting in a situation of rigid uniformity. Situation IIA is more serious than IB. In the former, the standard-setting group has expended resources and taken actions that were not required and indeed led to extremely serious problems in the case of purchase versus pooling.[24] In IB, the group restricted alternative treatments because the different circumstances were simply not verifiable.[25]

Exhibit 9.1   Uniformity and Relevant Circumstances in Practice

Policy Employed	Relevant Circumstances	
	Yes	*No*
Finite	IA ARB 51, APB 18, SFAS No. 94 and SFAS No. 115	IIA SFAS No. 115
	Ownership of common stock of other firms	Treatment of unrealized holding gains for trading securities as opposed to available-for-sale-securities
Rigid	IB SFAS No. 2	IIB APB 29
	Research and development costs	Assets acquired by donation

Finally, we stress once again that even though cell IA provides a "match" between the standard-setting body's action and the complexity of the situation, it is not necessarily the case that relevant circumstances have been defined and applied optimally—or, even if they have, that the benefits of the standard exceed its costs.

Formulating Accounting Policy

How can the concepts of finite uniformity, rigid uniformity, and flexibility be used for formulating accounting policy? Wherever possible, flexibility should be eliminated. In the various event categories, if it is possible to discern relevant circumstances and they can be measured and implemented in a cost-effective manner, finite uniformity should be implemented. On the other hand, if the event category is either a simple event or a complex event in which finite uniformity cannot be instituted in a cost-effective manner, rigid uniformity should be employed. These relationships are shown in Exhibit 9.2. We should also bear in mind that similarities of accounting methods within industries do exist, a situation that we examine next.

Uniformity Within Industries and Relevant Circumstances

A possible aid to standard setters, if they should attempt to bring about uniformity, is that within industries evidence exists that there is some degree of similarity relative to accounting method choices, particularly if they are of a similar size.[26] Numerous studies, with varying degrees of success, have also tried to categorize similarity of accounting method choices across industries to similarities of agency (contracting) theory conditions.[27] Both of these types of situations can interact or intersect with the type of uniformity analysis and policy being discussed here. For example, Dopuch and Pincus show that long-term FIFO users do *not* forgo large tax savings by remaining on FIFO.[28] On the other hand, if inflationary conditions were expected to impact a particular firm or industry, a firm might switch to LIFO to provide it with large tax savings. In addition, firms contemplating switching to LIFO would also have to consider agency implications. For example, LIFO would lower income, which

Exhibit 9.2   Instituting Uniformity

Broad Event Class		
Simple Event	Complex Event	
↓	Measurement and/or Cost Constraints	Measurable and Cost Effective
↓	↓	↓
Rigid Uniformity	Rigid Uniformity	Finite Uniformity

would affect debt covenants. The cash flow effects of the LIFO/FIFO choice create a relevant circumstance.

The Usefulness of Accounting Allocations

The previous discussion of uniformity and flexibility frequently involve another consideration, allocations, which have been an integral part of accounting. An *allocation* is a "slicing up" or dividing of costs or revenues arising in one period that are applicable to many periods. Some examples include depreciation, depletion, cost of goods sold, and bond premium/discount amortization.

Allocations have been criticized on the grounds that they are "incorrigible."[29] By this it is meant that there is no absolutely correct way to allocate costs because no single allocation method can be proved "scientifically" superior to another method. For this reason, it has been concluded that all accounting allocations are, in the end, arbitrary. In fact, many allocations, such as depreciation and cost of goods sold, presently fall under the category of flexibility as previously discussed.

However, to say that accounting allocations are arbitrary does not mean that they are not useful. We have already seen in Chapter 8 that accounting accruals can be useful in determining security prices, but, despite their "incorrigibility," more economically relevant accruals (i.e., accelerated depreciation for fixed assets that will be used more intensively in their earlier years) would improve the assessments of users in terms of both feedback and cash flow prediction.

One point that should be reiterated is that instituting fair value measurements (SFAS No. 157) could have important implications for accounting allocations. As a result, the market would largely determine allocations.

Disclosure

Broadly interpreted, disclosure is concerned with information in both the financial statements and supplementary communications—including footnotes, poststatement events, management's discussion and analysis of operations for the forthcoming year, financial and operating forecasts, the summary of significant accounting policies, and additional financial statements covering segmental disclosure and extensions beyond historical costs. *Financial reporting* is often used as an umbrella term to cover both financial statements themselves and the additional types of information mentioned before. SFAC No. 5 (para. 9) defines *disclosure* as presentation of information by means other than recognition in the financial statements, which is contrasted with *recognition* in the financial statements themselves; this is the aspect of disclosure on which we largely concentrate. Financial reporting is so complex that other forms of disclosure must supplement the financial statements themselves if an adequate picture of financial conditions and operations is to be available for user analysis. For example, attempts by management to remove liabilities from the balance sheet requires, at the least, better disclosure of liabilities and risks that have managed to escape the balance sheet.

The Disclosure Function of the SEC

It has always been implicitly recognized that disclosure as interpreted by the Securities and Exchange Commission (SEC) has two aspects.[30] One of these might be termed *protective disclosure* since the SEC has been concerned with protecting unsophisticated investors from unfair treatment. The other aspect is *informative disclosure*, the full range of information useful for investment analysis purposes. Obviously, there is some degree of overlap between these functions of disclosure.

In its earlier history, the SEC stressed protective rather than informative disclosure. The Securities Act of 1933 required the filing of a registration statement with the SEC prior to the sale of a new issue of securities. Included in the registration statement and the prospectus given to the purchaser is extensive information about the business of the issuer, the securities being sold, and the identity and relevant financial interests of those distributing the securities. In addition, extensive information about the underwriter's compensation and dealings between the corporation and its officers, directors, and principal shareholders must be provided in the registration statement. Much of this information is protective in nature, although there is certainly informative material in the registration statement and the prospectus. The Securities Exchange Act of 1934 extended most of these rules for new issues of securities to sales of existing issues. In effect, then, the intention was to keep the information on the initial registration current.

Several restrictions were put into effect when a firm filed a registration statement: a 20-day waiting period; delivery of the prospectus to purchasers; and the potential imposition of rather heavy civil liability damages upon the issuer, its officers, directors, and underwriters for filing inadequate or misleading information. It was thought that this package of restrictions would be a strong deterrent against blatant attempts to defraud investors. The SEC also had the authority to invalidate a registration or suspend it if it had already become effective if the information was either incomplete or inaccurate in any material respect.

The Shift Toward Informative Disclosure

Although the protective and informative aspects of disclosure tended to overlap, the SEC shied away from requiring disclosure of "soft information." However, since the early 1970s, the

SEC appears to have shifted its emphasis toward informative disclosure. For example, the commission had always shunned inflation accounting proposals—despite the presumed importance for informative purposes—very likely on the grounds that the data were not highly verifiable and the average investor would probably not understand the numbers. However, after the FASB exposure draft on general price-level statements came out, the SEC in ASR 190 required for most major firms supplementary disclosures of replacement cost information for depreciation expense, fixed-asset valuation, cost of goods sold, and inventories. It is possible that the movement toward informative disclosure has occurred as a result of studies of market efficiency.

The Advisory Committee on Corporate Disclosure to the SEC continued the SEC's movement toward informative disclosure. The committee prepared a voluminous report in 1977 summarizing the present state of disclosure and making further recommendations about disclosure. Although stating that the existing disclosure system was adequate and not in need of drastic change, it endorsed the shift away from hard information (as signified by objectively verifiable historical data) toward the soft information embodied in opinions, forecasts, and analyses.

Among the committee's informative-disclosure suggestions were earnings forecasts with a "safe harbors" provision that would protect management from the liability penalties of the federal securities laws, provided projections were reasonable and made in good faith.[31] Other forward-looking informative data recommended by the committee included planned capital expenditures and their financing, management plans and objectives, dividend policies, and policies relative to enterprise capital structure.[32] Other informative disclosures recommended by the committee included standard product-line classifications for segmental reporting, determined on an industry-by-industry basis, and disclosure of social and environmental information if it was expected to affect future financial performance, such as a constant violation of the law.[33]

The SEC acted on the recommendations of the committee in 1979 by adopting Rule 175, which provided safe harbor from the liability provisions of the federal securities laws for projections that are reasonably based and made in good faith.[34]

Imperfections of the Disclosure Process

The system of disclosure largely in effect today is called *differential disclosure.* The 10-K and 10-Q reports filed annually and quarterly by management with the SEC are used by professional financial analysts. The analysts act as intermediaries by interpreting the SEC filings for the investing public. Beaver believed that the emphasis on more disclosure in the annual report would downgrade the importance of the differential disclosure approach.[35] Differential disclosure should be distinguished from *selective disclosure.* The latter indicates more information available to some individuals, which would be information asymmetry. This constitutes insider information and raises the possibility that those in possession of the insider information may be able to earn an abnormal return.

Although informative disclosure should improve the evaluation of risk and return of enterprises, there are several important qualifications to bear in mind. An important channel of disclosure communication is that between the corporation and financial analysts representing brokerage firms and investment consultants. Several aspects of this arrangement were discussed in Chapter 4. Since financial analysts do not pay for this information, it is likely to be overproduced as compared to the information that would have been available if it were supplied on a market-oriented basis.

However, Brownlee and Young note that timely possession of financial information results in a benefit to the holder (and user) of that information as opposed to later users.[36] Brownlee and Young see financial analysts as aggressive seekers of information that can profitably be sold to consumers (who have an advantage over other consumers who do not have the information on as timely a basis). Thus, they do not see a need for extensive additional disclosures. In effect, through their aggressive information search, security analysts cause the market for financial information to act efficiently in terms of providing adequate and timely information (with those willing to pay for the information better off than those who do not pay, an equitable market-type solution to the problem).[37] However, the SEC passed Regulation FD in August 2000, which rejected selective disclosure and requires broad and equal access to management disclosures thus "leveling the playing field."

Regulation FD attempts to prevent the leaking of important information to favored financial analysts prior to announcing it to the general public. Hence the SEC is attempting to eliminate this source of insider trading information. This has created some consternation among corporate management ranks relative to using the communication process.

For example, before Regulation FD, firms could require analysts to use selective disclosure solely for improving their earnings-per-share forecasts.[38] Also, corporations could protect proprietary information more easily.[39] Nevertheless, opposition to Regulation FD was expressed on the grounds that information flows would be diminished because firms would be fearful of violating the regulation.[40]

Early research results on Regulation FD have been mixed. Irani and Karamanou, using univariate and multivariate analysis, find that analyst following was lower under Regulation FD and analyst forecast dispersion was higher, indicating the possibility of lower information availability.[41] Taking a different tack, Bushee, Matsumoto, and Miller examined analysts' phone calls to corporate management before and after Regulation FD.[42] Although there was a negative impact on the number of firms hosting "open" calls after Regulation FD was passed that had previously hosted only "closed" calls employing selective disclosure, they did not find a greater decrease in the information content of conference calls before and after Regulation FD.[43] Heflin, Subramanyan, and Zhang found that Regulation FD has not impeded information flow to financial analysts and may have actually increased voluntary disclosures on forward-looking data related to earnings.[44]

While the results are mixed, it is still too early to tell if Regulation FD will be successful. However, as more firms become used to Regulation FD with the passage of time, we expect the results to be more positive. Also, our own beliefs accord with a more "level playing field," more information symmetry, and a rejection of selective disclosure.

Another argument against regulations that would require the overproduction of disclosure information is the possibility of *information overload*: the inability of users to process and intelligently utilize all the information provided in financial reports. Still another problem with disclosure, mentioned previously in this chapter, is that of competitive disadvantage. For example, in an area such as segmental disclosure, firms may be somewhat reluctant to reveal information about product lines because they might give vital information to competitors and damage their own favorable market situations. Hence, an inequitable situation may be created, since some individuals will tend to be unfavorably affected, such as present owners of securities of firms whose competitive advantage is revealed. A situation like this would be an economic consequence of an accounting standard. In this particular case, as long as there were no bias relative to firms (in terms of the information being reported), neutrality (SFAC No. 2) should govern the disclosure: As long as the information required is relevant and reliable, the effect on a particular interest should not be considered.

There are other perceived limitations to the disclosure process. A point that has been mentioned in the disclosure literature is that adequate diversification by the investor may reduce the need for information at the firm-specific level.[45] The investor's concerns, it is argued, are with firm-specific information only insofar as it affects the portfolio. However, separating firm-specific information into categories—that which has no effect on the portfolio and that which is useful in terms of portfolio assessment—appears virtually impossible.

A complementary argument involves the undiversified investor.[46] Because unsystematic risk can be virtually eliminated by proper diversification, the question arises as to responsibilities owed to the undiversified investor in terms of disclosure, since the costs must be borne largely by others (costs passed on to customers of the firm or lower dividends for all stockholders, for example).[47] However, it is difficult to separate information useful specifically for undiversified portfolios and that which is also useful for diversified portfolios—not to mention the difficulty of separating information that is portfolio specific from that which is firm specific.

Lev, however, has also made a very strong argument in favor of additional disclosure.[48] Additional disclosure benefits all users. The problem with information asymmetry (which is defended by Brownlee and Young) is that those who do not have information will tend to take defensive measures, such as not dealing in securities where limited information is present, buying diversified portfolios, or even staying out of the market altogether. When this occurs, a "thin" market results, and those with additional information would not get the full benefit of their advantage. Hence, on the grounds of equity, Lev favors additional disclosure (such as management's forecast of earnings), which is beneficial to all parties—those having additional information as well as those not possessing this information.

Moreover, Lev believes that there is a complementarity relative to the favorable effects of disclosure for users that is also beneficial to the enterprise itself and its management. He believes that the firm should have an organized disclosure policy that dovetails with corporate policies in production, marketing, and investment.[49] These disclosures would involve areas such as new product announcements, earnings forecasts, and research and development budgets. Lev would not restrict disclosures to "good news" items only. He also advocates "bad news" disclosures, such as justifying dividend decreases, because forthright announcements over the long run should mitigate the adverse effect of the event itself. An organized disclosure policy is beneficial to all parties because uncertainty about the firm is reduced over the long run, leading to higher security prices, lower price volatility, and reduced spread between bid and ask prices, resulting in greater liquidity of the stock.[50] Certainly Regulation FD of the SEC, which tries to eliminate selective disclosure, represents an important step along the path that Lev would like to take.

Forms and Methods of Disclosure

In this section, we survey several forms of disclosure. We commence with Management's Discussion and Analysis in the annual report.

Management's Discussion and Analysis

Since 1968, the SEC has required firms to include in their annual report a Management's Discussion and Analysis (MD&A) section that would give readers a prospective view of future operations and cash flows.[51] "Safe harbors" have been provided for forward-looking information as long as it is determined on a reasonable basis and in good faith. Both retrospective and prospective information are required but the former basically serves as a benchmark for the latter. Specific information required includes

1. Results of operations including information on selling price changes, cost changes, and volume changes

2. Assessment of the enterprise's future liquidity

3. Capital resources and planned capital expenditures

4. Known trends, uncertainties, and future events which might have a material affect on numbers 1–3

Signaling and Management Earnings Forecasts

Signaling theory appears to be largely consistent with the advocacy of greater disclosure. It is posited in signaling theory that firms with undisclosed "good news" information will attempt to distinguish themselves from firms not having "good news" by informing the market of their situation. The market, in turn, should reward these firms by favorable price effects on their securities. The nondisclosing firms that are assumed to have "bad news" are then subject to price declines. Signaling theory is generally consistent with the semistrong form of the efficient-markets hypothesis. Forms of signaling include dividends and stock repurchases as well as specific accounting disclosures.[52] Dividends and stock repurchases require cash outflows, but they protect against the dispensing of important proprietary information (Lev would, of course, prefer disclosure of information relative to new products, research and development, and capital budgeting programs.)

A form of signaling is in the area of voluntary disclosure of earnings forecasts. Lev and Penman found that firms that disclosed expected favorable earnings were indeed rewarded by favorable changes in security prices.[53] However, they also found that nondisclosing firms in the same industry as forecasting firms were not negatively affected by not publishing their earnings forecasts.[54] Furthermore, some firms that did disclose "bad news" were subject to negative price reactions, which is also consistent with the efficient-markets hypothesis.[55] This is not, however, necessarily consistent in the short run with Lev's general ideas regarding additional voluntary disclosure, although Lev's disclosure ideas are more applicable to the long run.

Going beyond earnings forecasts, Kasznik and Lev are concerned with management disclosures in the face of a major earnings surprise.[56] This type of disclosure may take the form of conference calls with analysts or public announcements via news services such as the Associated Press. Approximately half of these firms did not provide any prior information whatsoever relative to the major earnings surprise. However, of those making announcements, firms with negative earnings were twice as likely to provide information as those having positive news. Those firms providing information of major earnings surprises were generally larger than firms not providing information. Also, the larger the surprise, the more likely is management to communicate the information. Of course, this communication would now take place under the constraints of Regulation FD.

SFAS No. 131

The American Institute of Certified Public Accountants issued a special committee report which led directly to SFAS No. 131.[57] The FASB implemented major parts of the special committee report in SFAS No. 131. As opposed to SFAS No. 14's broad choice among major segments including products, production processes, and marketing channels, SFAS No. 131 requires segment reporting by "management approach which . . . is based on the way that management organizes the segments within the enterprise for making operating decisions and assessing performance."[58] This is clearly intended to follow through on the committee's segmental disclosure recommendation. Assuming that there are no escape hatches from the intent of the standard, SFAS No. 131 represents an important advance in segment reporting.

There is a question, however, relative to measuring segmental profit or loss. Reconciliation of segment profit or loss to the enterprise's consolidated income may be done either to consolidated income before income taxes, extraordinary items, discontinued operations, and the cumulative effect of changes in accounting principles or to consolidated income after these items have been deducted. To what extent this diversity in financial reporting would effect comparability is an open question.[59]

An operating segment is constituted by having either 10% or more of combined revenue, both internal and external, of all operating segments; essentially 10% of combined profit of all operating segments; or 10% of the combined assets of all reporting segments.[60] At least 75% of total consolidated revenue must be included in the reportable segments.[61]

Segment assets must also be reported. Segment liabilities, however, are optional. In the balance sheet area, SFAS No. 131 falls short of the special committee's report. In addition, segment cash flows are not required.[62] As with SFAS No. 14, SFAS No. 131 requires, where applicable, information by major geographical segment and by major customers where any individual customers constitute 10% or more of corporate revenues. A new feature of SFAS No. 131 is that segmental information in interim periods must contain information on segment revenues, segment profit or loss, and segment assets.[63]

Early evidence indicates that SFAS No. 131 has been successful. In comparing 1997 segment reporting (SFAS No. 14) with 1998 segment reporting (SFAS No. 131), Street, Nichols, and Gray found a marked decline in the number of enterprises claiming that they operated in only one segment.[64] Also, the average number of reported segments increased from 1997 to 1998. Finally, the numbers of items reported in each segment increased from 1997 to 1998. Hermann and Thomas's study shows results that are largely in agreement with Street,

Nichols, and Gray.[65] In addition, Hermann and Thomas found that 68 of their 100 sample firms changed the definition of their segments after adopting SFAS No. 131.[66] However, this may be a two-edged sword. Ettredge, Kwon, and Smith found that many of the respondents to the exposure draft preceding the issuance of SFAS No. 131 were concerned that revealing information about their operating segments would give vital information to their competitors.[67] It is possible that in determining new segments some firms may really be trying to hide vital segment information. Be that as it may, recent research does indicate the usefulness of SFAS No. 131, because a higher association was found between current earnings and the earnings of the following year for firms using SFAS No. 131 than was found previously when the firms in their sample were multi-segment firms under SFAS No. 14. SFAS No. 131 is clearly an improvement over SFAS No. 14.

Finally, a question has been raised relative to the management approach for segmental reporting of SFAS No. 131. Data are supposed to be both relevant and comparable according to the conceptual framework. By emphasizing each firm's own managerial approach, has comparability of segmental units been sacrificed on an interfirm comparison basis?[68] The problem can, of course, be avoided by assuming that managements, whether by product group or geographic area, would generally be choosing similar risk–return qualities by segment.[69]

There are two real issues arising from the presumed split between relevance and comparability of SFAS No. 131. First, should intercompany comparisons be made of divisional segments or should they mainly be used for understanding the operations of the enterprise of which they form a subset? Second, if segments of an enterprise lack comparability, won't enterprises themselves lack comparability because they are often made up of disparate segments in varied industries? But accounting standards, at least ideally, are supposed to lead to both comparability and relevance, even though enterprises themselves are in numerous and varied industries, by providing information that is helpful for assessing risk and return as well as helping to predict future cash flows. We do not believe that comparability has been sacrificed by SFAS No. 131.

Quarterly Information

The SEC requires many publicly traded companies to disclose quarterly financial data. Interest in these reports has perked up significantly in our age of instant information and communication. We have already mentioned that in SFAS No. 131, in terms of revenues, profit or loss, and segment assets, segments must also disaggregate quarterly earnings.

Interim reports should include, among other items, income statement data and basic and fully diluted earnings-per-share numbers. Balance sheet and cash flow statements are encouraged but not required. We would also add that quarterly information reporting requirements have added pressure on management to meet analysts' forecasts, particularly in the area of earnings-per-share numbers.

Perhaps the principal theoretical issue underlying quarterly data is whether each interim period should be viewed as a separate period standing on its own, called the *discrete view,* as contrasted with the *integral view,* which sees each quarterly report as a link or portion of the annual report. APB Opinion No. 28 favors the integral approach, but the ground is not completely settled on this issue. From a theoretical standpoint, the integral view has more validity because a year is a natural period of time, and many actions and events occurring during the year are really parts of a greater whole. For example, pension expense, post-retirement benefits other than pension, bad debts, and management bonuses should be allocated among interim periods. In addition, interim income taxes should be determined based on the estimated annual effective tax rate. Nevertheless, there are items that are discrete to particular quarterly segments. Certainly sales and related cost of goods sold, as well as other types of revenues, are discrete to particular quarterly segments where recognition and matching occur. Similarly, extraordinary items should be charged or credited as incurred within particular quarters. Although there are many quarterly issues that still remain to be definitively solved, the integral approach should hold sway except where events are very specific to particular quarterly segments.

Despite the problems of the disclosure process, our value judgment is that, on balance, the operations of securities markets and investors, as a totality, will benefit by expanding the disclosure process. Sengupta provides one piece of evidence supporting this position.[70] He found in Financial Analysts Federation ratings of corporate disclosure practices that highly evaluated firms have a lower risk premium—owing to quantity and quality of disclosures—and a resultant lower cost of capital. Along the same line, Lang and Lundholm found that firms with more information disclosure policies have a greater analyst following, more accurate analyst earnings forecasts, and less volatility in forecast revisions (analysts revise their own forecasts in light of management's own forecasts).[71]

Small Firms Versus Larger Firms

A contention is that small firms incur significantly higher costs than large ones in carrying out complex accounting standards or disclosure requirements.[72] Hence, the FASB (and the SEC) has provided some relief to smaller firms.[73] (See Chapter 3 for more on this issue.) The FASB specifically considers implications of disclosures for smaller firms with the express purpose of requiring disclosures only where they are relevant and cost effective. Furthermore, the FASB established a Small Business Advisory Committee of the Financial Accounting Standards Advisory Council for facilitating communication concerning financial reporting for both small enterprises and small public accounting firms. Nevertheless, balancing costs against benefits in financial reporting for small firms is not an easy task. For example, SFAS No. 33 on current cost and constant dollar disclosures (essentially similar to general price-level adjustments) was applicable only to firms having either in excess of $125 million of property, plant, and equipment or a billion dollars in total assets; similarly, privately held companies—which are generally smaller than publicly held firms—are exempt from segmental disclosures and earnings-per-share requirements.

However, recent research suggests that the disclosures of small firms, such as earnings announcements as well as published financial statements, have more information content than the statements for larger firms.[74] The reason for this may be that much less information is publicly available on smaller firms, which makes their published financial statements and related disclosures relatively more important for investors and therefore more comprehensive.[75]

We can expect more disclosure in the future. One harbinger of this change is the FASB's Business Reporting Research Project and its subsequent report, parts of which were published in 2000 and 2001. Among other issues, this report is concerned with disclosures in selected industries, the use of the Internet for conveying financial information, and dealing with disclosure redundancies between FASB and SEC reporting requirements. This report should be closely monitored because it has long-term reporting implications.

Improving Accounting Standards

In later chapters we discuss potential standards, but we start here with disclosure. It would well behoove auditors to require better disclosure of related party transactions such as the now ill-famed special purpose entities (SPEs) used by Enron, among others. According to the *Wall Street Journal*, Enron's disclosures were "virtually indecipherable" and also offered reassurance to the arm's-length nature of the transaction that was clearly untrue.[76] Disclosures should show how SPEs affect the parent's financial position and the nature of the various interests in the SPE.

Summary

Under finite uniformity, policy-making organizations attempt to take into account relevant circumstances in broadly similar event situations. Policy-making bodies do not attempt to cope with relevant circumstances under rigid uniformity. Their chief concern under rigid uniformity is to limit alternatives, which, in turn, would lead to greater verifiability but less relevance. Relevant circumstances are different economic factors leading to potentially different patterns of cash flows in broadly similar types of event situations.

Although finite uniformity should lead to greater relevance because rule making attempts to take into account appropriate circumstances, it is not at all clear that the resulting additional benefits would exceed the incremental costs of implementation. Certainly a more extensive metatheoretical framework would be needed to delineate the accounting required for relevant circumstances. In addition, extensive empirical research would have to be focused on the search for relevant circumstances.

Finite and rigid uniformity are ideals. It is unlikely that either could ever be totally and consistently applied. At present, examples of both rigid and finite uniformity can be found in various pronouncements of rule-making bodies. Perhaps finite uniformity could be instituted in event situations in which alternatives can be measured with a high degree of reliability and in a cost-effective manner. Certainly one step that might be taken is to eliminate alternatives in event situations in which it does not appear that relevant circumstances exist. Accounting allocations, while often arbitrary, are still useful in measuring income and determining security prices.

The great complexity of business and financial and operating events means that financial statements must be supplemented by an increasing array of disclosures. These include Management's Discussion and Analysis, management earnings forecast (which is still optional), segment disclosure, and quarterly financial reporting. The first two look forward whereas the last two provide feedback. Relative to segment disclosure, SFAS No. 131 will hopefully provide an improvement over SFAS No. 14 because the disclosure is supposed to accord with management's own way of making operating decisions and assessing segmental performance.

In the realm of differential disclosure, small firms have received some amount of relief regarding financial reporting relative to large firms. Despite some shortcomings with the disclosure process, it can only become more important in the future.

Regulation FD of the SEC attempts to eliminate selective disclosure in terms of conveying information to financial analysts and the general public. The elimination of selective disclosure is complementary to efforts to increase the level of disclosure to the public.

QUESTIONS

1. Is Cadenhead's conception of circumstantial variables as the only permissible departure from prescribed accounting methods closer to finite or rigid uniformity? Explain.

2. Do you think management policies should be acceptable as potential relevant circumstances? Why or why not?

3. How do present magnitudes differ from future contingencies?

4. Are simple transactions really examples of rigid uniformity? Why or why not?

5. Finite and rigid uniformity would result in different information being received by users of financial statements. What difference would this make in terms of resource allocation when viewed from a macroeconomic standpoint?

6. Why does segment disclosure in SFAS No. 131 represent a potential improvement over segment disclosure in SFAS No. 14?

7. How do protective and informative disclosure differ?

8. Under previous disclosure requirements of the SEC, dividends paid during the past two years to shareholders must be stated in the annual report. This requirement has been broadened:
   a. There must be disclosure of any restrictions on the firm's present or future dividend-paying ability.
   b. If the firm has not paid dividends in the past despite the availability of cash, and the corporate intention is to continue to forgo paying dividends in the foreseeable future, disclosure of this policy is encouraged.
   c. If dividends have been paid in the past, the firm is encouraged to disclose whether this condition is expected to continue in the future.
   d. Do you think that this broadening of disclosure of dividend policy is primarily protective or informative? Discuss.

9. ASR 242 of the SEC states that relative to payments made to foreign governmental and political officials, "registrants have a continuing obligation to disclose all material information and all information necessary to prevent other disclosures made from being misleading with respect to such transactions." This ASR appeared shortly after the passage of the Foreign Corrupt Practices Act. Do you think this type of disclosure is primarily protective or informative in nature?

10. If *uniformity* means eliminating alternative accounting treatments, then surely comparability of financial statements of different enterprises would be improved. Do you agree with this statement? Comment.

11. Is the choice of LIFO a relevant circumstance compared to FIFO?

12. Do you agree that it is not necessary to provide information for undiversified investors? Discuss.

13. SFAC No. 6 defines *circumstances* as follows:

Circumstances are a condition or set of conditions that develop from an event or series of events, which may occur almost imperceptibly and may converge in random or unexpected ways to create situations that might otherwise not have occurred and might not have been anticipated. To see the circumstance may be fairly easy, but to discern specifically when the event or events that caused it occurred may be difficult or impossible. For example, a debtor's going bankrupt or a thief's stealing gasoline may be an event, but a creditor's facing the situation that its debtor is bankrupt or a warehouse's facing the fact that its tank is empty may be a circumstance.

How does this definition of circumstances relate to the definition of relevant circumstances presented in the chapter?

14. SFAS No. 13 in effect regards a lease period of 75% or more as a relevant circumstance in distinguishing between capital and operating leases. What economic factors (cash flow differentials) lie behind this policy choice?

15. An argument against additional disclosure is that financial analysts aggressively seek this information, which is then sold to their customers, resulting in an adequate market solution to the problem of providing timely and relevant information on securities. Do you agree?

16. What are the possible benefits of a disclosure process that is integrated with major policies in marketing, production, and finance? Do you think only "good news" items should be disclosed? Why or why not?

17. Do you think that disclosures of smaller firms have more information content than disclosures for larger firms?

18. What is meant by the phrase "degrees of representational faithfulness?"

19. Firms A and B are exactly the same size as Firm C and Firm D. Firm A acquires for cash 100% of the common stock of Firm C. Firm B acquires 100% of Firm D by exchanging one share of its own stock for each share of common stock of Firm D. Are there differences in relevant circumstances between these two transactions? Explain.

20. How do Lev's views on disclosure differ from the views of Brownlee and Young?

21. Distinguish between the discrete and integral views of quarterly information disclosure.

22. What evidence supports the statement that SFAS No. 131 is an improvement over SFAS No. 14?

CASES, PROBLEMS, AND WRITING ASSIGNMENTS

1. Refer to either a current intermediate accounting text or a guide to current generally accepted accounting principles. Give at least one example for each of the four cells of Exhibit 9.1 (your instructor may desire to modify this problem).

2. Compare and contrast the Hutton (2004) and Lev (1992) disclosure strategies.

3. Give as many examples as you can of flexibility under current generally accepted accounting principles.

4. SFAS No. 115 defines held-to-maturity securities as debt securities that the firm "has the positive intent and ability to hold . . . to maturity." Trading securities "are bought and held principally for the purpose of selling them in the near term. . . ." Available-for-sale securities are simply everything else.

   SFAS No. 115 requires held-to-maturity securities to be valued at amortized cost with the other two carried at fair value. Unrealized gains and losses on trading securities are recognized in net income, but for available-for-sale securities, unrealized gains and losses are recognized as other comprehensive income and as a separate part of owners' equity.

   Two members of the FASB voted against the standard. They wanted the three types of securities to be carried at market value and unrealized gains and losses of the three "types" to go through income.

   Required:

   Evaluate the Board's attempt to use a finite uniformity approach to the investments covered in the standard. How did the dissenters to SFAS No. 115 want to deal with the problem?

5. Cadenhead presented an approach to uniformity referred to as *circumstantial variables.* Circumstantial variables are *environmental conditions* (conditions beyond the control of the individual firm that are applicable to the particular industry that the firm is in). Circumstantial variables lead to problems relative to either (a) costliness of the prescribed method in the particular event situation or (b) a low degree of verifiability because estimates vary widely relative to the prescribed method. For example, Cadenhead notes that the existence of a ready market with regularly quoted prices would facilitate inventory valuation if realizable value were not used relative to inventories, but the absence of such a market would allow a firm to use another type of inventory/cost of goods sold measurement.

   In the four situations discussed here, classify each situation according to whether it involves finite uniformity, rigid uniformity, flexibility, or circumstantial variables.
   a. *Research and development costs:* SFAS No. 2 requires that all research and development costs (some of which will have future cash flow benefits and others will not) be written off to expense as incurred. Are there any other accounting principles that are present here? Discuss.
   b. *Unusual right of return by customers:* SFAS No. 48 covers those industries (of which there are not many) in which buyers have an unusual right of return due to industry practices that cannot be avoided by the individual firm. The "unusual right of return" arises where buyers have an unusually long time period during which purchase returns can be made. From the seller's standpoint, revenue is recognized at time of sale, *provided that the future returns can be*

reasonably estimated (there are five other conditions that must also be met, but they are of no concern here). If sales returns *cannot* be reasonably estimated, then sales revenues are not recognized until returns *can* be reasonably estimated or (more likely) the return privilege has substantially expired. Hence, it is not cash flow differences that are at issue but rather the ability to estimate the expected returns that is the key point.

    c. Investment tax credit (assume no investment tax credit carryforward problem): All of the cash benefits in the form of lower taxes are received in the year of asset acquisition. The enterprise may recognize benefit (in the form of lower tax expense) in the year of acquisition, or the benefits may be spread over the life of the asset in the form of lower annual depreciation.

    d. Oil and gas accounting: SFAS No. 19 tried to allow only "successful efforts." In successful efforts, the costs of dry holes must be written off once it is known that the holes are dry. If (and only if) a well were successful, drilling costs would be capitalized and amortized over future years.

6. Colleges and universities frequently get graduating seniors to donate money to them. A very common practice is to divide this money up over a number of years. Thus a $30 donation might be divided up over a five-year period (based on a *Wall Street Journal* article of March 2, 2007; the $30 contribution and the $6 division over five years was actually cited in the article).

Required:

    a. Is this an allocation? Discuss.
    b. Why do you think that colleges and universities follow this practice?
    c. What entry did the college make for the five-year division?
    d. Do you have any other comments you would like to make about this practice?

CRITICAL THINKING AND ANALYSIS

1. What is the relationship between uniformity (both finite and rigid) and disclosure?

Notes

    1. *Ijiri (1975, pp. 9–11).*
    2. *Solomons (1983, pp. 112–113) viewed a conceptual framework as a buffer against political attacks.*
    3. *Miller (1985, p. 71), a former faculty fellow at the FASB, takes a similar position.*
    4. *Fields, Lys, and Vincent (2001, p. 257).*
    5. *Sprouse (1978, p. 71).*
    6. *Krisement (1997) proposes a quantitative method for measuring uniformity, which he refers to as comparability, based on relative frequency of usage of a particular method. If the uniformity of two methods of depreciation was being measured (straight-line versus accelerated depreciation, for example) and all firms in the sample used straight-line depreciation, complete uniformity would result. If, on the other hand, 50% of the firms used straight-line depreciation and the other 50% used accelerated depreciation, the result would be a low level of uniformity.*

7. *FASB (1980a, p. 45).*

8. *Ibid. (p. 48).*

9. *FASB (1985, p. 46).*

10. *Sorter and Ingberman (1987, p. 106) have also attempted to classify events and establish the cash flow aspect as the key to event recognition. Event recognition centers on "an actual, required future, or hypothetical cash flow associated with the acquisition and disposition of rights and obligations."*

11. *Powell (1965, pp. 680–681).*

12. *A very extensive literature in the area of income smoothing or managing income developed during the 1970s. For an excellent summary, see Ronen and Sadan (1981) and also Chapter 12.*

13. *See Cadenhead (1970).*

14. *The use of LIFO would not be an environmental condition because those electing to use it for tax purposes must use it for financial reporting purposes. Hence, its use for financial reporting purposes is beyond managerial control and is applicable to all firms electing it for tax purposes.*

15. *Provided none of the other conditions held and there is no bargain lease renewal present. FASB (1976, para. 7).*

16. *For a graphic example, see Wyatt (1983, pp. 58–60).*

17. *FASB (1980a, p. 46).*

18. *Ibid. (p. 47).*

19. *Sterling (1985, pp. 21–34).*

20. *Flexibility is sometimes called diversity. See Grady (1965, p. 33) for one example.*

21. *AICPA (1958, para. 5).*

22. *Dye and Verrechia (1995) analyze agency theory issues that arise between managers and shareholders and also between current and prospective shareholders in situations of (a) rigid uniformity and (b) flexibility.*

23. *Powell (1965, pp. 680–681).*

24. *Now phased out by SFAS No. 141. See Chapter 18 for more details.*

25. *However, questions are being raised relative to the possible capitalization of some intangible costs. See Chapter 11 for further details*

26. *See Chung, Park, and Ro (1996) and Morse and Richardson (1983).*

27. *For example, Zmijewski and Hagerman (1981). For a summary of these studies, see Watts and Zimmerman (1986, pp. 244–283).*

28. *Dopuch and Pincus (1988, p. 52).*

29. *Thomas (1969 and 1974).*

30. *Much of the information on the SEC and the disclosure process was obtained from Anderson (1974).*

31. *SEC (1977, pp. 344–365).*

32. *Ibid. (pp. 365–379).*

33. *U.S. Government Printing Office (1977, pp. 380–398).*

34. *SEC (1979, p. 19).*

35. *Beaver (1978, p. 50).*

36. *Brownlee and Young (1987, p. 21).*

37. *Brownlee and Young argued against the need for mandated disclosure by a governmental agency such as the SEC. Benston (1973) argued that the information required by the Securities Acts of 1933 and 1934 could be inferred from other data sources and that voluntary information disclosure plays an important role in information-efficient markets.*

38. *McCarthy (2001). Using an information economics model, Arya et al. (2005) raise the issue of a "herding" instinct arising among analysts: a tendency to arrive at similar end results.*

39. *Arya et al. (2005).*

40. *Ibid.*

41. *Irani and Karamanou (2003).*

42. *Bushee, Matsumoto, and Miller (2004).*

43. *Ibid.*

44. *Heflin, Subramanyam, and Zhang (2003).*

45. *Beaver (1978, pp. 46–47).*

46. *Ibid. (p. 47).*

47. *Coffee (1988, pp. 82 and 119) points out that although finance theory states that rational shareholders should hold diversified portfolios, evidence indicates that significant numbers of investors do not, in fact, possess diversified portfolios. Coffee also points out that it is possible many of these individuals may diversify by owning other risky investments, such as real estate. The sad case of many Enron employees owning only Enron stock comes to mind here.*

48. *Lev (1988).*

49. *Lev (1992). Another advocate of an integrated corporate disclosure strategy is Hutton (2004). Gibbins, Richardson, and Waterhouse (1992) are in agreement with Lev that disclosure is an important function that needs to be carefully managed. They note that while the disclosure literature is quite extensive, little has been done on how the process of disclosure happens or on the organizational structure and deliberations involved in the process (p. 3). See also Healy and Palepu (1993) for more on the importance of disclosure strategies.*

50. *See Bloomfield and Wilks (2000).*

51. *See Bryan (1997) for further details on the information presented here.*

52. *See Gelb (2000) for the interplay among the various forms of signaling.*

53. *Lev and Penman (1990).*

54. *Frankel, McNichols, and Wilson (1995) show that, as might be expected, firms that go into the capital markets more frequently are more likely to furnish earnings forecasts but not necessarily in periods just prior to seeking external financing (possibly owing to avoiding potential litigation). Complementary to Frankel, McNichols, and Wilson, Baginski and Hassell (1997) find that managers provide more precise forecasts of earnings for firms with more extensive following by analysts and also for smaller firms for which less public information is available.*

55. *Lev and Penman (1990).*

56. *Kasznik and Lev (1995).*

57. *AICPA (1994).*

58. *FASB (1997, para. 4).*

59. *Ibid. (pp. 13–14). See the comments of James Leisenring in his dissent to the opinion.*

60. *Ibid. (para. 18).*

61. *Ibid. (para. 20).*

62. *Ijiri (1995, p. 63) would like segment reports to show investment in the segment, income generated by the segment, and the "cash recovery" in the segment (cash flow).*

63. *FASB (1997, para. 33.)*

64. *Street, Nichols, and Gray (2000).*

65. *Hermann and Thomas (2000).*

66. *Ibid. (p. 289).*

67. *Ettredge, Kwon, and Smith (2002).*

68. *See Emmanuel and Garrod (2002).*

69. *Ettredge, Kwon, Smith, and Zarowin (2005, pp. 774–775).*

70. *Sengupta (1998).*

71. *Lang and Lundholm (1996).*

72. *Atiase, Bamber, and Freeman (1988, p. 18).*

73. *Larger firms also receive disclosure benefits. For example, only very large firms can use shelf registration, the registration of equity securities for future sale, even though the firm has no present intention to issue the securities. See Atiase, Bamber, and Freeman (1988, p. 19). Differential standards for small firms have been supported in two studies: Murray and Johnson (1983) and Guterblet (1983).*

74. *However, two AICPA committees found that, in addition to it being costly for small enterprises to prepare financial statement information in areas such as tax allocation, leases, and pensions, these enterprises are also providing some information that users either do not need or find confusing. Atiase, Bamber, and Freeman (1988, p. 19).*

75. *Ibid. (p. 20).*

76. *Bryan-Low and Brown (2002, p. C1).*

References

American Institute of Certified Public Accountants (1958). Accounting Research Bulletin No. 50, *Contingencies*. AICPA.

———— (1994). *Improving Business Reporting—A Customer Focus: Meeting the Information Needs of Investors and Creditors*. AICPA.

Anderson, Alison Grey (January 1974). "The Disclosure Process in Federal Securities Regulation: A Brief Review," *Hastings Law Journal*, pp. 311–354.

Arya, Anil, J. Glover, B. Mittendorf, and G. Narayanamoorthy (May–June 2005). "Unintended Consequences of Regulating Disclosures: The Case of Regulation Fair Disclosure," *Journal of Accounting and Public Policy*, pp. 243–252.

Atiase, Rowland K., Linda S. Bamber, and Robert N. Freeman (March 1988). "Accounting Disclosures Based on Company Size: Regulations and Capital Markets Evidence," *Accounting Horizons*, pp. 18–26.

Baginski, Stephen, and J. M. Hassell (April 1997). "Determinants of Management Forecast Precision," *Accounting Review*, pp. 303–312.

Beaver, William (January 1978). "Future Disclosure Requirements May Give Greater Recognition to the Professional Community," *Journal of Accountancy*, pp. 44–52.

Benston, George J. (March 1973). "Required Disclosure and the Stock Market: An Evaluation of the Securities Act of 1934," *American Economic Review*, pp. 132–155.

Bloomfield, Robert, and T. Wilks (2000). "Disclosure Effects in the Laboratory: Liquidity, Depth and the Cost of Capital," *Accounting Review* (January 2000), pp. 13–42.

Brownlee, E. Richard, and S. David Young (September 1987). "The SEC and Mandated Disclosure: At the Crossroads," *Accounting Horizons*, pp. 17–24.

Bryan, Stephen (April 1997). "Incremental Information Content of Required Disclosures Contained in Management Discussion and Analysis," *Accounting Review*, pp. 285–301.

Bryan-Low, Cassell, and K. Brown (2002). "And Now, the Question Is: Where's the Next Enron?" *Wall Street Journal* (June 18), pp. C1 and C10.

Bushee, Brian, D. Matsumoto, and G. S. Miller (July 2004) "Managerial and Investor Responses to Disclosure Regulation: The Case of Reg FD and Conference Calls," *Accounting Review*, pp. 617–644.

Cadenhead, Gary (September 1970). "'Differences in Circumstances': Fact or Fantasy?" *Abacus*, pp. 71–80.

Chung, Kun, Taewoo Park, and Byung T. Ro (Spring 1996). "Differential Market Reactions to Accounting Changes Away From Versus Towards Common Accounting Practices," *Journal of Accounting and Public Policy*, pp. 29–54.

Coffee, John C., Jr. (1988). "Shareholders Versus Managers: The Strain in the Corporate Web," in *Knights, Raiders, and Targets,* eds. John C. Coffee, Jr., Louis Lowenstein, and Susan Rose-Ackerman. Oxford University Press, pp. 77–134.

Dopuch, Nicholas, and Morton Pincus (Spring 1988). "Evidence on the Choice of Inventory Accounting Methods: LIFO Versus FIFO," *Journal of Accounting Research*, pp. 28–59.

Dye, Ronald, and Robert Verrechia (July 1995). "Discretion vs. Uniformity: Choices Among GAAP," *Accounting Review*, pp. 389–415.

Emmanuel, C. R., and N. Garrod (2002). "On the Relevance and Comparability of Segmental Data," *Abacus* (Vol. 38, No. 2), pp. 215–234.

Ettredge, Michael, S. Y. Kwon, and D. Smith (2002). "Competitive Harm and Companies' Positions on SFAS No. 131," *Journal of Accounting, Auditing & Finance* (Vol. 17, No. 2), pp. 93–109.

Ettredge, Michael, S. Y. Kwon, D. Smith, and P. Zarowin (July 2005). "The Impact of SFAS No. 131 Business Segment Data on the Market's Ability to Anticipate Future Earnings," *Accounting Review*, pp. 773–804.

Fields, Thomas D., T. Lys, and L. Vincent (2001). "Empirical Research on Accounting Choice," *Journal of Accounting and Economics* (Vol. 31), pp. 255–307.

Financial Accounting Standards Board (1976). Statement of Financial Accounting Standards No. 13, *Accounting for Leases*. FASB.

——— (1980a). Statement of Financial Accounting Concepts No. 2, *Qualitative Characteristics of Accounting Information*. FASB.

——— (1985). Statement of Financial Accounting Concepts No. 6, *Elements of Financial Statements: A Replacement of FASB Concepts Statement No. 3 (incorporating an amendment of FASB Concepts Statement No. 2)*. FASB.

——— (1997). Statement of Financial Accounting Standards No. 131, *Disclosure About Segments of an Enterprise and Related Information*. FASB.

Frankel, Richard, M. McNichols, and G. P. Wilson (January 1995). "Discretionary Disclosure and External Financing," *Accounting Review*, pp. 135–150.

Gelb, David (2000). "Corporate Signalling With Dividends, Stock Repurchases and Accounting Disclosures," *Journal of Accounting, Auditing & Finance*, (Vol. 15, No. 2), pp. 99–120.

Gibbins, Michael, Alan J. Richardson, and John Waterhouse (1992). *The Management of Financial Disclosure: Theory and Perspectives.* The Canadian Certified General Accountants' Research Foundation.

Grady, Paul (1965). Accounting Research Study No. 7, *Inventory of Generally Accepted Accounting Principles for Business Enterprises.* American Institute of Certified Public Accountants.

Guterblet, Louis G. (Fall 1983). "An Opportunity—Differential Standards," *Journal of Accounting, Auditing & Finance*, pp. 16–28.

Healy, Paul M., and Krishna Palepu (March 1993). "The Effect of Firms' Financial Disclosure Strategies on Stock Prices," *Accounting Horizons*, pp. 1–11.

Heflin, Frank, K. R. Subramanyam, and Y. Zhang (January 2003). "Regulation FD and the Financial Information Environment: Early Evidence," *Accounting Review*, pp. 1–37.

Hermann, Don, and W. Thomas (September 2000). "An Analysis of Segment Disclosures Under SFAS No. 131 and SFAS No. 14," *Accounting Horizons*, pp. 287–302.

Hutton, Amy (Fall 2004). "Beyond Financial Reporting: An Integrated Approach to Corporate Disclsoure," *Journal of Applied Corporate Finance*, pp. 8–16.

Ijiri, Yuji (1975). Studies in Accounting Research #10, *Theory of Accounting Measurement*. American Accounting Association.

—— (September 1995). "Segment Statements and Informativeness Measures: Managing Capital Versus Managing Resources," *Accounting Horizons*, pp. 55–67.

Irani, Afshad, and I. Karamanou (March 2003), "Regulation Fair Disclosure, Analyst Following, and Analyst Forecast Dispersion," *Accounting Horizons*, pp. 15–30.

Kasznik, Ron, and Baruch Lev (January 1995). "To Warn or Not to Warn: Management Disclosures in the Face of an Earnings Surprise," *Accounting Review*, pp. 113–134.

Krisement, Vera (1997). "An Approach for Measuring the Degree of Comparability of Financial Accounting Information," *European Accounting Review* (Vol. 6, No. 3), pp. 465–486.

Lang, Mark, and R. Lundholm (October 1996). "Corporate Disclosure Policy and Analyst Behavior," *Accounting Review*, pp. 467–492.

Lev, Baruch (January 1988). "Towards a Theory of Equitable and Efficient Accounting Policy," *Accounting Review*, pp. 1–22.

—— (Summer 1992). "Information Disclosure Strategy," *California Management Review*, pp. 9–32.

Lev, Baruch, and Stephen H. Penman (Spring 1990). "Voluntary Forecast Disclosure, Nondisclosure, and Stock Prices," *Journal of Accounting Research*, pp. 49–76.

McCarthy, Ed (February 2001). "After Regulation FD: Talking to Your Constituents," *Journal of Accountancy*, pp. 28–33.

Miller, Paul B. W. (March 1985). "The Conceptual Framework: Myths and Realities," *Journal of Accountancy*, pp. 62–71.

Morse, Dale, and Gordon Richardson (Spring 1983). "The LIFO/FIFO Decision," *Journal of Accounting Research*, pp. 106–127.

Murray, Dennis, and Raymond Johnson (Fall 1983). "Differential GAAP and the FASB's Conceptual Framework," *Journal of Accounting, Auditing & Finance*, pp. 4–15.

Powell, Weldon (Autumn 1965). "Putting Uniformity in Financial Accounting Into Perspective," *Law and Contemporary Problems*, pp. 674–690.

Ronen, Joshua, and Simcha Sadan (1981). *Smoothing Income Numbers: Objectives, Means, and Implications*. Addison-Wesley.

Securities and Exchange Commission (1977). *Annual Report*. SEC.

—— (1979). Release No. 33-6084, *Safe Harbor Rule for Projections* (June 25; 44 FR 38810).

Sengupta, Partha (October 1998). "Corporate Disclosure Quality and the Cost of Debt," *Accounting Review*, pp. 459–474.

Solomons, David (Spring 1983). "The Political Implications of Accounting and Accounting Standard Setting," *Accounting and Business Research*, pp. 107–118.

Sorter, G., and M. Ingberman (Spring 1987). "The Implicit Criteria for the Recognition, Quantification, and Reporting of Accounting Events," *Journal of Accounting, Auditing & Finance*, pp. 99–114.

Sprouse, Robert (January 1978). "The Importance of Earnings in the Conceptual Framework," *Journal of Accountancy*, pp. 64–71.

Sterling, Robert R. (1985). *An Essay on Recognition*. University of Sydney: Accounting Research Centre.

Street, Donna, N. Nichols, and S. J. Gray (September 2000). "Segment Disclosures Under SFAS No. 131: Has Business Segment Reporting Improved?" *Accounting Horizons*, pp. 259–285.

Thomas, Arthur L. (1969). Studies in Accounting Research No. 3, *The Allocation Problem in Financial Accounting Theory*. American Accounting Association.

—— (1974). Studies in Accounting Research No. 6, *The Allocation Problem: Part 2*. American Accounting Association.

U.S. Government Printing Office (1977). *Report of the Advisory Committee on Corporate Disclosure to the Securities and Exchange Commission.* U.S. GPO.

Watts, Ross, and J. L. Zimmerman (1986). *Positive Accounting Theory.* Prentice Hall.

Wolk, Harry I., and Patrick Heaston (1992). "Toward the Harmonization of Accounting Standards: An Analytical Framework," *International Journal of Accounting* 27 (Vol. 27, No. 2), pp. 95–111.

Wyatt, Arthur R. (February 1983). "Efficient Market Theory: Its Impact on Accounting," *Journal of Accountancy*, pp. 56–65.

Zmijewski, Mark, and R. Hagerman (1981). "An Income Strategy Approach to the Positive Theory of Accounting Standard Setting/Choice," *Journal of Accounting and Economics* (Vol. 9, No. 3), pp. 129–149.

10

International Accounting

Learning Objectives

After reading this chapter, you should be able to:

- Understand why different countries have different approaches to financial accounting and reporting.
- Appreciate that multiple accounting classification models have been proposed, the Anglo-American and Continental models being the most recognized.
- Note the role of the European Union (EU) toward convergence.
- Understand the emergence of the International Accounting Standards Board (IASB) as a major player in the setting of the accounting standards.
- Understand the rules-based versus principles-based approach to standard setting and the true and fair override.

International trade and investment have grown at a staggering rate over the last quarter century. Accompanying the huge growth in trade has been an extensive increase in direct foreign investment in which a U.S. corporation acquires subsidiaries in, say, Norway or the converse. This type of firm is known as a multinational or a transnational corporation. In addition, cross-border financings have also increased dramatically. An example of a cross-border financing would involve, say, a Chicago hospital acquiring a new MRI machine by means of a loan from a bank in Reykjavik, Iceland.

Even more important than cross-border financings is the listing of equity securities of foreign corporations for trading on domestic exchanges. This is done to raise large amounts of equity capital in foreign nations. An example of this phenomenon was the registration of Daimler Benz securities, one of more than 450 non-U.S. listings registered for trading on the New York Stock Exchange (NYSE). Since its original listing, Daimler Benz merged with Chrysler, forming a major multinational corporation. (As of mid-June 2007, Daimler has agreed to sell an 80% stake in Chrysler to Cerberus Capital Management, a private equity firm.) These increasingly global business transactions have tested existing financial reporting systems, challenging them to translate these economic activities into understandable financial reports.

The chapter starts by reviewing approaches to developing accounting standards in selected European and Asian nations, most of which occur in first world nations. We then examine attempts to measure harmonization among the accounting standards of different countries and national groupings.[1] Finally, we emphasize the growth and development of the IASB in its quest for harmonization—now more frequently called convergence—of accounting standards. We also examine rules-based versus principles-based approaches to standard setting and the true and fair override.

National Accounting Differences

It is obvious that languages and cultures can differ between countries, but it may not be so evident that the "language of business," accounting, can vary as much as it does. We start this section by examining some of the reasons and conditions that underlie varying approaches to financial accounting among economically advanced nations. Our survey will not be exhaustive but will instead concentrate on a relatively few but very important economically advanced nations.[2] We also briefly examine a group of developing nations in Southeastern Asia. After examining the differences among nations, we will then turn our attention in the next major section to the "harmonization" of accounting standards: the attempt to make various accounting standards and modes of financial reporting of different countries as similar as possible.

There are two general financial reporting models that have evolved in the economically advanced countries. The Anglo-American model (also referred to as the Anglo-Saxon model) features the presence of a strong accounting profession, a somewhat limited role of government, the importance of securities markets for raising equity capital, and an emphasis on the true and fair view of audited financial statements. The true and fair view refers to the use of judgment to make financial statements useful instruments for making investment decisions, as opposed to ensuring that they have been presented correctly in accordance with legislative fiat. In other words, the true and fair outlook emphasizes economic substance over the legalistic form that prevails in the continental model.

To accomplish the true and fair view, the idea of an override or use of a different method or standard than the prescribed one has been suggested to bring about representational faithfulness. As an example, the EU's Fourth Directive calls for investment properties to be subject to depreciation, but economic reality might call for assets of this type to be accounted for by using mark-to-market.[3] Alexander and Archer fear that a preparer using the override option might be resorting to earnings management. They prefer that the override, if one is needed, be accomplished by a standard-setting body, not the preparer.[4] However, it is not clear that mere development of a new rule constitutes an override. For example, booking tax loss carry forwards (SFAS No, 109) replaced footnote recognition only of loss carry forwards (APB Opinion No. 11) because it is more representationally faithful. We do not view this as an override. However, we emphasize that there is no true and fair override under Financial Accounting Standards Board (FASB) rules.

The continental model generally presents a relatively weak accounting profession; reflects strong governmental influence on accounting regulation and organization, including the primacy of tax influences and the protection of creditors in financial statement presentation rather than for investor needs; and—as the latter implies—emphasizes the importance of debt financing through major banks rather than the raising of equity capital. Within the two basic models, important distinctions as well as interesting directions of change are present.

The Anglo-American Model

As the title indicates, this grouping includes the United Kingdom (England, Wales, Scotland, and Northern Ireland), many members of the British Commonwealth, and the United States, which was, of course, an English colony until 1776.

United Kingdom

The roots of accounting run very deep in the United Kingdom (UK). The oldest professional accounting societies arose in the UK in the middle of the 19th century in the Scottish cities of Edinburgh, Glasgow, and Aberdeen. However, the underlying core of British accounting has been found in the various Companies Acts beginning in 1844 and coming down to recent times (1989). Prior to 1981, the Companies Acts had largely been concerned with disclosures. In the acts since 1981, previous company acts were consolidated, and, in addition, several directives of EU have been passed. There is no United Kingdom equivalent of the Securities and Exchange Commission (SEC). The accounting profession in the United Kingdom consists of six major organizations:

1. Institute of Chartered Accountants in England and Wales
2. Institute of Chartered Accountants of Scotland
3. Institute of Chartered Accountants in Ireland
4. Association of Certified Accountants
5. Institute of Cost and Management Accountants
6. Chartered Institute of Public Finance and Accountancy

It is particularly interesting to note that the Institute of Chartered Accountants in Ireland, which was established prior to partition, still embraces both Northern Ireland and the Republic of Ireland. No standard-setting body existed in England prior to 1970, but several scandals occurring in the 1960s raised the possibility of government regulation of accounting standards. As a result, the accounting profession responded, thereby avoiding immediate regulation.

The first standard-setting organization, the Accounting Standards Steering Committee (ASSC), was organized by the Institute of Chartered Accountants in England and Wales (ICAEW) in 1970; the other five organizations later joined the ICAEW in its sponsorship. The ASSC (its name was later changed to the Accounting Standards Committee, or ASC) was somewhat unwieldy because its standards had to be approved by all six of the sponsoring organizations. The ASC resembled the APB more than the FASB, with members serving on a part-time basis without salary.

As a result of the Dearing Committee Report of 1988, the Accounting Standards Board (ASB) replaced the ASC in 1990. The ASB operates more along the lines of the FASB, with a full-time paid chairman, a full-time paid technical director, and seven salaried board members who serve on a part-time basis.[5] The ASB issues accounting standards on its own authority, thus avoiding the awkwardness of needing the approval of the six sponsoring organizations. The ASB, paralleling the FASB, is supervised by a group, the Financial Reporting Council, that is independent of the profession. The enforcement mechanism of the ASB is stronger than that of the ASC since the Companies Act of 1989 requires major companies to disclose in their annual reports any departures from accounting standards.[6] Assisting the ASB, the Urgent Issues Task Force (UITF), which largely corresponds to the Emerging Issues Task Force (EITF) in the United States, works to resolve unsatisfactory or conflicting interpretations of standards.

While the standard-setting apparatus in the UK has been somewhat influenced from across the Atlantic (and vice versa) for several years, there is a more recent, perhaps stronger, influence from continental Europe in the form of the European Union (EU). To a greater or lesser extent, standard setting in other countries in the British Commonwealth has been influenced by the UK model.

United States

At this point, little more needs to be said about the standard-setting arrangements in the United States (U.S.). While not quite as old as their British counterparts, American professional accounting organizations have shown significant influence and leadership over the years. Certainly, American standard setters have blazed the trail of regulation being centered in the private sector. The government/private sector "partnership" approach between the SEC and the FASB (or its predecessors) was first instigated in the U.S., with the SEC largely exerting oversight prerogatives. Historically, the U.S. Congress has on rare occasions threatened to directly legislate accounting standards (the famous investment credit case) but has not actually micro-managed the SEC. However, the Sarbanes-Oxley Act (SOX) of 2002, Section 108(d), suggests a failure in the SEC's oversight responsibilities with the act's direct instructions to the SEC regarding accounting standards.

One other point that should be made about accounting in the United States is that the term "present fairly" in opinions of American auditing firms is not the same as the "true and fair view." *Present fairly* basically means that the financial statements are in accordance with GAAP, with departures being extremely rare. Others outside of the accounting profession, including the legal profession, occasionally see the present fairly view as being similar to the true and fair view.[7] Zeff secs the infrequent departure from GAAP coming from SEC policy.[8] Of course, American standard setting is presumably oriented toward providing useful information for investors and creditors rather than toward a legalistic emphasis on creditor protection and income tax laws. However, the proliferation of rules and complexity in U.S. accounting standards seems to bring this presumption into question.

Canada

Canada, like several members of the British Commonwealth, originally looked to the UK for guidance in financial reporting, but over time it has become more influenced by the U.S. approach. Because of the importance of Ontario in the Canadian federation, Ontario Companies Acts have been essential in terms of financial statement disclosures. American influence can be noted from the Ontario Securities Act of 1966, which gave the Ontario Securities Commission oversight power over the Toronto Stock Exchange and a position similar to the SEC relative to the standard-setting function.

Since the 1940s, the Canadian Institute of Chartered Accountants (CICA) has used committees to establish accounting standards. In 1973, two important groups were established: the Auditing Standards Committee and the Accounting Research Committee. The accounting and auditing "recommendations" of these two groups are published in the CICA Handbook. CICA recommendations often parallel American standards. The CICA established an Emerging Issues Committee in 1988, which is similar to its American counterpart, the Emerging Issues Task Force (EITF).

The Accounting Research Committee includes members from Financial Executives International of Canada as well as the Society of Industrial Accountants of Canada. To this extent, it bears a resemblance to the FASB. Both Canadian committees also use a system of exposure drafts for the purpose of receiving input from affected parties. The two committees also require a two-thirds vote before a recommendation can be issued.

Australia

Australia is an interesting study. While relying on British Companies Acts, the various states of Australia also had their own Companies Acts. Their acts emphasized disclosures, not measurement rules, and were not always in agreement with one another. Agreement was finally achieved in 1987 by a Federal Companies Act, which was applicable to the Australian Capital Territory. Each of the states then adopted the Federal Companies Act. The true and fair view was required by these acts but has become less important since 1991, when a more legalistic outlook was adopted.

An equally complex duality has existed in the standard-setting arena. There are two major accounting organizations in Australia: Institute of Chartered Accountants in Australia and

Australian Society of Accountants. Both organizations issued their own statements independently until 1966. At that time, they jointly founded the Australian Accountancy Research Foundation (AARF), which is responsible for drafting and issuing accounting standards, called Australian Accounting Standards. The standards are issued in the name of both sponsoring organizations.

In 1984, the Accounting Standards Review Board (ASRB) was created and funded by the government, making yet another standard-setting agency. The ASRB was underfunded, and the government looked to the AARF as the primary drafter of standards, although the ASRB did not give automatic approval to AARF standards, creating a very confusing situation. The two agencies were merged in 1988 and the resulting body was renamed the Australian Accounting Standards Board (AASB) in 1991.

The ASEAN

The ASEAN (Association of Southeast Asia Nations) is a group of developing nations in Southeast Asia. The association was formed in 1967 with the charter members being Malaysia, Indonesia, Singapore, Thailand, and the Philippines. Newer members include Brunei Darussalam, Cambodia, Laos, Myanmar (also known as Burma), and Vietnam. The ASEAN is intended to foster trade and development both within and outside the region. Charter members are—generally speaking—more economically advanced and have stronger accounting organizations than the newer members.

In general, government agencies are more concerned with disclosure within the charter member group with both standard-setting and audit rules being made by private-sector organizations. Accounting standards have drawn heavily upon the United States, United Kingdom, and the International Accounting Standards Board (discussed later).[9] As a result, we classify the ASEAN nations with the Anglo-American group; however, individual members may not perfectly match this classification. Regional harmonization efforts within the ASEAN group have been mixed. Singapore and the Philippines have fully adopted international standards, but interest among the remaining members varies greatly.

Other Countries

Two other countries, the Netherlands and New Zealand, are of interest. The Netherlands, while a small country, has an interesting political and economic history. The country has been a colony of a major European nation (Spain) and has a sizable overseas empire located in the Dutch East Indies, the West Indies, and coastal South America. Furthermore, like Czechoslovakia, which broke apart resulting in the Czech Republic and Slovakia in 1993, the greater Netherlands separated from Belgium (which still has its own divisional problems between Flemings and Walloons), leaving the Netherlands now consisting of what we frequently call Holland.

While the Netherlands is a continental nation, its accounting situation is largely in the Anglo-American mold, with company law and the accounting profession playing important roles.[10] Of particular significance has been the influence of Dutch academics on financial reporting. As a result, the country has been at the vanguard of fair value reporting. Important Dutch companies, such as the giant NV Philips Gloeilampenfabrikien (a firm somewhat similar to General Electric in the United States), were essentially using the distributable income approach (no holding gains or losses recognized) in their published financial statements. The only company still using distributable income today is Heineken, Europe's largest brewery.

New Zealand is another important follower of the Anglo-American approach, although, unlike its larger neighbor, Australia, standard setting has remained within the private sector. New Zealand's professional body of accountants is the New Zealand Society of Accountants (NZSA). While a committee of this body had been issuing statements on accounting practice since 1951, a new group, the Board of Research, was formed in 1961, which issued Statements on Accounting Practice. Finally, in 1973 the council of the New Zealand Society began issuing its current series, called Statements of Standard Accounting Practice, the same title used in the United Kingdom.

In 1991, three major organizations—NZSA, the New Zealand Stock Exchange, and the Securities Commission—recommended the establishment of an accounting standards board, which would be somewhat similar to the FASB in its operations. New Zealand, unlike Australia, has not attempted to veer from the true and fair view of financial reporting. It has also been proposed that Australia and New Zealand should combine their standard-setting structures.[11]

The Continental Model

As the name implies, countries following the continental model include the major countries of Western Europe, such as France and Germany, as well as Japan, which is neither European nor continental. States of the former Soviet bloc, including Russia, are struggling either to return to the economic mainstream or to modernize both their economic and political systems, which can be particularly difficult since many of these countries historically lack both a free market and a democratic political system. Financial reporting, in the Western sense, is thus fairly primitive in these countries, so they are not included in our discussions.

France

France has the closest approach to a uniform national accounting system. The French approach—called the Plan Comptable General—includes a national uniform chart of accounts, explanations of technical terms, and explanations of accounts to be debited and credited.[12] The plan was originally conceived in 1947 and revised in 1957, with a further revision in 1982 (including the effect of the Fourth Directive of the EU) and an extension in 1986 (involving the Seventh Directive on consolidated financial statements). In addition to the plan, important influences on French accounting include the Code de Commerce and tax laws.[13]

France provides a good example of the continental model. The French accounting profession is relatively small and weak. It did not really begin to develop until after the Second World War. The principal stock exchange, the Paris Bourse, does not approach the importance of securities exchanges in other Western and advanced countries. Consequently, the main influences on accounting in France come from the national government and, more recently, the EU.[14]

Germany

A second example of the continental model is Germany. German banks are a more important source of corporate financing than are their Anglo-American counterparts. Financial accounting standard setting and GAAP in the American and English sense do not exist in Germany. Professional accounting activities are mainly concerned with the auditing function.

However, the 1965 Corporation Law moved somewhat toward Anglo-American approaches in terms of requiring more disclosures and a limited amount of consolidations for the largest corporations; nevertheless, Germany still remained solidly in the continental mold. Since that time, the Fourth, Seventh, and Eighth EU Directives have been codified into German accounting through the Comprehensive Accounting Act of 1985.

There are some signs of Germany moving toward the Anglo-American view resulting from the Fourth and Seventh Directives of the European Union (discussed later). More German corporations owning foreign subsidiaries are showing segment income and capital investment figures.[14] Furthermore, while not mandatory, more German firms are publishing cash flow statements. Although there has been an attempt to move away from conservative valuation principles in consolidated financial statements, this has been seen as a factor that could lead to erosion of the conservative German orientation resulting from differences between individual and consolidated financial statements.

Japan

Japan is a special example of the continental model. Located off the Asian mainland in the western Pacific, the country was quite insular and self-sufficient until Admiral Perry sailed into Tokyo Bay in 1853, eventually resulting in opening up Japan to Western trade, commerce, and other influences. Japan's recovery from the destruction of the World War II is nothing less than astounding, but the country has still maintained important aspects of its insularity and isolation, as expressed in the restrictive import policies that the United States and other countries have attempted to change.

Japan's rapid industrial expansion after Admiral Perry's expedition began in 1868 under the Meiji Restoration to the imperial throne. Large industrial consortia consisting of major firms and banks formed *zaibatsu*—vertically integrated relationships ending with a single family in control—that significantly influenced the economy through World War II. During the Allied occupation of Japan, most of these zaibatsu were disbanded. However, they have since been replaced by less formalized associations of horizontal relationships that form groupings referred to as *keiretsu*.

In the midst of this oligopolistic type of economic dominance, the Accounting Standards Board of Japan (ASBJ) has maintained a relatively low profile. Japan's government has dominated Japanese accounting. The first important laws affecting accounting were established in the late 19th century using France and Germany as their model.[16] Tax laws have probably been the most important influence on Japanese accounting. Protection of creditors rather than providing information to investors has resulted in the balance sheet taking precedence over the income statement.[17] Historically, debt financing through the Japanese banking system has been far more important than equity financing in Japan.

However, several corporate failures during the 1990s prompted the Ministry of Finance to initiate a subtle change in direction, placing an increased emphasis on the income statement. Reviews of multiple bankruptcies showed that companies had hidden losses by moving them to off-balance-sheet affiliates or by simply ignoring highly deflated real estate holdings. The resulting standards changes requiring consolidation of subsidiaries in which the firm has "effective control" were aimed at improving income statement quality for investors. Of course, the change caused Japanese firms to take income "hits."[18] A decade later another series of corporate scandals has raised questions about Japan's accounting practices. It is likely that the litany of Enron-like fraudulent reporting incidents by Japanese companies (e.g., Livedoor, Associant Technology, Surugayaa, Zanebo[19]) influenced the ASBJ to pursue a project with the IASB to reduce differences between International Financial Reporting Standards (IFRSs) and Japanese accounting standards. Perhaps this step will delay the inevitable call for increased governmental regulation, something akin to the U.S. SEC.

Overview of National Profiles

It should be clear from this brief survey of the Anglo-American and Continental models that major differences in accounting and financial reporting occur between these groups and that significant differences arise within groups. Key factors of difference appear to be between capital-based financial markets where long-term investment is dominated by individual and institutional investors in the capital market and credit-based financial markets where the bulk of long-term funds is provided by government or financial institutions. In the former situation, financial reporting would be geared more toward providing information useful to actual and prospective investors, whereas in the latter, protection of creditors is the stronger force.[20] Also important is the division between private and state regulation of the standard-setting process and the participation of the accounting profession in the setting of standards.

In addition, financial reporting is grounded in the legal system of the nation. For example, the Companies Acts dominate in the UK with the result that audited financial statements must be approved by the shareholders and that auditors must be appointed by the shareholders.[21] In continental Europe, however, conformity to tax laws has been a dominating factor. A brief list of differences between the United States and other countries before the movement toward IFRS adoption is shown in Exhibit 10.1.

Problems Stemming From National Accounting Differences

National differences in accounting have led to extensive research and discussion as to why they have arisen. Some researchers have looked at cultural factors and differences that often have sociological underpinnings.[22] Others have focused on economic/political/professional dimensions of national accounting differences that have had a direct impact on the accounting profession itself.[23] These national differences have been extremely important. Many securities exchanges throughout the world have been "going international" by listing the stocks of foreign countries for trading. The EU has already taken significant steps for listing

Exhibit 10.1   Some Differences in Accounting Between U.S. and Other Countries Before IFRS

Event	Country
Noncapitalization of leases	France
Partial income tax allocation	United Kingdom
Frequent revaluation of land and buildings	United Kingdom and Australia
Very limited consolidations (prior to the Seventh Directive)	France, Germany, and other continental countries
LIFO not used	United Kingdom and Australia
Direct adjustments to owners' equity for unusual gains and losses	Most continental countries
Some capitalization of development costs	United Kingdom
Capitalization of research and development costs if recovery is assured beyond a reasonable doubt	Australia
Very limited use of income tax allocation	Japan
Goodwill charged against stockholders' equity	United Kingdom
More extensive capitalization of software systems development costs (including systems analysis and systems design costs)[a]	Japan

[a] Scarbrough, McGee, and Sakurai (1993).

on the exchanges of each country the securities of major firms in other EU nations.[24] In the United States and Canada, a system of reciprocity is already in effect for listing the securities for trading of the other nation as well as raising capital through new issues. In addition, most Israeli and Japanese firms listed for trading on American securities exchanges use U.S. GAAP for their primary financial statements.[25] For other firms that wish to list their securities on American exchanges but whose primary financial statements are in their own domestic GAAP, a Form 20 F reconciliation must be made. This is an SEC form that requires a reconciliation of earnings and stockholders' equity between the firms' domestic financial statements and U.S. GAAP. However, in June 2007, the SEC voted unanimously to propose that the Form 20-F reconciliation be dispensed with for foreign firms filing on American security exchanges.

With the listing of stocks of foreign countries on domestic securities exchanges, research studies have looked at several issues and questions such as whether Form 20-F filings have information content and if securities that are listed on both domestic and foreign securities exchanges have similar or different returns.[26] One of the issues being raised is whether different national accounting standards and disclosure rules might lead to a different structure of security returns (as appeared to be the case with SmithKline Beecham), which would imply that world capital markets are neither well integrated nor informationally efficient.

Concurrent with the increasing levels of international trade, multinational corporations have become more important, and various entities have attempted to bring the world closer together. Consequently, efforts have been made to measure differences in accounting standards and practices in different nations and regional groupings. The FASB and the IASB have taken the lead in attempting to harmonize the accounting standards of different nations and groups, which we next examine.

International Harmonization of Accounting Standards

Revolutionary developments in transportation and communications have been bringing the world closer together, toward what has been called a "global village." Since the end of World War II, a large growth in international trade and other forms of interdependency among nations have had enormous significance for many facets of our lives. In a general way, these developments have a homogenizing effect on many customs, practices, and institutions. In business, several specific conditions have led to a desire to harmonize/converge accounting standards among nations.[27]

Harmonization refers to the degree of coordination or similarity among the various sets of national accounting standards and methods and formats of financial reporting.[28] Harmonization has been broken down into two aspects: (1) Material harmonization (also called de facto harmonization) refers to harmonization among accounting practices of different enterprises whether or not stemming from regulations, and (2) formal harmonization (also called de jure harmonization) refers to the process or degree of harmonization present among the accounting rules or regulations of different countries or groups.[29]

Among the factors underlying the desire for harmonization is the rise in importance of the multinational firm. General similarity of accounting standards and procedures would facilitate coordination among the parts of the multinational enterprise. In particular, consolidated financial reporting would certainly be made easier if the accounting rules applicable to the various parts of the multinational firm were more consistent. Complementary to the rise of the multinational corporation is the internationalization occurring within the public accounting profession. Many firms have offices and practices throughout the world. The greater the degree of harmonization, the more the auditing function is facilitated.

Finally, cross-border financings have increased as has the listing of securities of foreign enterprises for trading on the major stock exchanges in many countries. The International Organization of Securities Commissions (IOSCO), an organization of securities exchange commissions throughout the world, is actively concerned with promoting harmonization of accounting standards. In short, harmonization fosters both coordination and efficiency.

Many studies have attempted to measure the progress of harmonization.[30] Among the relatively recent studies, Emenyonu and Gray (1996) found a modest improvement in harmonization from 1971–1972 to 1991–1992. In their empirical tests, they examined 293 corporate annual reports in five countries (United States, United Kingdom, France, Germany, and Japan) involving a total of 26 issues covering both measurement and disclosure. Similarly, Archer, Delvaille, and McLeay found little increase in harmonization between 1986–1987 and 1990–1991 in the event areas of deferred taxes and goodwill with measures of harmonization being low.[31] Their study covered 89 enterprises in eight Western European countries.

Research through the 1990s concludes that harmonization is occurring, but its progress has been slow. However, the IASB and FASB's Norwalk Agreement of 2002 gives a second wind to harmonization/convergence, so we expect significantly faster progress toward harmonization, albeit slower than what many would like. The IASB's experience with the European Union (EU) is a strength that it brings to the IASB–FASB convergence project. So, before we discuss the IASB, we first look at the EU, an important political grouping that brought, in its wake, an attempt to harmonize accounting standards and reporting on a regional basis.

The EU

In the wake of two devastating world wars, major parts of which were fought in Western Europe, attempts were made to integrate the countries of this region both economically and politically. One of the first attempts at integration came in 1952 with the formation of the European Coal and Steel Community (ECSC). The purpose of ECSC was to allow an unfettered movement of labor and capital among the coal and steel industries of Belgium, the Netherlands, Luxembourg, Italy, France, and West Germany. Another significant economic grouping was the European Free Trade Association (EFTA), formed in 1960, which included Austria, Norway, Sweden, Switzerland, Great Britain, Portugal, and Denmark. These two groups were sometimes called "the inner six" and "the outer seven," respectively. EFTA nations agreed to mutual free-trade agreements with ECSC countries.

The European Community, now called the EU was formed in 1967 and eventually included the ECSC nations plus Great Britain, Portugal, Austria, and Denmark from EFTA as well as Ireland, Greece, Finland, and Spain. Norway, from the EFTA group, is not currently in the EU. Several nations from the former Soviet bloc in Eastern Europe are now in the EU. Turkey, Croatia, and the Former Yugoslav Republic of Macedonia are candidates for membership and may eventually qualify. As of 2007, at least 27 countries with 23 different official languages comprise the EU, a uniquely diverse collective.[32]

The EU, with its drive toward economic integration, has been concerned with harmonization of accounting standards of its member nations. The Council of Ministers of the EU nations has issued several directives with important implications for accounting. Directives become binding on the member countries, although they may not be implemented in exactly the same way by each nation since the national legislative body in each country must pass the directives. The directives also contain some degree of flexibility and choice that is left to each member nation's discretion.

Two directives, the Fourth Directive and the Seventh Directive, contain important accounting matters. The Fourth Directive, adopted in 1978, concerns basic issues of financial reporting that are applicable to companies within the EU community. In addition to providing standard formats for financial statements, the directive states that financial statements must be based on four concepts: consistency, going concern, prudence, and accrual accounting. This directive permits current value statements in addition to historical costs and also supports application of the true and fair view.[33] Since the true and fair view calls for going beyond accounting rules to portray economic reality, it is very questionable how it can be implemented given differences in definition, interpretation, and application among the countries constituting the EU.[34] Furthermore, it is contended that the true and fair view is being interpreted in EU nations in terms of their own particular cultures and traditions.[35] Increasingly, the true and fair view is seen as going from the need to "override" accepted accounting principles with full disclosures in order to show the facts and conditions of the enterprise truthfully to a diligent application of existing GAAP.[36]

The Seventh Directive, passed in 1983, extended consolidation accounting to firms within the member states of the EU under a very wide group of circumstances in which one firm has substantive control over one or more other firms. This directive, like the Fourth Directive, requires the true and fair view. Legislatures of member nations had all passed the Seventh Directive by 1992. While the national laws are not exactly the same, it is clear that the Seventh Directive has increased harmonization in the area of consolidations among the member nations.[37] However, there are options allowed under the Fourth and Seventh Directives that allow for differences in some areas such as the definition of a subsidiary and consolidation exemptions in which the ultimate parent is not an EU firm.[38]

As previously noted, while the Fourth and Seventh Directives helped to improve harmonization, the pace was not fast enough for the EU Commission. The EU Commission saw the need to give its members access to major equity capital sources—which means the New York Stock Exchange (NYSE). But SEC rules required either the adoption of American GAAP or of complex reconciliation forms such as Form 20-F discussed previously. As the end result of working with the IASB and other groups such as the International Organization of Securities Commissions (IOSCO), members of the EU adopted IASB standards for their consolidated financial reporting in 2005.[39] By deciding to incorporate IFRS into its statute law, the EU in effect turned over its accounting standard setting to the IASB. This adoption en masse increased IASB's stature and legitimacy in the global community. The EU itself or individual member nations may decline—for whatever the reason—to use specific IASB standards.[40]

The International Accounting Standards Board

In the late 1960s, three professional accounting organizations (AICPA, CICA, and ICAEW)[41] formed an International Study Group to review the need for international accounting standards. This group's work led to establishment of the Accountants International Study Group (AISG) and eventual founding of the International Accounting Standards Committee (IASC) in 1973 with charter members from nine countries: Australia, Canada, France, Germany, Japan, Mexico, the Netherlands, the United Kingdom and Ireland, and the United States.

Restructured and renamed in 2001, the IASC now calls itself the International Accounting Standards Board (IASB). Today, "nearly 100 countries currently require or permit the use of, or have a policy of, convergence"[42] with IASB standards, a clear indicator of its progress to-date. Its legitimacy as a credible world standard setter is no longer in question. "Rather than compete with the IASB, most national boards accept that they must work with IASB chairman Sir David Tweedie in order to remain relevant."[43]

The IASB operates within an organizational structure akin to the FASB. Its International Accounting Standards Committee (IASC) Foundation has 22 trustees who appoint IASB's 14 board members, oversee its operations, and are responsible for fund raising from approximately 200 contributors worldwide.[44]

Typically, the standards issued by the IASB are referred to as IFRS or IFRSs. The term, International Financial Reporting Standard(s), has both a narrow and a broad meaning. Narrowly, IFRS refers to the new numbered series of pronouncements that the IASB is issuing, as distinct from the International Accounting Standards (IAS) series issued by its predecessor. More broadly, IFRS refers to the entire body of IASB pronouncements, including standards and interpretations approved by the IASB–IASs, its Conceptual Framework, Standing Interpretations Committee (SIC) interpretations approved by the predecessor International Accounting Standards Committee, and International Financial Reporting Interpretations Committee (IFRIC) interpretations. So, IFRSs consists primarily of 41 IASs issued from 1973 to 2001 before the renaming of the board and the new series of IFRS standards (Exhibit 10.2) issued after IASB's formation in 2001. Some IASs have been revised and the old numbers kept. Others have been superseded. Therefore, only 29 of the original 41 IAS numbers are currently referenced as IASB standards (Exhibit 10.3, page 316).

After considerable work with organizations like IOSCO, the G4+1 (Australia, Canada, New Zealand, the United Kingdom, and the United States), and the FASB, the IASB has produced what are deemed to be high-quality financial standards. We previously mentioned that EU countries began using IASB standards for consolidated financial statements in 2005. Similarly, American stock exchanges began accepting IASB standards for domestic listing in 2005 without reconciliation.[45] The overwhelming number of adoptions in 2005 prompted the IASB to issue a moratorium on required implementation of new standards or revisions until January 1, 2009. This effectively allows companies to digest what may have been a very large meal of financial standards. It also allows for the inevitable problems from implementations to surface and be addressed.[46]

Convergence

The IASB has greatly reduced the allowed number of treatments in particular event areas and also increased disclosure requirements.[47] As a result, d'Arcy sees IASB standards as being quite close to U.S. GAAP from the standpoint of harmonization.[48] However, the work of harmonization, now being called convergence, with the U.S. is far from complete. In 2002, the IASB and FASB's Norwalk Agreement[49] stated their common goal of developing accounting standards usable for both domestic and cross-border financial reporting. They committed to convergence of IFRS and U.S. GAAP; they also committed to maintenance of the compatibility, once achieved.

The Memorandum of Understanding between the IASB and the FASB is reviewed and reaffirmed annually.[50] Assuming successful completion of their convergence work, the resulting standards applicable to the vast majority of public companies will indeed be powerful. Also, partnering with an organization (the FASB) that is not dependent on the financial resources of donors expecting influence in the standards-setting process mitigates some of the political lobbying that Zeff warns the IASB to expect.[51] The result should be higher quality IFRSs in both appearance and reality.

So, convergence of IASB and FASB standards will be a major step toward international harmonization for English-speaking countries. However, Evans provides an excellent discussion of a major obstacle toward international harmonization: language.[52] English, the official language of the IASB, contains terms developed over many years that are converted/translated

Exhibit 10.2   International Financial Reporting Standards (IFRS)

IFRS Number	Subject	Effective Year
1	First-time Adoption of International Financial Reporting Standards (revised 2005)	2004
2	Share-based Payment	2005
3	Business Combinations	2004
4	Insurance Contracts	2005
5	Noncurrent Assets Held for Sale and Discontinued Operations	2005
6	Exploration for and Evaluation of Mineral Resources	2006
7	Financial Instruments: Disclosures	2007
8	Operating Segments	2009

into a target language in which there may be no equivalent terms. This is especially difficult if the target language lacks a history of economic language and markets that more developed countries have experienced. The result may be misleading labels in financial reporting, especially if a special label already has meaning in the target language. A false sense of comparability in financial reporting between countries may develop during the purportedly routine translation of an IFRS from English into the target language. We next examine another important difference between the FASB and the IASB: rules-based versus principles-based standards.

Principles-Based Versus Rules-Based Standards

A contrast that has been made between FASB standards and IASB standards is that the former are rules based while the latter are generally principles based. *Rules-based standards* are highly detailed, often have many exceptions, require extensive implementational guidance, and often have "bright line" distinctions (e.g., 75% capitalization rules for leases and 50% ownership rules for consolidations). Frequently the bright line distinction can be subverted by management.

Principles-based standards are shorter than rules-based standards and rely heavily on judgment either by management or the auditor to carry out the intentions of the standard-setting agency in terms of relevance, reliability, or attaining "economic reality."[53] Historical cost depreciation provides an example of a principles-based standard. Paragraph 5 of Chapter 9 of ARB 43 mentions the now famous "systematic and rational" description of historical cost appreciation but provides no further guidance.

The Sarbanes-Oxley Act required the SEC to draft a report on principles-based accounting standards that would better align the interest of management and auditors with investors and creditors.[54] The report uses the term *objective oriented standards* for a true principles-based approach. Objectives oriented standards, according to the report, would not use bright line tests and would have very few exceptions. They would also provide adequate guidelines for

Exhibit 10.3   International Accounting Standards (IAS)

IAS Number	Subject	Effective Year
1	Presentation of Financial Statements (revised 2005)	2005
2	Valuation and Presentation of Inventories in the Context of the Historical Cost System (revised 2003)	2005
7	Cash Flow Statements (revised 1992)	1994
8	Profit or Loss for the Period, Fundamental Errors and Changes in Accounting Policies (revised 2003)	2005
10	Contingencies and Events Occurring After the Balance Sheet Date (revised 2003)	2005
11	Accounting for Construction Contracts (revised 1993)	1995
12	Accounting for Taxes on Income (revised 2000)	2001
16	Accounting for Property, Plant, and Equipment (revised 2003)	2005
17	Accounting for Leases (revised 2003)	2005
18	Revenue Recognition (revised 1993)	1995
19	Accounting for Retirement Benefits in the Financial Statements of Employers (revised 2004)	2005
20	Accounting for Government Grants and Disclosure of Government Assistance	1984
21	Accounting for the Effects of Changes in Foreign Exchange Rates (revised 2003)	2005
23	Capitalization of Borrowing Costs	1995
24	Related Party Disclosures (revised 2003)	2005
26	Accounting and Reporting by Retirement Benefit Plans	1998
27	Consolidated Financial Statements and Accounting for Investments in Subsidiaries (revised 2003)	2005
28	Accounting for Investments in Associates (revised 2003)	2005
29	Financial Reporting in Hyperinflationary Economies	1990
31	Financial Reporting of Interests in Joint Ventures (revised 2003)	2005
32	Financial Instruments: Disclosure and Presentation (revised 2005; disclosure provisions superseded on adoption of IFRS 7)	2005
33	Earnings Per Share (revised 2003)	2005
34	Interim Financial Reporting	1999
36	Impairment of Assets (revised 2004)	2004
37	Provisions, Contingent Liabilities, and Contingent Assets	1999
38	Intangible Assets (revised 2004)	2004
39	Financial Instruments: Recognition and Measurement (revised 2005; some revisions effective 2006)	2005
40	Investment Property (revised 2004)	2005
41	Agriculture	2003

implementation, but they would still require the use of judgment by accountants and auditors. Standards can never cover every possible situation and contingency, so judgment would be needed to best capture the underlying economic reality. There is thus a gray area between providing enough detail to allow a standard to be operationalized and providing sufficient information to cover virtually every contingency. Before the line of too much detail is crossed, judgment would come into play. Finding this happy medium will not be easy. In addition, when judgment comes into play we enter the arena of potential moral turpitude, a situation that accountants have become much too familiar with of late.

Orientations to Rules-Based Versus Principles-Based Standards. Schipper believes that a principles-based approach would need extensive implementational guidance to enable it to work well. This would, of course, result in eroding the differences between rules-based and principles-based approaches.[55] She also notes the importance of having a strong enforcement agency such as the SEC, which is not present in most other jurisdictions.[56]

Benston, Bromwich, and Wagenhofer believe that the principles-based approach would work better in tandem with the revenue–expense orientation than with the asset–liability orientation of SFAC No. 6.[57] Their reason for this view is that with fair value accounting increasingly coming on board, accounting standard setters would have an extremely complex mechanism with many rules and guidelines (this point is true relative to SFAS No. 157). They see the revenue–expense model as being able to produce more reliable and auditable numbers. However, there is an inconsistency between the revenue–expense approach and fair value measurement because fair value is primarily geared to the primacy of the balance sheet. Benston et al. would provide, under either principles-based or rules-based standards, a true and fair override that would give accountants more professional responsibility and provide more transparent numbers.

To bring about convergence, not only would there have to be a unified approach with either rules-based or principles-based standards, but the IASB would need a conceptual framework that would work in tandem with the FASB conceptual framework, a subject that we next examine.

Conceptual Framework

Agrawal et al. note that the IASB and FASB's respective conceptual frameworks are similar.[58] They find that the IASB identifies several user groups, but it emphasizes only those objectives that are common to all users. The principal qualitative characteristics are similar to those in SFAC No. 2.[59] Likewise, the IASB lists several possible measurement bases (e.g., historical cost, replacement cost, exit value, present value) and notes that historical cost is the most prevalent basis, although it may be combined with other approaches. Even though there are similarities between the two frameworks, differences exist, and both frameworks are rather old and in need of updating.

A major difference between the IASB's conceptual framework and the FASB's is that the primary user group in the FASB document (SFAC No. 1) is limited to investors and creditors. The IASB's framework considers more than just the business enterprise. A second difference relates to the authoritative nature of the two frameworks. Preparation of financial statements under IFRS explicitly requires that management consider IASB's *Framework for the Preparation and Presentation of Financial Statements* when guidance is needed for an issue not covered by IASB's pronouncements or interpretations. There is no such requirement in U.S. GAAP.[60]

Several points should be stressed relative to the IASB framework. First, the document is very similar to and was clearly based on the FASB document. In fact, the IASB and the FASB are now working together on a single "converged" conceptual framework. Second, the IASB work is considerably shorter than the FASB instrument, even excluding SFAC No. 7, which was not published until after the IASC framework appeared. Third, since talks about harmonization (now called convergence) of standards were already under discussion, the two frameworks had to be closely integrated. It is also safe to say that the then IASC genuinely wanted a theoretical document underlying the promulgation of their standards.

Although not included in the *Memorandum of Understanding,* in 2004, the IASB and FASB initiated a project to develop a converged conceptual framework. The resultant document will be a single framework, as is the IASB's current conceptual framework, not a series of concept statements as in U.S. GAAP. The intent of the project is to improve on the respective frameworks, not focus on those areas in which they already have similarity. As such, the project asks which, if any, additional qualitative characteristics might improve the framework (e.g., high quality, true and fair view, credibility, transparency). It also asks whether materiality is a constraint or more appropriately classified as a qualitative characteristic.[61] For convergence to be attained, the IASB and FASB need similar conceptual frameworks.

Fair Value

"The purpose of financial reporting is to give an understanding, which is not misleading, of the underlying economics of an enterprise."[62] To this end, development of principles-based standards that tell accountants *how to decide* what to do rather than dictating by *rule* what to do is generally seen as characteristic of IFRSs. So, what are the implications of this characteristic when considering standards for financial reporting? A major implication is that users make decisions based on fair value, not historical cost. So, how can the financial statements best communicate fair values to users? Clearly, to the delight of financial analysts, the trend is toward increasing the use of fair value in the balance sheet.[63] However, the changes have sparked mixed responses as companies attempt to implement IFRSs using fair values. Two issues stand out as problematic: measurement and accounting for the changes in fair value.

Measurement. The International Valuation Standards Committee (IVSC), a Non-Government Organization (NGO) member of the United Nations, has emerged as the international authority on asset valuation methodologies.[64] "The demand for valuations prepared under International Valuation Standards is being driven by the rapid adoption around the world of International Accounting Standards, the growing influence of International Public Sector Accounting Standards, and the increasing need for users of valuation reports to have a consistent and comparable measurement of assets wherever they may be."[65]

ISVC's membership consists of organizations such as The Appraisal Institute, American Society of Appraisers, The Royal Institution of Chartered Surveyors, and the Japanese Association of Real Estate Appraisers. It appears that an entire industry is ready to blossom, meeting the needs of accountants seeking fair values at period-end for financial reporting. Depending on the resultant frequency of updates for these fair values, fiscal year-end and perhaps interim reporting, the changes to accounting organizations will be far reaching.

Note that the IASB is following the FASB's lead in SFAS. No. 157, *Fair Value Measurements,* with plans to establish a single source of guidance for all IFRSs using fair value. In fact, IASB issued SFAS No. 157 as a discussion paper and invited comments before writing an exposure draft of its own standard.[66]

Accounting and Fair Value. Once fair values have been determined, the resultant write-up or write-down is recorded. By introducing these changes into the accounting books, increased earnings volatility may result. It is difficult to reason that when the underlying economics become more volatile they should be ignored simply because they would introduce that volatility into the financial reporting system. However, the introduction of a fair value option in IAS 39, *Financial Instruments: Recognition and Measurement,* prompted the financial services industry, primarily banks, to fiercely oppose its adoption in full by the EU.

The term "carved out" became associated with the elimination of 17 paragraphs from the standard as the EU temporarily did a partial adoption of IAS 39 as a compromise to proceed with the planned 2005 harmonization using IFRSs.[67] IAS 39 became a maelstrom, attracting complaints (earnings volatility, complexity of the standard) from a broad range of constituents.[68] As results from first-time reporters using IFRS were issued in 2005, total recognized income, including IAS 39 fair value adjustments, affected companies such as Reuters, BP, and Cadbury Schweppes. The effects ranged from positive to negative and from small to large.[69] So, the concerns of increased earnings volatility appear to be evidenced in actual reporting and may not be avoidable, so improvements to the standard may come by reduction of its complexities.[70]

International Federation of Accountants (IFAC)

IFAC, formed in 1977, strives to protect the public interest by encouraging high-quality practices by the world's accountants. Like the IASB, members of IFAC are accounting organizations from around the world, with over 150 members from 118 countries. IFAC, through its boards, produces international standards for auditing and assurance, ethics, education and public sector accounting, and guidance for accountants in business. Like the IASB, IFAC guidelines cannot be imposed on any member organization or nation.

Since the IASB and IFAC are so closely concerned with complementary international accounting issues, the possibility of their merger has arisen. Although this has not occurred, both organizations continue to cooperate and work together on their mutual interests.

United Nations (UN)

The UN has long had an interest in the operations of multinational corporations. It has not as yet come up with any significant regulations relative to financial reporting for multinationals. The UN has also shown interest in international accounting standards, but it has definitely played a secondary role to the IASB.

The UN, at a conference held in 1999, has shown an interest in prescribing an accounting curriculum and determining qualifications to sit for professional accounting exams. The reception was lukewarm, at best. IFAC felt that these matters should remain in the hands of local accounting boards.[71] Members from the United Kingdom, France, and the United States desired to have the work of the UN discontinued in the area of accounting curriculum and professional eligibility.

Organisation for Economic Cooperation and Development (OECD)

Another organization concerned with promoting convergence is the OECD. This group is made up of 24 members coming mainly from the large, industrialized Western nations. Although it has been mainly focused on fiscal and economic matters, OECD has begun taking an interest in accounting practices. In 1978 it formed the Ad Hoc Working Group on Accounting Standards, which was concerned with formulating standards for multinational enterprises. It has begun working with standard-setting agencies within its member nations and also the IASB, whose efforts it supports. One of the OECD's activities is to protect multinational businesses from extreme regulatory proposals that the UN might attempt to adopt.[72]

Summary

Significant differences exist among nations in terms of financial reporting and accounting systems. Among industrially advanced nations, a distinction can be made between Anglo-American countries and those in the Continental mold. Countries in the Anglo-American group feature strong professional accounting organizations and an orientation toward the true and fair view and believe in the importance of securities markets for raising equity capital and a somewhat limited role of government. The Continental countries, on the other hand, typically have weaker accounting organizations, a stronger presence of law in terms of setting accounting regulations, and financial reporting systems geared to income tax laws and the protection of creditors. They also place a greater importance of banks for debt financing with a lesser importance of securities markets for raising capital. In addition to economic and political differences among nations, social and cultural differences may also play an important role in financial accounting differences.

The journey toward harmonization/convergence of accounting standards is well underway with increasing speed and momentum. Clearly, there are two dominate sets of international GAAPs: IFRSs and U.S. GAAP. The 2002 Norwalk Agreement and the 2004 Conceptual Framework Project between the FASB and IASB are focused on convergence, eliminating differences in both current and future standards. The resultant compromises to attain convergence will likely spawn criticisms that the IASB standards are becoming too much like FASB standards and vice versa.

One significant difference between IASB and FASB standards is that the former are generally principles based, while the latter are generally rules based. The two groups will have to resolve their differences here, as well as regarding the use of the true and fair override.

Assuming the convergence project is successful, one may question the need for two standard-setting organizations. Furthermore, since the IASB has also simultaneously agreed to a convergence project with the Accounting Standards Board of Japan, one may also question the efficiency of approaching change through two convergence projects.

QUESTIONS

1. What does harmonization of accounting standards mean?

2. What is convergence and how does it differ from harmonization?

3. The EU opted to use exclusively IASB standards for consolidated financial statements beginning in 2005. What drove this decision?

4. Compare the true and fair view of the United Kingdom, the "present fairly" outlook of the United States, and the legalistic view of the continental model.

5. What are the different conceptions of the true and fair view?

6. Why has no continental model country developed a conceptual framework?

7. What is the relationship between the IFAC and IASB?

8. What are the main distinctions between the Anglo-American and the continental models?

9. How does the role of government differ in the United Kingdom and the United States relative to financial reporting?

10. What are the possible implications if accountants outsource the balance sheet to external appraisers (applying fair value accounting) for period-end financial statement reporting?

11. For years the FASB had little interest in pursuing international harmonization projects. What prompted its seemingly new interest in 2002 to work with the IASB in such a cooperative manner?

12. Evaluate the IASB's approach to convergence.

13. Why do the rules-based and principles-based approaches to standard setting tend to converge, as Schipper sees it?

14. How will the role of national standard-setting bodies be affected by adoption of IASB standards?

15. How do de facto harmonization and de jure harmonization differ from each other?

16. What are the advantages of convergence–harmonization of accounting standards?

17. Is the revenue–expense orientation consistent with fair value measurement?

CASES, PROBLEMS, AND WRITING ASSIGNMENTS

1. What are the main distinctions between the Anglo-American and the continental models relative to accounting and financial reporting? Within the Anglo-American group, how does the United States differ from other members of the group? What developments are leading to erosion of differences between at least some members of the Anglo-American and continental groups?

2. According to Alexander and Archer (2003), Anglo-American (or Anglo-Saxon) accounting is a "myth." Discuss their reasons for this. Do you agree with them?

CRITICAL THINKING AND ANALYSIS

1. Why do we need international accounting standards? Why not simply let each country develop and use its own standards and let it go at that?

2. The IASB and FASB are pursuing a single, converged conceptual framework. Develop what you consider to be a more complete model of accounting qualitative characteristics, taking the best from the two existing frameworks and addressing deficiencies with your individual proposals.

3. In 2003, South Africa was the first country to adopt IFRS with fair value accounting. The country does not allow for differential accounting treatment depending on size of enterprise. What type of response would you expect from this implementation?

Notes

1. *See Saudagaran and Diga (1999) for an extended discussion of research paradigms for examining international accounting. Many of these approaches were discussed here in Chapter 2.*

2. *Much of the information for this section was derived from Zimmerman (1992); Evans, Taylor, and Holzmann (1994); Mathews and Perera (1993); and—in particular—Choi and Mueller (1992) and Nobes and Parker (1995).*

3. *Alexander and Archer (2003).*

4. *Alexander and Archer do not mention the possibility of the override being instigated by the auditor. However, the auditor's tacit approval may be involved, if the preparer is the instigator of the override.*

5. *Parker (1995, p. 109).*

6. *Ibid. (p. 110).*

7. *See Zeff (1993, p. 128, and 1994, pp. 6–7). Alexander and Archer (2000) see the difference between the* true and fair view *and* present fairly *as leading to the conclusion that the Anglo-American model is a "myth." However, Nobes (1998) argues that the single most important factor used to develop a financial reporting classification system is the financing system. As such, Nobes's classification closely groups UK and U.S. systems, supporting the idea of the Anglo-American model's existence. On the other hand, d'Arcy (2001), in her harmonization paper that classifies countries by their accounting rules, not their accounting practices, places the UK closer to several continental countries than to the United States. Nobes (2004) questions the reliability of d'Arcy's UK placement in his subsequent analysis of her data. So, the search for the "best" agreed-upon classification system continues.*

8. *For further discussion, see Zeff (1987, p. 28).*

9. *Saudagaran and Diga (2000, p. 8).*

10. *Extensive discussion of the development of accounting regulation in the Netherlands appears in Zeff (1993).*

11. *Rahman, Perera, and Tower (1994).*

12. *Choi and Mueller (1992, pp. 90–91).*

13. *Eberhartinger (1999) notes that an absence of accounting regulation in France leads to expenses in French financial statements being the same as in tax returns.*

14. *A recent analysis of financial accounting and reporting in France that relates recent changes to cultural and environmental factors appears in Baydoun (1995).*

15. *Working Group on External Financial Reporting (1995).*

16. *Campbell and Nobes (1995, p. 288).*

17. *Ibid. (p. 290).*

18. *Landers (2000, p. A19).*

19. *Hayashi and Morse (2006).*

20. *See Rebmann-Huber (1990) and Nobes (1998).*

21. *See Most and Salter (1990).*

22. *Hofstede (1987) and Nobes (1998). Nobes sees the colonial inheritance of African nations from England, France, Belgium, and Germany as being very important.*

23. *For example Choi and Mueller (1992), Doupnik and Salter (1995), Gray (1988), Chanchani and MacGregor (1999), and Jaggi and Low (2000).*

24. *Choi and Mueller (1992, p. 310).*

25. *Amir, Harris, and Venuti (1993, p. 233).*

26. *For example Frost and Pownall (1996) and Adams, Weetman, Jones, and Gray (1999).*

27. *The term* du jour *for making both domestic and cross-border financial reporting standards compatible is referred to as "convergence," formerly called "harmonization." In our discussions, we see the terms as synonymous.*

28. *Meek and Saudagaran (1990, pp. 168–169) make a distinction between standardization and harmonization. The former refers to uniform standards in all countries. Harmonization, according to Meek and Saudagaran, refers to reconciling different national viewpoints as long as there are no logical conflicts. Wallace (1990, pp. 10–11) presents five degrees of harmonization within the context of the International Accounting Standards Board's limitations and goals.*

29. *Rahman, Perera, and Ganeshanandam (1996). See also van der Tas (1988).*

30. *Among relatively recent studies see Hermann and Thomas (1995). See van der Tas (1988) for approaches to measuring harmonization.*

31. *Archer, Delvaille, and McLeay (1995).*

32. *For an up-to-date membership list, see http://europa.eu.*

33. *Interestingly, the true and fair view approach results from UK requests that it be added to the Fourth Directive. When the UK joined the EU, the true and fair view was not yet included in the draft document (Roberts, Weetman, and Gordon, 2005, p. 460).*

34. *See Nobes (1993), Higson and Blake (1993), and Walton (1993).*

35. *Alexander (1993 and 1996) believes that the true and fair view is culture specific; whereas Ordelheide (1996) believes that the true and fair view can become an EU-wide concept because legal cases on it would ultimately be decided by the European Court of Justice, which would, presumably, be applying the concept on an EU-wide basis.*

36. *Stacy (1997, p. 708).*

37. *For an extensive analysis of the Seventh Directive, see Diggle and Nobes (1994).*

38. *Roberts, Salter, and Kantor (1996, p. 3).*

39. *For an extended discussion of the EU adoption of IASB standards, see Cañibano and Mora (2000) and, in particular, Haller (2002).*

40. *Whittington (2005).*

41. *American Institute of Certified Public Accountants (AICPA), Canadian Institute of Chartered Accountants (CICA), Institute of Chartered Accountants of England & Wales (ICAEW).*

42. *IASB (2007) Web site: www.iasb.org.*

43. *House (2005).*

44. *IASB (2007) Web site: www.iasb.org/About+Us/About+Us.htm for its current organizational structure.*

45. *Dye and Sunder (2001) discuss the possibility of allowing U.S. firms to choose either FASB or IASB standards. See also Sunder (2002) for the benefits of competition in accounting standards.*

46. *Implementation problems may range from translation of standards from the IASB's English language to the country's official language, into the country's laws, or conceptual issues that the standard may not have adequately considered.*

47. *For further details, see Garrido, Leon, and Zorro (2002).*

48. *d'Arcy (2001).*

49. *The Norwalk Agreement is named for the two boards' meeting location: Norwalk, Connecticut, also home of the FASB's offices.*

50. *For the most recent "Memo of Understanding With the FASB and the IASB," see www.iasb.org. This document details the short-term and longer-term convergence projects underway.*

51. *Zeff (2002).*

52. *L. Evans (2004).*

53. *Schipper (2003) states that most standards drafted by the FASB are really principles based. However, the number of scope and treatment exemptions make them appear to be rules based.*

54. *Securities and Exchange Commission (2003).*

55. *Schipper (2005).*

56. *Ibid.*

57. *Benston, Bromwich, and Wagenhofer (2006).*

58. *Agrawal et al. (1989, pp. 243–246).*

59. *Epstein and Mirza (2006, pp. 8–9). "The qualitative characteristics are understandability, relevance, reliability, and comparability. Reliability comprises representational faithfulness, substance over form, completeness, neutrality, and prudence. It suggests that these are subject to a trade-off between characteristics. The Framework does not specifically include a 'true and fair' requirement. . . ."*

60. *IASB (2006a).*

61. *Ibid.*

62. *Alexander and Jermakowicz (2006) conclude that wording such as "true and fair" or "not misleading" are necessary to the reporting of an enterprise's underlying economics. "Rules, by themselves, are inadequate."*

63. *Pizzani (2006).*

64. *Ibid.*

65. *IVSC (2005).*

66. *IASB (2006b).*

67. *Cairns (2006).*

68. *Jopson (2005a).*

69. *Jopson (2005b).*

70. *In this case, FASB appears to have learned from the IASB's experience with IAS 39. SFAS No. 159, The Fair Value Option for Financial Assets and Financial Liabilities—Including an Amendment of FASB Statement No. 115 , is similar, but not identical, to the fair value option in IAS 39. It allows for recognition of fair values without the complexity of hedge accounting provisions. Unrealized gains and losses are reported in earnings when the fair value option is selected. It allows for fewer alternatives when choosing to adopt the fair value option.*

71. *Aggestam (1999).*

72. *Nobes (1995, p. 134).*

References

Adams, Carol, P. Weetman, E. A. E. Jones, and S. Gray (1999). "Reducing the Burden of U.S. GAAP Reconciliations by Foreign Companies Listed in the United States: The Key Question of Materiality," *European Accounting Review* (Vol. 8, No. 1), pp. 1–22.

Aggestam, Caroline (1999). "Towards a Global Accounting Qualification?" *European Accounting Review* (Vol. 8, No. 4), pp. 805–813.

Agrawal, Surendra P., P. H. Jensen, A. L. Meador, and K. Sellers (1989). "An International Comparison of Conceptual Frameworks of Accounting," *International Journal of Accounting*, pp. 237–250.

Alexander, David. (1993). "A European True and Fair View?" *European Accounting Review* (Vol. 2, No. 1), pp. 59–80.

——— (1996). "Truer and Fairer, Uninvited Comments on Invited Comments," *European Accounting Review* (Vol. 5, No. 3), pp. 483–493.

Alexander, David, and S. Archer (2000). "On the Myth of 'Anglo-Saxon' Financial Accounting," *International Journal of Accounting* (Vol. 35, No. 4), pp. 539–557.

——— (2003). "On Economic Reality, Representational Faithfulness and the 'True and Fair Override,'" *Accounting and Business Research* (Vol. 33, No. 1), pp. 3–17.

Alexander, David, and E. Jermakowicz (2006). "A True and Fair View of Principles/Rules Debate," *Abacus* (Vol. 42, No. 2), pp. 132–164.

Amir, Eli, Trevor Harris, and Elizabeth Venuti (1993). "A Comparison of the Value Relevance of U.S. Versus Non U.S. GAAP Accounting Measures Using Form 20 F Reconciliations," *Studies on International Accounting, 1993* (Supplement to *Journal of Accounting Research*), pp. 230–264.

Archer, Simon, P. Delvaille, and S. McLeay (Spring 1995). "The Measurement of Harmonization and the Comparability of Financial Statement Items: Within Country and Between Country Effects," *Accounting and Business Research*, pp. 67–80.

Baydoun, Nabil (1995). "The French Approach to Financial Accounting and Reporting," *International Journal of Accounting* (Vol. 30, No. 3), pp. 189–207.

Benston, George, M. Bromwich, and A. Wagenhofer (2006). "Principles-Versus Rules-Based Accounting Standards: The FASB's Standard Setting Strategy," *Abacus* (Vol. 42, No. 2), pp. 165–188.

Cairns, David (2006). "Financial Reporting International Briefing—EU Adoption of IAS 39 Fair Value Option," *Financial Times Information Limited - Europe Intelligence Wire - Accountancy* (LexisNexis, January 1).

Campbell, Les, and Christopher Nobes (1995). "Financial Reporting in Japan" in *Comparative International Accounting*, eds. C. W. Nobes and R. H. Parker. Prentice Hall, pp. 288–308.

Cañibano, Leandro, and A. Mora (2000). "Evaluating the Statistical Significance of de Facto Accounting Harmonization: A Study of European Global Players," *European Accounting Review* (Vol. 9, No. 3), pp. 349–369.

Chanchani, Shalin, and A. MacGregor (1999). "A Synthesis of Cultural Studies in Accounting," *Journal of Accounting Literature* (Vol. 18), pp. 1–30.

Choi, Frederick, and Gerhard Mueller (1992). *International Accounting,* 2nd ed. Prentice Hall.

d'Arcy, Anne (2001). "Accounting Classification and the International Harmonization Debate—an Empirical Investigation," *Accounting Organizations & Society* (Vol. 26, Nos. 4–5), pp. 327–349.

Diggle, Graham, and Christopher Nobes (Autumn 1994). "European Rule Making in Accounting: The Seventh Directive as a Case Study," *Accounting and Business Research*, pp. 319–334.

Doupnik, Timothy, and Stephen Salter (1995). "External Environment, Culture, and Accounting Practice: A Preliminary Test of a General Model of International Accounting Development," *International Journal of Accounting* (Vol. 30, No. 3), pp. 189–207.

Dye, Ronald, and S. Sunder (2001). "Why Not Allow FASB and IASB Standards to Compete in the U.S.?" *Accounting Horizons* (Vol. 15, No. 3), pp. 257–271.

Eberhartinger, Eva (1999). "The Impact of Tax Rules on Financial Reporting in Germany, France, and the UK," *International Journal of Accounting* (Vol. 34, No. 1), pp. 92–119.

Emenyonu, Emmanuel, and Sidney Gray (1996). "International Harmonization and the Major Developed Stock Market Countries: An Empirical Study," *The International Journal of Accounting* (Vol. 31, No. 3), pp. 269-279.

Epstein, Barry J., and Abbas Ali Mirza (2006). IFRS 2006: *Interpretation and Application of International Financial Reporting Standards.* John Wiley and Sons.

Evans, Lisa (2004). "Language, Translation and the Problem of International Accounting Communication," *Accounting, Auditing & Accountability Journal* (Vol. 17, No. 2), pp. 210–248.

Evans, Thomas G., Martin Taylor, and Oscar Holzmann (1994). *International Accounting & Reporting.* South Western College Publishing.

Financial Accounting Standards Board (2007). Statement of Financial Accounting Standards No. 159, *The Fair Value Option for Financial Assets and Financial Liabilities—Including an Amendment of FASB Statement No. 115.* FASB.

Frost, Carol, and Grace Pownall (March 1996). "Interdependence in the Global Capital Markets for Capital and Information: The Case of SmithKline Beecham plc," *Accounting Horizons*, pp. 38–57.

Garrido, Pascual, A. Leon, and A. Zorro (2002). "Measurement of Formal Harmonization Progress: The IASC Experience," *International Journal of Accounting* (Vol. 37, No. 1), pp. 1–26.

Gray, S. J. (April 1988). "Towards a Theory of Cultural Influence on the Development of Accounting Systems Internationally," *Abacus*, pp. 1–15.

Haller, Axel (2002). "Financial Accounting Developments in the EU: Past Events and Future Prospects," *European Accounting Review* (Vol. 11, No. 1), pp. 153–190.

Hayashi, Yuka, and Andrew Morse (2006). "Livedoor Inquiry Prompts Focus on Japan's Accounting Rules: Despite Progress, Calls Rise to Rein in Aggressive Tactics," *Wall Street Journal* (January 26), p. C3.

Hermann, Don, and Wayne Thomas (Autumn 1995). "Harmonization of Accounting Measurement Practices in the European Community," *Accounting and Business Research*, pp. 253–265.

Higson, Andrew, and John Blake (1993). "The True and Fair View Concept—A Formula for International Disharmony: Some Empirical Evidence," *International Journal of Accounting* (Vol. 28, No. 2), pp. 104–115.

Hofstede, Gert (1987). "The Cultural Context of Accounting," in *Accounting and Culture.* American Accounting Association, pp. 1–11.

Holzer, H. Peter, ed. (1984). *International Accounting.* Harper and Row.

House, John (2005). "Financial Reporting World Standard-Setters Meeting—Remaining Relevant," *Financial Times Information Limited - Europe Intelligence Wire - Accountancy* (LexisNexis, November 1).

IASB (2006a). "Preliminary Views on an Improved Conceptual Framework for Financial Reporting: The Objectives of Financial Reporting and Qualitative Characteristics of Decision-Useful Financial Reporting Information," *International Accounting Standards Board,* Discussion Paper.

———— (2006b). "Fair Value Measurements: Project Summary," *International Accounting Standards Board* (December), pp. 1–5.

IVSC (2005). *International Valuation Standards 2005,* 7th ed. International Valuation Standards Committee Web site: www.ivsc.org/standards/index.html. Retrieved February 10, 2007.

Jaggi, Bikki, and P. Y. Low (2000). "Impact of Culture, Market Forces, and Legal System on Financial Disclosures," *International Journal of Accounting* (Vol. 35, No. 4), pp. 495–519.

Jopson, Barney (2005a). "Banks and IASB in Stalemate on Derivatives," *Financial Times* (London edition, September 16), p. 30.

———— (2005b). "New 'Fair Value' Rules Turn up Pounds 123M Loss," *Financial Times* (London edition, July 27), p. 21.

Landers, Peter (2000). "New Accounting Shows Weaknesses of Japanese Firms," *Wall Street Journal* (February 29), p. A19.

Mathews, M. R., and M. H. B. Perera (1993). *Accounting Theory and Development,* 2nd ed. Thomas Nelson Australia.

Meek, Gary, and S. Saudagaran (1990). "A Survey of Research on Financial Reporting in a Transnational Context," *Journal of Accounting Literature* (Vol. 9), pp. 145–182.

Most, Kenneth S., and Stephen B. Salter (1990). "Classification Research in International Accounting and Its Relevance to European Accounting Harmonization," presented at *Global Economic Alliances: The Implications for Accounting Education, Standard Setting and Practice* (Montreal), pp. 1–9.

Nobes, C. W. (Winter 1993). "The True and Fair View Requirement: Impact on the Fourth Directive," *Accounting and Business Research,* pp. 35–48.

———— (1995). "The Harmonization of Financial Reporting," in *Comparative International Accounting,* eds. C. W. Nobes and R. H. Parker. Prentice Hall, pp. 117–142.

———— (September 1998). "Towards a General Model of the Reasons for International Differences in Financial Reporting," *Abacus,* pp. 162–187.

Nobes, C. W., and R. H. Parker, eds. (1995). *Comparative International Accounting,* 4th ed. Prentice Hall.

Ordelheide, Deiter (1996). "True and Fair View: A European and a German Perspective II," *European Accounting Review* (Vol. 5, No. 3), pp. 495–506.

Parker, Robert (1995). "Regulating Financial Reporting in the United Kingdom, the United States, Australia, and Canada," in *Comparative International Accounting,* eds. C. W. Nobes and R. H. Parker. Prentice Hall, pp. 99–116.

Pizzani, Lori (May–June 2006). "A Fair Question: Will New Initiatives Lead to Global Acceptance of Fair Value?" *CFA Magazine,* pp. 62–63.

Rahman, Asheq, H. Perera, and S. Ganeshanandam (Autumn 1996). "Measurement of Formal Harmonization in Accounting: An Exploratory Study," *Accounting and Business Research,* pp. 325–339.

Rahman, Asheq, H. Perera, and G. Tower (1994). "Accounting Harmonization Between Australia and New Zealand: Towards a Regulatory Union," *International Journal of Accounting* (Vol. 29, No. 3), pp. 316–333.

Rebmann-Huber, Zelma (1990). "The Relationship Between Financial Markets and Financial Reporting Systems: Model and Empirical Test for 16 Countries of the OECD," presented at *Global Economic Alliances: The Implications for Accounting Education, Standard Setting and Practice* (Montreal), pp. 1–18.

Roberts, Clare B., Stephen Salter, and Jeffrey Kantor (March 1996). "The IASC Comparability Project and Current Financial Reporting: An Empirical Study of Reporting in Europe," *British Accounting Review*, pp. 1–22.

Roberts, Clare B., Pauline Weetman, and Paul Gordon (2005). *International Financial Reporting: A Comparative Approach*, 3rd ed. Prentice Hall.

Saudagaran, Sharokh, and J. Diga (1999). "Evaluation of the Contingency-Based Approach in Comparative International Accounting: A Case for Alternative Research Paradigms," *Journal of Accounting Literature* (Vol. 18), pp. 57–95.

——— (2000). "The Institutional Environment of Financial Reporting Regulation in ASEAN," *International Journal of Accounting* (Vol. 35, No. 1), pp. 1–26.

Scarbrough, Paul, Robert McGee, and Michiharu Sakurai (1993). "Accounting for Software Costs in the United States and Japan: Lessons From Differing Standards and Practices," *International Journal of Accounting* (Vol. 28, No. 4), pp. 308–324.

Schipper, Katherine (March, 2003). "Principles-Based Accounting Standards," *Accounting Horizons*, pp. 61–72.

——— (May 2005). "The Introduction of International Accounting Standards in Europe: Implications for International Convergence," *European Accounting Review*, pp. 101–126.

Securities and Exchange Commission (2003), "Study Pursuant to Section 108(d) of the Sarbanes-Oxley Act of 2002 on the Adoption by the United States Financial Reporting System of a Principles-Based Accounting System." Government Printing Office.

Stacy, Graham (1997). "True and Fair View: A UK Auditor's Perspective," *European Accounting Review* (Vol. 6, No. 4), pp. 705–709.

Sunder, Shyam (2002). "Regulatory Competition Among Accounting Standards Within and Across International Boundaries," *Journal of Accounting and Public Policy* (Vol. 21, No. 3), pp. 219–234.

van der Tas, Leon G. (Spring 1988). "Measuring Harmonization of Financial Reporting Practice," *Accounting and Business Research*, pp. 157–169.

Wallace, R. S. O. (June 1990). "Survival Strategies of a Global Organization: The Case of the International Accounting Standards Committee," *Accounting Horizons*, pp. 1–22.

Walton, Peter (1993). "Introduction: The True and Fair View in British Accounting," *European Accounting Review* (Vol. 2, No. 1), pp. 49–58.

Whittington, Geoffrey (May, 2005), "The Adoption of International Accounting Standards in the European Union," *European Accounting Review*, pp. 127–153.

Working Group on External Financial Reporting (September 1995). "German Accounting Principles: An Institutionalized Framework," *Accounting Horizons*, pp. 92–99.

Zeff, Stephen (December 1987). "Setting Accounting Standards: Some Lessons From the U.S. Experience," *The Accountant's Magazine*, pp. 26–28.

——— (August 1993). "The Politics of Accounting Standards," *Economia Aziendale*, pp. 123–142.

——— (June 1994). "A Perspective on the U.S. Public/Private Sector Approach to Standard Setting and Financial Reporting," *Inaugural Lecture, State University of Limburg*.

——— (2002). "'Political Lobbying' on Proposed Standards: A Challenge to the IASB," *Accounting Horizons* (Vol. 16, No. 1), pp. 43–54.

Zimmerman, V. K., ed. (1992). *Changing International Financial Markets and Their Impact on Accounting*. Center for International Education and Research in Accounting, University of Illinois.

11

The Balance Sheet

Learning Objectives

After reading this chapter, you should be able to:

- Appreciate the underlying approaches to balance sheet and income statement relationships.
- Understand the evolving definitions of assets, liabilities, and owners' equity.
- Appreciate the complexity of balance sheet valuation techniques and recent trends.
- Comprehend hybrid securities.
- Understand the nature of derivatives.
- Comprehend balance sheet classification issues.

The next three chapters examine the balance sheet, income statement, and cash flow statements, respectively, in order to review the conceptual foundation of current financial reporting practices. We emphasize the definitions of accounting elements and the rules of recognition and measurement applicable to each financial statement. It is not our intent to cover all extant accounting standards: Such an approach is taken in intermediate accounting textbooks. Rather, we wish to gain an overview of the principles of accounting measurement or calculation embodied in the three basic financial statements.

We commence this chapter by reviewing the relationship between the balance sheet and income statement. If the statements are articulated, they are linked together mathematically without any "loose ends," then either a revenue–expense view or an asset–liability view predominates. The revenue–expense view means that the income statement predominates, whereas an asset–liability view means that the balance sheet is primary. The nonarticulated view means that the two statements are independently defined.

The chapter then examines recognition and measurement problems in the three sections of the balance sheet: assets, liabilities, and owners' equity. We will see that a great many valuation methods exist and that sometimes revenue–expense predominates and sometimes asset–liability predominates. Nonarticulation is becoming scarce due to the concept of comprehensive income (Chapter 12). As we shall see, the asset–liability view is beginning to supplant the revenue–expense view for income determination. Many problems are relatively new, such as those involving derivatives and hybrid securities, and solutions are just beginning to emerge. The chapter concludes with a brief discussion of classification in the balance sheet.

The Relationship Between the Balance Sheet and the Income Statement

Two approaches, the articulated and the nonarticulated, have been advocated for defining accounting elements and the relationship between the balance sheet and income statement.[1] *Articulation* means that the two statements are mathematically defined in such a way that net income is equal to the change in owners' equity for a period, assuming no capital transactions or prior period adjustments. The nonarticulated approach severs the mathematical relationship between the balance sheet and income statement: Each statement is defined and measured independently of the other.

Articulation

The accounting elements identified in Statement of Financial Accounting Concept (SFAC) No. 6 are assets, liabilities, owners' equity, revenues, gains, expenses, and losses.[2] Income is calculated from revenues, gains, expenses, and losses. Under articulation, income is a subclassification of owners' equity. Exhibit 11.1 illustrates the articulated accounting model and classification system. For ease of presentation, we take a proprietary approach, in which the net assets are equal to owners' equity.

Under the articulated concept, all accounting transactions can be classified by the model in Exhibit 11.1. There are three subclassifications of owners' equity: contributed capital, retained earnings, and unrealized capital adjustments. Contributed capital is subclassified into legal capital (par value) and other sources of contributed capital (for example, premiums above par value and donated assets). Retained earnings has three main subclassifications: income statement accounts, prior period adjustments, and dividends. Because income is a subclassification of retained earnings, the income statement and balance sheet articulate.

There are further subclassifications within the income statement itself: the distinctions between revenues and gains, between expenses and losses, and the classification of gains and losses as either ordinary or extraordinary. Some accounting transactions bypass the income statement altogether because they are considered to be adjustments of previous years' income. These adjustments are made directly to retained earnings. Dividends represent a distribution of income. The third subclassification of owners' equity, unrealized capital adjustments, arises from a few specific accounting rules. These are fast disappearing as a result of SFAC No. 130 on comprehensive income (Chapter 12).

Exhibit 11.1 Accounting Classification System

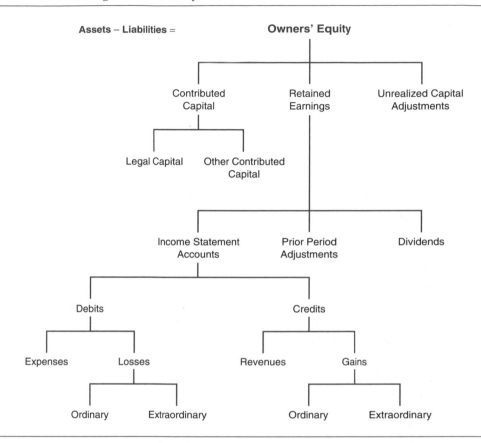

The accounting classification system is rather simple, but this simplicity causes some difficulty because complex transactions cannot always be neatly categorized into one of the classifications in Exhibit 11.1. New types of business transactions challenge the limits of the basic accounting model. For example, mandatory redeemable preferred stock, because it is stock, has definite ownership characteristics; however, since it must be redeemed, it also resembles bonds. Currently, the Securities and Exchange Commission (SEC) prohibits the inclusion of mandatory redeemable preferred stock in owners' equity; a case might be made for its classification as owners' equity. Such complex transactions exceed the limits of the accounting classification system. Even so, it is remarkable that the categorical framework used to classify accounting transactions is virtually unchanged since Pacioli's time. It may be that supplemental disclosure is the only way to deal with newer complexities—short of developing an entirely new accounting classification system.

Within the articulated system, there are two alternatives for defining accounting elements. One approach, referred to as the *revenue–expense* view, focuses on defining the income statement elements. It places primacy on the income statement, principles of income recognition, and rules of income measurement. Assets and liabilities are defined, recognized, and measured as a by-product of revenues and expenses. The other approach is referred to as the *asset–liability* view. It is the antithesis of the revenue–expense approach because it emphasizes the definition, recognition, and measurement of assets and liabilities. Income is defined, recognized, and measured as a byproduct of asset and liability measurement.

Revenue–Expense Approach

Since the 1930s, accounting policy has been mainly concerned with the definition, recognition, and measurement of income. Income is derived by matching costs (including arbitrary allocations such as depreciation) to recognized revenues. Both the income statement and balance sheet are primarily governed by accounting rules of revenue recognition and cost matching, and these rules represent a revenue–expense orientation.

One consequence of the revenue–expense approach is to burden the balance sheet with by-products of income measurement rules. As a result, the balance sheet contains not only assets and liabilities (defined later in this chapter) but also ambiguous debits and credits called deferred charges and deferred credits. These items do not conform to current definitions of assets and liabilities, yet they are included in the balance sheet because of deferred recognition in the income statement.

An example of a deferred charge is organizational startup costs. These costs are allocated to the income statement over a number of years rather than expensed immediately. Once incurred, organizational costs are a sunk cost and cannot be recovered. Therefore, it is questionable if such costs should be carried forward in the balance sheet. The same is true of some deferred credits. Many of these types of credit balances are not really liabilities; they are simply future income statement credits arising from present transactions that are deferred to future income statements. An example of this type of deferred credit—now largely gone—is the investment tax credit accounted for under the deferral method per Accounting Principles Board (APB) Opinion No. 2. Deferred investment tax credits are not a legal liability; rather, they simply arise from a difference between how the tax credits are treated in the firm's tax return and financial statements.

There are multiple examples of accounting standards that emphasize the effects of transactions on the income statement somewhat to the exclusion of their impact on the balance sheet. For example, pension accounting under APB Opinion No. 8 was mainly concerned with income statement recognition of pension expenses.[3] Virtually no consideration was given to the question of whether a pension liability exists. The recognition and amortization of intangible assets under APB Opinion No. 17 introduced a dubious debit into the balance sheet (arising from the purchase method of accounting for business combinations) and arbitrarily amortized it over a maximum of 40 years. However, this has been changed by SFAS No. 142 to an asset–liability orientation (see chapter 18).[4] The question of whether an intangible asset (goodwill) really exists is not addressed.

Asset–Liability Approach

The asset–liability approach is directly concerned with measuring and reporting assets and liabilities. In SFAC No. 6, the Financial Accounting Standards Board (FASB) defines comprehensive income as the change in the firm's net assets (assets minus liabilities) from nonowner sources. The income statement is regarded as simply a way of classifying and reporting certain changes that have occurred in the firm's net assets. Because assets and liabilities are real, it seems logical that measurement should focus on them. The owners' equity account is merely an invention to make possible the double-entry accounting system. Income and its components (revenues, gains, expenses, and losses) are thus regarded as secondary concepts that are simply a way of reporting on changes in assets and liabilities.

The asset–liability approach focuses on the measurement of net assets. This approach is arguably superior to a revenue–expense approach because, as we have noted, assets and liabilities are real. It is the increase in the value of net assets that gives rise to what we call income, not vice versa. The revenue–expense approach turns things around, implying that changes in net assets are the consequences of "income" measurement. The current value models presented in Appendix 1-A of Chapter 1 are examples of the asset–liability approach.

Although the revenue–expense approach has been the basic orientation of current financial reporting practices, some specific accounting standards reflect an asset–liability emphasis. SFAS No. 7 proscribes loss capitalization for companies that are in the development stage. Previous practice had been to capitalize losses while in the development stage and to write off the losses against future income. The requirement under SFAS No. 7 keeps a deferred charge out of the balance sheet. SFAS No. 109 focuses income tax accounting on the recognition of tax "assets" and "liabilities."

The Nonarticulated Approach

The possibility for nonarticulated financial statements has not been widely discussed in accounting literature. However, the idea appears to have merit. There is a great deal of tension between proponents of the traditional revenue–expense approach and the asset–liability approach because revenue–expense proponents are primarily concerned with stabilizing the fluctuating effect of transactions on the income statement—they are prepared to introduce deferred charges and deferred credits to smooth income measurement. On the other hand, asset–liability advocates are mainly concerned with reporting changes in the value of net assets, and they are prepared to tolerate a more volatile income statement that may include unrealized holding gains and losses.

It is evident that the two groups are polarized partly because the balance sheet and income statement are mathematically articulated. Since articulation exists only by custom, the two statements could be severed and both groups might be satisfied with a revenue–expense–based income statement and an asset–liability–based balance sheet. However, rather than going in the direction of nonarticulation, the comprehensive income approach required in SFAS No. 130 (Chapter 12) suggests that articulation will continue to be the accepted accounting paradigm in the near-term.

Assets

In discussing assets, liabilities, and owners' equity, we present the evolution of definitions first because definitions are necessary for classifying business transactions into the appropriate categories (as illustrated in Exhibit 11.1). The next step is to define the point in time when elements are recognized in the balance sheet. Finally, we review the attributes to be measured for specific types of assets, liabilities, and owners' equity.

Definition of Assets

The definition of assets is important because it establishes what types of economic factors will appear in the balance sheet. It identifies the elements to be recognized, measured, and reported in the balance sheet. A definition of assets should be solely concerned with the criteria for classifying accounting transactions as assets. As indicated in Chapter 1, the attribute to be measured should be stated independently of the object to be measured. Many definitions of assets can be found in accounting literature. However, the accounting profession in the United States has made only three formal attempts to define assets:

1. Something represented by a debit balance that is or would be properly carried forward upon a closing of books of account according to the rules or principles of accounting (provided such debit balance is not in effect a negative balance applicable to a liability), on the basis that it represents either a property right or value acquired, or an expenditure made which has created a property or is properly applicable to the future. Thus, plant, accounts receivable, inventory, and a deferred charge are all assets in balance sheet classification.[5]

2. Economic resources of an enterprise that are recognized and measured in conformity with generally accepted accounting principles. Assets also include certain deferred charges that are not resources but that are recognized and measured in conformity with generally accepted accounting principles.[6]

3. Assets are probable future economic benefits obtained or controlled by a particular entity as a result of past transactions or events.[7]

The first definition emphasizes legal property but also includes deferred charges on the basis that they are "properly" included with assets. A distinction is made between assets and deferred charges, but both are considered to be assets. The justification is that deferred charges relate to future-period income statements. They are included with assets solely because of income statement rules that defer the recognition of these costs as expenses until future periods. This aspect of the definition clearly represents a revenue–expense approach to the financial statements.

The second definition emphasizes that assets are economic resources, which are defined as "the scarce means available . . . for the carrying out of economic activity."[8] Assets are perceived to be more than legal property; anything having future economic value is an asset. For example, a lease agreement that grants the lessee property use rights (though not ownership rights) would satisfy this broader definition. Deferred charges are separately identified in this definition, but are still grouped with assets.

The third definition is a further evolution of the concept that assets are economic resources. Key characteristics of an asset are its capacity to provide future economic benefits, control of the asset by the firm, and the occurrence of the transaction giving rise to control and the economic benefits. The capacity to provide economic benefits has also been called future service potential. It means that an asset is something that will produce positive net cash flows in the future. These cash flows may occur in one of two ways: in a direct market exchange for another asset or through conversion in a manufacturing operation to finished goods (which are then exchanged for another asset in a market exchange). SFAC No. 6 also attempts to reconcile this definition with certain types of deferred charges. Some deferred charges, it argues, do benefit the cash flows of future periods. For example, prepaid costs are deferred charges that will reduce future-period outflows of cash. However, other deferred charges, such as organizational startup costs, are sunk costs and do not have any impact on future cash flows.

The "economic resources" approach represents a broader concept of assets than the legal property concept and is consistent with the economic notion that an asset has value because of a future positive net cash flows. The genesis of this broader definition can be found in both economic and accounting literature. It represents an emphasis on control of assets rather than legal ownership. Because the concept of economic resources is broad, it encompasses a wide variation in (a) methods of realizing the future benefits and (b) determining the probability of realizing future benefits. The only subclassification reported within the asset group is the current–noncurrent distinction. This tells very little, though, about how the benefits are to be realized and the probability of realizing the benefits. Classification of assets is discussed further in the final section of the chapter.

The breadth of the economic resources concept has led some accountants to prefer a narrower concept of assets based on the notions of exchangeability and severability.[9] According to this narrower viewpoint, an asset should represent only those economic resources that can be severed from the firm and sold. This narrower asset definition would reduce variation in the reporting of assets in terms of the realization of future benefits—because having value only from productive use would be excluded by this narrower definition. Assets held for use can be argued to have a higher risk of realizing future benefits than assets held directly for sale. It follows that a balance sheet that excludes such assets would have less uncertainty regarding the realization of future benefits.

The severability/exchangeability approach does highlight a weakness in economic value theory. Economic value is often reduced to the one dimension of market exchange prices. An asset may have value in use to its owner, but there may not be an external market due to the nature of the asset. For example, the relocation or installation costs of secondhand manufacturing equipment may preclude a market for such goods. However, assets held for use still have the potential to generate future cash flows even though they are not directly salable. The severability/exchangeability approach is very conservative and seems to restrict unnecessarily what is included in the balance sheet as an asset.

Definitions of assets have evolved from a narrow legal orientation to a broader concept of economic resources. As the definition has broadened, the boundary around what is and what is not an asset has become obscure. One might find it surprising that accountants have failed to more clearly define this basic accounting element. However, the legal profession has also had difficulty in defining assets. In law, the following terms have similar but distinctly different meanings: property, property rights, ownership, title, and possession. There is no clear, unambiguous asset concept in law. An FASB discussion memorandum expressed the opinion that legal definitions and concepts are not helpful in formulating accounting definitions of assets.[10]

Executory Contracts

A longstanding problem in accounting has been the question of how to account (if at all) for mutually unperformed executory contracts.[11] A mutually unperformed executory contract is a contract unperformed by both parties. The traditional accounting view is that no recognition is required in financial statements because a binding exchange has not yet occurred. The contract is prospective. Two examples of such contracts are employment contracts and long-term purchase agreements. In both cases, neither an asset nor a liability is recorded under present practices. However, it can be argued in the case of an employment contract that the employer incurs a liability to pay future wages and receives a benefit in the form of securing future employee services. Similarly, a long-term purchase agreement could be considered a liability for future payments and an asset for future purchases made under the agreement. However, conventional accounting wisdom regards such contracts as too uncertain and contingent for accounting recognition.

There is nothing in the asset definitions just presented that would exclude recognition of executory contracts. The exclusion is by custom and seems to rest on the belief that a binding transaction has not yet occurred. Solomons was not pleased with the FASB's inability to decide whether executory contracts should be booked, merely disclosed in footnotes, or simply omitted from the statements.[12] Indeed, the omission of executory contracts can lead to some rather strange entries when losses arise. For example, when a price decline occurs in the case of purchase commitments, a debit to a loss account is offset by a credit to a liability account. The credit is certainly unique because no liability exists for the amount of the obligation itself because of its executory nature. However, no other type of account obviously fits the credit, so the liability account is employed in the spirit of its being the least obnoxious type to use.[13] The suggestion to book executory contracts is certainly deserving of attention.

Recognition and Measurement of Assets

As noted in Chapter 7, SFAC No. 5 is more or less intended to be broad enough to encompass extant accounting practices. It says little that is new with respect to the complex issue of recognition. Thus Chapter 7, as does this chapter, draws on more theoretically grounded work in discussing the recognition of assets and liabilities. The discussion here is, of course, complementary to the discussion of revenue and expense recognition and future events analyzed in Chapter 12.

The following "pervasive principle" has been stated about the initial recognition and measurement of both assets and liabilities:

> Assets and liabilities generally are initially recorded on the basis of events in which the enterprise acquires resources from other entities or incurs obligations to other entities. The assets and liabilities are measured by the exchange prices at which the transfers take place.[14]

Hence, assets are initially recognized when the transaction transferring control occurs. At this point, a potential exists for future economic benefits. Assets are measured at the market value (exchange price) of the consideration exchanged or sacrificed to acquire the assets and place them in operating condition. This is called historical acquisition cost. However, in no case should an asset be recorded in an amount greater than its cash equivalent purchase price. When the consideration is nonmonetary, the market value of the asset received may provide a more reliable basis for measuring acquisition cost. This reflects a primary concern for measurement reliability.

The remainder of this section reviews how specific types of assets are measured in periods subsequent to acquisition. As will be seen, numerous attributes are measured, such as original acquisition cost (historical cost), historical cost less cumulative charges to income (book value), replacement cost, selling prices, net realizable value (selling price less disposal costs), and net realizable value less normal markups. This eclectic approach to accounting measurement violates the additivity principle of measurement theory. The resulting balance sheet may convey relevant information to users, but from the viewpoint of pure measurement theory it can be criticized for a lack of additivity. One often suggested solution to the additivity problem is multicolumn reporting, with each column representing a different attribute of measurement.[15] However, expanded reporting might confuse users because of information overload.

Receivables

Receivables are carried at historical cost, adjusted for an estimate of uncollectible amounts. The attribute being measured is an approximation of net realizable value. However, a true measure of net realizable value would be the selling price of receivables through factoring—less any estimated liability for recourse due to nonpayment by the debtors. Since factoring involves present value discounting, the accounting approximation of net realizable value is overstated by the amount of interest implicit in factoring.

Investments Not Subject to Equity Accounting

SFAS No. 115 brought major changes to investments in marketable securities. Its predecessor on this matter, SFAS No. 12, required that marketable equity securities be carried at lower of historical cost or current market value on a portfolio-wide basis with marketable debt securities continuing to be valued at cost unless a "permanent" decline in value occurred.

SFAS No. 115 is a move toward current values. Investments in equity and debt securities are classified in one of three ways:

1. Held to maturity, where the firm has both the positive intent and ability to hold to maturity

2. Trading, where the purpose is to sell the securities in the near term

3. Available for sale, where neither of the other two categories apply

For investments in equity securities where neither the equity method nor full consolidation applies, classification is done according to either the trading or available-for-sale categories. Both of these categories are to be valued at fair market value. As with SFAS

No. 12, fair value of equity securities must be readily available from a securities exchange or the over-the-counter market.

For bonds in the held-to-maturity category, the effective rate of interest method was used (as with bonds payable), resulting in a constant rate of return based on the historical cost of the bonds. However, SFAS No. 159 now allows firms to value held-to-maturity securities at market value.

Securities in both the trading and available-for-sale categories are carried on the balance sheet at fair (current) value. In both of these categories, interest and dividends are recognized according to the usual rules when earned. The big change comes in regard to unrealized holding gains or losses. Holding gains or losses are recognized in income at the end of the period for trading securities and were recognized as a separate component of stockholders' equity at the end of the period for available for sale securities. This is, of course, an example of nonarticulation. As a result of SFAC No. 130, unrealized holding gains and losses on available-for-sale securities are now part of comprehensive income.

Two FASB members dissented from the standard.[16] Sampson and Swieringa believe that all securities covered by this standard should be carried at fair value. The same security owned by different firms could receive three possible treatments if it is a bond and two possible treatments if it is a stock. More important, they are concerned with potential earnings management (e.g., selectively selling securities from the available-for-sale category to generate realized gains and not selling when that might be economically desirable to exclude losses from income).

A possible problem not mentioned by Sampson and Swieringa involves managing earnings by switching securities from one category to another. The standard states that transfers from held to maturity should be rare except for particular circumstances mentioned in the standard and also that "given the nature of a trading security, transfers into or from the trading category should be rare."[17] However, the available-for-sale category appears to be flexible enough to enable transfers between it and the trading category relatively easily.

Kathryn Means raises a totally different issue. The statement is vague about how income should be booked for debt securities in the available-for-sale category. She suggests that amortization of discount or premium in terms of the historical cost amortization rate would be inappropriate since the interest rate on current value would, therefore, fluctuate. Another possibility would be to adapt the historical rate of return to the new current value (this would be somewhat similar to the treatment of modification of terms in SFAS No. 114, where the historical rate of return is used to discount the restructured cash flows as discussed later in this chapter). She favors adapting the amortization of premium or discount to the current market interest rate, which would be a recognized time value of money component of income.[18] The difference between the time value of money adjusted value at the current interest rate and the fair value amount would be the unrealized holding gain or loss component, which would go to stockholders' equity but would now presumably be an item of other comprehensive income. (See Exhibit 11.2 for an illustration for $100,000 of bonds maturing in 3 years with a 10% nominal interest rate and a current market rate of 12%.) Means's suggestion would increase the representational faithfulness of SFAS No. 115, and the cost of implementation appears to be relatively small.

Exhibit 11.2 Available-for-Sale Debt Using Current Interest and Fair Value for Holding Gain

Year	Net Investment Beginning of Year	×	Current Interest Rate	=	Interest Income	−	Cash	=	Amortization		Net Investment End of Year	−	Fair Value End of Year	=	Unrealized Gain or (Loss)
1	$95,196a		12%		$11,424		$10,000		$1,424		$96,620b		$ 98,287c		$ 1,667d
2	98,287		11%		10,812		10,000		812		99,099e		95,653f		(3,446)g
3	95,653		15%		14,348		10,000		4,348		100,000h		100,000		0

a ($100,000 × 0.71178) + ($10,000 × 2.40183, present value of interest and principal at 12%) = $95,196
b $95,196 + $1,424 = $96,620
c ($100,000 × 0.81162) + ($10,000 × 1.71252, present value of interest and principal at 11%) = $98,287
d $98,287 − $96,620 = $1,667
e $98,287 + $812 = $99,099
f $110,000 × 0.86957 = $95,653
g $95,653 − $99,099 = ($3,446)
h $95,653 + $4,348 ($1 rounding error) = $100,000

339

Finally, Nobes mentions that classification of marketable securities in SFAS No. 115 is based on management intentions. Nobes takes issue with asset classifications being based on management's intentions:

> It is a poor principle because intentions can change, cannot directly be audited, and are sometimes unclear even to directors. This poor principle brings with it numerous rules about intermediate categories, changes of intentions, and the audit of intentions. This is what partly made the U.S. GAAP voluminous and led the IASB to publish 351 pages of rules as "Implementation Guidance."[19]

Nobes's criticism of this standard accords with our discussion in Chapter 9 of relevant circumstances not being based on management intentions.

Investments Subject to Equity Accounting

Equity securities in an amount of 20% to 50% of the outstanding voting stock are normally accounted for using the equity method under the requirements of APB Opinion No. 18.[20] When equity accounting is used, the investment no longer represents a real attribute of measurement. It is best described as adjusted historical cost, with the adjustment determined by the rules of equity accounting. The investment is increased for the equity share of investee income after eliminating any profit arising from investor–investee transactions and is reduced for amortization of any purchase differential and dividends paid by the investee company.

It can be argued that an investment accounted for by equity accounting may approximate the current selling price of the securities. However, there is no compelling reason to believe this to be true. The attribute being measured is a unique accounting concept. There is no direct measurement of the attribute by reference to a market price. The attribute does not exist in the real world; it can be derived only by applying the rules of APB Opinion No. 18. This peculiar effect on the balance sheet represents another example of the revenue–expense approach to accounting policy. The main emphasis of equity accounting is on the income statement, with less concern given to the introduction of a dubious measurement in the balance sheet. However, SFAS No. 157 on fair value measurement portends the end of the equity method, although it is not clear how soon this will happen.

Inventories

Ending inventory is calculated by first determining the quantity on hand, then multiplying this quantity by the unit acquisition cost. An arbitrary choice must be made as to the assumed unit cost, and this depends on the flow assumption selected. Major alternative flow assumptions are FIFO, LIFO, and weighted average. The attribute being calculated is historical cost in all methods. However, the result is arbitrary because unit prices will differ depending on the flow assumption. A FIFO pricing of inventory will price the cost of goods sold assuming the oldest stock is sold first. Ending inventory is priced at the most recent unit costs. The reverse is true with LIFO. Goods are assumed sold from the most recent purchases, leaving ending inventory as the oldest units on hand. It is not necessary that goods actually flow in the manner assumed by the inventory pricing system, and this is why the methods are arbitrary. Hence, flexibility is present in inventories and cost of goods sold accounting. The waters of inventory accounting are, of course, muddied by the tax benefits of LIFO and the concomitant requirement that LIFO inventories must be used for financial reporting purposes. Other inventory pricing systems exist in specialized industries—for example, dollar value LIFO, retail inventory, process costing, and job order costing.

Accounting Research Bulletin (ARB) No. 43 requires a lower of cost or market rule to be used in inventory calculation.[21] Market value is defined as replacement cost, but a range is established in which replacement cost must fall between the upper and lower limits. The upper limit is net realizable value, and the lower limit is net realizable value less a normal markup. The upper and lower limits are used only if replacement cost falls outside the range. These upper and lower limits reduce fluctuations in accounting income between periods when inventory is written down. This policy reflects a concern for the income statement effect resulting from inventory writedowns.

In summary, inventory is carried at the lower of historical cost or market (replacement) cost. However, historical cost is an arbitrary amount resulting from the required assumption concerning the flow of goods. If replacement cost is lower than historical cost, the actual calculation may be one of replacement cost, net realizable value, or net realizable value less a normal markup. This variety exists because there are upper and lower limits on the value of replacement cost that may be used in applying the lower of cost or market rule.[22]

SFAS No. 151 brought a minor modification to inventory accounting.[23] It requires that abnormal amounts of idle facility costs, freight, handling, and spoilage all be treated unequivocally as current period costs. Previously, under ARB No. 143, they were treated as current period costs if they were deemed to be "so abnormal" in size. This created a problem of whether to treat them as period costs or product costs. SFAS No. 151 clarifies a slightly ambiguous situation. The main reason underlying the standard was to eliminate a slight difference between FASB standard and International Accounting Standard (AIS) 2. The standard also requires the use of normal capacity for applying fixed overhead to product.

Self-Constructed Assets and Manufactured Inventories

The measurement problem with regard to self-constructed assets concerns the identification of the costs incurred to create the asset. The problem of cost identification applies to any type of asset that is self-constructed or manufactured rather than purchased. Two specific problem areas are inventory production and the treatment of interest costs.

A controversy surrounds the calculation of certain costs of manufactured inventory. Two methods are discussed in accounting literature: variable costing (sometimes called direct costing) and full-absorption costing. Only variable production costs are charged to inventory under variable costing. All fixed costs, such as overhead allocations and supervisory salaries, are expensed as period costs. Full-absorption costing, on the other hand, attempts to assign all manufacturing costs, both fixed and variable, to the production of inventory. This approach requires the development of arbitrary overhead rates based on assumed production levels.

ARB No. 43 requires the use of full-absorption costing, arguing that a better estimate of the total production cost is achieved with full-absorption costing using normal capacity (long-run average annual production) as noted above. From a measurement viewpoint, however, the attribute being calculated under full-absorption costing is not clear. Since some fixed costs are incurred over a wide range of production, it is questionable if fixed costs are part of the direct, unavoidable sacrifice required to produce inventory. This accounting debate is not resolved by the definition of assets presented in SFAC No. 6. However, a huge ferment in the cost and managerial accounting areas has led to improved methods of assigning fixed costs to products on bases such as causality and benefits received, resulting in full-absorption costing emerging as dominant over variable costing.

SFAS No. 34 requires the addition of interest costs on borrowed funds to the acquisition cost of self-constructed assets if the amount is significant.[24] The requirement applies to assets constructed for use or sale but not to routine inventory production. This policy is justified on the grounds that interest on borrowed funds is part of the total sacrifice required to acquire the asset. In addition, SFAS No. 34 mentions that the revenues of future periods will be benefited by the costs—such as interest—that are part of the acquisition of a resource. This view is very definitely a matching orientation, which, in turn, gives a revenue–expense orientation to the asset rather than the asset–liability view used in the conceptual framework.[25] Similar practices apply to the capitalization of property taxes and insurance costs on land and buildings that are being readied for production. In fairness, however, it should be noted that SFAS No. 34 preceded by a year SFAC No. 3, which first defined the elements.

One of the major criticisms of SFAS No. 34 is that it imputes an interest cost regardless of whether any specific debt has been incurred to finance the asset construction. In such cases, the interest cost is only a notional charge, or opportunity cost, rather than an actual incurred cost. Moreover, Means and Kazenski show that there are several possibilities for determining the amount of interest to be capitalized.[26] The problem does not lie in the flexibility of choice among different methods, however, but rather in establishing verifiability: too many means of calculating a specifically desired amount. Another criticism is that interest is not added to the acquisition cost of other assets. Interest is usually treated as a period expense and is classified as a financing cost. Therefore, SFAS No. 34 is inconsistent with general accounting policies for interest expense recognition, because it adopts a revenue–expense rather than an asset–liability orientation and does not resolve verifiability problems in the measurement of interest to be capitalized.

Assets Subject to Depreciation or Depletion

The historical acquisition cost of assets that are depreciated or depleted is allocated over the estimated useful life. Depreciation allocation is achieved by any of several arbitrary methods: straight line, sum of the years' digits, declining balance, and units of production. There are no relevant circumstances that dictate any one method in a particular situation. The policy choice is subject only to the constraint of consistency from year to year.

Specialized depreciation systems are used in certain situations. These systems include group and composite depreciation, the replacement and retirement methods, and the inventory depreciation system. All these systems are simpler to apply than regular methods and are acceptable only on the grounds that the results do not vary materially from conventional depreciation methods.

Costs of natural resources are depleted rather than depreciated. Depletion costs are allocated over the useful life in the same manner as depreciable assets. The units of production method is used, in which an estimate must be made of the total expected production. Yearly depletion cost is based on the pro rata amount of production. These depletion costs are charged to inventory and become expensed when the inventory is sold.

The balance sheet carrying value for assets subject to depreciation and depletion is historical cost less cumulative allocations of cost to the income statement. This amount is called book value and is the result of cost allocation. Book values do not represent real attributes and therefore cannot be directly measured. They can only be calculated by applying the rules specified in the depreciation or depletion method being used. This is another example of a unique accounting attribute and is the result once again of the revenue–expense orientation to the financial statements.

Impaired Assets

In SFAS No. 121, *Accounting for the Impairment of Long-Lived Assets and for Long-Lived Assets to Be Disposed Of*, the FASB examined the issue of writedown of long-lived assets—and possible related goodwill—arising from factors such as decreased market value, significant physical change in the asset or the manner of its usage, changes in the business climate that could affect the asset's operations, and declining cash flows from both current and prospective operations.[27] Future events can thus play an important role in determining whether impairment exists.

The Board used different recognition and measurement criteria for the impairment event. Given one or more of the conditions previously mentioned, recognition occurs if the projected undiscounted cash flows (net of the direct related cash outflows) expected to result from the asset's usage is less than the asset's carrying value.[28] Measurement of the loss writedown, however, is based on the excess of the carrying value of the asset over its fair value less costs of disposal.

Concerning the question of what level of aggregation should be employed in recognizing impairment, the Board stated that assets should be "grouped at the lowest level for which there are identifiable cash flows that are largely independent of the cash flows of other groups of assets."[29] In some circumstances in which cash flows are not specific to particular assets and a major identifiable segment of the firm is being disposed of within a year of the measurement date, APB Opinion No. 30 governs and the asset is carried at lower of carrying amount or net realizable value, but this has been changed in SFAS No. 144 (see below).

If the impairment test for recognition applies to fixed assets acquired in a business combination and goodwill was recognized when the acquisition occurred, goodwill is assigned to the assets on a pro rata basis using fair values of all of the assets in the purchase. If a writedown is necessary, goodwill is eliminated first.

There are two issues of verifiability underlying this standard. The first concerns estimating the future cash flows attributable to the asset; the second involves estimating the fair value of the asset. Concerning the former, the FASB desired the "best estimate" of future cash flows. This measurement can be either a modal single most likely outcome of expected future cash flows or an expected-value approach weighing the probabilities of possible outcomes.[30] The Board appeared to view this as not unlike a capital budgeting type of decision in which future cash flows must be estimated. Concerning fair values of assets, several possible sources can be utilized, such as industry-published list prices or quotations from online database services for similar assets.[31] If quoted fair values are not available, they can be estimated by discounting the future cash flows at an appropriate rate, taking into account the risk factors inherent in each situation.[32] The standard maintains an optimistic tone relative to verifiability when discussing these two measurements.

We believe that the Board's positive tone relative to the verifiability of the cash flows and fair values is warranted, although manipulation for earnings management purposes is a distinct possibility. The real issue may be why these valuations are not extended to a broader set of fixed assets. Since the measurements are restricted to impairments, we have yet another lower-of-cost-or-market-value situation. Of course, marketable securities in SFAS No. 115, *Accounting for Certain Investments in Debt and Equity Securities,* have emerged from lower of cost or market into a fair value mode. Perhaps SFAS No. 121 is a first step in this direction.

There are some other interesting theoretical issues relative to impaired assets. The use of undiscounted cash flows was advocated because the Board used the criterion of cost recoverability, which, in turn, leads to the lower-of-cost-or-market outcome: Either costs are recoverable or a loss is expected, a bimodal situation. A much more extensive movement toward current values would arise if fair value were used as both a recognition and measurement factor without regard to cost recoverability, a move that is now underway with SFAS No. 157.

While the FASB's usage of fair values is intended to be conservative, the cost recovery criterion is not conservative in one situation. No writedown occurs where undiscounted cash flows are greater than the carrying amount of the asset but the latter, in turn, exceeds the discounted cash flows. This situation is somewhat reminiscent of troubled debt restructuring prior to the passage of SFAS No. 114.

SFAS No. 144 brought refinements to SFAS No. 121 but did not change the basic measurement rules. In the case where several assets constitute a productive unit but the assets have different lives, then the undiscounted cash flow analysis is done in accordance with the principal asset: The principal asset is the most significant asset in terms of its cash flow generating capacity.[33] If an impairment results, it is allocated proportionately in accordance with the carrying values of the individual assets constituting the group.

Assets in discontinued segments were previously covered by APB Opinion No. 30. The presentation of the assets constituting these operations net of tax effects and below the continuing operations is still covered by APB Opinion No. 30. However, APB Opinion No. 30 is superseded by SFAS No. 144 in terms of the valuation of these assets.[34] Assets are no longer to be valued at their net realizable value with anticipation of further possible losses from operations from the statement date to the disposition date being deducted from the carrying value. Assets are now to be valued in accordance with the criteria developed in SFAS No. 121 with the refinements added by SFAS No. 144.

In computing the carrying value of impaired assets, proportionate goodwill was to be assigned and deducted in accordance with SFAS No. 121. Since SFAS No. 142 converted goodwill into a nonamortizable asset subject to its own impairment rules, goodwill is no longer assigned to individual assets. The one exception is if the assets themselves constitute a reportable segment or component that gave rise to goodwill when acquired.[35]

Nonmonetary Exchanges of Similar Assets

APB Opinion No. 29 establishes a unique rule to account for nonmonetary exchanges of similar assets. The rule is contrary to the general principle of using the value of the economic sacrifice to measure the transaction.[36] In a nonmonetary exchange, the sacrifice to obtain a new asset consists of a traded-in asset and possibly some cash. Under APB Opinion No. 29, the new asset was recorded at the book value of the traded-in asset (rather than market value), plus any additional cash consideration. As with other asset acquisitions, the cash equivalent purchase price sets an upper limit on the recorded value. The rationale for this policy was that an exchange of similar assets represents a continuation of the underlying earning process. It is as though the former asset is embodied in the new asset, thus justifying no recognition of a gain or loss on the disposal of the old asset. Any implied gain or loss is recognized indirectly through subsequent depreciation. This accounting policy was at variance with general accounting practices. One reason for its existence may be that Internal Revenue Service regulations follow a similar (though not identical) procedure.[37]

SFAS No. 153 amended APB Opinion No. 29. In the new standard, the exception for the exchange of similar productive assets in APB No. 29 is eliminated. Instead, the focus is on exchanges of nonmonetary assets that have "commercial substance." For commercial substance to exist, the exchanged assets must have significantly different cash flows. When this occurs, the new asset is booked at fair value. If there is no commercial substance, the newly acquired asset is carried forward at the book value of the old asset. SFAS No. 153 appears to have a more rigorous underlying economic sense than APB Opinion No. 29. This standard is part of the convergence project and is largely in line with IAS 16.

Intangible Assets

Assets can be classified as either tangible or intangible. Physical substance is the distinguishing criterion, but it is not a definitive characteristic because some assets (such as accounts receivable, investments, and capitalized lease rights) are legally intangible in nature yet are not so regarded by accountants. Assets more commonly thought of as intangible are copyrights, patents, and trademarks. Purchased franchise rights and purchased goodwill are also considered to be intangible assets.

All intangible assets are initially recorded at the sacrifice incurred to acquire the assets. Like assets subject to depreciation and depletion, intangible assets are calculated at historical cost less cumulative charges to income. As stated before, book value is a unique accounting attribute of measurement and represents the revenue–expense orientation. APB Opinion No. 17 brought some order to intangibles by requiring straight-line amortization of costs over a period not exceeding 40 years. If a shorter period of economic benefit exists, it should be used. Copyrights, patents, and franchise agreements all have finite legal lives that can be used to determine a more specific period of future economic benefit. In these circumstances, a specific amortization period that reflects useful economic life can be determined. It has also been shown that royalty income plays an important role in securities valuation and that royalty income signals to investors prospects relative to research and development expenditures (R&D).[38]

It can be argued that amortization of intangibles (such as trademarks and purchased goodwill) is not necessary because they have an unlimited life. APB Opinion No. 17 rejected this notion in favor of compulsory amortization. Prior to APB Opinion No. 17, it was common to not amortize goodwill. APB Opinion No. 17 can best be understood as an attempt to bring rigid uniformity to a subjective area of practice, one where flexibility resulted in poor comparability. In a 1999 exposure draft, it was proposed that goodwill amortization be set at a 20-year maximum from the previous 40-year period. SFAS No. 142 made an abrupt turnaround by not subjecting goodwill to amortization but by subjecting it to periodic tests of impairment (Chapter 18).

Until SFAS No. 2, research and development (R&D) costs were generally capitalized and classified as an intangible asset.[39] The justification was that future benefits existed in the form of probable future patents or products having economic value. However, the uncertainty of realizing these benefits led to the uniform policy in SFAS No. 2 of expensing all research and development costs as incurred. This is another example of a situation in which the concern about measurement reliability led to rigid uniformity.[40]

Obviously, some R&D expenditures would satisfy the asset definition in SFAC No. 6. The FASB's policy in SFAS No. 2 emphasizes verifiability over representational faithfulness or relevance. There is a movement afoot that is in a very early stage to capitalize intangibles such as R&D and certain restructuring costs.

Capitalizing Intangible Costs. Lev and Zarowin make a compelling argument that "the almost universal expensing of intangible investments in the United States is inconsistent with the FASB's conceptual framework." Current GAAP requires that intangibles such as restructuring costs and R&D be expensed in the period when incurred even though they may deliver significant benefits in future periods, resulting in a mismatching of costs with revenues. They argue that one of the contributing factors to the low correlation between reported earnings and stock returns may result from this period costing of intangibles that actually provide future economic benefits.[41] The issue at hand, of course, involves a clash between relevance and reliability, the most important tradeoff in SFAC No. 2 of the conceptual framework (Chapter 7).

As a result of changes in business operations, such as the information technology revolution, speed in bringing new products to market, and increasing deregulation, changes in the financial statement model are also in order. Specifically, Lev and Zarowin would extend capitalization for intangible costs in a fashion similar to software capitalization costs when they reach the point of technological feasibility as discussed in SFAS No. 86:

Given the uncertainty concerns, it makes sense to recognize intangible investments as assets when the uncertainty of benefits is considerably resolved. . . . Accordingly, a reasonable balance between relevance and reliability of information would suggest the capitalization of intangible investment when the project successfully passes a significant technological feasibility test, such as a working model for software or a clinical test for a drug.[42]

Lev and Zarowin also point out that the clash between relevance and reliability, which has been resolved by immediate write-off, also involves a conflict with the definition of assets provided in SFAC No. 6.

In arguing their proposal, they state that capitalization at the point of technological feasibility would provide relevant information for helping to predict future earnings. And, they would go even further by restating current and previous income statements for understatements of income in periods when costs were written off and for overstatements of income in subsequent periods.[43]

Lev and Zarowin attach a great deal of importance to restating past financial statements. Correction of the past helps to put the present into a more useful perspective. Past statements are presently changed on a pro forma basis for changes in accounting principle and are formally restated for material errors.

Though Lev and Zarowin do not discuss particulars, changes to the current income statement would be viable candidates to go through comprehensive income. Their proposal would result in an interesting compromise between relevance and reliability, which would replace the present victory of reliability over relevance for intangible costs. Their proposal deserves to be very seriously considered by accountants in general and the FASB in particular.[44]

Deferred Charges

There are two distinct types of deferred charges. One type represents prepaid costs, which provide a future benefit in the form of reduced future cash outflows for services—for example, prepaid insurance. Prepayments are normally allocated to the income statement on a straight-line basis over the period of future benefit. The other type of deferred charge represents a cost that is being deferred from expense recognition solely because of income measurement rules. This type includes organizational startup costs and deferred losses on sale leasebacks. Most deferred charges are amortized in the same manner as intangible assets except where specific requirements apply.

Summary of Asset Measurement

This is by no means a comprehensive review of all assets. Some topics were omitted because they are covered in later chapters—for example, deferred tax charges and leased assets. Individual assets in the balance sheet may represent one of many attributes, some of which are unique accounting concepts and have no real-world meaning. Book values of depreciable assets and investments accounted for under equity accounting are two examples of unique accounting attributes. Such a situation is uncomfortable, at least in terms of measurement theory. However, as stated at the outset of this section, an eclectic balance

Exhibit 11.3 Summary of Asset Measurement

Asset	Attribute(s)
Receivables	Approximation of net realizable value.
Investments (subject to APB Opinion No. 115)	Amortized historical cost if debt securities are intended to be held to maturity; otherwise, fair value.
Investments (subject to APB Opinion No. 18)	Unique accounting attribute (equity accounting).
Inventories	Cost, replacement cost, net realizable value, or net realizable value less normal markup.
Self-constructed assets	Full-absorption costing for inventory and capitalization of interest for noninventory assets.
Assets subject to depreciation or depletion	Unique accounting attribute (book value).
Nonmonetary exchanges of similar assets	Book value of old asset plus cash.
Intangible assets	Unique accounting attribute (book value). R&D presently not capitalized.
Deferred charges	Unique accounting attribute (book value).
Restructured receivables resulting from modification of terms	Newly restructured future cash inflows discounted at original rate.
Impaired assets	Fair value if less than carrying value, assuming undiscounted future cash flows are less than carrying value.

sheet may still convey relevant information to users. A summary of asset measurement is presented in Exhibit 11.3.

Three distinct types of assets appear in balance sheets: assets held for sale, assets that have economic value through use in production, and deferred charges. The benefits of these assets are derived differently and represent differing degrees of certainty and measurement reliability. Assets held for sale and measured at net realizable value (such as receivables) represent a high degree of certainty as to realization as well as measurement reliability. Assets held for production represent more uncertainty as to the realization of future economic benefits owing to the inherent risk of manufacturing. Furthermore, historical cost gives little indication of the productive value of such assets. Finally, certain types of deferred charges do not have any direct effect on future cash flows. Of course, we can expect significant changes once fair value measurements arrive.

Because of the wide variation in asset realization and measurement, it is very difficult to interpret assets in the aggregate. It is questionable if a balance sheet's numbers are really additive. Of course, they are summed to perform ratio analysis; however, relevance or usefulness should be suspect owing to the adding of these unlike numbers. Aggregation of data across separate legal entities to prepare a consolidated balance sheet further compounds this problem.

Liabilities

Definition of Accounting Liabilities

Definitions of accounting liabilities have evolved over time in a manner similar to that of definitions of assets. The three major statements on liabilities are:

1. Something represented by a credit balance that is or would be properly carried forward upon a closing of books of account according to the rules or principles of accounting, provided such credit balance is not in effect a negative balance applicable to an asset. Thus the word is used broadly to comprise not only items which constitute liabilities in the popular sense of debts or obligations (including provision for those that are unascertained), but also credit balances to be accounted for which do not involve a debtor and creditor relation. For example, capital stock and related or similar elements of proprietorship are balance sheet liabilities in that they represent balances to be accounted for, though these are not liabilities in the ordinary sense of debts owed to legal creditors.[45]

2. Economic obligations of an enterprise that are recognized and measured in conformity with generally accepted accounting principles. Liabilities also include certain deferred credits that are not obligations but that are recognized and measured in conformity with generally accepted accounting principles.[46]

3. Liabilities are probable future sacrifices of economic benefits arising from present obligations of a particular entity to transfer assets or provide services to other entities in the future as a result of past transactions or events.[47]

The first definition implies an entity theory view of the firm because no distinction is made between owners' equity and liabilities. The entity theory views the firm as a self-sufficient enterprise separate from its owners, and both liabilities and owners' equity are sources of external capital for which the firm is accountable. The other two liability definitions do not mention owners' equity, which seems to imply a proprietary view of the firm in which owners' equity represents owners' residual interest in the net assets.

The liability portion of the first definition emphasizes legal debts. In the second definition, the liability concept is broadened to mean economic obligations. APB Statement 4 defines economic obligations as the responsibility to transfer economic resources or provide services to another entity in the future. This parallels the change in the asset definition. In addition, deferred credits are identified separately but are still considered to be a part of liabilities.

The third and most recent definition continues the emphasis on economic obligations rather than legal debt and drops deferred credits.[48] Deferred charges were similarly dropped from the asset definition. SFAC No. 6 elaborates on the definition by listing three essential characteristics of an accounting liability:

1. A duty exists.

2. The duty is virtually unavoidable.

3. The event obligating the enterprise has occurred.

Most liabilities are contractual in nature. Contractual liabilities result from events in which a liability arises that is either expressly or implicitly contractual in the legal sense of the term. SFAC No. 6 indicates that a duty can also arise from constructive and equitable obligations as well as legal contracts. A constructive obligation is one that is implied rather than expressly written. SFAC No. 6 specifically mentions the accruals of noncontractual vacation pay and bonuses. An employer duty may exist if such payments have been made in the past even if there is no written agreement to pay them in the future. Equitable obligations are an ambiguous, gray area of common law in which a duty is not contractually present but which may nevertheless exist because of ethical principles of fairness (called equity). The example given in SFAC No. 6 concerns the responsibility of a monopoly supplier to deliver goods or services to dependent customers. In spite of their mention in SFAC No. 6, equitable obligations are not presently recognized in balance sheets.

Contingent liabilities are a subset of accounting liabilities. SFAS No. 5 defines these as "an existing situation, or set of circumstances involving uncertainty as to possible gain or loss to an enterprise that will ultimately be resolved when one or more future events will occur or fail to occur."[49] Only losses are recognized, owing to conservatism. A loss contingency (contingent liability) is accrued if (a) it is probable that a liability has occurred or an asset has been impaired and (b) it can be reliably measured. Examples of contingent liabilities given in SFAS No. 5 are product warranties and pending or threatened litigation. The definition of a contingent liability is consistent with the SFAC No. 6 definition, with the additional proviso concerning feasibility and reliability of measurement.

Finally, there are deferred credits. Although not specifically mentioned in the most recent definition, they continue to be part of the liability section in the balance sheet under present practices. There are two different types of deferred credits. The first type represents prepaid revenues; for example, magazine or newspaper subscriptions. There is a contractual duty to provide a future good or service, and a liability clearly exists in such a situation.

The second type of deferred credit is more ambiguous and arises from income rules that defer income statement recognition of the item. Two examples of this second type of deferred credit are investment tax credits (APB Opinion No. 2) and deferred gains on sale leaseback transactions (SFAS No. 13).[50] These types of items impose no obligations on the firm to transfer assets in the future. Rather, they are simply past transactions being deferred from the income statement until future periods.

In summary, accounting liabilities include five distinctly different types: contractual liabilities, constructive obligations, equitable obligations, contingent liabilities, and deferred credits. As with assets, there is considerable variety within the liability group, but not to the degree that occurs within assets. This is because most liabilities are contractual in nature. Of the remaining noncontractual liabilities, contingent liabilities are disclosed separately, and deferred credits are identifiable in the balance sheet. As a result, there is a natural subclassification of liabilities that can easily be inferred from the balance sheet. This is not the case with assets.

Recognition and Measurement of Liabilities

APB Statement 4 and SFAC No. 5 indicate that liabilities are measured at amounts established in the transaction, usually amounts to be paid in the future, sometimes discounted.[51] The general principle is that liabilities are measured at the amount established in the exchange. For current liabilities, such as accounts payable, this represents the face value of the obligation to be settled in the future. The nondiscounting of current liabilities is justified on the grounds of immateriality; that is, the present value is not materially different from the nondiscounted future value.

For noncurrent obligations, the measurement represents a present value calculation based on current interest rates. An example is bonds, which are recorded at the net proceeds received. The net proceeds represent the stream of interest payments and principal repayment discounted at the current market rate of interest. If the stated interest rate on the bonds is at the current rate, the present value, net proceeds, and face value are all equal at the time of issuance. If the stated interest rate differs from market rates, a premium or discount will occur.

Notes Payable With Below Market Rates of Interest

Under APB Opinion No. 21, notes payable with below market interest rates must be discounted.[52] The purpose of the discounting is to adjust the note to an equivalent note having the market rate of interest. The discount is then amortized over the life of the note to adjust periodic interest expense to a market rate. By this procedure, the real economic value of the transaction is measured at imputed market prices and is consistent with the general principle of discounting noncurrent liabilities at the market rate of interest. An identical procedure is required for notes receivable with below market interest rates.

Bonds Payable

As noted previously, bonds are initially recorded at the net proceeds of the transaction. The net proceeds are equal to the present value of future interest payments and principal repayment, discounted at the market rate of interest, less any bond issue costs. It is necessary to create a bond premium or discount account if the stated interest rate differs from the market rate. The carrying value of bonds in subsequent balance sheets represents the face value of the bonds plus unamortized premiums or minus unamortized discounts. This is the book value of bonds and is analogous to book value of depreciable assets.

Book value of bonds payable is another example of a unique accounting attribute. The book value of bonds must be calculated instead of measured directly. A direct measurement of bonds is not made after the bonds are initially recorded. Premiums and discounts are amortized to income over the term of the bonds by the effective interest method (APB Opinion No. 21). This has the effect of adjusting interest expense to the market rate that existed at the time of issue. Straight-line amortization is also permitted if the results are not materially different from the effective interest method.

Convertible Bonds

Bonds may have a feature permitting an exchange of bonds for common stock. It is typical for convertible bonds to have a lower coupon interest rate than conventional bonds. The reason for this is that investors are willing to pay a price for the conversion option, and the price is paid in the form of lower interest rates. For this reason, convertible bonds have elements of both debt and owners' equity. The forgone interest can be thought of as capital donated to the firm in exchange for this privilege.

Two policies have been used to account for convertible bonds. One approach is to treat convertible debt as conventional debt until conversion. This is the method required under APB Opinion No. 14.[53] The other approach is to segregate an amount of the debt as the price paid for the conversion privilege and to add this amount to contributed capital. Interest on the face amount of the debt is imputed using the market rate for nonconvertible debt that existed at the time of issue. This more complex approach was adopted in APB Opinion No. 10, suspended almost immediately in APB Opinion No. 12, and superseded in APB Opinion No. 14.[54] The reason for suspension was perceived measurement difficulties arising from the potential for subjectivity in choosing the market interest rate. So long as a subjective choice could be made, the results were of questionable reliability. Because of the perceived measurement problems, APB Opinion No. 14 established a simpler method of accounting by treating convertible debt as regular bonds.

Convertible debt highlights the limitations of the accounting classification system (see Exhibit 11.1). The balance sheet is incapable of subtle distinctions, such as those implied by convertible versus conventional bonds. However, APB Opinion No. 15 (and also SFAS No. 128) requires recognition of the conversion feature in earnings per share (EPS) calculations.[55] The limitations of accounting classification are more easily overcome with EPS rules, however, because EPS is a supplemental disclosure rather than part of the financial statements.

When convertible debt is converted, a gain or loss is not normally recognized. The rationale for not recognizing a gain or loss is that, since the security has both debt and equity characteristics, the conversion represents only a reclassification of the security from debt to equity. This procedure is inconsistent with SFAS No. 4, which deals with accounting for early retirement of debt.[56] Because convertible debt is initially accounted for as conventional debt, it would be logical to recognize a gain or loss on conversion. Conversion represents the equivalent of early debt retirement. In other words, two separate transactions are implied by APB Opinion No. 14. The first is the recording as conventional debt; then there is the equivalent of early retirement and the issue of common stock in exchange for debt retirement. Since no initial recognition is given to the conversion feature prior to conversion, it is inconsistent to ignore gains and losses on the grounds that the conversion merely represents a reclassification from debt to equity. APB Opinion No. 14 is therefore logically inconsistent.

Debt With Stock Warrants

APB Opinion No. 14 requires that a value be assigned to detachable stock warrants that may accompany the issue of debt. This policy is inconsistent with the treatment of convertible debt. The reason for the two different policies is that a convertible bond is argued to be either debt or equity at any one time; it cannot be both simultaneously. Detachable warrants, however, permit the holder to own simultaneously both debt and equity (if the warrant is exercised). Therefore, part of the proceeds can be thought of as a direct payment for the right to buy stock. And since a market price is readily determinable for stock warrants, the measurement problem encountered with convertible debt does not occur.

In theory, there is little distinction between convertible debt and debt with detachable stock warrants. In both cases, an amount of money is being paid in the transaction for the right to acquire stock. However, the money paid for this privilege is clearly identifiable in the case of detachable warrants traded in the market. It is a more subjective calculation in the case of convertible debt. Hence, considerations of verifiability have led to two different accounting policies for two similar areas of accounting.

Redeemable Preferred Stock and Other Hybrid Securities

Financial managers are constantly attempting to keep debt off the balance sheet. A relatively new twist in this area is redeemable preferred stock (which is, of course, an oxymoron). This is essentially debt that is attempting to pass as owners' equity. For example, Nair, Rittenberg, and Weygandt examined the redeemable preferred stock of the Toro Company.[57] This stock is nonvoting, has a mandatory schedule for periodic redemption at par, and is callable at the company's option; dividends are cumulative and have preference over common dividends, and the stock has a fixed annual dividend rate without further participation. The key point for Nair, Rittenberg, and Weygandt is the mandatory redemption feature; hence, they would classify this stock as debt. This is essentially the position of the SEC.

Newer issues of redeemable preferred stock have evidenced some softening of the mandatory redemption feature, such as allowing conversion into common stock. Kimmel and Warfield note that the conversion to common stock privilege was present in about 15% of redeemable preferred stock issues prior to 1980, but the percentage has increased to approximately 66 2/3% in 1988 and 1989.[58] The growth in common stock conversion privileges, voting rights, and other possible features may make it difficult to use the debt versus equity dichotomy.[59] This may be unavoidable if these securities truly fit into a "no man's land" between debt and equity, but it is to be hoped that this complication can be avoided. Unfortunately, breaking down the debt and equity characteristics of redeemable preferred stock in an objective quantifiable manner would be much more difficult than in the case of convertible preferred stock.

Another hybrid security is known as trust preferred stock.[60] First issued by Texaco in 1993, the issuing company created a wholly owned subsidiary, Texaco Capital, which sold the trust preferred stock to investors. In turn, the subsidiary sold subordinated bonds to the parent. These bonds are eliminated in the consolidation, but the interest that Texaco pays to Texaco Capital is tax deductible for tax purposes. The trust preferred certificates appear between debt and equity on the balance sheet. Bond rating agencies treat these certificates as "equity like" because of long maturities, deep subordination, and some ability to defer dividends.

Recent research has found that trust preferred securities accounted for approximately 60% of all new preferred security issues between 1993 and 1996.[61] While 72% of the "dividend" payments were classified as some type of expense, 7% were reported as preferred dividends with the remainder not clearly classified. Firms facing tight debt constraints relative to debt–equity ratios are most likely to classify trust preferred securities as equities. Hybrid securities could well pose difficulties for users to understand because they are not quite fish and not quite fowl. It behooves the FASB to very carefully set requirements for determining which trust preferred certificates are debt and which are equity.

Mandatorily Redeemable Financial Instruments. SFAS No. 150 covers mandatorily redeemable financial instruments.[62] This is a rules-based standard covering many nuances and contingencies. The general rule is that these instruments will be classified as debt, whether the firm will be issuing cash or its own equity shares in settlement. Flexibility was previously used in financial statement presentation, sometimes being classified as debt, sometimes as equity, and sometimes between the two categories.

We are generally in favor of this standard because the rigid uniformity approach should improve comparability. We also agree with the liability classification. If an instrument calls for a redemption in the firm's equity shares only—whether in terms of a specific number of shares or a specific dollar amount—under a proprietary theory approach, the interest of shareholders would be diluted and liability classification is appropriate. The liability classification, where common stock will satisfy the debt, has led to discussion of whether the liability definition in SFAC No. 6 should be broadened.

Securitizations

An increasingly common type of transaction involves the sale by a firm (called the transferor) of an asset or group of assets to another firm (called the transferee). The assets involved are usually financial assets such as mortgage receivables. The transferee finances the acquisition by issuing securities—backed by the acquired assets—to a group of outside investors.

The key issue arising in securitizations involves whether the transferor has relinquished all rights in the assets. If so, the transferor credits the assets and no debt appears on its balance sheet just like any other similar sale of assets. If, however, the transferor retains rights to the assets, such as a repurchase arrangement, then the transferor has not relinquished all rights to the assets and the transferee is not free to use or dispose of the assets as it sees fit. In this latter case, the transaction appears to be a collateralized loan and the transferor would have to credit an appropriate liability account.

The extremes of the securitization transaction are easy to understand. More complex transactions blur the issue of whether the transferor has really disposed of the assets. One of the transferor's objectives, of course, is to keep debt off of its balance sheet. Several examples of more complex transactions appear in SFAS No. 125.[63]

Summary of Liability Measurement

Like assets, liabilities are recognized when the transaction giving rise to the obligation occurs. There are many different types of accounting liabilities, just as there are many different types of assets. Unlike assets, however, the different types of accounting liabilities are more easily recognized in the balance sheet. The different types of accounting liabilities represent differing degrees of obligations for the firm. For example, not all accounting liabilities represent legal debt, so in the case of bankruptcy some accounting liabilities would be ignored. The certainty of differing types of obligations also differs, as well as the reliability of measurement. Legal debt has a high probability of being paid and has a high degree of measurement reliability as well. Certain types of deferred credits, on the other hand, do not represent future cash flows at all.

Contingent liabilities often have a lower degree of verifiability than other accounting liabilities. All these characteristics must be considered in evaluating accounting liabilities. As with assets, it is difficult to interpret liabilities in the aggregate because of these differences.

In the case of current liabilities, liabilities are initially measured at face value of the future obligation. There is no present value adjustment. Noncurrent liabilities are initially measured at the present value of future interest and principal repayments. The current market rate of interest is used as the discount rate. This is not a subjective measurement, because market values of debt are established in exactly the same manner—the discounting of a stream of payments at the market rate of interest. A premium or discount may exist that is amortized to the income statement over the term of the debt. Book value of debt is used in subsequent balance sheets. This is a unique accounting attribute representing face value of debt adjusted for any unamortized premiums or discounts. Once again, this book value represents the revenue–expense orientation and the historical cost allocation process (see Chapter 12).

Owners' Equity

Definition of Owners' Equity

Owners' equity is defined as the stockholders' residual interest in the net assets of the firm. This definition represents the proprietary theory according to which stockholders are perceived to be owners of the firm. From the liability definition in *Accounting Terminology Bulletin (ATB) No. 1,* no clear distinction was made between liabilities and owners' equity. However, APB Statement 4 and SFAC No. 6 do make distinctions between the two: APB Statement 4 offers a passive definition of owners' equity as the excess of the firm's assets over its liabilities. The same approach is also taken in SFAC No. 6. Both definitions imply a proprietary ownership of the firm by the stockholders.

In a sole proprietorship, owners' equity can be represented by a single owner's equity account. The corporate form of ownership gives rise to a legal distinction between contributed capital and earned capital (retained earnings). In most states in the past, dividends could be legally paid only from retained earnings, but the 1984 Revised Model Business Corporation Act—which many states have passed—will allow dividends to be paid out of either contributed capital (including the capital stock account) or retained earnings. For example, in 1987 Holiday Inn was able to declare a large dividend that exceeded the entire owners' equity in order to avoid an unfriendly takeover bid. Holiday Inn is incorporated in Delaware, which allows dividends to be paid as long as the fair value of the assets is greater than the fair value of the liabilities after the distribution. The 1984 act allows firms to pay dividends as long as insolvency is avoided. Insolvency means (a) the inability to pay debts as they come due or (b) fair value of liabilities exceeds fair value of assets.[64]

Sectional distinctions within owners' equity accounts may become less important than has been the case. We will maintain, however, the usual distinctions even though the owners' equity situation is in flux. So a typical breakdown of total owners' equity will include contributed capital and retained earnings.

Contributed capital may be subclassified into legal capital and other capital. Legal capital represents the limited liability of stockholders. If shares are fully paid up, there is no additional stockholder liability. Legal capital is measured at par value, or at the issue price in the case of no par value stocks. Other contributed capital includes stock premiums, donated capital, capital from the reissue of treasury stock, and capital from the issue of stock options and warrants.

A third component of owners' equity (see Exhibit 11.1) represents unrealized gains or losses. Most items representing net gains or losses that went to stockholders' equity (e.g., unrealized gains or losses on available for sale securities) now go to comprehensive income. One exception is deferred compensation expense related to employee stock ownership plans.[65]

Recognition and Measurement of Owners' Equity

Owners' equity transactions can be of two types—capital transactions or income-related transactions. Capital transactions represent the direct contributions or withdrawals of assets by owners. Income-related transactions represent income statement transactions and prior-period adjustments that pertain to income of previous periods. This chapter deals only with capital transactions. Income-related transactions are discussed in Chapter 12. The general principle of measurement for all capital transactions is the same as for assets and liabilities: the market value at the time of the transaction. These values are then carried forward unchanged in subsequent balance sheets.

Contributed capital is measured by the value of assets contributed to the firm by stockholders. It is possible to contribute services rather than assets, in which case the value of the services is used to measure contributed capital. If the value of contributed assets or services exceeds the legal capital of issued stock, the excess is recorded as a premium. Other sources of contributed capital include conversions of convertible debt and the issue of detachable stock warrants with debt (discussed earlier in the liability section of the chapter). Two other sources of contributed capital are the reissue of treasury stock and the issue of employee stock options.

Retained earnings is equal to the cumulative income or loss of the firm as measured by the rules of income determination, less cash dividends declared. Stock dividends also affect the balance of retained earnings and are discussed in a section that follows.

Treasury Stock

U.S. corporations are permitted to trade in their own securities. However, state laws and accounting policies prohibit companies from recognizing income on such transactions. This prohibition is intended to discourage stock price manipulations. Reacquired stock is classified as a contra account to outstanding stock. The stock is still legally issued but is not considered to be outstanding.

Treasury stock acquisition has been seen as a method of signaling future prospects to shareholders.[66] This would be especially the case where tender offers are made to shareholders as opposed to open-market reacquisition.[67] It would appear, under the signaling assumption, that the segment of the shareholder population that receives the "good news" signal does not resell its shares to the corporation. Other possible reasons for treasury stock purchases include (a) a desire for management to more strongly entrench itself by owning a greater proportion of stock, (b) the need to have stock available for the exercise of stock options, (c) a need to reduce the scope of investment by the firm because the cost of capital exceeds the marginal return on investment, (d) supporting the market price of the firm's stock, and (e) using stock repurchases for earnings per share management.[68]

Two methods may be used to account for treasury stock—(1) the cost method and (2) par value method. The methods differ only in terms of the accounts used, but the net effect on owners' equity is the same. This is an example of flexibility, since there is unconditional choice in the selection of the accounting policy. However, it makes very little difference since the only effect is on subclassifications within owners' equity. When treasury stock is reissued, the difference between the reissue price and carrying value of the treasury stock is recorded as contributed capital. In some situations retained earnings may be debited, but it can never be credited in treasury stock transactions.

Stock Dividends

ARB No. 43 discusses two separate accounting policies for stock dividends, depending on the size of the dividend.[69] Large stock dividends are defined as those over 25% and are accounted for by reclassifying retained earnings to contributed capital based on the par value of the stock issued. Small stock dividends are defined as those less than 20%. The accounting policy is to reclassify retained earnings to contributed capital on the basis of the market value of the stock and using pre-dividend market prices to value the dividend. A gray area exists from 20% to 25%, in which either method may be used. Accounting Series Release (ASR) No. 124 of the SEC sharpens the cutoff between small and large stock dividends to 25% in place of the "no man's land" of 20% to 25% where either method could be used.[70]

The contention has been made that the accounting for stock dividends arrived at by the Committee on Accounting Procedure (CAP) is really a matter of management intent.[71] The two purposes are whether management (1) desires to give shareholders evidence of their interest in retained earnings or (2) desires to lower the price of the shares with the stock dividend serving as a stock split, but without changing par value of the stock or the number of authorized shares. Even if this contention is correct, allowing accounting to be a matter of managerial intent would allow similar transactions to be booked differently.[72] This is, of course, the flexibility problem discussed in Chapter 9. In addition, ARB No. 43 also recognized that stock dividends as distributions of real wealth, from intention (a), is completely fallacious.[73]

Some attempts have been made to use the size of the dividend to define relevant circumstances. However, because total market value of outstanding stock should not change because of stock dividends, little support can be given to using the pre-dividend market price per share to value the transaction. All that has occurred is an increase in the total number of shares. The market price per share should decline exactly in proportion to the dilutive effect of the new shares. If the price is not diluted, other new information exists that causes investors to revise their assessment of the stock.[74]

Using the par value to measure a stock dividend makes more sense given that the total market value of outstanding stock should be unchanged. It can even be argued that a stock dividend is no different in principle from a stock split in which no change is recorded in owners' equity. This is unacceptable for stock dividends, though, because the dollar amount of legal capital has increased. So, reclassification of retained earnings to contributed capital is necessary because there has been an increase in legally issued capital.

While there is some evidence that both small stock dividends (below 20%) and large stock dividends may be a signal to shareholders of future dividends and earnings prospects, it is difficult to justify finite uniformity that is based on the size of the dividend.[75] There does not appear to be a relevant circumstance justifying two accounting methods. The future contingency of greater earnings and dividends is too tenuous to justify two methods of accounting. Furthermore, the two different methods do not affect income, assets, or liabilities. Only the composition within owners' equity is affected. For both large and small dividends, market price per share should fall in accordance with the dilutive effect of the stock dividend. Therefore, use of pre-dividend market prices is a policy that is difficult to defend.

Financial Instruments

Financial instruments are contracts involving a financial asset of one entity and a financial liability (or equity) of another entity. The FASB defines a financial instrument as cash, evidence of an ownership interest in an entity, or a contract that both

1. Imposes on one entity a contractual obligation (a) to deliver cash or another financial instrument to a second entity or (b) to exchange financial instruments on potentially unfavorable terms with the second entity.

2. Conveys to that second entity a contractual right (a) to receive cash or another financial instrument from the first entity or (b) to exchange other financial instruments on potentially favorable terms with the first entity.[76]

Some financial instruments are quite familiar and their accounting is straightforward; for example: cash held on demand deposit, trade receivables, notes, bonds, and common and preferred stock. Other instruments are highly complex and their use is motivated by management's desire to exploit tax laws, to hedge other assets/liabilities of the entity against market risks (for example, interest rate and foreign exchange hedges), and to achieve off-balance-sheet financing to "create" a more favorable-looking balance sheet (also one of the appeals of leasing).

Derivatives

Many of these latter financial instruments are known as derivatives. Derivatives are financial instruments whose value is based on (derived from) other financial instruments, stock indexes or interest rates, interest rate indexes, or some asset. Over the past decade, derivatives have received considerable attention—including an unenlightening 1994 segment on CBS's *60 Minutes*—because of spectacular losses by blue chip American companies, old-line British investment banks, and American municipalities. Among the reasons behind such large losses is a lack of understanding of what derivatives are and how they are legitimately used. Appendix 11-A illustrates a very simple example of a derivative.

Types of Derivatives

Derivatives can be classified into two general types: forward-based and option-based derivatives.

Forward-Based Derivatives. Forward-based derivatives arise between two parties where one party will realize a gain and the other party will realize a loss due to a change in value of the factor underlying the instrument. Forward contracts involve foreign currencies, debt contracts, or commodities that have a specific price at the contract date with a gain or loss arising from the change in price at the specified settlement date. For example, a commonly used forward type of instrument would be a futures contract either buying or selling foreign exchange.

Assume that an American firm has acquired a sizable inventory from a Norwegian firm and will be required to pay in Norwegian kroner (NOK). The firm, thus, has a "short" position in NOK. The firm's risk, of course, is that the dollar will decline relative to the NOK. To protect itself, the firm can acquire from a foreign exchange dealer a futures contract to receive kroner with maturities approximating when payments must be made to the firm's Norwegian suppliers. The objective is to hedge against the decline of the dollar against the NOK. If the dollar does decline relative to the NOK, the loss on paying the Norwegian creditors should be largely offset by the gain on the foreign currency transaction. Of course, if the dollar gains relative to the NOK, the gain from the payment of the creditor will be offset by the loss on the foreign currency transaction. The American firm has hedged by largely eliminating either gains or losses on its commercial transaction by means of the foreign exchange transactions going in the "opposite" direction. Another possibility is to obtain a forward exchange contract payable in NOK at the time the bill in NOK becomes due. This type of derivative locks in any gain or loss differential between the dollar and NOK as of the date the forward exchange contract is acquired.

A newer type of forward contract is the swap, which dates back only to 1982. Interest rate swaps arise when a customized deal is set up between two firms that exchange interest rates on a "notional" amount. A notional amount is a fictitious amount on which the parties base the interest rate swap. For example, Firm A has just borrowed $10,000,000 at a fixed interest rate of 7.6%. It then enters into an interest rate swap with Firm B based on a notional amount of $10,000,000. The terms of the interest rate swap call for A to receive from B the prevailing fixed interest of 7.6% (Firm A is, of course, also paying 7.6% on the accrual borrowing) and will pay B the variable or "floating" interest rate, which will be based on the London Interbank Offering Rate (LIBOR) plus 1%. The interest rate that values this contract, LIBOR plus 1%, is known as the underlying.

Exhibit 11.4   Interest Rate Swap Payoff Table

Date	Fixed Rate	LIBOR +1%	A's "Receipts" from B	A's "Payments" to B	Net Receipt or Payoff
June 30, 2000	7.60%	7.52%	$760,000	$752,000	$ 8,000
Dec. 31, 2000	7.60%	7.38%	760,000	738,000	22,000
June 30, 2001	7.60%	7.29%	760,000	729,000	31,000
Dec. 31, 2001	7.60%	7.21%	760,000	721,000	39,000
June 30, 2002	7.60%	7.33%	760,000	733,000	27,000
Dec. 31, 2002	7.60%	7.36%	760,000	736,000	24,000
					$151,000

An *underlying* may be a price or index of prices, but it is not the rate of an asset or liability itself. Underlyings would include exchange rates for currency futures and options and commodity prices for commodity futures and options. In our example, the contract is initiated on January 1, 2000, and matures on December 31, 2002, with settlement occurring on a six-month basis. The settlement table for this transaction is shown in Exhibit 11.4. The actual money changing hands is restricted to the differential shown in the last column.

By entering into a transaction to receive the fixed payments and pay the variable payments, Firm A has, in effect, turned its fixed-rate note into a variable-rate note since its net interest payments will now be equal to the variable payments column of Exhibit 11.4. Firm A has taken advantage of the decline that it expected in interest rates after the original transaction at a fixed rate was entered into (we presume new economic developments materialized leading A to believe interest rates would decline). A's total interest cost saving—without considering present values—would be $151,000, the sum of the last column in Exhibit 11.4.

Of course, A might not be so prescient. Given the same swap contract but with rising interest rates, the results might be as in Exhibit 11.5. In this case, Firm A has lost $202,000 by entering into the swap. Overall, however, Firm A has done well during the period of rising interest rates if most of its obligations are in the form of fixed rate borrowings. Therefore, its loss on this interest rate swap can be viewed as an insurance cost against declining interest rates at a time when it has largely fixed rate obligations. Notice also that Firm B's gain or loss is exactly the opposite of A's. When entering into a swap to pay fixed and receive variable, B loses when interest rates decline (Exhibit 11.4) and gains when interest rates rise (Exhibit 11.5). The interest rate swap is a zero-sum game: What one party gains, the other loses.

Since the original fixed payment note has now been turned into a variable rate, the original note plus the swap are referred to as a synthetic instrument. A *synthetic instrument* arises when more than one transaction or position is reviewed as a unit and that unit is economically similar to a particular financial instrument. Firm A may have believed that its balance sheet contained too many fixed liabilities with the move toward variable-rate-based liabilities being desirable. Firm B may well have had the opposite problem. Hence, both firms would be engaged in risk management by adjusting their interest schedules in accordance with their

Exhibit 11.5   Interest Rate Swap Payoff Table

Date	Fixed Rate	LIBOR +1%	A's "Receipts" From B	A's "Payments" to B	Net Receipt or Payoff
June 30, 2000	7.60%	7.71%	$760,000	$771,000	($11,000)
Dec. 31, 2000	7.60%	7.82%	760,000	782,000	(22,000)
June 30, 2001	7.60%	7.93%	760,000	793,000	(33,000)
Dec. 31, 2001	7.60%	8.02%	760,000	802,000	(42,000)
June 30, 2002	7.60%	8.05%	760,000	805,000	(45,000)
Dec. 31, 2002	7.60%	8.09%	760,000	809,000	(49,000)
					($202,000)

perceived financial needs. Both firms are also hedging: Firm A is hedging against declining interest rates, and Firm B is hedging against rising interest rates. Interest rate swaps may also provide some arbitraging opportunities by giving firms access to credit markets that they may not ordinarily engage in, giving them slightly lower interest rates. Of course, one or both parties may also be engaging in pure speculation.

The type of interest rate swap illustrated here is frequently called a plain vanilla swap. In this case, the plain vanilla swap consisted of an interest exchange of fixed for variable without any further complications. Derivatives transactions can be much more complex than those illustrated here.[77]

Without question, derivatives are an important tool for hedging and managing risk. The danger comes when hedging becomes speculation. This line is not always easy to find. For example, the German company Metallgesellschaft AG nearly went bankrupt in 1993. Its American subsidiary, MG Corporation, was selling gasoline and oil products on a fixed price basis for up to 10 years. It attempted to hedge by purchasing short-term oil futures. In case of price rises, the gains on the price rises would offset losses on their long-term supply contracts. Unfortunately, the company had large losses on its short-term futures contracts, and the gains on its regular business were essentially long term in nature and could not counteract its short-term losses of $1 billion. Opinion differed as to whether the firm was speculating or hedging.[78] At the least, it appears that the company's short-term oil futures contracts were not a good hedge relative to their long-term fixed price sale contracts. The latter may have been the real source of the company's problem. Hence, one of the answers to the derivatives problem may lie in better internal controls to make sure that the company is following prescribed policies adequately.

Option-Based Derivatives. Option holders pay a specific "up front" price that gives them the right to buy ("call") or sell ("put") a specific quantity at a specific price of a standard commodity or a financial or equity instrument. Common examples of call options would be stock options, convertible bonds, and convertible preferred stock. American options can be exercised during a specified period, while European options can be exercised only on a specific date. The option holder has the right—but not the obligation—to exercise the option, whereas forward types of contracts require performance.

Common stock options are quite popular. Call options would be acquired if it is expected that the price of a stock will increase. If ABC stock is presently selling for $60 and an option costs $5 allowing the holder to buy a share at $70, the holder may exercise the option when the price is above $70 and will make money if the stock price goes above $75.

Put options are acquired if the price of the stock is expected to drop. If CDE stock is presently selling for $50 and a put option costs $5 allowing the holder to sell a share at $40, the holder may exercise the put option when CDE goes below $40 and will make money if the price drops below $35. If the put option is exercised, the option holder can satisfy the contract by either using his/her share of CDE stock or acquiring it in the market for $35. One advantage of common stock options is that an active secondary market for options is provided by the Chicago Board Options Exchange if the holder wishes to sell the option prior to its expiration.

Options, both for common stock and commodities, give the holder flexibility and protection relative to either price increases or decreases of the particular common stock or commodity. One complex type of derivative combines interest rate swaps and options and is known as a swaption.

There are several other types of options that provide flexibility and protection. Interest rate caps give the holder protection against rising interest rates. If interest rates rise above a specified level, the cap holder receives cash equal to the excess of the interest rate above the cap rate times the notional premium. Interest rate floors are similar to caps, but they give the holder protection against declining interest rates. One problem with both caps and floors is that they are not exchange traded, leaving the option holder open to credit risk should the option writer fail to fulfill its obligation if actual rates either go above the cap or below the floor.

FASB Pronouncements on Derivatives

The FASB has issued several pronouncements dealing with specific financial instruments: SFAS No. 13 addresses the accounting for leveraged leases, SFAS No. 77 concerns the sale of receivables with recourse, and FASB Technical Bulletin No. 85-2 discusses accounting for collateralized mortgage obligations.[79] There are numerous instruments in existence, however, and new ones are being created with increasing frequency.[80]

Several earlier standards (SFAS Nos. 80, 105, and 119) pertaining to disclosure of derivatives have been superseded by SFAS No. 133. SFAS No. 133 now supplements SFAS No. 107. SFAS No. 107 requires fair value disclosures of all financial instruments, both assets and liabilities, whether or not recognized in the body of the balance sheet. This disclosure must be either in the balance sheet itself or in the footnotes thereto. If fair value cannot be determined, information such as the carrying amount, effective interest, and maturity—as well as why fair value cannot be determined—must be provided. SFAS No. 133 significantly extends SFAS No. 107.

SFAS No. 133. SFAS No. 133 finally took the step of valuing derivatives at fair value. Consider the example previously discussed in Exhibits 11.4 and 11.5. Assume that on December 31, 2000, a market appraisal indicates that the value of the swap has increased by $20,000 due to the fixed rate exceeding the variable rate through December 31, 2002 (this amount also might have been determined by discounting the difference between the fixed and projected variable interest rate amounts for the four settlement dates in 2001 and 2002). The following entry would be made on December 31, 2000:

Interest rate swap contract	$20,000	
Unrealized holding loss on bonds payable	$20,000	
Unrealized holding gain on swap		$20,000
Bonds payable		$20,000

The unrealized holding gain and loss would be shown in other income and would, of course, cancel each other. The interest rate swap contract would be a current asset. The notional value of the swap would not be considered. The credit to bonds payable is intended to show that account at its current value. The decline in the interest rate would cause the market value of the bonds to increase. If variable rates were higher than fixed rates, the debits and credits would reverse. The swap contract account would have a credit balance and would be a current liability. Bonds payable would be debited to reduce the market value because higher interest rates would drive the market value down. Notice that the swap contract has the capacity to be either an asset or a liability, depending on the structure of interest rates. This was noted in SFAS No. 105:

> An interest rate swap can be viewed as a series of forward contracts to exchange, for example, fixed cash payments for variable cash receipts computed by multiplying a specified floating rate market index by a notional amount. Those terms are potentially favorable or unfavorable depending on subsequent movements in the index, and an interest rate swap is a financial asset and a financial liability to both parties.[81]

In subsequent periods, the interest rate swap contract will be adjusted up or down from the balance of $20,000. If at the next statement date the contract is worth $15,000, bonds payable will be debited for $5,000 and the swap contract account credited for $5,000.

For actual net receipts or payoffs, interest expense will be debited or credited. For example, in Exhibit 11.4 the following entry would occur on December 31, 2000:

Cash	$22,000	
Interest expense		$22,000

SFAS No. 133 also requires a disclosure relative to the effectiveness of hedges.[82] Interest rate swaps are assumed to be *effective* if (a) the notional amount of the swap equals the principal amount of the asset or liability being hedged and (b) the fair value of the swap is zero at its inception.[83] In the interest rate swap illustration used previously, if the principal of the borrowing is $10,000,000 and the variable interest rate is also 7.6%, like the fixed rate, the hedge would be "effective." This appears to be the case whether the variable interest rate increases or declines. The effectiveness measurement itself appears to be most effective in certain forward contract hedge situations. Assume that a firm intends to buy 100,000 pounds of Brazilian coffee in six months. The firm desires protection against a rise in the U.S. dollar cost of Brazilian coffee. The company uses a cash flow hedge in the form of a six-month forward contract to acquire 100,000 pounds of Costa Rican coffee. If Brazilian coffee goes up $0.10 a pound during the six-month period and Costa Rican coffee goes up by $0.06 a pound, then we might say that the hedge was 40% effective $[1 - (0.06/0.10) = 0.4]$. The disclosure of hedge effectiveness will probably be quite useful. We may see further clarification and refinement of effectiveness measurements in the near future as firms cope with this problem.

Under SFAS No. 133, if a hedge is deemed to be "not effective," the gain or loss on the hedge and the related derivative goes directly to income. If the hedge is effective, gain or loss on the hedge and the derivative goes through other comprehensive income and is then transferred to earnings when actual realization occurs.

SFAS No. 133 is much tighter relative to hedging effectiveness than IAS 39. SFAS No. 133 has to have a virtual zero offset of derivative and hedge. It also allows only an individual pairing of each individual derivative and hedge, whereas IAS 39 allows "macro hedging": pairing a number of derivatives and offsetting hedges.[84]

SFAS No. 133 also requires that embedded derivative instruments should be valued separately from the host contract. Embedded derivatives are secondary aspects of the host (main) contract that may or will require cash flows upon the occurrence of a specific event that is separate from the host contract itself. For example, if Firm A borrows from Firm B and the instrument also allows B to buy a specific number of A's common shares at a bargain purchase price based on movements of the Dow Jones Index, then an embedded derivative is present and would have to be valued separately from the host contract (A's borrowing from B). The separate valuing of the host and embedded contract must be done by both parties. The option privileges in convertible bonds and convertible preferred stock are not considered to be embedded derivatives because their values are closely tied to the values of the issuer's common stock via the specific conversion ratios. However, SFAS No. 155 now allows the fair value option to be extended to both the host contract and the underlying derivative.[85]

In terms of disclosures, entities must indicate their objectives and policies for holding derivatives and hedging instruments. They are also encouraged to provide quantitative information about the various types of market risks that are involved.

SFAS No. 138. SFAS No. 138 provided clarifying amendments for a few issues that were providing implementation difficulties in SFAS No. 133.[86] For example, normal purchases and sales not involving financial instruments or derivatives were not subject to SFAS No. 133. However, if the price is based on an underlying that is not closely related to the asset being purchased or sold, it would come under SFAS No. 133.[87] SFAS No. 149 and SFAS No. 155 [88] primarily provide updates to incorporate recommendations from FASB's Derivatives Implementation Group (DIG) and to allow for broader application of fair value measurements.

SFAS No. 149. This Statement amends SFAS No. 133 by clarifying certain definitions and technical activities effecting some derivatives and hedges. The attempt was to require that contracts with similar characteristics be handled uniformly, which would improve comparability.

SFAS No. 156. SFAS Nos. 140 and 156 are technical standards dealing with the servicing of financial assets and liabilities, including securitizations.[89] A *servicing asset* involves financial assets where specified contractual servicing fees, late charges, and other auxiliary services are expected to yield a profit for the servicer. If the servicing revenues are not expected to exceed their costs, then the servicing firm has a servicing liability. SFAS No. 156 calls for fair value of servicing assets and servicing liabilities "where practicable."

Cornell and Landsman found SFAS No. 140 short in its disclosures relative to enabling users to determine cash flow risks of securitizations that are not determined to be sales.[90] This appears to be overcome in SFAS No. 156, since management must list its basis for classifying servicing assets and liabilities and the inherent risks by class (para. 4 amending para. 17 [e1] and [e2] of SFAS 140).

SFAS No. 159. SFAS No. 159 allows for practicality exceptions relative to fair value measurement of certain financial instruments.[91] SFAS No. 159 now allows a fair value choice for valuing many financial instruments. One purpose of this standard is to mitigate volatility in earnings measurement without resorting to hedging activities because some assets and liabilities are measured differently. However, in general, the fair value option can be selectively applied to one or more financial instruments rather than all of the members of a particular class. The fair value option is similar to, but not identical with, the fair value option in IAS 39.

Two FASB members dissented with SFAS No. 159. Their main point of disagreement is that an instrument-by-instrument application of the fair value option will not necessarily reduce earnings volatility, and it also reduces the relevance of the resulting measurement of income. We wholeheartedly agree with their dissent to this standard.

Classification in the Balance Sheet

ARB 43 requires classification of assets and liabilities based on liquidity. Two classifications are used—current and noncurrent.[92] *Current* is defined as the firm's operating cycle or one year, whichever is longer. The operating cycle is the time required to go from materials acquisition to cash collection from revenues. Operating cycles will differ from firm to firm and industry to industry. A liquidity ranking within the current and noncurrent groups is also normally made, although it is not required by any specific accounting standard.

The current/noncurrent approach gives only a crude indication of a firm's liquidity. Current assets cannot be used to assess critical cash flow capacity because the operating cycle may be a year or even longer. In addition, the current asset grouping contains some assets that do not affect current cash flows at all—for example, deferred charges and credits. Other classifications might be better for the assessment of liquidity. For example, a monetary/nonmonetary classification system combined with a current/noncurrent classification would give a better understanding of future cash flows. The problems of liquidity measurement are considered further in Chapter 13 in terms of the cash flow statement.

Another way of subclassifying assets would be according to those held for exchange (sale), those held for use, and those representing deferred charges. This would provide some additional information about how economic benefits will be realized and the uncertainty surrounding realization. As indicated earlier in the chapter, considerable variation exists in the asset group. As a general rule, the realization of future benefits will be more uncertain from production than from exchange. A classification system based on this approach would communicate relevant information about how the benefits will be realized and give some awareness of the relative risks concerning the realization of the benefits. A case could also be made that the most relevant information to report would be net realizable values for assets held for sale and replacement costs for assets held for production (assuming replacement would, in fact, occur).

More detailed reporting could also be made of liabilities. There are five distinctly different types of accounting liabilities: contractual, constructive, equitable, contingent, and deferred charges. Separate classifications by type would assist in evaluating the nature of the different types of obligations. As mentioned earlier in the chapter, it is relatively easy to group liabilities into these classifications. It would also aid the reader of balance sheets to know which liabilities are legally enforceable in the event of bankruptcy and which are not. As with assets, liabilities also have differing degrees of certainty concerning realization.

Finally, from a pure measurement viewpoint, classifying assets by the attribute being measured might aid in understanding the eclectic nature of measurement in the balance sheet. Numerous asset attributes are measured and reported in a balance sheet. It is not always clear from reading a balance sheet just how much variation there is in asset measurement. By custom, a balance sheet is added. In terms of measurement theory, the accounting elements in a balance sheet are not additive because of the different attributes being measured. This does not mean that balance sheets or financial ratios lack relevance, but the additivity question does raise an important issue concerning usefulness.

- The distinction between available-for-sale securities and trading securities should be eliminated. All realized gains and losses should go through income. All unrealized gains and losses should go through comprehensive income.
- Held-to-maturity securities should be carried at fair value if it is readily determinable. Unrealized gains and losses should go through comprehensive income until realized.
- All convertible bonds should be separated into their debt and equity components at issuance.

Summary

Definitions of accounting elements determine the types of economic events that are recognized as accounting transactions and how they are classified in the accounting classification system illustrated in Exhibit 11.1. Yet it is apparent that the definitions are of a general nature and that the transactions we recognize in accounting are derived as much from tradition as from the definitions of elements themselves. This may be inevitable. However, the value of good definitions from a policy-making perspective is that they enable policy makers to categorize and understand new types of transactions. Definitions should also aid in identifying those areas of existing practice that are inconsistent. Classification is fundamental in any science to understanding the nature of the discipline. The same is true of accounting classification and the understanding of economic events reported in the financial statements.

Historical cost is widely considered to be the basis of measurement in accounting, but it is very clear that many other types of measurement are embodied in current practices.

The many attributes involved in asset measurement were summarized in Exhibit 11.3. Liability measurement is less eclectic than asset measurement, but it too has variation. Face amount of debt is measured for current liabilities, and noncurrent debt is initially measured at discounted present values. Capital transactions in owners' equity basically represent the historical amounts of the transactions. However, as was evident, there are different ways of determining the values of some capital transactions—for example, treasury stock transactions and stock dividends. A troubling new type of financial instrument is the debt–equity hybrid instrument. Included here would be redeemable preferred stock and trust preferred certificates. The economic consequence involved with these instruments is an attempt to keep debt off of the balance sheet or at least out of the liabilities section.

This chapter should make it clear that accounting policy and practice are pragmatic. There is no single valuation model on which accounting practice is based. Departures from historical costs are frequent and are made for many reasons. The lower-of-cost-or-market rule represents balance sheet conservatism. Some accounting practices have come about because of verifiability (reliability) problems—for example, the treatment of convertible debt. Other departures are undertaken because more relevant information may be conveyed by the reporting of current values—for example, the use of current exchange rates to translate foreign operations. A point brought out in the chapter is that fair value measurement is here and will be further applied in future standards. Relevance is now the guiding concept.

One problem not raised in this chapter is the inconsistent use of discounting future cash flows.[93] As stated throughout this chapter, the balance sheet violates the concept of being additive. However, it must be remembered that accounting policies are the result of a political process and inevitable compromises. Finally, measurement purity per se does not ensure that accounting information will be useful or relevant.

Among financial instruments, derivatives are particularly difficult to account for. Derivatives sometimes have elements of both assets and liabilities. The two principal types of derivatives are forward-based and option-based derivatives, though the two types can be combined in extremely complex forms. As a result of SFAS No. 133, we are now attempting to value derivatives at fair (current) value.

Appendix 11-A: A Simple Example of a Weather Derivative

This appendix presents an extremely simplified example of a weather derivative. In this example the Wolozin-Buffett (W-B) Company, a medium-sized manufacturer in Minneapolis, would like to avoid the high power costs of a cold winter. On the other hand, the Northern States Power Company would have lower revenues and income if the winter is warm. Clearly there is an area where W-B and Northern States could work together and hedge their opposing interests. The assumptions are shown in Exhibit 11.6 for January 2004.

Exhibit 11.6   Weather Derivative Assumptions

Average Temperature	Probabilitiy	Power Cost to Wolozin-Buffett
12°–20°	1/3	$10,000
8°–12°	1/3	$15,000
0°– 8°	1/3	$20,000

With the weather averaging 0 to 8 degrees, Northern States does well but W-B does not. If the temperature averages between 12 and 20 degrees, the opposite situation occurs. Should the temperature average between 8 and 12 degrees, both parties are satisfied. Assume that W-B and Northern States contact a financial intermediary such as Bankers Trust or Marsh-McLennan. The financial intermediary sets up a weather derivative. If the temperature is between 12 and 20 degrees, W-B pays Northern States $5,000. If the temperature is between 0 and 8 degrees, Northern States pays W-B $5,000. Nobody pays if the temperature is between 8 and 12 degrees.

Notice that both parties have successfully hedged against risk. Payment of $15,000 a month by W-B is okay, and receipt of $15,000 a month is likewise presumed to be okay for Northern States. Each has hedged against the opposite danger: a cold winter for W-B and a warm winter for Northern States.

Obviously this is an extremely simple example. Average temperature does not go above 20 degrees or below zero. Also, costs are considered to be the same within the three ranges. Finally, the probabilities are equal. While weather derivatives may seem like an arcane example, they are widely used for exactly the reasons and purposes illustrated here. Despite its simplicity, this hypothetical example shows the power of derivatives when properly used.

QUESTIONS

1. What are the characteristics of assets, liabilities, and owners' equity, and how have they evolved over time?

2. Why is it difficult to define the basic accounting elements?

3. Why are asset and liability definitions important to the theoretical structure of accounting? Why are definitions important to policy-setting bodies?

4. Numerous attributes are measured in the balance sheet. What are the different attributes? Why is this practice criticized?

5. What do aggregated balance sheet totals represent? These balance sheet data are used for ratio analysis. How useful do you think ratio analysis is? Explain.

6. Multiple approaches have been advocated concerning the definition of accounting elements and the relationship between the balance sheet and income statement. What are these approaches and how do they differ?

7. What is the meaning of "owners' equity" in the balance sheet? Why are certain unrealized gains or losses included in owners' equity?

8. What are deferred charges and deferred credits, how do they come about, and do they conform to asset and liability definitions?

9. Why have mutually unperformed executory contracts traditionally been excluded from financial statements? Can this practice be justified in terms of asset and liability definitions? How relevant is this approach for professional sports franchises? Explain.

10. What is the purpose of balance sheet classification? How useful is the information produced from a classified balance sheet? What are some alternative classification systems that could be used?

11. As a potential investor, what do you feel would be the most useful attribute of measurement for each of the following: inventories held for sale, inventories held for production, and long-term debt? Would your answer differ if you were a potential lender? What if you were a manager of a company? What measurement problems are illustrated by this question?

12. Why is it difficult to determine the historical acquisition cost of self-constructed assets? Do definitions of accounting elements and general principles of recognition and measurement resolve the controversy over full-absorption costing and variable costing of manufactured inventory? Explain.

13. The limitation of the accounting classification system depicted in Exhibit 11.1 was referred to throughout the chapter. What is meant by this? Give some examples. Why is the accounting classification system the foundation of the accounting discipline?

14. Is the "available for sale" category for debt and equity securities used in SFAS No. 115 a homogeneous category? Explain.

15. Based on your reading of this chapter, plus your general knowledge of accounting standards, identify five examples of measurement flexibility in the statement of financial position.

16. SFAS No. 133 (213 pages), 149 (78 pages), and 155 (27 pages) define standards for derivatives in 318 pages. How do you think a principles-based approach to setting standards would affect their length? Explain.

17. Discuss the bright line that does or does not distinguish debt and equity classifications.

18. Why is there an implicit recognition of fair value in the 1984 Revised Model Business Corporation Act?

19. How does the asset impairment measurement approach of SFAS No. 121, *Accounting for the Impairment of Long-Lived Assets and for Long-Lived Assets to Be Disposed Of,* compare to deprival value?

20. Why are interest rate swaps a zero-sum game?

21. What is a securitization and why do firm's use this technique?

22. Of the various reasons that a firm might deal in its treasury stock, are there any that you might think are questionable? Discuss.

23. Are disclosures of hedging effectiveness effective?

24. Why are convertible bonds and convertible preferred stock not examples of embedded derivatives?

25. How does the term "embedded derivatives" compare with the term "embedded journalists" (from the Iraq War)?

26. Traditional measures of net assets do not capture the value of human capital in an organization. Which trends, if any, suggest that intellectual capital may eventually be a candidate for inclusion as an intangible on the balance sheet?

CASES, PROBLEMS, AND WRITING ASSIGNMENTS

1. Review a recent annual report and consider the following: Identify all attributes of measurement explicitly identified in the balance sheet and accompanying notes. Notice which items are not specified. Group the accounting elements by attribute. How thorough is the explanation of measurement in the balance sheet? Identify any unusual assets or liabilities. How useful is the current/noncurrent distinction for assessing liquidity? Based on your review, what level of user sophistication do you think is necessary to understand how the balance sheet numbers have been derived? How useful do you think the balance sheet is? What are its limitations and how might it be improved, especially from a communication viewpoint?

2. Assume that an asset is being examined and it is determined that its cash flows would be $10,000 per year for four years (assume that all cash flows are received at the end of the year). The carrying value of the asset is $35,000 and its replacement cost is $30,000. The firm's cost of capital is 10%.

   Required:
   a. What would be the amount, if any, that should be written off because the asset is impaired under SFAS No. 121?
   b. Why is your answer in part (a) anomalous and how does SFAS No. 121 justify it?
   c. Would your answer to part (a) be different if the cash flows were $8,000 rather than $10,000? Explain.
   d. Is there anything unusual about your answer to part (c) since accounting rules are frequently concerned with conservatism?

3. Assets A, B, and C constitute an asset group. Asset B is considered to be the principal asset in this group. Asset B has a three-year estimated life and A and C have remaining lives of four years. Data

on the expected undiscounted cash flows of the three assets, their book values (carrying values), and their fair values less costs to dispose are shown below:

Undiscounted cash flows by year	A	B	C
1	$18,000	$80,000	$12,000
2	15,000	70,000	10,000
3	12,000	65,000	9,000
4	10,000		6,000
Book value	$60,000	$220,000	$20,000
Fair value less Disposal costs	$65,000	$18,000	$25,000

Required:

a. Determine the amount of impairment according to SFAS Nos. 121 and 144.

b. By how much should each of the assets be written down?

c. What theoretical problems do you see with the application of SFAS Nos. 121 and 144 to asset impairments?

4. Assume an interest rate swap with a notional value of $1,000,000. Firm A receives fixed and pays variable. The fixed rate on December 31, 2000, is 8%. The swap has two years to run with variable interest rates of 7.8% and 7.6% expected on December 31, 2001, and 2002, respectively (annual settlements are assumed for simplicity). Firm A's cost of debt is 8%.

Required:

a. Determine the fair value of the derivative and state whether it would be an asset or a liability.

b. Assume that the swap occurred prior to December 31, 2000, and the interest rate swap contract had a debit balance of $1,000. Under this circumstance, make the entry for the fair value as of December 31, 2000.

5. Shown below are paragraphs 8–10 of ARB 43, Chapter 7 on stock dividends.

a. Para. 8. The question as to whether or not stock dividends are income has been extensively debated; the arguments pro and con are well known. The situation cannot be better summarized, however, than in the words approved by Mr. Justice Pitney in *Eisner v. Macomber*, 252 U.S. 189, wherein it was held that stock dividends are not income under the Sixteenth Amendment, as follows:

A stock dividend really takes nothing from the property of the corporation and adds nothing to the interests of the stockholders. Its property is not diminished and their interests are not increased . . . the proportional interest of each shareholder remains the same. The only change is in the evidence which represents that interest, the new shares and the original shares together representing the same proportional interests that the original shares represented before the issue of the new ones.

Para. 9. Since the shareholder's interest in the corporation remains unchanged by the stock dividend or split up except as to the number of share units constituting such interest, the cost of the shares previously held should be allocated equitably to the total shares held after receipt of the stock dividend or split up. When any shares are later disposed of, a gain or loss should be determined on the basis of the adjusted cost per share.

Para. 10. As has been previously stated, a stock dividend does not, in fact, give rise to any change whatsoever in either the corporation's assets or its respective shareholders' proportionate interests therein. However, it cannot fail to be recognized that, merely as a consequence of the expressed purpose of the transaction and its characterization as a dividend in related notices to shareholders and the public at large, many recipients of stock dividends look upon them as distributions of corporate earnings and usually in an amount equivalent to the fair value of the additional shares received. Furthermore, it is to be presumed that such views of recipients are materially strengthened in those instances, which are by far the most numerous, where the issuances are so small in comparison with the shares previously outstanding that they do not have any apparent effect upon the share market price and, consequently, the market value of the shares previously held remains substantially unchanged. The committee therefore believes that where these circumstances exist the corporation should in the public interest account for the transaction by transferring from earned surplus to the category of permanent capitalization (represented by the capital stock and capital surplus accounts) an amount equal to the fair value of the additional shares issued. Unless this is done, the amount of earnings which the shareholder may believe to have been distributed to him will be left, except to the extent otherwise dictated by legal requirements, in earned surplus subject to possible further similar stock issuances or cash distributions.[94]

Required:

    a. From a logical standpoint, evaluate the CAP's argument involving situations in which market value of common stock should be capitalized in certain stock dividend situations.

    b. Do you see a possible "hidden agenda" here involving certain economic consequences that the CAP was trying to bring about relative to stock dividends? Explain.

6. Leeson Company entered into an interest rate swap with Morley Corporation on January 1, 2003. The notional amount of the swap is $20,000,000. Leeson will pay Morley a fixed annual rate of 8%. Morley will pay Leeson LIBOR plus 1%. Settlement is to be made every six months and the contract lasts for three years. The annual variable rates based on LIBOR plus 1% are:

July 1, 2003	8.26%
January 1, 2004	8.32%
July 1, 2004	8.18%
January 1, 2005	7.92%
July 1, 2005	7.90%
January 1, 2006	8.06%

Required:

    a. Set up a schedule showing the net receipts or payments for Leeson.

    b. Why would Leeson enter into a strategy of this type?

    c. Has Leeson benefited from this transaction?

    d. What dangers are present?

7. On January 1, 2000, $1,000,000 of 10% debenture bonds were acquired by Means Corporation at $927,908, which would yield a 12% rate of return. The bonds mature on December 31, 2004. Interest is paid annually on December 31. Means Corporation classifies these securities as available-for-sale securities. Shown below are the effective interest rate and market value of the securities at various dates.

Date	Effective Interest	Market Value
December 31, 2000	11%	$968,975
December 31, 2001	9%	$1,025,310
December 31, 2002	12%	$966,195
December 31, 2003	9%	$1,009,173

Required:

    a. Using the method suggested by Kathryn Means (i.e., use the current interest rate for the recognition of income and determination of fair value with the holding gain component going to owners' equity), determine the income and unrealized holding gain components for the years 2000 through 2004 (assume that the interest rate change occurs on each December 31).

    b. Make the entries that result from assuming that these debenture bonds were Means Corporation's only available-for-sale securities.

CRITICAL THINKING AND ANALYSIS

1. It might be said that we are slowly moving toward an asset–liability approach in the balance sheet. Which event situations support this statement?

2. In July 2003, the SEC submitted to Congress its *Study Pursuant to Section 108(d) of the Sarbanes-Oxley Act of 2002 on the Adoption by the United States Financial Reporting System of a Principles-Based Accounting System*. A year later, FASB issued its reply, *FASB Response to the SEC Study on the Adoption of a Principles-Based Accounting System* (July 2004). The SEC recommended that FASB when setting standards "avoid the use of percentage tests ('bright-lines') that allow financial engineers to achieve technical compliance with the standard while evading the intent of the standard." Identify where bright lines currently exist in the statement of financial position, areas in which we might expect revisions in the future. What is the argument for use of bright-line tests?

Notes

1. FASB (1976b).
2. FASB (1985).
3. APB (1966a). This has been superseded by SFAS No. 87 and SFAS No. 158, which do take the balance sheet into consideration.
4. APB (1970a).
5. Committee on Terminology (1953, para. 26).
6. APB (1970a, para. 132).
7. FASB (1985, para. 25).
8. APB (1970a, para. 57).
9. Chambers (1966) and Arthur Andersen and Co. (1974).
10. FASB (1976b, para. 122).
11. Executory contracts were discussed in accounting literature as early as Canning (1929).
12. Solomons (1986, p. 116).
13. The inapplicability of the credit to a liability in the case of purchase commitments as well as examples of how to book this type of executory contract appears in Gujarathi and Biggs (1988). For other arguments in favor of recognizing executory contracts as part of general accounting practice, see Hughes (1978), Ijiri (1975, pp. 129–140), and Ijiri (1980).
14. APB (1970a, para. 145). See also FASB (1984, para. 67).
15. American Accounting Association (1966) and Stamp (1980).
16. FASB (1993, pp. 10–11).
17. Ibid. (para. 15).
18. Means (1994).
19. Nobes (2005)
20. APB (1971a).
21. Committee on Accounting Procedure (1953).
22. In an exhaustive analysis of possible lower-of-cost-or-market techniques, Ijiri and Nakano (1989) demonstrate that in addition to conservatism, these measurements may improve verifiability of accounting numbers and have informational value arising from disclosing prospective negative events more rapidly than would occur under normal economic conditions.
23. FASB (2004a).
24. FASB (1979).
25. However, Mozes and Schiff suggest that comparability does not result from this standard because of capitalization inconsistencies. They would not capitalize interest unless a direct link existed between the asset and debt. See Mozes and Schiff (1995).
26. Means and Kazenski (1988).
27. FASB (1995, para. 5). For an in-depth review of asset writedowns, see Alciatore et al. (1998).
28. Zucca and Campbell (1992) found evidence that some firms attempt to smooth earnings (earnings were higher than expected prior to the write-off) and others took a "big bath" (other losses occurred when earnings were already below normal). Out of 77 writedowns examined between 1978 and 1983, they found 22 examples of income smoothing and 45 big bath examples.
29. FASB (1995, para. 8).
30. Ibid. (paras. 9 and 89).
31. Ibid. (para. 72).
32. Ibid. (para. 92).

33. *FASB (2001, para. 18).*

34. *Ibid. (paras. 41–44).*

35. *Ibid. (para. 12).*

36. *APB (1973).*

37. *FASB (2004b).*

38. *Gu and Lev (2004).*

39. *FASB (1974).*

40. *For a discussion of R&D disclosure in Canada, see Entwistle (1999). Of particular interest is the fact that 17 of 21 executives opposed capitalization of R&D charges. Many of these individuals felt that immediate expensing is favorably viewed by the investment community.*

41. *Recent articles largely concurring with Lev and Zarowin (1999) that immediate write-off of intangibles lowers the correlation between earnings and security prices include Lee and Sami (1998), Lev (2002a, and Lev and Sougiannis (1996).*

42. *Lev and Zarowin (1999, p. 377). See also Aboody and Lev (1998). Eccher (1998) points out that using the technological feasibility standard would result in only a relatively small proportion of R&D costs being capitalized.*

43. *Ibid. (p. 380).*

44. *Lev (2002a and 2002b) sees organizational infrastructure as the key to generating the value of intangible assets.*

45. *Committee on Terminology (1953, para. 27).*

46. *APB (1970, para. 132).*

47. *FASB (1985, para. 35).*

48. *However, the definition of probable varies within the conceptual framework itself as noted by Botosan, Koonce, Ryan, Stone, and Wahlen (2005, p.161). They point out that in the definition given above in SFAC No. 6, a liability may, in reality, have a low probability of actual future sacrifice, whereas in SFAC No. 5 probable means more likely to be incurred than not.*

49. *FASB (1975b).*

50. *APB (1962) and FASB (1976a).*

51. *APB (1970, para. 181) and FASB (1984, para. 67).*

52. *APB (1971b).*

53. *APB (1969a).*

54. *APB (1966b), APB (1967b), and APB (1969a).*

55. *APB (1969b).*

56. *FASB (1975a).*

57. *Nair, Rittenberg, and Weygandt (1990).*

58. *Kimmel and Warfield (1993, p. 35).*

59. *Kimmel and Warfield (1995).*

60. *Engel, Erickson, and Maydew (1999).*

61. *Frischmann, Kimmel, and Warfield (1999).*

62. *FASB (2003b).*

63. *FASB (1996, paras. 31–46).*

64. *Roberts, Samson, and Dugan (1990, p. 38).*

65. *FASB (1997, para. 112).*

66. *Ho, Liu, and Ramanan (1997). Gelb (2000) provides evidence that firms in industries with relatively low entry barriers tend to signal "good news" by either cash dividends or treasury stock purchases rather than conveying potentially damaging proprietary information through disclosures.*

67. *Vafeas (1997).*

68. *Hribar, Jenkins, and Johnson (2006) examine firms that marginally fall short of analysts' earnings per share (EPS) forecasts and subsequently repurchase shares. As a result, EPS increases. This EPS management is not earnings management per se but is closely related.*

69. *Committee on Accounting Procedure (1953).*

70. *SEC (1972).*

71. *Foster and Scribner (1998).*

72. *This evidently is what actually does occur in practice. For an enumeration of the various ways that stock dividends are treated, see Zucca and Kirch (1996).*

73. *Committee on Accounting Procedure (1953, Ch. 7).*

74. *Capital market research supports the argument that there is no theoretical change in the value of the firm due to the dividend per se. See Foster (1986) for a review of this research.*

75. *Peterson, Millar, and Rimbey (1996) and Rankin and Stice (1997).*

76. *FASB (1990, p. 3).*

77. *For a good presentation of a yen-for-dollar currency swap intended to lower the cost of borrowing, see Cerf and Elmy (1998).*

78. *See Lowenstein (1995).*

79. *A collateralized mortgage obligation is a debt security that is secured by a "pool" of mortgage loans receivable. Interest and principal payments on the mortgages are then accumulated to pay interest/principal on the collateralized mortgage obligations.*

80. *See Stewart and Neuhausen (1986) for a listing of some of the current financial instruments.*

81. *FASB (1990, p. 36).*

82. *FASB (1998, p. 243).*

83. *Ibid. (paras. 62–103).*

84. *Wood (2006, p. 50).*

85. *FASB (2006a).*

86. *FASB (2000).*

87. *FASB (2000, para. 4a).*

88. *FASB (2003a) and FASB (2006a).*

89. *FASB (2006b).*

90. *Cornell and Landsman (2006, p. 52).*

91. *FASB (2007, para. C21b).*

92. *SFAS No. 6 (FASB, 1975c) allows current liabilities to be reclassified as long term if the firm has the intention and ability to refinance the loan on a long-term basis. Gramlich, McAnally, and Thomas (2001) find that firms reclassify to the long-term category in order to smooth the current ratio: The current ratio may be too low or too high prior to the reclassification.*

93. *A full discussion of discounting in financial reporting appears in Weil (1990).*

94. *Reprinted by permission.*

References

Aboody, David, and B. Lev (1998). "The Value Relevance of Intangibles: The Case of Software Capitalization," *Studies on Enhancing the Financial Reporting Model, 1998* (Supplement to *Journal of Accounting Research*), pp. 161–191.

Accounting Principles Board (1962). APB Opinion No. 2, *Accounting for the Investment Credit.* AICPA.

———— (1966a). APB Opinion No. 8, *Accounting for the Cost of Pension Plans.* AICPA.

———— (1966b). APB Opinion No. 10, *Omnibus Opinion—1966*. AICPA.

———— (1967a). APB Opinion No. 11, *Accounting for Income Taxes*. AICPA.

———— (1967b). APB Opinion No. 12, *Omnibus Opinion—1967*. AICPA.

———— (1969a). APB Opinion No. 14, *Accounting for Convertible Debt and Debt Issued With Stock Purchase Warrants*. AICPA.

———— (1969b). APB Opinion No. 15, *Earnings per Share*. AICPA.

———— (1970). APB Statement No. 4, *Basic Concepts and Accounting Principles Underlying Financial Statements of Business Enterprises*. AICPA.

———— (1971a). APB Opinion No. 18, *The Equity Method of Accounting for Investments in Common Stock*. AICPA.

———— (1971b). APB Opinion No. 21, *Interest on Receivables and Payables*. AICPA.

———— (1973). APB Opinion No. 29, *Accounting for Nonmonetary Transactions*. AICPA.

Alciatore, Mimi, C. Dee, P. Easton, and N. Spear (1998). "Asset Write-Downs: A Decade of Research," *Journal of Accounting Literature* (Vol. 17), pp. 1–39.

American Accounting Association (1966). *A Statement of Basic Accounting Theory*. AAA.

Arthur Andersen and Co. (1974). *Accounting Standards for Business Enterprises Throughout the World*. Arthur Andersen.

Botosan, Christine, L. Koonce, S. G. Ryan, M. Stone, and J. Wahlen (Sept. 2005). "Accounting for Liabilities: Conceptual Issues, Standard Setting, and Evidence From Academic Research," *Accounting Horizons*, pp. 159–186.

Canning, John B. (1929). *The Economics of Accountancy*. Ronald Press.

Cerf, Douglas C., and F. J. Elmy (November 1998). "Accounting for Derivatives: The Case of a Currency Rate Swap Used to Hedge Foreign Exchange Rate Exposure," *Issues in Accounting Education*, pp. 931–955.

Chambers, Raymond J. (1966). *Accounting, Evaluation and Economic Behavior*. Prentice Hall.

Committee on Accounting Procedure (1953). ARB No. 43, *Restatement and Revision of Accounting Research Bulletins*. AICPA.

Committee on Terminology (1953). Accounting Terminology Bulletin No. 1, *Review and Resume*. AICPA.

Cornell, Bradford, and W. Landsman (Fall 2006). "Accounting and Valuation: How Helpful Are Recent Accounting Rule Changes?" *Journal of Applied Corporate Finance*, pp. 44–52.

Eccher, Elizabeth A. (1998). "Discussion of the Value Relevance of Intangibles: The Case of Software Capitalization," *Studies on Enhancing the Financial Reporting Model, 1998* (Supplement to *Journal of Accounting Research*), pp. 193–198.

Engel, Ellen, M. Erickson, and E. Maydew (Autumn 1999). "Debt Equity Hybrid Securities," *Journal of Accounting Research*, pp. 249–274.

Entwistle, Gary M. (December 1999). "Exploring the R & D Disclosure Environment," *Accounting Horizons*, pp. 323–341.

Financial Accounting Standards Board (1974). Statement of Financial Accounting Standards No. 2, *Accounting for Research and Development Costs*. FASB.

———— (1975a). Statement of Financial Accounting Standards No. 4, *Reporting Gains and Losses From Extinguishment of Debt*. FASB.

———— (1975b). Statement of Financial Accounting Standards No. 5, *Accounting for Contingencies*. FASB.

———— (1975c). Statement of Financial Accounting Standards No. 6, *Classification of Short-Term Obligations Expected to Be Refinanced*. FASB.

———— (1976a). Statement of Financial Accounting Standards No. 13, *Accounting for Leases*. FASB.

———— (1976b). FASB Discussion Memorandum: *An Analysis of Issues Related to Conceptual Framework for Financial Reporting: Elements of Financial Statements and Their Measurement*. FASB.

——— (1979). Statement of Financial Accounting Standards No. 34, *Capitalization of Interest Cost*. FASB.

——— (1984). Statement of Financial Accounting Concepts No. 5, *Recognition and Measurement in Financial Statements of Business Enterprises*. FASB.

——— (1985). Statement of Financial Accounting Concepts No. 6, *Elements of Financial Statements*. FASB.

——— (1990). Statement of Financial Accounting Standards No. 105, *Disclosure of Information about Financial Instruments With Off Balance Sheet Risk and Financial Instruments With Concentrations of Credit Risk*. FASB.

——— (1993). Statement of Financial Accounting Standards No. 115, *Accounting for Certain Investments in Debt and Equity Securities*. FASB.

——— (1995). Statement of Financial Accounting Standards No. 121, *Accounting for the Impairment of Long Lived Assets to Be Disposed Of*. FASB.

——— (1996). Statement of Financial Accounting Standards No. 125, *Accounting for Transfers and Servicing of Financial Assets and Extinguishment of Liabilities*. FASB.

——— (1997). Statement of Financial Accounting Standards No. 130, *Reporting Comprehensive Income*. FASB.

——— (1998). Statement of Financial Accounting Standards No. 133, *Accounting for Derivative Instruments and Hedging Activities*. FASB.

——— (2000). Statement of Financial Accounting Standards No. 138, *Accounting for Certain Derivative Instruments and Certain Hedging Activities*. FASB.

——— (2001). Statement of Financial Accounting Standards No. 144, *Accounting for the Impairment or Disposal of Long-Lived Assets*. FASB.

——— (2003a). Statement of Financial Accounting Standards No. 149, *Amendment of Statement No. 133 on Derivative Instruments and Hedging Activities*. FASB.

——— (2003b). Statement of Financial Accounting Standards No. 150, *Accounting for Certain Financial Instruments With Characteristics of Both Liabilities and Equity*. FASB.

——— (2004a). Statement of Financial Accounting Standards No. 151, *Inventory Costs: An Amendment of ARB No. 43, Chapter 4*. FASB.

——— (2004b). Statement of Financial Accounting Standards No. 153, *Exchanges of Nonmonetary Assets: An Amendment of APB Opinion No. 29*. FASB.

——— (2006a). Statement of Financial Accounting Standards No. 155, *Accounting for Certain Hybrid Financial Instruments*. FASB.

——— (2006b). Statement of Financial Accounting Standards No. 156, *Accounting for Servicing of Financial Assets: An Amendment of FASB Statement No. 140*. FASB.

——— (2007). Statement of Financial Accounting Standards No. 115, *The Fair Value Option for Financial Assets and Liabilities—Including an Amendment of FASB Statement No. 115*. FASB.

Foster, George (1986). *Financial Statement Analysis*. Prentice Hall.

Foster, Taylor W. III, and E. A. Scribner (February 1998). "Accounting for Stock Dividends and Stock Splits: Corrections to Textbook Coverage," *Issues in Accounting Education*, pp. 1–13.

Frischmann, Peter J., P. D. Kimmel, and T. D. Warfield (September 1999). "Innovation in Preferred Stock: Current Developments and Implications for Financial Reporting," *Accounting Horizons*, pp. 201–218.

Gelb, David S. (2000). "Corporate Signaling With Dividends, Stock Repurchases, and Accounting Disclosures: An Empirical Study," *Journal of Accounting, Auditing, & Finance* (Vol. 15, No. 2), pp. 99–120.

Gramlich, Jeffrey, M. L. McAnally, and J. Thomas (September 2001). "Balance Sheet Management: The Case of Short-Term Obligations Reclassified as Long-Term Debt," *Journal of Accounting Research*, pp. 283–295.

Gu, Feng and B. Lev (March 2004), "The Information Content of Royalty Income," *Accounting Horizons*, pp. 1–12.

Gujarathi, Mahendra R., and Stanley F. Biggs (September 1988). "Accounting for Purchase Commitments: Some Issues and Recommendations," *Accounting Horizons*, pp. 75–82.

Ho, Li Chin Jennifer, C. S. Liu, and R. Ramanan (1997). "Open Market Stock Repurchase Announcements and Revaluation of Prior Accounting Information," *Accounting Review* (July 1997), pp. 475–487.

Hribar, Paul, Nicole Thorne Jenkins, and W. Bruce Johnson (2006). "Stock Repurchases as an Earnings Management Device," *Journal of Accounting and Economics* (Vol. 41, Issue 1–2), pp. 3–27.

Hughes, John S. (October 1978). "Toward a Contract Basis of Valuation in Accounting," *Accounting Review*, pp. 882–894.

Ijiri, Yuji (1975). "Theory of Accounting Measurement," *Studies in Accounting Research #10.* American Accounting Association.

———— (1980). *Recognition of Contractual Rights and Obligations: An Exploratory Study of Conceptual Issues.* FASB.

Ijiri, Yuji, and Isao Nakano (September 1989). "Generalizations of Cost or Market Valuation," *Accounting Horizons*, pp. 1–11.

Kimmel, Paul, and Terry Warfield (June 1993). "Variations in Attributes of Redeemable Preferred Stock: Implications for Accounting Standards," *Accounting Horizons*, pp. 30–40.

———— (January 1995). "The Usefulness of Hybrid Security Classifications: Evidence From Redeemable Preferred Stock," *Accounting Review*, pp. 151–167.

Lee, Buryung B., and H. Sami (August 1998). "Informativeness of Earnings for Firms With Unrecorded Intangible Assets," *Accounting Enquiries*, pp. 85–140.

Lev, Baruch (2002a). "Intangibles at a Crossroads: What's Next?," *Financial Executive* (March/April), pp. 35–39.

———— (2002b). "The Importance of Organizational Infrastructure (OI)," *Financial Executive* (July/August), pp. 33–36.

Lev, Baruch, and T. Sougiannis (February 1996). "The Capitalization, Amortization, and Value-Relevance of R & D," *Journal of Accounting and Economics*, pp. 107–138.

Lev, Baruch, and P. Zarowin (Autumn 1999). "The Boundaries of Financial Reporting and How to Extend Them," *Journal of Accounting Research*, pp. 353–385.

Lowenstein, Roger (1995). "Is Corporate Hedging Really Speculation?" *Wall Street Journal* (July 20), p. C1.

Means, Kathryn M. (June 1994). "Effective Interest . . . On What Basis," *Accounting Horizons*, pp. 71–79.

Means, Kathryn M., and Paul M. Kazenski (September 1988). "SFAS 34: A Recipe for Diversity," *Accounting Horizons*, pp. 62–67.

Mozes, Haim, and A. I. Schiff (March 1995). "A Critical Look at SFAS 34: Capitalization of Interest Cost," *Abacus*, pp. 1–17.

Nair, R., Larry Rittenberg, and Jerry Weygandt (June 1990). "Accounting for Redeemable Preferred Stock: Unresolved Issues," *Accounting Review*, pp. 33–41.

Nobes, Christopher W. (March 2005). "Rules Based Standards and the Lack of Principles in Accounting," *Accounting Horizons*, pp. 25–34.

Peterson, Craig A., J. A. Millar, and J. N. Rimbey (April 1996). "The Economic Consequences of Accounting for Stock Splits and Large Stock Dividends," *Accounting Review*, pp. 241–253.

Rankin, Graeme, and Earl K. Stice (January 1997). "Accounting Rules and Signalling Properties of 20 Percent Stock Dividends," *Accounting Review*, pp. 23–46.

Roberts, Michael, William Samson, and Michael Dugan (December 1990). "The Stockholders' Equity Section: Form Without Substance?" *Accounting Horizons*, pp. 35–46.

Securities and Exchange Commission (1972). Accounting Series Release No. 124, *Pro Rata Stock Distributions to Shareholders.* SEC.

Solomons, David (June 1986). "The FASB's Conceptual Framework: An Evaluation," *Journal of Accountancy*, pp. 114–124.

Stamp, Edward (1980). *Corporate Reporting: Its Future Evolution.* Canadian Institute of Chartered Accountants.

Stewart, John E., and Benjamin S. Neuhausen (August 1986). "Financial Instruments and Transactions: The CPA's Newest Challenge," *Journal of Accountancy*, pp. 102–112.

Vafeas, Nikos (Spring 1997). "Determinants of the Choice Between Alternative Share Repurchase Methods," *Journal of Accounting, Auditing & Finance*, pp. 101–124.

Weil, Roman (December 1990). "Role of the Time Value of Money in Financial Reporting," *Accounting Horizons*, pp. 47–67.

Wood, Duncan (March 2006). "The Grass May Look Greener, but Each Side Has Problems," *Treasury & Risk Management*, pp. 48–50.

Zucca, Linda C., and David R. Campbell (September 1992). "A Closer Look at Discretionary Writedowns of Impaired Assets," *Accounting Horizons*, pp. 30–41.

Zucca, Linda C., and D. P. Kirch (June 1996). "A Gap in GAAP: Accounting for Midrange Stock Distributions," *Accounting Horizons*, pp. 100–112.

12

The Income Statement

Learning Objectives

After reading this chapter, you should be able to:

- Understand the significance of the evolving definitions of revenues, expenses, gains, and losses.
- Appreciate the importance of future events relative to revenue and expense recognition.
- Understand the complexities underlying the income statement and its organization and presentation.
- Understand the importance of comprehensive income.
- Grasp the significance of the simplified approach to earnings per share.
- Comprehend the significance of earnings management and how it is manifested.
- Understand the relationship between manipulation of management compensation plans and income smoothing.
- Become familiar with new proposals in income measurement.

The income statement has been—and will continue to be—an extremely important and basic financial statement. We have seen its importance in previous chapters relative to predicting future cash flows and assessment of management performance. In this chapter, we will look back at the development of the income statement as well as examine current developments.

We start by exploring the development of basic terminology such as *income, revenues,* and *expenses* and the standards for recognition of the latter two. We then review an important and newly emerging topic, the role of future events in revenue and expense recognition. Next, we turn to the controversy over current operating versus all-inclusive income—an old argument that is still developing. The all-inclusive approach has led to comprehensive income, which is next examined. We also discuss the classifications comprising the extended format of the income statement: extraordinary items, accounting changes, discontinued operations, and prior period adjustments (for completeness). We then examine earnings per share and the recent changes that have affected it. After that, we look at some specialized topics involving income measurements: development stage enterprises, troubled debt restructuring, early extinguishment of debt, and stock options. Subsequently, we address an extremely important topic, earnings management, and its two principal manifestations: (1) managing income to affect management compensation and (2) income smoothing. Finally we address some new developments in the income statement.

Income Definitions

Accounting income has been formally defined in the following ways:

- Income and profit . . . refer to amounts resulting from the deduction from revenues, or from operating revenues, of cost of goods sold, other expenses, and losses.[1]
- Net income (net loss)—the excess (deficit) of revenue over expenses for an accounting period.[2]
- Comprehensive income is the change in equity (net assets) of an entity during a period of transactions and other events and circumstances from nonowner sources.[3]

The first two definitions, from Accounting Terminology Bulletin (ATB) 2 and Accounting Principles Board (APB) Statement 4, clearly represent the revenue–expense approach. When the primary emphasis is on revenue and expense measurement, it is necessary to have standards that define those elements and specify their recognition and measurement. The third definition, from Statement of Financial Accounting Concept (SFAC) No. 6, represents a clear change in direction to the asset–liability approach. This appears to be the direction that the Financial Accounting Standards Board (FASB) is taking and will take in the future. The impact, if any, on the income statement of the apparent change in direction cannot be foreseen, but it should begin gathering steam in the years immediately ahead.

Revenues and Gains

However net income is defined, it is convenient to separate it into components for reporting. These components have been defined as revenues, expenses, gains, and losses. Revenues have been defined in the following ways:

- Revenue results from the sale of goods and rendering of services and is measured by the charge made to customers, clients, or tenants for goods and services furnished to them.[4]
- Revenue—gross increases in assets and gross decreases in liabilities measured in conformity with generally accepted accounting principles that result from those types of profit-directed activities . . .[5]

- Revenues are the inflows or other enhancements of assets of an entity or settlements of its liabilities (or a combination of both) during a period from delivering or producing goods, rendering services, or other activities that constitute the entity's ongoing major or central operations.[6]

The first definition, from ATB 2, reflects a revenue–expense approach and emphasizes the direct identification of revenue-producing activities. A difference can be detected in the second definition, which is from APB Statement 4. Revenues are defined as an increase in net assets arising from income-producing activities. At first glance, this appears to represent a shift to the asset–liability orientation; however, measurement is said to be based on generally accepted accounting principles, which still implies the revenue–expense orientation. Finally, the third definition, from SFAC No. 6, does clearly define revenue as an increase in net assets. This represents an asset–liability approach and is consistent with the SFAC No. 6 definition of comprehensive income.

The definition from ATB 2 is similar to the presentation of revenues in Chapter 5, in which revenues were defined as the output of the enterprise in terms of its product or services. However, all three of these definitions, by introducing the issue of how to measure revenues, interject the issue of recognition into the definition. How to measure an element should conceptually be kept separate from the definition since questions of recognition and measurement may well supersede the issue of what is being measured. Recognition is examined in more detail shortly.

Gains and revenues typically have been displayed separately on financial statements. Gains have been defined in the following manner:

- Revenues . . . from other than sales of products, merchandise, or services. . . .[7]
- Gains are increases in equity (net assets) from peripheral or incidental transactions . . . except those that result from revenues or investments by owners.[8]

The distinction between a revenue and gain once was a subject of considerable controversy. One school of thought believed that only revenues should be reported on income statements. The secondary or peripheral nature of gains means that they did not represent recurring income from the entity's main area of income-producing activities and therefore should be excluded from the income statement. This school of thought has been called the *current operating income concept*. The competing position was called the *all-inclusive income concept*. Its proponents believed that all revenues and gains, regardless of source, should be included in the income statement. There has been an evolution away from the current operating concept to the all-inclusive concept, which is reviewed later in the chapter.

Revenue Recognition

When is a revenue a revenue? From a theoretical point of view, the answer to this question is clear: "[Revenues] should be identified with the period during which the major economic activities necessary to the creation and disposition of goods and services has been accomplished."[9] The practical problem with this definition, however, is the inability to make an objective measurement of the results of those economic activities. Until a verifiable measurement can be made, no revenue can be recognized. Unfortunately, the accomplishment of the "major economic activities necessary to the creation and disposition of goods and services" and the ability to measure those accomplishments objectively frequently occur at different times and in different reporting periods. Finally, as noted in Chapter 7, SFAC No. 5 is of little help to the general problem of recognition. Although SFAC No. 5 purports to be the piece of the conceptual framework dealing with recognition, it does little more than reiterate, in an ad hoc manner, concepts from prior SFACs (that is, element definitions, measurability, relevance, and reliability).

Four alternative points in time for recognizing revenue are discussed in the accounting literature and used in accounting practice:

1. During production

2. At the completion of production

3. At the time of sale

4. When cash is collected

Revenue is recognized during production for certain long-term contracts (see Accounting Research Bulletin (ARB) 45 and SOP 81-1); it is recognized at the completion of production for certain agricultural and mining operations (see ARB 43, Chapter 4, paragraphs 15–16); and it is recognized at the time of cash collection when the installment method is used for sales of real estate (see SFAS No. 66).

Although the topic of revenue recognition has been lively and provocative, the fact remains that revenues generally are recognized at the point of sale when legal title is transferred.[10] This norm is clearly expressed in Chapter 1 of ARB 43: "Profit (revenue) is deemed to be realized when a sale in the ordinary course of a business is effected, unless the circumstances are such that collection of the sales price is not reasonably assumed."[11]

This rule was one of the six originally adopted by the American Institute of Certified Public Accountants (AICPA) in 1934 (see the discussion in Chapter 3). Exceptions are sanctioned in the accounting rules, as previously mentioned, but the general principle is that revenues are recognized at the time of sale.

The vast majority of exceptions to recognizing revenue at the point of sale have evolved because new transactions have emerged that do not fit the mold of traditional transactions. In many instances, but not all, these transactions are peculiar to specific industries. As noted in Chapter 3, the AICPA has been the primary source of the development of accounting standards, particularly revenue recognition standards, as new transactions emerge. Its Accounting Standards Division periodically issues accounting guides (Guides) and used to issue Statements of Position (SOPs). These documents, however, do not have to be followed in practice as do FASB Statements and Interpretations. Perhaps this is why Jaenicke found the accounting practices for revenue recognition that have evolved for these new transactions to be inconsistent in rationale and, often, in outcomes.[12]

In SFAS No. 32, issued in 1979, the FASB announced that it was embarking on a program of extracting standards from the Guides and SOPs, modifying them, if necessary, to be internally consistent with FASB Statements and Concepts, and issuing them as SFASs. Thirteen SFASs in this program have been issued: franchise fee revenue (No. 45), revenue recognition when right of return exists (No. 48), product financing arrangements (No. 49), the record and music industry (No. 50), cable television companies (No. 51), motion pictures (No. 53), insurance enterprises (No. 60), title plant (No. 61), broadcasters (No. 63), mortgage banking (No. 65), sales of real estate (No. 66), costs and initial rental operations of real estate projects (No. 67), and an omnibus statement applying to securities dealers, employee benefit plans, and banks (No. 83).

Exceptions to the general rule of recognizing revenue at the point of sale have been sanctioned by the professional literature. Revenue may be recognized during production for long-term construction contracts if reliable estimates of the extent of progress and of the cost to complete can be made and if reasonable assurance of collectibility exists. If immediate marketability at a quoted price exists for a product whose units are interchangeable, revenue may be recognized at the completion of production. Recognizing revenue on a cash basis, either installment or cost recovery, is allowed if no reasonable basis exists for estimating collectibility.

Two additional bases for recognizing revenue have been suggested by many but are not permitted by authoritative literature. Some support recognizing revenue on an accretion basis where product marketability at known prices exists and it is desirable to recognize changes in assets, such as growing timber.[13] Regarding material resources, particularly natural gas and petroleum, many support a view of recognizing revenue on a discovery basis because of the significance of discovery on the earnings process.

Although the norm for revenue recognition is the point of sale, the primary criterion for revenue recognition applied in practice is the completion of the earnings process. In other words, revenue should be recognized when the transaction or event that culminates the earnings process has occurred. Measurement problems must be resolved, however, before revenue is recognized. Attributes that must be measurable are (a) sales price, (b) cash collections, and (c) future costs. If all three can be measured or estimated with reasonable accuracy, then revenue is recognized when the earning process is complete; otherwise, recognition must be delayed until reasonable measurements can be made.

Revenue recognition has been something of an Achilles' heel where attempts to manage earnings (see below) arise. For example, companies in the telecommunications industry, on occasion "swap" fiber optics capacity with other carriers. In this type of transaction, a company such as Qwest would book all of the "revenue" immediately whereas the fiber optic acquired was capitalized and is being expensed over several years.[14] Industry practice appears to be recognizing the revenues over time. Furthermore, this type of practice really appears to be a swap of assets with revenue generation being highly questionable.

Possible New Developments in Revenue Recognition

The FASB and International Accounting Standards Board (IASB) are involved in a long-range project involving revenue recognition.[15] The traditional rules of revenue recognition are income statement oriented although standard-setting emphasis, particularly with the passage of SFAS No. 157 on fair value measurements, has swung toward the balance sheet. Consequently, the FASB (and IASB) are at a very early stage of viewing revenue recognition in terms of changes in assets and liabilities.

Revenue recognition, as noted above, has long been cited as one of the principal problems in accounting.[16] Further evidence of the problem is found in some recent research done by Altamuro, Beatty, and Weber.[17] Altamuro et al. found a considerable number of violations of revenue recognition rules that they connected with earnings management. As a result of numerous violations of the revenue recognition process, the Securities and Exchange Commission (SEC) issued Staff Accounting Bulletin (SAB) 101, *Revenue Recognition,* which provides guidance to firms for applying our present revenue recognition rules.

Interestingly, the FASB has been critical of SAB 101, arguing that it provides too tight a rein on revenue recognition and results in making income statements less useful for predicting future cash flows. The FASB project that could change revenue recognition rules more toward balance sheet valuations and away from completion of the earnings process could have enormous repercussions, both theoretically and institutionally, with a possible showdown looming between the FASB and the SEC.

Expenses and Losses

Expenses have been defined in the following ways:

- Expense in the broadest sense includes all expired costs which are deductible from revenues. . . . [18]
- Expenses—gross decreases in assets or gross increases in liabilities recognized and measured in conformity with generally accepted accounting principles that result from those types of profit-directed activities of an enterprise. . . . [19]
- Expenses are outflows or other using up of assets or incurrences of liabilities (or a combination of both) during a period from delivering or producing goods, rendering services, or carrying out other activities that constitute the entity's major or central operations.[20]

The first definition, from Accounting Terminology Bulletin (ATB) 4, represents the traditional revenue–expense orientation. In the second definition, from APB Statement 4, a relationship is established between expense and net assets. However, measurement is still based on rules of the revenue–expense orientation. The third definition, from SFAC No. 6, represents a strong asset–liability approach. Again, the FASB may be looking forward in applying this definition. In practice, though, expense recognition continues to be guided by a strong revenue–expense orthodoxy in which expenses are "matched" to recognized revenues.

Losses are defined in APB Statement 4 and SFAC No. 6 in a parallel manner to gains. Losses represent a reduction in net assets, but not from expenses or capital transactions. As with gains, the distinction between expenses and losses is not important under the all-inclusive income concept. At one time, however, this was a major issue in accounting.

A good review of the matching-concept literature can be found in a 1964 American Accounting Association committee report.[21] A summary of current expense-recognition rules is found in APB Statement 4. Expenses are classified into three categories:[22]

1. Costs directly associated with the revenue of the period

2. Costs associated with the period on some basis other than a direct relationship with revenue

3. Costs that cannot, as a practical matter, be associated with any other period

A hierarchy exists and the matching concept is based on it. If possible, costs should be matched against the revenues directly produced. If a direct cause-and-effect relationship does not exist, costs should be matched to revenue in a rational and systematic manner. Finally, if there is not even an indirect cause-and-effect relationship, the costs are recognized as period expenses when incurred.

Typically, the third category is the only one that does not give accountants significant recognition problems. Costs incurred in the current period that provide no discernible future benefit as well as costs incurred in past periods that no longer provide discernible future benefits are expensed immediately. The relevant event generally is recognizable: no future benefit. For example, when a building is destroyed by fire, there is no future benefit; thus, an expense (loss) is recognized immediately.

The first and second categories do provide recognition problems. The first category is basically the application of the matching concept—that is, match costs against revenues that they helped to generate. Some items, such as direct material and labor are relatively clear. Others, however, such as overhead items, require allocation on some basis to the products manufactured. In the absence of a direct means of associating expenses with revenues (cause and effect), costs must be associated with accounting periods on the basis of a "systematic and rational allocation" (category two). The major expense-recognition problem, then, concerns those costs that are clearly not expired in the period incurred but are not associated with the revenues of a particular period.[23]

The standard of expense recognition through allocation does not provide guidance to the events that trigger accounting recognition as does the standard of revenue recognition. Revenue-recognition standards specify not only the amount of revenue to recognize (sales price) but also the period for which the revenue should be recognized (period of sale). Expense-recognition standards aid in determining the amount of expense to be allocated over future years, the cost to be amortized. Those standards, however, prescribe neither how the assets provide their benefit nor when the benefit is provided; thus, they give little practical guidance.

The need for systematic and rational cost allocation over multiple periods cannot be avoided in the existing accounting model. The model based on historical cost, unlike the one based on measuring current value, must allocate the costs incurred. Some examples of these costs include depreciation, organizational startup costs, goodwill amortization, bond premium/discount amortization, and the inventory method (FIFO, LIFO, etc.) used to allocate inventory costs to cost of goods sold. Most accountants share the view that the method of allocation used is nothing more than an arbitrary decision. After extensive study of the subject, Thomas concluded that selection of a particular allocation method over alternative methods is meaningless because the superiority of one allocation method over another can be neither verified nor refuted.[24] This means that there is no obviously correct way to allocate the costs because no single allocation method can be proved superior to another. For example, it cannot be logically demonstrated that straight-line depreciation is any more appropriate than accelerated depreciation methods or that FIFO is more appropriate than LIFO.

Another way of describing this dilemma is to say that no allocation is completely defensible against other methods. For this reason all accounting allocations are, in the end, arbitrary, which is a very disturbing idea that strikes at the logical core of historical cost accounting. Because of the arbitrariness of accounting allocations, allocation-free financial statements have been advocated as a better way of reporting useful information. Allocation-free accounting can be accomplished by using cash flow statements, exit-price systems, and certain types of replacement-cost systems (discussed in Appendix 1-A).

Although it is the case that allocations are arbitrary, income statements—which contain allocations—have information content. Capital market research, discussed in Chapter 8, provides strong evidence that this is the case. The usefulness of accounting information is an empirical issue that transcends the deductive logic of the allocation problem.

Nevertheless, the calculation aspect of most expense measurements is one that cannot be easily resolved under historical cost accounting. Perhaps rigid uniformity should be pursued in the absence of meaningful finite uniformity applications. The main point to remember, however, which was discussed in Chapter 8 and noted before, is that accounting income numbers—despite the presence of numerous allocations—have information content for external users.

Future Events and Accounting Recognition

As accounting concepts and definitions in the areas of both revenues and expenses have evolved, more attention has been paid to the nature and role of future events and the recognition process.[25] Our reporting process is grounded in recording events that have occurred, but these past events and their recording are very dependent upon our interpretation of future events either happening or not happening. Every accrual and deferral is to a greater or lesser extent dependent upon future events. For example, calculation of depreciation is dependent upon future events such as the estimated years of asset life and the expected salvage value of the asset. Indeed, recording the acquisition of the fixed asset strongly implies that the cost of the asset will be recovered from favorable future operations.

A good starting point for coming to grips with the future-events problem is to understand the nature of asset and liability definitions. In SFAC No. 6, the asset definition states that control over the asset derives from a past transaction or event that will result in future economic benefits. Similarly, the obligation from a liability stems from a past transaction that will require future sacrifice of cash or other assets. Asset and liability definitions are virtually balanced between past and future. The asset and liability definitions provided in the United Kingdom, Australia, and Canada and by the International Accounting Standards Board have a similar balance between past and future.

Some Aspects of Future Events

At the present time, our treatment of future events in asset, liability, expense, and revenue recognition has not been well systematized. National and international accounting standard-setting bodies began to examine the problem at a 1994 conference.

Perception of the Past Event

Occasionally, recognition of the past event is governed by whether a "one-event view" or a "two-event view" is held.[26] For example, assume that an employer makes an offer of incentives to employees to encourage early retirement. Single-event-view adherents would recognize a transaction occurring when the offer is made, whereas dual-event backers would not recognize the liability until employees actually accept the offer. The single-event partisans would be much more reliant on probabilistic estimates of the degree of acceptance of the offer. Dual-event recognition is both slower and less reliant on probabilistic estimates (even with the two-event view, estimates must still be made of the present value of the actual resources that will be expended). The one-event view and the two-event view are both consistent with the asset and liability views of SFAC No. 6.

Probabilistic Nature of Future Events

The probabilistic nature of future events is clearly the major problem underlying future events and their impact on event recognition. In most cases of asset recognition, it is assumed that cost will be, at the least, recovered from future operations. With liabilities, it is assumed that they will be paid when due. In the case of assets in which full cost recovery may not occur and in the case of contingent liabilities, questions of probability can be quite fuzzy. One example of this occurs in SFAS No. 5 relative to loss contingencies, which should be recognized when the loss becomes "probable" (over 50%?) as opposed to being merely "reasonably possible" or "remote."

The conference of standard-setting bodies mentioned previously also examined recognition using a modal concept (single-most-likely event to occur), a weighted probability approach (sum of the various outcomes multiplied by the expected probability of the event occurring), and a cumulative probability approach. The cumulative probability approach is an extension of the modal approach because it would combine all successful outcomes and compare their combined probabilities with unsuccessful outcomes, going with the combined outcomes that exceeded 50%. Obviously, the probability question is also closely related to measurement issues. If these problems could be solved, we would make enormous progress in the event recognition area.

Management Intent

The role of management intent as a basis of event recognition was rejected by conference participants.[27] Not only can management intent change, but its interpretation can be subject to agency theory considerations. If two firms own similar assets, both of which have values that are considerably less than their cost, the fact that one firm's management may intend to shortly get rid of the asset whereas the other firm's management does not (or at least says that it does not) should not lead to a different event recognition. Both firms should either write the asset down or not write it down until a specific event—the sale of the asset—occurs. Opening the door to managerial intent could result in lower comparability.

Market Values

Beaver has observed that market values are a rich repository of information about future events.[28] Security prices are often viewed as a market consensus of present values of expected future cash flows of securities. The problem is that many market prices may result from thinly traded securities or assets, leading to questions concerning representational faithfulness or verifiability of the resulting numbers.

Conservatism

Beaver made a very astute observation about conservatism. He stated that there may be a comparative advantage to reporting "bad news" (conservatism) through financial reporting as opposed to other sources for disseminating financial information.[29] There could, for example, be an overall favorable bias built into reports of financial analysts. Hence, accounting conservatism could be adding balance to the totality of financial information flowing to users. Examples of conservatism are, of course, legion and would include reporting inventories at lower-of-cost-or-market and the recognition of probable loss contingencies but not probable gain contingencies. Beaver also notes the great difficulty of building conservatism on a consistent basis across standards. While Beaver's analysis of conservatism is quite interesting, progress in solving the future-events problem could minimize the role of conservatism. On the other hand, it could increase the role of conservatism as a counterweight against the increased role of future events (see also the discussion of conservatism in Chapter 5).

Future Economic Conditions

Changes in future economic conditions can frequently increase or decrease the value of assets. If current conditions impair the value of an asset, the question arises as to whether conditions will improve, which would allow avoidance of an asset writedown. Clearly, no one can guarantee an economic prediction. As a result, the consensus of participants at the standard setters' conference was to avoid predicting changes in future economic conditions unless compelling evidence was present relative to future changes.

Future Legal Requirements

Like future economic conditions, participants in the standard-setters' conference were against predicting future legal changes unless these revisions have already been enacted. A good example of this arises in SFAS No. 109 on income tax allocation. Unless future tax rate changes have been enacted into law, future tax rates are assumed to be the same as current tax rates.

Summary of Future Events

We are only at the threshold of examining how to consistently treat the role of future events in accounting recognition. The problem is fraught with many measurement difficulties and will undoubtedly require a careful trade-off of qualitative characteristics such as relevance and reliability. The answers, as with so many other factors, may be largely qualitative in nature, which may add to the ever-burgeoning role of disclosure.

Current Operating Versus All-Inclusive Income

Until 1968, whether certain components of comprehensive income should be displayed in the income statement or the retained earnings statement was a controversial issue, especially with regard to the display of unusual (nonoperating) and infrequently occurring gains and losses. The current operating school of thought held that the income statement should contain only normal operating items and that nonoperating items should be reported in the retained earnings statement. The all-inclusive school of thought maintained that all components of comprehensive income should be in the income statement and that, as a corollary, the retained earnings statement should reflect only total earnings as reported in the income statement and dividend distributions, in addition to beginning and ending balances.

Current operating advocates contended that the income statement is more useful in assessing management's performance and predicting future years' performance if items extraneous to current management decisions are excluded. They believed that most financial statement users look only to bottom-line net income to assess current performance and to make predictions regarding subsequent years' performance. If material, extraneous, nonoperating, and infrequently occurring items are reported in the income statement, financial statement users would be seriously misled and might, as a result, make incorrect decisions.

Those favoring the all-inclusive concept cited several reasons for their position. First, current operating lends itself to easy manipulation by management because it makes the decision on whether or not an item is extraordinary. Second, financial statement users may be misled because they may not realize that substantial gains or losses have been "hidden" in the retained earnings statement. Third, the summation of all income displayed in the income statement for a period of years should reflect the reporting entity's net income for that period. Finally, they pointed out that proper classification within the income statement allows both normal recurring items and unusual, infrequently occurring items to be displayed separately within the same statement.

Historically, the American Accounting Association (AAA) favored the all-inclusive concept. In 1936, the AAA's *A Tentative Statement of Accounting Principles Underlying Corporate Financial Statements* contained the following statement: "The income statement for any given period should reflect all revenues properly given accounting recognition and all costs written off during the period, regardless of whether or not they are the results of operations in that period. . . ."[30]

Conversely, the AICPA consistently favored the current operating concept until APB Opinion No. 9. For example, in ARB 43, the Committee on Accounting Procedure indicated that all extraordinary items should be carried directly to the surplus account.[31] However, in December 1966, the APB leaned strongly toward the all-inclusive concept in APB Opinion No. 9, which as amended requires that all nonoperating, infrequently occurring items except for prior period adjustments be included in the computation of net income and reported separately on the income statement.[32]

There is empirical research to support the primacy of the current operating income concept. Gonedes, in a capital market study, found that the nonoperating income items had no information content, which suggests that the relevant information for stock valuation is captured by the operating income number.[33] Research on the smoothing of year-to-year income (reviewed later in the chapter) suggests that operating income is better predicted by operating rather than all-inclusive income, which is also supportive of the current operating income concept. However, a later stock market study found that some nonoperating income items were significantly associated with changes in security prices, although the effect was opposite of what was expected in that nonoperating items representing "bad news" were positively associated with stock prices.[34] One interpretation for these results is the so-called big bath theory. The idea here is that when firms come clean with bad news, there is a positive response by the market because the firm has finally recognized in the financial statements that a major problem exists and it is moving to redress the problem. For example, in 1987 Citicorp unexpectedly recognized an enormous $3 billion loss on its foreign loans. The day after the announcement, the firm's stock increased in value by about 5%.

Comprehensive Income

SFAC No. 5 (Chapter 7) proposed a statement of earnings and comprehensive income to cover all changes in equity except for investments by and distributions to owners.[35] Hence comprehensive income pushes the all-inclusive approach toward its logical conclusion. It also falls under the scope of proprietary theory because, in theory at least, all changes in equity (except for capital transactions with owners) enter into the calculation of comprehensive income, which affects the interests of owners.[36] Comprehensive income is also seen as highly appropriate for predictive purposes and equity valuation.[37]

Elements of Comprehensive Income

In addition to net income as presently defined, comprehensive income includes those elements of profit and loss that bypassed the income statement. These items, listed in SFAS No. 130, include foreign currency translation adjustments where the functional currency is not the U.S. dollar and unrealized holding gains and losses on available-for-sale securities.[38] In addition, minimum pension liability adjustments, which were classified as intangible assets, are now part of comprehensive income. The Board did not change the place or positioning in the income statement of discontinued operations, extraordinary items, and gains or losses arising from cumulative changes in accounting principle. While these items might be considered components of comprehensive income, it is likely that the FASB did not want to excessively disturb the existing order of the income statement. Nor did the Board change the place of prior period adjustments going directly to retained earnings. The rationale for keeping prior period adjustments in their place is that the retroactive restatement of income of prior years results in comprehensive income of prior affected periods being effectively restated.[39] The FASB also stated that earnings per share should not be calculated for comprehensive income.[40] Part of the reason for this lies in flexible reporting policies: If comprehensive income is shown within a statement of changes in equity, then earnings per share calculation would be inconsistent and confusing.[41] While the FASB's move into comprehensive income is appropriate and timely, it appears to be fairly cautious and is probably intended to be evolutionary in nature.

Reporting Comprehensive Income

SFAS No. 130 allows three methods of reporting comprehensive income: (1) in a combined statement of financial performance (income in which the comprehensive income elements and total would appear below net income), (2) in a separate statement of comprehensive income, which would begin with net income, and (3) reported within a statement of changes in equity.[42] However, the Board's preference is for method (a), the combined statement of financial performance.[43] Two members of the FASB dissented from SFAS No. 130. It was their belief that most firms would use approach (c), reporting comprehensive income within a statement of changes in equity.[44] This would result, in their belief, in a diminishment of importance and visibility of comprehensive income. Certainly this criticism has validity and is consistent with our observations. Three possible reporting formats with one quite likely blurring the presumed importance of comprehensive income is simply too much flexibility. Despite conservatism in what to display and flexibility in how to display it, SFAS No. 130 should have a net beneficial effect on income presentation.[45]

Nonoperating Sections

The nonoperating section of the income statement has expanded since APB Opinion No. 9 and now includes three subdivisions: (1) extraordinary items, (2) accounting principle changes, and (3) discontinued operations. Furthermore, a fourth item, prior-period adjustments, is reported in the retained earnings statement. This, of course, represents the continuing dilemma between the current operating versus all-inclusive concepts.

Extraordinary Items

How to report extraordinary items has been controversial for many years. The controversy is a good example of the shift away from finite uniformity to rigid uniformity in accounting standards. As we will see, this shift was necessitated because the concept of finite uniformity was thought to be abused in accounting practice; to circumvent that abuse, rigid uniformity became the rule.

The basis of the controversy is the impact that extraordinary items may have on financial statement users' perceptions of the results of operations and projections of future operations for the reporting entity. Evaluating the results of current and past operations and projecting future operations relies heavily on an ability to separate normal, recurring components of comprehensive income from those that are not recurring.

Prior to APB Opinion No. 9, the prevailing standard covering extraordinary items was Chapter 8 of ARB 43, which was a reprint of ARB 32, issued in 1947. The ARBs were vague, as the following quote illustrates:

> [There] should be a general presumption that all items of profit and loss recognized during the period are to be used in determining the figure reported as net income. The only possible exception to this presumption relates to items which in the aggregate are material in relation to the company's net income and are clearly not identifiable with or do not result from the usual or typical business operations of the period.[46]

With no more guidance than the above for the 19 years prior to APB Opinion No. 9, accounting practice for extraordinary items was not uniform. APB Opinion No. 9 attempted to bring order out of disarray. It required display of all extraordinary items in a specifically designated section of the income statement—as opposed to leaving the decision up to the reporting entity. Also it provided a new definition of *extraordinary items*: "Events and transactions of material effect which would not be expected to recur frequently and which would not be considered as recurring factors in any evaluation of the ordinary operating processes of the business."[47]

Unfortunately, the new definition still proved to be ambiguous. As a result, the APB restudied the problem in 1973 and issued APB Opinion No. 30. This opinion resorted to rigid uniformity and virtually eliminated the existence of extraordinary items because the definition of and criteria for an extraordinary item were so restrictive. In fact, the APB expressly stated that extraordinary items should occur in only rare situations.[48] For an item to qualify as extraordinary, it had to be both unusual in nature and infrequent in occurrence. The APB defined these terms as follows:

- *Unusual nature*—The underlying event or transaction should possess a high degree of abnormality and be of a type clearly unrelated to, or only incidentally related to, the ordinary and typical activities of the entity, taking into account the environment in which the entity operates.
- *Infrequency of occurrence*—The underlying event or transaction should be of a type that would not reasonably be expected to recur in the foreseeable future, taking into account the environment in which the entity operates.[49]

The environment in which the entity operates is often the controlling factor in applying the two criteria. For example, frost damage to a citrus grower's crop in north or central Florida would not qualify as extraordinary because frost damage there is normally experienced every three or four years. Conversely, similar damage to a citrus grower's crop in south Florida or Southern California probably would qualify as extraordinary because frost damage there is not experienced on a recurring basis. As a result of APB Opinion No. 30, extraordinary items, other than those specifically allowed (gains and losses from early extinguishment of debt, including gains by debtors from troubled debt restructurings), have practically disappeared from the scene.

An extraordinary item, should one occur, is displayed in the income statement in a specified section entitled extraordinary items. This section appears just above net income. All items are shown net of tax. Events or transactions that are unusual or infrequent but not both must be displayed with normal recurring revenues, costs, and expenses. If these items are not material in amount, they are not shown separately from other items. If they are material in amount, they are exhibited separately above the caption income (loss) before extraordinary items. They may not be displayed net of tax. However, normal disclosure practices include a footnote explanation of the item.

Accounting Changes

Changes in accounting methods employed by a reporting entity may affect significantly the financial statements of both the current reporting period and any trends reflected in comparative financial statements and historical summaries of the reporting entity. Accounting changes are classified in three broad categories:[50]

- *Change in accounting principle*—Results from adoption of a generally accepted accounting principle different from a generally accepted accounting principle previously used for reporting purposes. A characteristic of a change in accounting principle is that the change is from one generally accepted that *has been used previously* to another that is *also* generally accepted—for example, changing from straight-line depreciation to an accelerated-depreciation method, as discussed in APB Opinion No. 20.
- *Change in accounting estimate*—Results when a change in a previously estimated item occurs because, through the passage of time, more information for making the estimate is known—for example, the change in estimated life of a depreciable asset where previous depreciation was based on a 10-year life and after five years it is estimated the asset will be used only an additional two years.
- *Change in reporting entity*—Results when there has been a material change in the reporting entity since the last financial statements were compiled—for example, when the specific group of subsidiaries comprising the reporting entity is significantly different from the specific group reported in the previous reporting period.

Prior to APB Opinion No. 20, there was no comprehensive, consistent standard dealing with accounting changes. That document established standards to be followed for accounting changes.

SFAS No. 154 replaced APB Opinion No. 20 and SFAS No. 3 (relative to presentation of accounting changes on interim financial statements). Instead of including the cumulative effect of the change in accounting principle just below extraordinary items in the current income statement, as done under APB Opinion No. 20, SFAS No. 154 requires retrospective changes in all affected income statements unless it is impractical to carry out.[51] Balance sheet accounts will be adjusted to reflect the cumulative effect of the change in accounting principle as of the beginning of the first period presented. The retrospective changes do not apply to accounts that would have been affected by the change in accounting principle except for income taxes. As with APB Opinion No. 20, the reason underlying the change must be disclosed in the footnotes.

In the event that it is impractical to carry out the desired treatment for changes in accounting principle, the changes are carried back into the balance sheet accounts—assets, liabilities, and owners' equity—of the earliest date at which retrospective application is applicable.[52]

A change in accounting estimate is not reported separately, as is a change in accounting principle. Effects of the change are accounted for in the period of change if that is the only period affected, or in the period of change and future periods if the change affects both on a prospective basis. For example, assume a 10-year life has been used to depreciate an asset, and in the sixth year the life is adjusted to eight years. Depreciation expense for the sixth through eighth years is simply the underappreciated cost at the beginning of the sixth year spread over the remaining three years. In essence, an overstatement of depreciation for the last three years will offset the understatement of the first five years.[53] A major change brought about by SFAS No. 154 affects depreciation, depletion, and amortization where a change in principle arises, such as a change from straight-line depreciation to sum-of-the-years-digits depreciation. These changes are now to be handled on a prospective basis as a change in estimate.[54] This now makes them, in effect, a change in accounting principle handled as if it were a change in estimate.

For a change in reporting entity, APB Opinion No. 20 requires that financial statements of all prior periods be restated to show financial information as if the new reporting entity had existed for all periods. Financial statements of the period of change should describe the nature of and reasons for the change. Furthermore, the effect of the change on income before extraordinary items, net income, and corresponding per share amounts is disclosed for all periods.[55]

The FASB increasingly appears to favor retroactive restatement for accounting principle changes it promulgates in new SFASs. In a majority of its major SFASs, the FASB has either required or encouraged retroactive restatement for a change in accounting principle rather than the method of accounting required by APB Opinion No. 20.

The main reason underlying SFAS No. 154 is that it is part of the convergence project with the International Accounting Standards Board (IASB). SFAS No. 154 is closer to IAS No. 8 than was its predecessor, APB Opinion No. 20. Whether SFAS No. 154 is really preferable, on its own account, to APB Opinion No. 20 is questionable. Whether a "restatement" is, like Coca-Cola, the "real thing" in relation to pro forma presentations under APB Opinion No. 20 is questionable. This is particularly the case since indirectly affected accounts, except for income taxes, are not restated as they were under the pro forma presentations.

Prior Period Adjustments

SFAS No. 154 did not make any major changes to either APB Opinion No. 20 or SFAS No. 16 for prior period adjustments. Accounting for (and the display of) prior period adjustments is quite straightforward. The amount of prior period adjustments is charged or credited to the beginning retained earnings balance. They are exhibited net of tax in the retained earnings statement and are thereby excluded from the determination of net income for the current period.

APB Opinion No. 9 was the first to deal with prior period adjustments and was fairly restrictive. To be classified as a prior period adjustment under APB Opinion No. 9, an event or transaction had to be (a) identified specifically with particular prior periods, not attributable to economic events occurring subsequent to the prior period, (b) primarily determined by persons other than management, and (c) not susceptible to estimation prior to determination.[56]

The criteria were thus quite definitive. However, the Securities and Exchange Commission (SEC) staff increasingly began to question the application of APB Opinion No. 9. In SEC staff administrative interpretations of APB Opinion No. 9 and later in Staff Accounting Bulletin No. 8, it excluded charges or credits resulting from litigation from being treated as prior period adjustments, even though this item was illustrated in APB Opinion No. 9 as a specific example of a prior period adjustment. As a result of this and other problems, the FASB reconsidered the concept of prior period adjustments. SFAS No. 16 is the result of the FASB's reconsideration. It limits prior period adjustments to the following:

- Correction of an error in the financial statements of a prior period
- Adjustments that result from realization of income tax benefits of preacquisition operating loss carryforwards of purchased subsidiaries[57]

SFAS No. 16 does not affect the manner of reporting certain accounting changes that are treated, for accounting purposes, like prior period adjustments. This treatment is required for a few specified changes in accounting principle, including changes from LIFO to another inventory method, changes in accounting for long-term construction contracts, and changes to or from the full-cost method used in the oil and gas industry. As mentioned earlier, frequently the FASB requires or permits changes in accounting principle that result from adoption of a new SFAS to be treated like prior period adjustments. Examples of these include SFAS No. 2, research and development cost; SFAS No. 4, early extinguishment of debt; SFAS Nos. 5 and 11, contingencies; SFAS No. 7, development stage enterprises; SFAS No. 12, marketable securities; SFAS No. 19, oil and gas; SFAS No. 35, reporting by defined benefit pension plans; SFAS No. 43, compensated absences; SFAS No. 45, franchise fee revenue; SFAS No. 48, revenue recognition when right of return exists; SFAS No. 50, records and music; SFAS No. 52, foreign currency; SFAS No. 53, motion pictures; SFAS No. 60, insurance; SFAS No. 61, title plant; SFAS No. 63, broadcasters; and SFAS No. 65, mortgage banking activities.

Earnings per Share

The term *summary indicator* was coined by the FASB in its 1979 discussion memorandum entitled *Reporting Earnings*.[58] When information is summarized in such a way that a single item can communicate considerable information about an enterprise's performance or financial position, that item is a summary indicator. Examples of summary indicators include earnings per share (EPS), return on investment, and the debt-to-equity ratio. The most used summary indicator to date, and the one that has received the most attention from accounting policymaking bodies, is undoubtedly EPS.

Reporting EPS has been commonplace for many years. However, the decision to report it, the manner in which it was calculated, and where it was reported were entirely at management's discretion prior to APB Opinion No. 9. This opinion strongly recommended, but did not require, that EPS be calculated and reported in the income statement. It also suggested how hybrid securities, such as convertible debentures, should be handled in the calculation. However, without specific rules, EPS calculations can be manipulated and thus mislead users. Because of the potential for manipulation and the apparent reliance on reported EPS, the APB restudied the subject and, in 1969, issued APB Opinion No. 15.

APB Opinion No. 15, as amended, was a set of rigid rules that accountants had to follow to calculate and report EPS. Those rules were designed to result in an EPS number that reflected the underlying economic substance of the capital structure of the reporting enterprise rather than its legal form. The calculations were complex and necessitated the APB's publishing of an interpretative, 116-page booklet. Subsequently, the FASB, in SFAS No. 21, suspended APB Opinion No. 15 for nonpublic enterprises.

SFAS No. 128

The FASB issued a prospectus in 1993 on EPS. Three principal reasons underlay the FASB's desire to evaluate APB Opinion No. 15: (1) increasing comparability with other nations in the EPS area, (2) simplifying the computational aspects of EPS, and (3) revising disclosure requirements.[59] The FASB and the IASB cooperated on this project together.

The principal change from APB Opinion No. 15 to the new standard, SFAS No. 128, was the elimination of the computation of *primary earnings per share* (PEPS). This category, which might be called "partially diluted earnings per share," was both difficult to calculate and difficult for users to understand. PEPS included convertible preferred stock and convertible bonds in the denominator calculation of shares outstanding if at date of issue the effective interest rate was equal to or less than two-thirds of the Aa bond rate. The supposition was that the effective interest rate on these securities was so low that conversion was imminent. The date of the comparison of interest rates remained as of the date of issuance of the convertible shares, which ignored changing interest rate conditions.

The main change brought about by SFAS No. 128 was simply to eliminate the PEPS category. Now required are basic EPS where no dilution is present and diluted EPS where dilution is at its greatest. Users can thus comprehend the effect on EPS of the full amount of dilution without the presence of the artificial and confusing PEPS calculation.[60] Elimination of PEPS also brought the United States into alignment with virtually all other nations in terms of EPS requirements.

Another change from APB Opinion No. 15 is that the 3% rule has been eliminated. That rule stated that if fully diluted earnings per share had a 3% or less decline from "simple" EPS where no dilution was present, then only simple EPS had to be published. Under SFAS No. 128 both basic and diluted EPS must be exhibited.[61] This not only accords with how other nations generally require EPS calculations but also enables the user to assess the full effect of dilution on EPS.

EPS calculations have to be shown right on the income statement itself for both basic and diluted EPS (for both income before discontinued operations and extraordinary items as well as for the "bottom line" net income itself but not comprehensive income). SFAS No. 128 also requires a reconciliation of both the numerators and denominators between basic and diluted EPS.[62]

SFAS No. 128 is a distinct improvement over APB Opinion No. 15. The elimination of PEPS is definitely a case of less information leading to more usefulness.

Specialized Subjects Concerning Income Measurement

Several specialized topics provide important examples of the evolution and development of a consensus in accounting standards. As will be seen, this evolutionary process frequently takes several years and may have a significant impact on reported earnings. Moreover, these examples will reflect how the lack of a consistent accounting theory framework hinders the establishment of accounting standards.

Development Stage Enterprises

A development stage enterprise is any enterprise that "is devoting substantially all of its efforts to establishing a new business" and either has not commenced principal operations or, if principal operations have commenced, has generated no significant revenues as yet.[63] A theoretical question exists as to whether certain costs incurred in the development stage should be expensed or deferred.

There is some theoretical justification for deferring costs and operating losses incurred in the development stage because these costs (a) have not generated revenue and (b) provide a future benefit such as the very existence of the enterprise and its ability to operate. Costs incurred in the development stage typically will be in connection with financial planning, exploring for natural resources, developing products and channels of distribution, and establishing sources of supply for raw material. Prior to January 1, 1976, costs of this nature generally were deferred by enterprises in the development stage, while operating enterprises expensed most of these costs. Thus, a dual set of accounting standards existed—one for development stage enterprises and another for operating enterprises— even though there is no relevant circumstance separating the two (the future benefit idea is much too tenuous). SFAS No. 7 requires that costs of a similar nature be accounted for similarly, regardless of the stage of development of the entity incurring the cost. In other words, the FASB said the nature of the cost, not the nature of the enterprise, determines the appropriate accounting.

Costs incurred by development stage enterprises provide an interesting example of a setting in which multiple accounting theories, although all perhaps equally supportable, can lead to different answers. The FASB certainly made a wise choice in terms of the issue here particularly because it (a) required complete disclosure by the development stage enterprise to avoid misleading financial statement users by heavy initial losses, while at the same time it (b) achieved uniformity on the basis of the nature of the transaction or event that has occurred rather than the nature of the enterprise experiencing the transaction or event. It is interesting to note, however, that this problem is yet another allocation problem. The FASB obviously opted for rigid uniformity in selecting a solution as opposed to finite uniformity, where a relevant circumstance might be viewed as the development stage of the enterprise. However, this would be a broad interpretation of the notion of relevant circumstances.

Troubled Debt Restructuring

A troubled debt restructuring occurs whenever "the creditor for economic or legal reasons related to the debtor's financial difficulties grants a concession to the debtor that it would not otherwise consider."[64] SFAS No. 15, on troubled debt restructuring, was a triumph of economic consequences over representational faithfulness. The calculation of the impact (gain or loss) was measured by both the debtor and creditor as the difference between the carrying amount of the obligation immediately prior to restructuring and the undiscounted total future cash flows after restructuring. Since APB Opinion No. 21 required discounting, the concept of present value is commonly accepted and used in accounting. However, it did not apply to the restructuring of debt.

When terms of the debt were modified, but it continued as an obligation (such as a reduction in interest rate, extension of maturity date, reduction in face amount, or similar modifications), the FASB concluded that no transaction or event occurred as long as the total undiscounted future cash flows are equal to or greater than the carrying amount of the obligation. Thus, in this situation no gain or loss was recorded by either party. If total undiscounted future cash flow were less than the carrying amount of the debt, the obligation would be reduced to the cash flow amount. The creditor recorded a loss for the reduction (not extraordinary), while the debtor recorded an extraordinary gain for the reduction.

SFAS No. 114 has changed the rules for the creditor in the case of a modification of terms. The restructured cash flows are now discounted by the original effective interest rate at the inception of the transaction. Any reduction in the carrying value of the loan would be written off as additional bad debt expense. The change in present value of the expected future cash flows of the instrument would then have been recognized as either interest income or reduction of bad debt expense.[65]

There are two major problems with SFAS No. 114. The conception of the restructuring appears to be that the original transaction is still in effect when clearly it is not. The discount rate applicable to the newly restructured cash flows should be the new market-determined rate—not the historical—rate of interest. As a result, two FASB members voted against passage of SFAS No. 114 for this very reason. They believed that the newly restructured cash flows should be discounted by the current market interest rate rather than the inapplicable historical rate.

The second major problem is that SFAS No. 114 is applicable only to creditors. Debtors are still governed by SFAS No. 15, and therefore they do not discount the restructured cash flows. Consequently, they will not recognize a gain if the undiscounted cash flows exceed the carrying value of the original debt. As with SFAS No. 15, they find the effective interest rate that equates the newly restructured cash flows with the existing carrying value of the debt. Thus, the accounting for debtors and creditors relative to modification of terms is totally asymmetrical; one discounts and generally takes a loss whereas the other does not discount and does not reflect a gain (unless the undiscounted, newly restructured cash flows are *less* than the carrying value of the debt prior to restructuring). Clearly there is a lot of unfinished business with troubled debt restructurings. Evolution can be a slow and painful process.

Early Extinguishment of Debt

The early extinguishment of debt provides an interesting example of changing standards and their effect on the income statement. Prior to APB Opinion No. 26, there were three acceptable methods of accounting for the gain or loss on early extinguishment: (1) amortize over the remaining life of the original issue, (2) amortize over the life of a new issue, or (3) recognize currently on the income statement. The APB opted for the third alternative and stated that criteria of APB Opinion No. 9 apply in determining whether the gain or loss is extraordinary.

The consensus of the accounting profession was that the gain or loss met the extraordinary classification requirements. Nine months after APB Opinion No. 26, APB Opinion No. 30 was issued. This opinion altered the criteria for extraordinary status established in APB Opinion No. 9. Under APB Opinion No. 30, the gain or loss from early extinguishment of debt definitely was not considered extraordinary. Thus, in the short period of nine months an item that typically was not given immediate income statement recognition became a mandatory extraordinary item and then a mandatory operating item. The amount involved is frequently very significant in relation to comprehensive income for a given period.

Finally the FASB settled the issue. In SFAS No. 4, it declared that gains and losses from the early extinguishment of debt, if material, are reported like, and along with, extraordinary items net of the applicable tax effects. Reporting of a gain or loss from early extinguishment of debt provides a good example of where the standard-setting agency gave in to its constituency on a single-line financial statement item but did not change the overall standard (of what qualifies as extraordinary). Obviously, the reason for the concession is the magnitude of the numbers involved.

Stock Options

Stock options are a management compensation tool that have received an inordinate amount of media attention. By providing compensation to management in the form of rights to buy stock—provided the share price exceeds the strike (exercise) price after a holding period of usually three to five years—stock options were seen as a tool for aligning management interests with general shareholder interests. This, of course, is an application of agency theory (Chapters 2 and 4) to an actual industry setting.

In practice, stock options have become a very destabilizing instrument. Problems arise because, in many cases, options are extremely large and they can be exercised in a relatively short period of time without any requirement that the newly acquired shares must be held for any period of time after acquisition. As a result, managers frequently attempt to influence share prices by means of income manipulation (a worst case scenario would be WorldCom's capitalization of ordinary expenses to the tune of at least $7 billion). Hence, stock options have frequently led to dysfunctional management behavior rather than the original goal of aligning management and shareholder interests.

Furthermore, the question of whether stock options are an expense led to a bruising battle between FASB and preparers. The latter, led largely by emerging high-tech firms, did not want stock options recorded as an expense because it would lower income—often making it negative—and thus raise the cost of capital. The FASB wanted stock options recorded as expenses, hence the stock options fight largely boiled down to a question of economic consequences (Chapter 4). The FASB was forced to retreat, but it did pass SFAS No. 123 requiring footnote disclosure of stock options expense. Therefore, the key question that we examine next is whether stock options are an expense and, if so, how to show them on the income statement.

At present, stock options are viewed from the perspective of finite uniformity.[66] Nonqualified stock options where market price exceeds the strike price are treated as an expense equal to the difference between market value and strike price times the number of shares at the measurement date (see below). However, if strike price equals or exceeds market price at measurement date, no expense is presently recorded.

The difference and relationship between market price and strike price at measurement date is seen to be a present magnitude–type relevant circumstance (Chapter 9). We do not believe that this is a viable distinction. After all, when exercised, both types of options will have market values in excess of strike prices, and even the degree of difference is not necessarily a function of the type of option granted. Nor do we accept the argument that the stock option is a nonreciprocal equity transaction (Chapter 7), on the assumption that the firm is not giving up anything at the present time and therefore has no obligation.[67] To the contrary, the recipient receives a potentially valuable option and has given up cash consideration to obtain the option. This means that the firm, of necessity, has given up something of value.

In the following sections, we discuss nonqualified stock options and incentive stock options, and finally we attempt to reconcile the problem by means of the equity theories discussed in Chapter 5.

Nonqualified Stock Options

Employee stock ownership plans (ESOPs) are considered a form of deferred compensation to employees if there is a bargain purchase price established in the plan. If a bargain purchase does exist, the accounting recognition and measurement focus on the value of the bargain purchase option. The value represents additional compensation, and a corresponding amount is credited to other contributed capital. Employee services are deemed to be exchanged for the right to buy stock below market price. Measurement at four different points in time has been discussed in the literature. The four dates are the grant date, receipt date by the employee, first exercisable date, and actual exercise date. The actual value to the employee is known with certainty only on the exercise date. If measurement occurs any earlier, it must be based on the estimated value of the option to the employee.

APB Opinion No. 25 requires the bargain amount of stock options, known as nonqualified stock options, to be allocated as a periodic expense from the grant date through the period of service required to receive the benefits. The bargain amount is measured by the difference between market price and the stock option exercise price on the measurement date with the former being greater. The measurement date is defined as the point in time when both the number of options and exercise price are known. Usually the grant date and measurement date are one and the same, in which case the measurement is straightforward. A deferred compensation expense account is debited and contributed capital is credited for the total bargain purchase. The deferred compensation expense is amortized over the number of periods required to exercise the options. The debit is an owner's equity contra account.

If either the number of shares or exercise price is unknown at grant date, a yearly estimate must be made of both. In such a situation, it is also necessary to estimate the market price of the stock at the future measurement date. Having made these necessary estimates, one must make a yearly accrual of the estimated additional compensation expense arising from the options. This results in a debit to expense and a credit to contributed capital, just for an estimate of the current period cost.[68] The entire bargain purchase is not recognized because it is not yet determinable. However, an estimate is made of the bargain purchase and the pro rata effect on yearly compensation expense. At the measurement date (the point when both number of shares and exercise price is known), the actual compensation cost is measured by subtracting the option price from the market price on that date. The actual bargain value of the ESOP at the measurement date, less previous yearly expense recognition based on estimates, is debited to deferred compensation expense and amortized over the remaining service period required to exercise the options. A corresponding amount is credited to contributed capital. This procedure represents a change in accounting estimate, and any adjustment is made prospectively as required under APB Opinion No. 20.

Contributed capital is credited for the bargain purchase element in an ESOP. The rationale for this policy is that employee services are being exchanged for the opportunity to buy stock below market price. This amount is considered to be part of the consideration given by these shareholders for the right to buy stock under an ESOP.

Incentive Stock Options

In 1986, the FASB announced its intention to review accounting for ESOPs. The underlying rationale of the FASB's exploration has been to extend expense recognition to incentive stock option plans. In incentive stock options, market price equals or exceeds the exercise price at date of grant; hence, no expense is calculated under APB Opinion No. 25. The FASB's underlying reasoning was that an incentive stock option plan, like a nonqualified stock option plan, is a form of compensation; therefore, expense should be recognized.[69]

In June 1993, the FASB issued an exposure draft. Since the option has value to the employee, an asset was to be recognized on the measurement date, which would continue to extend from the grant date to the exercise date.

One of the key issues in this exposure draft concerns how to measure the asset value at the date of grant. The exposure draft relied on the Black-Scholes option pricing model, although more recently developed binomial models were also allowed.[70] Extensive criticism was raised relative to the representational faithfulness and also the comparability of these models for valuing employee stock options, as well as questions of verifiability of the resulting measurements.[71] Without doubt, however, the biggest controversy concerned the perceived economic consequences of the prospective standard. Many financial executives believed that the expense treatment of all stock options would significantly cut down on their use, making it difficult to attract high-quality executive talent, particularly in newly developing high-technology industries. In addition, it was also believed that the new treatment would raise the cost of capital.[72] After a stormy year and a half of debate and argument, the Board withdrew the exposure draft in December 1994 by a five-to-two vote.

The FASB, however, licked its wounds and decided to push for footnote disclosure of what the effect of stock options would have been on income and earnings per share. This was accomplished in SFAS No. 123, which is largely similar to the withdrawn exposure draft. For the time being, at least the FASB appeared to be resigned to the footnote disclosure resolution of the problem, although recognition in the income statement is encouraged.

However, the FASB pushed on and finally, in 2004, issued SFAS No. 123R, which required the recording of expense for incentive stock options.[73] The FASB deserves a lot of credit for finally passing a standard that many segments of business fought against passionately, if not bitterly.

The measurement date for determining the value of the stock option is usually the grant date. The value of the stock option is determined by using models such as the Black-Scholes option pricing models or lattice-type models. The inputs to these models include: the stock price, strike price, volatility (standard deviation of rate of return), time to expiration, and risk-free rate of interest. Note that the volatility has to be estimated, raising issues of reliability of the measurement. The service period, over which the options will be expensed, runs from the grant date till the date that the option(s) can be exercised. Straight-line amortization of the value of stock options is to be used. Compensation expense is debited, and stock options, a contributed capital item on the balance sheet, is credited. A liability can be credited if the employee is to receive mandatorily redeemable shares (para. 32). When stock options are exercised, stock option warrants are closed out to capital stock and paid in capital accounts.

SFAS 123R is also part of the convergence project with the International Accounting Standards Board (IASB). SFAS 123R and IFRS 2 are very close to each other since both use similar fair value methods to determine share-based expense methods.

Backdating Stock Options

Another problem in the stock options area receiving enormous attention recently involves backdating stock options. This practice involves backdating stock options to the point in the year when stock prices of the firm are at a low or lowest point for the year, increasing employees' profit when the shares are exercised. The backdating itself may not be illegal; however, the lack of appropriate disclosure *is* because it violates SEC rules. The backdating problem has affected approximately 130 firms as of the beginning of 2007. Suffice it to say that the practice—which violates the intent underlying stock options to provide performance-based compensation—could be an illegal conversion of shareholders' assets to members of management.[74]

Stock Options and Equity Theories

A key to understanding whether stock options are an expense is to note how they relate to the entity and proprietary theories (Chapter 5). Unquestionably, stock options are compensation to employees. However, under entity theory, dividends and interest are distributions to capital providers. The same treatment should apply to stock options since the recipients are, by definition, among the firm's owners. The only cost to the firm is an opportunity cost equal to the difference between the market value per share and the strike price per share times the number of shares exercised during the period. At present, however, since we are still largely under the historical cost approach, opportunity costs are not generally viewed as expenses.

The situation is different under the proprietary theory. Stock options represent a very real cost to outside shareholders because the value of their shares is diluted owing to the option price being less than market value.

Consequently, we recommend that the income statement be reformatted. The present "bottom line" would be maintained with one exception: Interest expense should not be deducted to calculate net income. The result from this change would be entity income (income to the firm itself). From entity income, deduct interest costs and stock option costs (however measured) to arrive at proprietary income. Users would benefit from seeing both entity and proprietary theory income numbers. This new approach highlights the difference between income to the firm and income to the shareholder; it should not be difficult to educate users on what the two incomes mean.

An additional benefit to separating entity and proprietary income would be improved articulation between the income statement and the statement of cash flows. In the statement of cash flows (Chapter 13), interest expense would be shown in its rightful place as a financing activity rather than as an item of cash flow from operations as is presently the case under a purely proprietary approach. The present misplacement of interest expense is intended to make cash flows from operating activities articulate with the income statement.

If the verifiability problem of measuring stock option costs can be overcome, we believe the approach recommended here can be quite beneficial. Many companies, even prior to SFAS No. 123R, had been expensing stock options (e.g., Coca-Cola, Computer Associates International, Cendant, Amazon.com). A minor measurement problem involves whether nonqualified and incentive stock options should be measured using the Black-Scholes (or a similar) option model or whether nonqualified options should still be measured according to APB Opinion No. 25.

Earnings Management

Earnings management has been defined by Schipper as "purposeful intervention in the external financial reporting process, with the intent of obtaining some private gain (as opposed to, say, merely facilitating the neutral operation of the process)."[75] Agency theory studies frequently fall under the category of earnings management since a firm's management may attempt to influence earnings to (a) maximize its compensation, (b) avoid the breaching of debt covenants of bond liabilities, which would prevent payment of dividends, and (c) minimize reported income to lessen the possibility of governmental interference if the enterprise has high political visibility.

Another important example of earnings management involves attempts to meet or beat financial analysts' quarterly earnings predictions. Recent studies have shown a very large number of examples of quarterly income announcements just beating analyst forecasts and a relatively small number of cases in which quarterly earnings announcements just fell short of analyst predictions.[76] Still within the income statement, McVay has uncovered a subtle form of earnings management.[77] She has found what she refers to as *classification shifting*, whereby components of core earnings costs (cost of goods sold and general, selling, and administrative expenses) are shifted to a lower segment of the income statement, thus improving gross profit margins with total income remaining the same. An anecdotal example of this involved Borden Incorporated's 1992 SEC filings: The SEC determined that $192 million of marketing expenses showed up on the income statement as a restructuring charge.[78] By reclassification within the income statement, classification shifting avoids the difficult problem of shifting dollars between years.[79]

McVay's model uses a statistical approach whereby actual core earnings exceed predicted core earnings and special expense items likewise increase owing to the downward shifting of core expenses. For her study she used 76,901 firm-year observations extending from 1989 to 2003.[80] She estimates that 2.2% of reported special items are, in reality, current period operating expenses.[81]

The accounting literature has many examples of purported earnings management for a variety of reasons. In mergers where stock is exchanged between enterprises, Erickson and Wang find evidence that acquiring firms attempt to increase income prior to the acquisition in the hope that higher income will raise the acquiring firm's stock price thus lowering the number of shares needed for the acquisition (the share exchange ratio is based on the prices of the two securities).[82] In a similar vein (but going in the opposite direction), Wu found evidence that earnings were manipulated downward just prior to leveraged management buyouts.[83] However, Wu's study contradicted previous work by DeAngelo, who did not find understatement of earnings by means of accrual manipulations, possibly because of potential intense scrutiny of management prior to buyouts and the severe penalties that could result.[84] In addition, some evidence has been found of firms lowering income in situations in which import protection is being sought through means such as tariffs, quotas, and marketing agreements.[85]

Kasznik has found evidence that firms that provide voluntary earnings forecasts tend to increase earnings by decreasing discretionary accruals (see following) if earnings forecasts are overestimated.[86] However, he did not find evidence that actual earnings are decreased if earnings forecasts are underestimated. If these and other earnings management effects are present, the management of earnings constitutes inside information because the market would not be aware of the manipulation. However, researchers concede that whether earnings have been managed is difficult to detect.[87] Nevertheless, earnings management is seen as a very serious problem by the SEC.[88]

In a very interesting study of earnings management, Nelson, Elliott, and Tarpley questioned auditors in a then Big Five firm about recalled perceived attempts to manage earnings.[89] The most frequently recalled attempts occur when standards are imprecise or nonexistent, requiring judgment by the auditor. These would include reserves such as bad debts and warranties and restructuring charges where rates are changed or reversals occur.

Where "precise standards" exist and earnings management occurs, transactions are frequently "structured." For example, a lease might be set up to cover just under 75% of the estimated economic life (assuming no other capitalization criteria applies).[90]

Perhaps the most common earnings management situations involve management compensation and income smoothing. Unfortunately, earnings management for compensation purposes often overlaps with income smoothing, so these two topics cannot be easily separated. We commence with the management compensation problem.

Management Compensation

Management compensation contracts attempt to align management behavior with the interests of shareholders because the interests of these two groups can conflict. Compensation contracts of management can be quite complex. In addition to cash compensation, they often include bonus incentives based on income and/or share price and longer term incentives often utilizing stock option plans. For bonuses, earnings are generally more important than security prices.

Bonus plans that are based on earnings often have a top or ceiling and a floor or bogey. Between the ceiling and the floor, the bonus is often a percentage of income. At the ceiling, the bonus is maximized, and below the floor there is no bonus. Healy, in an often cited study, found that above the ceiling and below the floor, income was deferred until the following periods.[91] In particular, the timing of transactions, especially year-end accruals, can be used to shift income from one period to the next. Holthausen, Larcker, and Sloan largely agreed with Healy except that they did not find income-decreasing tactics being used when firms were below the floor.[92] Another study, by Gaver, Gaver, and Austin, was also largely in agreement with Healy except that they found the presence of earnings-increasing discretionary accruals when firms were below the floor.[93]

Income might be managed by manipulating discretionary accruals. *Discretionary accruals* are accruals that management would have the ability to control in the short run. These include changing bad debt expense percentages, increasing production to inventory fixed manufacturing overhead (which involves real costs of carrying inventories), and changing estimates of warranty expense. Discretionary accruals are somewhat limited and they are also difficult to estimate and differentiate from nondiscretionary accruals: accruals not easy to change in the short run. A group of costs that are not discretionary accruals are expenses where control can be changed somewhat in the short run. These include advertising and research and development costs. Unlike discretionary accruals, these costs are performance oriented: Real factors are involved rather than simply allocations between periods. It is quite likely that the distinction between these two types of costs cannot easily be made in accounting research.[94] Earnings management for compensation purposes cannot be easily distinguished from income smoothing, a topic to which we next turn.

Income Smoothing

Given the importance of reported accounting income, one hypothesis has been that managers seek to smooth income over time so that a more stable earnings stream with less year-to-year variance would lead to higher firm valuation. In some ways, this argument suggests a naive stock market that cannot unravel accounting data correctly. Income smoothing diminishes unsystematic risk that a diversified portfolio can also eliminate (Chapter 8). However, Ronen and Sadan suggest alternatively that managers smooth income to facilitate better predictions (by outsiders) of future cash flows on which firm value is based.[95]

There are three ways that smoothing can be achieved:

1. Timing of transactions
2. Choice of allocation methods/procedures
3. Classificatory smoothing between operating and nonoperating income

The timing of transactions is a managerial choice rather than an accounting choice, but it is probably the most direct and influential method of manipulating accounting income. Accounting research has focused mainly on the other two approaches. Smoothing can be achieved through the choice of accounting allocation methods and, prior to APB Opinion No. 30, through the classification of income as operating/nonoperating (it is assumed that the desire is to smooth operating income). After APB Opinion No. 30, little discretion existed in classifying operating and nonoperating income. Several empirical studies have supported the hypothesis that income smoothing is achieved through both accounting method choice (allocations) and classifications. This latter finding may help to explain why the APB elected to use rigid uniformity in APB Opinion No. 30 concerning nonoperating items rather than the finite uniformity approach used in APB Opinion No. 9.

Chaney and Jeter find that income-smoothing firms tend to be larger than nonsmoothing enterprises. They have higher stock market returns and larger absolute discretionary accruals.[96] Firms in the lowest industry deciles, Chaney and Jeter find, are least likely to smooth. Other researchers have also found smoothing-type behavior. DeFond and Park, for example, found that where current earnings are poor, the tendency was to "borrow" from the future by adjusting accruals.[97] They also found the converse occurring: If current earnings are good and future prospects are poor, current earnings are "saved" for the future. Yet questions exist about the income-smoothing literature.

Although empirical tests have confirmed income-smoothing behavior, there are several problems with this body of research.[98] First, the underlying theory or motivation for smoothing is not specified clearly enough to make strong predictions as to what smoothed income would look like. Thus, the approach has been to use fairly simple time-series models of income trends, but this could misspecify the smoothed income series and produce misleading results. Second, we cannot readily determine what the unsmoothed income series looks like since the firm's entire set of accounting methods, as well as transaction timing, produces the aggregate income results. If we cannot calculate unsmoothed income, it is not easy to determine how, if at all, income has been smoothed. Third, there may be a built-in bias that overstates income smoothing owing to inflation. That is, there is likely to be an upward year-to-year drift in the income series due solely to general inflationary effects. So, in light of these possible problems, the evidence in support of widespread income-smoothing practices is less convincing than it appears to be at first glance.

More general studies of the time-series properties of accounting income numbers indicate that the series are best described as a random walk with slight upward drift.[99] This means that although there is a slight upward trend from year to year, the best prediction of current-period income is last-period income. These more general time-series studies are not supportive of the smoothing hypothesis. If smoothing were occurring, the trend-line effect should dominate and random-walk prediction models would be inferior to moving-average time-series models in explaining accounting income series.

Income Statement Developments

While it hardly appears that the area of income measurement and determination is undergoing a ferment, there are some interesting developments that merit attention. We examine several of them in this section.

Cash Earnings

Howell has suggested a "cash earnings" operating statement to replace the income statement.[100] Operating income would consist of cash revenues less operating cash flows such as costs to service customers, costs of conversion (presumably manufacturing costs), and development and administration costs. Noncash flow expenses and accruals, such as depreciation and amortization and gains and losses, would be deducted from operating income to arrive at "cash earnings." Since noncash flow items are deducted from operating income, cash earnings is a poorly chosen title. Howell would not deduct interest charges on the operating statement because it is a financing cost. Operating income would agree with the similarly titled first section on the statement of cash flows. Interest expense would become a part of debt financing costs on the statement of cash flows, a recommendation similar to one made in Chapter 13 and previously in this chapter.

Howell emphasizes the importance of cash flows, which we agree with (see Chapter 13). However, it should be noted that accruals (along with cash flows) are important for predicting future earnings (Chapter 8). Perhaps a better approach would be to improve methods of writing off long-lived assets rather than employing the system of flexibility in place today. Howell's approach has some appeal but it de-emphasizes the importance of accrual accounting measurements of income, which can certainly be improved.

Pro Forma Earnings and Offshoots

A supplementary measure to GAAP income is known as pro forma earnings, which are provided to financial analysts. The idea underlying pro forma earnings is that, for predictive purposes, the exclusion of unique, one-time events can be useful to investors.[101] The pro forma earnings approach appears to be an outgrowth of the current operating idea discussed previously. Unfortunately, management has frequently viewed the pro forma idea as a way to eliminate bad news events and maintain favorable events, making the statement biased and misleading.[102]

This was the situation as it stood until approximately 2001. In a study covering the years 1998–2000, the conclusion was reached that firms using pro forma earnings announcements tended to be "young" firms coming largely from the tech and business services industries.[103] These firms tended to be marginal in terms of profits and have high debt levels. These firms often attempted to beat analysts' expectations.

However, an important change, largely brought about by the SEC in 2001 and 2002, changed pro forma reporting. The SEC provided cautionary advice on pro forma reporting in 2001 and issued Regulation G in 2002, which requires that GAAP information be presented with the same prominence as non-GAAP information in pro forma earnings. In addition, the SEC has required reconciliation of pro forma earnings to GAAP-based earnings with adequate discussion and disclosure in the Management Discussion and Analysis section of the corporate annual report. Two studies have largely confirmed the improvement in reporting pro forma earnings since 2002.[104]

Indeed it appears that "irrational exuberance" in pro forma earnings reporting has been largely tamed. As a result, pro forma earnings releases have gone down significantly.

A G4+1 report takes an opposite tack to pro forma earnings, even though it also has the underlying purpose of enhancing the predictive ability objective. The G4+1 report proposes a single income statement with three components:

1. results of operating or trading activities;
2. result pertaining to financing and other treasury activities;
3. other gains and losses.[105]

The G4+1 report would include items of comprehensive income, presumably in other gains and losses. Since the G4+1 report is concerned with predictive ability objectives, it is interested in what might be called *earnings sustainability*. This means separating permanent and transitory (one time) elements of income, which can also confound differences between operating and nonoperating elements of income. The AAA committee report makes it clear that this task is not easily accomplished. For example, a necessary restructuring of an enterprise's operating activities would pertain to operations even though it is a one-time charge that is not capitalizable.[106]

Matrix Approaches

Barker has a similar earnings sustainability orientation as the G4+1, but he would accomplish it using a matrix format.[107] He would first show comprehensive income with breakdowns between earnings sustainability items and other categories such as infrequently occurring items and noncontrollable items. He then breaks out of the totals what he refers to as "remeasurement" items, which are not useful for predictive purposes because they are either not sustainable or not controllable.

Thus he would make sure that inventory impairment costs were not included in cost of goods sold, for example. Similarly, with financial instruments, interest costs would be separated from fair value changes with the latter appearing in the remeasurement column. The result would be three columns: (1) a total column with an arrangement of operating items first and nonoperating items below, (2) a "before remeasurement" column with continuing items of both an operating and nonoperating nature, and (3) the "remeasurement" column consisting of nonrecurring items. This breakdown would aid prediction of future cash flows from the before remeasurement column. Also, this breakdown might aid in assessing some accounting practices of management. For example, persistent actuarial losses might indicate a continuing underestimation of pension service costs.

Another recent matrix approach by Glover et al. has been suggested.[108] The Barker approach that we just examined was based on the recurring–nonrecurring dichotomy, whereas the Glover et al. approach is based on a fact versus forecast distinction. Glover et al. have several possible approaches to the fact versus forecast distinction. These include cash only, cash plus deferrals, and cash plus deferrals including amounts without "uncertainty." The third case would include depreciation measurement (determined by policy) but not salvage value (determined by estimation). In discussing fair value measurements and the fact versus forecast dichotomy, Glover et al. do see difficulties in applying their matrix approach.

Of the two matrix approaches discussed, the recurring versus nonrecurring distinction appears to be the most promising. However, the point is that researchers are still carefully examining issues of format and presentation of the income statement. We make progress only by carefully examining new possibilities.

Retrospective Reports

While other developments have tried to improve the predictive objective of accounting information or bring income closer to cash flow measurements, Lundholm has taken a retrospective approach.[109] He proposes to report on the ex post (after the fact) accuracy of various accounting estimates appearing on the financial statements. These include—among others— bad debt expenses, warranty expenses, and projected pension benefit obligations (in other words, future events). One problem recognized by Lundholm is that charges and credits for various accruals may actually take longer than a year to clear. Nevertheless, the idea is a good one and should be further examined because it provides a possible way to check management estimates and accruals. Increasing management accountability would be a welcome development.

Quality of Earnings

There has been an increasing emphasis on quality of earnings. One definition of the term emphasizes income before extraordinary items, assuming that it is a good indicator of future earnings.[110] Thus, this definition is concerned with earnings sustainability, as previously discussed. The other definition of quality of earnings identifies it with the opposite of earnings management. Hence, quality of earnings is indirectly defined in terms of what it is not.[111] At a time when we are concerned with earnings quality, we are faced with an enormous number of restatements (see next section).[112] Of course, it may not be fair to compare these phenomena, since one is in the theoretical area and the other is in the so-called real world.

The presence of multiple acceptable accounting methods (inventories and depreciation, for example) as well as considerable freedom even with selected methods (such as estimating number of years of life and salvage value under straight-line depreciation) brings us right back to questions involving uniformity (Chapter 9). Quality of earnings appears to involve economically relevant accruals and an attempt to arrive at an income number that would be a good representation of "true income." This is impossible at the present time, but we must continue to take slow and steady steps to keep improving the quality of income.

Financial Statement Restatements

Finally, we note an alarming growth in financial statement restatements. The number was up to a staggering 1,420 in 2006.[113] The initial increase in 2002 through 2004 was due to internal control shortcomings, which came to light as a result of applying Section 404 of the Sarbanes-Oxley Act.[114] However, a large part of the problem has arisen because of difficulties in applying complex accounting standards, particularly in the area of leases.[115]

Some of the restatements may also be due to Staff Accounting Bulletin 99 of the SEC, which removed the quantitative bound of 5% of net income as a threshold for determining material errors (Chapter 5). As a result, the boundary may have effectively moved much lower, causing many more restatements.

Summary

The income statement is based on the historical cost model of revenue recognition and expense matching. That does not mean, however, that it will not change. Some of the changes in the income statement that have occurred in the past 15 years provide a hint as to what might be expected in the future. It is safe to say, regarding the recognition of revenue, that the FASB is moving toward rigid uniformity. Likewise, in expense recognition, which is largely based on a system of arbitrary allocation, it would also not be surprising to see the FASB move toward rigid uniformity. However, the role of future events in revenue and expense recognition needs to be more closely examined. Although too flexible in presentation, the FASB's requirement for a comprehensive income measure pushes us further down the all-inclusive income statement track. However, pro forma earnings, one view of quality of earnings, and a G4+1 report are looking at the importance of the predictive objective and lean toward a current operating view of income.

For the past 50 years, the income statement has been viewed by users of financial statements, as well as by standard setters, as the predominant financial statement. A review of past ARBs and APBs clearly indicates that more time and effort was placed on refining the income statement to the detriment of the balance sheet. Since the inception of the FASB, however, there appears to have been a shift toward "cleaning up" the balance sheet and a movement toward more of an asset–liability approach to the financial statements consistent with the conceptual framework project.

Earnings management has become an important subject for researchers. A vital aspect of earnings management is income smoothing, by which management attempts to reduce the variance in year-to-year measurements of reported income with the hope of raising security prices. Although some evidence supports the smoothing hypothesis, it is an extremely difficult phenomenon to measure, so we cannot be certain of how widespread the practice is. Manipulation by management of earnings to maximize compensation is another important aspect of earnings management.

QUESTIONS

1. Describe how definitions of income, revenues, and expenses have changed in statements issued by successive standard-setting bodies.

2. Four points in the revenue cycle, from production through to cash collection, are possible events for revenue recognition. What *relevant circumstances* would justify finite uniformity rather than rigid uniformity for revenue recognition, and which approach is used in practice? Explain.

3. What is the matching concept, and why is there an implied hierarchy for expense recognition?

4. Why is there no matching problem for periodic costs, and what are some examples?

5. What types of costs present matching problems, how are they dealt with, and what are some examples of such costs?

6. There has been a trend toward rigid uniformity in the format of the income statement. Explain how and why this has occurred.

7. Why might the distinction between revenues and gains, and between expenses and losses, be important to report yet unimportant as to how they are reported?

8. Research, while inconclusive, has shown that earnings are manipulated downward prior to a management buyout. What is the logic of this and why do management buyouts present a difficult agency theory problem?

9. Why is comprehensive income an application of proprietary theory?

10. If a separate statement of comprehensive income is presented, do all elements of comprehensive income appear in this statement?

11. Why is less really more with SFAS No. 128 on earnings per share?

12. Describe the incentives that might motivate income smoothing and the ways it could be done.

13. Why is income smoothing difficult to research, and what are the research findings to date?

14. Why may interindustry income uniformity be more difficult to achieve than intra-industry uniformity, and what are the implications of this in terms of a conceptual framework project, specific accounting standards, and comparability of accounting income numbers?

15. What is the relationship between earnings management and income smoothing?

16. Is earnings per share an example of finite or rigid uniformity?

17. Why is the handling of troubled debt restructuring under SFAS No. 114 illogical?

18. Why are future events so important to the issue of revenue and expense measurement?

19. Which factor discussed under future events is the most important and why?

20. From the standpoint of management, are there any differences between attempting to control bad debt expense percentages and research and development expenses?

21. Why do you think earnings are managed when it appears that actual income might be less than management's voluntary forecasts of earnings?

22. Is the FASB correct in attempting to separate stock options from stock appreciation rights that are payable in cash?

23. Should incentive and nonqualified stock options be treated the same on the financials?

24. In what two different senses is the term *pro forma* used?

25. In SFAS No. 154, changes in accounting principle result in a restatement, whereas under APB Opinion No. 20, a change in accounting principle was handled in a pro forma manner. How does a restatement differ from a pro forma presentation?

26. What is classification shifting?

CASES, PROBLEMS, AND WRITING ASSIGNMENTS

1. Revenue recognition, when the right of return exists, was standardized in 1981 by SFAS No. 48. Prior to this, SOP 75-1 provided guidance but was not mandatory (which is why the FASB has brought various SOPs into the accounting standards themselves). As a result, three methods were widely used to account for this type of transaction: (1) no sale recognized until the product was unconditionally accepted, (2) sale recognized along with an allowance for estimated returns, and (3) sale recognized with no allowance for estimated returns. SFAS No. 48 mandated revenue recognition for such sales subject to six conditions: (1) price is substantially fixed or determinable at sale date; (2) buyer has paid or is obligated to pay the seller, and payment is not contingent on resale of the product; (3) buyer's obligation would not be changed in the event of theft of or physical damage to the product; (4) buyer acquiring the product for resale has economic substance apart from the seller; (5) seller has no significant obligations to bring about resale by the buyer; and (6) future returns can be reasonably estimated.

Required:

    a. Discuss the underlying conceptual issues concerning revenue recognition when the right of return exists. Can any (or all) of the pre–SFAS No. 48 methods be justified?

    b. Indicate the rationale for each of the SFAS No. 48 tests before a revenue is recognized.

    c. Is SFAS No. 48 an example of finite uniformity or of circumstantial variables as developed by Cadenhead (see Chapter 9)?

    d. Discuss the role of future events in SFAS No. 48.

2. Accounting for the transfer of receivables with recourse has been problematic. At issue is whether such a transaction is, in substance, a sale, in which case a gain/loss would be recognized, or a financing transaction, in which case any gain/loss should be amortized over the original life of the receivable. (The receivable could be long-term; for example, a sale of an interest-bearing note.) SOP 74-6 concluded that most transfers with recourse are financing transactions based on the argument that a transfer of risk (i.e., no recourse) must exist for a sale to have occurred. In 1983, the FASB reached a different conclusion in SFAS No. 77. A sale is now recognized if (a) the seller surrenders control of future economic benefits embodied in the receivable and (b) the seller's obligation under the recourse provisions can be reasonably estimated. If these conditions are not met, the proceeds from a transfer are reported on the balance sheet as a liability.

Required:

    a. What is the critical issue in interpreting the nature of this transaction? How does interpretation of the critical issue lead to the two different viewpoints?

    b. Explain why the SOP 74-6 view represents a revenue–expense orientation, while the SFAS No. 77 represents an asset–liability orientation.

3. In its 1994 monograph on future events, the FASB discussed several orientations that might be related to asset valuation. As an example of its thinking, assume that we are assessing future sales of a product for the purpose of determining the value of the asset that is used to manufacture the product. The product is expected to sell for $25 per unit. Probability and unit sales are shown here.

Probability	Estimated Sales
.45	0
.10	5000
.30	6000
.15	8000

Required:

Part 1

    Determine (a) the modal (most likely individual unit sales), (b) the cumulative probability (summed probability of sales being either positive or negative), and (c) the weighted probability number (expected value of probability times estimated sales times sales price).

Part 2

How might these approaches be utilized to value the asset that is used to manufacture the product?

4. In 1983, a number of computer software companies reported use of an accounting procedure that was investigated by the SEC. The accounting policy is to capitalize the cost of developing computer software and amortize it over the life of the software (usually three to five years). This procedure is used by large and small companies, but the impact is more pronounced on smaller, new companies, in which a greater portion of their activity is devoted to software development.

   An official of Comserv, a small company that specializes in software, said that small companies would be in deep trouble because of SFAS No. 86. He said smaller companies would be under strong pressure to keep costs down if development costs had to be expensed. He also said, relative to the immediate write-off of these costs, that smaller companies would not be able to put as much cash into their own growth and development because of SFAS No. 86.

   The SEC's concern was whether this accounting policy was consistent with SFAS No. 2 concerning the expensing of research and development costs as incurred. In 1985, SFAS No. 86 treated software-related research and development costs the same as in SFAS No. 2.

Required:

   a. Evaluate the software capitalization argument with reference to SFAS No. 2.
   b. Why is the choice of accounting policies (expensing vs. capitalization) more likely to affect smaller companies?
   c. Comment on the claim that small companies wouldn't be able to invest as much cash in their own growth if they couldn't capitalize many costs. Is this a real economic consequence?
   d. If you were a FASB member, how would you have voted on this issue? Explain.

5. Discuss the role of future events in the following revenue and expense recognition situations.
   a. Modification of terms under troubled debt restructuring in SFAS No. 114
   b. Pension accounting relative to measuring current expense in SFAS No. 87
   c. Other postretirement benefits under SFAS No. 106
   d. Full costing and successful efforts in oil and gas accounting as well as the SEC's reserve recognition accounting proposal

6. Shown below is the bottom part of the income statement of Waste Management, Inc., for the year ending December 31, 1998. Also shown below is a note from its financial statements showing the elements of its comprehensive income items, which were shown as part of the statement of changes in equity.

Required:

   a. Recast the income statement for December 31, 1998, so that it includes comprehensive income.
   b. Even though not allowed by the FASB, compute the EPS for comprehensive income.

Waste Management, Inc.
Summarized Consolidated Financial Statements

Year Ended December 31	1998	1997	1996
Income (loss) from continuing operations	(766,802)	(1,025,838)	287,532
Discontinued operations:			
Income from operations of discontinued businesses, net of applicable income tax and minority interest of $17,490 in 1996	—	—	22,620
Income (loss) on disposal or from reserve adjustment, net of applicable income tax and minority interest of $100,842 in 1997 and $(18,640) in 1996	—	95,688	(285,921)
Income (loss) before extraordinary item and cumulative effect of change in accounting principle	(766,802)	(930,150)	24,231
Extraordinary loss on refinancing or retirement of debt, net of applicable income tax and minority interest of $2,600 in 1998 and $4,962 in 1997	(3,900)	(6,809)	—
Cumulative effect of change in accounting principle, net of income tax of $1,100 in 1997	—	(1,936)	—
Net income (loss)	$(770,702)	$(938,895)	$24,231

	Foreign Currency Translation Adjustment	Minimum Pension Liability Adjustment	Accumulated Other Comprehensive Income
Balance, December 31, 1996	$(95,056)	$(18,885)	$(113,941)
Current-period change	(180,744)	11,492	(169,252)
Balance, December 31, 1997	$(275,800)	$ (7,393)	$(283,193)
Current-period change	(77,842)	(59,769)	(137,611)
Balance, December 31, 1998	$(353,642)	$(67,162)	$(420,804)

c. Do you think that elements specific to comprehensive income should be shown only in the statement of changes in equity?

d. Do you think there are circumstances in which Waste Management might desire to show comprehensive income elements within the income statement itself?

7. Utilizing the stock options proposal made in this chapter, show entity and proprietary income in the following situation for the Ethan Neil Corporation:

Income before taxes	$4,810,000
Interest expense	182,000
Stock options expense (incentive)	240,000
Income tax rate	40%

CRITICAL THINKING AND ANALYSIS

1. The question of the usefulness of cost allocations was discussed in Chapter 9 and this chapter (discretionary accruals and management compensation plans). What, if anything, would you do about (fixed) cost allocations? Don't forget to consider political costs.

Notes

1. *Committee on Terminology (1955, para. 8).*
2. *APB (1970, para. 134).*
3. *FASB (1985, para. 70).*
4. *Committee on Terminology (1955, para. 5).*
5. *APB (1970, para. 134).*
6. *FASB (1985, para. 78).*
7. *APB (1970, para. 198).*
8. *FASB (1985, para. 82).*
9. *Sprouse and Moonitz (1962, p. 177).*
10. *See complete discussion of revenue recognition concepts in AAA (1965a).*
11. *Committee on Accounting Procedure (1953, Chapter 1, para. 1).*
12. *Jaenicke (1981, pp. 6–10).*
13. *Philips (1963).*
14. *Solomon and Pulliam (2002).*
15. *Graziano (2005, (p. 29).*
16. *Ibid. (p. 28).*
17. *Altamuro, Beatty, and Weber (2005).*
18. *Committee on Terminology (1957, para. 3).*
19. *APB (1970, para. 134).*
20. *FASB (1985, para. 80).*
21. *AAA (1965b).*
22. *APB (1970, para. 155).*
23. *Jaenicke (1981, pp. 117–118).*
24. *Thomas (1969 and 1974).*
25. *See Kirk (1990), Beaver (1991), and FASB (1994a).*
26. *FASB (1994a, pp. 7–8).*
27. *Ibid. (p. 6).*
28. *Beaver (1991, pp. 128–129).*
29. *Ibid. (p. 131).*
30. *AAA (1936, section 8).*
31. *Committee on Accounting Procedure (1953, Chapter 8, para. 13).*
32. *APB (1966, para. 16).*
33. *Gonedes (1978).*

34. *Hoskin, Hughes, and Ricks (1986).*

35. *FASB (1984, para, 39).*

36. *AAA's Financial Accounting Standards Committee (1997, p. 124) believes that under comprehensive income, preferred dividends should be deducted from income, which would be the residual income approach. However, a proprietary theory orientation is also possible with preferred dividends not being deducted from income.*

37. *Ibid. (p. 122).*

38. *For a complete list, see FASB (1997b, para. 39).*

39. *Ibid. (para. 106).*

40. *Ibid. (paras. 76 and 77).*

41. *Ibid. (para. 77).*

42. *Ibid. (para. 22).*

43. *Ibid. (para. 23).*

44. *Ibid. (p. 10). The AAA Financial Accounting Standards Committee (2000, p. 366) agrees (along with a G4+1 report) that comprehensive income should be shown in one financial statement.*

45. *Hirst and Hopkins (1998) perceived problems for financial analysts who worked the income statement containing both net income and comprehensive income, but this might have been attributable to their lack of familiarity with the format. In an experiment involving nonprofessional investors, Maines and McDaniel (2000) found that the most effective way to present comprehensive income data was in the statement of comprehensive income.*

46. *Committee on Accounting Procedure (1953, Chapter 8, para. 11).*

47. *APB (1966, para. 21).*

48. *APB (1973, para. 23).*

49. *Ibid. (paras. 19–20).*

50. *APB (1971, paras. 7–8).*

51. *FASB (2005). May and Schneider (1988) report strong evidence indicating that changes in accounting principle occur not for reasons of representational faithfulness but rather to manage earnings. Their evidence suggests that discretionary changes in accounting principle are more likely to be taken if the effect on earnings is positive rather than negative.*

52. *Ibid. (paras. 8 and 9).*

53. *Ibid. (paras. 31–32). Nurnberg (1988, pp. 18 and 21–22) notes that it is often difficult to determine from annual reports whether the cumulative or prospective basis of correction has been used. His preference for changes in accounting estimates would be to use the retroactive method as long as it appears that benefits exceed costs.*

54. *Ibid. (para. 20).*

55. *Ibid. (paras. 34–35).*

56. *APB (1966, para. 23).*

57. *FASB (1977b, para. 11).*

58. *FASB (1979).*

59. *FASB (1997a, para. 75).*

60. *Core, Guay, and Kothari (2002) show that the treasury stock method of computing diluted EPS understates the dilutive effect of outstanding EPS and therefore overstates the measure of fully diluted EPS.*

61. *FASB (1997a, paras. 126 and 132).*

62. *Ibid. (paras. 137 and 138).*

63. *FASB (1975, para. 11).*

64. *FASB (1977a, para. 1).*

65. *SFAS No. 118 broadened, and possibly muddled, methods for recognizing the loss on impairment and other value changes in the restructured instrument. See FASB (1994b).*

66. *Differences in tax treatment for the firm between incentive and nonqualified options provide a stronger basis for finite uniformity, but we do not believe that the tax tail should wag the accounting transaction dog. In other words, tax differences alone are not enough to justify using finite uniformity, as they are in the case of FIFO versus LIFO.*

67. *Newberry (2001) discusses this point on nonreciprocal transactions and, similar to the discussion here, rejects the nonreciprocity interpretation of stock options. However, nonreciprocity of equity transactions as opposed to liability transactions is not as prevalent as she seems to be implying.*

68. *Using Staubus's residual equity approach as a framework, Wiseman (1990) concludes that stock options are a form of nonresidual equity. See also Cheung (1992) and Wiseman (1992) for additional coverage of this argument.*

69. *Not surprisingly, Hill, Shelton, and Stevens (2002) find that the higher the value of stock options held by the top five officers of a firm, the more strongly is disclosure of stock option information opposed.*

70. *FASB (1993, para. 113).*

71. *Hemmer, Matsunaga, and Shevlin (1994) argue that the FASB's recommendation to use the expected term of the option leads to an overstating of option value when applying the Black-Scholes model to incentive stock options. See also Aboody (1996).*

72. *Dechow, Hutton, and Sloan (1996) reject the idea that charging stock options to expense would raise the cost of capital. Their evidence, which is indirect, is based on comment letters to the FASB on the stock option exposure draft of 1993. They did not feel that firms that submitted letters against the exposure draft were in significant need of new capital nor did they find that firms needing new capital are extensive users of stock options.*

73. *FASB (2004).*

74. *Another desultory practice with stock options involves earnings management practices. Cheng and Warfield (2005) find that managers with "high equity incentives" (relatively large numbers of stock options, for example) are more likely to engage in earnings management to increase the value of shares to be sold in the future. However, Bartov and Mohanram (2004) show that disappointment may result from this behavior in the post-exercise period owing to the reversal of earnings management techniques employed in the pre-exercise period.*

75. *Schipper (1989, p. 92).*

76. *Dechow and Skinner (2000) summarize these studies. For further corroborating evidence, see Payne and Robb (2000). Moehrle (2002) shows that firms reverse restructuring charges to beat analysts' quarterly earnings forecasts.*

77. *McVay (2006).*

78. *Ibid. (p. 502).*

79. *Increasing income through earnings management leaves future net assets inflated. Barton and Simko (2002) show that this behavior constrains managers' ability to maintain this form of behavior, the larger the overstatement of net assets. See also footnote 74.*

80. *McVay (2006, p. 502).*

81. *Ibid. (p. 503).*

82. *Erickson and Wang (1999). There is some evidence that earnings are manipulated upward prior to initial public offerings. See DuCharme, Malatesta and Sefcik (2001).*

83. *Wu (1997).*

84. *DeAngelo (1986).*

85. *Jones (1991).*

86. *Kasznik (1999).*

87. *See the comments of DeAngelo (1988) and Dechow, Sloan, and Sweeney (1995).*

88. *Healy and Wahlen (1999, p. 366).*

89. *Nelson, Elliott, and Tarpley (2002). For further discussion see Nelson, Elliott, and Tarpley (2003).*

90. *Nelson, Elliott, and Tarpley (2002). See also the excellent criticism of this paper by Gibbins (2002).*

91. *Healy (1985). For a good discussion of management compensation arrangements within an accounting framework, see Scott (1997), pp. 263–283.*

92. *Holthausen, Larcker, and Sloan (1995).*

93. *Gaver, Gaver, and Austin (1995).*

94. *For more on the difficulties in distinguishing between discretionary and nondiscretionary accruals, see Bernard and Skinner (1996) and Dechow, Sloan, and Sweeney (1995).*

95. *Ronen and Sadan (1981).*

96. *Chaney and Jeter (1997).*

97. *DeFond and Park (1997).*

98. *For more on the difficulties in predicting aggregate (total) accruals in earnings management studies, see McNichols (2000) and Thomas and Zhang (2000).*

99. *See Watts and Leftwich (1977) and Albrecht, Lookabill, and McKeown (1977).*

100. *Howell (2002).*

101. *Arnold and Duggan (2002, p. 38).*

102. *Ibid. (p. 39).*

103. *Bhattacharya, Black, Christensen, and Mergenthaler (2004). Lougee and Marquardt (2004) are largely in agreement with these results in their own study.*

104. *See Entwistle, Feltham, and Mbagwu (2006) and Bowen, Davis, and Matsumoto (2005).*

105. *American Accounting Association (2000, p. 366).*

106. *Ibid. (pp. 370–371).*

107. *Barker (2004).*

108. *Glover, Ijiri, Levine, and Liang (2005).*

109. *Lundholm (1999).*

110. *Penman and Zhang (2002, p. 237).*

111. *See Teets (2002).*

112. *See Reilly (2006) for the SEC's attempt to gain more transparency and to come to grips more quickly with misstatements.*

113. *Pozen (2007, p. A11).*

114. *Ibid.*

115. *Ibid.*

References

Aboody, David (August/December 1996). "Market Value of Employee Stock Options," *Journal of Accounting and Economics*, pp. 357–391.

Accounting Principles Board (1966). APB Opinion No. 9, *Reporting the Results of Operations*. AICPA.

——— (1970). APB Statement No. 4, *Basic Concepts and Accounting Principles Underlying Financial Statements of Business Enterprises*. AICPA.

——— (1971). APB Opinion No. 20, *Accounting Changes*. AICPA.

——— (1973). APB Opinion No. 30, *Reporting the Results of Operations*. AICPA.

Albrecht, W. Steve, Larry L. Lookabill, and James C. McKeown (Autumn 1977). "The Time-Series Properties of Annual Earnings," *Journal of Accounting Research*, pp. 226–244.

Altamuro, Jennifer, A. Beatty, and J. Weber (April 2005). "The Effects of Accelerated Revenue Recognition on Earnings Management and Earnings Informativeness: Evidence From SEC Staff Accounting Bulletin No. 101," *Accounting Review*, pp. 373–401.

American Accounting Association (1936). *A Tentative Statement of Accounting Principles Underlying Corporate Financial Statements*. AAA.

———— (1965a). "The Matching Concept," *Accounting Review* (April), pp. 368–372.

———— (1965b). "The Realization Concept," *Accounting Review* (April), pp. 312–322.

———— Financial Accounting Standards Committee (June 1997). "An Issues Paper on Comprehensive Income," *Accounting Horizons*, pp. 120–126.

———— (September 2000). "Response to the Special Report of the G4+1, 'Reporting Financial Performance: A Proposed Approach,'" *Accounting Horizons*, pp. 365–379.

Arnold, Jerry, and J. W. Duggan (May 2002). "Making Pro Forma Information More Useful," *Financial Executive*, pp. 38–41.

Barker, Richard (June 2004). "Reporting Financial Performance," *Accounting Horizons*, pp. 157–172.

Barton, Jan, and P. Simko (2002). "The Balance Sheet as an Earnings Management Constraint," *Accounting Review Supplement*, pp. 1–33.

Bartov, Eli, and P. Mohanram (October 2004). "Private Information, Earnings Manipulations, and Executive Stock-Option Exercises," *Accounting Review*, pp. 889–920.

Beaver, William H. (December 1991). "Problems and Paradoxes in the Financial Reporting of Future Events," *Accounting Horizons*, pp. 122–134.

Bernard, Victor L., and D. J. Skinner (August–December 1996). "What Motivates Managers Choice of Discretionary Accruals?" *Journal of Accounting and Economics*, pp. 313–325.

Bhattacharya, Nilabhra, E. Black, T. Christensen, and R. Mergenthaler (March 2004). "Empirical Evidence on Recent Trends in Pro Forma Reporting," *Accounting Horizons*, pp. 27–43.

Bowen, Robert, A. Davis, and D. Matsumoto (October 2005). "Emphasis on Pro Forma Versus GAAP Earnings in Quarterly Press Releases: Determinants, SEC Intervention, and Market Reactions," *Accounting Review*, pp. 1011–1038.

Chaney, Paul K., and D. C. Jeter (August 1997). "Income Smoothing and Firm Characteristics," *Accounting Enquiries*, pp. 1–50.

Cheng, Qiang, and T. Warfield (April 2005). "Equity Incentives and Earnings Management," *Accounting Review*, pp. 441–476.

Cheung, Joseph K. (June 1992). "An Option-Theoretic Argument Favoring EPS Dilution Over Holding Gain/Loss," *Accounting Horizons*, pp. 86–89.

Committee on Accounting Procedure (1953). ARB No. 43, *Restatement and Revision of Accounting Research Bulletins*. AICPA.

Committee on Terminology (1955). Accounting Terminology Bulletin No. 2, *Proceeds, Revenue, Income, Profit, and Earnings*. AICPA.

———— (1957). Accounting Terminology Bulletin No. 4, *Cost, Expense and Loss*. AICPA.

Core, John, W. Guay, and S. P. Kothari (July 2002). "The Economic Dilution of Employee Stock Options: Diluted EPS for Valuation and Financial Reporting," *Accounting Review*, pp. 627–652.

DeAngelo, Linda (July 1986). "Accounting Numbers as Market Valuation Substitutes: A Study of Management Buyouts of Public Stockholders," *Accounting Review*, pp. 400–420.

———— (1988). "Discussion of Evidence of Earnings Management From the Provision for Bad Debts," *Studies of Management's Ability and Incentives to Affect the Timing and Magnitude of Accounting Accruals, 1988* (Supplement to *Journal of Accounting Research*), pp. 32–40.

Dechow, Patricia, A. P. Hutton, and R. G. Sloan (1996). Economic Consequences of Accounting for Stock Based Compensation," *Studies on Recognition, Measurement, and Disclosure Issues in Accounting* (Supplement to *Journal of Account Research*), pp. 1–20.

Dechow, Patricia, and D. J. Skinner (June 2000). Earnings Management: Reconciling the Views of Accounting Academics, Practitioners, and Regulators," *Accounting Horizons*, pp. 235–250.

Dechow, Patricia, Richard Sloan, and Amy Sweeney (April 1995). "Detecting Earnings Management," *Accounting Review*, pp. 193–225.

DeFond, Mark L., and C. W. Park (July 1997). "Smoothing Income in Anticipation of Future Earnings," *Journal of Accounting and Economics*, pp. 115–140.

DuCharme, Larry L., P. Malatesta, and S. Sefcik (2001). "Earnings Management: The Effect of Ex Ante Earnings Expectations," *Journal of Accounting, Auditing, and Finance* (Vol. 16, No. 4), pp. 369–400.

Entwistle, Gary, Glenn Feltham, and C. Mbagwu (March 2006). "Financial Reporting Regulation and the Reporting of Pro Forma Earnings," *Accounting Horizons*, pp. 39–55.

Erickson, Merle, and S. Wang (April 1999). "Earnings Management by Acquiring Firms in Stock for Stock Mergers," *Journal of Accounting and Economics*, pp. 149–176.

Financial Accounting Standards Board (1975). Statement of Financial Accounting Standards No. 7, *Accounting and Reporting by Development Stage Enterprises*. FASB.

——— (1977a). Statement of Financial Accounting Standards No. 15, *Accounting by Debtors and Creditors for Troubled Debt Restructuring*. FASB.

——— (1977b). Statement of Financial Accounting Standards No. 16, *Prior Period Adjustments*. FASB.

——— (1979). *Reporting Earnings*. FASB.

——— (1984). Statement of Financial Accounting Concepts No. 5, *Recognition and Measurement in Financial Statements of Business Enterprises*. FASB.

——— (1985). Statement of Financial Accounting Concepts No. 6, *Elements of Financial Statements*. FASB.

——— (1993). Exposure Draft, *Accounting for Stock-Based Compensation*. FASB.

——— (1994a). *Future Events: A Conceptual Study of Their Significance for Recognition and Measurement* (L. Todd Johnson, principal author). FASB.

——— (1994b). Statement of Financial Accounting Standards No. 118, *Accounting by Creditors for Impairment of a Loan—Income Recognition and Disclosures*. FASB.

——— (1997a). Statement of Financial Accounting Standards No. 128, *Earnings per Share*. FASB.

——— (1997b). Statement of Financial Accounting Standards No. 130, *Reporting Comprehensive Income*. FASB.

——— (2004). Statement of Financial Accounting Standards No. 123R, *Share-Based Payment*. FASB.

——— (2005). Statement of Financial Accounting Standards No. 154, *Accounting Changes and Error Corrections: A Replacement of APB Opinion No. 20 and FASB Statement No. 3*. FASB.

Gaver, Jennifer J., K. M. Gaver, and J. R. Austin (February 1995). "Additional Evidence on Bonus Plans and Income Management," *Journal of Accounting and Economics*, pp. 3–28.

Gibbins, Michael (2002). "Discussion of Evidence From Auditors About Managers' and Auditors' Earnings Management Decisions," *Accounting Review Supplement*, pp. 203–211.

Glover, Jonathan, Y. Ijiri, C. Levine, and P. Liang (December 2005). "Separating Facts From Forecasts in Financial Statements," *Accounting Horizons*, pp. 267–282.

Gonedes, Nicholas J. (Spring 1978). "Corporate Signaling, External Accounting, and Capital Market Equilibrium: Evidence on Dividends, Income, and Extraordinary Items," *Journal of Accounting Research*, pp. 26–79.

Graziano, Cheryl (July/August 2005). "Revenue Recognition: A Perennial Problem," *Financial Executive*, pp. 28–31.

Healy, Paul M. (April 1985). "The Effect of Bonus Schemes on Accounting Decisions," *Journal of Accounting and Economics*, pp. 85–107.

Healy, Paul M., and J. Wahlen (December 1999). "A Review of the Earnings Management Literature and Its Implications for Standard Setting," *Accounting Horizons*, pp. 365–383.

Hemmer, Thomas, Steve Matsunaga, and Terry Shevlin (December 1994). "Estimating the 'Fair Value' of Employee Stock Options With Expected Early Exercise," *Accounting Horizons*, pp. 23–42.

Hill, Nancy Thorley, S. W. Shelton, and K. T. Stevens (2002). "Corporate Lobbying Behavior on Accounting for Stock-Based Compensation: Venue and Format Choices," *Abacus* (Vol. 38, No. 1), pp. 78–90.

Hirst, D. Eric, and P. E. Hopkins (1998). "Comprehensive Income Reporting and Analysts' Valuation Judgments," *Studies on Enhancing the Financial Reporting Model, 1998* (Supplement to *Journal of Accounting Research*), pp. 47–75.

Holthausen, Robert, D. Larcker, and R. Sloan (February 1995). "Annual Bonus Schemes and the Manipulation of Earnings," *Journal of Accounting and Economics*, pp. 29–74.

Hoskin, Robert E., John S. Hughes, and William E. Ricks (1986). "Evidence on the Incremental Information Content of Additional Firm Disclosures Made Concurrently With Earnings," *Studies on Alternative Measures of Accounting Income, 1986* (Supplement to *Journal of Accounting Research*), pp. 1–32.

Howell, Robert A. (March/April 2002). "Fixing Financial Reporting: Financial Statement Overhaul," *Financial Executive*, pp. 40–42.

Jaenicke, Henry R. (1981). *Survey of Present Practices in Recognizing Revenues, Expenses, Gains, and Losses.* FASB.

Jones, Jennifer J. (Autumn 1991). "Earnings Management During Import Relief Investigations," *Journal of Accounting Research*, pp. 193–228.

Kasznik, Ron (Spring 1999). "On the Association Between Voluntary Disclosure and Earnings Management," *Journal of Accounting Research*, pp. 57–81.

Kirk, Donald J. (June 1990). "Future Events: When Incorporated Into Today's Measurements," *Accounting Horizons*, pp. 86–92.

Lougee, Barbara, and C. Marquardt (July 2004). "Earnings Informativeness and Strategic Disclosure: An Empirical Eranunation of 'Pro Forma' Earnings," *Accounting Review*, pp. 769–795.

Lundholm, Russell J. (December 1999). "Reporting on the Past: A New Approach to Improving Accounting Today," *Accounting Horizons*, pp. 315–322.

Maines, Laureen, and L. S. McDaniel (April 2000). "Effects of Comprehensive-Income Characteristics on Nonprofessional Investors' Judgments: The Role of Financial-Statement Presentation Format," *Accounting Review*, pp. 179–207.

May, Gordon S., and Douglas Schneider (September 1988). "Reporting Accounting Changes: Are Stricter Guidelines Needed?" *Accounting Horizons*, pp. 68–74.

McNichols, Maureen (2000). "Research Design Issues in Earnings Management Studies," *Journal of Accounting and Public Policy* (Vol. 19, No. 4), pp. 313–345.

McVay, Sarah (May 2006). "Earnings Management Using Classification Shifting: An Examination of Core Earnings and Special Items," *Accounting Review*, pp. 501-531.

Moehrle, Stephen R. (April 2002). "Do Firms Use Restructuring Charge Reversals to Meet Earnings Targets?" *Accounting Review*, pp. 397–413.

Nelson, Mark, J. A. Elliott, and R. L. Tarpley (2002). "Evidence From Auditors About Managers' and Auditors' Earnings Management Decisions," *Accounting Review Supplement*, pp. 175–202.

——— (2003). "How Are Earnings Managed? Examples From Auditors," *Accounting Horizons* (Supplement), pp. 17–35.

Newberry, Susan (2001). "Reciprocal and Non-Reciprocal Transactions: The FASB's Stock-Based Compensation Project," *Abacus* (Vol. 37, No. 2), pp. 177–187.

Nurnberg, Hugo (September 1988). "Annual and Interim Financial Reporting of Changes in Accounting Estimates," *Accounting Horizons*, pp. 15–25.

Payne, Jeff L., and S. Robb (2000). "The Effect of Ex Ante Earnings Expectations," *Journal of Accounting, Auditing, and Finance* (Vol. 15, No. 4), pp. 371–392.

Penman, Stephen H., and X-J Zhang (April 2002). "Accounting Conservatism, the Quality of Earnings, and Stock Returns," *Accounting Review*, pp. 237–264.

Philips, G. Edward (January 1963). "The Accretion Concept of Income," *Accounting Review*, pp. 14–25.

Pozen, Robert (2007). "The SEC's Fuzzy Math," *Wall Street Journal* (March 23), p. A11.

Reilly, David (2006). "No More 'Stealth Restating,'" *Wall Street Journal* (September 21), pp. C1 and C3.

Ronen, Joshua, and Simcha Sadan (1981). *Smoothing Income Numbers: Objectives, Means, and Implications.* Addison-Wesley.

Schipper, Katherine (December 1989). "Earnings Management," *Accounting Horizons*, pp. 91–102.

Scott, William R. (1997). *Financial Accounting Theory.* Prentice Hall.

Solomon, Deborah, and S. Pulliam (2002). "SEC Takes a Hard Line on Qwest," *Wall Street Journal* (June 26), pp. A3 and A8.

Sprouse, Robert T., and Maurice Moonitz (1962). Accounting Research Study No. 3, *A Tentative Set of Broad Accounting Principles for Business Enterprises.* AICPA.

Teets, Walter R. (November 2002). "Quality of Earnings: An Introduction to the *Issues in Accounting Education* Special Issue," *Issues in Accounting Education*, pp. 355–360.

Thomas, Arthur L. (1969). "The Allocation Problem," *Studies in Accounting Research #3.* American Accounting Association.

———— (1974). "The Allocation Problem: Part Two," *Studies in Accounting Research #9.* American Accounting Association.

Thomas, Jacob, and X-J Zhang (2000). "Identifying Unexpected Accruals: A Comparison of Current Approaches," *Journal of Accounting and Public Policy* (Vol. 19, No. 4), pp. 347–376.

Watts, Ross L., and Richard W. Leftwich (Autumn 1977). "The Time Series of Annual Accounting Earnings," *Journal of Accounting Research*, pp. 253–271.

Wiseman, Donald E. (December 1990). "Holding Loss/Gain as an Alternative to EPS Dilution," *Accounting Horizons*, pp. 18–34.

———— (June 1992). "Reply to 'An Option-Theoretic Argument Favoring EPS Dilution Over Holding Gain/Loss,'" *Accounting Horizons*, pp. 90–93.

Wu, Y. Woody (Fall 1997). "Management Buyouts and Earnings Management," *Journal of Accounting, Auditing & Finance*, pp. 373–390.

13

Statement of Cash Flows

Learning Objectives

After reading this chapter, you should be able to:

- Understand the basic construction of the statement of changes in financial position.
- Understand the motivation for the FASB's move from the statement of changes in financial position to the cash flow statement.
- Understand the requirements of the cash flow statement and the nonarticulation problem that arises when the indirect method is used.
- Comprehend the classification problems that exist in the FASB's trichotomy of operating, investing, and financing activities.
- Appreciate the analytical usefulness of the cash flow statement for different users.
- Understand the importance and usefulness of free cash flow.

The opening setting of Meredith Willson's popular musical *The Music Man* is a passenger car of a train bound for River City, Iowa, sometime during the early 20th century. Several salesmen are found advocating cash terms of sale.[1] "Cash for the merchandise, cash for the button hooks. . . . Cash for the crackers and the pickles and the flypaper. . . ." The salesmen had it right. Ultimately, bills, investments, debts, dividends, etc., are paid with cash, not earnings. If a firm does not generate sufficient cash in the course of its business, it will face extinction. It is that simple. What is not so simple is the best way of conveying a firm's historical cash flows to users. The good news is that we have made much progress over the past forty years. The bad news is that we have more work to do.

In 1971, the Accounting Principles Board (APB) mandated the Statement of Changes in Financial Position (SCFP) for financial reporting.[2] This "funds flow" statement reported changes in assets, liabilities, and owners' equity account balances. In 1987, the Financial Accounting Standards Board (FASB) mandated a statement of cash flows (SCF), SFAS No. 95.[3] This statement superseded the SCFP. The transition from a funds flow statement to a cash flow statement reflected the FASB's interest in cash-basis reporting as an important supplement to the accrual-based income statement and balance sheet.

In the next section, we discuss the SCFP. Next, we discuss the motivation and structure of the SCF. We highlight two major problems: (1) the nonarticulation problem arising from usage of the indirect method in the operating section of the SCF and (2) classification problems and inconsistencies with the FASB's three-way classification within the SCF. Even though some parts of the SCF are viewed to be more important than others, we emphasize that the SCF should be considered in its entirety.

Subsequently, we introduce and explain the concept of free cash flow (FCF), a non-GAAP measure that has arisen partially because of shortcomings in the SCF. We conclude with a review of related theoretical and empirical research, and we make recommendations for changes to the SCF.

The Statement of Changes in Financial Position

To appreciate fully the significance of the statement of cash flows, it is necessary to understand the structure and motivation of its predecessor, the Statement of Changes in Financial Position (SCFP).

The SCFP itself is successor to a prior financial statement, the *funds flow statement*. In a funds flow statement, working capital accounts are defined as comprising the *fund balance*. The purpose of this statement was to show how the fund balance accounts increased from income and other sources and decreased from losses and other uses. The funds flow concept represented the liquid and readily available resources of the firm.

APB Opinion No. 19 stated that the reporting objectives of the SCFP are to (a) complete the disclosure of changes in financial position, (b) summarize financing and investing activity, and (c) report funds flow from operations. The information from these three items cannot be *directly* obtained from an income statement and comparative balance sheets because of the manner in which data are aggregated. Thus, the SCFP provided a different way of classifying and reporting accounting transactions than occurs in a balance sheet and income statement. However, since it relies on definitions and measurements of accounting elements from the other two financial statements, it may be described as a *derivative* financial statement. The underlying logic is summarized as follows:

$$\text{transaction credits} = \text{transaction debits} \tag{13.1}$$

There are two balancing sections in the statement of changes in financial position. These are called *sources of resources* and *uses of resources,* respectively. Sources of resources are defined as transaction credits. These arise from increases in equities and decreases in assets. Increases in equities reflect financing from external sources (e.g., debt and stock issues), as well as internal sources (e.g., net income and proceeds from the disposal of assets).[4]

Exhibit 13.1   Standard Format of the Statement of Changes in Financial Position

Sources of Resources (transaction credits)

1. Increases to the "fund balance" accounts
    a. From net income
    b. From other sources

2. Other sources of resources

3. Decrease, if any, in the fund balance for the period

Uses of Resources (transaction debits)

1. Decreases to the "fund balance" accounts
    a. From net losses
    b. From other sources

2. Other uses of resources

3. Increase, if any, in the fund balance for the period

Uses of resources are defined as transaction debits. These arise from decreases in equities and increases in assets. Decreases in equities reflect a reduction in the firm's financing, including debt retirement, treasury stock purchases, dividend payments, and net losses. Asset increases are uses of the firm's resources. In all cases, the firm's available resources decrease because of debit transactions.

In both the sources and uses sections of the SCFP, transactions are classified into those affecting the fund balance and those affecting other accounts. The effect of net income on the fund balance is reported separately. The structure of the SCFP is illustrated in Exhibit 13.1, which provides a system of classifying transaction debits and credits.[5]

SCFP's predecessor, the funds flow statement, included only the transactions listed under points 1a and 1b in Exhibit 13.1. Transactions not affecting fund accounts were excluded. The result was a report on the change in fund balance and how this change came about. The emphasis in funds flow reporting focused much more narrowly on liquidity. By adding the transactions listed under point 2 in Exhibit 13.1, a comprehensive summary is made of all changes in financial position, not just those pertaining to fund balance accounts. This approach is referred to as the *all-inclusive* or *all-resources* SCFP. The types of transactions listed under point 2 pertain to investment and financing activities not affecting fund accounts. Examples include the conversion of convertible debt to common stock, stock issued for non-monetary assets, dividends paid in property rather than cash, and nonmonetary exchanges of assets. APB Opinion No. 19 opted for the all-inclusive approach rather than the narrower funds flow statement. However, it is apparent that a funds flow statement is still contained within the SCFP.

As part of the preparation of the SCFP, it was necessary to define those balance sheet accounts making up the fund balance accounts. APB Opinion No. 19 permitted any one of four definitions: cash, cash plus near cash (short-term marketable securities and other temporary investments), quick assets, and working capital, an example of flexibility. In any case, all transactions in nonfund accounts are to be included in the statement of changes in financial position. This is true even if the transactions have no direct effect on fund accounts.

When funds are defined as working capital, nonfund transactions are restricted to non-monetary transactions, such as nonmonetary exchanges of assets and the conversion of convertible debt to common stock. Defining funds as cash leads to additional complications as there are many accounting transactions that do not affect cash. This results in additional nonfund transactions that need to be reported separately. Hence, a working capital definition of funds minimized the cost of producing an SCFP. Given that APB Opinion No. 19 allowed flexibility on this point, most firms elected to define funds as net working capital.

The recognition of the importance of the SCFP was gradual. In 1963, APB Opinion No. 3 *recommended* inclusion of an SCFP in the annual report.[6] The Securities and Exchange Commission (SEC) made it mandatory for statutory filings beginning in 1971.[7] In response to the SEC action, the APB issued APB Opinion No. 19 in 1971 and made the statement *mandatory* for financial reporting.[8]

The Motivation for a Cash Flow Statement

What prompted the FASB to rediscover cash-basis accounting as an important supplement to accrual-based financial statements, and why did cash flow supplant the more general concept of funds flow and changes in financial position?[9] During the FASB's deliberations that led to the adoption of an SCF, a consensus emerged that funds should be defined as cash rather than as net working capital. Net working capital came to be viewed as a poor measure of liquidity for three reasons. First, deferred charges and credits are included in net working capital but have no cash flow consequences. Second, the conversion of current assets into cash can take a year or longer for firms with a long operating cycle. And third, items such as inventory are carried on a cost basis and thus do not explicitly measure the cash flow potential of the inventory. In light of these ambiguities, cash flow reporting is appealing because of its straightforwardness and literal interpretation—cash is cash is cash.

Objectives of Financial Reporting

SFAC No. 1 lists three general objectives of financial reporting. The first of these is very broad and states, "Financial reporting should provide information that is useful to present and potential investors and creditors and other users in making rational investment, credit, and similar decisions."[10] Two additional objectives can be thought of as specific ways of meeting the first objective. These are (1) reporting information about the firm's net resources and changes in those resources and (2) reporting information useful in assessing future cash flows. These two reporting goals have motivated the FASB's adoption of an SCF.

Objectives of the Statement of Cash Flows

In SFAC No. 5, the FASB makes the following claims about an SCF:

It provides useful information about an entity's activities in generating cash through operations to repay debt, distribute dividends, or reinvest to maintain or expand operating capacity; about its financing activities, both debt and equity; and about its investing or spending of cash.

Important uses of information about an entity's current cash receipts and payments include help-ing to assess factors such as the entity's liquidity, financial flexibility, profitability, and risk.[11]

An earlier FASB discussion memorandum suggested that cash flow data are a useful sup-plemental disclosure because they:

1. Provide feedback on actual cash flows

2. Help to identify the relationship between accounting income and cash flows

3. Provide information about the quality of income

4. Improve comparability of information in financial reports

5. Aid in assessing flexibility and liquidity

6. Assist in predicting future cash flows[12]

In one way or another, all of the preceding points deal with the limitations of accrual accounting.[13] This suggests that cash flow data can supplement the accrual data provided in the income statement and balance sheet.

It is obvious that cash flow data are necessary in assessing past cash flows (point 1). It fol-lows that cash flow data are also necessary for understanding the cash flow being generated from *operations* (point 2).[14] The third point, *quality of income,* is a term used by financial ana-lysts to describe the relationship between cash flow and accounting income (compare with *quality of earnings* in Chapter 12). The higher the correlation between accounting income and cash flows, the higher the quality of income. The quality-of-income concept reflects an aware-ness that accounting income comprises many noncash accruals and deferrals and does not necessarily give a good indication of liquidity.

The fourth point deals with the uniformity problem. Owing to flexibility in the choice of some accounting policies, comparability between companies may not be achieved. As indicated in Chapter 9, many areas of accounting fail to achieve uniformity. Cash flow from operations is subject to fewer arbitrary choices of accounting policy. It is more uniform than income measure-ment and results in a higher level of comparability. For this reason, the SCF has been advocated as a way of dealing with the arbitrariness of income measurement. There is an appealing clarity and directness to cash flow when contrasted with the abstractness of accounting income.[15]

The fifth point concerns the use of cash flow data to assist in assessing a firm's financial flexibility and liquidity. *Financial flexibility* is the ability of the firm to adapt to new situations and opportunities. *Liquidity* is the capability for quick conversion of assets to cash without loss. Cash being generated internally from operations gives an indication of both liquidity and flexibility. Cash flow represents internal resources available for debt servicing and repay-ment, new investment, and distributions to stockholders. This was the original reason for requiring a funds flow statement.

Liquidity information is also contained in the balance sheet. However, as we noted in Chapter 11, the current–noncurrent classification system is a poor guide to liquidity. Some current items are deferred charges or credits that have no impact on future cash flows. In addition, assets such as inventory may not be readily converted into cash. Furthermore, within the current group of assets, very few are actually convertible to cash within a short period. Finally, since the attribute of measurement reported in the balance sheet is normally something other than net realizable value, it is not possible to determine how much cash will be generated from assets. In essence, a balance sheet presents nothing more than a crude ranking of liquidity, and in its present form it reveals very little about liquidity and flexibility. An SCF, on the other hand, gives insight into the cash-generating potential of operations.

The *exit-price* accounting system illustrated in Appendix 1-A is intended to measure flexibility of the firm in terms of the amount of cash that could be realized from nonforced liquidation of assets.[16] However, even exit-price measurement is only a crude indicator of liquidity and flexibility. Although such a measurement system might provide an estimate of the cash conversion value of a firm's resources, it is the speed of conversion that ultimately determines both liquidity and flexibility. How useful exit-price accounting is for assessing a firm's flexibility is therefore questionable. In addition, a firm is more likely to raise capital incrementally rather than by selling all its assets. Normally, a firm would not sell its productive assets to raise new capital for new investment opportunities. A firm is more likely to use either new capital or cash realized from assets being held for sale, such as inventories.

The sixth and final point suggests that cash flow data are useful for predicting future cash flows. It makes sense that past cash flow data would be useful for predicting future cash flows. However, it remains unsettled if cash flow, funds flow, or accounting income is the best predictor of future cash flows. It is also unclear what the prediction period should be. Holding aside the question of costs, the expanded disclosure philosophy maintains that firms should disclose all potentially useful information.

Requirements of the Cash Flow Statement

Structure of the SCF

The SCFP used a very general sources and uses framework. This binary framework focuses mechanically on the narrow accounting debit–credit relation illustrated in Exhibit 13.1. In contrast, the SCF classifies cash receipts and payments into more meaningful categories relating to operating, financing, and investing activities.

Cash is defined as literal cash on hand or on-demand deposit, plus cash equivalents. *Cash equivalents* are short-term, highly liquid investments, which are convertible into known amounts of cash. Like APB Opinion No. 19, the SCF requires all *noncash* investing and financing transactions to be reported as a supplement to the SCF, either in a schedule or in a narrative format. This approach represents the all-inclusive or all-resources concept of funds flow reporting. It presumably assures that *all* of the firm's transaction debits and credits are accounted for and presented in the SCF. An example of the suggested format is illustrated in Exhibit 13.2.

In the SCF, cash flows are segregated into those stemming from operating activities, investing activities, and financing activities. This organization provides more classificational

Exhibit 13.2   Illustration of the SCF in Accordance with SFAS No. 95 (Direct Method)

COMPANY M
CONSOLIDATED STATEMENT OF CASH FLOWS
FOR THE YEAR ENDED DECEMBER 31, 2000
Increase (Decrease) in Cash and Cash Equivalents

Cash flows from operating activities:	
Cash received from customers	$13,850
Cash paid to suppliers and employees	(12,000)
Dividend received from affiliate	20
Interest received	55
Interest paid (net of amount capitalized)	(220)
Income taxes paid	(325)
Insurance proceeds received	15
Cash paid to settle lawsuit for patent infringement	(30)
Net cash provided by operating activities	$1,365
Cash flows from investing activities:	
Proceeds from sale of facility	$6,001
Payment received on note for sale of plant	150
Capital expenditures	(1,000)
Payment for purchase of Company S, net of cash acquired	(925)
Net cash used in investing activities	$(1,175)
Cash flows from financing activities:	
Net borrowings under line-of-credit agreement	$300
Principal payments under capital lease obligation	(125)
Proceeds from issuance of long-term debt	400
Proceeds from issuance of common stock	500
Dividends paid	(200)
Net cash provided by financing activities	$875
Net increase in cash and cash equivalents	$1,065
Cash and cash equivalents at beginning of year	600
Cash and cash equivalents at end of year	$1,665

SOURCE: FASB Statement No. 95, Statement of Cash Flows, page 44. Used with permission of FASB. Method of Presentation.

consistency, which should lead to greater comparability than the SCFP (see footnote 5). However, three of the seven members of the FASB dissented from the statement. They maintained that interest and dividends *received* arise from investing activities rather than from operating activities, as stated in paragraph 22 of the standard. This is in line with current thinking in finance. Similarly, interest paid is an element of financing activities rather than an operating cost, as noted in paragraph 23.[17]

SFAS 95 states that operating cash flows may be presented using either the direct or the indirect method. The *direct method* reports literal cash flows related to income statement classifications (revenues, cost of sales, etc.). By contrast, the *indirect* or *reconciliation method* starts with accrual income and adjusts it for the associated noncash items. More information is reported with the direct method, and the FASB appears to favor it. However, in both the exposure draft and the eventual accounting standard, the FASB acknowledged that the direct method might be more costly, since not all companies organize their accounting records in such a way that produces the necessary data.

If the direct method is used, a separate schedule shall reconcile net operating cash flow with net income, as illustrated in Exhibit 13.3. Thus, the indirect or reconciliation method must be used either alone or as a supplement to the direct method. Several members of the FASB believe that allowing the use of the indirect method will impede user understanding and will diminish the quality of financial reporting.[18]

Exhibit 13.3 also shows the supplemental schedule of noncash investing and financing activities required whether the direct or the indirect method is the primary vehicle for displaying net cash from operating activities.

The great bulk of American firms use the indirect method. It would appear that preparers have been influenced by the cost issue, given their very strong preference for the indirect method. Both methods result in the same cash flow from operations number. The information in arriving at this number, however, is different: (a) cash flow numbers for sales, cost of goods sold, and the like versus (b) a reconciliation adjusting accrual accounting income to its cash flow analog. The issue involved is one of costs versus benefits of information. There has been a limited amount of empirical research indicating that the direct method is preferred to the indirect, particularly by outside users. In a study involving 282 respondents who were financial analysts, investment advisers, accounting professors, and "accountants," McEnroe found that 56% favored the direct method as opposed to 44% favoring the indirect method.[19]

The Nonarticulation Problem

An important problem has surfaced relative to the indirect method. An extensive study by Bahnson, Miller, and Budge found that where the indirect method is employed in determining cash flow from operations, *nonarticulation* occurs when the cash flows arising from the changes in the working capital accounts of consolidated enterprises are not equal to the working capital adjustments listed in the operations section of the SCF.[20] Nonarticulation can create confusion in understanding the underlying numbers in the operating section of the SCF because it appears to make the SCF inconsistent with the underlying balance sheet. Furthermore, these discrepancies occurred in 75% of the situations covered in the researchers' sample.

Exhibit 13.3   Indirect or Reconciliation Method of Presenting Net Cash Flows From Operating
Activities

Reconciliation of net income to net cash provided by operating activities:

Net income		$760
Adjustments to reconcile net income to net cash provided by operating activities:		
Depreciation and amortization	$445	
Provision for losses on accounts receivable	200	
Gain on sale of facility	(80)	
Undistributed earnings of affiliate	(25)	
Payment received on installment note receivable for sale of inventory	100	
Change in assets and liabilities net of effects from purchase of Company S:		
Increase in accounts receivable	(215)	
Decrease in inventory	205	
Increase in prepaid expenses	(25)	
Decrease in accounts payable and accrued expenses	(250)	
Increase in interest and income taxes payable	50	
Increase in deferred taxes	150	
Increase in other liabilities	50	
Total adjustments		$605
Net cash provided by operating activities		$1,365
Fair value of assets acquired	$1,580	
Cash paid for the capital stock	(950)	
Liabilities assumed	$630	

SOURCE: FASB Statement No. 95, Statement of Cash Flows, page 45. Used with permission of FASB.

We might add that the discrepancies are not trivial. As an example, in Exhibit 13.4, we calculated the change in the balance sheet accounts for accounts receivable, inventories, and accounts payable for 3M Company and compared those changes to the working capital adjustments provided in the SCF. Note especially the percentage difference for accounts receivable. We have even observed instances in which even the signs are different.

One important reason for nonarticulation is because of acquisitions of subsidiaries during the year. When a firm acquires a subsidiary, beginning-of-year working capital balances of acquired

Exhibit 13.4   Comparison of Balance Sheet Changes and Working Capital Adjustments for 3M Company ($000,000)

	2005	2004	Change in Balance Sheet Account	Working Capital Adjustment in the SCF	Percentage Difference
Accounts receivable	$2,838	$2,792	$(46)	$(184)	300.0%
Inventories	$2,162	$1,897	$(265)	$(294)	10.9%
Accounts payable	$1,256	$1,168	$88	$113	28.4%

SOURCE: 3M Company 10-K annual report for fiscal year December 31, 2005, pp. 38, 40.

firms are not included in beginning consolidated balance sheets. To articulate, these missing balances would have to be included in the beginning-of-year balances for the consolidated firm.

In addition to nonarticulation caused by mid-year acquisitions, nonarticulation is also caused by transactions involving working capital accounts that do not affect cash. These types of transactions affect nonconsolidated firms as well as consolidated ones. Some examples of these kinds of transactions include:

- Writeups or writedowns of working capital items—typically inventories—when firms are acquired by purchase
- Depreciation allocations within manufactured inventories
- Any type of reclassification of working capital accounts between current and noncurrent categories[21]

Finally, nonarticulation can occur when one accounts payable account is used for the purchase of both working capital assets (e.g., inventories), as well as for the purchase of non-working-capital assets (e.g., equipment). For example, the purchase of inventory on account is an operating activity. It leads to an increase in accounts payable and to a positive (cash inflow) working capital adjustment in the operating section of the SCF. In contrast, the purchase of equipment on account is an *investing* activity. When the SCF is constructed, the deferred payment for the equipment should be reflected in the investing section. As such, the change in balance sheet accounts payable will not equal the accounts payable adjustment in the operating section of the SCF.

These situations abound when the indirect method is used and unfavorably affect the utility of the method. As a result, Bahnson, Miller, and Budge strongly favor the direct method.[22]

Classification Problems of SFAS No. 95

In addition to three dissents by FASB members, significant questions have been raised about the structure of the SCF as specified by SFAS No. 95. Relative to the operating, financing, investing trichotomy, Nurnberg states that this breakdown is in accordance with the finance literature and is supposed to provide information that is useful for investment and credit decisions.[23] However, Nurnberg notes that the SCF classifies interest and dividend *receipts* as operating inflows and interest *payments* as operating outflows. According to the finance literature, these are investing activities in the former situation and financing activities in the latter case.[24]

In SFAS No. 95, the FASB followed the income statement format with a proprietary orientation—interest revenue and expense and dividend revenue as reflected as operating items. This contrasts with showing these elements as investing activities (interest and dividend revenues) or financing activities (interest expense) as in an entity theory approach (Chapter 5). While the FASB may have had a difficult choice between following the accounting income (proprietary theory) approach and the finance orientation (entity theory), more practical considerations may have influenced the FASB. Banking institutions favored classifying interest receipts and interest payments as operating items—which they may well be for banks—to avoid reporting negative cash flows from operations.[25] Hence, maintaining consistency with the income statement as well as the problem of the banking industry may have influenced the FASB's decision to split interest expense (operations) and the receipt and repayment of principal (financing activities).

International Accounting Standards (IAS)

IAS 7 of the International Accounting Standards Board (IASB) takes a flexible view toward interest and dividends received or paid. They may be classified as operating, investing, or financing cash flows, provided that they are classified consistently from period to period. The treatment conflicts with the present proprietary orientation of SFAS No. 95 and the entity theory approach suggested in this chapter and Chapter 12.

For banks, interest and dividends can be viewed as operating cash flows. If IAS 7 were changed to allow this classification by banks, then the IASB will have attained uniformity within industries as discussed in Chapter 9.

Premium and Discount on Bonds and Notes

The split between interest and dividend revenues (operating) and purchasing stock of other firms (investing) and borrowing or repaying principal (financing) leads to further problems. In the case of bonds payable or long-term notes payable, the question arises as to how to handle any discount or premium, which are interest adjustments but are part of principal borrowed: a positive amount in the case of a premium or a shortfall in the case of a discount.

Vent, Cowlings, and Sevalstad have found four ways to deal with this situation in published annual reports.[26] Consider a situation in which a firm issues four-year 8% coupon bonds with a total face value (par value) of $10,000. The bonds are sold for $11,000 on December 31, 2000. For simplicity, assume straight-line amortization of the premium. Annual interest expense would be $550 ($800 minus $250 of premium amortization). The four methods are shown in Exhibit 13.5. Method 1 is probably the easiest to follow and would probably be the one used with the direct method. Notice that the sum of the operating flows does not equal the accrual accounting interest expense because the $1,000 premium is part of the financing flow in the year 2000. Methods 2 and 3 break out the premium from the investment flow and put it into the operating flow category. Method 2 assigns the premium to the operations in the year of

Exhibit 13.5 Premium Allocation Between Operating and Financing Cash Flows[a]

| | Method 1 | | | Method 2 | |
| | Operating Flow | Financing Flow | | Operating Flow | Financing Flow |
Year					
2000		$11,000			$11,000
2001	$(800)			$(800)	
2002	(800)			(800)	
2003	(800)			(800)	
2004	(800)	(10,000)		(800)	(11,000)
2004				1,000	

| | Method 3 | | | Method 4 | |
| | Operating Flow | Financing Flow | | Operating Flow | Financing Flow |
Year					
2000	$1,000	$10,000			$11,000
2001	(800)			$(550)	(250)
2002	(800)			(550)	(250)
2003	(800)			(550)	(250)
2004	(800)	(10,000)		(550)	(250)
2004					(10,000)

SOURCE: Based on Vent, Cowlings, and Sevalstad (1995).

payment, 2004, whereas Method 3 makes assignment in 2000, the year of issue. Method 4 allocates the premium over the life of the bonds.

Our preference is for Method 1 despite the lack of agreement between the accrual and cash flow amounts. Method 4 makes the least sense because it allocates the premium over the four years as a financing outflow (which it is not), thereby breaking up the annual cash flow from 2001 through 2004 into two $800 segments. While Method 1 is almost assuredly going to be used with the direct method, Methods 1–3 would all be possible under the indirect method. Notice that we are dealing with yet another example of the allocation problem.

Munter raises several similar issues. If interest payments are capitalized in accordance with the provisions of SFAS No. 34, they will be excluded from operating activities and included in investing activities as part of the acquisition costs of the fixed asset.[27] This raises the question of whether events should be classified by the basic nature of the receipt or expenditure (interest payment) or on the basis of the ultimate purpose of the event (asset acquisition).

A similar division arises in lease transactions with differences between capital leases and operating leases.[28] In the case of operating leases, the entire amount of the cash expenditures is classified as a cash outflow deriving from operating activities. For capital leases, the interest portion is classified as an operating activity, whereas the reduction of principal portion is a financing activity. Whether the basic nature of the event or the ultimate classification of the transaction should govern in the SCFs remains an unanswered question.

Increased Flexibility of Presentation

In SFAS No. 95, hedging activities were considered to be investing activities. The standard presented a strict classification by the nature of the hedge transaction as an investment-type transaction (the rigid uniformity concept).

In contrast, SFAS No. 104, which amends SFAS No. 95, allows association with the balance sheet account to which the hedge pertains. If it is identifiable with a particular balance sheet item such as inventories (protecting against inventory price increases, for example), SFAS No. 104 allows the hedge (forward contracts, futures contracts, and options or swaps) to be classified either with that item on the balance sheet as an element of operations or as an investing activity.[29] Nurnberg and Largay believe that the increased flexibility in accounting for hedge transactions in SFAS No. 104 will generally lead to less comparability but may be justified as an increase in "fineness" in some situations.[30]

Analytical Usefulness of the Cash Flow Statement

Despite classification and nonarticulation problems, the SCF is clearly a very useful statement. This is nicely demonstrated in a unique example of research by Ingram and Lee, in which they use the income statement and the SCF together.[31] They posited that over time, growing firms will have *higher* income and *lower* cash flows from operations. This is because growing firms will have increasing inventories and accounts receivable as they expand. To some extent the inventories and receivables will be offset by increases in payables, but the net effect of the growth in working capital is that each year, the change in income will exceed the change in operating cash flows in actual and most likely relative terms. Furthermore, as a firm expands, there will be net investment outflows as fixed assets are acquired and cash inflows from financing as new debt and equity are floated and dividends remain low or nonexistent.

For a firm that is contracting, the relationships will largely run in reverse; sales and income decline but operating cash flows will usually increase as accounts receivable and inventory are contracted. In addition, cash outflows for investment will decline. Similarly, in the financing category, cash outflows will increase as stock repurchases (treasury stock), debt retirements, and cash dividends increase.

Notice the similarity between Ingram and Lee's work and the use of cash flows and accruals for predictive purposes as discussed in Chapter 8. Ingram and Lee's statistical analysis, which involved almost 1,000 firms over the period 1974–1992, largely supported their deductive analysis. Consistent with the above, their analysis also found that expanding firms are more likely to have more financial leverage than contracting enterprises.

Issues Relating to Rules for Classifying Cash Flows

While the SCF is less manipulable than income, it is not exempt from the problem.[32] Cash flow from operations is considered by many to be the most important part of the SCF, and many users focus on it. Consequently, considerable activity is devoted to increasing cash flows from operations by shifting cash outflows from operating activities to investing activities, or by shifting cash inflows from investing activities to cash inflows from operating activities.[33] While the overall effect on cash remains unchanged, without further scrutiny, users will undoubtedly view this realignment favorably.

Maremont offers an example of this problem involving Tyco International, a seller of home security alarm systems.[34] Customers pay approximately $30 a month for these services, and the contracts often extend beyond a year. Tyco sells these services itself, but it also buys service contracts from other dealers. It would seem that cash expended by Tyco to develop home security alarm sales versus money spent by Tyco to acquire service contracts from other firms should be treated similarly: (a) cash outflows from operations for portions applicable to home security alarm sales recognized in income in the current year and (b) cash outflows for investments for the portion attributable to revenues to be recognized in future periods. Similar treatment of purchased contracts and contracts sold directly by Tyco would be an example of a well-merited rigid uniformity.

However, Tyco evidently treats these similar cash flow situations differently. The dealer contracts purchased by Tyco are treated as "acquisitions" and these cash flows are recognized on the SCF as cash outflows from operations on a considerably slower basis than cash outflows from internally generated home security alarm systems. Classificational inconsistencies of this type on the SCF are not unusual.

Another example of using flexibility in applying FASB's classification rules comes from the automotive industry. In an article from the *Wall Street Journal,* Mulford relates three such examples from the automotive industry.[35] In these situations, Ford Motor Co., General Motors Corp., and Harley-Davidson Inc. lent money to dealers in the form of notes receivable so that the dealers could purchase inventories. The companies recognized the revenue from the sales but classified the loans as investing activities. This increased reported cash flow from operating activities by a nontrivial amount. In the General Motors case, reported cash flow from operating activities was $7.6 billion. If the notes receivable had been treated as an operating activity instead of as an investing activity, cash flow from operating activities would have been $3.5 billion.

Contrast this approach with that of Navistar International Corp. While the company's captive subsidiary shows the notes receivable as an investing activity, Navistar's consolidated results reclassifies the notes receivable as a part of cash flow from operating activities. Mark Oberle, Navistar's director of investor relations, notes: "At the end of the day, we define ourselves as a manufacturing company with a finance subsidiary. . . . [The] sale and the associated change in receivables . . . [is] part of our core business."[36]

The upshot is that even when the rules for classifying cash flows are not violated, the vagueness or flexibility in applying the rules allows companies in the same industry to give vastly different perspectives to investors and creditors. A partial solution to this problem is given below.

The SCF Is More Than Cash Flow From Operating Activities

The previous section highlights how flexibility in classification (or even deliberate misclassification) can affect the perception of the firm's financial strength. As we indicated previously, cash flow from operating activities is considered by many to be the most important part of the SCF, and many users focus on it.[37] The undue attention to one section of the SCF is problematic. The statement of cash flows consists of three parts, and they are all important. The following example using WorldCom Inc. illustrates the point.

On July 21, 2002, WorldCom Inc. filed voluntary petitions for reorganization under Chapter 11 of the U.S. Bankruptcy Code in the United States Bankruptcy Court for the Southern District of New York. Prior to filing for bankruptcy, WorldCom had engaged in accounting irregularities, capitalizing expenses that should have been classified as operating activities. This misclassification boosted reported cash flow from operating activities and lent credibility to its net income. While many investors were fooled by WorldCom's shenanigans, the SCF—in its entirety—gave enough hints to cause investors to be skeptical.

Exhibit 13.6 presents selected items from WorldCom's SCF until approximately six months before the company filed for bankruptcy. Note that net income was positive for the three years before the firm filed for bankruptcy. A closer look at the SCF gives a different picture, in spite of the fact the company inflated cash flow from operating activities by misclassifying operating expenses as investments. If the cash flow from investing activities reflects *necessary* investments in the business, the difference between cash flow from operating activities and cash flow from investing activities provides information on how much cash is (or will be) available for investors. In WorldCom's case, this difference indicates that the company was hemorrhaging cash in three of the four years before bankruptcy. The cumulative effects indicate that by December 31, 2001, the company had dug itself a $12 billion hole.

While it is not uncommon for new and growing companies to invest more than they generate from operations, one might wonder if WorldCom was this kind of company. Furthermore, even if one assumed that all of the investing activities were legitimate, it would have been logical to question how long this kind of investing activity could continue. In essence, when would the "hole" stop getting deeper and how would WorldCom climb out?

Unfortunately, investors who unduly focused on net income or even cash flow from operating activities would probably not have asked that question. *In its entirety,* the SCF paints a valuable picture of the net cash flow generating ability of a business. Investors who ignore one or more parts do so at their peril.

Cash Flow Needs of Different Users

In his 1988 letter to the shareholders of Berkshire Hathaway (BRKA), Warren Buffett summarized what needs to be reported for users of financial statements.

What needs to be reported is data . . . that helps financially-literate readers answer three key questions: (1) Approximately how much is this company worth? (2) What is the likelihood that it can meet its future obligations? and (3) How good a job are its managers doing, given the hand they have been dealt?[38]

Exhibit 13.6   Selected Items From WorldCom's Statement of Cash Flows ($000,000)

As Reported	12/31/98	12/31/99	12/31/00	12/31/01
Net income (loss)	$(2,669)	$4,013	$4,153	$1,501
Cash flow from operating activities (CFO)	$4,085	$11,005	$7,666	$7,994
Cash used in investing activities (CFI)	(9,433)	(9,555)	(14,385)	(9,690)
CFO –CFI	$(5,348)	$1,450	$(6,719)	$(1,696)
Cumulative CFO - CFI	$(5,348)	$(3,898)	$(10,617)	$(12,313)

SOURCE: Mergent Online (http://www.mergentonline.com, accessed Thursday, November 23, 2006).

In essence, the financial statements need to provide the information for valuing the company, making credit decisions, and assessing managerial performance. Assessing managerial performance requires accurate measures of *historical* cash flows.[39] Credit and valuation decisions require unbiased predictions of *future* cash flows, in line with Statements of Financial Accounting Concepts (SFAC) No. 1.[40]

Investment decisions are particularly dependent on *predicting* future cash flows.[41] Investing is a capital allocation decision. In principle, the accepted decision criterion is the same criterion used for capital budgeting decisions. For capital budgeting purposes, firms should accept an investment if the present value of the expected net cash flows is positive.[42] That is, accept the investment if the net present value (NPV) is positive.

Similarly, a stock purchase is acceptable if the per-share present value of the future expected cash flows—intrinsic value—is greater than the current market price. Most investment professionals recognize this.[43] For example, in discussing intrinsic value in Berkshire Hathaway's "An Owner's Manual," Warren Buffett, one of the world's best and best known investors, notes:

> Intrinsic value is an all-important concept that offers the only logical approach to evaluating the relative attractiveness of investments and businesses. Intrinsic value can be defined simply: It is the discounted value of the cash that can be taken out of a business during its remaining life. The calculation of intrinsic value, though, is not so simple. As our definition suggests, intrinsic value is an estimate rather than a precise figure, and it is additionally an estimate that must be changed if interest rates move or forecasts of future cash flows are revised.[44]

The question is: What cash flows do we use to determine intrinsic value? In principle, the definition of the cash flows used for valuing the business enterprise is the same as that used for capital budgeting purposes. However, in the case of the firm, the cash flows are called *free cash flows* (FCFs). Mulford and Comiskey note that "The term 'free' refers to an absence of a superior claim. It is cash flow that is available for use with no strings attached. Spending it will not affect the firm's ability to generate more."[45]

They document the increasing attention to free cash flow in the financial press, most likely due to a "reaction to the numerous and well-publicized accounting problems and examples of egregious acts of earnings management witnessed in recent years." Mulford and Comiskey view the increasing popularity of free cash flows positively:

We welcome the growing attention placed on free cash flow. We think that it provides evidence that investors and creditors are emphasizing what really matters to analysis and valuation. . . .[46]

Mulford and Comiskey point out that there are several definitions of free cash flow used by companies and in the financial press. Following the entity theory of the firm, we focus on cash flow to the firm.[47] Unfortunately, FCFs cannot be obtained directly from the SCF. They are defined as follows.

$$FCF = NOPLAT - investment\ in\ operating\ invested\ capital \qquad (13.2)$$

NOPLAT is net operating profit less adjusted taxes. In a simple case, NOPLAT is after-tax operating income.[48] Investment in operating invested capital is typically broken down into investment in net operating working capital and investment in noncurrent assets.

Note that FCFs do not include interest expense, a financing expense.[49] Furthermore, consistent with the notion of an ongoing firm, *operating cash* is regarded as part of net operating working capital, much the same as accounts receivable and inventories.[50]

We illustrate the construction of FCF and its comparison to the SCF by introducing the ABC Company. Exhibit 13.7 presents ABC's income statement and balance sheet. From these two statements, we construct an SCF in Exhibit 13.8 on page 445 and a statement of free cash flows in Exhibit 13.9 on page 446.

In Exhibit 13.10 on page 447, we show how FCFs can be computed from the SCF. Note that we add back after-tax interest expense to cash flow from operating activities to eliminate the effects of financing flows in cash flow from operating activities. We also subtract the increase in operating cash as part of invested capital.

Exhibit 13.11 on page 447 presents a comparison of four performance or valuation measures for ABC Company. The choice of measure depends on time, resources, and the use to which it is put. In the interest of time, some users might only consider net income. To obtain a better understanding of the firm's operations, and to assess the quality of net income, users might focus on cash flow from operating activities (CFO). To avoid any potential problems with classifying operating expenses as investing activities, and to get a sense of the *net* cash-generating ability of the firm, it makes sense to subtract cash from investing activities (CFI). As we have noted previously, CFO is "contaminated" with interest expense (financing).[51] To focus on the operations of the enterprise, and to recognize operating cash itself as a part of invested capital, we can compute FCFs. Investors can estimate the intrinsic value of the firm by discounting forecasted FCFs using the firm's weighted average cost of capital.[52]

Unfortunately, when considered with net income, we now have four performance measures that give potentially different views. The real world is never simple.

Cash and Funds Flow Research

Two long-standing advocates of cash flow reporting, Lawson and Lee, have argued that cash flow reports are necessary to report on the firm's performance.[53] That is, liquidity (cash flow) is an integral part of the firm's performance. Lee puts it even more strongly: "Cash flow and not profit is the end result of entity activity. Profit is an abstraction; cash is a physical

Exhibit 13.7   Income Statement and Balance Sheet for ABC Company

Income Statement	2004	2005	2006	2007
Sales		$6,100	$6,466	$6,789
Cost of goods sold (excluding depreciation)		(4,209)	(4,462)	(4,684)
Gross profit		1,891	2,004	2,105
Selling, general and administrative expense		(1,098)	(1,229)	(1,290)
Depreciation and amortization		(215)	(220)	(228)
Operating income		578	555	587
Interest expense		(44)	(35)	(36)
Pre-tax income		534	520	551
Provision for taxes (40%)		(214)	(208)	(220)
Net income (loss)		$320	$312	$331

Balance Sheet as of December 31	2004	2005	2006	2007
Cash and equivalents	$300	$244	$323	$339
Accounts receivable	930	915	1,035	1,018
Inventories	1,010	1,037	970	1,154
Total current assets	2,240	2,196	2,328	2,511
Property, plant, and equipment	2,500	2,562	2,651	2,783
Total assets	$4,740	$4,758	$4,979	$5,294
Accounts payable	$850	$854	$841	$883
Notes payable	73	58	60	67
Total current liabilities	923	912	901	950
Long-term debt	657	524	539	606
Total liabilities	1,580	1,436	1,440	1,556
Common stock	860	830	860	860
Retained earnings	2,300	2,492	2,679	2,878
Total common equity	3,160	3,322	3,539	3,738
Total equities	$4,740	$4,758	$4,979	$5,294

resource."[54] Although there is some debate as to whether cash flow reports are superior to accrual statements or just an important supplement to them, Lawson and Lee have neverthe- less made a strong case. As discussed in Chapter 8, the cash flow valuation model from the financial economics literature presents a similar viewpoint: Cash flows of the firm are the

Exhibit 13.8   Statement of Cash Flows for ABC Company

Statement of Cash Flows (SCF)	2005	2006	2007
Cash flow from operating activities (CFO)			
Net income	$320	$312	$331
Depreciation	215	220	228
Adjustment for accounts receivable	15	(120)	17
Adjustment for inventories	(27)	67	(184)
Adjustment for accounts payable	4	(13)	42
Cash flow from operating activities	$527	$466	$434
Cash flow from investment activities (CFI)	$(277)	$(309)	$(360)
Cash flow from financing activities (CFF)			
Notes payable	$(15)	$2	$7
Long-term debt	(133)	15	67
Cash dividends	(128)	(125)	(132)
Common stock repurchases	(30)	30	–
Cash flow from financing activities	$(306)	$(78)	$(58)
Net increase in cash	$(56)	$79	$16
Cash at beginning of year	300	244	323
Cash at end of year	$244	$323	$339

ultimate determinant of firm value, not accrual accounting income. However, there is also a growing body of capital market research evidence that accounting accruals provide information over and above literal cash flows vis-à-vis the firm's security prices.[55]

One interpretation of this body of research is that cash flows and accruals are more useful together than either one is alone; that is, both are useful in evaluating the firm's performance and prospects. From this perspective, then, the SCF is complementary to accrual statements, and the decomposition of accrual data into its cash flow and accrual components provides *new* information.

A number of surveys of investors and analysts have consistently shown that cash (funds) flow data are used for investment analysis but that conventional profitability analysis based on accrual data dominates over the liquidity focus of cash or funds flow.[56] However, a survey commissioned by the Financial Accounting Foundation found that funds flow data were increasing in importance while accrual data were decreasing in importance.[57] Empirical analysis indicating the importance of information content of both accrual accounting income and cash flows was discussed in Chapter 8. All of this suggests that cash flow plays an important and perhaps increasing role in assessing overall firm performance and prospects.[58]

Exhibit 13.9   Statement of Free Cash Flows for ABC Company

Free Cash Flows	2005	2006	2007
Taxes (cash basis) on operating income			
Provision for taxes	$214	208	220
Add tax shield for interest expense	18	14	14
Taxes (cash basis) on operating income	$232	222	234
Free cash flow from operating assets			
Operating income	$578	$555	$587
Taxes (cash basis) on operating income	(232)	(222)	(234)
Net operating profit less adjusted taxes (NOPLAT)	$346	333	353
Depreciation and amortization expense	215	220	228
Gross cash flow	$561	553	581
Investment in net operating working capital	$48	(145)	(141)
Investment in net property, plant, and equipment	(277)	(309)	(360)
Total investment	$(229)	(454)	(501)
Free cash flows from operating assets	$332	$99	$80
Free cash flows to equities			
After-tax cash flows to interest bearing debt			
Interest expense, after tax	$26	$ 21	$22
Repayment (issuance) of interest-bearing debt	148	(17)	(74)
After-tax cash flows to interest bearing debt	$174	$4	$(52)
Cash flows to common equity			
Cash dividends	$128	$125	$132
Repurchase (issuance) of common stock	30	(30)	–
Cash flows to equity	$158	$95	$132
Free cash flows to equities	$332	$99	$80

Improving the SCF

It is clear that the SCF is an important tool for investors, creditors, and managers. While recognizing its value in its current form, we are convinced that there is room for improvement. We are not alone.

Broome notes that the SCF plays a crucial role in securities analysis. However, reflecting on the events surrounding the accounting debacles of Adelphia, Dynegy, Qwest, Tyco,

Exhibit 13.10   Computing Free Cash Flow From the SCF for ABC Company

	2005	2006	2007
Cash flow from operating activities (CFO)	$527	$466	$434
Add: After-tax interest expense	26	21	22
Less: Increase in operating cash	56	(79)	(16)
Net cash flow from investing activities	(277)	(309)	(360)
Free cash flow	$332	$99	$80

Exhibit 13.11   A Comparison of Performance Measures for ABC Company

Performance measure	2005	2006	2007
Net income	$320	$312	$331
Cash flow from operating activities (CFO)	$527	$466	$434
Cash flow from investing activities (CFI)	(277)	(309)	(360)
CFO –CFI	$250	$157	$74
Free cash flow	$332	$99	$80

WorldCom, and others, he convincingly argues that the SCF can and should be improved. SFAS No. 95's flexibility in allowing either the direct or the indirect method creates confusion.

> "The complicated adjustments required by the indirect method are hard for the reader to under-stand and . . . provide corporate managers more leeway for manipulating the statement of cash flows. . . . In many cases, these adjustments cannot be reconciled to observed changes in balance sheet accounts . . ."[59]

Another issue, which we have already noted, deals with the classification of specific cash flows among the SCF's three sections. Given these shortcomings, Broome makes three major recommendations. First, in light of the fact that the both indirect and direct methods might have valuable information content, he recommends that "the FASB require the direct method *and* [italics added] the associated reconciliation of net income to operating cash flow for the operating section."[60] Second, the FASB should provide more guidance on classification of cash flows for the three sections. Finally, he recommends that "the supplementary reconcilia-tion should begin with cash flow from operations and proceed to net income, which is the reverse of the current practice in statements of cash flows."[61]

We agree with Broome, that the direct method should be required.[62] However, if the present system of choice between the direct and indirect method is kept, we think that firms should be required to provide a schedule showing the noncash flow transactions that affect working capi-tal accounts. This should allow the user to understand the differences between balance sheet changes and the SCF. Furthermore, in the case of mid-year acquisitions, firms should provide a schedule that reconciles the working capital adjustments in the operating section of the SCF with the respective balance sheet changes. In general, a firm should explain the source of any nonarticulation that occurs in the operating section of the SCF.

Summary

The Statement of Changes in Financial Position was mandated by APB Opinion No. 19 in 1971. The purpose of the statement was to disclose changes in financial position, summarize financing and investing activity, and report funds flow from operations.

The Statement of Cash Flows is a special case of the more general Statement of Changes in Financial Position, with funds simply defined to be cash. It is a derivative statement because it is based on the accounting transactions already summarized in the income statement and balance sheet. However, new information is reported through the decomposition of the data into cash flow and accrual components, and through reclassifying the data into operating flows, net financing flows, and net investment flows.

In SFAS No. 95, the FASB chose to follow the traditional income statement, proprietary approach, rather than the entity model. This has led to issues relating to classification. Interest expense, interest revenue, and dividend revenue all appear in the operating section, whereas the related balance sheet items (bonds payable, stock investments, and long-term notes receivable) are either financing or investing elements. While the entity approach, on its own, might be more useful, the FASB chose to stay with the traditional income statement model.

Two issues associated with the SCF are nonarticulation and misclassifications. Nonarticulation refers to the fact that working capital adjustments in the operating section frequently differ from the changes in the respective balance sheet accounts. It can occur when the indirect method is used.

One type of misclassification results in mixing financing cash flows (interest expense) with operating cash flows. Another type of misclassification increases cash flow from operating activities by shifting certain cash flows to investing activities. International accounting standards allow flexibility in presentation as long as consistency is maintained.

Research concerning the usefulness to investors of cash and funds flow data is supportive of the contention that they are informative above and beyond accrual data. Indeed, some argue that that the SCFs are more useful in investment analysis than earnings reports.[63] Yet there are problems with the SCF. Either the direct or indirect method of presenting cash flows from operations can be chosen. If the direct method is selected, an indirect reconciliation must also be presented. This has led to an almost unanimous selection of the indirect method.

Free cash flows are growing in usage. They might be considered a variant of the statement of cash flows and are consistent with classifying interest expense as a financing activity.

In spite of the above-mentioned problems, we think that the change from the SCFP to the SCF has brought about a greater consistency among firms. In addition, we think that it provides information that is useful for predictive purposes and enhances comparability. We expect the SCF to become increasingly more important to users because it does not contain the "arbitrariness" of the income statement.

QUESTIONS

1. How did the all-inclusive or all-resources approach to the SCFP with funds defined as working capital differ from the older funds flow statement?

2. SFAS No. 95 allows a choice between the direct and the indirect method for calculating the operations section of the SCF. Do you think this is a case of flexibility? Explain.

3. What is the "fineness" issue raised by Nurnberg and Largay relative to accounting for hedging transactions in SFAS No. 104?

4. Does the "fineness" issue arise in the handling of capitalized interest costs (SFAS No. 34) relative to the treatment of this item in SFAS No. 95? Explain.

5. What advantages do you see for classifying interest expense as an investing cash flow rather than an operating cash flow? What is the advantage of classifying it as an operating cash flow? What is the advantage of classifying it as a financing cash flow?

6. Explain how cash flow data complement the income statement and balance sheet.

7. What is the "quality of income" concept, and how does cash flow reporting relate to it?

8. What attribute is being measured in the SCF, and how well is representational faithfulness achieved? Compare this to when funds are defined as working capital.

9. Why is the three-way classification system in the SCF more informative than the two-way source/use classification?

10. How does the source/use classification reflect the structure of double-entry accounting?

11. What is the purpose of reporting noncash items in the SCF?

12. Why is the SCF called a *derivative statement?*

13. What do research findings indicate concerning the relevance of cash and funds flow data?

14. What does it mean to classify a cash flow according to the basic nature or function of the event as opposed to the ultimate purpose of the transaction? Which method do you prefer?

15. Reexamine Exhibit 13.11. Explain the purpose of each performance measure. As a manager, which performance measure would you want to use? Which measure would you want used to evaluate you? Why? How would your decision change if your firm were experiencing a boom? A recession? How would your decision change if your firm's plant and equipment needed to be replaced? What if plant and equipment were new?

16. Should a CEO be evaluated based on one year's cash flows? Why or why not? (Your answer might be affected by your definition of cash flow.)

17. The value of the firm is equal to the discounted value of the firm's free cash flows. Is it possible to forecast distant free cash flows? If not, what is the alternative?

18. Comment on the following statement: Cash flow from operating activities is the most important section of the SCF. Hence, analysis should be focused on this section.

19. Does the statement of cash flows obviate the possible need for exit price financial statements?

CASES, PROBLEMS, AND WRITING ASSIGNMENTS

1. Presented in the exhibit for Case 1 is a graph of accounting income, cash flows from operations, and working capital flows from operations for W. T. Grant Company, a retailer that filed for bankruptcy in 1976. As late as 1973, the company's stock was selling for 20 times earnings. What does the chart indicate concerning the usefulness of income, cash, and funds flows? What could explain the significant differences between working capital flows and cash flows?

Exhibit for Case 1   W. T. Grant Net Income, Working Capital, and Cash Flow From Operations for fiscal Years Ending January 31, 1966 to 1975

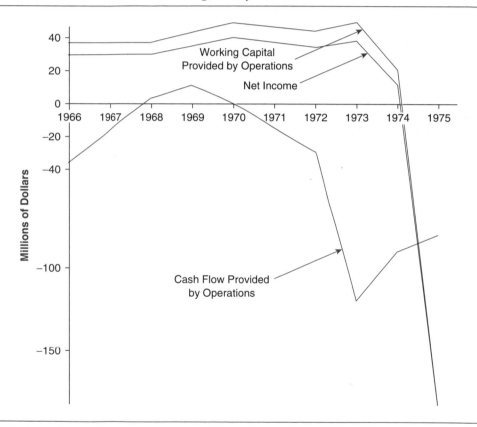

2. This case is adapted from Appendix B of the exposure draft leading up to the FASB's standard on cash flow reporting.[64] Prepare in good form an SCF. Use the direct format. The following information is about the activities of Company D, a diversified multinational corporation with interests in manufacturing and financial services, for the year ending December 31, 20XX:

a. Company D purchased new property, plant, and equipment for $4,000. The company also sold some of its equipment with a book value of $1,900 for $2,500.

b. Company D entered into capital lease transactions for the use of new equipment, and the related lease obligation was $750.

c. Company D purchased all the common stock of Company ABC for $900 in cash. Company D thereby acquired Company ABC's working capital other than cash (a net current liability of $100) and its property, plant, and equipment valued at $3,000, while assuming Company ABC's long-term debt of $2,000.

d. Cash borrowed by Company D for the year consisted of short-term debt of $75 and long-term debt of $1,250.

e. Company D paid $300 on its short-term debt and $125 on capital lease obligations during the year.

f. Company D issued $750 in common stock during the year, $250 of which was issued to settle long-term debt and $500 of which was issued for cash.

g. Company D paid $450 as dividends to its stockholders during the year.

h. Company D's financial services activities during the year included purchases and sales of investment securities amounting to $4,700 and $5,000, respectively. Lending activities produced new loans of $7,500 and collections of loans of $5,800. Customer deposits in its banking subsidiary increased by $1,100.

i. The following are the results of Company D's operations for the year.

Net income	$3,000
Depreciation and amortization	1,500
Deferred taxes	150
Changes in operating working capital items other than cash:	
Increase in inventory	4,000
Decrease in accounts receivable	2,000
Increase in accounts payable	1,150
Changes in interest accruals:	
Increase in interest earned but not received	350
Increase in interest accrued but not paid	100
Cash received from customers for sales of goods10,000	
Cash dividends received	700
Cash paid to suppliers, employees	6,000
Cash paid for interest, taxes	1,750

j. The effect on cash and cash equivalents of changes in the exchange rate for the year was $100.

3. The adjacent balance sheets represent the beginning and end-of-year for 2000 for the N-M Company and the income statement for 2000. Other information:

a. The leased property rights and liability arose from a four-year lease on December 31, 1999. Annual lease cost is $10,000. Payments are due annually beginning on December 31, 2000. Discount rate is 10%.

b. The 8% debenture bonds were sold on December 31, 1999, for $49,500. Bonds have a five-year life. Straight-line amortization is to be used.

c. Leased property is being depreciated on a straight-line basis over four years.

d. Depreciation on owned property is $7,075 for the year.

N-M Company
Balance Sheet as of December 31

	1999	2000
Assets		
Cash	$ 47,000	$79,828
Accounts receivable (net)	160,000	154,000
Stock investment (cost)	10,000	10,000
Fixed assets (gross)	180,000	160,000
Less: Accumulated depreciation	72,000	71,075
Fixed assets (net)	108,000	88,925
Leased property rights	31,700	23,775
Total Assets	$356,700	$356,528
Liabilities		
Accounts payable	$83,000	$80,000
Debenture bonds payable (8%)	50,000	50,000
Less: Unamortized discount	500	400
Debenture bonds payable, net	49,500	49,600
Capital lease liability	31,700	24,870
Total liabilities	$164,200	$154,470
Owners' Equity		
Common stock	$50,000	$50,000
Retained earnings	142,500	152,058
Total owners' Equity	192,500	202,058
Total Liabilities and Owners' Equities	$356,700	$356,528

N-M Company
Income Statement for Year ending December 31, 2000

Sales	$120,000
Operating expenses	
Depreciation	15,000
Salaries and wages	35,000
Miscellaneous	37,000
Total operating expenses	87,000
Operating Income	33,000
Other revenues and expenses	
Interest revenue	(1,000)
Interest expense	7,270
Gain on fixed asset disposal	(2,200)
Total other revenues and expenses	4,070
Income Before Income Taxes	28,930
Income Tax Expense (40%)	11,572
Net Income	$17,358

e. Fixed assets having a cost of $20,000 were sold during the year.

f. Dividends of $7,800 were declared and paid during the year.

Required:

a. Do a conventional SCF in accord with SFAS No. 95. (Use the indirect method.)

b. Do a second SCF in accordance with the modifications suggested in the section of the chapter entitled "Classification Problems of SFAS No. 95."

c. Discuss the underlying reason for the two approaches.

4. Ventius Company issued $10,000 of four-year bonds on December 31, 2000. The coupon rate on the bonds is 7½%. The bonds were sold for $9,400.

Required:

a. Show four possible ways that the interest, principal, and discount can be distributed (allocated) between operating and financing cash flows for the years 2000–2004.

b. Discuss these four approaches and state your preferences.

5. On January 1, 2006, P Company had the following balance sheet (in thousands):

P Company Balance Sheet as of January 1, 2006	
Cash	$200
Accounts Receivable (net)	87
Inventory	96
Fixed Assets (net)	267
Total	$650
Accounts Payable	$160
Capital Stock	300
Retained Earnings	190
Total	$650

On July 1, 2006, P Company bought 100% of S Company for $80. S Company's balance sheet on that date was as follows:

S Company Balance Sheet as of July 1, 2006	
Cash	$20
Accounts Receivable (net)	30
Inventory	35
Fixed Assets (net)	40
Total	$125
Accounts Payable	$45
Capital Stock	20
Retained Earnings	$60
Total	$125

Income statements for P and S for the year 2006 for each entity (from July 1 for S) are shown here.

Income Statements
Year Ending December 31, 2006

	P	S
Sales	$325	$120
Cost of Sales	187	65
Gross Margin	$138	$55
Operating Expenses		
Salaries	40	24
Depreciation	20	10
Net Income	$78	$21

Balance sheets for P and S Companies and the consolidated balance sheet on December 31, 2006 are shown here:

	P	S	Eliminations	Consolidated
Cash	$225	$39		$264
Accounts Receivable (net)	105	24		129
Inventory	73	48		121
Fixed Assets (net)	247	30		277
Investment in S	80		$(80)	
Total	$730	$141		$791
Accounts Payable	177	40		217
Capital Stock	300	20	$(20)	300
Retained Earnings	253	81	(60)	274
Total	$730	$141		$791

Company P paid dividends of $15. Company S had no investing or financing transactions.

Required:

a. Show separate SCFs for P and S for the year 2006 (for S it will be from July 1, 2006 to December 31, 2006) using the indirect method.

b. Show a consolidated SCF for 2006 (from January 1, 2006 to December 31, 2006). Hint: Your cash flow will not show the correct cash increase for 2006.

c. Where does the discrepancy in b. lie and what is it an example of? How might the situation be remedied?

d. In b., show how you think the SCF would be done in actual practice.

6. Select a publicly traded company (your instructor may do this for you). Over a 10-year period trace the following elements:
   a. Net income with depreciation and amortization added back to make it more comparable to cash flows.
   b. Cash flows from operations (from the SCF).
   c. Cash flows from investing activities.
   d. Cash flows from financing activities.

Required:

Assess how closely the company adheres to the Ingram-Lee model in absolute and relative terms: If income increases, does cash flow increase at a lesser rate? Does investing have net outflows and financing have net cash inflows?

7. WorldCom, Inc. improperly capitalized $3.8 billion dollars of expense from January 1, 2001 through the first quarter of 2002 ($3.04 billion occurred in 2001). Its balance sheets for the years ending December 31, 2000 and 2001 showed the following selected balances (in millions):

	2000	2001	Change
Other current assets	$2,007	$2,230	$223
Accounts receivable (net of allowance for bad of $1,532 in 2000 and $1,086 in 2001)	6,815	5,308	(1,507)
Accounts payable	6,022	4,844	(1,178)
Other current liabilities	4,005	3,576	(429)

On the SCFs (indirect method) for the year ended December 31, 2001, WorldCom showed the following adjustments to reconcile net income to cash flow from operations (I = increase to income and D = decrease to income):

Accounts receivable (net)	$281	(I)
Other current assets	164	(I)
Accounts payable and other current liabilities	1,154	(D)

Required:

   a. What effect did WorldCom's misclassification have on cash flows (a) in total and (b) by classification?
   b. Why is it difficult to accept the effects on cash flow from operations of the working capital items listed above?
   c. WorldCom's long-term debt went up by approximately $13 billion during 2001. Is it possible that some of WorldCom's current liabilities were reclassified as long-term during 2001?

CRITICAL THINKING AND ANALYSIS

1. Do you think that the indirect method of reporting cash flows from operations should be eliminated, allowing only the direct method in the SCFs? Discuss.

2. What is cash flow? In your answer, be sure to reference the use to which it is put.

3. Why is the use of free cash flows increasing?

4. Broome (2004) recommends that the FASB should provide more guidance on classification of cash flows for the three sections. What guidance would you suggest?

Notes

1. *In those days, salesmen traveled the country on trains, peddling their wares.*

2. *APB (1971).*

3. *FASB (1987).*

4. *We use "equities" to include both liabilities and owners' equity.*

5. *Ketz and Largay (1987) noted difficulties in determining whether an event or transaction fell into the operating, investing, or financing category on the SCFP. Moreover, intrafirm inconsistencies arise relative to classification on the income statement and the SCFP. For example, Ketz and Largay (p. 13) note that a $946,000 gain on the sale of marketable securities by Evans & Sutherland in 1985 was included in operating income on the income statement but was deducted from funds provided by working capital on the SCFP.*

6. *APB (1963).*

7. *SEC (1970).*

8. *APB (1971).*

9. *See Most (1992) for a strong criticism of the move away from a funds flow statement to a cash flow statement.*

10. *FASB (1978, para. 34).*

11. *FASB (1984, para. 52).*

12. *FASB (1980).*

13. *Rappaport (1998, p. R6) said it succinctly: "Cash is a fact, earnings an opinion."*

14. *The term* cash flow *is often used indiscriminately in the financial press and in analysts' reports, frequently referring to net income plus depreciation. Our usage reflects a much richer definition, which includes the various sources and uses of cash.*

15. *This is due to arbitrary allocations in the determination of accounting income. See Thomas (1969) and the discussion in Chapter 9.*

16. *Chambers (1966) used the term* adaptability, *but it means the same thing as* flexibility *in the context being used here.*

17. *FASB (1987, p. 9).*

18. *Ibid. (p. 13).*

19. *McEnroe (1996). See also Jones and Widjaja (1998) and Jones, Romano, and Smyrnios (1995). The latter two studies show respondents having a preference for the direct method in Australia, where the direct method is required. Recent survey evidence by Brahmasrene, Strupeck, and Whitten (2004) indicates that 82% of CEOs, CFOs, and managers preferred the indirect method, compared with 70.3% of investors and analysts.*

20. *Bahnson, Miller, and Budge (1996).*

21. *This could happen when operating notes payable that are currently due are expected to be refinanced by a firm that has the ability and intention to do so.*

22. *Bahnson, Miller, and Budge (1996).*

23. *Nurnberg (1993, pp. 61–62).*

24. *Ibid. (p. 65).*

25. *Nurnberg and Largay (1998, p. 410).*

26. *Vent, Cowling, and Sevalstad (1995).*

27. *Munter (1990, pp. 55–56).*

28. *Ibid.*

29. *For further discussion, see Nurnberg and Largay (1996, pp. 126 and 127); FASB (1987, para. 14, footnote 4); and FASB (1989, para. 35).*

30. *Nurnberg and Largay (1996, p. 127). They also point out similar discrepancies and inconsistencies in sale-leasebacks, purchase and sale of rental assets, and loan securitizations.*

31. *Ingram and Lee (1997).*

32. *Mulford and Comiskey (2005, chapters 3 and 4) provide an excellent discussion of misstatements of operating and investing cash flows. The entire text provides a comprehensive treatment of cash flows and is an excellent resource for anyone using cash flows for making credit, compensation, or valuation decisions.*

33. *See Sender (2002) and Frigo and Graziano (2003).*

34. *See Maremont (2002).*

35. *Cited in Weil (2004, p. C3).*

36. *Weil (2004, p. C3).*

37. *See, for example, Randerson (2004, p. 49).*

38. *Buffett (1988).*

39. *To counteract negative cash flows, Ericsson, the Swedish telecommunications company, established a managerial bonus system that made the 300 top managers' bonuses dependent on meeting cash flow objectives. See Corporate Finance (2001). Howell (2002) discusses the importance of free cash flows as a tool for management teams to create value.*

40. *Sharma and Iselin (2003) present evidence that cash flow data lead to more accurate solvency assessments than accrual information. Billings and Morton (2002) find that "cash flow disclosures . . . are incrementally related to debt ratings after controlling for other profitability and risk measures."*

41. *Chen, Conover, and Kensinger (2002) note that "share values are often substantially greater than the amount that could be justified based on expected cash flows from existing [italics added] operations." This makes the prediction problem particularly challenging.*

42. *For capital budgeting purposes, net cash flows are equal to operating cash flow less investment in net operating working capital and noncurrent assets. Operating cash flow is defined as after-tax operating income plus depreciation.*

43. *While we wish that were the end of the story, Rappaport (2005, p. 65) notes that some analysts believe that estimating cash flows far in the future is "too time-consuming, costly, and speculative to be useful." Because of asymmetric information, analysts tend to attach substantial weight to recent reported short-term performance, particularly for younger companies.*

44. *Buffett (June 1996, p. 4)*

45. *Mulford and Comiskey (2005, p. 358).*

46. *Ibid. (pp. 347, 348).*

47. *FCFs are a non-GAAP measure. Our definition is consistent with the definition of net cash flows used for determining the NPV for capital budgeting purposes. See Mulford and Comiskey (2005, p. 359–361) for a discussion of different definitions.*

48. *See Koller, Goedhart, and Wessels (2005, p. 162). In practice, constructing FCFs is much more complex. For example, it involves converting the provision for taxes to cash-basis taxes paid on operating income. We ignore such complexities for our simple examples.*

49. *This is consistent with the arguments made by the three dissenting members of the FASB when SFAS No. 95 was put to a vote. See the previous discussion regarding classification problems of SFAS No. 95.*

50. *Operating cash is that amount of cash necessary for the operations of the business. For valuation purposes, analysts distinguish between operating cash and excess cash.*

51. *It makes sense to focus on the operations of a firm without the distortions of financing. Financing is an activity that can change over time; it can easily be modified to suit the owners. In contrast, capital allocation decisions (investing activities) are very long-term decisions, not easily reversed.*

52. *For a comprehensive treatment of valuation from both a theoretical and practical viewpoint, see Koller, Goedhart, and Wessels (2005). Harrison (2003) provides an informal thumbnail sketch.*

53. *The seminal works are Lawson (1971) and Lee (1972). For later work, see Lawson (1985) and Lee (1985).*

54. *Lee (1985, p. 93).*

55. *The intrinsic value of the firm is an estimate and is not observable. In the presence of efficient capital markets, a firm's intrinsic value would be equal to its market value. Capital markets research does not typically focus on valuation per se. Rather, it deals with security returns (percentage changes in market values). In the presence of efficient capital markets, security returns can also be viewed as percentage changes to the firm's intrinsic value due to new information. See Chapter 8 for a review of this research.*

56. *For example, Clarkson (1962), Hawkins and Campbell (1978), Backer and Gosman (1978), and Lee (1983).*

57. *Louis Harris and Associates, Inc. (1980), cited in FASB (1980, p. 31).*

58. *For additional discussion in this area, see Lorek and Willinger (1996).*

59. *Broome (2004, p. 18).*

60. *Ibid. (p. 20).*

61. *Ibid. (p. 20).*

62. *Miller and Bahnson (2002, p. 51.) note that "Contrary to today's conventional wisdom, the direct method isn't hard to apply."*

63. *See MacDonald (1999).*

64. *Adapted with permission of the Financial Accounting Foundation.*

References

3M Company (2005). Form 10-K Annual Report to the United States Securities and Exchange Commission (December 31).

Accounting Principles Board (1963). APB Opinion No. 3, *The Application and Source of Funds.* AICPA.

Accounting Principles Board (1971). APB Opinion No. 19, *Reporting Changes in Financial Position.* AICPA.

Backer, Morton, and Martin L. Gosman (1978). *Financial Reporting and Business Liquidity.* National Association of Accountants.

Bahnson, Paul R., P. B. W. Miller, and B. P. Budge (December 1996). "Nonarticulation in Cash Flow Statements and Implications for Education, Research, and Practice," *Accounting Horizons*, pp. 1–15.

Billings, Bruce K., and Richard M. Morton (June/July 2002). "The Relation Between SFAS No. 95 Cash Flows From Operations and Credit Risk," *Journal of Business Finance and Accounting*, pp. 787–805.

Brahmasrene, Tantatape, C. David Strupeck, and Donna Whitten (October 2004). "Examining Preferences in Cash Flow Statement Format," *CPA Journal*, pp. 58–60.

Broome, O. Whitfield (March/April 2004). "Statement of Cash Flows: Time for Change!" *Financial Analysts Journal*, pp. 16–22.

Buffett, Warren E. (1988). "Letter to Shareholders," Berkshire Hathaway Inc. Annual Report to Shareholders. Available at www.berkshirehathaway.com; accessed June 15, 2006.

———— (1996). "An Owner's Manual," Berkshire Hathaway Inc., Official Home Page, Available at www.berkshirehathaway.com; accessed June 15, 2006.

Chambers, Raymond J. (1966). *Accounting, Evaluation and Economic Behavior.* Prentice Hall.

Chen, Andrew H., James A. Conover, and John W. Kensinger (Spring/Summer 2002). "Proven Ways to Increase Share Value," *Journal of Applied Finance*, pp. 89–97.

Clarkson, Geoffrey P. E. (1962). *Portfolio Selection: A Simulation of Trust Investment.* Prentice Hall.

Corporate Finance (June 2001), "Ericsson links executive performance to cash flow," p. 14.

Financial Accounting Standards Board (1978). Statement of Financial Accounting Concepts No. 1, *Objectives of Financial Reporting by Business Enterprises.* FASB.

———— (1980). FASB Discussion Memorandum: *An Analysis of Issues Related to Reporting Funds Flows, Liquidity, and Flexibility.* FASB.

———— (1984). Statement of Financial Accounting Concepts No. 5, *Recognition and Measurement in Financial Statements of Business Enterprises.* FASB.

———— (1987). Statement of Financial Accounting Standards No. 95, *Statement of Cash Flows.* FASB.

———— (1989). Statement of Financial Accounting Standards No. 104, *Statement of Cash Flows—Net Reporting of Certain Cash Receipts and Cash Payments and Classification of Cash Flows From Hedging Transactions.* FASB.

Frigo, Mark L., and Ron Graziano (July 2003). "Strategic Decisions and Cash Flow," *Strategic Finance*, pp. 8–11.

Harrison, David S (February 2003). "Business Valuation Made Simple," *Strategic Finance*, pp. 45–48.

Hawkins, David F., and Walter J. Campbell (1978). *Equity Valuation: Models, Analysis and Implications.* Financial Executives Research Foundation.

Howell, Robert A. (May 2002). "Tying Free Cash Flows to Market Valuations," *Financial Executive*, pp. 17–20.

Ingram, Robert W., and T. A. Lee (September 1997). "Information Provided by Accrual and Cash-Flow Measures of Operating Activities," *Abacus*, pp. 168–185.

Jones, Stewart, Claudio Romano, and Kosmas Smyrnios (Spring 1995). "An Evaluation of the Decision Usefulness of Cash Flow Statements by Australian Reporting Entities," *Accounting and Business Research*, pp. 115–129.

Jones, Stuart, and Loura Widjaja (September 1998). "The Decision Relevance of Cash-Flow Information," *Abacus*, pp. 204–219.

Ketz, J. Edward, and James A. Largay III (June 1987). "Reporting Income and Cash Flows From Operations," *Accounting Horizons*, pp. 9–17.

Koller, Tim, Marc Goedhart, and David Wessels (2005). *Valuation: Measuring and Managing the Value of Companies*, 4th ed. John Wiley & Sons.

Largay, James A., and Clyde P. Stickney (July–August 1980). "Cash Flows, Ratio Analysis and the W. T. Grant Company Bankruptcy," *Financial Analysts Journal*, pp. 51–54.

Lawson, G. H. (October and November 1971). "Cash-Flow Accounting," *Accountant*, pp. 586–589 (October); pp. 620–622 (November).

———— (Spring 1985). "The Measurement of Corporate Performance on a Cash Flow Basis: A Reply to Mr. Egginton," *Accounting and Business Research*, pp. 99–112.

Lee, T. A. (Summer 1972). "A Case for Cash Flow Reporting," *Journal of Business Finance*, pp. 27–36.

———— (Spring 1983). "A Note on Users and Uses of Cash Flow Information," *Accounting and Business Research*, pp. 103–106.

———— (Spring 1985). "Cash Flow Accounting, Profit and Performance Measurement: A Response to a Challenge," *Accounting and Business Research*, pp. 93–97.

Lorek, Kenneth, and G. Lee Willinger (January 1996). "A Multivariate Time-Series Prediction Model for Cash-Flow Data," *Accounting Review*, pp. 81–102.

Louis Harris and Associates (1980). *A Study of the Attitudes Toward and an Assessment of the Financial Accounting Standards Board.* Louis Harris and Associates.

MacDonald, Elizabeth (1999). "Analysts Increasingly Favor Using Cash Flow Over Reported Earnings in Stock Valuation," *Wall Street Journal* (April 1), p. C2.

Maremont, Mark (2002). "How Is Tyco Accounting for Its Cash Flow?" *Wall Street Journal* (March 5), pp. C1 and C2.

McEnroe, John (1996). "An Examination of Attitudes Involving Cash Flow Accounting: Implications for the Content of Cash Flow Statements," *International Journal of Accounting* (Vol. 31, No. 2), pp. 160–174.

Miller, Paul B. W., and Paul R. Bahnson (February 2002). "Fast Track to Direct Cash Flow Reporting," *Strategic Finance*, pp. 51–57.

Most, Kenneth (February 1992). "SFAS 95: The Great Mystery," *Accounting Enquiries*, pp. 199–214.

Mulford, Charles W., and Eugene E. Comiskey (2005). *Creative Cash Flow Reporting: Uncovering Sustainable Financial Performance.* John Wiley & Sons.

Munter, Paul (September 1990). "Form Over Substance: Another Look at the Statement of Cash Flows," *CPA Journal*, pp. 54–56.

Nurnberg, Hugo (June 1993). "Inconsistencies and Ambiguities in Cash Flow Statements Under FASB Statement No. 95," *Accounting Horizons*, pp. 60–75.

Nurnberg, Hugo, and James A. Largay III (December 1996). "More Concerns Over Cash Flow Reporting Under FASB Statement No. 95," *Accounting Horizons*, pp. 123–136.

———— (December 1998). "Interest Payments in the Cash Flow Statement," *Accounting Horizons*, pp. 407–418.

Randerson, Erik (September 2004). "In an Era of Full Disclosure, What About Cash?," *Financial Executive*, pp. 48–50.

Rappaport, Alfred (1998). "Three Ways Stock-Market Investors Can Stack the Odds in Their Favor," *Wall Street Journal* (February 26) p. R6.

———— (May/June 2005). "The Economics of Short-Term Performance Obsession," *Financial Analysts Journal*, pp. 65–79.

Securities and Exchange Commission (1970). Accounting Series Release No. 117, *Adoption of Article 11A of Regulation S-X.* SEC.

Sender, Henny (2002). "Cash Flow? It Isn't Always What It Seems," *Wall Street Journal* (May 7), pp. C1 and C3.

Sharma, Divesh S., and Errol R. Iselin (September/October 2003). "The Relative Relevance of Cash Flow and Accrual Information for Solvency Assessments: A Multi-Method Approach," *Journal of Business Finance and Accounting*, pp. 1115–1140.

Thomas, Arthur L. (1969). "The Allocation Problem," in *Studies in Accounting Research #3.* American Accounting Association.

Vent, Glenn A., J. F. Cowling, and S. Sevalstad (December 1995). "Cash Flow Comparability: Accounting for Long-Term Debt Under SFAS 95," *Accounting Horizons*, pp. 88–96.

Weil, Jonathan (2004). "Outside Audit: 'Cash Flow Never Lies'—Or Does It?" *Wall Street Journal* (April 16), p. C3.

14

Accounting for Changing Prices and Inflation

Learning Objectives

After reading this chapter, you should be able to:

- Comprehend the historical background of accounting for changing prices in the United States.
- Understand the essence of purchasing power gains and losses and holding gains and losses.
- Understand why SFAS No. 33 failed.
- Understand SFAS No. 157, its complexities, and its extension in SFAS No. 159.

I nflation can be defined very simply as a rise in the average price level for goods and ser- vices in an economy. Many of us are painfully aware of this phenomenon. It has racked the United States fairly continually since the end of World War II and particularly since 1973 (in the wake of the OPEC oil boycott). Inflation finally began moderating in the early 1980s. As of the year 2007 inflation appears to be under control, although it is always under careful scrutiny. Over the years, inflation has posed the single greatest problem that we face in accounting theory. Finally, it should also be noted that, even in the absence of inflation, indi- vidual prices are always changing because of shifts in supply and demand for individual products and services.

While inflation has abated, it is important to remember the recent words of two prominent accounting theorists: "The issue of price changes remains fundamental to accounting mea- surement, as do the associated issues raised by price change accounting. . . . This raises many issues, such as the appropriate concept of capital maintenance."[1]

Under a historical cost-based system of accounting, inflation leads to two basic problems. First, many of the historical numbers appearing on financial statements are not economically relevant because prices have changed since they were incurred. This might impede the use of financial statements for predicting future cash flows and assessing managerial performance. This is, of course, the problem of representational faithfulness discussed in Statement of Financial Accounting Concept (SFAC) No. 2, *Qualitative Characteristics of Accounting Information*, as an element of the primary quality of reliability. Second, since the numbers on financial statements represent dollars expended at different points of time and, in turn, embody different amounts of purchasing power, they are simply not additive. Hence, adding cash of $10,000 held on December 31, 2007, to $10,000 representing the cost of land acquired in 1955 (when the price level was significantly lower) is a dubious operation because of the significantly different amount of purchasing power represented by the two numbers.

Because of these two underlying problems, several aspects of the relevance quality are badly impaired under historical costing. It is quite likely that predictive value is diminished as a result of using and combining dollars of different purchasing power. Using financial reporting to determine accountability is similarly restricted owing to the basic shortcomings of historical costing, as is comparability among financial statements of different firms. Another deficiency resulting from the fundamental weaknesses of historical costs lies in the area of capital maintenance. Under historical costing, income is usually overstated relative to amounts that can be distributed to stockholders without reducing the beginning balance of the enterprise's net assets in real terms. Thus, many "dividends" are really liquidating in nature, rather than derived from earnings (as they appear to be under historical costing).

We commence by first giving a brief history of inflation accounting in the United States prior to the passage of Statement of Financial Accounting Standards (SFAS) No. 33. We then briefly examine some basic elements of inflation accounting including purchasing power gains and losses and holding gains and losses. SFAS No. 33, a then monumental standard, will next be analyzed. The bulk of the chapter will then be devoted to the recently enacted SFAS No. 157, and its extension in SFAS No. 159. We close by analyzing some important theoretical issues raised by SFAS No. 157.

Institutional Aspects of Inflation Accounting Prior to SFAS No. 33

Accountants in the United States have realized for more than 75 years the potential impact on reported accounting numbers of the effects of changing prices, whether specific or general in nature.[2] In fact, some corporations restated their primary financial statements for the effects of changes in specific prices during the 1920s. Accounting organizations, such as the American Accounting Association (AAA) and the American Institute of Certified Public Accountants (AICPA), have discussed accounting for the effects of changing prices in their publications for approximately a half century. Both organizations strongly supported the historical cost model in the mid-1930s. The AAA made this statement: "Accounting is . . . not essentially a process of valuation, but the allocation of historical costs and revenues to the current and succeeding periods."[3] The AICPA adopted the following as one of its first six rules: "Profit is deemed to be realized when a sale in the ordinary course of business is effected, unless the circumstances are such that the collection of the sale price is not reasonably assured."[4]

By the early 1950s, however, both the AAA and AICPA began to modify their positions. In 1951, the AAA issued Supplementary Statement No. 2, *Price Level Changes and Financial Statements*. The statement recommended that financial statements should be stated in units of general purchasing power as a supplement to the primary historical cost statements.[5] In 1950, the AICPA sponsored a study on changing concepts of income. One paper noted: "Comparisons of income over time are possible only if adjustments are made for changes in the purchasing power of money income."[6]

The AAA continued to support price-level-restated financial statements in its 1957 and 1966 reports. Likewise, the AICPA in Accounting Research Study No. 6 in 1961 and Accounting Principles Board Statement No. 3 supported general price-level adjusted statements. Without making any commitments to either general price-level or current value concepts, the Trueblood Committee reaffirmed the need to recognize changing prices in financial statements.[7]

Shortly after its inception, the Financial Accounting Standards Board (FASB) issued an exposure draft entitled "Financial Reporting in Units of General Purchasing Power." The draft proposed to require the presentation, as supplementary information, of the balance sheet and income statement restated in units of general purchasing power. The FASB deferred action on its exposure draft because the Securities and Exchange Commission (SEC) issued Accounting Series Release (ASR) 190, which reversed the SEC's long-standing position of forbidding the presentation of information other than historical cost.

ASR 190 required certain registrants (approximately the nation's 1,000 largest enterprises) to disclose as supplementary information in their Form 10-K:

> The estimated current replacement cost of inventories and productive capacity at the end of each fiscal year for which a balance sheet is required and the approximate amount of cost of sales and depreciation based on replacement cost for the two most recent full fiscal years.[8]

The replacement cost disclosures required by ASR 190 differed from the requirements of SFAS No. 33. In general, the SEC required that replacement cost information reflect the probable effect of replacement by new, more efficient, productive assets. For example, if replacement of current equipment would probably result in lower labor costs, those anticipated lower labor costs should be reflected in the supplementary disclosures.

At first glance, it seems the need to consider the effects of changing prices in financial reports has followed a rather evolutionary development; actually, the opposite is true. For nearly 40 years, the majority of the literature on the subject dealt with the possibility of restating historical cost financial statements for changes in general price levels, not the adoption of a new measurement system. Price-level-restated financial statements continue to use historical cost as the measurement system but alter how historical cost is reported—that is, units of constant dollars rather than units of nominal dollars. A current cost approach, however, changes the basic measurement system to one of current values (now called *fair value*) rather than historical costs.

Accountants in general and accounting organizations, such as the AAA, AICPA, and FASB, tended to favor price-level-restated historical cost until the SEC's rather dramatic action of issuing ASR 190. Why the accounting profession tended to favor price-level-restated historical cost over current cost is purely conjecture, but several possible reasons exist. The methodology of restating historical cost for changes in units of currency is generally easier than measuring current cost. It involves obtaining an externally derived price level index, such as the Consumer Price Index (CPI), and multiplying the historical cost by the current index level divided by the past index level at the previous date of measurement.

The SEC's action, however, altered the evolution of accounting for changing prices in the United States. ASR 190 resulted in the FASB immediately reconsidering its position (general price-level restatement at that time) and led to the dual approach adopted in SFAS No. 33. This release (ASR 190) moved the development of accounting for changing prices significantly forward. It was not an evolutionary step but more a reflection of the thinking of the then chief accountant of the SEC, John C. Burton. Burton's background was academic, and he firmly believed that if any changes in financial reporting were needed because of changing prices, those changes should be made to the measurement system itself to permit the system to report more useful information to the users of financial reports. His desire was for a measurement system using current economic costs. Under such an approach, expenses would be based on the current cost of replacement of particular assets sold or used. In this way, the matching process would show a long-run average cash flow figure based on current costs at the times transactions occur. Although the ease of application (of general price-level adjustments) cannot be denied, since no new economic measurements must be made, Burton had serious doubts as to whether any significant benefit would be achieved from such a system. Certainly, the impact of Burton's position on accounting for changing prices cannot be overemphasized. It is quite possible that the FASB would not have considered current cost had Burton not been the SEC's chief accountant.

An Overview of Inflation Accounting

In discussing responses to inflation, one distinction must immediately be stressed: that between general purchasing power adjustment and current valuation. The difference in purpose and approach was briefly discussed in Chapter 1 and in the brief institutional background of inflation accounting in this chapter. General price-level adjustment is concerned with the change in purchasing power of the monetary unit over time relative to goods and services produced and sold in the economy. To measure the change in the level of prices occurring during a particular time period, a price index must be constructed. A *price index* is a weighted average of the current prices of goods and services; these averages are related to prices in a base period, and their purpose is to determine how much change has occurred. Adjustment is accomplished by taking the historical cost of an item and multiplying it by a fraction consisting of the general price index for the current period in the numerator divided by the general price index existing at the time of acquisition. Hence, if the price of land acquired for $10,000 in 1954, when the price index was 80, were being restated in 2008 dollars, when the index was 220, the calculation would be:

$$\$10,000 \times 220/80 = \$27,500$$

The $27,500 does not in any sense, except by pure coincidence, represent the value of the land in 2008. The cost has simply been translated into the number of 2008 dollars having purchasing power equivalent to the number of dollars originally expended in 1954.

In this example, we assumed that the land was adjusted by a *general price index:* one attempting to measure the changes in the prices of all goods and services available in the economy. SFAS No. 33 used the consumer price index for general price-level purposes. Though a broad index, it is not a true general price-level index. Narrow price-level indexes, called *specific price-level indexes,* can also be used to simulate the prices of various assets. For example, a specific price index for capital equipment in the steel industry could be used to estimate the cost of capital equipment there.

Current valuation—also called current cost and fair value—represents an attempt to derive the specific value or worth for a particular point or period in time of assets, liabilities, expenses, and revenues. The FASB, in SFAS No. 107, has defined fair value as the amount that an asset could be exchanged for in a current transaction between willing parties.[9] This transaction could not be a forced liquidation. As we shall shortly see, except in complete and perfect markets, differences exist between seller and buyer conceptions of current or fair valuation. The two types of current valuation, referred to in Chapter 1, are called entry and exit values.[10] *Entry value* refers to replacement cost in markets in which the asset, liability, or expense is ordinarily acquired by the enterprise. *Exit value* refers to the net realizable value or disposal value of the firm's assets and liabilities in what has been termed a system of "orderly liquidation."[11] Both measures are examples of opportunity costs, and both are certainly relevant in some decision situations, such as capital budgeting. Before we examine SFAS No. 157 (and its predecessors), we examine two other components of inflation-adjusted income: purchasing power gains and losses and holding gains and losses. We also examine a complex—but very useful—current value approach called deprival value.

Purchasing Power Gains and Losses

Purchasing power gains and losses arise as a result of holding net monetary assets or liabilities during a period when the price level changes. *Monetary assets and liabilities* include cash itself and other assets and liabilities that are receivable or payable in a fixed number of dollars. These include accounts and notes receivable and payable and also long-term liabilities.

Purchasing power gains and losses arise because monetary items, which are fixed in terms of the number of dollars to be received or paid, gain or lose purchasing power as the price level changes.[12] The potential for gains and losses is summarized in Exhibit 14.1 on page 466, where "net monetary assets" refers to total monetary assets exceeding monetary liabilities and the converse is true for "net monetary liabilities."

Exhibit 14.1   Purchasing Power Gains and Losses

	State of the Economy	
State of the Enterprise	Inflation	Deflation
Net Monetary Asset Position	Purchasing Power Loss	Purchasing Power Gain
Net Monetary Liability Position	Purchasing Power Gain	Purchasing Power Loss

Purchasing power gains and losses are determined by measuring the purchasing power of the monetary items available to a firm and comparing it with the actual amount of the net monetary accounts. A simple example should clarify the method of measurement. Assume a firm's activity in its monetary elements is summarized in the T-account that follows:

	Net Monetary Assets		
Beginning balance	$10,000		
1st quarter net inflows	8,000	2nd quarter net outflows	$12,000
3rd quarter net inflows	13,000		
4th quarter net inflows	6,000		
	$37,000		$12,000
Ending balance	$25,000		

The general price index shows the following for the year:

Beginning index	180
1st quarter	192
2nd quarter	197
3rd quarter	205
4th quarter	210

To measure the purchasing power gain or loss for the year stated in terms of the purchasing power of the dollar during the 4th quarter, the beginning balance and the subsequent changes in net monetary items are restated in terms of their purchasing power measured in 4th-quarter terms. This is done by multiplying these elements by a fraction consisting of the 4th-quarter index in the numerator, divided by the index at the time the net change occurred or when the item was on hand (in the case of the beginning balance). This is shown in the following T-account:

Net Monetary Assets (in terms of 4th-quarter purchasing power)			
$10,000 \times 210/180 =$	$11,667		
$8,000 \times 210/192 =$	8,750	$12,000 \times 210/197 \ =$	$12,792
$13,000 \times 210/205 =$	13,317		
$6,000 \times 210/210 =$	6,000		
	$39,734		
	$26,942		

The ending balance in the price-level-adjusted T-account shows the monetary purchasing power available to the firm measured in 4th-quarter dollars. Since this is more than the actual amount of net monetary assets at the end of the year, the firm has lost $1,942 of purchasing power by holding net monetary assets during a period when the general price level index was rising.

All systems of both general purchasing-power adjusted income and current value income include purchasing power gains and losses as an element of income. The measurement itself, however, may be in either general or specific purchasing-power terms.[13] Classification would be as a nonoperating component of income or might possibly go to other comprehensive income.

Purchasing power gains and losses are not discussed in SFAS No. 157, nor are they part of that standard's income measurement system. It was part of the supplementary data presented in SFAS No. 33. However, if inflation were to become severe, it might be included in the measurement of income or, as with SFAS No. 33, shown as a supplementary measurement.

Holding Gains and Losses

Just as monetary items are subject to a gain or loss as the price level changes, nonmonetary assets (which we will call real assets) are subject to a gain or loss as a result of change in their value. Holding gains and losses on real assets can be divided into two parts: (1) monetary holding gains and losses, which arise purely because of the change in the general price level during the period, and (2) real holding gains and losses, which are the difference between general price-level-adjusted amounts and current values. Monetary holding gains and losses are capital adjustments only; they are not a component of income. The disposition of real holding gains and losses would be an important theoretical issue affecting the determination of income, but it is not considered in SFAS No. 157.

Holding gains and losses can also be classified from the standpoint of being realized or unrealized in the conventional accounting sense.[14] A simple example should clarify these relationships. Assume that a piece of land was acquired for $5,000 on January 2, 2007, when the general price index was 100. One-tenth of the land was sold on December 31, 2007, for $575. The entire parcel of land was valued at $5,750 on December 31, 2007. The total real and monetary holding gains are computed in the following manner:

Current value on December 31, 2007	$5,750
General price-level-adjusted historical cost on December 31, 2007 [$5,000 × (110/100)]	5,500
Total real holding gain	$250
General price-level-adjusted historical cost on December 31, 2007	$5,500
Historical cost	5,000
Total monetary holding gain	$500

The total holding gain comprises the algebraic sum of the real and monetary holding gains or losses. Hence, if all the facts were the same except that the current value of the land was $5,400 on December 31, 2007, there would have been a total real holding loss of $100. Holding gains and losses are realized by the process of selling the asset or, in the case of a depreciable asset, using it up over time.[15] The decomposition of the holding gains in the example is summarized in Exhibit 14.2.

Deprival Value

Deprival value is a measurement of current or fair value (see Chapter 2). It is obtained as follows. Let A be the *higher* of net realizable value (essentially exit value) or the present value of future cash flows, and let B be replacement cost. Then, deprival value is the *lower* of A or B.

By taking the lower of the two, deprival value measures the opportunity cost to the enterprise of being "deprived" of the asset. Van Zyl and Whittington show that if the *higher* of A or B is taken, we essentially go from deprival value to fair value.[16] We think that it would have been appropriate for the FASB to have carefully considered deprival value earlier in SFAS No. 33 and more recently in SFAS No. 157, since it provides an excellent estimate of the firm's opportunity cost.

The use of deprival value may create problems relating to verifiability. In addition, it might also be subject to deliberate overstatement or understatement if managers desired to manipulate their holding gains and losses on asset dispositions.[17] This would particularly apply if holding gains and losses were to become part of income determination.

Exhibit 14.2   Analysis of Holding Gains

	Holding Gain Type		
State	*Real*	*Monetary*	*Total*
Realized	$ 25	$ 50	$ 75
Unrealized	225	450	675
Total	$250	$500	$750

Provisions of SFAS No. 33 and Rejection in SFAS Nos. 82 and 89

SFAS No. 33

In SFAS No. 33, the FASB decided to keep nominal historical costs as the basis of primary financial statements. SFAS No. 33 specified that the effects of changing prices should be presented as supplementary information in annual reports.[18] The FASB realized that a consensus could not be obtained on which method of accounting should be adopted. The proponents of a constant dollar approach as well as those of a current cost (the term *current cost* was used in place of *current value* and *fair value*) approach both held quite strong views about the usefulness of one to the exclusion of the other. As a result, the FASB concluded that enterprises should report supplementary information under both of these fundamentally different measurement approaches.

Not all enterprises had to comply with SFAS No. 33; those to which it applied were

Public enterprises that prepare their primary financial statements in U.S. dollars and in accordance with U.S. generally accepted accounting principles and that have, at the beginning of the fiscal year for which financial statements are being presented, either:
a. Inventories and property, plant, and equipment [excluding goodwill or other intangible assets] (before deducting accumulated depreciation, depletion, and amortization) amounting in aggregate to more than $125 million; or
b. Total assets amounting to more than $1 billion (after deducting accumulated depreciation).[19]

SFAS No. 33 defined a "public enterprise" as one

(a) whose debt or equity securities are traded in a public market on a domestic stock exchange or in the domestic over-the-counter market (including securities quoted only locally or regionally) or (b) that is required to file financial statements with the Securities and Exchange Commission.[20]

Approximately 1,200 enterprises were affected directly by SFAS No. 33. In addition, the FASB encouraged those not affected to experiment with disclosing changing price information.

For constant dollar reporting, the SFAS required disclosure of

a. Information on income from continuing operations for the current fiscal year on a historical cost/constant dollar basis . . .
b. The purchasing power gain or loss on net monetary items for the current fiscal year. . . .

The purchasing power gain or loss on net monetary items shall not be included in income from continuing operations.[21]

Regarding current cost, the following had to be disclosed:

a. Information on income from continuing operations for the current fiscal year on a current cost basis . . .
b. The current cost amounts of inventory and property, plant, and equipment at the end of the current fiscal year . . .

c. Increases or decreases for the current fiscal year in the current cost amounts of inventory and property, plant, and equipment, net of inflation. . . . [22]

The overall format adopted in SFAS No. 33 of disaggregation rather than aggregation of information is significant. It indicates that the Board itself had not decided whether real holding gains and losses and purchasing power gains and losses are part of income from continuing operations. Also, it points out the Board's confidence in the disclosure mechanism, possibly based on a belief in market efficiency as opposed to a particular aggregation of information. It leaves the problem of aggregating information to the user.

In brief, SFAS No. 33 failed for several reasons. First, there was a dramatic decline of inflation during the early 1980s. In addition, measurement problems were present, as were questions of understandability and usefulness for predictive purposes.

SFAS No. 82

SFAS No. 82, issued in late 1984, eliminated the constant dollar income disclosures that had previously been required by SFAS No. 33. It appears that this information confused users and may have caused "information overload" because of the presence of similar current cost income disclosures. As a result, the Board obviously felt that the cost of the constant dollar income disclosures exceeded the benefits of the information.

SFAS No. 89

The other shoe dropped, so to speak, on the remaining part of SFAS No. 33 approximately two years after the appearance of SFAS No. 82. The parts of SFAS No. 33 that remained in effect—current cost income measurement, purchasing power gain or loss, and holding gain information (as well as the five-year summary of selected financial disclosure) were "encouraged" but not required. Thus, the Board beat a hasty retreat from the problem of accounting for changing prices.[23] As a possible sop to those advocating the need for financial reporting to take into account changing prices, the standard, in Appendix A, included a guide for those firms still desiring to present supplementary information showing the effects of changing prices. Little that was new appeared in Appendix A that had not previously appeared in Appendix E of SFAS No. 33 or in the academic literature.

The most interesting aspect of SFAS No. 89 is that it passed only by a four-to-three vote. The comments of the dissenters were extremely enlightening. David Mosso stated his belief that the issue of changing general and specific prices is the most important problem that will be faced by the FASB during this century.[24] He was against the passage of SFAS No. 33 but was also against making the remaining sections of it voluntary in SFAS No. 89. Despite SFAS No. 33's shortcomings, Mosso saw it as a base on which to build in future years. Making it voluntary would essentially destroy this hard-won base. Raymond Lauver agreed with these sentiments. In addition, given the shortcomings of SFAS No. 33, Lauver felt it quite understandable that SFAS No. 33 was not being widely used after only five years of dissemination. Robert Swieringa agreed with both Mosso and Lauver and also saw a loss of systems and data continuity: essentially the fixed costs of installing and capturing current cost data.[25] Hence, if inflation returns, systems that were removed would have to be installed once again.

SFAS No. 157

Main Elements of SFAS No. 157

SFAS No. 157, *Fair Value Measurement,* is a major new standard that affects accounts that "require or permit fair value measurement" on the balance sheet though the standard has little to say about related income statement considerations.[26] The statement is grounded in the belief that current values (now called fair values) are more relevant for decision-making purposes than historical costing for all users and user groups.

Included in the coverage of this standard would be the following:

1. Leases under SFAS No. 13 (para. C9)

2. Impaired assets under SFAS No. 144, which would still be a lower-of-cost-or-market type of valuation

3. Exchanges of nonmonetary assets under APB Opinion No. 29 and SFAS No. 153, with an exception allowed if fair value is not "reasonably determinable" (para. C21c)

4. Derivatives under SFAS No. 133 with unrealized gains or losses recognized in earnings, but more disclosure is to be provided (para. C13–16)

5. Loan impairments under SFAS No. 114, provided that observable market prices are used (para. C18)

6. Zero interest rate loans under APB Opinion No. 21 (para. C19)

7. Assets and liabilities acquired in a business combination (para. C21e)

This is a motley assortment of assets and liabilities, but we believe that SFAS No. 157 is basically providing a beachhead for a much wider usage of fair value measurements.

Clear exceptions to this standard are raw material and merchandise inventories (still governed by Accounting Research Bulletin No. 43, Chapter 4), share-based payment transactions (SFAS No. 123R), and accounting standards allowing measures based on "vendor-specific evidence of fair value" (paras. 2 and 3), as well as fixed assets, except those specifically mentioned above.

The fair value system of SFAS No. 157 is basically an exit-value system, but one that is grounded in revenue generating potential rather than a liquidity measurement in an orderly liquidation circumstance.[27] SFAS No. 157 defines fair value as "the price that would be received to sell an asset or paid to transfer a liability in an orderly transaction between market participants at the measurement date" (para. 5) at the highest and best value for an asset and at the lowest price for a liability.

Market participants are assumed to be independent of the reporting enterprise, knowledgeable, and able and willing to enter into the transaction (para. 10).

Asset prices are supposed to be derived for the asset in the market where the asset has "the highest and best use" (para. 8). Similarly, liability prices would pertain to where liabilities have the lowest prices. The asset price should come from the asset's principal market, but there is some confusion if a higher price comes from an auxiliary market.

The standard itself gives an example of land "currently developed for industrial use" (para. A10). However, in the example, it has a higher value if used for a high-rise condominium. The standard would take into account the value in-use if developed for industrial use and in-exchange if used for condominiums. The standard recommends using the highest value, but if it will definitely be used for industrial purposes, than we believe that that is the only value that should be used. We do not believe that the standard is clear on this issue. However, markets are fairly limited for fixed and other operating types of assets.

The issue is less confusing in the case of liabilities. For example, some financial instruments might be sold either in brokered markets or in dealer markets. The lowest price would govern without any of the complexities that may surround different asset markets.

Prices for both assets and liabilities do not include deductions (or increases in the case of liabilities) for transaction costs with the exception of transportation costs to ship the asset to market (para. 9). Transaction costs are "direct incremental costs" such as advertising costs to notify market participants of the asset's specifications and availability.

Transaction costs are not deducted (with the exception, as noted, of transportation costs), but they can influence the highest and best selling price. For example, assume that in one market an asset can be sold for $25 with transaction costs of $5 whereas in another market the selling price would be $24 with transaction costs of $3. The reselling (highest and best) fair value price would be $24 since the net receivable ($21) is higher than the net of $20.

Measurement Considerations

SFAS No. 157 attempts to establish the highest and best use for assets. In establishing highest and best use, the standard distinguishes between two categories: in-use and in-exchange. This distinction applies strictly to assets. *In-use* refers to the asset being used in combination with other assets by a purchaser (para. 13a). *In-exchange* pertains to an asset being used on a separate or stand-alone basis by the buyer (para. 13b). Relative to liabilities, the lowest cost of eliminating the liability would be the analog of highest and best use for assets.

Prices of both assets and liabilities are tempered by an important factor. Asset prices can be reduced by risk factors, which could lower the price in the asset's highest or best use. If, for example, potential obsolescence pertained to an asset, it would have to be factored into the selling price if not already included therein.

In the case of liabilities, nonperformance risk would have to be considered. *Nonperformance risk* pertains to the possibility of the firm itself not being able to pay its debts as they mature. In terms of the valuation process, this would result in raising the discount rate and lowering the carrying value of the debt, which would result in a gain to the enterprise.

Finally, fair value generally applies to specific assets and liabilities, but it can apply to a larger aggregation of assets such as a business owned by the reporting entity (para. 6).

Valuation Techniques

There are three valuation techniques or approaches within both the in-exchange and in-use categories for assets and also for liabilities.

The *market approach* involves determining current prices for identical—or at least comparable—assets and liabilities (para. 18a).

The *income approach* uses future earnings or cash flows that are then discounted to a simulated selling price (para. 18b). This method would also appear to pertain to liabilities such as bonds payable, which require future periodic outlays of cash for interest purposes. Other valuation techniques of a more indirect nature also fall under the income approach category. These include the Black-Scholes model and binomial models. These indirect methods are frequently referred to as *mark-to-model* models.

A third technique is the *cost approach.* This approach involves determining the current cost to replace the service capacity of an asset (para 18c). Notice that this is a replacement cost or entry value and not an exit price!

These valuation techniques should be consistently applied (para. 20). Change, however, may be made if newer markets open up or other factors arise leading to more representative measures of fair value.

The Fair Value Pricing Hierarchy

The fair value pricing hierarchy pertains to the process or mechanics of securing prices. There are three levels for securing prices, labeled Level 1 through Level 3.

Level 1 prices are quoted prices in active markets for *identical* assets or liabilities (para. 24). If a Level 1 price is available for an asset or liability but the firm owns a large number of units of the asset and putting them all on the market at once would lower the per unit price from the quoted Level 1 price, the Level 1 quoted price would be used. This is because aggregated values are intended to be market specific rather than entity specific under SFAS No. 157.[28]

Level 2 prices pertain to quoted prices for *similar* assets and liabilities priced in active markets (para. 28a). Because they are for similar rather than identical assets, they are below Level 1. However, they could be for identical as well as similar assets (or liabilities) in markets that are relatively inactive (para. 28b). Within Level 2, prices might also be derived from other than quoted prices from sources such as interest rates and yield curves.

Level 3 inputs are derived in situations in which there is little market activity (para. 30). Hence these inputs are called *unobservable inputs.* Information from unobservable inputs is to be based on the best available information, and they involve assumptions that the reporting enterprise makes relative to how market participants would establish prices. Clearly issues of comparability and verifiability become very important relative to Level 3 inputs.

A diagram illustrating the relationships among these various concepts is shown in Exhibit 14.3.

Disclosures

Numerous disclosures for interim and year-end disclosures must be made under SFAS No. 157. This is especially the case for measurements using unobservable inputs (Level 3). Fair value measurements at the reporting date plus a breakout of details pertaining to the usage of the three levels must be shown (para. 32). For Level 3 measurements, beginning and end-of-year balances and the composition of the changes must be shown. In addition, gains and losses on Level 3 measurements must be shown, including where these amounts went. These are the main disclosures.

Evaluating SFAS No. 157

SFAS No. 157 is indeed a far-reaching standard. Suffice it to say that 24 FASB standards and three Accounting Principles Board opinions were affected by this standard. We break our critique into two parts: omissions and theoretical issues.

Omissions

The Income Statement. There is virtually no mention of the income statement in SFAS No. 157. We, therefore, would most likely conclude that for fixed assets, depreciation would most likely be equal to the decline in the value of the asset between two points in time. This would also leave the possibility that a fixed asset could appreciate if its overall market value increased more than the decline owing to usage. Appendix E of SFAS No. 157 indicates some changes to SFAS No. 144 on impairment of long-lived assets. One wonders why the later standard did not render the earlier standard totally null and void since the subject matter of SFAS No. 157 totally encompasses SFAS No. 144.

Holding Gains and Losses. We previously commented on the fact that SFAS No. 157 is a balance-sheet oriented standard with little said about the income statement, including the determination of fair value depreciation. Nor is anything said about what to do with holding gains, whether monetary or real, or realized versus unrealized, except that disclosures should be made about where they are shown in income (para. 32c and d). Even if monetary and real proportions are not broken out, holding gains provide an excellent case for running unrealized amounts through other comprehensive income and then bringing realized portions into income. While no mention is made of purchasing power gains and losses, this issue may have to be faced if inflation increases sharply.

Theoretical Issues

The Exit Value Choice. Most conceptions of net realizable value or exit value would take into account transaction costs.[29] Fair value as defined in SFAS 157 does not. It therefore becomes

Exhibit 14.3   Hierarchy Employed in SFAS No. 157

Category	SFAS No. 157 Classification	Comments
How assets are used	In-use versus in-exchange	Applicable only to assets. Joint costs may impede in-use category.
Valuation techniques	Market, income, cost approaches	This category provides an overview of valuations.
Fair value hierarchy	Level 1, Level 2, Level 3	This category provides the specifics of pricing going from higher to lower verifiability.

difficult to interpret the meaning of exit value as fair value if transaction costs (save for transportation costs) are not deducted. The measurement seems to be incomplete and overstated without taking transaction costs into account.

Market-Based Versus Entity-Specific Prices. In the Summary of the SFAS No. 157 (on the very first page, which is unnumbered and also without paragraph numberings), the statement declares "that fair value is a market-based measurement not an entity-specific measurement." Certainly in perfect competition we can say that as a result of interaction between buyers (demanders) and sellers (suppliers) prices are determined by the market. As we relax the perfect competition assumption, it is not quite as easy to draw this conclusion. In the case of monopoly, for example, the seller sets the price and accepts the quantity demanded. Thus, in less than perfect competition, the price may be largely determined in the marketplace, but the seller may have more influence over it.

This less than perfect competition case is recognized in the standard in the situation in which the firm owns a large number of securities. Hypothetically putting them all on the market would lower the price (paras. C71 and C72). In this situation, the standard would use the existing market price, without considering the effect of the firm putting the shares on the market. This would be a true market-determined price. In contrast, the lower hypothetical price would be the entity-specific price.

In addition, asset prices are negatively affected by the risk associated with the asset. Liability prices must consider nonperformance risk (para. A31) by the seller, which would likewise affect the price. These are examples that show that market-based versus entity-specific prices are by no means mutually exclusive categories.

Pricing Approaches and Techniques. SFAS No. 157 employs a complex pricing hierarchy. For assets, the "in-use" and "in-exchange" categories are viewed to see where the "highest and best" use lies. However, if the asset is valued from an in-use perspective, its value is based on its use in combination with other assets. However, this could easily lead to a joint cost situation in which individual asset values are indeterminable. Hence the in-exchange approach would really govern.

The valuation techniques or approaches listed in paragraph 18 (market approach, income approach, and cost approach) provide a broad array of overall costing techniques for determining fair value. While the first two are based on exit markets, the cost approach is clearly an entry value.

This brings up a number of problems and issues. Firstly, unlike the very precise exit-value approach of Chambers and Sterling, it is unlikely that under SFAS No. 157 financial statement amounts will be additive. Secondly, there is such a wide variety of approaches and techniques for measurement that reliability (verifiability) for individual firm measurements may be improved but comparability among firms may be decreased. This may be a worthwhile tradeoff, but we wonder if it was considered by the Board. Furthermore, we question this complex current value mechanism because it will leave individual balance sheets with a graveyard of mixed valuations, both current values and historical costs. Thirdly, the Board chose exit values because "it embodies current expectations about the future inflows associated with the asset . . ." (para. C26). If this were really the case, it is puzzling why transaction costs (except for transportation costs) are not deducted. Finally, this standard is apt to create problems for users analyzing profitability, leverage, and efficiency ratios over time.

Finally, the actual pricing mechanisms themselves go from Level 1 to Level 3 (paras. 24–30). There is much useful detail here. Level 3 inputs, using unobservable inputs, will probably not be highly verifiable, but that can be expected at some point in current value systems.

Capital Maintenance. We come again to the issue of capital maintenance. It represents the amount that can be distributed to shareholders as dividends without breaching capital. The maximum dividend declaration is represented by the income generated during the period.

How useful a gauge of capital maintenance a particular income system provides is another issue. It has often been said, for example, that during periods of steep inflation, historical cost income overstates the firm's dividend possibilities owing to understating expenses such as depreciation and cost of good sold. Hence general price-level adjustment (Chapter 1) provides an income measurement for capital maintenance possibilities that takes into account the declining purchasing power of the monetary unit. From an entity theory perspective, capital maintenance can be geared to the firm itself, taking into account the cost of productive assets in the industry in which the firm competes.[30]

The capital maintenance gauge provided by applying SFAS No. 157 is questionable. Using historical costs for inventories as opposed to fair values for other assets is one problem. Another problem arises from not deducting transaction costs from the fair value determinations of enterprise assets. Finally, questions of reliability of fair value determinations using Level 3 measurements are another consideration. Hence the use of income measured under SFAS No.157 for capital maintenance purposes has to be somewhat questionable.

Comparability and Reliability. If measurements are not reliable (verifiable), we question whether a high degree of comparability can result. Level 3 measurements using unobservable inputs certainly raise this issue. Another potential problem arises where some firms use markets having higher fair values than those determined for principal markets. These are some potential problems, but it is clearly too early to tell how important they are. The FASB is to be commended for finally coming to grips again with the current value problem. We fear, however, that many interpretations and modifications will arise before the fair value issue becomes truly settled.

Other Points. There are two other points that we would make. First, the standard states (para. 17) that frequently the initial cost or transaction price will be equal to the exit value at the initial recognition. This will be true of financial instruments but not for fixed and other operating assets (see Appendix 1-A).

Secondly, fair value measurements are supposed to occur "in the principal market for the asset or liability, or in the absence of a principal market, the most advantageous market for the asset or liability" (para. 8). This is clear and unambiguous, but in para. 10 emphasis appears to have shifted to the highest and best use: "A fair value measurement assumes the highest and best use of the asset by market participants, considering the use of the asset that is physically possible, legally permissible, and financially feasible at the measurement."

Final Assessment of SFAS No. 157

The FASB is certainly to be commended for taking on a very difficult task. The camel is sometimes said to be similar to a horse designed by a committee. The same thing might be said of SFAS No. 157. However, we question whether SFAS No. 157 will ever have the utility of the fabled "ship of the desert." We foresee many amendments and revisions forthcoming for this standard.

SFAS No. 159

SFAS No. 159, *The Fair Value Option for Financial Assets and Financial Liabilities—Including an amendment of FASB Statement No. 115*, extends fair value measurement as an "option" to several new areas.[31] The option is extended to more financial asset and financial liability events, except for the following:

1. Subsidiaries that the firm is required to consolidate (para. 8a)

2. Variable interest entities (para. 8b), which are discussed in Appendix 18-A

3. Overfunded pension plan benefits, other postretirement benefits and post employment benefits, and various deferred compensation arrangements and plans (para. 8c)

4. Leased assets and liabilities (para. 8d), although these were *included* in SFAS No. 157[32]

5. Various bank deposits and liabilities (para. 8e)

6. Financial instruments that are part of owners' equity (para. 8f)

The fair value option may be applied instrument by instrument. It is irrevocable and must be applied in totality to individual financial instruments (para. 5). One FASB member disagreed with the instrument-by-instrument approach, which would decrease comparability among enterprises (p. 15). We agree.

In addition, this standard is supposed to reduce income volatility by allowing similar valuation measurement across the spectrum of financial instruments. We would question whether it is the FASB's job to reduce income volatility. Furthermore, SFAS No. 159 would also presumably reduce unnecessary hedging to smooth income, by allowing similar valuation for all financial instruments.[33]

Statement No. 159 also amends SFAS No. 115 on marketable securities (paras. 28 and 29). It allows available-for-sale and held-to-maturity securities to be measured at fair value. For securities measured at fair value, unrealized gains and losses would presumably go through income.

One potential side effect of SFAS No. 159 is that buyout firms may attempt to recognize their management fees "upfront" when they buy companies with the intent to later take them public. Indeed, in an April 18, 2007, article in the *Wall Street Journal*, it was noted that the buyout firm, Blackstone Group, may be planning "to apply market-value accounting to the management and performance fees that it will receive for being general partner of its investment funds."[34] However, SFAS No. 159 says nothing about the upfront income recognition of management fees and similar revenue sources. We are concerned that any attempt to book management fees upfront may be symptomatic of the return of "Enronitis," a fatal disease suffered by that disgraced giant (see Appendix 18-A).

Summary

Coping with inflation and changing prices has presented an extremely serious challenge to accounting theory. The literature has discussed numerous methods for grappling with these problems.

The first major standard to deal with this problem was SFAS No. 33. SFAS No. 33 was a probationary standard that required both constant dollar and current-cost-adjusted income from continuing operations to be published as supplemental to the primary historical cost statements. In addition, it required purchasing power gains and losses on monetary items and total holding gains, broken into the inflationary component and the real component, to be disclosed separately. Questions of usefulness, understandability, and the abatement of inflation caused it to be withdrawn.

While bits and pieces of fair value accounting were dealt with for derivative instruments (SFAS No. 133 and 149) and impaired assets (SFAS No. 144), a broad standard was not passed until September 2006, when SFAS No. 157 was finally passed. This standard basically uses an exit-value system but without taking into account transaction costs, aside from transportation costs. However, the purpose of SFAS No. 157 is not to determine the liquidity available to the firm if the assets were disposed of in an orderly liquidation. Entry-value systems are concerned with measuring replacement costs of the firm's assets. The specific purpose of the fair value measurement appears to be concerned with determining the net fair value of the firm's revenue-generating potential, although this is not explicitly stated in the standard.

Fair value prices pertain to the firm's principal or most advantageous market. Asset markets can be either in-use or in-exchange. The former pertains to situations in which the asset is used in combination with other assets and the latter in which the asset is used alone.

SFAS No. 157 has a complex system for determining "highest and best" use of assets. It uses valuation techniques that are first grounded in the market approach, then the income approach (present values of future cash flows), and thirdly, a cost approach, which would apply strictly to assets and would determine the cost of acquiring a similar asset (an entry value).

Finally there are three "levels" for the actual determination of prices. Level 1 involves quoted prices in active markets for identical assets and liabilities. Level 2 is less specific, involving prices for similar assets (but not identical assets), prices for identical assets but in markets that are not overly active, and, finally, inference from indirect factors such as yield curves and interest rates. Level 3 prices come from "unobservable" inputs developed from the firm's own data and information.

Finally, asset prices have to be tempered for risk factors such as obsolescence (if not already in the price). Liabilities must take into account "nonperformance" factors, which refers to the firm's ability to pay its debts.

This is an immense standard, and there are many other issues to consider. Capital maintenance measurement is not very clear and precise. How comparable and reliable (verifiable) these numbers are is open to question.

This standard will probably be very useful, but it is highly likely it will be changed and amended in the future.

QUESTIONS

1. How would you explain a purchasing power loss to someone who says you have not really lost either money or real assets?

2. What is the relationship between fair value and deprival value?

3. In addition to inflation subsiding, what other reasons underlie why SFAS No. 33 would most likely have failed?

4. How did the SEC undercut the FASB's general price-level approach?

5. Do you think there is any reason to distinguish between in-use and in-exchange categories in SFAS No. 157?

6. Are observable inputs always specific prices? Explain.

7. Does the nonperformance factor relative to the firm work against it or for it?

8. SFAS No. 157 is exit-value oriented; hence no entry value numbers may be used. Is this statement correct?

9. Is it correct that transaction costs play no role in determining highest and best use for an asset in SFAS No. 157? Explain.

10. Costs of identical assets will always be a Level 1 measurement under SFAS No. 157. Is this statement correct? Explain.

11. In-use and in-exchange categories play no role relative to liability measurement in SFAS No. 157. Is this statement correct? Explain.

12. What is the additivity problem?

13. Why do we get a poor measure of capital maintenance under historical costing?

14. What is a "market specific" versus an "entity specific" measurement, and does this distinction hold? Explain.

15. Why, under deprival value, do we compare exit-value and present-value numbers taking the *higher* of the two?

16. Should capital stock be valued at fair value?

CASES, PROBLEMS, AND WRITING ASSIGNMENTS

1. A firm has a net monetary liability balance of $10,000 on January 1, 2001. During the first third of the year, the balance decreased to $7,500. During the second third of the year, the balance increased to $12,500. During the last third of the year, the balance increased to $20,000. The general price index was 100 during the first third of the year, 110 during the second third, and 106 during the last third. Compute the purchasing power gain or loss for the year.

2. A plot of land costing $200,000 was acquired on January 1, 2001. The price level was 120 on that date. One-quarter of the land was sold on December 31, 2001, for $60,000 when the general price level was 180. Compute the following holding gains:
   a. Realized real holding gain
   b. Unrealized real holding gain
   c. Realized monetary holding gain
   d. Unrealized monetary holding gain

CRITICAL THINKING AND ANALYSIS

1. How does the traditional conception of exit value differ from that presented in SFAS No. 157?

2. Would you prefer remaining with historical cost or would you prefer to shift to SFAS No. 157?

Notes

1. *Whittington and Zeff (2001, pp. 228–229).*
2. *Specific price changes refer to particular price changes for individual assets or classes of assets.*
3. *AAA (1936, p. 61).*
4. *AICPA (1953, Ch. 1). The six rules were adopted by the institute membership in 1934 and reprinted as part of Chapter 1 of Accounting Research Bulletin (ARB) 43.*
5. *AAA (1951).*
6. *Fabricant (1950, p. 154).*
7. *AICPA (1973, p. 14)*
8. *SEC (1976).*
9. *FASB (1991, para. 5).*
10. *The terms appear to have first been used by Edwards and Bell in their classic work with regard to three different time dimensions: past, current, and future. See Edwards and Bell (1961, pp. 74–80). Today the terms* entry value *and* exit value *used alone refer to the present time dimension.*
11. *Orderly liquidation refers to disposal of assets in the usual course of business operations where the firm is not forced to accept heavily discounted prices. See Chambers (1966, p. 204). Of course, it would be impossible, by definition, to have an orderly liquidation of an enterprise's entire stock of nonmonetary assets.*
12. *For an in-depth discussion of the complexities of measuring purchasing power gains and losses, see Hall and Tippett (1996).*

13. *For a discussion of the choice, see Gynther (1966, pp. 155–158).*

14. *A good example is shown by Edwards (1954).*

15. *See Edwards and Bell (1961, pp. 112–114) for further details.*

16. *van Zyl and Whittington (2006). The one exception would be if replacement cost exceeds the other two values, which indicates that the asset should be sold and not replaced.*

17. *Barth and Landsman (1995, pp. 101–102). See also Solomons (1995, pp. 47–48 for a defense of deprival value.*

18. *While research on the usefulness of SFAS No. 33 varies considerably, two studies have found usefulness in the current cost disclosures. Brown, Huefner, and Sanders (1994) examined 28 corporate acquisitions between 1976 and 1985 and found a significant positive correlation between sellers current cost disclosures under SFAS No. 33 just before sale and buyers recorded values for these assets right after acquisition. Sami and White (1994) found that predictive values of current cost disclosures under SFAS No. 33 when used in conjunction with historical cost figures led to reduced forecast errors of security returns when compared with the use of historical cost figures alone.*

19. *FASB (1979, para. 23).*

20. *Ibid. (para. 22).*

21. *Ibid. (para. 29).*

22. *Ibid. (paras. 29 and 30).*

23. *While SFAS No. 89, in effect, ended current cost accounting in published financial statements. Nevertheless, research has continued in terms of attempting to improve and refine specific index and current value measurements. Two examples are Hall and Shriver (1990) and Lim and Sunder (1991). Little, if any, research has been done on the constant dollar approach discussed in SFAS No. 82.*

24. *FASB (1986, p. 2).*

25. *Ibid. (p. 3).*

26. *FASB (2006).*

27. *Edwards and Bell (1961, p. 76) and van Zyl and Whittington (2006).*

28. *We believe that most aggregated values are a combination of market prices and entity considerations. For example, the value of a fixed asset would be based on the market price for an asset in a specific condition.*

29. *Edwards and Bell (1961, p. 76) denote exit value as being net of removal costs and transport and installation costs that the seller might have to bear. For major fixed-asset installations, these costs might be considerable. Sterling, in his conception of exit value, attempts to measure the net amount of cash that would be received from the immediate sale of an asset (Sterling, personal correspondence). Hence, for a major asset such as a printing press, exit value would be the firm's selling price less any tearing-out costs. On the other hand, for an asset such as an oil deposit, exit value would consist of the selling price of the asset as it is in the ground. See Sterling (1979, p. 220). Chambers does not appear to treat the issue in his major work. His definition of current cash equivalent does not take these reductions into account. See Chambers (1966, pp. 201–202, 208–209, and 218), for example. For exit values to be representationally faithful to the concept of measuring the total funds available to the firm, selling price net of costs of disposition appears to be the most appropriate measure.*

30. *This can be done by using an entry-value approach and not closing any holding gains to income.*

31. *FASB (2007).*

32. *Interestingly, SFAS 159 does not mention that leases were included in SFAS No. 157.*

33. *The unnecessary hedging to mitigate income volatility is reminiscent of foreign currency translation under SFAS No. 8, which was succeeded by SFAS No. 52 (see Chapter 18).*

34. *Pulliam and Reilly (2007, p. C1).*

References

American Accounting Association (1936). *A Tentative Statement of Accounting Principles Underlying Corporate Financial Statements.* AAA.

——— (1951). Supplementary Statement No. 2, *Price Level Changes and Financial Statements.* AAA.

American Institute of Certified Public Accountants (1953). Accounting Research Bulletin No. 43, *Prior Opinions,* Chapter 1. AICPA.

——— (1973). *Objectives of Financial Statements.* AICPA.

Barth, Mary, and Wayne Landsman (December 1995). "Fundamental Issues Related to Using Fair Value Accounting for Financial Reporting," *Accounting Horizons,* pp. 97–107.

Brown, Larry, R. Huefner, and R. Sanders (March 1994). "A Test of the Reliability of Current Cost Disclosures," *Abacus,* pp. 2–17.

Chambers, Raymond J. (1966). *Accounting, Evaluation and Economic Behavior.* Prentice Hall.

Edwards, Edgar (April 1954). "Depreciation Policy Under Changing Price Levels," *Accounting Review,* pp. 267–280.

Edwards, Edgar, and Philip Bell (1961). *The Theory and Measurement of Business Income.* University of California Press.

Fabricant, Solomon (1950). "Business Costs and Business Income Under Changing Price Levels: The Economist's Point of View," in *Five Monographs on Business Income.* AICPA.

Financial Accounting Standards Board (1979). Statement of Financial Accounting Standards No. 33, *Financial Reporting and Changing Prices.* FASB.

——— (1984). Statement of Financial Accounting Standards No. 82, *Financial Reporting and Changing Prices: Elimination of Certain Disclosures.* FASB.

——— (1986). Statement of Financial Accounting Standards No. 89, *Financial Reporting and Changing Prices.* FASB.

——— (1991). Statement of Financial Accounting Standards No. 107, *Disclosure About Fair Values of Financial Instruments.* FASB.

——— (2006). Statement of Financial Accounting Standards No. 157, *Fair Value Measurements.* FASB.

——— (2007). Statement of Financial Accounting Standards No. 159, *The Fair Value Option for Financial Assets and Liabilities.* FASB.

Gynther, R. S. (1966). *Accounting for Price-Level Changes: Theory and Procedure.* Pergamon Press.

Hall, Thomas, and Keith Shriver (July 1990). "Econometric Properties of Asset Valuation Rules Under Price Movement and Measurement Errors: An Empirical Test," *Accounting Review,* pp. 537–556.

Hall, Thomas, and M. Tippett (Spring 1996). "The Estimation of Monetary Gains and Losses in Diverse International Economic Environments," *Abacus,* pp. 91–105.

Lim, Suk, and S. Sunder (October 1991). "Efficiency of Asset Valuation Rules Under Price Movement and Measurement Errors," *Accounting Review,* pp. 669–693.

Pulliam, Susan, and D. Reilly (2007). "Blackstone Tests Fairness of Using 'Fair Value' Rule," *Wall Street Journal* (April 18), pp. C1 and C2.

Sami, Heibatollah, and Richard A. White (Fall 1994). "Incremental Information Content of SFAS No. 33 Earnings Disclosures: Some New Evidence," *Journal of Accounting and Public Policy,* pp. 253–279.

Securities and Exchange Commission (1976). Accounting Series Release No. 190, *Notice of Adoption of Amendments to Regulation S-X Requiring Disclosure of Certain Replacement Cost Data.* SEC.

Solomons, David (March 1995). "Criteria for Choosing an Accounting Model," *Accounting Horizons,* pp. 42–51.

Sterling, Robert (1979). *Toward a Science of Accounting*. Scholars Book Company.

van Zyl, Tony, and Geoffrey Whittington (2006). "Deprival Value and Fair Value: A Reinterpretation and a Reconciliation," *Accounting and Business Research* (Vol. 36, No. 2), pp. 121–130.

Whittington, Geoffrey, and S. A. Zeff (2001). "Mathews, Gynther and Chambers: Three Pioneering Australian Theorists," *Accounting and Business Research* (Vol. 31, No. 3), pp. 203–234.

15

Income Taxes and Financial Accounting

Learning Objectives

After reading this chapter, you should be able to:

- Understand the many possible interpretations of income tax allocation.
- Comprehend why discounting of deferred tax assets and liabilities is warranted.
- Interpret the shift from SFAS No. 96 to SFAS No. 109.
- Understand why tax loss carryforwards should be booked.

Accounting has become considerably more complex as a result of the federal government's attempt to influence such macroeconomic factors as corporate investment by means of the income taxation process. In this chapter, we examine income tax allocation, a topic that has been extremely controversial for many years but finally may be beginning to attain closure in SFAS No. 109.

The income tax law of 1913 established business income as a basis for taxation. Because *income* for tax purposes was defined differently than *income* for accounting purposes, the law resulted in many items being recognized in different time periods for tax and book purposes. The efforts to "synchronize" tax and book accounting go back to the 1930s, but it was ARBs 43 and 44 (revised) (1953 and 1958, respectively) that firmly established income tax allocation as a canon of financial accounting. After examining the basic elements of tax allocation, we analyze extensively the principal timing difference: accelerated depreciation for tax purposes and straight-line depreciation for published financial reporting. Various positions on income tax allocation within the context of book-tax timing differences arising from depreciation are explored. We also examine how discounting of deferred taxes would work. The chapter concludes with an analysis of the major aspects of SFAS No. 109, including the booking of tax loss carryforwards.

Income Tax Allocation

The allocation of corporate income taxes is one of the most controversial issues that has ever arisen in financial accounting theory. ARB 43 put it into practice in words that today have an almost archaic-sounding innocence when viewed with the hindsight of 50 years of heated debate:

> Income taxes are an expense that should be allocated, when necessary and practicable, to income and other accounts, as other expenses are allocated. What the income statement should reflect under this head . . . is the expense properly allocable to the income included in the income statement for the year.[1]

Tax allocation is made necessary by the timing differences between when a revenue or expense item reaches the published financial statements as opposed to when it appears on the tax return. In these situations, tax expense is based on the published before-tax income figure. The problem can also be viewed from the perspective of the balance sheet, where the tax basis and book basis of assets and liabilities differ. Hence, the income tax allocation process acts like a balance wheel between income tax expense and income tax liability numbers, with the difference appearing on the balance sheet. We will closely scrutinize the meaning of the income tax expense number and the balance sheet account arising from the income tax allocation process.

APB Opinion No. 11 continued the thrust of ARBs 43 and 44 (revised). As long as timing differences arise, tax allocation must take place, despite the possibility of relevant circumstantial differences. This requirement is known as *comprehensive allocation*.

After many years in process, SFAS No. 96 appeared in 1987. It continued the comprehensive allocation approach of APB Opinion No. 11, but it was unduly conservative in terms of recognizing deferred tax assets on the balance sheet. SFAS No. 109 succeeded SFAS No. 96 in 1992 and restored consistency in terms of a largely evenhanded treatment relative to the balance sheet recognition of deferred tax assets and liabilities.

Permanent differences between published statements and tax returns are not subject to the allocation process. In the case of a nontaxable item, such as municipal bond interest, there is no effect on either tax expense or tax liability.

Another aspect of the tax picture is called *intrastatement* or *intraperiod tax allocation*. Where prior period adjustments, extraordinary items, changes in accounting principle, or operations of discontinued segments of a firm have tax effects, these items are shown net of the tax effect. The balance of the total tax expense figure then appears below net income before income taxes and extraordinary items. Intrastatement allocation is relatively easy to employ and probably has relevance for users, so the benefits appear to outweigh the costs. Nothing else of a theoretical nature is involved in intrastatement tax allocation.

There are numerous examples of timing differences (now called *temporary differences*). The tax liability would be greater than tax expense where either revenues are recognized for tax purposes earlier than for published reporting purposes or expenses are recognized more rapidly on the financial statements than on the tax return. Examples include the following:

- Receipt of cash for rent or subscriptions prior to the period in which services are performed
- Warranties recognized for financial accounting purposes when goods are sold and for tax purposes when work is performed
- Postretirement benefits other than pensions recognized prior to cash payment
- Bad debt expense is recognized in the period of sale for financial reporting purposes and in the period when the actual write-off occurs for tax purposes

Conversely, tax expense is greater than tax liability when either revenues are recognized more slowly or expenses more rapidly for tax purposes than for book purposes. These situations would include:

- Income from long-term construction contracts using the percentage-of-completion approach for financial accounting and the completed-contract approach for income taxes
- Installment sale income recognized for financial purposes at the time of sale and when cash is collected for taxes
- Accelerated depreciation for taxes and straight-line depreciation for financial accounting
- Intangible drilling and development costs deducted when incurred for taxes and capitalized for financial accounting

The Rationale of Income Tax Allocation

As the name explicitly states, income tax allocation is indeed an allocation. Thomas, in fact, has characterized it in very pithy terms:

> Tax allocation embodies the allocation problem in one of its most pathological forms. . . . Tax allocation may be perceived as an attempt to make allocation consistent, and its allocation problems are the consequences of other allocations.[2]

Although the language of ARB No. 43 is not explicit, it appears that income tax allocation is grounded in the matching concept. However, matching, as it is employed in tax allocation, differs from all other applications of matching. In the usual situation, expenses are matched against revenues. The result is expected at least to roughly portray efforts (expenses) that have given rise to accomplishments (revenues). However, the matching that occurs under income tax allocation attempts to normalize income tax expense with pre-tax accounting income. Hence, after-tax income is also correlated with pre-tax income. The matching brought about by tax allocation literally occurs at a lower point on the income statement than that of any other expense. Viewed from the perspective of the 1990s, matching provides a weak rationale for income tax allocation. However, within the framework of the historical cost approach, and in an era when the arbitrariness of the allocation process was not questioned, a strong case could have been made for income tax allocation.

Income tax allocation may smooth income, but because its use is mandatory where timing differences exist, it cannot be construed as a smoothing instrument—since management has no choice but to use it under both APB Opinion No. 11 and SFAS No. 109.[3] Comprehensive allocation is thus an example of rigid uniformity.

The FASB overhaul of income tax allocation in SFAS No. 96 and then again in SFAS No. 109 kept the comprehensive aspect of APB Opinion No. 11 but switched from the revenue–expense (matching) orientation to the asset–liability viewpoint. Prior to examining this switch-over, we examine the workings of income tax allocation in its most important application: the use of accelerated depreciation for tax purposes and straight-line depreciation for financial reporting.

Tax Allocation and Accelerated Depreciation

In the early years of the income tax allocation debate, the case favoring allocation was often made by using what was, in effect, a single-asset situation.[4] For example, assume that an asset with a five-year life and a cost of $15,000 and no salvage value is depreciated with a 40% tax rate by the sum-of-the-years' digits for tax purposes and by straight-line depreciation for financial accounting. The results are shown in Exhibit 15.1. The fifth column shows an increase in deferred taxes in the first and second years and reversal and elimination in the fourth and fifth years. If this model were representative of real circumstances, the tax allocation situation would present few problems. The extra tax benefits above those stemming from straight-line depreciation received in the early years of the asset's life are paid back in the later years.

Another situation is depicted in Exhibit 15.2, where a new asset acquisition is made each year until the firm reaches a stable point. It is assumed that beyond 2010 the pattern of acquiring a new asset each year and the disposal of an old one continues as before.

Cost and depreciation methods are the same as in the first example. Beyond 2009, total accelerated and straight-line depreciation are equal, so the tax benefits occurring in Years

Exhibit 15.1   Tax Deferral With a Single Asset

(1) Year	(2) Sum-of-the-Years'-Digits Depreciation	(3) Straight-line Depreciation	(4) Excess Tax Depreciation	(5) Deferral of Taxes (40% Tax Rate × Column 4)
1	$5,000	$3,000	$2,000	$800
2	4,000	3,000	1,000	400
3	3,000	3,000	0	0
4	2,000	3,000	(1,000)	(400)
5	1,000	3,000	(2,000)	(800)
	$15,000	$15,000	$0	$0

Exhibit 15.2   Tax Deferral in a Multiasset Situation

	Year 1	Year 2	Year 3	Year 4	Year 5	Year 6
Sum-of-the-Years'-Digits Depreciation						
Asset A	$5,000	$4,000	$3,000	$2,000	$1,000	
Asset B		5,000	4,000	3,000	2,000	$1,000
Asset C			5,000	4,000	3,000	2,000
Asset D				5,000	4,000	3,000
Asset E				5,000	5,000	4,000
Asset F						5,000
Total	$5,000	$9,000	$12,000	$14,000	$15,000	$15,000
Straight-Line Depreciation						
Asset A	$3,000	$3,000	$3,000	$3,000	$3,000	
Asset B		3,000	3,000	3,000	3,000	$3,000
Asset C			3,000	3,000	3,000	3,000
Asset D				3,000	3,000	3,000
Asset E					3,000	3,000
Asset F						3,000
Total	$3,000	$6,000	$9,000	$12,000	$15,000	$15,000
Excess of sum-of-the-years'-digits over straight-line depreciation	$2,000	$3,000	$3,000	$2,000	$0	$0
Deferral (excess × 40% tax rate)	$800	$1,200	$1,200	$800	$0	$0

1 through 3 become permanent when viewed in the aggregate sense. Of course, if the firm continues to expand or if costs of new assets increase, the amount of deferred taxes will continue to increase.[5] In fact, the great bulk of empirical evidence appears to indicate that the deferred tax account does indeed increase over time.[6]

The situation of virtually permanent deferral has presented an enigma to accounting standard setters and theoreticians in terms of interpreting the credit and even calling into question the whole process of tax allocation where the potential for permanent deferral exists.

Interpreting Deferred Tax Credits

Unquestionably, no legal liability arises as a result of using accelerated depreciation for income tax purposes. The federal government's desire in allowing accelerated depreciation as well as shorter guideline lives (the Modified Accelerated Cost Recovery System [MACRS]) prescribing the number of years of tax life for the various classes of assets has been to stimulate economic growth and modernize the nation's productive capacity by raising the internal rate of return on capital investment projects. Nothing is owed the government as a result of "excess" depreciation allowances taken for tax purposes. Moreover, the problem simply disappears if the enterprise uses accelerated depreciation for both tax and book purposes. The definition of legal liability, however, is too narrow for accounting purposes, which are, of course, concerned with portraying economic reality in accordance with user objectives and needs.

Another way of looking at the problem is to view each asset individually rather than looking at *the aggregate balance* of the deferred tax credit account. This is often referred to as the *rollover* method.[7] From the individual asset standpoint, the "liability" is paid off even though a new "loan" is received when a new asset is acquired, thereby offsetting the payback on the older asset as its tax depreciation diminishes. Thus, rollover proponents might say that accounts payable are recognized even though accounts that are paid off may be replaced with new payables. However, the rollover view has been strongly criticized because the payoff of each loan on older assets cannot be compared to the accounts payable situation because the debts are paid off individually, which, of course, is not the case with income taxes.[8]

The argument that deferred taxes are not the same as accounts payable weakened the case for comprehensive tax allocation with deferred taxes interpreted as liabilities. Because of this indeterminate status, deferred taxes were viewed as deferred credits in APB Opinion No. 11. As a result, the income statement, under the mantle of the matching concept, took precedence over the balance sheet (which now contained deferred charges that might not be assets and deferred credits that might not be liabilities).[9] The deferred credit approach differs from the liability interpretation under comprehensive allocation in the sense that the deferred credit account is not adjusted if tax rates change, whereas it is adjusted under the liability method if tax rates change. This distinction is in addition to the interpretation of the account itself.

Orientations to Income Tax Allocation

There are several policy positions possible on the income tax allocation issue. One is that allocation is not appropriate. In other words, tax expense equals tax liability. Some theoretical justification for advocating no allocation has been derived from the interpretation that income tax payments are a distribution of income rather than being an expense.[10] However, this has not been a popular position and cannot be strongly defended.

Somewhat related to the idea that income taxes are a distribution of profits rather than an element deducted in arriving at profits is the new form of equities position of Graul and Lemke.[11] According to their interpretation, the credit arising under income tax allocation represents a subordinated equity investment in the firm by the federal government. The reason the government makes this investment in the enterprise is to stimulate business investment. Deferred tax credits would be listed as an element of invested capital in the owners' equities section of the balance sheet. There is indeed some logic to this position, but it is simply one possible interpretation and nothing more. The fact that macroeconomic policy has led to certain tax benefits for business does not make government an investor in the firm except in the most limited sense.

Another possibility is the net-of-tax method, in which income tax expense is equal to the tax liability. However, the book depreciation is increased (or reduced) according to the following formula in any year by the excess tax benefits received above (or below) those that would have been derived from straight-line depreciation:

$$D_t = S + r(A_t - S) \tag{15.1}$$

where

$$D_t = \text{net of tax depreciation for period } t$$
$$S = \text{straight-line depreciation}$$
$$r = \text{tax rate}$$
$$A_t = \text{accelerated depreciation for period } t$$

Hence, if accelerated depreciation were $500 for a particular year and straight-line were $400 with a 40% tax rate, net-of-tax depreciation would be $440, determined by

$$\$440 = \$400 + .40(\$500 - \$400) \tag{15.1a}$$

Net-of-tax depreciation gives the same bottom-line net income effect as comprehensive allocation but moves the deferred credit over to the asset side as an additional element of accumulated depreciation. This certainly eliminates a large stumbling block of comprehensive allocation—interpreting deferred tax credits. Moreover, there is some theoretical justification for net-of-tax depreciation in a historical cost context.[12] Assume that amortization should concur with benefits received. In the case of fixed assets, two benefits can be postulated: (1) revenue-producing or cost-avoidance potential from productive utilization and (2) tax reduction. Therefore, if an asset renders relatively even service over its life and accelerated depreciation benefits are taken, there is certainly some justification for net-of-tax depreciation. However, the procedure is still an allocation and not a method of valuation. Along the same line, the numbers cannot be transformed or related to any current value measurements. They might, however, be transformed into general price-level-adjusted depreciation numbers.

Still another possible orientation to the timing difference problem is called *partial allocation.* Under partial allocation, only those deferred credits that can reasonably be expected to reverse in the foreseeable future on an aggregate basis are recorded on the books.[13] Thus, income tax expense for a given year is defined as the total tax costs attributable to the given year's operations, costs that will be levied against the firm, both in the current and future years, on a gross or aggregate basis. Hence, the deferred tax credit is clearly definable as a liability. The balance of the deferred tax liability account represents the amount expected to be paid in the future, which is attributable to the current and past years' operations on a gross basis.

An example should clarify the partial allocation approach. Assume that a firm's income before depreciation is $20,000 each year and the tax rate is 40%. Depreciation is the only timing difference between tax and book figures. The planning horizon is a five-year period. Depreciation figures are shown in Exhibit 15.3 (assets are designated $A_1 \ldots A_n$). All predictions are assumed to be accurate. For comparison and completeness, the numbers are also

Exhibit 15.3   Partial and Comprehensive Income Tax Allocation

Year	Tax Depreciation			Book Depreciation			Comprehensive Allocation	Partial Allocation
	A_1	A_2	A_3	A_1	A_2	A_3	40% (TD–BD)	
2005	$8,000			$5,000			$1,200	$1,120
2006	6,000			5,000			400	
2007	4,000	$2,400		5,000	$1,500		(40)	
2008	2,000	1,800		5,000	1,500		(1,080)	
2009		1,200	$8,000		1,500	$5,000	1,080	
2010		600	7,000		1,500	5,000	440	

shown for comprehensive allocation. Beyond 2009, tax depreciation is expected to exceed book depreciation.

Notice that the liability in 2005 under partial allocation is based on the fact that tax depreciation in 2007 and 2008 is less than book depreciation. This results in an anticipated obligation, because tax payments in those years would be greater than the anticipated "normal" amount based on book depreciation. This liability under partial allocation is consistent with the definition of liabilities in SFAC No. 6, which defines them as "probable future sacrifices of economic benefits arising from present obligations of a particular entity to transfer assets . . . as a result of past transactions or events."[14] Whether deferred tax credits arising under comprehensive allocation are liabilities consistent with the previous definition is not entirely clear.[15] Partial allocation is, of course, an example of finite uniformity. The relevant circumstance is whether tax depreciation will be less than book depreciation in any given year. Allocation occurs only if this condition is expected to exist over the period of the planning horizon. In accordance with the previous example, entries for the first four years that would arise under partial allocation are shown in Exhibit 15.4 along with entries under comprehensive allocation.

The obvious question about partial allocation concerns the issue of verifiability, since the method predicts a cash flow variable. Buckley has made some progress in this area.[16] He has

Exhibit 15.4   Entries Under Partial and Comprehensive Tax Allocation

Allocation					
Partial Allocation			*Comprehensive Allocation*		
Year 2005			*Year 2005*		
Income tax expense	5,920		Income tax expense	6,000	
Deferred tax liability		1,120	Deferred tax credit or liability		1,200
Income tax liability		4,800	Income tax liability		4,800
Tax liability is .4 ($20,000 – $8,000)					
Year 2006			*Year 2006*		
Income tax expense	5,600		Income tax expense	6,000	
Income tax liability .4 ($20,000 – $6,000)		5,600	Deferred tax credit or liability		400
			Income tax liability		5,600
Year 2007			*Year 2007*		
Income tax expense	5,400		Income tax expense	5,400	
Deferred tax liability	40		Deferred tax credit or liability	40	
Income tax liability .4 ($20,000 – $6,400)		5,440	Income tax liability		5,440
Year 2008			*Year 2008*		
Income tax expense	5,400		Income tax expense	5,400	
Deferred tax liability	1,080		Deferred tax credit or liability	1,080	
Income tax liability .4 ($20,000 – $3,800)		6,480	Income tax liability		6,480

developed a predictive model embracing the appropriate variables of anticipated capital investment over the planning horizon; tax and book depreciation differentials, including different lives; and expected changes in the tax rate. After setting up matrices for these variables, matrix algebra is used to solve for the predicted annual change in the deferred tax liability account. Tested by five firms in the Los Angeles area, the model had a high degree of predictive accuracy; not surprisingly, the firms found the results useful for cash budgeting and planning. There has been some support in the literature for partial allocation.[17] In addition, the United Kingdom essentially adopted it for years beginning after January 1, 1979, although it was abandoned in 1999.

Agency theory must also be considered in regard to partial allocation. How likely is it that management will favor an accounting method that lowers the current year's income based on a future contingency? Furthermore, management could also use the problem of verifiability as an additional argument to support any desire not to lower income in the current year.[18]

Another significant theoretical consideration relative to partial allocation is the *future events* problem. Notice in Exhibit 15.3 that assets A_2 and A_3 partially block the repayment of accelerated depreciation benefits received in earlier years. However, as of the end of 2005, the acquisition of assets A_2 and A_3 has not as yet occurred. The acquisitions of the assets are wholly executory events as of the end of 2005, even though their effect is taken into account in the allocation entries. The impact of future events on financial reporting could become an extremely important topic in accounting theory deliberations (future events were discussed in Chapter 12).

One more question remains in terms of partial allocation and comprehensive liability. Since the resulting credits are interpreted as liabilities that mature beyond a year, is discounting of these values appropriate?

Discounting Deferred Tax Liabilities

Long-term liabilities, such as bonds payable and noncancellable leases, are carried at their present values. This is accomplished by discounting future payments by the effective or implicit interest rate. Similarly, APB Opinion No. 21 requires that noninterest-bearing notes receivable must be discounted at their implicit interest rate. Consistency would, therefore, appear to dictate that tax liabilities (not deferred credits, however) under either the comprehensive or partial approaches should likewise be discounted.

Guenther and Sansing attempt to make the case that deferred tax liabilities arising from the use of accelerated depreciation for tax purposes and straight-line depreciation for financial reporting should not be discounted.[19] Their reason is that the deferred tax liability is not a "true" cash flow. We disagree with their position because (a) it has been defined as a liability and (b) the amount involved is a *fragmented cash flow*. By this term, we mean that deferred tax liabilities arise as a result of "paying back" on a rollover basis excess amounts of tax depreciation taken over "normal" amounts of financial reporting depreciation (times the tax rate). It should also be remembered that the deferred tax liability will be part of an overall liability that will arise in future periods.

In reality, the tax liabilities under either of the two interpretations are interest-free loans. However, the opportunity cost doctrine from economics has been advocated as a justification for discounting by the implicit interest rate: If the funds were not received from the government in the form of lower income taxes through higher depreciation allowances, borrowing from another source would have been necessary.[20] The interest rate on the funds from the next best source would be their opportunity cost. The opportunity cost doctrine is occasionally used in financial accounting. If an asset is donated to a firm, for example, it is booked at its fair market value with a credit to donated capital. Therefore, from the economic standpoint, it appears to be quite reasonable that deferred tax liabilities should be shown at their present value using the interest rate for a loan of similar duration, repayment schedule, and risk borne by the lender. The implicit interest rate should be on an after-tax basis.[21] We will assume that it is 10%. Entries for discounting deferred tax liabilities under partial and comprehensive allocation are shown in Exhibit 15.5 for 2005 through 2008.

Under comprehensive allocation, the tax expense consists of current tax liabilities and the present value of future obligations using an individual-asset rollover interpretation. Where partial allocation is employed, the tax expense includes the present value of future obligations where an actual payment above the future years' liabilities is involved, because book depreciation of presently owned assets is expected to exceed tax depreciation without a shielding effect from assets to be acquired in the future. This would, of course, be in addition to the current year's tax liability.

Summary of Orientations to Income Tax Allocation

In this section, we have reviewed and analyzed a bewildering number of possible approaches to the income tax allocation question. The various positions are shown in Exhibit 15.6 on page 497. The tax allocation debate can be approached only in terms of such criteria as consistency with other areas of valuation, relevance to users, and verifiability of measurements. Pure deductive logic alone cannot resolve this very perplexing issue. Prior to examining the workings of SFAS No. 109, we briefly examine the MACRS of the federal government.

Modified Accelerated Cost Recovery System

Prior to the 1981 tax act, corporate balance sheets in the United States were encumbered by hundreds of billions of dollars of deferred tax credits under the comprehensive deferral approach required by APB Opinion No. 11. Whatever its economic merits might have been, the deferred tax credit situation became further aggravated under the 1981 tax act because the period of tax recovery was further shortened.

The new system, called MACRS (Modified Accelerated Cost Recovery System), came about in the 1986 tax act and changed the percentages from the 1981 act. MACRS eliminates the concept of useful depreciable life. Instead, it substitutes six classes of capital assets with prescribed lives. Furthermore, salvage values are not considered. As a result, controversies over useful life between the IRS and corporations have been eliminated. The classes of capital assets as set out in the Tax Reform Act of 1986 are

Exhibit 15.5   Entries Under Discounting Deferred Tax Liabilities

Partial Allocation			*Comprehensive Allocation*		
Year 2005			**Year 2005**		

Income tax expense	5,644		Income tax expense	5,731	
Deferred tax liability		844	Deferred tax credit		931
Income tax liability		4,800	Income tax liability		4,800

As shown in Exhibit 15.3, reversal occurs for Years 3 and 4 which are 2 and 3 years after Year 1:

$$.826 \times \$40 \quad = \quad \$ 33$$
$$.751 \times 1{,}080 \quad = \quad \underline{811}$$
$$\$844$$

As shown in Exhibit 15.3, reversal occurs for asset A, in Years 3 and 4 after Year 1:

$$.826 \times .40 \times \$1{,}000 \quad = \quad \$330$$
$$.751 \times .40 \times \$2{,}000 \quad = \quad \underline{601}$$
$$\$931$$

Year 2006			**Year 2006**		

Income tax expense	5,600		Income tax expense	5,930	
Interest on deferred tax liability	84		Interest on deferred tax liability	93	
Deferred tax liability		84	Deferred tax liability		423
Income tax liability		5,600	Income tax liability		5,600

Interest at 10% on the balance of the deferred tax liability is (.10 × $844)

Interest at 10% on the balance of the deferred tax liability is (.10 × $931). The current liability on A_1 reverses in 2 years in Year 2008: $.826 \times .40 \times \$1{,}000 = \$330$

Year 2007			**Year 2007**		

Income tax expense	5,400		Income tax expense	5,319	
Interest on deferred tax liability	93		Interest on deferred tax liability	135	
Deferred tax liability		53	Deferred tax liability		14
Income tax liability		5,440	Income tax liability		5,440

Deferred tax liability is credited for interest (.10 × $928) and debited for the $40 reversal

Interest at 10% on the balance of deferred tax liability is (.10 × $1,354). The reversal on A_1 is $400. Present value of additional liabilities on A_2, which reverses in Years 2009 and 2010, is

$$.826 \times .40 \times \$300 = \$ 99$$
$$.751 \times .40 \times \ 600 = \underline{180}$$
$$\$279$$

Year 2008			**Year 2008**		

Income tax expense	5,400		Income tax expense	5,379	
Interest on deferred tax liability	98		Interest on deferred tax liability	137	
Deferred tax liability	982		Deferred tax liability	964	
Income tax liability		6,480	Income tax liability		6,480

Deferred tax liability is debited for the $1,080 reversal and credited for interest (.10 × $981). The account has a zero balance except for the $1 rounding error.

Interest at 10% on the balance of deferred tax liability is (.10 × $1,368).The reversal on A_1 is $1,200. Present value of additional liabilities on A_2, which reverses in 2008, is $.826 \times .40 \times \$300 = \$99$

Exhibit 15.6   Summary of Tax Allocation Positions

Major Positions and Variants	Designation of Balance as Asset or Liability	Discounting of Balance
No Allocation	No	No
Partial Allocation	Yes	Yes, it can be
Comprehensive Allocation		
New Form of Equities	No (becomes owners equity)	No
Net of Tax	No (becomes increased accumulated depreciation)	
Deferred	No	No
Liability	Yes	Yes, it can be

Class (Years) Types of Assets

3 years: Short-lived special manufacturing tools and handling devices in some industries. Examples include rubber manufacturing, glass products, fabricated metals, and manufacture of motor vehicles.

5 years: Cars, light trucks, and certain manufacturing equipment: oil drilling, construction, chemical manufacturing, and some clothing manufacturing. Also special tools for selected industries such as boat building.

7 years: Most heavy manufacturing equipment.

10 years: Includes railroad track, electrical generating and transmission equipment, cement manufacturing equipment, and food processing equipment for grain, sugar, and vegetable oil.

15 years: Includes gas pipelines and nuclear plants.

20 years: Includes sewer pipes and phone cables.

Cost recovery schedules for the various classes are shown in Exhibit 15.7 on page 498.

The Asset–Liability Orientation of SFAS No. 109

Dissatisfaction with APB Opinion No. 11 led to the reconsideration of income tax allocation by the FASB.[22] SFAS No. 96 appeared in December 1987, after almost five years of assessment and analysis. The standard kept the comprehensive income tax orientation of APB Opinion No. 11 but substituted a liability (asset–liability) approach in place of the deferred approach of APB Opinion No. 11. However, SFAS No. 96 employed some unusual restrictive assumptions in moving to the balance sheet focus and away from the matching concept underlying the comprehensive–deferred approach of APB Opinion No. 11. Dissatisfaction with the conservative recognition of deferred tax assets in SFAS No. 96 led to its replacement by SFAS No. 109.[23] SFAS No. 109 relaxed some of SFAS No. 96's restrictive conditions for recognizing deferred tax assets.

Exhibit 15.7   MACRS Allowances Under the 1986 Tax Act

Year	3-Year	5-Year	7-Year	10-Year	15-Year	20-Year
1	33.00	20.00	14.28	10.00	5.00	3.75
2	45.00	32.00	24.49	18.00	9.50	7.22
3	15.00[a]	19.20	17.49	14.40	8.55	6.68
4	7.00	11.52[a]	12.49	11.52	7.69	6.18
5		11.52	8.93[a]	9.22	6.93	5.71
6		5.76	8.93	7.37	6.23	5.28
7			8.93	6.55[a]	5.90[a]	4.89
8			4.46	6.55	5.90	4.52
9				6.55	5.90	4.46[a]
10				6.55	5.90	4.46
11				3.29	5.90	4.46
12					5.90	4.46
13					5.90	4.46
14					5.90	4.46
15					5.90	4.46
16					3.00	4.46
17						4.46
18						4.46
19						4.46
20						4.46
21						2.25
	100	100	100	100	100	100

[a] Indicates the year of switchback to straight-line depreciation.

An Illustration

Exhibit 15.8 on page 500 provides an overview of how SFAS No. 109 would ordinarily work. We assume that there have been no temporary differences prior to the current year, 1995. Also assumed is a tax rate schedule showing declining enacted tax rates. The deferred tax assets projected to arise in 1997 and 2003 are recognized at the rates that have been legislatively enacted for those years. If future changes in tax rates have not been legislated, then the current rate must be used.

Deferred tax assets in Exhibit 15.8 in 1996 and beyond are indicated by parentheses; deferred tax liabilities are shown without parentheses. The $135 deduction expected in 1997 could be recognized only by (a) carrying it back against the taxable income of a current or preceding year or (b) carrying it forward against a deferred tax liability of a future year arising from an event that has already occurred. In this case, the $135 could be "carried back" to 1994 (when the tax rate was 46% as opposed to the enacted 34% of 1997). If the $135 deduction was not exhausted by the taxable income of 1994 and 1995, it could be applied against the deferred tax liabilities of 1996, 1998, and 1999. The $30 deduction of 2003 would not have been recognized under SFAS No. 96 because there are no existing carrybacks or carryforwards to apply it against (an amount can be carried back for three years).

In addition to carryback of deferred tax assets and the allowed carryforward against deferred tax liabilities of future years, SFAS No. 109 also allows recognition of deferred tax assets if realization is *more likely than not*," which means a probability of more than 50%.[24] Thus, if a firm has constantly had taxable income, the judgment could be made that it will continue to have taxable income and the deferred tax asset should be recognized. Notice that taxable incomes of future years are future events that have not yet occurred. SFAS No. 109 also allows tax planning strategies to be utilized as a possible means for recognizing deferred tax assets. Thus, if a firm has a prospective deferred tax asset of $20,000, it might offset this amount against the taxable income arising from the planned sale of an asset if the deferred tax asset cannot be carried back against taxable income or deferred tax liabilities, carried forward against existing deferred tax liabilities, or if the probability is less than 50% that future taxable income will be generated to absorb the deferred tax asset. If, from the best available evidence, all of a deferred tax asset will not be realized, a valuation allowance for the amount that is not expected to be realized should be set up.[25]

While these rules may be occasionally cumbersome, the broader recognition of deferred tax assets of SFAS No. 109 restores a consistency between deferred tax assets and liabilities, which should be beneficial for financial statement users. One important benefit of SFAS No. 109 is that if a firm has been successfully generating taxable income and realization of deferred tax assets is "more likely than not," the extensive type of scheduling that had to be done under SFAS No. 96 can be avoided.

Another major change between SFAS No. 96 and SFAS No. 109 occurred in regard to the classification of current versus noncurrent deferred tax assets and liabilities. In SFAS No. 96, items originating or reversing in the next year were considered current while those originating or reversing beyond a year were noncurrent. In SFAS No. 109, the current or noncurrent designation is derived from the classification of the related asset or liability. In Exhibit 15.8, depreciation and deferred compensation (stock options) would be noncurrent; bad debts, warranty expense, and the installment sale would be current. The tax entry for 1995 would be:

Income tax expense	441	
Current deferred tax asset ($300 × .34)	102	
Noncurrent deferred tax asset ($210 × .34)	71	
Current deferred tax liability ($400 × .34)		136
Noncurrent deferred tax liability ($230 × .34)		78
Income taxes payable ($1,000 × .4)		400

Exhibit 15.8   Complex Income Tax Allocation Under *SFAS No. 109*

	Prior Years		Current Year	Future Years					
	1993	1994	1995	1996	1997	1998	1999	. . .	2003
Accounting income	$1,000	$1,000	$1,120						
Temporary differences									
Depreciation			(50)^O	$(120)^O	$(60)^O	$100^R	$130^R		
Bad debts			100°	(100)^R					
Warranty expense			200°	(125)^R	(75)^R				
Installment sale			(400)^O	400^R					
Deferred compensation			30°						$(30)^R
Subtotals (taxable income for 1995)	$1,000	$1,000	$1,000	$55	$(135)	$100	$130		$(30)
× Enacted tax rates	46%	46%	40%	34%	34%	34%	34%		34%
= Tax liability for 1993, 1994, and 1995 and deferred tax assets (in parentheses) or deferred tax liabilities beyond 1995	$460	$460	$400	$19	$(46)	$34	$44		$(10)

SOURCE: Adapted with changes courtesy KPMG Pear Marwick.

O = Originating

R = Reversing

The current deferred tax asset stems from the reversals of $100 and $125 for bad debts and warranty expense during 1996 and the warranty reversal of $75 expected in 1997. The non-current deferred tax asset is based on the originating depreciation amounts of $120 and $60 during 1996 and 1997 and the $30 reversing amount for deferred compensation during 2003. The current deferred tax liability comes from the $400 reversal of the installment sale during 1996. The noncurrent deferred tax liability stems from the depreciation reversals of $100 and $130 during 1998 and 1999. The two current and noncurrent accounts would be netted and shown as either a net asset or net liability but are shown separately for illustrative purposes. A current deferred tax liability of $34 and a noncurrent deferred tax liability of $7 would result ($136 minus $102 and $78 minus $71, respectively). In future years, as balance sheet accounts, adjustment would be made from the balances of the four deferred tax accounts.

Unfortunately, SFAS No. 109, like SFAS No. 96, does not allow discounting of deferred tax assets and liabilities. This position is inconsistent with numerous other events such as pensions, other postretirement benefits, leases, and notes receivable and payable without stipulated interest rates. Although there are some difficulties, such as predicting reversals or drawdowns of deferred tax assets and liabilities and determining an appropriate interest rate, these problems are by no means insurmountable.[26]

Net Operating Losses and Income Tax Allocation

SFAS No. 96 also took a negative view of treating tax-loss carryforwards as assets as did its predecessor, APB Opinion No. 11. It did allow them to reduce existing deferred tax liabilities with a reduction of the operating loss on the income statement. Any excess of the tax-loss carryforward over the deferred tax liabilities could not have been booked.

SFAS No. 109 has taken a complete turnaround on booking tax-loss carryforwards from its two predecessors. Tax-loss carryforwards will now be booked subject to the same valuation allowance procedures discussed previously for deferred tax assets.[27] The thinking of the Board—and correctly so—is that a close relationship exists between deferred tax assets and tax-loss carryforwards and the fact that both have the characteristics of assets as defined by the conceptual framework.[28]

A net operating loss arises if deductions exceed gross income for a taxable year. In the 1954 Internal Revenue Code, Congress recognized that it was unfair to tax firms in profitable years without allowing any benefits in loss years. Consequently, the 1954 code included provisions for carryback and carryforward of net operating losses. The carryback now covers a two-year period, and the carryforward period encompasses 20 years.

Since 1986, the Internal Revenue Service (IRS) has become more restrictive in terms of recognizing tax-loss carryforwards coming from acquired corporations. Continuity-of-business enterprise requirements are the key. To use tax-loss carryforwards, the loss corporation or the acquiring corporation must either continue the traditional business of the loss corporation or use a significant portion of the loss corporation's assets in a business. Despite the more restrictive treatment of the IRS, the 20-year carryforward provides a strong justification for treating tax-loss carryforwards as assets in most cases, as occurs in SFAS No. 109.[29] If there are uncertainties of realization, a valuation account can be set up, reducing both the deferred tax asset receivable and the income tax credit.

Empirical Research on Income Tax Allocation

Over the years, there has been a fairly extensive amount of empirical research on various aspects of income tax allocation. Two early studies were done by Beaver and Dukes.[30] In their first study, they found that income using income tax allocation had a higher degree of association with security price behavior than income determined without income tax allocation. Their second study suggested that the net-of-tax method using a tax rate significantly higher than current rates then existing had a higher association with security prices than income tax allocation using existing rates.

More recent research has also generally proved to be favorable to the usage of income tax allocation in its present asset-liability orientation of SFAS No. 109. Using cross-sectional regression analysis, Ayers found that SFAS No. 109 provides additional value-relevance above that of APB Opinion No. 11 when relating security prices to financial statement determinations of assets, liabilities, and net deferred tax liabilities and several other balance sheet measurements.[31] He likewise found better association of net deferred tax liabilities to firm value under SFAS No. 109 rather than its predecessor when tax rates increased under the Revenue Reconciliation Act of 1993. Ayers attributes the improved value relevance of SFAS No. 109 over APB Opinion No. 11 to separate recognition of deferred tax assets, adjustment for tax rate changes, and the creation of the valuation allowance for deferred tax assets.[32]

Somewhat complementary to the Ayers study is one done by Espahbodi, Espahbodi, and Tehranian.[33] They were concerned with security price reactions to the lowering of corporate income tax rates in the 1980s followed by the prospect of going from APB Opinion No. 11 to an asset–liability approach, which would give firms a one-time significant income increase owing to the potential lowering of deferred tax liabilities. The prospective one-time increase in income would also lower the probability of debt covenant violation, although there could be increased political costs to firms and also the prospect of increased compensation for corporate officers. The authors used an events study, tracking security prices just before and after the exposure draft releases preceding the issuance of SFAS Nos. 96 and 109. As would be expected, they found favorable price reactions to these events, which outweighed the potential increase in political costs and increased compensation for corporate officers.

A different aspect of income tax allocation was explored by Cheung, Krishnan, and Min.[34] They were interested in cash flow predictions using deferred tax allocations. They demonstrated that for one-year-ahead predictions of cash payments for income taxes, a model taking into account the previous year's tax payments plus net increases in deferred taxes (embracing both deferred tax assets and liabilities whether current or noncurrent) would predict the following year's income tax payments better than a model simply using the previous year's taxes paid relating to the taxes paid for the following year. They also used the predictions from their model in the Lorek-Willinger multivariate cash flow prediction model (Chapter 13), which improved that model's cash flow predictions. While it is intuitively obvious that predictions of the following year's tax payments will be improved by including increases in deferred tax liabilities along with cash payments for taxes in the current year, particularly if income tax expense and tax payments are increasing, this in no way detracts from the importance and usefulness of their study.

Another important finding was made by Givoly and Hayn.[35] They also used cross-sectional analysis centering on important announcements relative to the Tax Reform Act of 1986. The authors found that individuals do view the deferred tax liability as a real liability. The decline in the deferred tax liability resulting from the anticipated passage of the 1986 tax act was seen as leading to a significant increase in corporate equities. Thus, investors appear to view deferred taxes as a liability. Note that in the period encompassed by the study, 1984 to 1986, APB Opinion No. 11 with its deferred credit approach was in effect. Also note the complementary nature of this study to the one by Espahbodi, Espahbodi, and Tehranian discussed previously.

Two somewhat narrower studies concern the valuation allowance that can be used to offset deferred tax assets. Miller and Skinner found that valuation allowances tended to be smaller given either larger deferred tax liabilities or greater expected future taxable income, both of which would be available to absorb the reversal of deferred tax assets.[36] Behn, Eaton, and Williams have generally similar findings to those of Miller and Skinner in their study. Also note the conflict between relevance and reliability arising from booking valuation allowances.[37]

Some empirical research has also questioned the usefulness of income tax allocation. Chaney and Jeter found a negative association existing between deferred taxes and security returns.[38] They found high variation in deferred tax balances, which they thought might indicate the presence of earnings management. Chandra and Ro had somewhat similar results in their research.[39] Their interpretation was that the market appeared to view deferred tax liabilities as a permanent transfer; hence it was really disguised equity. The market may well be rewarding firms with large deferred tax liability balances because these firms appear to be minimizing their tax payments. It should be pointed out that the years examined in both these studies did not go beyond 1986, a time when APB Opinion No. 11 was still in force.

While there is some disagreement, it appears on balance that SFAS No. 109 is both (a) useful and (b) an improvement over APB Opinion No. 11.

International Accounting Standards (IAS)

IAS 12, *Income Taxes*, is based on the balance sheet liability approach, the same as the FASB's approach using deferred tax assets and liabilities for recognizing temporary differences. Since IASB and FASB's underlying approaches to income taxes are the same, a short-term convergence project was included in the Memorandum of Understanding, the agreement to pursue convergence between IFRSs and U.S. GAAP. A Discussion Memorandum was targeted for release in 2008.[40]

Under FASB, deferred tax accounts are classified as either current or noncurrent, depending on the account to which they pertain. In contrast, IAS 12 classifies *all* deferred tax assets and liabilities as noncurrent. The tax effect of intercompany transactions is recognized at the buyer's tax rate, not the seller's tax rate as U.S. GAAP requires.[41]

Improving Accounting Standards

Deferred tax assets and liabilities should be discounted to their present value. As discussed previously, the discount rate for deferred tax liabilities should be for a loan of similar duration, repayment schedule, and risk undertaken by the lender. For deferred tax assets, a single rate might be prescribed since the government is the payer. Therefore, since the firm's risk is low, the rate should be determined based on a very high-quality investment having a very low rate of risk.

Summary

Income tax allocation appears to be based on the matching concept. Relevance to users of the allocation process is, however, open to serious question. APB Opinion No. 11 required comprehensive allocation using the deferred method of presentation. Comprehensive allocation is a form of rigid uniformity because the question of loan repayment, a potentially important relevant circumstance, is ignored. The deferral approach simply begs the question of balance sheet interpretation and has been rejected as an appropriate classification in SFAC No. 3. SFAS No. 96 adopted a modified asset–liability view, which is unfortunately hindered by very conservative asset-recognition criteria.

Perhaps the principal problem of comprehensive allocation is the growth of the balance sheet credit when accelerated depreciation is used for tax purposes and straight-line for financial reporting purposes. A possible defense of the liability approach is the rollover view, which employs an individual-asset interpretation for tax liabilities. This outlook has been criticized on the grounds that tax liabilities are not like accounts payable. The latter are paid off on an individual basis, whereas the former are not.

Consequently, another view, partial allocation, arose. In this situation, allocation is employed only if it is foreseen that there will be a real payback of loans received as a result of total book depreciation exceeding total tax depreciation in specific future years. Hence, partial allocation is really a form of finite uniformity. The main problem with partial allocation is the question of verifiability, since future tax and book depreciation as well as the tax rate must be estimated. Other drawbacks are agency theory problems and the role of future events in the recognition of assets and liabilities.

SFAS No. 109 has taken a strong departure from its predecessors by providing a much more liberal recognition policy for both deferred tax assets and tax-loss carryforwards. Both have been justified on the grounds of falling within the conceptual framework definition of assets. In both cases, valuation allowances may be in order if it is thought that either asset will not be fully realized. SFAS No. 109, like SFAS No. 96, does not allow the discounting of deferred tax assets and liabilities. Finally, while answers are not yet final, empirical research has shown that SFAS No. 109 has more relevance than APB Opinion No. 11. Cash flow prediction appears to be enhanced by income tax allocation.

QUESTIONS

1. As a type of allocation, why is income tax allocation unique?

2. Relative to depreciation, why is comprehensive allocation an example of rigid uniformity and partial allocation an example of finite uniformity?

3. Although net-of-tax depreciation gives the same bottom-line result as comprehensive allocation, are there any financial ratios that would be affected by the choice between these methods?

4. How do the deferral and liability methods of implementing comprehensive allocation differ?

5. What is the rollover defense of the liability interpretation of deferred taxes, and how has it been attacked?

6. What is the justification for discounting deferred tax liabilities under either comprehensive or partial allocation?

7. What is the interpretation of income tax expenses under partial allocation?

8. What is permanent deferral?

9. How did SFAS No. 96 differ from APB Opinion No. 11?

10. How does SFAS No. 109 differ from SFAS No. 96?

11. Refer to Exhibit 15.8. Under SFAS No. 96, there was a "conservative" recognition of deferred tax assets. As a result, the $135 deferred tax asset in 1997 would need to be "carried back" to 1994. Why would this result not be conservative?

12. If discounting were used in the area of deferred tax assets and liabilities (as this chapter advocates), would there be any particular difficulty relative to tax-loss carryforwards?

13. Do you think that income tax allocation can improve the prediction of future tax payments in the short run?

14. Do deferred tax liabilities arising from using tax depreciation for tax purposes and straight-line depreciation for financial reporting lead to true future cash flows?

15. What are the weaknesses of partial allocation?

16. How are valuation allowances used in income tax allocation?

17. Should tax-loss carryforwards be booked? Explain.

CASES, PROBLEMS, AND WRITING ASSIGNMENTS

1. Refer to Exhibit 15.8. Assume that in 1996 accounting income is $2,000. There is one new temporary difference: Installment sale income of $350 is recognized in 1996 but will not be taxed until 1997 when the cash is collected.

Required:

Prepare the tax entries for 1996 in accordance with SFAS No. 109.

2. Nowell Company is experimenting with comprehensive-liability income tax allocation called for in SFAS No. 109 but, in addition, they are employing discounting. No temporary differences exist up to the year 2000. Shown here is a schedule of tax depreciation, book depreciation, and income before depreciation.

	Tax Depreciation		Book Depreciation		Income Before Depreciation
Year	A1	A2	A1	A2	
2005	$50,000		$35,000		$300,000
2006	40,000	$60,000	35,000	$50,000	400,000
2007	30,000	50,000	35,000	50,000	420,000
2008	20,000	40,000	35,000	50,000	440,000

The tax rate is 45%. The discount rate is 8%.

Required:

Prepare income tax entries for 2005, 2006, 2007, and 2008, discounting deferred tax liabilities at 8%. Why would using discounting be a stronger asset–liability orientation than not discounting deferred tax liabilities?

3. Accounting income for the Kolbow Company for 2005 (its first year of operations) was $1,700,000. Differences between book and income were as follows:

Municipal bond interest (permanent)	$ 75,000
Excess of tax over book depreciation	240,000
Excess of installment sales over collections	30,000
Compensatory stock option expense	37,000

Scheduled temporary differences over the next several years are:

	2006	2007	2008	2009
Depreciation	$(160,000)	$100,000	$140,000	$160,000
Excess of installment collections over sale	20,000	10,000		
Compensatory stock option expenses				(37,000)

Parentheses indicate a deduction in the previous schedule. Enacted tax rates are as follows:

2005	40%
2006	40%
2007	35%
2008	30%
2009	30%

Required:

a. Determine the taxable income for 2005.

b. Prepare a schedule and do the tax entries for 2005.

c. Taxable income in 2006 is $1,400,000. One new temporary difference has arisen. Bad-debt expense of $22,000 occurred during 2001, but the actual write-off (which is when the tax deduction is taken) is not expected to occur until 2002. Prepare a schedule and do the tax entries for 2006.

4. Gillette Company, maker of shaving products and many other personal products, showed a net income of $1.428 billion in 1998 and $1.427 billion in 1997 on page 1 of its 1998 annual report. A note to the 1998 income said that the 1998 income of $1.428 billion was to be reduced $347 million owing to reorganization and realignment expenses. Consistent with this, the net income in the consolidated statement of income for 1998 was $1.081 billion.

	1998	1997
Noncurrent deferred tax assets:		
Benefit plans	$180	$163
Merger-related costs	13	12
Operating loss and credit carryforwards	31	33
Valuation allowance	(29)	(31)
Net noncurrent deferred tax assets	$195	$177

In addition, following information appeared in the footnotes for the 1998 corporate annual report (figures are in millions).

Required:

a. Why do you think Gillette initially showed its income for 1998 to be $1.428 billion? Discuss.

b. Is the expensing of the reorganization and realignment costs of $347 million after taxes for 1998 correct? Explain.

c. What is the valuation allowance?

d. Why do you think Gillette maintains this account?

e. Do you think that earnings management is being used by Gillette?

5. WorldCom in 2001 and 2002 capitalized basic switching costs from expenses to capital assets to the tune of $3.8 billion dollars with approximately $3.04 billion occurring in 2001. The corporate tax rate is 35%. For 2001, WorldCom's income before taxes was $2.432 billion and its income tax expense was $0.943 billion for 2001. Assume that WorldCom, on its tax return, expenses the entire $3.04 billion.

Required:

a. Would WorldCom's actions have led to a situation of income tax allocation? Explain.

b. Do you think, based on the numbers shown above, that WorldCom allocated the income taxes stemming from the incorrect capitalization of the switching expenses?

6. Nortel Networks, the Canadian telecommunications equipment manufacturer, has recently suffered large losses, creating very large tax loss carryforwards. The company also has a very sizable

valuation allowance, which it deducts from the tax loss carryforwards on the balance sheet. During the last quarter of 2005, it reduced the valuation allowance by $111 million. In the first quarter of 2006, however, it added back $90 million to the valuation allowance.

Required:

What do you think may have been the underlying reason for Nortel's behavior relative to the manipulation of the valuation allowance?

CRITICAL THINKING AND ANALYSIS

1. What are the strengths and weaknesses of (a) no allocation, (b) comprehensive allocation with an income statement orientation, (c) comprehensive allocation with a balance sheet orientation, and (d) partial allocation? Which would you choose?

2. Is the deferred tax "liability" really a liability? Explain.

Notes

1. *Committee on Accounting Procedure (1953, p. 88).*
2. *Thomas (1974, pp. 146–147).*
3. *SFAS No. 109 discusses tax-planning strategies to prevent net operating loss carryforwards from expiring and also strategies resulting in realization of deferred tax assets. FASB (1992, p. 9). This is not done in APB Opinion No. 11 (APB 1967).*
4. *For example, see Moonitz (1957, p. 177).*
5. *The classic article discussing the multiasset case and its ramifications is by Davidson (1958).*
6. *See Livingstone (1967a, 1967b, and 1969) and Price Waterhouse & Co. (1967). For an opposing view, see Herring and Jacobs (1976). For a refutation of Herring and Jacobs, see Davidson, Skelton, and Weil (1977). The Davidson, Skelton, and Weil (1977) study was updated by Davidson, Rasch, and Weil (1984). Using Compustat data for 3,108 firms, all of them listed on the major exchanges, plus additional data for approximately 2,000 smaller firms for the years 1974–1982, they found that on the average only 7.5% of the firms that experienced a change in the deferred taxes account paid additional taxes as a result of a decline in the account resulting from depreciation timing differences. Skekel and Fazzi (1984) replicated the Davidson, Rasch, and Weil (1984) paper but restricted their sample to capital-intensive firms for the years 1974–1982. They found that only 4.5% of this group, on the average, paid additional taxes as a result of a decline in the deferred taxes account resulting from depreciation timing differences.*
7. *For a discussion, see Black (1966, pp. 69–72).*
8. *See the comments of Davidson, in Black (1966, pp. 117–119).*
9. *See the discussion of APB Statement 4 in Chapter 6.*
10. *Suojanen (1954, p. 393). For a broad discussion of this question, see Wheeler and Galliart (1974, pp. 51–56).*
11. *Graul and Lemke (1976). For a somewhat similar argument, see Watson (1979).*
12. *See Bierman (1990) for an extended discussion of the rationale underlying the net-of-tax method.*
13. *See Jeter and Chaney (1988) and Chaney and Jeter (1989) for further discussion of partial allocation.*
14. *FASB (1985, p. 13).*

15. *Nair and Weygandt (1981, p. 100) do not think that deferred tax liabilities arising under comprehensive allocation are consistent with the liability definition of SFAC No. 3. However, the statement itself appears to admit the possibility that the comprehensive liability approach is consistent with the liability definition presented there. See FASB (1980, p. 71). It appears that both partial allocation and the comprehensive liability approaches may result in the credits qualifying as liabilities according to SFAC No. 6.*

16. *Buckley (1972, pp. 71–101).*

17. *See Nair and Weygandt (1981, p. 100).*

18. *An aspect of the agency theory problem with partial allocation that Gordon and Joos (2004) found was that avoiding booking deferred tax liabilities occurred for the purpose of understating leverage. However, they did not find understating or avoiding deferred tax liabilities for the purpose of smoothing (managing) income.*

19. *Guenther and Sansing (2004). See also Amir, Kirschenheiter, and Willard (2001).*

20. *See Nurnberg (1972, pp. 657–658).*

21. *For more background on the appropriate rate, see Nurnberg (1972, pp. 659–665) and Williams and Findlay (1975), Wolk and Tearney (1980, pp. 126–127), Findlay and Williams (1981), and Collins, Rickard, and Selby (1990).*

22. *See Nair and Weygandt (1981) and Rosenfield and Dent (1983), for example.*

23. *For an analysis of the weaknesses and inconsistencies of SFAS No. 96, see Wolk, Martin, and Nichols (1989).*

24. *FASB (1992, paras. 95 and 96). In assessing earnings management via income tax allocation, Phillips, Pincus, and Rego (2003) find earnings increased through factors such as manipulating (increasing) useful lives of depreciable assets for financial reporting. Hence current tax liabilities would be unaffected.*

25. *In an events study, Kumar and Visvanathan (2003) find that changes in the deferred tax valuation account provide useful information relative to the current year concerning realization of the deferred tax asset itself and also changes in earnings prospects for the following year.*

26. *For difficulties in implementing discounting, see Stepp (1985). For difficulties of predicting reversals that affect the liability method as well as discounting, see Robbins and Swyers (1984, pp. 108–110 and 114–118). For a proposal on how to handle discounting, see Bublitz and Zuckerman (1988).*

27. *Generally, firms having large tax-loss carryforwards (and little else) are the subject of acquisitions by profitable firms. An exception is Aether Holdings, a company with tax-loss carryforwards of nearly a billion dollars and cash of $130 million as a result of selling off wireless communications and data operations holdings in 2004. Aether was attempting to buy Athlete's Foot in 2006 to utilize its tax-loss carryforwards against profitable operations. For further details, see Jones (2006).*

28. *FASB (1992, paras. 80–85).*

29. *Not surprisingly, Amir and Sougiannis (1999) find that tax loss carryforwards have value to investors positively affecting share prices.*

30. *Beaver and Dukes (1972 and 1973).*

31. *Ayers (1998).*

32. *Guenther and Sansing (2000, pp. 2–3), based on their analytical model, state that the timing of the reversal of deferred tax liabilities on an aggregate basis has no relevance to firm valuation because future fixed asset acquisitions could shield or delay the reversal of deferred tax liabilities. But this is intuitively obvious because future fixed asset acquisitions can hardly expect to influence present valuations of the firm prior to the fixed asset acquisitions.*

33. *Espahbodi, Espahbodi, and Tehranian (1995).*

34. *Cheung, Krishnan, and Min (1997).*

35. *Givoly and Hayn (1992). For an analytical (deductive) study showing a similar outcome, see Sansing (1998).*

36. *Miller and Skinner (1998).*

37. *Behn, Eaton, and Williams (1998). Petree, Gregory, and Vittray (1995) discuss the complexities of calculating deferred tax asset valuation allowances.*

38. *Chaney and Jeter (1994).*
39. *Chandra and Ro (1997).*
40. *See www.iasb.org for more information.*
41. *Epstein and Mirza (2006, pp. 526–575).*

References

Accounting Principles Board (1967). Accounting Principles Board Opinion No. 11, *Accounting for Income Taxes.* AICPA.

Amir, Eli, and T. Sougiannis (1999). "Analysts' Interpretations and Investors' Valuation of Tax Carryforwards," *Contemporary Accounting Research* (Vol. 16, No. 1), pp. 1–33.

Amir, Eli, M. Kirschenheiter, and K. Willard (2001). "The Aggregation and Valuation of Deferred Taxes," *Review of Accounting Studies* (Vol. 6), pp. 275–97.

Ayers, Benjamin (April 1998). "Deferred Tax Accounting Under SFAS No. 109: An Empirical Investigation of Its Incremental Value-Relevance Relative to APB No. 11," *Accounting Review*, pp. 195–212.

Beaver, William, and Roland Dukes (April 1972). "Interperiod Tax Allocation, Earnings Expectations, and the Behavior of Security Prices," *Accounting Review*, pp. 320–332.

——— (July 1973). "Interperiod Tax Allocation and d-Depreciation Methods: Some Empirical Results," *Accounting Review*, pp. 549–559.

Behn, Bruce, Tim Eaton, and Jan Williams (March 1998). "The Determinants of the Deferred Tax Allowance Account Under SFAS No. 109," *Accounting Horizons*, pp. 63–78.

Bierman, Jr., Harold (June 1990). "One More Reason to Revise Statement 96," *Accounting Horizons*, pp. 42–46.

Black, Homer (1966). Accounting Research Study No. 9, *Interperiod Allocation of Corporate Income Taxes.* AICPA.

Bublitz, Bruce, and Gilroy Zuckerman (1988). "Discounting Deferred Taxes: A New Approach," *Advances in Accounting* (Vol. 6), pp. 55–70.

Buckley, John (1972). *Income Tax Allocation: An Inquiry Into Problems of Methodology and Estimation.* Financial Executives Research Foundation.

Chandra, Uday, and B. T. Ro (Fall 1997). "The Association Between Deferred Taxes and Common Stock Risk," *Journal of Accounting and Public Policy*, pp. 311–333.

Chaney, Paul K., and Debra C. Jeter (June 1989). "Accounting for Deferred Income Taxes: Simplicity? Usefulness?" *Accounting Horizons*, pp. 6–13.

——— (Winter 1994). "The Effect of Deferred Taxes on Security Prices," *Journal of Accounting, Auditing & Finance*, pp. 91–116.

Cheung, Joseph, G. Krishnan, and C. Min (December 1997). "Does Interperiod Income Tax Allocation Enhance Prediction of Cash Flows," *Accounting Horizons*, pp. 1–15.

Collins, Brett, John Rickard, and Michael Selby (Winter 1990). "Discounting of Deferred Tax Liabilities," *Journal of Business Finance and Accounting*, pp. 757–758.

Committee on Accounting Procedure (1953). Accounting Research Bulletin No. 43, *Restatement and Revision of Accounting Research Bulletins.* AICPA.

Davidson, Sidney (April 1958). "Accelerated Depreciation and the Allocation of Income Taxes," *Accounting Review*, pp. 173–180.

——— (1966). "Comments," in H. Black, Accounting Research Study No. 9, *Interperiod Allocation of Corporate Income Taxes.* AICPA, pp. 117–119.

Davidson, Sidney, S. F. Rasch, and R. L. Weil (October 1984). "Behavior of the Deferred Tax Credit Account, 1973–82," *Journal of Accountancy*, pp. 138–142.

Davidson, Sidney, Lisa Skelton, and Roman Weil (April 1977). "A Controversy Over the Expected Behavior of Deferred Tax Credits," *Journal of Accountancy*, pp. 53–56.

Epstein, Barry J., and Abbas Ali Mirza (2006). Wiley IFRS 2006: *Interpretation and Application of International Financial Reporting Standards*. John Wiley and Sons.

Espahbodi, Hassan, P. Espahbodi, and H. Tehranian (October 1995). "Equity Price Reaction to the Pronouncements Related to Accounting for Income Taxes," *Accounting Review*, pp. 655–668.

Financial Accounting Standards Board (1980). Statement of Financial Accounting Concepts No. 3, *Elements of Financial Statements of Business Enterprises*. FASB.

——— (1985). Statement of Financial Accounting Concepts No. 6, *Elements of Financial Statements*. FASB.

——— (1987). Statement of Financial Accounting Standards No. 96, *Accounting for Income Taxes*. FASB.

——— (1992). Statement of Financial Accounting Standards No. 109, *Accounting for Income Taxes*. FASB.

Findlay, M. Chapman, III, and E. E. Williams (Winter 1981). "Discounting Deferred Tax Liabilities: A Reply," *Journal of Business Finance and Accounting*, pp. 593–597.

Givoly, Dan, and Carla Hayn (April 1992). "The Valuation of the Deferred Tax Liability: Evidence From the Stock Market," *Accounting Review*, pp. 94–110.

Gordon, Elizabeth A., and P. Joos (January 2004). "Unrecognized Deferred Taxes: Evidence From the U.K.," *Accounting Review*, pp. 97–124.

Graul, Paul, and Kenneth Lemke (June 1976). "On the Economic Substance of Deferred Taxes," *Abacus*, pp. 14–33.

Guenther, David, and Richard Sansing (January 2000). "Valuation of the Firm in the Presence of Temporary Book-Tax Differences: The Role of Deferred Tax Assets and Liabilities," *Accounting Review*, pp. 1–12.

——— (April 2004). "The Valuation Relevance of Reversing Deferred Tax Liabilities," *Accounting Review*, pp. 437–452

Herring, Hartwell, and Fred Jacobs (August 1976). "The Expected Behavior of Deferred Tax Credits," *Journal of Accountancy*, pp. 52–56.

Jeter, Debra C., and Paul K. Chaney (December 1988). "A Financial Statement Analysis Approach to Deferred Taxes," *Accounting Horizons*, pp. 41–49.

Jones, Steven D. (2006). "Aether Tries to Fit Glass Slipper on Athlete's Foot," *Wall Street Journal* (Sept. 11), p. C3.

Kumar, Krishna, and G. Visvanathan (April 2003). "The Information Content of the Deferred Tax Valuation Allowance," *Accounting Review*, pp. 471-490.

Livingstone, John L. (1967a). "Accelerated Depreciation and Deferred Taxes: An Empirical Study of Fluctuating Asset Expenditures," *Empirical Research in Accounting: Selected Studies, 1967* (Supplement to *Journal of Accounting Research*), pp. 93–105.

——— (1967b). "A Behavioral Study of Tax Allocation in Electric Utility Regulation," *Accounting Review* (July), pp. 544–552.

——— (Autumn 1969). "Accelerated Depreciation, Tax Allocation, and Cyclical Asset Expenditures of Large Manufacturing Firms," *Journal of Accounting Research*, pp. 245–256.

Miller, Gregory S., and Douglas Skinner (April 1998). "Determinants of the Valuation Allowance for Deferred Tax Assets Under SFAS No. 109," *Accounting Review*, pp. 213–233.

Moonitz, Maurice (April 1957). "Income Taxes in Financial Statements," *Accounting Review*, pp. 175–183.

Nair, R. D., and Jerry J. Weygandt (November 1981). "Let's Fix Deferred Taxes," *Journal of Accountancy*, pp. 87–102.

Nurnberg, Hugo (October 1972). "Discounting Deferred Tax Liabilities," *Accounting Review*, pp. 655–665.

Petree, Thomas, George Gregory, and Randall Vittray (March 1995). "Evaluating Deferred Tax Assets," *Journal of Accountancy*, pp. 71–77.

Phillips, John, M. Pincus, and S. O. Rego (April 2003). "Earnings Management: New Evidence Based on Deferred Tax Expense," *Accounting Review,* pp. 491–522.

Price Waterhouse & Co. (1967). *Is Generally Accepted Accounting for Income Taxes Possibly Misleading Investors?* Price Waterhouse & Co.

Robbins, Barry P., and S. O. Swyers (September 1984). "Accounting for Income Taxes: Predicting Timing Difference Reversals," *Journal of Accountancy,* pp. 108–118.

Rosenfield, Paul, and William C. Dent (February 1983). "No More Deferred Taxes," *Journal of Accountancy,* pp. 44–55.

Sansing, Richard (Autumn 1998). "Valuing the Deferred Tax Liability," *Journal of Accounting Research,* pp. 357–363.

Skekel, Ted, and C. Fazzi (1984). "The Deferred Tax Liability: Do Capital-Intensive Companies Pay It?" *Journal of Accountancy* (October 1984), pp. 142–150.

Stepp, James O. (November 1985). "Deferred Taxes: The Discounting Controversy," *Journal of Accountancy,* pp. 98–108.

Suojanen, Waino (July 1954). "Accounting Theory and the Large Corporation," *Accounting Review,* pp. 391–398.

Thomas, Arthur (1974). "The Allocation Problem: Part Two," *Studies in Accounting Research* #9. AAA.

Watson, Peter L. (Autumn 1979). "Accounting for Deferred Tax on Depreciable Assets," *Accounting and Business Research,* pp. 338–347.

Wheeler, James, and Wilfred Galliart (1974). *An Appraisal of Interperiod Income Tax Allocation.* Financial Executives Research Foundation.

Williams, E. E., and M. Chapman Findlay III (Spring 1975). "Discounting Deferred Tax Liabilities," *Journal of Business Finance and Accounting,* pp. 121–133.

Wolk, Harry I., Dale R. Martin, and Virginia A. Nichols (June 1989). "Statement of Financial Accounting Standards No. 96: Some Theoretical Problems," *Accounting Horizons,* pp. 1–5.

Wolk, Harry I., and M. G. Tearney (Spring 1980). "Discounting Deferred Tax Liabilities: Review and Analysis," *Journal of Business Finance and Accounting,* pp. 119–133.

16

Pensions and Other Postretirement Benefits

Learning Objectives

After reading this chapter, you should be able to:

- Understand defined benefit and defined contribution pension plans.
- Understand the evolution of accounting for defined benefit pension plans.
- Understand the implications of cash balance plans.
- Understand the nature of economic consequences pertaining to pensions and other postretirement benefits.
- Understand the accounting for postretirement benefits other than pensions and distinguish it from pension accounting.

The central questions in accounting for the effects of pension plans and other postretirement benefits involve the recognition and measurement of pension expenses and liabilities for the sponsoring company. Pension accounting provides an excellent illustration of the revenue–expense and asset–liability orientations to the financial statements. Previous accounting standards were based on a revenue–expense approach, which emphasized the recognition and measurement of annual pension expense. In SFAS No. 87, more rigid uniformity has been achieved in expense measurement, and the asset–liability orientation is evident in both expense measurement and the balance sheet recognition of unfunded pension benefits. Postretirement benefits are now subject to accrual accounting as a result of SFAS No. 106. In most areas, accounting for postretirement benefits is similar to pension accounting.

This chapter reviews the nature of pension plans in the first section. Pension plans are complex, so the review is meant to provide the necessary background for analysis of pension accounting. The second section examines in detail the 60-year development of pension accounting standards. The economic consequences of pension accounting standards are then discussed. After a simple illustration and a discussion of the main facets of SFAS No. 106, the economic consequences and theoretical aspects of other postretirement benefits are discussed in the final section of the chapter. Appendix 16-A gives an overview of pension expense calculations and actuarial funding methods.

Overview of Pension Plans

A pension plan is an arrangement between an employer and employee for the payment of postretirement income, hereafter called *pension benefits*.[1] There are many characteristics of pension plan design and funding, some of which are very complex. It is not feasible to review all of them, but we will briefly discuss significant areas that bear on pension accounting.

Defined Contribution and Defined Benefit Plans

An important feature of pension plans concerns the benefit formula and specification of contributions. There are two broad types of plans, and they differ as to how benefits are specified and funded. *Defined contribution* plans are those in which the benefit is defined as the future value of pension fund contributions made on an employee's behalf. The exact value is unknown prior to retirement because it depends on future earnings of pension fund investments. Benefits are solely a function of accumulated contributions, and for this reason the plans are called *defined contribution*. The value of benefits is variable; it is dependent on contribution levels and earnings made on invested contributions.

Contribution rates for defined contribution plans are normally stated as a percentage of wages or salaries. Plans may be either *noncontributory*, in which all contributions are made by the employer, or *contributory*, in which funding is shared by the employer and employee. Mandatory contributions must be made to a pension fund for most plans.[2] This means that assets are set aside for the sole purpose of paying pension benefits. The technical arrangements for accomplishing this are through either the establishment of a formal pension plan trust fund or the purchase of insured annuity contracts from insurance companies on behalf of employees. The term *pension fund* will be used to refer to both situations.

The other type of pension plan is called defined benefit. In *defined benefit* plans, the pension benefit is defined either as a specific dollar amount or by a general formula based on salary. Benefits may be expressed as a specific dollar amount, normally multiplied by years of membership in the plan (hereafter called *years of service*) to determine the value of the benefit. When benefits are defined by a general formula, two alternatives exist. Benefits can be based on career average salary: In this type of plan, pension benefits are based on career average salary multiplied by years of service. Another type of plan is referred to as *final pay:* pension benefits are based on final salary (usually the average of regular compensation a few years prior to retirement) multiplied by years of service. In all types of defined benefit plans, the value of pension benefits is directly related to the employee's years of service.[3] Membership in defined benefit plans is declining relative to membership in defined contribution plans. The number of insured defined benefit pension plans in the United States has gone from just under 50,000 in 1996 to just under 30,000 in 2005.[4] We can expect a further decline in defined benefit plans as a result of the Pension Reform Bill of 2006, which is encouraging 401(k) and other types of defined contribution plans. However, there are still approximately 44 million workers in America covered by defined benefit plans.

Benefits in a defined benefit plan may be paid in one of two ways: The benefit may be paid as a single lump sum amount at retirement date, or, alternatively, the benefit may be paid as a life annuity. Some plans permit the employee to elect either form of payment. When the benefit is lump sum, the payment represents a multiple of the defined base; for example, final regular salary averaged over five years, multiplied by 15% for each year of service. An employee with 40 years of service would receive 40 times .15 (which is six times final average salary). When benefits are defined as life annuity, the same principle is used. However, the benefit is paid each regular pay period and represents a fraction of the final average salary. For example, a rate of 1.5% per year of service and 40 years of service would create a lifetime monthly pension equal to 60% of final average monthly salary.

Vesting

Vesting refers to a qualifying period of pension plan membership that must be met before pension benefits legally exist. Pension benefits do not come into legal existences before vesting requirements are satisfied. Once benefits vest, there is a formal obligation between the plan and employees as set out in the terms of the plan.

Vested benefits are calculated as follows. The salary base, as defined in the benefit formula, is multiplied by the credited years of plan membership. For example, in a final pay plan, the salary base would be the most recent average salary, rather than final average salary. Because the benefits are not payable until retirement, actuaries compute the present value of vested benefits by discounting them at the assumed rate of interest earned on pension fund investments. Since pension benefits increase with each year of service, the value of vested benefits also increases with each additional year of service after becoming vested. At retirement date, the value of vested benefits will of course be equal to retirement benefits. If an employee withdraws from a plan prior to retirement, statutory requirements dictate that benefits must be frozen in the fund and paid when the employee retires. A permissible alternative is to transfer assets equal to the actuarial present value of vested benefits into the employee's new pension plan.

Single- and Multiemployer Plans

Another characteristic of pension plans is that they can be either single-employer or multiemployer plans. A multiemployer pension plan is subject to collective bargaining agreements in which two or more employers are plan sponsors. Under statutory requirements, one employer can contribute no more than 50% of initial contributions and no more than 75% thereafter. There are regulatory differences between the two types of sponsorship, and this does have some accounting implications, which are discussed later.

Actuarial Funding of Defined Benefit Plans

When benefits in a defined benefit plan are based on either career average or final average salary, it becomes something of a guess as to the value of future benefits. Actuaries are consulted to determine annual contribution levels. The principle of actuarial funding is to derive a time series of annual pension fund contributions that will accumulate to produce a projected pension fund balance sufficient to meet the cost of projected pension benefits. There is no single correct way of doing this. Many different actuarial funding models exist, and each one derives a different funding pattern over time. However, given the same set of plan conditions and actuarial assumptions, each method builds up a pension fund to the same future balance needed to meet expected retirement benefits. The extreme opposite of actuarial funding is called *terminal funding*. With terminal funding, the sponsor funds benefits only at the time of retirement. Actuarial funding achieves a more even cash flow. The methods developed by actuaries to determine contribution levels are referred to as either *actuarial funding methods* or *actuarial cost methods*. The term *actuarial funding method* will be used for the remainder of the chapter.

Actuarial funding methods are analogous to depreciation methods. A depreciation method allocates a given amount over a specified period of years. Each depreciation method produces a different time series of depreciation expense, but they all sum to the same amount (asset cost less estimated salvage). In a slightly more complicated way, the same thing happens with actuarial funding. Each actuarial funding method produces a time series of future contributions that compound to the same future amount. The mathematical differences between actuarial funding methods are in how benefits are assumed to accumulate (increase) with each year of employee service. It is important to emphasize that this is an arbitrary assumption made solely for the purpose of orderly pension funding. Pension benefits do not legally accumulate or increase in value with each year until vesting requirements are met. For funding purposes, however, benefits are assumed to accumulate each year, even prior to vesting. Actuarial terminology refers to the increase in accumulated benefits each period as *service cost* or *normal cost* and the accumulated benefits to date as *actuarial liability*. A very important point to reiterate, though, is that the actuarial calculation of both yearly service cost and actuarial liability is arbitrary and that each actuarial method produces different amounts.

Funding Complexities

Funding becomes more complex in three situations: (1) when a plan is started and past service credit is given to employees; (2) when plan amendments are made that alter benefit levels, and the amendments are made retroactive for past years of service credits; or (3) when actuarial assumptions differ from the subsequent experience of the plan (a situation giving rise to actuarial gains and losses). In all three cases, accumulated benefits will exist (as calculated by the actuarial funding method in use) but are not fully funded. Each of the three situations is explained here.

When a pension plan commences, credit is often granted to employees for past years of service. From an actuarial funding viewpoint, accumulated benefits exist for past service, but no funding has occurred. This gives rise to *unfunded past service cost.* It is also called *unfunded benefits* and *unfunded actuarial liability.* The identical situation is encountered when benefit improvements are made; this gives rise to what are called *prior service costs.* For example, the rate of benefit accumulation per year of service might be increased. If the increased rate is applied to prior service as well as future service, accumulated benefits will exist that have not been funded. In both cases, accumulated benefits exceed the existing pension fund balance.

Actuaries deal with the problem of unfunded accumulated benefits in one of two ways. One way is to assume that pension funding dates from the earliest past service credit granted and to continue calculating future contributions (future service costs) as though this were true. When this is done, however, a supplemental contribution is necessary because future service costs will be insufficient to fund expected retirement benefits. The total contribution, therefore, will be service cost plus a yearly supplement (until the deficiency is fully funded). The other solution is to compute a new time series of yearly contributions (service costs) over the remaining service life—to accumulate a pension fund sufficient to meet expected retirement benefits. Supplemental contributions are not necessary because future service costs are recalculated to make up the deficiency.

Actuarial gains and losses present a similar problem. In applying actuarial funding methods, actuaries must make assumptions about (a) future withdrawals from the plan, (b) effects of future salary levels on the value of expected retirement benefits (although this is not always done), and (c) the rate of interest to be earned on pension fund investments. If the pension plan experience differs from these assumptions, the pension fund will be either too high or too low. This difference is an *actuarial loss* if the fund is less than needed and an *actuarial gain* if the fund is greater. Actuarial gains and losses are treated in the same general way as other unfunded accumulated benefits. For example, if an actuarial loss exists owing to lower-than-expected earnings on fund investments, a supplemental annual contribution could be made over an arbitrary period of years to make up the deficiency. Alternatively, the loss could be funded implicitly by the calculation of a new time series of future contributions that will fully fund the expected retirement benefits.

Actuarial Funding Methods

There are two broad types of actuarial funding methods: *accumulated benefit* and *projected benefit.* The accumulated benefit method can be used in either of the two ways discussed to deal with unfunded accumulated benefits: A separate contribution may be calculated to supplement service cost, or service cost can be recalculated in such a way that the deficiency is implicitly funded as part of future service costs. The accumulated benefit method is so named because the accumulation of benefits is measured using current salary levels and years of service to value current benefits. This approach is a literal measurement of the value of current accumulated benefits based on the benefit formula in a plan. The method has been criticized for not incorporating future salary increases into the calculations. Eventual benefits will be based on future rather than current salaries. However, one variation of the method does use projected future salaries to calculate service costs.

Projected benefit funding methods are more complex. Each one represents an alternative way of spreading the cost of projected benefits over time. Within this group of methods, the first distinction is between individual and aggregate methods. Individual methods develop contribution rates for individuals, which are then summed to derive the total contribution for the plan. Aggregate methods make funding calculations for the plan as a whole. The other distinction concerns the manner in which unfunded accumulated benefits are funded. Different names have been given to projected benefit methods, depending on whether a supplemental contribution is required to deal with unfunded accumulated benefits.

It is essential to distinguish between actuarial funding methods and pension expense recognition methods. Prior to SFAS No. 87, any one of five accumulated benefit methods could be used for pension expense recognition purposes. SFAS No. 87 switched to one type of projected benefit method that must be used for pension expense recognition purposes. Appendix 16-A illustrates two pension expense recognition approaches (one accumulated benefit approach and the required projected benefit approach) and two projected benefit funding methods (projected accrued benefit cost method and the entry age normal method).

In general, the accumulated benefit method assigns more cost to later years of employment and a smaller amount to earlier years compared to projected benefit methods. There is a more even distribution of contribution levels with projected benefit methods. Differences between the two are less pronounced for stable, mature pension plans because the mixture of young and old employees tends to even out the results. But the differences become pronounced for very young pension plans or very old pension plans. For very young plans, the accumulated benefit method would recognize substantially less each year than projected benefit methods, and the reverse would be true for very old plans.

Employee Retirement Income Security Act of 1974 (ERISA)

ERISA was a landmark piece of social legislation that was intended to improve both access to and the security of pension benefits for employees.[5] The legislation affected four areas: (1) membership eligibility and vesting requirements, (2) mandatory funding requirements, (3) investment diversification requirements, and (4) the guarantee of certain vested benefits in the event of plan terminations. The first area (1) was intended to increase participation levels and to improve the probability of receiving benefits. This was achieved by setting maximum time periods on qualifying years of employment—first to join the plan and then to qualify for pension benefits. Membership eligibility cannot require a higher minimum age than 25 and a longer term of service than three years.

Vesting must follow one of three alternative formulas: (1) 100% vested after 10 years of membership; (2) graded vesting, in which benefits are 25% vested after five years, increasing 5% for the next five years, and increasing 10% per year thereafter—so that 100% vesting occurs in 15 years; (3) the "rule of 45," in which benefits of an employee with five or more years of membership must be 50% vested when the sum of age and years of membership are

45, with 10% additional vesting for each year of service (subject to a requirement that vesting be 50% after 10 years and 100% after 15 years).

The objective in the second area (2) was to override discretionary funding clauses in pension plans. ERISA requires that annual funding must occur and be based on an acceptable actuarial funding method. In addition, unfunded accumulated benefits must be funded over a maximum of 40 years for single-employer plans in existence on January 1, 1974; 30 years for plans established after that date; and 40 years for multiemployer plans. Unfunded accumulated benefits attributable to actuarial losses must be funded over a maximum of 15 years.

The third area (3) concerns portfolio diversification. ERISA states that pension fund managers should be concerned with diversification of investments. However, the only specific requirement is to limit investments in the sponsoring company to 10% of the total pension fund. This rule is designed to make a plan financially independent of the sponsor. If a sponsoring company fails, accumulated benefits of the company's pension plan should not be in jeopardy. In a general way, diversification also reduces investment risk and increases the security of assets held in the pension fund.

Finally, in the fourth area (4), ERISA created the Pension Benefit Guaranty Corporation (PBGC) as a national insurer of pension plans and empowered it to collect premiums from plans to pay for guaranteed termination benefits. Vested benefits of participants are partially guaranteed by the PBGC if a plan is terminated. There are different guarantees for single-employer and multiemployer plans.[6] If a pension fund cannot meet guaranteed vested benefits, any shortfall is paid by the PBGC. The PBGC, then, has a statutory lien against the sponsor for this shortfall up to a maximum of 30% of the sponsor's net worth. Premiums collected by the PBGC are intended to cover termination benefits that are not recouped from the sponsors of terminated plans. The PBGC, like defined benefit pension plans themselves, is experiencing financial difficulties. In mid-2006, the PBGC had a $23 billion deficit with potential new defined benefit terminations estimated at $108 billion.[7]

Much of the pension controversy centers on whether ERISA has had any effect on the nature of pension plans and the appropriate accounting for pension plans by sponsoring companies. The impetus for review of pension accounting by the Financial Accounting Standards Board (FASB) came in response to the passage of ERISA.

While ERISA has certainly been beneficial, pension funds are not always as well protected as they should be. During the 1980s, overfunded pension plans often attracted corporate raiders whose major purpose was to gain control of surplus pension assets. Congress slapped a 50% excise tax on these "reversions," but a loophole remained. If one-quarter of the surplus pension assets are put into a "replacement plan," the excise tax is only 20%. For example, Dillard's Inc., acquired Mercantile Stores, which had a $194 million pension surplus. Twenty-five percent of the existing surplus was put into Dillard's existing 401(k) plan, and after the 20% excise tax, Dillard's was left with $117 million of free cash.[8]

Cash Balance Plans

Pension plans of numerous American businesses have been modified or eliminated recently, particularly in the airline and automobile businesses.[9] The wrenching changes occurring as a result of this process are undoubtedly helping to make American business more competitive with foreign corporations but at a painful cost to the American worker.[10] Indeed Ford Motor Company's buyout plan of employees was brought about by the high cost of their pension plans. It was an attempt to make the company more competitive with its foreign competition.

An increasingly common practice is to modify pension plans by converting existing plans into *cash balance plans*. These plans redistribute benefits away from older employees whose benefits would have sharply increased as they entered the last phase of their employment and shift them to younger employees.[11] Another advantage to younger employees is that cash balance plans are more "portable": These plans can generally be moved with the employee to new employment. This type of redistribution brings about a decline in total pension benefits and a reduction in pension liabilities. Older employees may have to wait several years before catching up to where they previously were because their initial cash balance was below their accrued benefit in the previous defined benefit plan.[12] Furthermore, as a result of the switch to cash balance plans, older employees will not get the increased benefits in later years that generally arise from defined benefit plans. However, cash balance plans have been challenged on the grounds of age discrimination under the Age Discrimination in Employment Act of 1967.[13] As a result, IBM allowed employees who were both (a) at least 40 years of age and (b) with at least 10 years of service to opt for either the new cash balance plan or to remain with the old plan.

Legal Relationships in Defined Benefit Plans

The parties to a defined benefit pension plan are the sponsoring employer, a pension fund, plan participants (the sponsor's present and past employees or their beneficiaries), and the PBGC for plans subject to ERISA. Pension plans are governed by a formal document that sets out the rights and obligations of the employer and employee. Plans have clauses obligating the sponsor to make annual pension fund contributions. The typical requirement is that funding must be based on the advice of actuaries. However, exculpatory clauses usually exist that give the sponsor the right to determine its own contribution levels, to suspend contributions altogether, and to even terminate the plan with no obligation for further contributions. The effect of these clauses is to shelter the sponsor from a legal pension liability.

Pension plans also state that the payment of benefits is to be made solely from pension fund assets, not from the sponsor's assets. This is one reason for establishing a pension fund. Exculpatory clauses limit the payment of pension benefits to the existing assets of the pension fund, regardless of how much may be earned according to a plan's benefit formula. These clauses also shelter the sponsor from a legal pension liability. ERISA has not changed this basic relationship between sponsors and employees. Sponsors still have a right to terminate plans. Exculpatory clauses still shelter the sponsor from a direct legal liability to employees for pension benefits. However, there is now a minimum level of annual funding and a legal obligation for vested benefits that are guaranteed by the PBGC.

The PBGC is a fourth party to the plan, guaranteeing certain pension benefits upon plan termination and having a claim against the plan's sponsor for reimbursement if there is a shortfall in the pension fund at termination. For continuing plans, a funding obligation also exists because of the PBGC guarantee. If the plan continues, unfunded pension benefits will eventually become funded through statutory annual contributions. Either way, then, guaranteed pension benefits must be funded. The significance of this is that the sponsor has a legally unavoidable funding obligation for pension benefits guaranteed by the PBGC.

In a voluntary termination, the sponsor has a legal liability under ERISA for *all* accrued benefits, both vested and unvested.[14] It is only with involuntary plan terminations that the liability is restricted to PBGC-guaranteed *vested* benefits. Involuntary terminations generally occur only when the sponsor is insolvent or in bankruptcy, and they can be initiated either by the company or the PBGC. As mentioned previously, the PBGC is presently coming under intense financial pressure stemming from a wave of corporate bankruptcies.

Accounting Issues Relating to Defined Benefit Pension Plans

Defined contribution plans do not present difficult accounting problems. An expense is recognized for the sponsor's contribution made in accordance with the terms of the plan. No further obligation exists because pension benefits attributable to employee service to date are restricted to the accumulation of past contributions. In other words, accumulated benefits are fully funded by the sponsor as long as each year's required contribution is made. An expense and liability should be accrued for the current year's required contribution, and the liability is discharged when the contribution is made.

The major accounting question that emerges in a defined benefit pension plan is this: When the benefits are defined independent of contribution levels, does the sponsor have an obligation (either contractual or implied) to meet the *projected* cost of pension benefits arising from employee service to date? The implication is that existing contributions (pension fund assets) may be less than *accumulated* benefits relating to years of service worked to date. Any underfunding of accumulated benefits will need to be made up in future periods for the fund to have sufficient assets to meet expected retirement benefits. It can be argued, then, that unfunded accumulated benefits give rise to an accounting liability that should be recognized. In fact, SFAS No. 158, to be discussed shortly, now requires a liability to be booked for unfunded projected liability benefits.

Another accounting question concerns the recognition and measurement of yearly pension expense: Is it simply the cash contributed to the pension fund, or is it a more complex accrual based on the yearly increase in accumulated benefits? If a complex accrual is to be made, the problem is one of defining how pension benefits are assumed to accumulate in each period.

The recognition and measurement of pension expenses and liabilities as specified in accounting standards are examined in detail in the next section, which provides a historical perspective on the development of pension accounting.

Development of Pension Accounting Standards

ARB 36 (Codified as Chapter 13, Section A of ARB 43)

A cash basis for pension accounting existed prior to any accounting standards. Pension expense was equated with cash contributions to pension funds. The first pension accounting standard was ARB 36, issued in 1948. It was later codified as ARB 43, Chapter 13, Section A.[15] ARB 36 was concerned with the recognition of unfunded accumulated benefits (arising from plan startups) in the financial statements. There were three possible methods that could be used to account for unfunded accumulated benefits. One was to make a prior period adjustment— the reason being that the accumulated benefits were related to service given in the past. An alternative followed the same basic argument, but the adjustment was charged to current income and classified as an extraordinary item. These two methods represented the current operating and all-inclusive income concepts, respectively. ARB 36 adopted a third approach, which allocated unfunded accumulated benefits over current and future periods.

The argument in ARB 36 was that the cost of providing pension benefits should be spread over the remaining service life of employees. If unfunded accumulated benefits exist because of a plan startup, the employer's cost of meeting these benefits should be matched against future revenues to be generated from employees' labor. The matching concept is the underlying principle of ARB 36. Since the employer's future costs will increase because of future funding of unfunded accumulated benefits, future sales revenue will have a markup based on these higher pension contributions. The fact that service giving rise to the benefits occurred in the past is unimportant. It is future contributions and revenues that will be affected by the decision of the firm to incur unfunded accumulated benefits.

ARB 36 would not necessarily have changed the cash basis of pension accounting. If firms were expensing the amount of pension fund contributions and if the cash contribution included an element for unfunded accumulated benefits, a cash basis of accounting would still have existed. All ARB 36 did was reduce flexibility in how the cost relating to unfunded accumulated benefits was dealt with in the income statement.

ARB 47

A pension liability concept was introduced for the first time in ARB 47.[16] The standard recommended that the balance sheet report unfunded vested benefits. It also implied that the income statement should report the increase in unfunded vested benefits as the minimum pension expense for the period. In spite of the change, a de facto cash basis of accounting continued for most companies under ARB 47 because pension funds would normally have been in excess of vested benefits at the time of the standard. Prior to the pension reform movement, which began in the 1960s, it was not uncommon for pension plans to have lengthy vesting periods.[17] As a result, plans would normally have been adequately funded for vested benefits. This was because accumulated benefits would be predominantly unvested if lengthy vesting periods existed. A plan would need to have been grossly underfunded to be affected by ARB 47.

APB Opinion No. 8

A major change in pension accounting occurred with APB Opinion No. 8.[18] In this, standard pension expense was computed using any one of five acceptable accumulated benefit methods, regardless of cash contributions. Hence, APB Opinion No. 8 represented an example of flexibility. APB Opinion No. 8 represented a move from simple cash accounting to a more complex accrual basis. For companies following actuarial funding recommendations, the cash basis of accounting posed no problem. The real concern in APB Opinion No. 8 was for companies not consistently following actuarial funding advice. APB Opinion No. 8 was an attempt to make pension expense recognition consistent between those companies following actuarial funding advice and those that were not.

As has been pointed out, annual pension funding was potentially discretionary prior to ERISA. Using a cash basis of accounting, pension expense could vary from year to year, depending on management funding decisions. Companies might fund more in good years and less in bad years. That this happened has been supported by one research study based on data preceding adoption of APB Opinion No. 8.[19] The reason for mandating an accrual rested on the premise that a quantifiable portion of future pension benefits accumulates with each period of employment, regardless of how much is actually funded. The accountant's task is to make a reasonable estimate of the yearly cost of these accumulating pension benefits. Since this is exactly what actuarial funding methods do, it is understandable that APB Opinion No. 8 endorsed their use for pension expense estimation.

APB Opinion No. 8 was regarded as a successful accounting standard. It utilized a research study as the basis of the accounting standard and brought some order to pension accounting.[20] At the time of its adoption, APB Opinion No. 8 affected companies that were extremely discretionary in funding. However, a major uniformity problem still existed in the measurement of accrued pension expense—because APB Opinion No. 8 permitted flexibility in the choice of actuarial funding methods used to accrue pension expense. Funding methods vary significantly in the calculation of yearly normal cost. These differences are material under certain conditions and can materially affect reported income.[21] Appendix 16-A illustrates the yearly variation between actuarial funding methods.

APB Opinion No. 8 was consistent with the revenue–expense approach and with general principles of expense measurement. The accrual method achieved a "rational and systematic" recognition of pension costs over the working lives of employees, the exact words used in APB Opinion No. 8. Expenses are recognized in a rational and systematic manner if direct matching to revenue cannot be achieved. Under APB Opinion No. 8, pension costs were allocated to the periods of employee service, and in this way an indirect matching of costs to revenues was considered accomplished.

FASB Interpretation 3

FASB Interpretation 3 was issued in response to the passage of ERISA.[22] It reaffirmed APB Opinion No. 8 and concluded that ERISA did not create a pension liability except in the likelihood of plan termination. A liability accrual was required only if termination was probable and if guaranteed termination benefits exceeded pension fund assets. This requirement was a reiteration and interpretation of APB Opinion No. 8, paragraph 18, which required balance sheet recognition of legally unavoidable pension liabilities.

This interpretation was *incorrect,* however, because ERISA created an unavoidable obligation to fund unfunded accumulated benefits. The obligation exists whether the plan is terminated or not. If a plan is not terminated, an obligation still exists in the form of future annual statutory funding requirements (which include an element representing the funding of unfunded accumulated benefits).

SFAS No. 35

SFAS No. 35 defines the pension plan as a reporting entity and establishes accounting standards for the measurement and reporting of plan assets and plan obligations.[23] This is considered a landmark standard because it set accounting and reporting standards for a new entity, the pension plan, as separate and distinct from the sponsoring company. Assets are measured at current market values. Plan obligations are defined as accumulated benefits (both vested and unvested) and are measured using the accumulated benefit funding method, without taking future salary increases into consideration.

Great care is taken in SFAS No. 35 to separate clearly the plan (and pension fund) from the sponsor. The nature of the relationship between the sponsor and employee for the payment of pension benefits is carefully avoided. SFAS No. 35 represents a subtle way of reporting the sponsoring company's pension obligations. It is far less controversial to report a pension obligation of a plan than to report the obligation of a sponsor. This indirect approach to the liability question carried through in SFAS No. 36, which required information about the "plan's" obligations to be reported as a note in the sponsor's financial statements.

SFAS No. 36

SFAS No. 36 amended the supplemental disclosure requirements of APB Opinion No. 8, paragraph 46. The specific disclosure requirements of SFAS No. 36 were as follows:[24]

1. Basic plan description

2. General statement of funding policy (actuarial method not required)

3. Any significant matters affecting comparability between periods; for example, change in accounting methods, changes in actuarial assumptions or funding methods, plan amendments, and actuarial gains or losses

4. Plan assets, as measured under SFAS No. 35 requirements (market values)

5. Actuarially calculated accumulated benefits as measured under SFAS No. 35, separated into vested and unvested amounts

6. Interest rates used in making the actuarial calculations

7. Date at which the actuarial calculations were made

The most significant change was the disclosure of accumulated benefits as measured under SFAS No. 35 and the segregation of this amount into vested and unvested benefits. It was left to the reader to interpret the significance of the data, and how, if at all, they related to the sponsor. Disclosure was thus used as an effective way of dealing with a controversial topic.

SFAS No. 87 and SFAS No. 88: Shifting to a Liability Orientation

A revenue–expense orientation dominated pension accounting standards up to and including APB Opinion No. 8. Largely because of ERISA, most firms were funding and accruing similar amounts.[25] In a cash flow sense, then, the accounting can be said to have been uniform among companies. However, in an accrual sense there was no uniformity because the accruals could be based on any of five different actuarial methods—in addition to the effects of differing actuarial assumptions used in applying the methods. Each actuarial funding method accrues accumulated benefits in a different (and arbitrary) manner. The situation is analogous to the arbitrary allocation of costs under alternative depreciation methods.

The present standard, SFAS No. 87, has achieved greater uniformity in measuring accrued pension expense by mandating use of one actuarial method, *the benefits/years-of-service approach* (with projected future salaries). SFAS No. 87 uses *service cost* rather than the term *normal cost*. Accrued periodic pension expense is defined as the sum of:

1. Service (normal) cost for the year using the accrued benefit actuarial method (with projected future salaries).

2. Interest cost for the year relating to the actuarial present-value increase in accumulated benefits measured using the accrued benefit actuarial method (with projected future salaries) and the assumed discount rate.

3. A reduction for the increase in the fair value of plan assets over the period net of contributions and payments (or an increase in expense if fair value decreased), or, more simply, the effect of the expected return on plan assets.

4. Systematic amortization of unrecognized prior service cost (arising from plan adoptions and amendments), with such costs allocated over the remaining period of employee service.

5. Systematic amortization of actuarial gains/losses, with the minimum rate being one divided by the average service of active employees, or the average remaining life expectancy if most of the plan's participants are not active. Amortization occurs only if cumulative actuarial gains/losses exceed 10% of the greater of plan assets at fair value or the projected benefit obligation. This method is called corridor amortization.

6. Straight-line amortization of a transitional "net unrecognized obligation" or "net unrecognized asset" at the time of adopting SFAS No. 87, amortized as in the preceding number (5) subject to election of an alternative 15-year period if average service is less than 15 years.

The last three items—initial recognition of prior service costs, actuarial gains and losses, and transitional gain or loss—are now initially recognized as other comprehensive income prior to becoming part of accrued periodic pension expense under SFAS No. 130. This will be illustrated later in the chapter when SFAS No. 158 is discussed.

A pension liability is recognized if yearly funding is less than periodic expense, as computed before, and a pension asset is recognized if yearly funding exceeds the periodic expense.

In calculating the first component of pension expense, *service cost*, several important assumptions are necessary. First, future salary levels must be estimated. Second, actuarial assumptions are required with respect to turnover, mortality, early retirement, etc.—all of which relate to the probability of there being a pension obligation. Third, a discount rate (the time value of money) must be assumed for the calculation. The FASB requires that the assumed discount rate be based on the current interest rate required to settle pension benefits. The PBGC publishes such rates on a monthly basis, and these may be used as a guide in selecting the assumed discount rate.

The second component of pension expense, *interest cost*, also requires use of the assumed discount rate in accruing interest on accumulated pension benefits.

The third component of pension expense, *expected return on plan assets*, requires an estimate of the fair value of pension assets. Fair values are defined as market prices in a nonliquidation setting and estimates of market value for assets with no active market. Any difference between expected and actual return on plan assets becomes part of *actuarial gains/losses* subject to corridor amortization. Also, the rate of return on plan assets is a long-run average rate that has remained high despite the decline in interest rates since 2000.[26]

The fourth component of pension expense, *amortization of unrecognized prior service cost*, is not narrowly specified. Instead, systematic allocation is required and simple straight-line amortization is one acceptable algorithm. The fifth component of pension expense, *amortization of actuarial gains/losses*, is similarly specified in general terms of systematic amortization. In addition, amortization is only required if unrecognized gains/losses exceed the greater of 10% of the fair value of plan assets or 10% of accrued pension benefits. Frustration has been expressed over the fact that the corridor amortization method, which is intended to smooth out actuarial gains and losses, really results in hiding them.[27] It has, in fact, been suggested that actuarial gains and losses not be included in operating income.[28] This would certainly make it easier to reduce or eliminate smoothing techniques.

The fifth and final component of pension expense, the *transition net asset*, would result (at the time of adoption of SFAS No. 87) from an excess of plan assets at fair value exceeding the projected benefit obligation. A *transition net liability* would result from the reverse situation. The balance of the prepaid or accrued pension cost account is also factored into the transition amount. The transition net asset or obligation can either be recognized immediately as a cumulative effect change in accounting principle (APB Opinion No. 20) with a corresponding debit or credit to prepaid or accrued pension cost, or it can be amortized over the longer of 15 years or the average remaining service life of covered employees. Pension expense would be charged or credited if amortization of the transition amount is elected. At the end of the amortization period, the prepaid or accrued pension cost account should have the same balance that would have resulted from the firm using projected future salaries (required by SFAS No. 87) rather than accumulated salaries (required by APB Opinion No. 8).

The consequence of the last three components of pension expense is to smooth the annual accrual of pension expense and reduce the variability caused by unfunded past/prior service costs, actuarial gains/losses, transitional adoption of SFAS No. 87, and amortization of the intangible asset related to minimum pension liabilities recognized in the balance sheet. One important point to keep in mind, however, is that the booming stock market of the 1990s frequently created such a large credit for the return on plan assets that a pension credit rather than a pension expense resulted. For example, in 1998 General Electric's pre-tax income was increased more than a billion dollars from its pension plan.[29] Bell Atlantic's pre-tax profits were increased by $627 million, GTE Corporation had a $473 million pre-tax credit, and Caterpillar, Inc., came in with a $183 million dollar credit, among others.[30]

The FASB refers to three distinct types of pension obligations in SFAS No. 87: *projected benefit obligations* using the benefits/years of service approach, *accumulated benefit obligations* (measured using current salaries), and *vested benefit obligations* (which are a subset of accumulated benefit obligations). A shift to an asset–liability orientation was evident from the requirement to recognize a minimum pension liability when accumulated benefit obligations exceeded the fair value of plan assets (including those at the time of adopting SFAS No. 87). Note the conservatism, though, in that an asset was not recognized if accumulated benefits were less than the fair value of plan assets. In addition, the minimum balance sheet liability was measured using only *current* rather than projected future salary levels, which understated the liability relative to the actuarial calculation of service cost. SFAS No. 158 brought changes which will be discussed shortly.

The disclosures of SFAS No. 87 are oriented toward pension plan assets and obligations. The funded status of plans must be reported showing separately the fair value of plan assets and all three measures of pension benefit obligations (and a reconciling schedule). Also required are disclosures of unrecognized prior service cost, unrecognized actuarial gains/losses, and unamortized net obligations/assets. These disclosures are informative in that they convey information about likely future levels of funding required to meet pension obligations.

In the event of a pension plan being terminated or substantially curtailed, SFAS No. 88 sets out separate rules for recognizing and measuring a gain or loss to the sponsor after incurring the costs of settlement.[31] The accounting gain or loss is the net effect of closing out balance sheet balances arising from SFAS No. 87 plus any assets recaptured from the pension plan less any corporate assets required to settle or curtail the pension obligations.

Two aspects of SFAS No. 87 require further examination. The first involves the switch from APB Opinion No. 8, which required the use of current salaries in normal (service) cost calculation, to future (projected) salaries required in SFAS No. 87. The second concerns the extent to which pension liabilities should appear on corporate balance sheets.

The first problem (current versus future salaries) was discussed in Chapter 7 on the conceptual framework. Future salaries are executory in nature. They are based on factors such as promotions of existing personnel and increases in employees' skills and capabilities. Determination of these future salaries will likely not be the responsibility of current management. However, current management is being evaluated on the basis of present expenses being based on these future events. The underlying reason for the switch was for the purpose of enabling users to better predict future cash flows. Hence, two important theoretical issues arose. First, it is questionable whether a current liability can be based on future events that are executory in nature (the liability arises from the increase to the pension expense account relative to the credit to the cash account for contributions to the pension fund).[32] Second, the use of future salaries aimed at abetting prediction of future cash flows conflicts with accountability usage of the financial statements because of current management's lack of control over future salary costs, which are executory in nature.[33]

However, Wyatt, in his dissent to the opinion (p. 25) points out that the discount rate, which is the current interest rate to settle pension benefits, does include a general inflation factor. Hence, with an accumulated benefit approach, the discount rate includes a general inflation factor that is not present in the accumulated pension obligation amount, making the present value too small. If the accumulated pension obligation approach is accepted, a general inflation factor should be built in, which would be eliminated by the discounting process, or the inflation factor could be removed from the discount rate itself.

SFAS No. 132

SFAS No. 132 amended SFAS Nos. 87, 88, and 106 relative to certain disclosures.[34] These disclosures were intended to implement the prediction of future cash flows and future net income as well as analyzing the quality of current net income. These disclosures include:

- Reconciliation of beginning and ending balances of projected benefit obligation and fair value of plan assets
- Components of pension and other postemployment benefits (OPEB) expenses
- Balances of unamortized prior service costs and unrecognized gains or losses
- Discount rates, expected return on plan assets, and health care trend rates

These disclosures pertain to both pensions and OPEBs where applicable. The Board retained from SFAS No. 106 disclosure of the effects of both a one-percentage-point increase and decrease on the assumed health care cost trend rates. Additional disclosure required by SFAS No. 132 should be beneficial for users.

SFAS No. 132 (R)

SFAS No. 132 (R) is called a "revision" of that standard because it continued and increased pension disclosures.[35] The main additional disclosures were the following:

- Information about the composition of pension plan assets, including portions invested in equity securities, debt securities, and real estate
- The targeted composition of the investment in plan assets, if one exists
- The accumulated benefit obligation of the liability must be shown (previously it was shown only if it exceeded the plan's assets)
- A discussion of the anticipated return on plan investments
- Information relative to the forthcoming annual contribution to the pension plan
- Anticipated plan payments over the forthcoming 10-year period

These disclosures appear to be important and useful. Presumably the benefits provided by SFAS No. 132 (R) will exceed their costs.

SFAS No. 158

The main change brought about by SFAS No. 158, which is applicable to single-employer plans, is to bring the overfunded or underfunded status of a defined benefit pension plan from the footnotes to the body of the balance sheet.[36] In accomplishing this, the FASB went from the minimum liability using the accumulated benefit obligation against the fair value of plan assets to an asset or liability in the balance sheet using the projected benefit obligation measurement against the fair value of plan assets. This is done on a net-of-tax basis. In addition, the measurement of the overfunded or underfunded asset or liability is done at the year-end statement date.

Another important part of SFAS No. 158 involves certain costs or credits that arise during the period but are not recognized as part of net periodic pension expense until subsequently amortized. In the period when these items arise, they are charged or credited to other comprehensive income. These items comprise actuarial gains or losses, prior service costs, and the transition asset or obligation arising under SFAS No. 87. These are likewise done on a net-of-tax basis.

Finally, disclosures have to be made relative to those elements of accrued net pension cost that are originally recognized as part of other comprehensive income. These disclosures include newly recognized amounts, portions being amortized through net periodic pension costs, remaining balances of the aforementioned prior service costs, actuarial gains and losses, and the transition obligation.

A simple example should illustrate the main aspects of SFAS No. 158. Assume that on December 31, 2006, Russell Company has the following balances as well as other pertinent information ($000 omitted).

Cash paid to the insurance plan trustees is $540. Tax rate is 40%. The three entries follow.

Projected benefit obligation	$3,000	
Plan assets at fair value	1,800	
Accrued/prepaid pension cost	250	(cr)
Actuarial gain or loss arising during the year	75	(cr)
Transition obligation previously recognized in other comprehensive income	180	
Prior service cost previously recognized in other comprehensive income	135	
Net periodic pension expense:		
Service cost	640	
Interest on projected benefit obligation	240	
Expected return on plan assets	180	(cr)
Amortization of transition obligation	30	
Amortization of prior service cost	20	
Total	$750	

(1)

Accrued Net Pension cost	750	
Deferred Tax Asset	300	
Deferred Tax Benefit		300
Other Comprehensive Income		50
Cash		540
Accrued/Prepaid Pension Cost		160

     Recognition of net pension expense, deferred taxes,
     and a credit to other pension income for amortized
     transition obligation and prior service cost

(2)

Accrued/Prepaid Pension Cost	75	
Deferred Tax Cost	30	
Deferred Tax Liability		30
Other Comprehensive Income		75

     Recognition of actuarial gain arising during year

(3)

Other Comprehensive Income		865	
Deferred Tax Asset		346	
Deferred Tax Benefit			346
Additional Pension Liability			865
Ending required balance of pension			
liability accounts ($3,000 - $1,800)	$1,200		
Less beginning balance of accrued/			
prepaid Pension cost $250 (cr) plus			
net increase of $85	335		
Net increase to bring pension liability			
accounts up to $1,200	$865		

Evaluation of SFAS No. 158

On the whole, we believe that more useful information is conveyed to users by this standard. By showing either the overfunded or underfunded amount in the balance sheet itself, the standard brings an important number onto the balance sheet from the footnotes and also eliminates the conservatism of the old approach. Another aspect of this standard is that an overfunded or underfunded amount for OPEBs must also be shown as an asset or liability.

Empirical Research on Pensions

Prior to SFAS No. 158, a number of studies investigated whether a firm's unfunded pension benefits are interpreted "as if" they are liabilities. If they are, then stock prices should be lower in the presence of unfunded benefits since they would lessen the value of residual stockholder claims. Several studies have reported this to be the case.[37] If unfunded pension benefits are interpreted "as if" they are liabilities, then their presence should also affect corporate bond ratings and bond interest rates. There is evidence that bond ratings are lower and interest rates are higher in the presence of unfunded benefits, which is consistent with the market acting as if they are liabilities.[38]

Given the results of these studies, it might appear that there would be little economic consequence from SFAS No. 87 vis-à-vis balance sheet recognition of pension liabilities. However, Francis documents the balance sheet impact of the original 1982 FASB pension proposal for 218 companies that lobbied against liability recognition: On average, the new debt would have been about 8.9% of balance sheet assets, a finding similar to that reported in other studies.[39] Such a large increase could very easily have affected debt covenants in existing lending agreements.

The income statement is also affected by SFAS No. 87, mainly through a loss of flexibility. Beidleman reported evidence that pre–APB Opinion No. 8 pension expense was used to smooth yearly income, and Hagerman and Zmijewski found that the choice of amortization periods for unfunded prior service cost under APB Opinion No. 8 was associated with an income-increasing strategy for firms with high leverage levels and an income-decreasing strategy for large-sized firms.[40] These findings are supportive of economic consequences vis-à-vis debt contracting and political costs. Finally, Francis and Reiter found that long-term pension expense policy, not just the portion of expense pertaining to prior service cost, was associated with the hypothesized income-increasing and income-decreasing incentives of debt and political costs, respectively.[41] Given these research findings, it is not surprising that a loss of flexibility was of concern to many companies lobbying against the FASB's pension proposals that led up to SFAS No. 87. It was for these reasons that the FASB modified its original proposals and smoothed the effect of actuarial gains/losses in pension expense calculation.

Another aspect of pension accounting is the discount rate that firms use in determining service costs as well as off-balance-sheet accounts for vested benefits, projected benefit obligations, and accumulated benefit obligations (which were used for the minimum liability calculation that, if applicable, is in the body of the balance sheet). During the period 1987–1993, Blankley and Swanson found that discount rates used by 306 corporations for these purposes remained *above* surrogates suggested by the FASB, such as the PBGC recommended rates (annuity rates, high-quality corporate bonds, and 30-year treasury bonds).[42] The higher discount rate, of course, results in lower service costs and liability amounts. Complementary to the Blankley and Swanson work, another study found that interest rate changes are frequently used as an earnings management tool when firms face lower earnings and higher leverage conditions.[43]

The FASB's pension project that culminated in SFAS No. 87 can be seen as an object lesson in the politics of standard setting. The FASB's initial 1982 proposal was so controversial that it was issued under the unique title of "Preliminary Views." It generated more than 500 comment letters and two rounds of public hearings even before an exposure draft was issued. The exposure draft was also controversial and resulted in a similar level of negative reaction. Compromises were made, and these, along with a fortunately rebounding stock market that increased the value of pension fund assets, made the standard more acceptable to affected companies.[44] And, as with leases in SFAS No. 13, a long four-year transition period was allowed regarding minimum liability recognition. This would permit companies to mitigate potential adverse financial statement consequences prior to mandatory liability recognition under SFAS No. 87. After the stock market crash in late 1987, many pension plans found themselves underfunded once again, and many companies delayed the minimum liability provisions of SFAS No. 87 as long as possible.

Picconi has found that analysts have not fully assimilated observed relationships between accounting information and earnings when generating forecasts.[45] He believes that relevant information has been available to analysts to generate better forecasts, but the difficulty and complexity of the task may block their efforts. In particular, the size of the firm's pension liability and the unfounded liability have not been taken into account (these were in the footnotes when he did his research). His research was done prior to passage of SFAS No. 132 (R), so it remains to be seen if this standard will close the gap.

Postretirement Benefits Other Than Pensions

Like pensions, OPEBs had been handled on a cash basis of accounting prior to SFAS No. 106, which was passed in 1990. OPEB benefits include health care, life insurance outside of pension plans, and additional welfare benefits such as legal services, housing subsidies, tuition assistance, and day care, although the first two are undoubtedly the most important. Several estimates have been made of the total OPEB liability of American enterprises; the amount is not small, ranging between $140 billion and $2 trillion.[46] The FASB concluded that OPEB costs are a form of deferred compensation in which the employer receives current services in exchange for future benefits. As a result, the FASB took an enormous step in SFAS No. 106 by requiring the recognition and measurement of OPEB costs and obligations. Previously, SFAS No. 81 had required only minimum disclosures relative to OPEBs: a description of benefits provided and groups covered, the accounting and funding policies used for those benefits, and the cost of those benefits recognized for the current period.[47] However, as early as 1981 respondents to the discussion memorandum on pensions and other employment benefits and participants at the public hearing believed that OPEBs should be accounted for similarly to pensions. This may account for why relatively few changes were made in SFAS No. 106 from the exposure draft, unlike the many modifications that were made in SFAS No. 87, the pension standard. We begin by briefly examining the core of SFAS No. 106, the need to predict future health care costs. Next, we give a very simple example of the workings of SFAS No. 106 and then review the major features of the standard. Also, we cover SFAS No. 112. Finally, we follow this with a critique from a theoretical perspective of the standard.

Explicit Health Care Trending

The technical heart of the FASB proposal lies in the explicit approach to estimating future health care costs and then discounting these costs back to their present value to determine

OPEB expense and liability growth for the year. The process is described in the field test of the FASB proposal. Health service categories as well as demographic categories must be established. Six health service categories were finally established: (1) inpatient hospital care, (2) outpatient hospital care, (3) physician services and independent laboratory services, (4) drugs and medical sundries, (5) other professional services, and (6) all other items.[48] Demographic categories are then established, and costs for each service category are estimated. This process, an extremely complex one, entails estimating per capita spending by service and demographic categories, taking into account utilization rates for each category as measured by service units such as patient days in hospitals or doctor visits, service intensity that involves the mix or content of specific units of service such as hospital days or physician visits, specifically enacted Medicare policies, and health care prices.[49] Estimations are then made for future years by taking into account estimated changes in annual utilization, services intensity, and enacted Medicare policies and applying a specific health care price index to each future year. The results would then be discounted back to the current year to determine OPEB expense and the increase in the liability. As part of the calculation process actuarial estimations for factors such as mortality, morbidity (prediction of occurrences of nonfatal diseases and accidents that will require health care payments), turnover, and early retirement would have to be applied. Clearly OPEB accounting involves important issues of verifiability.[50]

Explicit health care trending (para. 39) makes OPEB accounting somewhat similar to the projected benefit obligation approach to pensions discussed previously. However, one important difference exists between the two. With pensions, future salary increases are wholly executory: Future salary increases will be granted by management in the future, and the benefits provided to the firm by employees in exchange for these future salary increases will likewise be received in the future. In the case of OPEBs, future health care cost increases are totally beyond the control of both present and future management, hence they do not have a two-sided executory nature.

Two other points should be made about OPEB accounting. Firstly, the discount rate should contain an element for general inflation (para. 42), which means that after discounting, only the pure anticipated health care cost increases should remain in the OPEB liability, with general inflation increases eliminated through the discounting process.

Secondly, the standard refers to the OPEB obligation as the *accumulated postretirement benefit obligation* (paras. 45 and 48), even though specific future health care cost increases are included therein. The OPEB liability appears to be of the projected-obligation-type—like pensions.

The Mechanics of OPEB

Assume that a firm has one employee who will be covered by OPEB. The plan is dated January 1, 1999, and goes into effect immediately. There is one active plan participant (covered employee); she is 58 years old and becomes fully eligible for benefits on January 1, 2002, when she will have performed all necessary service to qualify for postretirement benefits.

The employee is expected to retire on December 31, 2002. Postretirement benefits are expected to be $5,000 on December 31, 2003, and $7,716.83 on December 31, 2004 (end-of-year dates are assumed for convenience). The applicable discount rate is 10%. Discounting the two payments back to December 31, 2001, results in a value on that date of $9,930 ([$5,000 × .8264] + [$7,716.83 × .7513]). The $9,930 is then discounted back to its present value on both December 31, 1999 and 2000. One-third of the present value on December 31, 1999, and the following two years on the same date becomes the *service cost*. Interest on the same dates is then added in to arrive at the total OPEB expense, as illustrated in Exhibit 16.1.

Notice that service costs are not equal each year but are one-third of the present value at year end (see Case 1A of Appendix C of SFAS No. 106) even though paragraphs 43 and 246 talk about equal amounts per year during the *attribution period*. The year 2002 has only interest costs. The full eligibility date is analogous to the vesting date under pensions. However, pension service costs would run through 2002, the year when the employee retires. Hence, relative to OPEB the FASB has attempted an asset–liability approach. However, there is a legitimate question concerning whether the entire working period up to the point of retirement should bear its share of OPEB costs.[51]

Hence, a strong case can be made that OPEB benefits should be spread over the working life of employees and not merely to the full eligibility date because it is the act of retirement that "triggers" the OPEB obligation. In other words, the employee must actually retire to qualify for OPEB coverage. Thus, the interpretation of the OPEB transaction is that the benefit is offered in exchange for service to retirement date. In most pension plans, full benefits are not earned until retirement, whereas full benefits in some OPEB plans are earned at a date prior to retirement (the full eligibility date); hence, the FASB saw the attribution periods in SFAS Nos. 87 and 106 as being consistent. Moreover, in many cases the date of retirement and the full eligibility date may coincide.[52] Let us next examine the major aspects of SFAS No. 106.

Major Features of SFAS No. 106

We first examine whether there is a liability for postretirement benefits and then discuss actuarial assumptions, including interest and discount rates, prior service costs, and disposition of gains or losses.[53]

Postretirement Benefit Obligations Are Liabilities

The first issue is the question of whether postretirement benefits are liabilities. Paragraphs 152–158 make it clear that this is indeed the case. Even though the obligation is equitable in nature rather than a legal liability, there is a duty or requirement to sacrifice assets in the future. Furthermore, even though employers may terminate OPEB plans, they cannot do so very easily without incurring real costs, such as negative employee goodwill. Most corporate respondents to the exposure draft on OPEBs recognized that they are a liability, but questions relative to verifiability were also strongly voiced.[54] The assumption that OPEBs are part of the total compensation package for covered employees clearly stamps them as being attributable to past transactions or events.

Exhibit 16.1   Postretirement Benefit Illustration.

	Jan. 1, 1999	Dec. 31, 1999	Dec. 31, 2000	Dec. 31, 2001	Dec. 31, 2002	Dec. 31, 2003	Dec. 31, 2004
				Attribution Period			
				Full Eligibility Date	*Retirement Date*		
Expected benefit payments						$5,000	$7,717
Present value factor of obligation						×0.8264	×0.7513
						$4,132	$5,798
Present value on Dec. 31, 1999, 2000, 2001		$8,206c	$9,027b	$9,930a			
Service cost for year		2,735d	3,009e	3,310f			
Interest for year		—	274g	602h	$993i		
Total OPEB expenses		$2,735	$3,283	$3,912	$993		

a $4,132 + $5,798 = $9,930
b $9,930 × .9091
c $9,930 × .8264
d 1/3 × $8,206
e 1/3 × $9,027
f 1/3 × $9,930
g .10 × $2,735
h .10 × $6,018
i .10 × $9,930

Actuarial Assumptions

Our example is obviously as simple as possible. Not only will typical OPEB plans be much more complex, but they must be based on numerous actuarial assumptions. Postretirement benefits should take into account trends in health care costs, for example, as well as projected changes in Medicare benefits that may increase costs. Medical costs are generally going up, but changes in medical technology may reduce some costs. For example, triglycerides and other fatty substances in the blood may be eliminated in the future by means of pills rather than by costly angioplasty ("balloon") techniques. Clearly, OPEB costs will not be easy to determine in terms of both the cost of measurement and the reliability of the estimates.

If OPEB levels are based on wages, they should reflect expected wage levels rather than those in effect at the current time. SFAS No. 106 thus agrees with pension accounting since SFAS No. 87 employs the projected benefit approach rather than the accumulated benefit method.

Total OPEB expenses may be reduced by earnings from plan assets. *Plan assets* consist of stocks, bonds, and other investments that are segregated—presumably in a trust—for the exclusive purpose of providing for OPEB benefits. The expected long-term rate of return on plan assets should be based on their market value. If fund earnings are taxable, this should also be taken into account. Few OPEB plans are funded at this time because tax laws do not generally provide for a deduction for plan contributions, unlike the pension situation.

The discount rate used to show the OPEB obligation at present value should be based on rates of return for high-quality, fixed-income investments that are currently available on the market and whose cash flows are generally similar in amount and timing to OPEB payments (para. 31). The AAA Financial Accounting Standards Committee points out that OPEB obligations are largely unsecured and that the discount rate should thus concur with the employer's borrowing rate for unsecured debt with a similar payment structure.[55] This latter rate would most likely be higher than what SFAS No. 106 calls for, resulting in a lower present value for the firm's OPEB obligation. Paragraph 42 also notes that discount rates should include an inflationary component geared to the expected general rate of inflation. Another important issue that was previously discussed is whether OPEB costs should be spread over each employee's total working period or just to the full eligibility date, with the FASB opting for the latter.

Finally, there are many other actuarial assumptions that must be considered, including employee turnover, mortality, and dependency status. Once again, it must be stated that measurement costs will not be inexpensive and verifiability and other aspects of reliability should not be taken for granted.

Plan Amendments and Prior Service Costs

When plan amendments increase (or possibly reduce) employee benefits, and these costs are clearly attributable to future periods for active plan participants, they are to be charged to future periods. If plan amendments improve benefits based on service prior to the plan amendment itself or even the plan initiation, as with pensions, these are called *prior service costs.* Paragraph 51 provides for these costs to be recognized over the remaining years of service to full eligibility dates of active plan participants. These costs can be amortized over future periods on either a straight-line basis or on the basis of the remaining years of service of active plan participants to their full eligibility, an accelerated method of amortization (illustrated in paragraphs 451–454). Where employees are already retired or are beyond their full eligibility dates, prior service costs are amortized on the basis of the remaining life expectancy of these participants (para. 52). The retroactive basis is used, however, where prior service costs are involved relative to measuring the OPEB obligation. That is, prior service is taken into account in measuring the OPEB obligation when the plan is amended.

Gains and Losses

Gains and losses from OPEB plans arise from either differences from assumed experience or changes in plan assumptions. Net gains or losses are not recognized immediately but are amortized to the extent that the net amount exceeds 10% of the greater of the accumulated postretirement benefit obligation or the market-related value of plan assets as of the beginning of the year (para. 59). This amortization process for OPEB gains and losses, called the *corridor* approach, is quite similar to accounting for net gains or losses for pensions under SFAS No. 87.

SFAS No. 112

This standard applies to former or inactive employees who have not yet retired. Hence, this standard applies to *postemployment* benefits, whereas SFAS No. 106 applies to *postretirement* benefits, although the acronym OPEB applies to both.[56] Postemployment benefits apply to inactive employees who are not currently working but who have not been terminated as well as to former employees. Inactive employees may or may not be expected to return. Prior to SFAS No. 112, several methods were used to recognize any applicable postemployment costs. SFAS No. 112 reiterates that postemployment costs must be handled on an actuarial basis and not on a terminal funding or cash-type basis.

Theoretical Aspects of OPEB Accounting

Several theoretical considerations of OPEB have already been discussed. Pervading the whole postretirement benefit situation are issues of cost and reliability. There is, however, little question that OPEBs are indeed a liability. The FASB was rather adamant about the importance of recognition of OPEB costs and obligations in the financial statements as opposed to footnote disclosure (para. 164). Hence, the efficient-markets hypothesis was not used as a dodge to avoid responsibilities.[57] It is certainly desirable that the benefits of SFAS No. 106 will be greater than the costs of preparation and will outweigh problems of reliability.

As with pensions, there is a transition period for OPEB obligations. Transition assets or liabilities—the difference between the accumulated postretirement benefit obligation (actuarial present value of benefits earned to date) and the fair value of plan assets (if any)—can be recognized immediately as a change in accounting principle or amortized over the average remaining service period of active plan participants. If the latter is under 20 years, a 20-year amortization period can be used, as opposed to a 15-year minimum transition amortization period used for pensions. Similar to pensions, if transition is used, the charge or credit (usually the former) becomes a part of OPEB expense.

Economic Consequences of OPEB Recognition

Financial statement preparers strongly opposed OPEB recognition. In addition to costs of preparation, OPEB obligations on the balance sheet mean higher debt-to-equity ratios, which threaten debt covenants on bond issues. In addition, management compensation is affected by SFAS No. 106. While we are very sympathetic to the need to recognize OPEB costs and obligations, the blow might have been much more palatable to business if discounting had also been permitted with deferred tax liabilities. The need to be as consistent as possible in recognizing and measuring different liabilities is extremely important. It is not too late, we hope, to use the conceptual framework more effectively particularly now that SFAC No. 7 recommends wider use of present value techniques.

Another point is that the booking of OPEB obligations may well lead to an extensive scaling back of this benefit when the size of the liability is understood. This would be a classic example of shooting the messenger who brings bad news. Wyatt has quite correctly focused on the issue of liability recognition and accrual accounting for OPEB as one of accountability.[58] The FASB's job in examining OPEB costs and obligations is to be neutral while taking into account the benefits/costs matrix. We believe that they have done this. Whether OPEB benefits will be reduced is a separate issue that should not be linked to the FASB's responsibilities. There is some evidence that this has occurred. Mittelstaedt, Nichols, and Regier found 71 firms that cut OPEB benefits between 1989 and 1992.[59] Many of these firms reduced health insurance coverage owing to contracting cost problems (possible violation of debt covenants) although other problems, independent of SFAS No. 106 (such as general financial weakness and large firm-specific increases in health care costs), also played a role.

A last economic consequence to be considered is whether SFAS No. 106 will put American firms at a competitive disadvantage relative to foreign firms in such areas as cost of capital and pricing of products.[60] We tend to view this issue from a perspective similar to the question of the potential for the reduction of OPEB benefits as a result of SFAS No. 106. The real issue should not be one of bad economic consequences; it should be one of harmonization or convergence of accounting standards. That is, other nations should be using recognition and measurement techniques similar to those of SFAS No. 106, where applicable.

Empirical Research on OPEBs

We have already discussed verifiability problems relative to OPEB measurements. Choi, Collins, and Johnson, using a cross-sectional equity valuation model, show that OPEB measurements are "noisier" (have more measurement error) than pension measurements.[61] There is also some evidence that firms with larger OPEB obligations and greater leverage choose estimation parameters that reduce the OPEB liability (higher discount rates and lower health care trend rates), thereby reducing the probability of violating debt care covenants.[62]

Research has also been conducted in the area of early adoption of SFAS No. 106. Research has shown that early adopters of SFAS No. 106 had smaller OPEB liabilities and had less involvement with plan amendments than later adopters.[63] This was translated as "good news," and the market did react favorably to early adoptions.[64] Late adopters, on the other hand, tended to have relatively larger liabilities than early adopters and frequently had to renegotiate contractual arrangements. Late adoption was interpreted as "bad news" and was frequently accompanied by security price declines.

Finally, D'Souza has found evidence that regulated enterprises have incentives to select expense increasing parameters for the measurement of OPEBs because these can be passed through to consumers in the form of rate increases.[65]

International Accounting Standards (IAS)

IAS 19, *Accounting for Retirement Benefits in the Financial Statement of Employees,* which was revised in 2004, is under a four-year review by the International Accounting Standards Board (IASB) (2006–2010) to study pensions and other postretirement benefits related to (a) presentation and disclosures, (b) definitions of deferred benefit, defined contribution plans, and cash balance plans, (c) smoothing and deferred mechanisms, and (d) the treatment of settlements and curtailments. Under the Memorandum of Understanding, the agreement to pursue convergence includes this project.[66] The FASB and the IASB are scheduled to complete their review of pension accounting by 2014.

IASB 19, unlike SFAS No. 87, requires that past service costs be expensed immediately rather than amortized over the service period or life expectancy of employees. Actuarial gains and losses under IAS 19 can be recognized in equity, thereby smoothing earnings. This is in contrast to SFAS Nos. 87 and 158, in which actuarial gains and losses flow through comprehensive income. *Anticipated* changes in future postemployment benefits based on expected changes in the law are allowed under the IASB but not the FASB.[67]

Improving Accounting Standards

- OPEB benefits should be spread over the working life of employees and not just to the full eligibility date. Hence, the expense would be recognized in accordance with how benefits are received. Any differences between the OPEB expense and liability can be easily handled as a noncurrent asset.

(Continued)

(Continued)

> • There is a conflict between cash flow prediction and accountability in measuring pension service costs, discussed in this chapter and Chapter 7. The use of projected benefits required by SFAS No. 87 entails questions of verifiability, and the executory nature of future salaries makes it very questionable for accountability purposes. We would therefore return to the use of the accumulated benefit method (current salaries) for determining pension service costs because of its clearer applicability for the accountability objective.

Summary

Pension accounting for the sponsors of defined benefit pension plans has been one of the long-standing issues faced by accounting policy makers. The traditional approach has been based on a revenue–expense orientation in which the objective is to accrue yearly pension expense. This leads to the problem of determining how benefits accumulate with the passage of time and how these benefits should be measured. APB Opinion No. 8 sanctioned flexibility by permitting one of five actuarial methods to be used to measure yearly pension expense. This resulted in the same kind of arbitrariness as occurs with multiple depreciation and inventory methods.

In SFAS No. 87, the FASB has achieved more rigid uniformity regarding pension expense measurement. Only one actuarial method can be used, although some flexibility remains with respect to actuarial assumptions. A shift toward the asset–liability orientation is evident with both expense measurement and the new requirement to recognize a minimum balance sheet liability for unfunded pension benefits.

Institutional problems still remain in the pension area. Overfunded pension plans can still be "raided" with a relatively small excise tax of 20% if 25% of the surplus plan assets are put into a "replacement plan." Also, pension funds can be diverted from older employees toward younger employees through cash balance plans.

SFAS No. 106 brought accrual accounting to OPEB. Like pension costs, these costs are clearly a liability. In many respects, accounting for OPEB is very similar to pension accounting. Perhaps the most contentious issue for OPEB is the FASB's decision to amortize costs only to the full eligibility date rather than to the retirement date. The costs and reliability of OPEB measurements are important issues, as are several other questions involving the economic consequences.

SFAS No. 158 has brought the pension liability or asset on to the balance sheet. In addition, actuarial gains and losses, transition asset or liability, and prior service costs are recognized in the period when incurred, going through other comprehensive income (they are still recognized as part of net pension cost as amortized or recognized through the corridor rule). SFAS No. 132 and 132 (R) provide useful disclosures for analysts and other users.

Appendix 16-A: Illustration of Pension Expense Determination and Actuarial Funding Methods

The following illustration shows how service cost is determined by using (a) future salaries, which is required by SFAS No. 87, and (b) present salaries, which was required prior to SFAS No. 87. In addition, two methods are shown for determining plan funding. Interest cost and the interest credit for earnings on plan assets are also illustrated.[68] This illustration is extremely simplified to give the user a solid overview of the complexities of pension accounting while downplaying actuarial complexities.

The Killarney Company was formed on January 1, 2000. The firm hired 10 employees, all of whom were 62 years old during 2000. On January 1, 2001, Killarney established a defined benefit pension plan. Of the 10 employees, not all were expected to be with the firm until retirement. The firm's actuary estimated that there was a 100% chance of an employee staying with the firm for a year, an 80% probability that an employee would remain with the firm for two years, and a 50% probability that an employee would be with the firm until retirement in three years, when Killarney will cease operations. The actuary estimated that each employee would live for two years after retirement.

Each year, Killarney planned to contribute a certain amount to the pension fund. It was expected that the fund would earn a 12% rate of return each year. This rate is commensurate with the risk of the securities in the fund's portfolio. In contrast, the pension obligation was calculated using a discount rate of 10%. This rate is assumed to be the "settlement rate" for annuity contracts that could be used for settling the obligation (SFAS No. 87, para. 44). The lower discount rate for the liability reflects the lower risk of the fund payments. Another allowable discount rate mentioned in paragraph 44 is the rate of return on high-quality, fixed-income investments that are expected to be available in the market. This background information, as well as wage rates, is summarized in Exhibit 16.2 on page 542.

Most pensions base the salary on an expected average over the last few years of employment prior to retiring. In our illustration, the annual pension plan benefits for each employee were determined by the following *benefit formula:*

$$\text{Annual benefit per employee} = (10\%)(\text{expected final salary}) (\text{no. of years of service}) \tag{16.1}$$

Hence, after one year:

$$\text{Annual benefit per employee} = (0.10)(\$50,000)(1) = \$5,000 \tag{16.1a}$$

Exhibit 16.2   Background Information

Time		Working Period				Retirement Period	
		12-31-00	12-31-01	12-31-02	12-31-03	12-31-04	12-31-05
1	Current age	62	63	64	65	66	67
2	Applicable years of service	0	1	2	3		
3	Years to retirement, n	3	2	1	0		
4	Salary per employee for the year		$30,000	$40,000	$50,000		
5	Annual benefits proportion applied to final salary		0.10	0.10	0.10		
6	Probability today of surviving to time t		1.00	0.80	0.50		
7	Expected number of employees at time t	10	10	8	5	5	5
8	Settlement rate (discount rate, k)	0.10					
9	Expected return on pension fund investments, R	0.12					

The plan gave no credit for prior years of service, and employees were entitled to a pension only if they retired from the company. Employees were expected to retire at age 66. The total annual benefits paid by the plan were:

Total annual benefits

$$= \begin{pmatrix} \text{annual benefit} \\ \text{per employee} \end{pmatrix} \begin{pmatrix} \text{number employees predicted} \\ \text{to be with the firm at retirement} \end{pmatrix} \qquad (16.2)$$

Hence, after one year:

$$\text{Total annual benefits} = (\$5,000)(5) = \$25,000 \qquad (16.2a)$$

We next use the background information to determine the annual pension expense for the firm.

Accounting for Defined Benefit Plans

SFAS No. 87 made an important departure from its predecessor, APB Opinion No. 8. In the latter, service cost was determined by using current salaries, whereas in the former, estimated final salaries, which will underlie actual pension payments, are used for computing the current year's service cost. Exhibit 16.3 shows these two methods of calculating the firm's pension expense: the projected benefit obligation method and the accumulated benefit obligation approach.

Projected Benefit Obligation (PBO)

SFAS No. 87 requires the use of the PBO method. The periodic service cost and pension obligation are determined using the *future* projected salaries that will be used to determine the expected pension benefits with this method. One problem with using future salaries is that they are executory in nature; neither party has, as yet, fulfilled their obligations.

The components of the PBO approach are detailed in Panel A of Exhibit 16.3.

Killarney's management promised to provide its employees upon retirement with an annual pension payment specified by Equation 16.1. The cumulative annual benefits per employee are listed on line 1. Notice that the firm expected only 5 of the 10 employees to retire from the company. This projection is reflected on line 2. The PBO is the present value of the expected cumulative benefits as of the current year. The expected future benefits are discounted using the settlement rate (10% in our example). For example, Exhibit 16.3 indicates that after one year of service to the company, the employees as a whole have earned $25,000 per year (payable at the end of the year) for each of their two

Exhibit 16.3a   Panel A: Determination of Pension Cost Using the Projected Benefit Obligation (PBO)

Time		Working Period				Annual Benefits Earned Through 12-31-03	
	12-31-00	12-31-01	12-31-02	12-31-03		12-31-04	12-31-05
1 Cumulative annual benefits per employee		$5,000	$10,000	$15,000			
2 Expected number of employees at retirement		5	5	5			
3 Expected total annual retirement benefits as of time *t*	25,000	25,000	50,000	75,000		$75,000	$75,000
4 Projected benefit obligation		35,858	78,888	130,165			
5 Interest cost (10%)		–	3,586	7,889			
6 Service cost		35,858	39,444	43,388			
7 Pension cost		$35,858	$43,030	$51,277			

544

retirement years. The present value of these two cash flows as of December 31, 2001, is shown here.

12–31–00	12–31–01	12–31–02	12–31–03	12–31–04	12–31–05
				$25,000	$25,000
	$35,858	←	←	↵	↵

After two years of service, the employees have earned $50,000 per year for each of their two retirement years. The present value of these two cash flows as of December 31, 2002, is depicted here.

12–31–00	12–31–01	12–31–02	12–31–03	12–31–04	12–31–05
				$50,000	$50,000
		$78,888	←	↵	↵

From the PBO, we can calculate the interest cost (IC) and the service cost (SC). The IC reflects the increase in the value of the PBO over the period owing to interest on the obligation. It is computed by multiplying the prior year PBO by the settlement interest rate, or:

$$IC_t = (PBO_{t-1})(\text{settlement interest rate}) \tag{16.3}$$

The SC is that portion of the pension expense associated with an additional year of service. It is the incremental present value of the benefits earned in a given period. It is calculated by subtracting the interest cost from the incremental change in the projected benefit obligation, or:

$$SC_t = PBO_t - PBO_{t-1} - \text{interest cost}_t \tag{16.4}$$

Accumulated Benefit Obligation (ABO)

The ABO was used for measuring pension cost prior to the passage of SFAS No. 87. It is still required by SFAS No. 87 for determining the enterprise's minimum pension liability. The ABO is determined using *current* salaries as follows:

$$\text{Cumulative annual benefit per employee} = (10\%)(\text{current salary})(\text{no. of years of service}) \tag{16.5}$$

For example, after two years of service, the cumulative annual benefit per employee is equal to:

$$\text{Cumulative annual benefit}$$
$$\text{per employee} = (0.1)(\$40,000)\,(2) = \$8,000 \qquad (16.5a)$$

Panel B of Exhibit 16.3 b on page 547 details the ABO approach.

Several observations are in order when we compare pension cost using ABO or PBO. Notice that the sum of the total pension cost for 2001 through 2003 is the same for both methods. The pension cost under ABO has much more of a delayed effect, with larger service costs being packed into later years because the measurement is based upon current salaries, and with a "catch-up" effect in later years. This catch-up effect is similar to accounting changes using the prospective approach (changes in depreciation rates, for example).

Funding for Defined Benefit Plans

Funding of the obligation is separate and distinct from the accounting treatment of the firm's pension obligation. We illustrate two funding methods: the projected accrued benefit cost method and the entry age normal cost method.

Projected Accrued Benefit Cost Method (PABC)

With the PABC method, the contribution to the pension trust fund is designed to increase each year at a rate determined by the expected rate of return on the trust fund itself. This type of funding might be appropriate for a growing firm whose cash flows are expected to be significantly higher in the future than in the present. Panel A of Exhibit 16.4a on page 548 details the components of this type of funding.

First, the annual benefit stream based on *final* salaries is estimated. In our example, five employees were expected to retire from the company. They were expected to be paid a total of $75,000 per year for each of two years. The present value (at retirement) of this payment stream is $126,754. Note that each cash flow has been discounted using the *expected rate of return on the trust assets* (12%), as opposed to the lower settlement rate (10%). Each year, the portion of the present value of the benefit stream accrued annually is equal to the present value of the retirement stream divided by the number of years to retirement, or:

$$\text{Portion accrued annually until retirement}$$
$$= \frac{\text{PV(benefit stream at retirement)}}{\text{number of years to retirement}} \qquad (16.6)$$

In our example, $42,251 is accrued annually (126,754 ÷ 3). To obtain the expected contribution to the fund, each accrued portion is discounted back to the current year using the

Exhibit 16.3b   Panel B: Determination of Pension Cost Using the Accumulated Benefit Obligation (ABO)

| Time | Working Period | | | | Annual Benefits Earned Through 12-31-03 | |
	12-31-00	12-31-01	12-31-02	12-31-03	12-31-04	12-31-05
1 Cumulative annual benefits per employee		$3,000	$8,000	$15,000		
2 Expected number of employees at retirement		5	5	5		
3 Expected total annual retirement benefits as of time t		15,000	40,000	75,000	$75,000	$75,000
4 Accumulated benefit obligation		21,515	63,110	130,165		
5 Interest cost (10%)		—	2,151	6,311		
6 Service cost		21,515	39,444	60,744		
7 Pension cost		$21,515	$41,596	$67,055		

547

Exhibit 16.4a Panel A: The Projected Accrued Benefit Cost Method (PABC)

		Working Period				Retirement Period	
Time		12-31-00	12-31-01	12-31-02	12-31-03	12-31-04	12-31-05
1	Expected annual pension payments					$75,000	$75,000
2	PV, at retirement, of the annuity of annual pension payments				$126,754		
3	Portion accrued annually until retirement		$42,251	$42,251	42,251		
4	Discount factor for 12%, number of years to retirement		0.7972	0.8929	1.0000		
5	Contribution to pension fund		33,682	37,724	42,251	–	–
6	Pension fund balance at beginning of year		–	33,682	75,449	126,754	66,964
7	Interest on prior year fund balance at 12%		–	4,042	9,054	15,210	8,036
8	Disbursement of benefits		–	–	–	(75,000)	(75,000)
9	Pension fund balance at end of year*		$33,682	$75,449	$126,754	$66,964	$0

*Numbers may not add exactly due to rounding.

Exhibit 16.4b Panel B: Entry Age Normal Cost Method (EANC)

Time		Working Period				Retirement Period	
	12-31-00	12-31-01	12-31-02	12-31-03	12-31-04	12-31-05
1	Expected annual pension payments					$75,000	$75,000
2	PV, at retirement, of the annuity of annual pension payments				$126,754		
3	Annual contribution to pension fund = $126,754 ÷ FVIFA12%, 3 years = $126,754 ÷ 3.3744		$37,563	$37,563	37,563		
4	Pension fund balance at beginning of year		–	37,563	79,634	126,754	66,964
5	Interest on prior year fund balance at 12%		–	4,508	9,556	15,210	8,036
6	Disbursement of benefits		–	–	–	(75,000)	(75,000)
7	Pension fund balance at end of year*		$37,563	$79,634	$126,754	$66,964	$0

549

expected rate of return on the trust funds. From Panel A of Exhibit 16.4a for December 31, 2002, we have:

$$(\$42,251)(\text{PVIF}_{12\%,1}) = (\$42,251)(0.8929) = \$37,724 \tag{16.7}$$

where PVIF12%,1 is the present value interest factor for 12%, one year

Finally, the pension fund balance at the end of the year is equal to the contribution to pension fund, plus the beginning balance, plus interest earned over the year on the beginning balance, less the disbursement of benefits. For December 31, 2002, we have the following calculation:

	12–31–02
Plan assets at beginning of year	$33,682
Plus contribution to pension fund	37,724
Plus interest on prior year fund balance	4,042
Less disbursement of benefits	–
Plan assets at end of year	$75,448

See Panel A of Exhibit 16.4a for other years.

Entry Age Normal Cost Method (EANC)

This method starts with the present value (at retirement) of the retirement benefits stream ($126,754 in our example). It treats this amount as the future value of a level annuity of contributions to the fund. If each of these payments is invested at the expected rate of return, the pension fund will have exactly the funds necessary, at retirement, to make the payments promised to the employees. Specifically, the annual contribution to the fund under the entry age normal cost method is shown in Equation 16.8.

$$\text{Annual contribution to the fund} = \frac{\text{PV(annuity of annual pension payments)}}{\text{FVIFA}_{R\%,N}} \tag{16.8}$$

where FVIFA $_{R\%,N}$ is the future value interest factor of an annuity for R% and N years to retirement. In our case, with an expected rate of return of 12% and three years to retirement, we have:

$$\text{Annual contribution to the fund} = \frac{\$126,754}{3.3744} = \$37,563 \tag{16.8a}$$

See Panel B of Exhibit 16.4a on page 549 for other years.

Note again that each cash flow has been discounted using the *expected rate of return on the trust assets* (12%), as opposed to the lower settlement rate (10%). The pension fund balance for the EANC method is calculated the same way as the projected accrued benefit cost method. The pension fund balance increases faster with the EANC method than with the PABC method. For this reason, the EANC method may be preferred by employees over the PABC. There are other actuarial funding methods, but the two illustrated here are widely used.

QUESTIONS

1. What do the following actuarial terms mean: *accumulated benefits, actuarial liability, vested benefits, service cost,* and *unfunded accumulated benefits?* How are they measured? How are projected benefit obligations, accumulated benefit obligations, and vested benefit obligations defined in SFAS No. 87, and how are they actuarially calculated?

2. Why is there a pension accounting problem with defined benefit pension plans but not with defined contribution plans?

3. Explain how previous pension accounting standards were based on a revenue–expense approach to the financial statements.

4. Why did APB Opinion No. 8 only minimally improve uniformity between companies?

5. Is the treatment of unrecognized prior service cost and actuarial gains/losses in SFAS No. 87 an example of the asset–liability or revenue–expense orientation?

6. How has ERISA affected pension accounting?

7. Given the evidence from the research in the stock market, does it matter whether pension information is disclosed in the formal financial statements or as supplemental disclosure?

8. What economic consequences of SFAS No. 87 were suggested in the chapter?

9. Research has shown that discount rates used by firms are generally *above* rates suggested by the FASB. Will this make the interest cost portion of pension expense higher or lower than if discount rates were lower? Why do you think firms favor using a higher rate?

10. Is SFAS No. 87's argument favoring recognition of a pension liability for accumulated benefits consistent with the conceptual framework project?

11. If actuarial gains and losses and prior service costs, in line with SFAS No. 158, are to be recognized in the period when incurred, is there a double-counting effect when these elements are recognized as part of net pension expense?

12. How did the "give-and-take" differ between the FASB and its constituents in the drafting of SFAS No. 87 on pensions versus on SFAS No. 106?

13. Voluntary pension plan terminations have been increasing (see Stone [1987]) in which surplus plan assets are recaptured by sponsoring companies after deferred annuities (of equivalent value to accrued benefits) are purchased for plan participants. Why do you think this practice has been criticized by some employee groups, and how might SFAS No. 87 affect voluntary terminations?

14. What issues of qualitative characteristics of accounting information (SFAC No. 2) are important relative to accrual accounting for OPEBs?

15. What types of economic consequences may arise from accrual accounting for OPEBs in SFAS No. 106?

16. According to a *Wall Street Journal* article from February 1, 1996 (Lowenstein, p. C1), pension fund assets in the United States grew dramatically—by approximately 29%—during 1995, an excellent year in the stock market. However, underfunding of pension plans increased by a very sizable amount. Why do you think that this occurred?

17. While ERISA has been helpful, how well are employees protected in situations in which over-funded pension plans exist?

18. What is the danger, particularly to older employees, of restructuring pension plans into "cash benefit plans?"

19. What differences exist, relative to the use of future costs and future salaries, in the case of OPEBs (SFAS No. 106) and pensions (SFAS No. 87)?

20. Is it inconsistent to use future salaries for service cost calculations and current salaries for minimum liability calculation purposes?

❖

CASES, PROBLEMS, AND WRITING ASSIGNMENTS

1. Refer to Appendix 16-A. Assume that the firm is using projected accrued benefit cost funding. Suppose that a plan amendment was introduced during 2002 granting one year of prior service (for the year 2000) to each employee.

Required:

Determine the contribution to the pension fund for 2002 and 2003.

2. Smurfit-Stone Container Corporation's 2004 annual report shows the following information pertaining to its minimum pension liability (this is before SFAS No. 158; 000's omitted):

	12–31–02
Accumulated benefits obligation	$3,336
Fair value of plan assets	2,466
Underfunded status	870
Unrecognized actuarial loss	762
Unrecognized prior service cost	79
Net unrecognized costs	841
Net minimum liability	$29

Required:

How do you think Smurfit-Stone would justify their calculation of the minimum liability and do you agree with them?

3. Using SFAS No. 87 and SFAS No. 106 for additional background, list and briefly discuss as many similarities and differences as you can between pension accounting and OPEB accounting.

CRITICAL THINKING AND ANALYSIS

1. To qualify as a liability, a past transaction must exist. Is this the case with pensions and OPEBs? How does the use of financial statements for predicting future cash flows as opposed to evaluating management performance enter the picture?

Notes

1. *There are other benefits in a pension plan; for example, death and disability. These are normally paid for through group insurance contracts. Therefore, pension funding is assumed to refer just to the funding of retirement benefits.*

2. *Funding requirements established by the Internal Revenue Service and the Employee Retirement Income Security Act would be applicable to most pension plans.*

3. *Service credit is normally weighted evenly per year of service, although some plans do weight later years more heavily to reward long service. The Employee Retirement Income Security Act sets a limit on the weighting of later years. Backloading is the technical term for uneven weighting.*

4. *Jones (2006).*

5. *United States Public Law 93-406 (1974).*

6. *The guarantee for single-employer plans was set at $750 a month in 1974, to be adjusted upward annually by a ratio based on the Social Security income base. In 1988, the guarantee level was a monthly pension of $1,909.09. For multiemployer plans, the guarantee is $5 of monthly pension benefit per year of service, with the*

next $15 of monthly pension benefit only 75% guaranteed. In 1988, the PBGC charged an insurance premium of $16 and $2.60 per employee for single- and multiemployer plans, respectively. The charge is intended to cover operating costs and guaranteed benefits from plan terminations.

7. *Solomon (2006).*

8. *Schultz (1999b, p. C19).*

9. *See Jones (2006) for a good overview.*

10. *However, pensions of many top American executives are flourishing. See Schultz and Francis (2006) and Schroeder (2006).*

11. *Schultz (1999a, p. A6).*

12. *Briner and Pitman (2003, p. 34).*

13. *Schultz, Auerbach, and Burkens (1999, p. A1).*

14. *Although there is no direct obligation to employees, the PBGC does superimpose an obligation to make up the difference if fund assets are deficient at termination.*

15. *Committee on Accounting Procedure (1948).*

16. *Committee on Accounting Procedure (1956).*

17. *Davis and Strasser (1970) cite a large Department of Labor survey that indicated that most plans (and particularly larger plans) would not have been radically affected by the vesting requirements of ERISA. However, some plans were significantly affected.*

18. *APB (1966).*

19. *Beidleman (1973).*

20. *APB Opinion No. 8 successfully utilized the two-pronged approach advocated by the Accounting Principles Board. The standard was based on a study of pension accounting by Hicks (1965).*

21. *Numerical examples of differences may be found in Hicks (1965), FASB (1981), and Schipper and Weil (1982). Francis (1982) evaluated the yearly differences under a range of simulated conditions and concluded that there can be material effects on the income statement resulting from the choice of actuarial funding method.*

22. *FASB (1974).*

23. *FASB (1980a).*

24. *FASB (1980b).*

25. *Evidence of this is found in Francis and Reiter (1987), who report that only 29 of 297 firms in their study indicated a divergence between the two policies.*

26. *McCafferty (2003).*

27. *Babington (2003).*

28. *Ibid.*

29. *Schultz (1999a, p. A1).*

30. *Ibid.*

31. *FASB (1985b).*

32. *Robert Sprouse took this position in his dissent to SFAS No. 87 (FASB 1985a, p. 24).*

33. *For further background on these problems, see Wolk and Vaughan (1993).*

34. *FASB (1998).*

35. *FASB (2003).*

36. *FASB (2006).*

37. *See Daley (1984), Dhaliwal (1986), Feldstein and Seligman (1981), Kemp (1988), Landsman (1986), and Stone (1982) for a review of earlier studies.*

38. *Reiter (1985).*

39. *Francis (1987). See also Morris and Nichols (1984) and Rue and Volkan (1984).*

40. *Beidleman (1973) and Hagerman and Zmijewski (1979).*

41. *Francis and Reiter (1987).*

42. *Blankley and Swanson (1995).*
43. *Godwin, Goldberg, and Duchac (1996).*
44. *For details, see Saemann (1995).*
45. *Picconi (2006).*
46. *Wright (1990). See also the discussion of SFAS No. 112 later in this chapter.*
47. *FASB (1984, p. 2).*
48. *Dankner et al. (1989, p. 70).*
49. *Ibid. (pp. 69–71).*
50. *For further discussion of verifiability issues, see Fogarty and Grant (1995, pp. 29–31).*
51. *This point has also been made by the AAA Financial Accounting Standards Committee. See AAA (1990, p. 113).*
52. *Thomas and Farmer (1990, p. 103).*
53. *All paragraphs mentioned refer to FASB (1990).*
54. *Wolk, Vaughan, and Clapham (1998, p. 272).*
55. *AAA (1990, p. 114).*
56. *FASB (1992).*
57. *This has, to some extent, been corroborated in the research of Davis-Friday et al. (1999). They show that OPEB liability information has more value relevance in the financial statements relative to security prices than the same information shown in footnote disclosures only. The footnote disclosure information was elicited just prior to the passage of SFAS No. 106. See also Harper, Mister, and Strawser (1991).*
58. *Wyatt (1990).*
59. *Mittelstaedt, Nichols, and Regier (1995).*
60. *See Wright (1990) for further examples of economic consequences as applied to OPEB.*
61. *Choi, Collins, and Johnson (1997).*
62. *Amir and Gordon (1996). Landsman (1996) notes that measurement error owing to age structures of covered employees in the firms in the Amir and Gordon (1996) sample may not have been appropriately considered.*
63. *See Amir and Livnat (1996) and Amir and Ziv (1997).*
64. *Similar findings relative to early adoption of SFAS Nos. 87 and 88 were found by Langer and Lev (1993). Early adoption of these pension standards appears to be strongly related to increasing earnings over what they would have been under APB Opinion No. 8.*
65. *D'Souza (1998).*
66. *Epstein and Mirza (2006).*
67. *Ibid.*
68. *This example is based on Wolk and Rozycki (1996). That paper uses a more extensive example and also illustrates accounting for unrecognized prior service costs, corridor amortization of gains and losses, minimum liability, and the transition gain or loss.*

References

AAA Financial Accounting Standards Committee (March 1990). "Other Post-Employment Benefits," *Accounting Horizons*, pp. 111–116.

Accounting Principles Board (1966). APB Opinion No. 8, *Accounting for the Cost of Pension Plans*. AICPA.

Amir, Eli, and Elizabeth Gordon (Summer 1996). "Firms' Choice of Estimation Parameters: Empirical Evidence From SFAS No. 106," *Journal of Accounting, Auditing & Finance*, pp. 427–448.

Amir, Eli, and Joshua Livnat (October 1996). "Multiperiod Analysis of Early Adoption Motives: The Case of SFAS No. 106," *Accounting Review*, pp. 505–519.

Amir, Eli, and A. Ziv (Spring 1997). "Recognition, Disclosure or Delay: Timing the Adoption of SFAS No. 106," *Journal of Accounting Research*, pp. 61–81.

Babington, Deepa (2003). "Pension Accounting Discontent Surfaces in Meeting," *Reuters* from Forbes.com (February 13).

Beidleman, Carl R. (October 1973). "Income Smoothing: The Role of Management," *Accounting Review*, pp. 653–667.

Blankley, Alan, and Edward Swanson (December 1995). "A Longitudinal Study of SFAS No. 87 Pension Rate Assumptions," *Accounting Horizons*, pp. 1–21.

Briner, Russell, and M. Pitman (August 2003). "Disclosing Cash Balance Formulas," *CPA Journal*, pp. 33–37.

Choi, Byeonghee, Daniel Collins, and W. B. Johnson (July 1997). "Valuation Implications of Reliability Differences: The Case of Nonpension Postretirement Obligations," *Accounting Review*, pp. 351–383.

Committee on Accounting Procedure (1948). ARB No. 36, *Pension Plans—Accounting for Annuity Costs Based on Past Services*. AICPA.

——— (1956). ARB No. 47, *Accounting for the Cost of Pension Plans*. AICPA.

Daley, Lane Alan (April 1984). "The Valuation of Reported Pension Measures for Firms Sponsoring Defined Benefit Pension Plans," *Accounting Review*, pp. 177–198.

Dankner, Harold, B. Bald, M. Akresh, J. Bertko, and J. Wodarczyk (1989). *Retiree Health Benefits: Field Test of the Proposal*. Financial Executives Research Foundation.

Davis, Harry, and Arnold Strasser (July 1970). "Private Pension Plans 1960 to 1969—An Overview," *Monthly Labor Review*, pp. 45–56.

Davis-Friday, Paquita, L. B. Folami, C-S, Liu, and H. F. Mittelstaedt (October 1999). "The Value Relevance of Financial Statement Recognition vs. Disclosure: Evidence From SFAS No. 106," *Accounting Review*, pp. 403–423.

Dhaliwal, Dan S. (October 1986). "Measurement of Financial Leverage in the Presence of Unfunded Pension Obligations," *Accounting Review*, pp. 651–661.

D'Souza, Julia (July 1998). "Rate Regulated Enterprises and Mandated Accounting Changes: The Case of Electric Utilities and Post-Retirement Benefits Other Than Pensions (SFAS No. 106)," *Accounting Review*, pp. 387–410.

Epstein, Barry J., and Abbas Ali Mirza (2006). *Interpretation and Application of International Financial Reporting Standards*. John Wiley & Sons.

Feldstein, Martin, and Stephanie Seligman (September 1981). "Pension Funding, Share Prices, and National Savings," *Journal of Finance*, pp. 801–824.

Financial Accounting Standards Board (1974). FASB Interpretation No. 3, *Accounting for the Cost of Pension Plans Subject to the Employee Retirement Income Security Act of 1974*. FASB.

——— (1980a). Statement of Financial Accounting Standards No. 35, *Accounting and Reporting by Defined Benefit Pension Plans*. FASB.

——— (1980b). Statement of Financial Accounting Standards No. 36, *Disclosure of Pension Information*. FASB.

——— (1981). FASB Discussion Memorandum: *An Analysis of Issues Related to Employers' Accounting for Pensions and Other Postemployment Benefits*. FASB.

——— (1984). Statement of Financial Accounting Standards No. 81, *Disclosure of Postretirement Health Care and Life Insurance Benefits*. FASB.

——— (1985a). Statement of Financial Accounting Standards No. 87, *Employers' Accounting for Pensions*. FASB.

——— (1985b). Statement of Financial Accounting Standards No. 88, *Employers' Accounting for Settlements and Curtailments of Defined Benefit Pension Plans and for Termination Benefits*. FASB.

——— (1990). Statement of Financial Accounting Standards No. 106, *Employers' Accounting for Post-Retirement Benefits Other Than Pensions*. FASB.

———— (1992). Statement of Financial Accounting Standards No. 112, *Employers' Accounting for Post-Employment Benefits*. FASB.

———— (1998). Statement of Financial Accounting Standards No. 132, *Employers' Disclosures About Pensions and Other Postretirement Benefits: An Amendment of FASB Statements No. 87, 88, and 106*. FASB.

———— (2003). Statement of Financial Standards No. 132 (R), *Employers Disclosures About Pensions and Other Postretirement Benefits: An Amendment of FASB Statements No. 87, 88, 106, and 132*. FASB.

———— (2006). Statement of Financial Accounting Standards No. 158, *Employers' Accounting for Defined Benefit Pension and Other Postretirement Plans: An Amendment of FASB Statements No. 87, 88, 106, and 132 (R)*. FASB.

Fogarty, Timothy, and Julia Grant (September 1995). "Impact of the Actuarial Profession on Financial Reporting," *Accounting Horizons*, pp. 23–33.

Francis, Jere R. (1982). "An Analysis of Pension Cost Accruals by Actuarial Methodology" (PhD. diss., University of New England).

———— (Spring 1987). "Lobbying Against Proposed Accounting Standards: The Case of Employers' Pension Accounting," *Journal of Accounting and Public Policy*, pp. 35–57.

Francis, Jere R., and Sara Ann Reiter (March 1987). "Determinants of Corporate Pension Funding Strategy," *Journal of Accounting and Economics*, pp. 35–59.

Godwin, Joseph, Stephen Goldberg, and J. Duchac (Spring 1996). "An Empirical Analysis of Factors Associated With Changes in Pension Plan Interest-Rate Assumptions," *Journal of Accounting, Auditing & Finance*, pp. 305–322.

Hagerman, Robert L., and Mark Zmijewski (August 1979). "Some Economic Determinants of Accounting Policy Choice," *Journal of Accounting and Economics*, pp. 141–161.

Harper, Robert M., Jr., William Mister, and Jerry Strawser (September 1991). "The Effect of Recognition Versus Disclosure of Unfunded Postretirement Benefits on Lenders' Perceptions of Debt," *Accounting Horizons*, pp. 50–56.

Hicks, Ernest L. (1965). Accounting Research Study No. 8, *Accounting for the Cost of Pension Plans*. AICPA.

Jones, Steven D. (2006). "Pensions Likely to Stay Dying Breed," *Wall Street Journal* (August 29), p. C3.

Kemp, Robert S., Jr. (1988). "An Examination of the Relationship of Unfunded Vested Pension Liabilities and Selected Elements of Firm Value," *Advances in Accounting* (Vol. 5), pp. 59–72.

Landsman, Wayne (October 1986). "An Empirical Investigation of Pension Fund Property Rights," *Accounting Review*, pp. 662–691.

Langer, Russell, and B. Lev (July 1993). "The FASB's Policy of Extended Adoption for New Standards: An Examination of SFAS No. 87," *Accounting Review*, pp. 515–533.

Lowenstein, Roger (1996). "Intrinsic Value," *Wall Street Journal* (February 1), p. C1.

McCafferty, Joseph (2003). "Funding Funhouse," *CFO* magazine (January 1), pp. 65–67.

Mittelstaedt, H. Fred, William Nichols, and Philip Regier (October 1995). "SFAS No. 106 and Benefit Reductions in Employer-Sponsored Retiree Health Care Plans," *Accounting Review*, pp. 535–556.

Morris, Michael H., and William D. Nichols (Summer 1984). "Pension Accounting and the Balance Sheet: The Potential Effect of the FASB's Preliminary Views," *Journal of Accounting, Auditing & Finance*, pp. 293–305.

Picconi, Mark (July 2006). "The Perils of Pension: Does Pension Accounting Lead Investors and Analysts Astray?" *Accounting Review*, pp. 925–955.

Reiter, Sara Ann (1985). "The Effect of Defined Benefit Pension Plan Disclosures on Bond Risk Premiums and Bond Ratings" (PhD. diss., University of Missouri–Columbia).

Rue, Joseph E., and Ara G. Volkan (Summer 1984). "Financial and Economic Consequences of the New Pension Accounting Proposals: Is the Gloom Justified?" *Journal of Accounting, Auditing & Finance*, pp. 306–322.

Saemann, Georgia (Summer 1995). "The Accounting Standard-Setting Due Process, Corporate Consensus and FASB Responsiveness: Employers' Accounting for Pensions," *Journal of Accounting, Auditing & Finance*, pp. 555–564.

Schipper, Katherine, and Roman L. Weil (October 1982). "Alternative Accounting Treatments for Pensions," *Accounting Review*, pp. 806–824.

Schroeder, Michael (2006). "Congress Seeks to Rein in Special Executive Pensions," *Wall Street Journal* (January 25), pp. A1 and A9.

Schultz, Ellen (1999a). "Companies Reap a Gain off Fat Pension Plans: Fattened Earnings," *Wall Street Journal* (June 15), pp. A1 and A6.

——— (1999b). "Pension Terminations: '80s Replay," *Wall Street Journal* (June 15), pp. C1 and C19.

Schultz, Ellen, J. G. Auerbach, and G. Burkens (1999). "Controversy Besetting New Pension Plan Rises With IBM's Retreat," *Wall Street Journal* (September 20), pp. A1 and A8.

Schultz, Ellen, and T. Francis (2006). "As Workers Pensions Wither, Those for Executives Flourish," *Wall Street Journal* (June 23), pp. A1 and A8.

Solomon, Deborah (2006). "Pension Measure to Enact Changes Over Several Years," *Wall Street Journal* (August 5–6), p. A4.

Stone, Mary S. (Spring 1982). "A Survey of Research on the Effects of Corporate Pension Plan Sponsorship: Implications for Accounting," *Journal of Accounting Literature*, pp. 1–32.

——— (Autumn 1987). "A Financing Explanation for Overfunded Pension Plan Terminations," *Journal of Accounting Research*, pp. 317–326.

Thomas, Paula B., and Larry Farmer (November 1990). "OPEB: Improved Reporting or the Last Straw?" *Journal of Accountancy*, pp. 102–112.

United States Public Law 93-406 (1974). Employee Retirement Income Security Act.

Winklevoss, Howard E. (1977). *Pension Mathematics With Numerical Illustrations*. Richard D. Irwin.

Wolk, Harry I., and John Rozycki (July 1996). "An Integrated Illustration for Teaching Defined Benefit Pension Accounting," *Accounting Education: A Journal of Theory, Practice, and Research*, pp. 163–187.

Wolk, Harry I., and Terri M. Vaughan (February 1993). "A Conceptual Framework Analysis of Pension and Other Postretirement Benefit Accounting," *Accounting Enquiries*, pp. 228–261.

Wolk, Harry I., Terri M. Vaughan, and Stephen Clapham (1998). "Accountability and Decision Making: Analyzing Corporate Responses to the Exposure Draft for Postretirement Benefits Other Than Pensions," *Advances in Public Interest Accounting* (Vol. 7), pp. 263–293.

Wright, David W. (Fall 1990). "Accounting Pedagogy Based on Extant Authoritative Rules Versus Decision-Oriented Analysis: The Case of Other Postemployment Benefits," *Journal of Accounting Education*, pp. 183–205.

Wyatt, Arthur (March 1990). "OPEB Costs: The FASB Establishes Accountability," *Accounting Horizons*, pp. 108–110.

17

Leases

Learning Objectives

After reading this chapter, you should be able to:

- Understand the nature of the lease contract.
- Understand the arguments surrounding lease capitalization.
- Comprehend the evolution of lease accounting.
- Grasp the economic consequences of lease capitalization.
- Understand the G4+1 proposal on leases.

Leases have been the subject of more accounting standards than any other single topic. The Committee on Accounting Procedure (CAP) issued one standard, the Accounting Principles Board (APB) issued five standards, and the Financial Accounting Standards Board (FASB) issued ten. The attention given to leases in accounting standards reflects the increased use of leasing in the business community and the need to clarify and standardize the accounting for this complex transaction. The first accounting lease standard, Accounting Research Bulletin (ARB) 38, was issued in 1949; however, it was only in the 1960s and 1970s that accounting policy makers responded to the lease accounting problem.[1] The basic accounting requirements are unchanged since the comprehensive Statement of Financial Accounting Standard (SFAS) No. 13 was issued in 1976, although lease accounting continues to be controversial in the standards-overload debate.

Leasing has become popular for a number of operating and financial reasons. From an operating viewpoint, some assets are available only under lease; others are too expensive for outright purchase. Two significant financing aspects are the tax advantages (lease payments are fully deductible) and the possibility of off-balance-sheet financing, which occurs when leased assets and lease obligations are not reported in the financial statements. Off-balance-sheet financing results in better debt ratios and higher accounting rates of return than a purchase alternative could produce.

The accounting controversy about leases has focused on distinguishing between the economic substance of leases and their legal form. Prior to ARB 38, the accounting procedure for lease payments was to record them as periodic revenues for lessors and as expenses for lessees. Increasingly, however, some leases came to be viewed as the equivalent of purchases with debt financing. This view now dominates, and the focus of accounting standards has been on defining those situations in which a lease is considered to be a purchase equivalent and in making such leases look like a purchase with debt financing. These types of leases are called *capital leases,* and the accounting procedure for them is called *capitalization.* Noncapitalized leases are called *operating leases,* and the lease payments are treated as periodic expenses.

From a lessor's viewpoint, capital leases may be one of two types, sales or financing. A *sales-type lease* arises when a manufacturer or seller of merchandise uses leasing as a financing instrument to effect what is considered to be the equivalent of a sale. In these situations, the accounting standards have first been concerned with defining the criteria for sales recognition and then making the transaction look like the equivalent of a sale with vendor financing. A *financing-type lease* (also called a *direct financing lease*) occurs when a third party, typically a financial institution rather than a manufacturer or seller, finances a lease. In such situations, the financing party is the lessor and the accounting attempts to make the lease look like a loan with income realized through implicit interest in each lease payment. If a lease is not capitalized by a lessor, the payments are recognized as revenues when received.

This chapter begins with an examination of lease contracts and the capitalization argument and then reviews the evolution of lease accounting in the accounting standards, revealing an ever-finer attempt to achieve finite uniformity vis-à-vis operating and capital leases. Separate accounting rules have been developed for the two types. This approach is defended on the grounds of representational faithfulness, in which a lease is interpreted to be either a simple rental agreement or a more complex capital lease. The economic consequences of lease accounting standards are then considered. We then examine a very important lease proposal made by the G4+1 standard-setting organizations.

The Lease Contract

A *lease* is a legal document conveying use of property for a fixed period of time in exchange for rent or other compensation. From a legal viewpoint, a lease is both a conveyance and a contract, with the contractual element dominating.[2] It is a conveyance because the lessee acquires an interest in property for a fixed period of time. It is a contract because the lessor promises the lessee *quiet enjoyment* of the property during the lease term in exchange for the promise of periodic payments. Although it is not possible to define unambiguously a *true lease* in law, Exhibit 17.1 lists characteristics regarded as indicators of a true lease. Material variations from the characteristics listed in Exhibit 17.1 may result in a lease being regarded as a conditional sale agreement or a debt instrument rather than a true lease. Capitalization criteria in accounting standards have been concerned with many of these characteristics.

The Executory Nature of Lease Contracts

The legal form of a lease contract is an executory (unperformed) contract. A lessor (legal owner) transfers possession of a leased asset to a lessee for a fixed period of time in exchange for a series of rents. A lessee's performance is executory because future rents are due one period at a time. However, the performance question can be argued both ways with respect to the lessor. The distinction is important because it determines whether the contract is mutually unperformed or unilaterally unperformed. As indicated in Chapter 11, mutually unperformed executory contracts have traditionally been excluded from the balance sheet.

It can be argued that a lease contract is fully executed by a lessor when possession of the leased asset is transferred to a lessee. This would make a lease contract unilaterally unperformed by the lessee in the case of default. Such contracts are recognized in the balance sheet

Exhibit 17.1   Characteristics of a True Lease

The following factors are considered to be indications that a lease agreement is without doubt a true lease:

1. The absence of a provision for the transfer of the title to the lessee.

2. The absence of any mention of interest as a factor in rental charges.

3. Rental charges that are competitive with those charged by other lessors of similar equipment.

4. Rental charges that are reasonably related to the loss of value due to the lessee's use of the equipment or that are based on production or use and not necessarily related to purchase price.

5. The assumption of the risk of loss by the lessor.

6. The lessor is required to bear the cost of insurance, maintenance, and taxes.

7. The lessor retains the right to inspect the equipment during the term of the lease.

8. If the lessee has an option to purchase:
   a. The option price approximates the predicted fair market value of the equipment at the time the option may be exercised.
   b. Rentals are not applied to the option price.

9. The rentals charged under leasing plans without an option to purchase approximate the rental charged under plans with such an option.

10. Government agencies recognize the lessor as the owner of the leased asset.

11. The lessee considers by his action that he is a lessee and not a purchaser.

SOURCE: Financial Executives Research Foundation, Inc. (FERF) Accounting for Leases by David M. Hawkins and Mary M. Wehle (1973). Reprinted with permission by Financial Executives Research Foundation, Inc., http://www.fei.org

because possession of a leased asset is both an obligation and asset of the lessee. SFAC No. 6 defines assets as probable future economic benefits and liabilities as probable future sacrifices of economic benefits, both arising from past transactions.[3] A fixed-term lease contract grants property use rights, which may create future economic benefits even though property ownership does not exist. In the same manner, a lease contract also obligates the lessee to make future payments.

If a lease is interpreted as a mutually unperformed executory contract, it can be argued that an asset and liability do not exist for the lessee. In such a situation, the lessor would be permitting use for each period at a time only if the rentals are paid by the lessee. This would simply result in expensing current-period lease payments. Mutually unperformed future promises would be excluded from the balance sheet on the grounds that these are future transactions that have not yet occurred.

Legal remedies available to lessors in the event of lessee default treat leases like mutually unperformed executory contracts. A lessee is not liable for future lease payments in the event of default. A lessor must first mitigate the loss of rents by selling the asset or leasing it again. The lessee has a legal obligation to the lessor only for any residual losses after the lessor mitigates the loss. This makes leases significantly different from other debt agreements—for example, corporate bonds in which the borrower is obliged for the full amount of unpaid principal plus any accrued interest in the event of default.

The importance of the executory aspect of lease contracts is attested to in the second lease accounting standard, APB Opinion No. 5. The fundamental assumption underlying lease capitalization was noncancellability of the lease contract or other material equity factors such as the presence of a bargain purchase option or a bargain lease renewal option.[4] The existence of noncancellability clauses, it could be argued, supersedes the executory nature of lease contracts. If the promises under a lease contract are noncancellable, the executory nature still exists, but it has been mitigated to some extent, and additional legal rights have been created for both lessee and lessor in the event of nonperformance by the other party.

Although the executory nature of lease contracts is an important legal characteristic, its importance has been supplanted by an overriding concern with the economic substance of lease contracts. This basic approach is the one taken by policy makers since the first lease accounting standard in 1949. ARB 38 recommended that where it was obvious a lease contract was in substance a purchase, both an asset and an obligation should be recognized in the lessee's balance sheet. This general theme has continued in subsequent lease accounting standards.

Leases Compared With Purchase Arrangements

There are legal differences between true leases and purchase arrangements.[5] Purchase arrangements include outright cash sales, credit sales, installment sales, secured credit sales, or conditional sales. Title passes to the user of the property in all instances except leases and conditional sales. So a lease and a conditional sale are very similar in this respect. Title passes in a conditional sale when final payment is made, but this does not necessarily occur with a lease. Leases in which the title passes at the end of the lease term or in which a bargain purchase option exists are virtually the same as conditional sales with respect to legal ownership. Also, leases that exist for substantially all of a leased asset's economic life are virtually identical with conditional sales agreements calling for installment payments over the economic life of the asset.

A strong argument for capitalization can be made for leases that resemble conditional sales agreements. Of course, many of these leases would not be considered true leases in the eyes of the law. Even in law, however, the distinction is not always clear between a true lease and a sale. Both the Internal Revenue Service and the courts often deal with disputes about this issue. They interpret some lease contracts as conditional sales agreements, and vice versa. Capitalization of leases that are virtually conditional sales agreements would be consistent with the true legal nature of the transaction rather than with their superficial resemblance to a lease. Capitalization would treat disguised conditional sales like other conditional sales.

In the event of bankruptcy or default, credit sales and installment sales are identical. With both credit and installment sales, the seller is simply a general creditor of the buyer. A secured credit sale gives the seller a preferred claim or lien on the asset and a general creditor status for any amount of the obligation not covered by the value of the asset. In bankruptcy or default, the seller under a conditional sales agreement has a legal right to recover the property because title has not passed. In addition, the seller has a general creditor status for any difference between the unpaid obligation and the asset value. A lessor's claim is limited to provable damages (loss of lease payments), but the lessor must first mitigate these losses either through sale or a new lease of the repossessed property. In this latter way, a lease differs from a conditional sales agreement.

Lease Capitalization

From a lessee's viewpoint, a lease must be accounted for as either (1) a rental agreement or (2) a purchase equivalent with debt financing. For a lessor, the transaction must be treated as either (1) a rental agreement or (2a) a sale equivalent with debt financing (if it is a sales-type lease) or (2b) a loan equivalent (if it is a financing-type lease). Choice (1) for both lessee and lessor interprets the lease contract as an operating lease and recognizes the mutually unperformed executory nature of lease contracts. Choice (2) treats the lease as a capital lease and recognizes the conveyance and financing aspects of leases. The simplicity of the basic accounting classification system forces a lease to be accounted for in one of these two ways.

The choice of accounting policy has been described in the following manner:

> At one extreme, there is the case of two physically identical items of equipment used by a business, one financed or partly financed by borrowing, and the other financed by a lease that is non-cancellable for a period equal to the equipment's useful life. Most every informed person would agree that it doesn't make much sense to report one of these items on the balance sheet and omit the other. At the other end there are ephemeral leases . . . which most everyone agrees should not give rise to a balance sheet item. The problem is to state a principle that will provide a conceptually sound and practical way of drawing a line somewhere between the two extremes.[6]

The heart of the present policy is classification of leases as either operating or capital leases—a classic example of attempting to establish finite uniformity and to account representationally for the real substance of the lease transaction rather than its superficial legal form.

One of the major arguments against lease capitalization was verifiability. Specifically, some believed that the use of present value discounting techniques introduced less reliable accounting numbers into the financial statements. This concern was exaggerated, however, because present value calculations are only used to make lease financing look like the equivalent of a loan with an equal repayment schedule. The present value technique as applied to lease accounting is illustrated later in the chapter, and, as we will see, only one verifiability problem exists: the choice of interest rate used to discount the lease payments. There is some inevitable subjectivity in determining a lessee's rate, but it is certainly susceptible to close approximation. For a lessor, there is no subjectivity because the interest rate implicit in the lease is used. Verifiability is not considered to be a major issue with lease accounting today.

Capitalization for Lessees

Numerous criteria have been proposed to support lease capitalization. A very good survey is found in the FASB's discussion memorandum on leases and is summarized in Exhibit 17.2.[7] In general terms, the arguments for lease capitalization invoke the reasoning that certain leases are, in substance, purchases with debt financing. A lease is simply another type of legal instrument to accomplish this end. Different arguments and criteria have been used to define purchase equivalents, but the differences really are little more than alternative points where the line is drawn between operating and capital leases. The many viewpoints can be simplified into three broad approaches: legal, material equity, and substantial transfer of ownership benefits and risks. These represent increasingly broader interpretations of capital leases.

Exhibit 17.2   Lease Capitalization Criteria

1. Lessee builds up a material equity in the leased property.
2. Leased property is special purpose to the lessee.
3. Lease term is substantially equal to the estimated useful life of the property.
4. Lessee pays costs normally incident to ownership.
5. Lessee guarantees the lessor's debt with respect to the leased property.
6. Lessee treats the lease as a purchase for tax purposes.
7. Lease is between related parties.
8. Lease passes usual risks and rewards to lessee.
9. Lessee assumes an unconditional liability for lease rentals.
10. Lessor lacks independent economic substance.
11. Residual value at end of lease is expected to be nominal.
12. Lease agreement provides for lessor's recovery of investment plus a fair return.
13. Lessee has the option at any time to purchase the asset for the lessor's unrecovered investment.
14. Lease agreement is noncancellable for a long term.

Legal Approach

One way to resolve the lease classification problem is to treat true leases as described in Exhibit 17.1 as operating leases and to capitalize leases that are not true leases. This approach to lease capitalization resolves the problem by resorting to legal definitions and concepts. However, such an approach does not address the more fundamental question of whether true leases should be capitalized. It has been argued that all noncancellable leases create legal property rights and obligations that should be in a lessee's balance sheet even if they do arise from a lease contract.[8] It was pointed out in Chapter 11 that accounting theory and policy are not confined to legal definitions of accounting elements.

Material Equity

Historically, the argument for lease capitalization has relied on the concept of material equity. This means that the terms of the lease are such that the lessee is clearly paying for more than the current period rental value of the asset. In other words, the lessee is acquiring an implicit equity in the leased asset through the periodic lease payments. Evidence for such a situation would be rental payments in excess of yearly economic value or a bargain purchase option. The excess represents payment for the implicit property rights created by the lease. Also, noncancellability and a lease term for a significant portion of the asset's economic life would support the material equity argument. Material equity, as applied in accounting standards in the past, limited capitalization to a small number of leases that were virtually conditional sales agreements with installment payments. As a result, there was very little difference between the legal and material equity approaches.

Transfer of the Benefits and Risks of Ownership

SFAS No. 13 took a broader approach to the capitalization argument. Leases that substantially transfer "all of the benefits and risks incident to the ownership of property should be accounted for as the acquisition of an asset and the incurrence of an obligation by the lessee and as a sale or financing by the lessor."[9] The current definition has dropped noncancellability as a prerequisite for capitalization and de-emphasized the concept of material equity. In spite of the attempt in SFAS No. 13 to disassociate the standard from earlier standards, the essence of the capitalization argument remains the same as it has been since ARB 38—that a purchase equivalent has occurred. The difficulty, of course, has been in agreeing on when this occurs. The material equity concept has simply been superseded by a somewhat broader concept and set of tests.

Capitalization for Lessors

A basic issue with lessor capitalization is symmetry with lessee accounting. *Symmetry* means consistent accounting by lessees and lessors for capital and operating leases. Some feel that symmetry, per se, is not necessary.[10] Others believe that the basic characteristic of a capital lease should be consistently recorded by both lessor and lessee.[11] The absence of symmetry suggests that the basic classification of leases as operating and capital is inconsistent. Accounting standards have moved toward symmetry.

For sales-type leases, the same set of criteria applicable to lessees has been proposed for capitalization by lessors because if a sales-type lease is a purchase equivalent to the lessee, it must be a sale equivalent to the lessor. However, additional criteria must also exist before a sale is recognized. These criteria involve the usual assumptions underlying revenue recognition—mainly the certainty of cash collection and the absence of uncertainties regarding unincurred costs relating to the sale.

Financing-type leases present a different situation. The capitalization analogy treats such leases as the equivalent of debt financing. There is no sale revenue with financing-type leases, only interest revenue earned from the debt equivalent. Arguments for capitalization of finance-type leases have related more to the debt characteristic of the lease than to the sale characteristic. The main criterion proposed is the concept of *full payout*, which refers to a set of lease payments that returns a lessor's investment in the leased asset plus a reasonable interest on the investment.[12]

The Evolution of Lease Accounting Standards

A number of standards have been issued since 1949. We review them chronologically, first as they relate to lessees and then as they affect lessors.

Lessee Accounting

ARB 38

The first lease accounting standard, issued in 1949, was ARB 38. It was subsequently codified as Chapter 14 of ARB 43.[13] The standard recommended capitalization for certain leases that were, in substance, installment purchases. Although it referred specifically to the installment purchase analogy, it was more applicable to leases that were de facto conditional sales agreements. The capitalization criteria were any of the following: (a) the existence of a bargain purchase option at the termination of the lease, (b) covenants that permitted the application of lease rentals to the purchase price, or (c) rental payments so high that a purchase plan was evident. The first criterion deals with lease terms that make a lease almost indistinguishable from a conditional sale. The second and third criteria refer to the material equity argument and could be analogous to either an installment sale or conditional sale, though in legal terms the resemblance is closer to a conditional sale. No details were given in the standard concerning the measurement of either the leased asset or lease obligation.

APB Opinion No. 5

As part of the research approach initially adopted by the APB, a study was commissioned on leases. This resulted in Accounting Research Study (ARS) 4, issued in 1962.[14] ARS 4 took a legalistic approach to determining whether a lease was in substance a purchase. ARS 4 argued that noncancellability of the lease contract creates legal property rights warranting capitalization. The next accounting standard, issued in 1964, was APB Opinion No. 5. APB Opinion No. 5 did not accept the basic argument in ARS 4 and reaffirmed the material equity argument of ARB 38. However, it did introduce noncancellability, except upon the occurrence of some remote contingency, as a precondition for capitalization. As suggested earlier in the chapter, this condition could be interpreted as mitigating the executory nature of lease contracts.

APB Opinion No. 5 also modified criteria for capitalization, although the stated objective was to clarify ARB 43, Chapter 14, not change it. The intent was to capitalize any lease creating a material equity interest. Either of two primary criteria was listed: (1) a renewal option covering the useful economic life or (2) existence of a bargain purchase option. Some secondary indicators were also identified: (a) the property was specially acquired by the lessor to meet the needs of the lessee, (b) the lease term corresponded to the useful life, (c) the lessee incurred executory costs (insurance, taxes, and maintenance), (d) the lessee guaranteed any lessor obligation with respect to the leased asset, or (e) the lessee treated the lease as a purchase under tax law. Apparently these secondary criteria were ignored in practice because of the way the standard was worded. As a result, APB Opinion No. 5 caused little change in the number of leases that were capitalized, even though it intended the opposite effect.[15]

APB Opinion No. 10

APB Opinion No. 10, issued in 1966, was an omnibus opinion.[16] One paragraph dealt with leases and required the consolidation of certain subsidiaries that were principally engaged in leasing assets to parent companies. This standard was partially an amendment of APB Opinion No. 5, paragraph 12, and was concerned with lease contracts between related entities, such as parent and subsidiary companies. APB Opinion No. 10 required that subsidiaries engaged in sales-type leases to the parent company must be consolidated. In this way, it was not possible to avoid the reporting of leased assets by having unconsolidated subsidiaries write lease contracts. However, the consolidation of subsidiaries engaged in financing-type leases was left unresolved. As a result of APB Opinion Nos. 5 and 10, financing-type leases could be treated differently by the lessee, depending on whether the lessor was a subsidiary or an independent entity. Some leases were capitalized and some were not. The Securities and Exchange Commission (SEC) attempted to resolve this inconsistency with ASR 132, issued in 1972.[17]

APB Opinion No. 31

The next accounting standard for lessees was APB Opinion No. 31, issued in 1973.[18] This standard expanded disclosure of noncapitalized leases. APB Opinion No. 5 had been criticized on the grounds that it excluded many leases that should be capitalized. The disclosures required by APB Opinion No. 31 included the amounts of future rentals at both undiscounted amounts and present values. The effect of this disclosure requirement was to create adequate supplemental disclosure to permit users to informally capitalize noncapitalized lease obligations if they so desired. Although this disclosure expanded the reporting of information concerning noncapitalized lease obligations, it did not go so far as to formally place them on the balance sheet.

The SEC pressured the newly formed FASB to review lease accounting. Shortly after APB Opinion No. 31 was released (it was the last APB opinion), the SEC issued ASR 147.[19] The SEC was critical of existing lease accounting standards, and ASR 147 amended lease disclosure for statutory SEC filings. ASR 147 was mainly concerned with financing-type leases. As mentioned before, APB Opinion Nos. 5 and 10 were thought to have resulted in inconsistent capitalization of financing-type leases. ASR 147 required supplemental disclosure of noncapitalized financing-type leases on a basis that was equivalent to capitalization.

SFAS No. 13 (as Amended Through SFAS No. 98)

The FASB issued a discussion memorandum on leases in 1974, and after deliberations, SFAS No. 13 was issued in 1976. Criteria for lessee capitalization were revised again. This time there was a change in both concept and capitalization criteria. Noncancellability and material equity were abandoned in favor of broader tests representing substantive transfers of ownership benefits and risks—although, as indicated earlier, the underlying objective still seems to be the recognition of purchase equivalents. Perhaps the difference between APB Opinion No. 5 and SFAS No. 13 is better described as a change in where the line is drawn between operating and capital leases. SFAS No. 13 is quite clearly intended to capitalize more leases. There are four capitalization tests now applicable to both lessees and lessors:

1. Title passes to the lessee at the end of the lease term.

2. The lease contract contains a bargain purchase option.

3. The lease term is for at least 75% of estimated useful life, including any bargain lease renewal option (with the lease term covering more than 25% of the original economic life when new if the lease pertains to an older asset).

4. The present value of minimum lease payments (the sum of minimum rentals excluding executory costs, a bargain purchase payment if one exists, penalty payment for nonrenewal if renewal is unlikely, and any guaranteed residual value at the end of lease term—plus unguaranteed residual value for lessors) is 90% of the fair market value of the lease property at the inception of the lease, less any applicable investment tax credit.

The discount rate to be used by the lessee is the incremental borrowing rate. However, the lessor's implicit rate in the lease shall be used if it is obtainable and if the implicit rate is lower than the lessee's incremental borrowing rate. This represents conservatism because a lower interest rate will cause a higher present value and could result in lease capitalization under the 90% rule. The lessor's implicit rate is defined in SFAS No. 13, paragraph 5k, and is illustrated later in the chapter. If *any* one of these four tests or conditions is met, the lease must be treated as a capital lease by the lessee.

SFAS No. 13 also details how leases should be capitalized. The present value of minimum lease payments (defined in test 4) is computed using the interest rate determined as before. This amount is debited to leased assets and credited to lease obligations, subject to an upper limit of the asset's fair market value at lease inception. The asset is depreciated over its useful life if tests (1) or (2) are met. Otherwise, the depreciation period is the lease term with total amortization equal to the capitalized amount less any guaranteed residual value at the end of the lease term. During the lease term, each payment is allocated between interest expense and reduction of the lease obligation. The effective interest method described in APB Opinion No. 21 is used.[20] Finally, any executory costs (taxes, maintenance, and insurance) are expensed as incurred. If lease payments include an amount for these costs, it is separated and expensed directly each period.

In this manner, the prescribed accounting seeks to make the lease resemble a purchase of the asset with debt financing. The leased asset is depreciated over its useful life if it is being leased for substantially all its useful life. If the asset is leased for a shorter period, the shorter period is used as the amortization period. Executory costs are separated and expensed in the same manner as would occur with a purchase. Finally, lease payments are separated into the equivalent of principal and interest each period. The purchase analogy is illustrated with a numerical example in Exhibit 17.3 on pages 570 and 571.

Real estate leases are accounted for somewhat differently. Leases involving only land are capitalized if either test (1) or test (2) in SFAS No. 13 is satisfied. Otherwise, land leases are classified as operating. Land under lease is not treated as a purchase equivalent unless title is expected to transfer. The reason for this more restrictive test is due to the nondepreciable nature of land. When a lease includes both land and buildings, the capitalization test is more complicated. If test (1) or (2) is not met, an allocation is made between land and building based on relative fair market values. They are capitalized separately. If a real estate lease involving land does not meet test (1) or (2), but the fair market value of the land component is less than 25% of the total, the lease is treated as entirely attributable to the building for the purpose of applying tests (3) and (4) of SFAS No. 13. If either test (3) or (4) is met, the lease is capitalized. In other words, the land component is considered to be immaterial relative to the building component and the entire lease is capitalized. If the land component is 25% or more, the land and building are treated separately, with the land being an operating lease and the building being a capital lease if test (3) or (4) is met. These rules represent somewhat arbitrary ways of dealing with nondepreciable land in real estate leases.

In addition to the prescribed accounting for capital leases, a number of supplemental disclosures are required by SFAS No. 13: (a) gross amounts of assets under capital lease, (b) future minimum lease payments (excluding executory costs) in aggregate and for each of the five succeeding years, (c) total minimum sublease rentals to be received under noncancellable subleases, and (d) total contingent rentals as they are incurred each period. Lease assets and lease obligations are to be reported separately from other assets and liabilities in the balance sheet. Lease obligations are subject to current and noncurrent classification requirements.

A very important question whenever there is a major change in accounting policy is how it will be implemented. With lease capitalization, a generous phase-in period was permitted. For new leases written after 1976, capitalization was required if the new tests were met. However, for existing leases, companies were given until December 31, 1980, to retroactively capitalize the leases and restate prior years' financial statements. Supplemental disclosures were required

Exhibit 17.3 Lease Purchase Analogy

A company may purchase an asset outright for $100,000 with vendor financing. The note payable would be paid off with three year-end payments of $41,634.90. This represents an effective interest of 12 percent. An alternative is to lease the asset for three years with lease payments of $41,634.90 at the end of each year. The asset's economic life is three years, and no salvage is expected.

Loan/Lease Repayment Schedule

	(Col. 1) Beginning Principal	(Col. 2) Payment	(Col. 3) Interest (Col. 1 × .12)	(Col. 4) Principal (Col. 2 − Col. 3)	(Col. 5) Ending Principal (Col. 1 − Col. 4)
Year 1	$100,000.00	$41,634.90	$12,000.00	$ 29,634.90	$70,365.10
Year 2	$70,365.10	$41,634.90	$8,443.81	$ 33,191.09	$37,174.01
Year 3	$37,174.01	$41,634.90	$4,460.89	$ 37,174.01	–0–

Purchase Alternative

Year 1

	Debit	Credit
Asset	100,000	
Note payable		100,000
Note payable	29,634.90	
Interest expense	12,000.00	
Cash		41,634.90
Depreciation expense	33,333.33	
Accumulated depreciation		33,333.33

Lease Alternative

Year 1

	Debit	Credit
Leased asset	100,000	
Lease obligation		100,000
Lease obligation	29,634.90	
Interest expense	12,000.00	
Cash		41,634.90
Depreciation—Lease	33,333.33	
Accumulated lease depreciation		33,333.33

Loan/Lease Repayment Schedule

	(Col. 1) Beginning Principal	(Col. 2) Payment	(Col. 3) Interest (Col. 1 × .12)	(Col. 4) Principal (Col. 2 − Col. 3)	(Col. 5) Ending Principal (Col. 1 − Col. 4)
Year 2				**Year 2**	
Note payable	33,191.09		Lease obligation	33,191.09	
Interest expense	8,443.81		Interest expense	8,443.81	
Cash		41,634.90	Cash		41,634.90
Depreciation expense	33,333.33		Depreciation—Lease	33,333.33	
Accumulated depreciation		33,333.33	Accumulated lease depreciation		33,333.33
Year 3				**Year 3**	
Note payable	37,174.01		Lease obligation	37,174.01	
Interest expense	4,460.89		Interest expense	4,460.89	
Cash		41,634.90	Cash		41,634.90
Depreciation expense	33,333.34		Depreciation—Lease	33,333.34	
Accumulated depreciation		33,333.34	Accumulated lease depreciation		33,333.34

of what the pre-1977 lease assets and obligations would have been during the phase-in period if they had been capitalized. The reason for a long transition period was owing to the potential material effects of lease capitalization on some companies. SFAS No. 13 was less dramatic than expected because the new standard permitted companies some flexibility in complying with the new requirements. There was time to mitigate the impact on the balance sheet of lease capitalization. The final section of the chapter presents some evidence that this type of behavior (avoiding lease capitalization) did in fact occur.

A criticism of lessee accounting under SFAS No. 13 is that some leases that should be capitalized still are not. It can be argued that all leases in excess of one year should be capitalized, because assets and liabilities are created that are consistent with definitions of assets and obligations in SFAC No. 6.[21] One reason for avoiding this policy may be the costs that would be imposed on companies if all leases were capitalized, although we believe that the benefits to users would exceed the costs thereof. An apparent compromise exists on this point in the form of supplemental disclosure. For noncancellable operating leases in excess of one year, SFAS No. 13 requires the following supplemental disclosures:

- Future minimum rental payments in aggregate and for each of the succeeding five periods
- Total minimum rentals to be received under noncancellable subleases
- Rental expense with separate totals for minimum rentals, contingent rentals, and sublease rentals
- A general description of the lessee's lease contracts

Supplemental disclosure of noncapitalized leases is not as great under SFAS No. 13 as it was under APB Opinion No. 31. The noncancellability requirement will exclude some operating leases, and present value information is not required under SFAS No. 13. It is unclear why noncancellability was introduced as the overriding criterion for supplemental disclosure of operating leases since it was dropped as a capitalization criterion. Because many more leases will be capitalized under SFAS No. 13, it may be that the need for supplemental information is not as great as it was prior to the issuance of SFAS No. 13. Still, it is puzzling why the supplemental disclosures of noncapitalized leases were reduced so much. The weak disclosures of noncapitalized leases create incentives to structure leases in such a way as to avoid both capitalization and supplemental disclosure. If this can be done, off-balance-sheet financing through leases would still be possible. This issue is discussed later in the chapter.

Lessor Accounting

The initial impetus for lease capitalization was caused by a concern over lessee balance sheets. In particular, there was a desire to disclose lease obligations as debt equivalents. It was only belatedly that the lessor side of lease transactions was considered in accounting standards.

APB Opinion No. 7

APB Opinion No. 7, issued in 1966, was the first standard to address lessor accounting.[22] The equivalent of lease capitalization was required, but the criteria differed from APB Opinion No. 5. In addition, separate criteria existed for sales-type and financing-type leases. Sales-type leases were capitalized if three conditions were satisfied: (1) credit risks were reasonably predictable, (2) the lessor (seller) did not retain sizable risks of ownership, and (3) there were no important uncertainties regarding either costs or revenues under the lease contract. These three conditions differed from the lessee tests established under APB Opinion No. 5. As a result, it was possible for a lease contract to be capitalized by either the lessee or lessor, but not by both. This asymmetry between lessee and lessor accounting was criticized.

Financing-type leases are those that involve a third party who writes the lease contract. The lessor is the third party, typically a financial institution that provides the financing. The other two parties are the lessee and the manufacturer (or seller) of the leased asset. *All* financing-type leases were capitalized by lessors under APB Opinion No. 7; however, some financing-type leases were not capitalized by lessees under APB Opinion Nos. 5 and 10. As indicated earlier in the chapter, lessee accounting for financing-type leases was inconsistent under APB Opinion Nos. 5 and 10.

Leases capitalized under APB Opinion No. 7 were recognized as aggregate future rentals less the interest implicit in each rental. This represented the net present value of lease payments receivable. The effective interest method, as described in APB Opinion No. 21, was prescribed as the basis of interest revenue recognition. Each payment was separated into principal and interest, just as was required for lessees under APB Opinion No. 5.

Initial direct costs incurred by the lessor in originating a lease contract were deferred and recognized on a proportional basis consistent with the recognition of lease revenue. This applied to all leases and was an attempt to match lease-related costs to the revenue generated over the lease term.

APB Opinion No. 27

Criticisms of APB Opinion No. 7 regarding the noncapitalization of many sales-type leases led to the issuance of APB Opinion No. 27 in 1972.[23] The intent in APB Opinion No. 27 was to broaden the criteria for capitalization. The new criteria were

1. The collectibility of payments was reasonably assured.

2. No important uncertainties surrounded costs yet to be incurred on the lease.

3. Any one of the following:
   a. Title passed at end of lease term.
   b. A bargain purchase option existed.
   c. The leased property or similar property was for sale and the present value of required rentals (excluding executory costs) plus any investment tax credits was equal to or greater than normal selling price.
   d. The lease term was substantially equal to the remaining economic life of the property.

Two of the requirements under both APB Opinion Nos. 7 and 27 were similar and dealt with general revenue recognition criteria. Collectibility and the absence of uncertainties are generally assumed when accruing revenue in advance of cash collection. The third requirement of APB Opinion No. 27 replaced the second criterion of APB Opinion No. 7, the transfer of ownership risk, and was satisfied by any one of four conditions. The first two conditions reiterated the capitalization criteria of APB Opinion No. 5 for lessees. The last two were new and provided additional conditions that suggested the lease was a sale equivalent from the lessor's viewpoint. The addition of these two conditions was important because it represented a departure from the material equity argument and looked more broadly at the economic substance of the transaction. However, the newly broadened criteria for lessors were at variance with the narrower criteria for lessees established in APB Opinion No. 5.

SFAS No. 13

Finally, lessee and lessor accounting achieved near symmetry in SFAS No. 13. The four capitalization tests discussed earlier, which were only a slight modification of APB Opinion No. 27, were applied to both lessees and lessors. For lessor accounting, the two additional revenue recognition tests of APB Opinion Nos. 7 and 27 were also retained in SFAS No. 13. The existence of these two additional criteria means that it is possible for some leases that are capitalized by lessees to be treated as operating leases by lessors. However, it is unlikely that this would occur very frequently. Inconsistent capitalization of financing-type leases was also eliminated by SFAS No. 13. It will be recalled that APB Opinion Nos. 5, 7, and 10 created the potential for inconsistency.

Some asymmetry still exists between lessor and lessee accounting with respect to the choice of interest rate for calculating the capitalized value of leases. The lessor uses the implicit rate, which equates minimum lease payments plus unguaranteed residual value in excess of any guaranteed amounts with the sales price of the asset less any applicable investment tax credit. The lessee uses the lower of its incremental borrowing rate or the lessor's implicit rate (if it is obtainable), and only the guaranteed residual value is used. As a result, it is possible for the same lease to be measured differently in the financial statements of lessees and lessors. This disparity would be justified on the grounds of conservatism since a lower interest rate will increase the amount of the capitalized lease obligation. It can also be defended on the grounds that each party may not have the same interest rates, owing to the different risks involved. Different residual values can also be justified because they represent different values to the lessor and lessee.

An area of apparent inconsistency in lessor accounting concerns initial *direct lease costs,* costs incurred in arranging the lease. SFAS No. 13 requires expensing of initial direct lease costs if the lease is a sales type. However, for financing-type leases, these costs are amortized over the lease term indirectly through the effective interest method.[24] A new implicit interest rate must be calculated that will recognize the remaining unearned interest using the effective interest method. The justification is that these costs are best matched against interest revenue in the case of financing-type leases because the lessor earns revenue from lease financing.

On the other hand, with a sales-type lease, the costs are considered to be selling costs attributable to the arranging of debt finance. The costs are considered necessary to make the sale. This is another example of finite uniformity, in which the same costs are treated differently because of different circumstances. In this case, the circumstances have to do with the nature of the lessor's operations and the classification of initial direct lease costs as either selling costs or as reductions of future interest revenue.

Measurement of capitalized leases for lessors is specified in SFAS No. 13. The first step is to calculate the implicit interest rate in the lease: the rate of interest that equates minimum lease payments with the asset's fair market value at lease inception, reduced for any lessor investment tax credit. Minimum lease payments are defined as the sum of future rentals (less any amounts for executory costs paid by the lessor), plus amounts to be paid under bargain purchase options, plus penalty payment for nonrenewal if renewal is unlikely, plus guaranteed residual value if the asset reverts to the lessor, plus any unguaranteed residual value. The fair market value of the leased asset would normally be the cash selling price for both sales-type and financing-type leases. Minimum lease payments receivable plus unguaranteed residual value are recognized at the gross amount, and a contra-account is created to recognize unearned interest. The net balance represents the present value of minimum lease payments receivable. Unearned interest is recognized each period, as the interest component is separated from the lease payment through the effective interest method. Lessor accounting for a financing-type lease is illustrated in Exhibit 17.4 on pages 576 and 577 and for a financing-type lease with initial direct costs in Exhibit 17.5 on page 578.

The same procedures are used with a sales-type lease to account for the financing aspect of the lease. The present value of minimum lease payments receivable is computed and recognized in the balance sheet. Payments are separated into principal and interest components. However, in addition, revenue is recognized in an amount equal to the fair market value of the asset at lease inception. Normally this would be the cash selling price. The cost of the leased asset is recognized as cost of goods sold. So gross profit on the sales-type lease is recognized in addition to the present value of minimum lease payments receivable and interest revenue on lease payments.

For all noncapitalized leases, the lessor must disclose the cost and book value of leased property (the assets are still recorded in the lessor's balance sheet if they are operating leases). Other supplemental disclosures required of lessors are the same required of lessees and reflect the reciprocal nature of capitalized lease contracts. These are minimum future rentals from noncancellable leases, in aggregate and for each of the five succeeding years, and contingent rental income as it is recognized.

The FASB has issued a number of amendments and interpretations to SFAS No. 13, all of which are concerned with technical and specific issues.[25] In general, these additional rules have clarified the implementation of lease capitalization arising from complex terms in lease contracts. These additional rules are not reviewed since they pertain to narrower technical issues rather than general standards.[26]

Sale and Leaseback

A sale and leaseback occurs when the owner of an asset legally sells it and enters into a lease agreement to lease the asset back. The lessor (new legal owner) and lessee (original legal owner) both use the standard criteria for classifying such a lease as operating or capital. A principle was established in APB Opinion No. 5 that no immediate recognition should be given to any book gains or losses that the lessee might record in such a transaction. The general rule was that any gain or loss should be amortized by the lessee as an adjustment of the lease rental if the lease is

Exhibit 17.4   Financing-Type Lease

Assume the following:

1. Fair market value at lease inception is $131,540.53.

2. Lease payments are $50,000 at the end of each of the next three years and include $2,000 for executory costs.

3. Estimated residual value is $13,000, of which $5,000 is guaranteed by the lessee.

4. There are no siginficant initial direct lease costs.

Step 1—Calculate implicit interest rate.

Fair Market Value = Present Value of minimum lease payments exclusive of executory costs, guaranteed residual value, and unguaranteed residual value.

$$\$131{,}540.53 = \frac{\$48{,}000}{(1+i)^1} + \frac{\$48{,}000}{(1+i)^2} + \frac{\$48{,}000 + \$5{,}000 + \$8{,}000}{(1+i)^3}$$

$i = .09$

Step 2—Record gross amounts of minimum lease payments exclusive of executory costs, plus guaranteed and unguaranteed residual value, and the unearned interest calculated by the implicit rate.

Lease Payments Receivable	157,000.00	
Unearned Interest		25,459.47
Cash		131,540.53

To record asset payment and capital lease

Step 3—Record yearly interest revenue and lease payments.

Year 1

Cash	48,000	
Lease payments receivable		48,000
Unearned interest[a]	11,838.65	
Interest revenue		11,838.65

Year 2

Cash	48,000	
Lease payments receivable		48,000
Unearned interest[a]	8,584.13	
Interest revenue		8,584.13

Year 3

Cash	48,000	
Lease payments receivable		48,000
Unearned interest[a]	5,036.69	
Interest revenue		5,036.69
Asset	13,000	
Lease payment receivable		13,000

a See schedule on following page.

Exhibit 17.4   (Continued)

	Implicit Principal Repayments Schedule					
					Net Lease Investment	
	Beginning Net Lease Investment (Lease payments receivable less unearned interest)	*Payment*	*Interest*	*Principal*	*Ending Unearned Interest*	*Ending Lease Payment Receivable*
Year 1	$131,540.53	$48,000	$11,838.65	$36,161.35	$13,620.82	$109,000
Year 2	$95,379.18	$48,000	$8,584.13	$39,415.87	$5,036.69	$61,000
Year 3	$55,963.31	$48,000	$5,036.69	$42,963.31	–0–	$13,000

an operating lease and as an adjustment of lease depreciation if the lease is capitalized. The deferred gain or loss was reported in the balance sheet as a deferred credit or charge, respectively. One exception to this rule was that a loss was recognized if the asset's book value exceeded the fair market value at the time of the sale-leaseback. This, however, is nothing more than the application of conventional accounting conservatism through the lower-of-cost-or-market rule.

The reason for not recognizing a gain or loss is that the sale and leaseback are considered to be one transaction rather than two. Any book gains or losses therefore arise artificially from the accounting necessity of treating the transaction as having two separate parts. Since the lessee has the same asset as before (but leasing rather than owning), it is argued that no gain or loss should be recognized. To recognize such a gain or loss would be the virtual equivalent of selling something to yourself and recognizing a gain or loss on the transaction. This approach was retained in SFAS No. 13. If a lease is an operating lease, the deferred gain or loss is recognized proportionally to lease payments. If the lease is capitalized, the deferred gain or loss is recognized proportionally to lease depreciation. An example of a sale and leaseback involving book gains and losses is illustrated in Exhibit 17.6 on page 579.

SFAS No. 13 did establish conditions under which a gain or loss might be immediately recognized in a sale and leaseback. These tests are concerned with leases in which the original owner retains usage of a substantially smaller part of the total asset. It is argued that there really are two separate and distinct transactions when this occurs because the lessee would no longer have the same asset as before.

Leveraged Leases

Leveraged leases are a special type of financing lease involving three parties instead of the usual two. With this type of lease, the lessor acquires an asset by borrowing money from a third party and combining it with its own capital. The third party is typically a group of lenders, and the financing is usually in excess of 50% of the cost of the asset. The lessor then leases the asset to the lessee. The debt to the third party is nonrecourse, but the lessor assigns a portion of the lease payments to cover the debt and interest payments. The debt to the third

Exhibit 17.5   Financing-Type Lease With Initial Direct Costs

Assume the same facts as in Exhibit 17.4, expect that initial direct lease costs of $1,500 are incurred. The following entry would be made in Year 1:

| Lease payments receivable | 1,500 | |
| Cash | | 1,500 |

It is then necessary to calculate a new interest rate using the effective interest method:

$$133,040.53 = \frac{\$48,000}{(1+i)^1} + \frac{\$48,000}{(1+i)^2} + \frac{\$48,000 + \$5,000 + \$8,000}{(1+i)^3}$$

By interpolation, $i = .08395$.

Revised Principal Repayment Schedule

| | Beginning | | | | Net Lease Investment | |
| | | | | | Ending | Ending Lease |
	Net Lease Investment	Payment	Interest	Principal	Unearned Interest	Payment Receivable
Year 1	$133,040.53	$48,000	$11,168.75	$36,831.25	$12,790.72	$109,000.00
Year 2	$96,209.28	$48,000	$8,076.77[a]	$39,923.23	$4,713.95	$61,000.00
Year 3	$56,286.05	$48,000	$4,713.95	$43,286.05	–0–	$13,000.00

a   Includes adjustment for rounding error due to approximation of the effective interest rate.

Exhibit 17.6   Sale-Leaseback

Assume the same facts as in Exhibit 17.3. In addition, assume that the lessee was the original owner and sold the asset for $100,000 to the new owner, who is now the lessor.[a] Assuming the asset had a book value of $79,000 to the original owner (now lessee), the following entries would be required by the lessee in addition to those illustrated in Exhibit 17.3.

1. At Sale date:

Cash	100,000	
Asset (book value)		79,000
Deferred gain on sale-leaseback		21,000

2. For each of the three years during the lease term:

Deferred gain on sale-leaseback	7,000	
Depreciation—Lease		7,000

a. Normally, any gain or loss would be the difference between the original owner's book value and the selling price. In such cases, losses would always be recognized immediately and the gains deferred. However, it is possible for the sales price to be set at some amount other than market value. For example, suppose in this example the selling price was $85,000 and the estimated market value was $75,000. The following entry would be made by the original owner at the time of sales.

Loss on asset	4,000	
Cash	85,000	
Asset (book value)		79,000
Deferred gain on sale-leaseback		10,000

The effect of this entry is to recognize a loss of $4,000 ($79,000 − $75,000) for the adjustment to market value, and to defer the gain of $10,000 representing the payment in excess of market value by the buyer.

party may also be secured by the leased asset and sometimes by a guarantee from the lessee. At issue is whether this transaction should be accounted for as a conventional financing-type lease with an additional debt transaction or as a unique transaction warranting separate treatment.

From a lessee's viewpoint, a leveraged lease is not any different from other leases. The more difficult question concerns the effect of a leveraged lease on the lessor. One possible effect is that a leveraged lease is the same as a conventional financing-type lease with an additional debt transaction between the lessor and the third party. The other possibility is to regard a leveraged lease as a unique type of lease warranting special rules applicable to its special circumstances. The FASB concluded in SFAS No. 13 that the financing-type lease plus debt transaction analogy was inadequate to report leveraged leases. It argued that reporting leveraged leases as two separate transactions, a financing lease and a loan, failed to portray the lessor's net investment in the lease. What is required by SFAS No. 13 is a complex procedure of reporting all aspects of a leveraged lease in a net amount as if it were one transaction. This represents another example of finite uniformity in which relevant circumstances determine the appropriate accounting procedures. The requirements are illustrated in SFAS No. 13, Appendix E.

Assessing SFAS No. 13

The long-standing criticism of lease accounting is that many leases are not being capitalized but should be. This is no less true under SFAS No. 13 than it was under ARB 38 or APB Opinion No. 5. An inherent weakness of the finite uniformity approach is that some accounting methods may be preferred by management over others. In these instances, companies will be motivated to manipulate the relevant circumstances to get the desired accounting result. With leases, lessees continue to believe that there are advantages to off-balance-sheet financing through leases. This will always motivate companies to try to defeat the capitalization tests of lease accounting standards. Of course, debt covenants may be an issue motivating lessees to avoid capitalization.

It is not very difficult to structure a lease contract to defeat the four tests of SFAS No. 13 because the four tests are not stringent. A more challenging task, though, is to defeat lease capitalization tests for the lessee while satisfying them for the lessor. Lessors normally desire to capitalize leases and recognize sales revenue, but lessees prefer the effects of off-balance-sheet financing. One innovative method to accomplish both objectives is the use of third parties to guarantee residual values to the lessor: Such a procedure reduces the lessee's obligation under test (4) of SFAS No. 13 and, if significant enough, could lead to noncapitalization. However, there is no effect on the lessor because the lessor's accounting deals with the estimated residual value in total. No distinction is made between guaranteed and unguaranteed residual value.

Whenever accounting policies force unwanted results on companies, there will be creative activity to circumvent the unpopular policy. This is certainly the case with lease accounting. Because of the existing "let's beat SFAS No. 13" attitude, a strong case can be made for rigid uniformity. One solution would be to capitalize all leases that exceed one year. We already have suggestions for constructively capitalizing operating leases.[27] This unambiguous policy would eliminate the game playing and would also eliminate the somewhat artificial distinction still being made between capital and operating leases. As has been indicated throughout the chapter, it is somewhat arbitrary where the line is drawn between capital and operating leases. Therefore, a rigid policy of capitalizing all leases is an arguable improvement because it eliminates both the arbitrariness of where the line is drawn and the motivation to circumvent the finite uniformity established in SFAS No. 13. Moreover, there is growing sentiment for this position within standard-setting circles.[28] The G4+1 report, discussed below, provides an example of the way the wind may be blowing relative to wider lease capitalization.

Economic Consequences of Lease Capitalization

From the viewpoint of a company preparing financial statements, there are at least two types of economic consequences of lease accounting. One is the costs of complying with lease capitalization. More detailed analyses will be required by a company and its auditor in classifying leases as operating and capital. Recall that in Chapter 9 we saw that finite uniformity may impose a higher compliance cost than rigid uniformity. In addition, the accounting entries for each period will be more complicated if leases are capitalized. There has been no direct study of these types of costs; however, in 1973, one large company estimated it would cost $40,000 to install a lease capitalization system and $25,000 to $35,000 a year to operate it.[29]

The more critical concern has been whether lease capitalization might provide disincentives for leasing itself. From a lessee's perspective, leasing offered the possibility of off-balance-sheet financing for most leases prior to SFAS No. 13. A survey of lessees indicated that the effect on financial statements was a major reason for leasing.[30] Recent evidence from Australia indicates that when the Australian standard requiring lease capitalization was enacted, firms cut down on lease financing and substituted other forms of debt and used more equity financing.[31] Noncapitalization of leases improves debt ratios and accounting rate of return compared with a purchase/debt alternative. Some lessees also believed that noncapitalization of leases increased available capital because these leases do not affect borrowing restrictions in debt covenants and that the lower debt ratios that would be achieved by noncapitalization would result in better debt ratings and lower interest rates in the capital market. A study of pre–SFAS No. 13 lease accounting found that companies with high leverage levels were more likely to have reported their leases as operating rather than capital leases, which is consistent with the arguments above favoring off-balance-sheet financing.[32]

The argument against lease capitalization was presented to accounting policy makers in the following manner:

> The effects of treating leases as debt would extend beyond lessees to consumers and other parts of the economy. Increases in reported debt would tend to lead to an increase in interest rates and require an increased investment of equity capital requiring an even greater rate of return. This could contribute to inflationary pressures and act as a deterrent to investment in modernized or expanded plant and equipment.[33]

Neutrality tends to mitigate the preceding argument. Commenting on lease accounting, a former SEC chairman made these remarks:

> We recognize the usefulness of leases as a financing device. Economic objectives—including tax considerations—of two parties are frequently better satisfied by a lease arrangement than a purchase or sale. But leasing should not be made more attractive than it really is simply because of the way it is accounted for.[34]

It should not be the accounting per se that makes leasing attractive. If it is, the arguments favoring leasing are specious. The alleged advantages of off-balance-sheet financing have not been entirely supported by research evidence. For example, a survey of analysts indicated that the debt implication of noncapitalized leases is factored into the evaluation of companies.[35] In particular, the debt equivalent of leasing for lease-intensive industries was very well understood by analysts, even prior to SFAS No. 13. The general feeling was that lessees were usually within reasonable debt limits, even when lease effects were considered. So the survey evidence suggests that analysts were not fooled by off-balance-sheet lease financing even though company management seemed to believe otherwise. Consistent with these views, there is empirical evidence to support the view of leases "as if" they are debt equivalents in the pricing of stocks and bonds.[36]

The FASB commissioned a comprehensive research study of the economic and behavioral effects of SFAS No. 13.[37] One finding was that financial ratios and accounting rate of return of companies showed the expected changes owing to increased lease capitalization, although the change was smaller than anticipated. It was suggested that SFAS No. 13 had less impact than anticipated because pre-1977 leases did not have to be capitalized until 1980. This gave companies time to restructure leases as operating and to alter their capital structures to lessen the effects of capitalization on ratios. There was strong evidence that this type of behavior occurred; it reflects a belief in the naïveté of the market. Yet analysts surveyed in the same study professed not to be fooled by lease accounting differences (operating and capital) having no cash flow differences. The sophisticated-user viewpoint is also supported by a capital market study included in the assessment of SFAS No. 13 that showed no evidence of new information content in lease capitalization; that is, there was no abnormal security price response to the lease capitalization requirement. This is consistent with the efficient-markets hypothesis, particularly since similar information was required as a footnote disclosure under APB Opinion No. 31 prior to SFAS No. 13. In other words, the form of disclosure (footnote as in APB Opinion No. 31 or balance sheet as in SFAS No. 13) is not as important as the existence of disclosure per se.

Two other capital market studies offer additional evidence on lease accounting. One found that APB Opinion No. 31 disclosure requirements caused prices of affected companies to drop.[38] This can be interpreted to mean that the new lease disclosures of APB Opinion No. 31 had information content and that investors responded negatively to the revelation of hidden debt through lease financing. Such a finding is not surprising since the debt equivalent of most leases was not reported very well prior to APB Opinion No. 31. The second study found a negative price response during the time of the FASB's public hearings on leases in late 1974.[39] It was argued that the negative price response may have been caused by restrictive debt covenants that would have been violated if leases were capitalized. Such a situation was hypothesized to have possible adverse indirect cash flow consequences on the firm and its stockholders. This is an agency theory type of argument, and it does contradict survey evidence that analysts are not fooled by alternative accounting policies. The explanation may be that, prior to APB Opinion No. 31, analysts were really unaware of leases because there was very little reporting of them. But after APB Opinion No. 31, it mattered very little if the disclosures were made in footnotes or in the body of the balance sheet.

Another study evaluated the usefulness of lease capitalization in bankruptcy prediction.[40] Financial ratios, with and without lease capitalization, were compared to determine if the lease-adjusted ratios were better predictors. The study was made prior to both APB Opinion No. 31 and SFAS No. 13, so the effects of lease capitalization had to be approximated from rather limited footnote information. The results are interesting because they suggest that for bankruptcy prediction, at least, lease capitalization had no significant effect on the usefulness of accounting information. This finding partly contradicts survey research indicating that users believe lease capitalization is useful in predicting future cash flows and assessing debt-paying ability.[41]

Concerns about the adverse effects of lease capitalization seem to have been exaggerated, although the four-year phase-in period may have permitted companies to mitigate the anticipated adverse balance sheet effects. Management often continues to believe that noncapitalization offers some advantage, although user surveys and one capital market study suggest that lease capitalization has had no adverse impact. Holding aside the possible impact of lease capitalization on debt covenants, it could be argued that it is irrelevant whether lease information is disclosed as a footnote or in the body of the balance sheet. However, one prominent academic observed that footnote disclosure can give the impression that accountants do not know how to account for leases, so they absolve themselves of the problem through extensive disclosures.[42] Difficult accounting problems should not be dealt with through disclosure simply because disclosure is expedient and less controversial. The mandate of standard-setting bodies exists because of their technical competency and expertise in deciding controversial accounting issues. That mandate could easily be revoked if they fail to demonstrate competence and resolve.

The ferment over leases remains quite strong with respect to the so-called standards-overload problem. In a survey of private companies, the FASB reports that SFAS No. 13 is by far the most objectionable accounting standard to owners and auditors of the private companies surveyed.[43] The FASB has also hinted at a comprehensive review of lease accounting from time to time, but so far this has not occurred, although a recent study sponsored by major standard-setting organizations is bound to receive attention. We turn to this report next.

The G4+1 Report on Leases

Nailor and Lennard prepared a position paper on leases for the G4+1.[44] The G4+1 consist of the major standard-setting bodies from Australia, Canada, New Zealand, the United Kingdom, United States, and the International Accounting Standards Board. A *position paper* indicates that the topic is of great interest and importance, although there is no guarantee that the paper's recommendations will be put into effect by any of the member organizations. Nevertheless, as a position paper of the G4+1, the report occupies a very prominent place, even though the G4+1 was terminated in 2001.

The report can be summarized by saying that it would eliminate the distinction between operating and capital leases by making all leases capital leases. It would move leases from the area of finite uniformity to rigid uniformity. In addition, for the lessee it would result in showing what are now classified as operating leases as assets, which would certainly be the case since they embody the definition of assets from the conceptual framework (See definitions of SFAC No. 6 in Chapter 7) as containing "probable future economic benefits . . . controlled by a particular entity. . . ." Also, leases are liabilities since they result in "probable future sacrifices of economic benefits. . . ." Hence the ability of the enterprise to tailor lease contracts as operating leases with the nonappearance of debt in the balance sheet would be curtailed. Without the ability to hide debt, balance sheets would be more truthful and comparability would be enhanced.

Nailor and Lennard begin by separating leases from their possible classification as executory contracts discussed earlier. Once the lessor has delivered the property to the lessee, he or she has performed his or her portion of the contract, and the lessee has an obligation to pay for the property, hence a liability is created.[45] Other aspects of their approach also require scrutiny.

Renewal and Purchase Options of Lessees

Nailor and Lennard are generally against including renewal and purchase options in the initial asset and liability valuations of the lessee.[46] The reason for this, according to Nailor and Lennard, is that valuable options will be reflected in the lease rentals themselves.

In the case of an option to purchase at estimated fair market value, the option would not be overly valuable, although it would have some usefulness for the lessee. We would agree with Nailor and Lennard on not booking this type of option.

However, we would disagree with them on bargain purchase options. It is true that lease payments would reflect this type of option, but not wholly. If no bargain purchase option were included, lease payments would certainly be lower; but if the property reverted to the lessee at the end of the lease period, lease payments would certainly be higher. Of course, it is not clear at the inception of the lease whether the option will be exercised, but the presence of a bargain purchase option certainly indicates a high probability of exercise. Obviously we are in the realm of future events (Chapter 12) but usefulness of financial statements requires, we believe, inclusion of these values where a relatively high probability of exercise is present. Our position on booking the expected value of lease options where the probability of exercise is relatively high is in agreement with the American Accounting Association (AAA) Financial Accounting Standards Committee.[47]

Lessor Accounting

Lessor accounting, as envisaged by Nailor and Lennard, is generally the mirror image of lessee accounting. Operating leases would, of course, be gone. Where a residual interest in the asset exists for the lessor, the assets would include a financing asset—the lease receivable—and a property-type asset for the residual value. Different interest rates would prevail based on whether the residual value was guaranteed or unguaranteed. Unguaranteed residual values would require a higher interest rate owing to greater risk borne by the lessor pertaining to the value of the asset at the end of the lease period.

Other Aspects of the G4+1 Report

The interest rate used by the lessee for discounting the asset would be its incremental borrowing rate, which would reduce the lease asset and liability to fair market value because the rate includes risk inherent to the lessee.[48] The report does not state that the lessee should use the lessor's rate if (a) it is known to the lessee and (b) it is lower than the lessee's rate. This second aspect of the lessee's discount rate is used in SFAS No. 13 and attempts to promote conservatism (higher carrying value of the liability) rather than comparability, which results from the one rate.

Nailor and Lennard continue the single-transaction view of the sale-leaseback transaction discussed previously. Gains and losses arising from the sale by the lessee appear to be recognized immediately by the lessee rather than the SFAS No. 13 conservative approach of losses being recognized immediately but gains being amortized over the life of the lease.

One additional consequence would arise from the Nailor and Lennard lease proposal. No longer would corporations need to hire a battalion of consultants to help them structure leases so that they qualify as operating leases. From our viewpoint, capitalization via rigid uniformity is the best way to go. Operating lease consultants represent an uneconomic use of resources from the public standpoint. However, while lease accounting is back on the FASB's agenda, an exposure draft may not be out until 2009.[49]

Nailor and Lennard (and the G4+1) have made a signal contribution to lease accounting. While we disagree with the nonbooking by the lessee of significant option values held by the lessee, it is clear that this is an important report, which, hopefully, will lead to a careful scrutiny of the entire spectrum of lease accounting.[50]

Lease Accounting Under the IASB

Lease accounting under the IASB is similar—and different—than under the FASB. The difference is that the FASB, as we have just seen, has a rules-based orientation (Chapter 10) with "bright lines" carefully laid out (the 75% rule).

In IAS 17, a considerably shorter document than SFAS No. 13, a capital lease results when the lease is for "the major part" of an asset's economic life or the present value of the minimum lease payments are "substantially all" of the leased asset's economic value. Hence, IAS 13 requires more judgment than SFAS No. 13, but manipulation can occur under either standard.

To help bring about convergence, in December 2006, the IASB and FASB announced formation of the International Working Group on Lease Accounting. The first step in the project is the development of a discussion paper, scheduled for publication in 2008.

Improving Accounting Standards

In line with the G4+1 report, eliminate the distinction between operating and capital leases. All leases should become capital leases. We would not, however, eliminate valuable lease options from lessee asset and liability measurements.

Summary

Lease accounting represents a classic example of the search for meaningful finite uniformity. Using a broad classification of leases as operating or capital, the search has taken the direction of defining the criteria for classification. This has led to an emphasis on economic substance rather than legal form. The substance of capital leases is argued to be a purchase equivalent with debt financing for the lessee. For the lessor, a capital lease is analogous to a sale with vendor financing if it is a sales-type lease, and to a loan equivalent if it is a financing-type lease. It is somewhat arbitrary where the line is drawn between operating and capital leases. Over time, the criteria have changed, which clearly reflects the subjective nature of the criteria and the difficulty in achieving finite uniformity.

Because the distinction between operating and capital leases is somewhat arbitrary, the economic consequences of lease capitalization are very important in evaluating lease accounting standards. Management attitudes frequently show a belief in the market's naïveté—specifically, the advantages of off-balance-sheet financing. The evidence, however, supports the supposition that users are sophisticated with respect to lease reporting and that they are not fooled by lease accounting differences, at least after APB Opinion No. 31. Finally, there is survey and capital market research to support the position that the reporting of capital leases is useful and relevant. However, a strong case can be made for capitalizing all leases extending beyond one year. This type of rigid uniformity would eliminate the attempts to circumvent SFAS No. 13. This is exactly what the recent G4+1 special report has advocated. This move is long overdue.

QUESTIONS

1. What is the argument for finite uniformity in accounting for leases? Why is finite uniformity difficult to achieve? Explain what the relevant circumstances are in accounting for different types of leases.

2. Why is the conveyancing aspect of leases emphasized in capital leases and the contractual element emphasized in operating leases?

3. What are the similarities and differences between leases and other means of property acquisition? How can these similarities and differences be reported in the financial statements?

4. Is the executory nature of lease contracts important in assessing lease accounting? How have leases been interpreted? Why might noncancellability override the executory nature?

5. Review the evolution of capitalization criteria in lease accounting standards. Why did APB Opinion No. 5 have little impact? What impact has SFAS No. 13 had? Has there been an underlying theme in the development of lease accounting?

6. Does it matter if capital leases are reported in a footnote or in the body of the balance sheet? What research evidence exists to help evaluate this question?

7. Does symmetry exist between lessors and lessees under SFAS No. 13? Should symmetry be a goal of lease accounting?

8. How is representational faithfulness achieved in the capitalization requirements of SFAS No. 13?

9. Is there a measurement reliability (verifiability) problem with lease capitalization?

10. Evaluate the manner in which initial direct lease costs are accounted for under SFAS No. 13 for sales-type and financing-type leases.

11. Why was there some reason to expect negative economic consequences arising from lease capitalization? What is the role of neutrality in such a situation? What has been the response based on research findings to date?

12. Does the reporting of capital leases appear to have value to users of financial statements? Why are there costs of reporting capital leases?

13. What considerations may have motivated the FASB to grant a four-year transitional period in capitalizing pre-1977 leases meeting the capitalization tests of SFAS No. 13? What other political behavior is evident in the evolution of lease accounting?

14. Should valuable lease options of lessees be capitalized?

15. Why is the G4+1 like the Big Ten (a.k.a. Western Athletic Conference)?

16. Why is the IASB standard on leases (IAS 7) substantially shorter than the FASB's standard (SFAS No. 13)?

CASES, PROBLEMS, AND WRITING ASSIGNMENTS

1. Human Genome Sciences, Inc., a biopharmaceutical company, discovers, develops, and markets new gene and protein-based drugs. Its 1998 annual report showed property, plant, and equipment net of accumulated depreciation of $20,965,000 with total net assets of $244,247,000.

   A note on operating leases revealed the following:

   Operating Leases

   The Company leases office and laboratory premises and equipment pursuant to operating leases expiring at various dates through 2017. The leases contain various renewal options.

   Minimum annual rentals are as follows:

   Years Ending December 31,

1999	$5,990,790
2000	6,074,955
2001	6,197,186
2002	6,278,051
2003	5,353,707
Thereafter (2004–2017)	35,001,144
	$64,895,833

Required:

    a. Assume that the company's cost of debt is 10% and that operating lease payments between 2004 and 2017 are equal amounts per year. By how much would Human Genome Sciences' property, plant, and equipment and its total net assets increase by on December 31, 1998, if these leases were capitalized?

b. Assume that the company's net income for 1998 was $20 million. What was its return on assets (ROA) (1) before and (2) after capitalizing the operating leases? Use straight-line depreciation over 14 years for the capitalized leases. Operating lease expense for 1998 is $5,900,000.

2. Wright Company leases an asset for five years on December 31, 2000. Annual lease cost of $10,000 is payable on each December 31 beginning with the year 2001. In addition to the annual lease cost, the lease contract calls for a guaranteed residual value of $3,000. The asset has an economic life of seven years. Wright's incremental borrowing rate is 8%. The asset has an acquisition cost of $45,000. There are no purchase options.

Required:

a. As things now stand, is this a capital lease or an operating lease? Show figures.
b. What can Wright do to convert this lease to an operating lease? Explain and show figures.
c. Will lessee and lessor's accounting for this lease be symmetrical (capital lease for both lessor and lessee or operating lease for both lessor and lessee)? Explain.
d. Do you think that Wright's action in (b) represents a loophole to avoid capitalization or is it a useful part of the present leasing rules? Explain.

3. Assume the following facts concerning a sales-type lease:
   - The lease term is three years and qualifies as a capital lease for both lessor and lessee. The asset reverts to the lessor at the end of the lease term. Assume straight-line depreciation by the lessee.
   - Payments are $50,000 at the beginning of each year, plus a guaranteed residual value of $10,000 at the end of the lease term. The lessor estimates a total residual value of $15,000. Lease payments include $4,000 for executory costs under a maintenance agreement.
   - Initial direct costs associated with the lease are $2,700.
   - Cash sales price of the asset is $137,102.50. Lessor's manufacturing cost is $100,000.
   - The lessee does not know the lessor's implicit rate, but its own incremental borrowing rate is 11%.

Required:
a. Prepare the accounting entries for both lessor and lessee for the three years. What happens in Year 3 if residual value is only $8,000?
b. Assume the same facts as before except that the asset is first sold to a finance company, which then leases the asset to the lessee. Prepare the required entries in all three years for lessor and lessee.
c. Evaluate the differences between requirements (a) and (b) as well as the differences between lessor and lessee.

4. One of the four capitalization tests of SFAS No. 13 is that the lease term is 75% or more of the asset's remaining economic life. *Lease term* is defined as follows in SFAS No. 13 (as amended by SFAS No. 98, para. 22a):

The fixed noncancellable term of the lease plus (i) all periods, if any, covered by *bargain renewal options*, (ii) all periods, if any, for which failure to renew the lease imposes a penalty on the lessee in an amount such that renewal appears, at the *inception of the lease*, to be reasonably assured, (iii) all periods, if any, covered by ordinary renewal options during which a guarantee by the lessee of the lessor's debt related to the leased property is expected to be in effect, (iv) all periods, if any, covered by ordinary renewal options preceding the date as of which a *bargain purchase option* is exercisable, and (v) all periods, if any, representing *renewals or extensions* of the lease at the lessor's option; however, in no case shall the lease term extend beyond the date a *bargain purchase option* becomes exercisable. A lease which is cancellable (i) only upon the occurrence of some remote contingency, (ii) only with the permission of the lessor, (iii) only if the lessee enters into a new lease with the same lessor, or (iv) only upon payment by the lessee of a penalty in an amount such that continuation of the lease appears, at *inception,* reasonably assured shall be considered "noncancellable" for purposes of this definition. [All italics added.]

Required:

How can this test be circumvented through either the structuring of the lease contract or interpretation of the test? What are other ways in which lease capitalization could be avoided through the structuring of lease terms or interpretation of the tests? What problem does this exercise illustrate?

5. This problem shows the importance of considering the importance of converting operating leases to capital leases for the purpose of financial statement analysis. It is based on the techniques developed and illustrated in Imhoff, Lipe, and Wright (1991 and 1997), although it is much simplified from their presentation.

McAdoo Restaurants is a large franchise. Their balance sheet showed the following on December 31, 2000 (in thousands).

Assets (net)	$80,000	Liabilities	$45,000
		Owners' equity	35,000
Assets	$80,000	Liabilities and equities	$80,000

Net income after taxes was $6,500 for 2001. McAdoo's marginal tax rate is 35%. On December 31, 2000, McAdoo entered into several major lease contracts. These leases were all for 10 years and were operating leases. Starting in 2001, total annual lease payments, due on each December 31, are $3,000. McAdoo's marginal cost of capital rate is 10%. No change in liabilities occurred during the year, and there were no transactions with owners.

Required:

a. Convert the operating lease to a capital lease that is one year old. (Hint: Use the present value of a 10-year ordinary annuity.) Assume that straight-line depreciation is used for both book and tax purposes. There would be a zero salvage value.
b. Determine the net income after taxes if the leases are treated as capital leases.
c. Determine the return on assets under the (1) operating lease assumption and (2) capital lease assumption.
d. Determine the debt-equity ratio under the (1) operating lease assumption and (2) capital lease assumption.

   e. Do you think it is useful to convert operating leases to capital leases for financial statement analysis purposes? Discuss.

6. SFAS No. 98, which contained some amendments to SFAS No. 13, passed by a 4 to 3 vote. The following dissent to the opinion was made:

Messrs. Beresford, Lauver, and Swieringa dissent because this Statement prescribes different accounting for certain sale-leaseback transactions based on a distinction between active (as defined) and other use of leased property by a seller-lessee. That distinction is without economic substance and is used to arbitrarily preclude sale-leaseback accounting when a seller-lessee subleases the leased property.

Paragraph 48 acknowledges that a leaseback is a form of continuing involvement with leased property but argues that the form of that involvement is different if the seller-lessee intends to sublease that property. In a sale-leaseback transaction, the seller-lessee has exchanged ownership rights for lease rights, and the rights to use the leased property and to benefit from that use are the same regardless of how that property is used. Moreover, any guarantee of the cash flows related to the leased property is lodged in the lease contract and is not altered by what the seller-lessee does with that property.

An objective of financial reporting is to achieve greater comparability of accounting information. Paragraph 119 of *FASB Concepts Statement No. 2, Qualitative Characteristics of Accounting Information,* states that this objective is not to be attained by making unlike things look alike any more than by making like things look different. The moral is that in seeking comparability accountants must not disguise real differences nor create false differences.

Messrs. Beresford, Lauver, and Swieringa believe that this Statement makes like things look different by prescribing different accounting for certain sale-leaseback transactions based on the distinction between active and other use of leased property, a distinction not relevant to the accounting. Because that distinction arbitrarily limits the extent to which sale-leaseback accounting is permitted, the effects of accounting for identical sale-leaseback transactions will be different.

The majority's position was expanded upon in Paragraph 48 of *SFAS No. 98* in the section on "Basis for Conclusions":

48. Some respondents to the Exposure Draft noted that the nature of the continuing involvement associated with a normal leaseback does not change because of the seller-lessee's intent to occupy the property. The Board acknowledges that the leaseback is a form of continuing involvement with the property that serves as support for the buyer-lessor's investment.

Accordingly, the Board believes that transactions accounted for as sales should be limited when a sale-leaseback of property exists; otherwise, the effectiveness of paragraph 28 of Statement 66 would be compromised. Occupancy of the property by the seller-lessee provides a basis for distinguishing among sale-leaseback transactions involving real estate, including real estate with equipment.

The Board believes that the intent to sublease the property represents a different form of continuing involvement than does the intent to occupy and use the property in the seller-lessee's trade or business. When the property is subleased, the form and consequences of the seller-lessee's continuing involvement are equivalent to those of a real estate investor or developer whose ultimate source, timing, and amount of cash flows from the use of the property are different from those realized by a tenant. Based on those differences, the Board decided to reaffirm the Exposure Draft's provision to allow sale-leaseback accounting when the seller-lessee occupies the leased property.

The positions of both the majority and the dissenters center on issues of uniformity and comparability.

Required:

a. Using the perspective on uniformity developed in Chapter 9, analyze the rigid versus finite uniformity approach to the distinction between the two positions.

CRITICAL THINKING AND ANALYSIS

1. Should all leases beyond a year be capitalized?

Notes

1. *Committee on Accounting Procedure (1949).*
2. *Hawkins and Wehle (1973, p. 51).*
3. *FASB (1985).*
4. *APB (1964, para. 10).*
5. *Cook, D. C. (1963) and Zises (1973).*
6. *Anthony (1962).*
7. *FASB (1974, pp. 40–41).*
8. *This view is attributed to Myers (1962).*
9. *FASB (1976, para. 60).*
10. *Hawkins (1970).*
11. *Alvin (1970).*
12. *FASB (1974, pp. 95–97).*
13. *Committee on Accounting Procedure (1953, Chapter 14).*
14. *Myers (1962).*
15. *FASB (1974, pp. 159–160) indicates that there was only a modest increase in the number of leases capitalized after APB Opinion No. 5 was issued and that most of the increase was due to a new type of lease related to Industrial Development Bonds, which met the capitalization criteria.*
16. *APB (1966b).*
17. *SEC (1972). This requirement extended the reporting of capitalized leases between related parties and represented an interpretation of APB Opinion No. 5, paras. 10–12.*
18. *APB (1973).*

19. *SEC (1973).*

20. *APB (1971).*

21. *FASB (1985, paras. 25–40). This argument is substantially used by Nailor and Lennard (2000).*

22. *APB (1966a).*

23. *APB (1972).*

24. *FASB (1976, para. 18b) as amended by FASB (1986).*

25. *Other standards include SFAS Nos. 17, 22, 23, 26, 27, 28, and 29. These have been compiled in a single publication (FASB, 1980). A number of technical bulletins related to leases have been issued since 1980, but only two standards: SFAS Nos. 91 and 98.*

26. *For example, see Means and Kazenski (1987) for an inconsistency in SFAS No. 91 in the handling of initial direct costs in financing-type leases. This was subsequently corrected in para. 22, item i, of SFAS No. 98.*

27. *See Imhoff, Lipe, and Wright (1991 and 1997).*

28. *See McGregor (1996).*

29. *This evidence is anecdotal but was reported in Hawkins and Wehle (1973, p. 100).*

30. *Hawkins and Wehle (1973).*

31. *Godfrey and Warren (1995).*

32. *El-Gazzar, Lilien, and Pastena (1986).*

33. *Committee on Corporate Reporting of the Financial Executives Institute (1971, p. 237). This group is now called Financial Executives International.*

34. *Cook, G. B. (1973).*

35. *Hawkins and Wehle (1973).*

36. *Abdel-khalik, Thompson, and Taylor (1978), Bowman (1980), Imhoff, Lipe, and Wright (1993), and Ely (1995).*

37. *Abdel-khalik (1981). For a summary of recent empirical accounting research on leases, see Lipe (2001).*

38. *Ro. (1978).*

39. *Pfeiffer (1980).*

40. *Elam (1975).*

41. *Abdel-khalik (1981).*

42. *Anthony (1962).*

43. *FASB (1983).*

44. *Nailor and Lennard (2000).*

45. *Ibid. (p. 13).*

46. *Ibid. (p. 31).*

47. *AAA Financial Accounting Standards Committee (2001, p. 294).*

48. *Nailor and Lennard (2000, p. 71).*

49. *Heffes (2006).*

50. *Monson (2001) has embraced an aspect of lessee accounting that has been rejected by Nailor and Lennard. He would use the "whole asset" approach, which would book the entire value of an asset even though it may be leased for only a fraction of its expected operating life. We believe that this approach attempts to make the lease as similar as possible to a purchase, which it is not. We do not believe that the whole asset approach is representationally faithful, more useful, or would lead to greater comparability than the "financial components" approach, which books the asset just for its lease period plus additional periods where valuable options have been acquired.*

References

Abdel-khalik, A. Rashad (1981). *The Economic Effects on Lessees of FASB Statement No. 13*, Accounting for Leases. FASB.

Abdel-khalik, A. Rashad, Robert B. Thompson, and Robert E. Taylor (1978). "The Impact of Reporting Leases off the Balance Sheet on Bond Risk Premiums: Two Exploratory Studies," *Economic Consequences of Financial Accounting Standards.* FASB, pp. 103–155.

Accounting Principles Board (1964). APB Opinion No. 5, *Reporting of Leases in the Financial Statements of Lessee.* AICPA.

———— (1966a). APB Opinion No. 7, *Accounting for Leases in Financial Statements of Lessors.* AICPA.

———— (1966b). APB Opinion No. 10, *Omnibus Opinion.* AICPA.

———— (1971). APB Opinion No. 21, *Interest on Receivables and Payables.* AICPA.

———— (1972). APB Opinion No. 27, *Accounting for Lease Transactions by Manufacturer or Dealer Lessors.* AICPA.

———— (1973). APB Opinion No. 31, *Disclosure of Lease Commitments by Lessees.* AICPA.

Alvin, Gerald (March 1970). "Resolving the Inconsistency in Accounting for Leases," *New York Certified Public Accountant*, pp. 223–230.

American Accounting Association Financial Accounting Standards Committee (September 2001). "Evaluation of the Lease Accounting Proposed in the G4+1 Special Report," *Accounting Horizons*, pp. 289–298.

Anthony, Robert N. (1962). Letter to Weldon Powell, Chairman of the Accounting Principles Board (October 25). Cited in Financial Accounting Standards Board (1974, p. 39).

Bowman, Robert G. (April 1980). "The Debt Equivalence of Leases: An Empirical Investigation," *Accounting Review*, pp. 237–253.

Committee on Accounting Procedure (1949). ARB No. 38, *Disclosure of Long-Term Leases in Financial Statements of Lessees.* AICPA.

———— (1953). ARB No. 43, *Restatement and Revision of Accounting Research Bulletins.* AICPA.

Committee on Corporate Reporting of the Financial Executives Institute (1971). Cited in *Proceedings of the Accounting Principles Board of the American Institute of Certified Public Accountants: Public Hearing on Leases.* AICPA.

Cook, Donald C. (January–February 1963). "The Case Against Capitalizing Leases," *Harvard Business Review*, pp. 145–162.

Cook, G. Bradford (1973). "The Commission and the Regulation of Public Utilities" (Paper presented to the Financial Forum of the American Gas Association, Monterey, CA, 1974), cited in Financial Accounting Standards Board (1974, p. 38).

Elam, Rick (January 1975). "The Effect of Lease Data on the Predictive Ability of Financial Ratios," *Accounting Review*, pp. 25–43.

El-Gazzar, Samir, Steve Lilien, and Victor Pastena (October 1986). "Accounting for Leases by Lessees," *Journal of Accounting and Economics*, pp. 217–237.

Ely, Kirsten (Autumn 1995). "Operating Lease Accounting and the Market's Assessment of Equity Risk," *Journal of Accounting Research*, pp. 397–415.

Financial Accounting Standards Board (1974). FASB Discussion Memorandum: *An Analysis of Issues Related to Accounting for Leases.* FASB.

———— (1976). Statement of Financial Accounting Standards No. 13, *Accounting for Leases.* FASB.

———— (1980). *Accounting for Leases.* FASB.

———— (1983). *Financial Reporting by Privately Owned Companies: Summary of Responses to FASB Invitation to Comment.* FASB.

———— (1985). Statement of Financial Accounting Concepts No. 6, *Elements of Financial Statements.* FASB.

———— (1986). Statement of Financial Accounting Standards No. 91, *Accounting for Nonrefundable Fees and Costs Associated With Originating or Acquiring Loans and Initial Direct Costs of Leases.* FASB.

———— (1988). Statement of Financial Accounting Standards No. 98, *Accounting for Leases: Sale-Leaseback Transactions Involving Real Estate; Sales-Type Leases of Real Estate; Definition of the Lease Term; Initial Direct Cost of Direct Financing Leases.* FASB.

Godfrey, Jayne, and Susan Warren (September 1995). "Lessee Reactions to Regulation of Accounting for Leases," *Abacus*, pp. 201–228.

Hawkins, David M. (November 1970). "Objectives, Not Rules, for Lease Accounting," *Financial Executive*, pp. 30–38.

Hawkins, David M., and Mary M. Wehle (1973). *Accounting for Leases*. Research Foundation of Financial Executives Institute.

Heffes, Ellen (October 2006). "Leasing Back on FASB's Agenda; ED Likely in '09," *Financial Executive*, pp. 16–17.

Imhoff, Eugene, Robert Lipe, and David Wright (March 1991). "Operating Leases: Impact of Constructive Capitalization," *Accounting Horizons*, pp. 51–63.

——— (Fall 1993). "The Effects of Recognition Versus Disclosure on Shareholder Risk and Executive Compensation," *Journal of Accounting, Auditing & Finance*, pp. 335–368.

——— (June 1997). "Operating Leases: Income Effects of Constructive Capitalization," *Accounting Horizons*, pp. 12–32.

Lipe, Robert C. (September 2001). "Lease Accounting Research and the G4+1 Proposal," *Accounting Horizons*, pp. 299–310.

McGregor, W. (1996). *Accounting for Leases: A New Approach*. FASB.

Means, Kathryn M., and Paul M. Kazenski (December 1987). "SFAS 91: New Dilemmas," *Accounting Horizons*, pp. 63–67.

Monson, Dennis (September 2001). "The Conceptual Framework and Accounting for Leases," *Accounting Horizons*, pp. 275–287.

Myers, John H. (1962). Accounting Research Study No. 4, *Reporting of Leases in Financial Statements*. AICPA.

Nailor, Hans, and A. Lennard (2000). *Leases: Implementation of a New Approach*. Special Report prepared for the G4+1. FASB.

Pfeiffer, G. (1980). "The Economic Effects of Accounting Policy Regulation; Evidence on the Lease Accounting Issue" (PhD diss., Cornell University).

Ro, Byung T. (Autumn 1978). "The Disclosure of Capitalized Lease Information and Stock Prices," *Journal of Accounting Research*, pp. 315–340.

Securities and Exchange Commission (1972). Accounting Series Release No. 132, *Reporting Leases in Financial Statements of Lessees*. SEC.

——— (1973). Accounting Series Release No. 147, *Notice of Adoption of Amendments to Regulation S-X Requiring Improved Disclosure of Leases*. SEC.

Zises, Alvin (August 1973). "The Pseudo-Lease—Trap and Time Bomb," *Financial Executive*, pp. 20–25.

18

Intercorporate
Equity Investments

Learning Objectives

After reading this chapter, you should be able to:

- Comprehend relevant circumstances in intercorporate equity investments.
- Understand the change to goodwill brought about by Statement of Financial Accounting Standards (SFAS) No. 142.
- Understand purchase and pooling methods of consolidation and understand why pooling was eliminated.
- Understand the new entity approach to consolidation.
- Understand proportionate consolidation.
- Understand the equity method and why it is called a "one-line consolidation."
- Understand the fair value method where "significant" influence is absent.
- Understand the nature of special purpose entities and variable interest entities.
- Grasp the significance of defining the reporting entity.
- Understand why the Financial Accounting Standards Board (FASB) moved from the temporal method of SFAS No. 8 to the functional currency approach of SFAS No. 52.

Mergers and acquisitions have been an important part of the business scene for many years, with the 1980s and 1990s being periods of particularly high activity. At their best, mergers and acquisitions have resulted in important efficiencies and synergies. However, many mergers and acquisitions have not been well thought out and many corporate leaders appear to have become addicted to them. For example, companies such as AutoNation, Tyco, U.S. Office Products, and AT&T each acquired more than 100 firms between June 1995 and August 2001.[1] In a study conducted by *Business Week* of 302 mergers and acquisitions for this same period, it was found that the least successful acquisitions resulted from acquirers paying excessive premiums for the stock of acquired firms.[2] As a result, shareholders of acquiring firms suffered serious decreases in the value of their shares, whereas shareholders of the acquired firms generally made at least modest gains. In addition to excessive premiums being paid, many cost savings and synergies that were expected simply did not pan out, adding to subsequent stock price declines of acquiring corporations.[3]

Extensive changes have recently occurred in the United States in business combinations accounting. Pooling of interests, which brought the assets of acquired firms forward at historical cost as if a purchase transaction did not occur, simply bit the dust. A major change also occurred in purchase accounting situations in which goodwill was created owing to a premium being paid for an acquisition above the fair value of the net assets being acquired. Instead of goodwill being amortized over a period not to exceed 40 years, goodwill is not to be written down unless it becomes "impaired." Both the elimination of pooling and the change to goodwill will be discussed in this chapter. We shall also discuss the now infamous special purpose entity, in Appendix 18-A, a vehicle conceived to move liabilities off of the balance sheet but was additionally used, in some cases, to defraud both the shareholders and the firm itself.

Accounting standards for intercorporate equity investments represent the most extensive application of finite uniformity in accounting practice. The basic framework is set out in Exhibit 18.1. There are three ways to report on intercorporate equity investments: (1) consolidated reporting as if the two separate legal entities are one accounting entity using the purchase method, (2) nonconsolidation using the equity method of accounting, and (3) nonconsolidation using the fair (market) value approaches discussed in Chapter 11. However, we foresee further changes coming to intercorporate equity investments arising as a result of the movement toward fair values in SFAS No. 157. This should eventually result in the equity method becoming obsolete. We discuss the relevant circumstances that determine the method of reporting in the first section of the chapter and then go into detail on each of the methods. Under consolidation we discuss pooling of interests, even though it is no longer allowed for new acquisitions.

Exhibit 18.1   Finite Uniformity for Intercorporate Equity Investments

Ownership of Voting Stock	Accounting Method
>50%	Consolidate per ARB 51 (as amended by SFAS No. 94) and SFAS Nos. 141 and 142.
*20% to 50%	Equity accounting per APB Opinion No. 18.
<*20%	Fair (market) value for both trading securities and available-for-sale securities where unrealized gains and losses go to comprehensive income per SFAS No. 130 for the former and to income for the latter per SFAS No. 115.

*20 percent is only a guideline, not a rigid rule.

We also mention two other methods of consolidation that have received some support: (1) the new entity approach and (2) proportionate consolidation. After discussing the equity and fair value methods for less-than-full consolidation situations, we examine the nature of the reporting entity and how it might change in the future. We conclude the body of the chapter by examining foreign currency translation under Statements of Financial Accounting Standards (SFASs) Nos. 8 and 52. Appendix 18-A discusses special purpose entities and their successor, variable interest entities, and closes with a few words on the Enron fiasco.

Relevant Circumstances

The relevant circumstances that justify differential accounting for intercorporate equity investments depend on the level of influence held by the investor. In a seminal study, Moonitz evaluated several criteria, such as percentage of voting stock owned, controlling influence on the board of directors, and operating or managerial control.[4] He concluded that no one dimension can be used to determine the level of investor influence that exists. Not surprisingly, however, standard-setting bodies have focused on a single quantitative criterion—percentage of voting stock owned—as the basis for evaluating the level of influence. For convenience, we shall refer to this as *level of control*.

Three levels of control have been defined along with three distinctly different reporting methods for each level. Traditionally, outright control of the majority of voting stock has been the criterion for consolidated reporting. In fact, the Securities and Exchange Commission (SEC) prohibits consolidation of a subsidiary company unless majority ownership exists. Accounting Research Bulletin (ARB) 51 took a more cautious view that majority ownership per se did not indicate control if ownership were temporary or if for some reason control did not reside with the majority owner. In addition, ARB 51 specifically permitted separate reporting for *heterogeneous* subsidiaries instead of consolidation, and Chapter 12 of ARB 43 permitted a similar exception for foreign subsidiaries. The rationale for these two exclusions was based on the argument that (a) a heterogeneous subsidiary—such as a finance company subsidiary of a manufacturing firm (General Motors Acceptance Corporation and General Motors, for example)—would only distort the reporting of the main operations of the consolidated entity and (b) in the case of foreign operations, most foreign assets are in some degree of jeopardy as far as their ultimate realization by U.S. owners is concerned. These exceptions represented a further finite uniformity based on the circumstances of homogeneity versus heterogeneity of operations and whether a domestic or foreign subsidiary is involved.

In SFAS No. 94, the Financial Accounting Standards Board (FASB) rejected these exclusionary arguments and now requires *all* majority-owned companies to be consolidated except when control is only temporary or if the majority owner does not have effective control. The effect of SFAS No. 94 is to bring large amounts of debt onto the consolidated balance sheet that had previously been transferred to the subsidiary, an important economic consequence.[5]

SFAS No. 94 does not elaborate on the issue of temporary control, but it says that noncontrol by a majority owner may occur if the subsidiary is in legal reorganization or bankruptcy, or operates under foreign exchange restrictions or other governmentally imposed uncertainties that are so substantial as to cast doubt on the owner's ability to exercise control. In defense of SFAS No. 94, the FASB asserts that investors of a parent company are really investing in a group of affiliated companies as a whole, that consolidated statements are thus more relevant in reporting on the group, and that the omission of certain subsidiaries therefore fails to faithfully represent (representational faithfulness) the group of affiliated companies as a whole.[6] Beatty and Hand found some evidence that the FASB was attempting to "level the playing field" in SFAS No. 94 by requiring companies to provide more information to financial statement users who might not have been aware of debt levels carried by unconsolidated subsidiaries prior to SFAS No. 94.[7] We return to these issues at the end of the chapter when examining the problem of defining the reporting entity.

For less-than-majority-owned companies, the appropriate reporting is either the equity method or the fair value method. The relevant circumstance is whether the investor can exercise *significant influence* over operating and financial policies. In other words, *effective control* leads to consolidated reporting as if the two companies were one entity. But a lesser level of control can also exist in which there is significant influence but not effective control. In Accounting Principles Board (APB) Opinion No. 18, it was presumed that ownership of 20% to 50% of voting stock was prima facie evidence of the ability to exercise significant influence. However, FASB Interpretation No. 35 clarified that the relevant circumstance is the ability to exercise significant influence and that the 20% ownership level is only a guideline, not a hard and fast rule.[8] If there is no significant influence, then the fair value method of accounting is required under SFAS No. 115.

Consolidation

Consolidated reporting is a technique in which two or more entities are reported as if they are one common accounting entity. This is also called a *business combination.* To prepare consolidated financial statements, separate sets of individual entity accounting records must be combined and certain other adjustments made to arrive at the consolidated totals. Adjustment procedures are covered at length in advanced financial accounting textbooks. The focus here is on the conceptual foundation of accounting for business combinations, not on the consolidation adjustment procedures themselves. Terminology regarding business combinations is not uniform throughout the accounting literature. In this chapter, the following terms suggested by the FASB are used:

- *Combined enterprise:* The accounting entity that results from a business combination
- *Combinee:* A constituent company other than the combinor in a combination in which a combinor is identifiable
- *Combinor:* A constituent company entering into a combination whose stockholders (owners) as a group end up with control of the voting stock (ownership interests) of the combined enterprise
- *Constituent companies:* Separate business enterprises that enter into a business combination[9]

The central accounting issue in a business combination is the valuation of the assets and liabilities of the separate entities being combined for reporting purposes. In a 1976 discussion memorandum, the FASB outlined three possible methods of accounting. One is to use the book values of the combining entities. This method is called *pooling of interests accounting.*

A second method assumes that one entity, the parent company, "purchases" another entity, the subsidiary company. Assets and liabilities of the subsidiary are valued at market value at the time of purchase, and the parent's assets and liabilities are valued at book value. This is called *purchase accounting*. The third method, sometimes referred to as the *new entity approach*, results in all entities' assets and liabilities being revalued to market values at the time the combination originates. The central problem faced by standard-setting bodies is whether there are relevant circumstances to justify the use of more than one method to account for different types of business combinations.

While our emphasis is on consolidation accounting, a few words should be said about divestitures—disposals of the controlling interest in a subsidiary. There are four types of divestitures, as described by Cumming and Mallie.[10]

1. A *sell-off* occurs when the subsidiary's stock is sold for cash, assets, or in settlement of a debt.

2. A *spin-off* occurs when the subsidiary's stock is distributed to the combinor's shareholders as a dividend.[11]

3. A *split-off* occurs when the subsidiary's shares are distributed to the combinor's shareholders in exchange for shares of the parent's stock.

4. A *split-up* occurs when the shares of two or more subsidiaries are distributed to the combinor's shareholders in exchange for all of the parent's shares, with the parent then liquidated.

Pooling of Interests

The pooling of interests concept of a business combination is based on the premise that no substantive transaction occurs between the constituent companies. Rather, they merely unite their respective ownership interests and continue as if they are a single enterprise. The first applications of the pooling of interests concept resembled an internal reorganization more than a business combination—for example, the combination of two subsidiaries of the same parent enterprise. In such a situation, no new entity was established by the combination; the two already-related entities merely added together their previously separate financial statements to effect the combination. Pooling of interests started just that way, but eventually the method began to be applied to the combination of unrelated constituent companies. It was at this juncture that questions about pooling accounting began to arise.

What is the conceptual justification for pooling accounting? A pooling of interests is argued to be simply the formal unification of two previously separate ownership groups. The two agree to combine, or pool, their equity interests and continue as if they are a single enterprise. That is, there is a swap of equity shares in which the combinor company exchanges its shares for the outstanding shares of the combinee company. There is no purchase by one constituent of the other; thus, the assumption is that no exchange transaction occurs but that assets and liabilities are combined at their book values. Pooling is analogous to the concept of a nonmonetary exchange of similar fixed assets under APB Opinion No. 29, and as a result, the pooled assets and liabilities have the same basis of accounting in the combination as they did separately before the combination. The book values of the combined enterprise's assets and liabilities after the combination will be equal to the summation of the combinor's and combinee's respective book values just prior to the combination. Total stockholders' equity of the combined enterprise will also be equal to the sum of the constituent corporate stockholders' equities immediately prior to the combination. There may be some changes in individual components, depending on the exchange ratio, but in aggregate the combined stockholders' equity is the sum of the precombination totals. Of course, one might equally well argue that as a result of the pooling a new entity exists and a totally new basis of accounting should be used in the consolidated accounting for this new entity (see following discussion).

The justification for pooling is, we believe, largely a fiction. The desirability of pooling is to avoid certain ramifications of purchase accounting: (a) By combining assets at historical costs, future income would be higher because it would avoid booking acquired assets at the purchase price (which would usually be higher than the combinee's historical cost) and (b) it would avoid booking goodwill.

A whole series of accounting standards attempted to differentiate poolings from purchases. These included ARB 40 (codified as ARB 43, Chapter 7C), ARB 48, and—most extensively—APB Opinion No. 16. APB Opinion No. 16 set up an extensive set of qualifying criteria that differentiated pooling from purchases.

While pooling of interests has been eliminated for new acquisitions by SFAS No. 141, older acquisitions accounted for as poolings will not be changed; this would have been an onerous job. Thus, consolidated statements will have some discrepancies by combining assets of subsidiaries acquired using two different methods: purchase and pooling. The same applies for segmental analysis (SFAS No. 131). Of course, the only way to eliminate these discrepancies would be to go to fair value accounting (Chapter 14), in which assets are continually updated to their current values.

The Purchase Method

In purchase accounting, the assumption is that the combinor is a parent company that purchases the combinee (subsidiary) and must account for the purchase as it would for the acquisition of any asset. The asset, investment in the combinee company, is recorded by the combinor at the latter's cost determined as of the date the combination is consummated.[12] This results in the consolidated reporting of the combinee's net assets at their fair market value at the date of combination. Accounting for the combination, however, may be complicated for several reasons:

- If part of the price paid is of a noncash nature, the total cost of the combinee may not be readily obvious.
- The fair value of the combinee's assets and liabilities probably is not readily available because its statement of financial position reports only book values and, in fact, may not report all assets, such as internally developed assets.
- In consolidations where the combinee acquires less than 100% of the common stock of the combinee, a minority interest is created.[13]
- Frequently, the total cost of the combinee is not equal to the summation of the fair values of its individual assets less liabilities, and the purchase differential must be dealt with in some manner. Traditionally, this difference has been called *goodwill*.

SFAS No. 141

With the elimination of pooling, SFAS No. 141 stated that comparability between firms would be improved as would prediction of future cash flows because newly acquired assets would be booked at fair market value rather than historical cost of the combinee.[14] Prior to SFAS No. 142, the FASB actually considered shortening the write-off period of goodwill from a maximum of 40 years to 20 years in the exposure draft of September 7, 1999. We turn next to SFAS No. 142, which reversed course on goodwill write-off.

SFAS No. 142 and Goodwill

Coming out simultaneously with SFAS No. 141 was SFAS No. 142 on goodwill. The essence of SFAS No. 142 is that goodwill is converted into an intangible asset with an indefinite life but is subject to write-off as an expense if it becomes "impaired." Tests of impairment must be made on an annual basis.

SFAS No. 142 requires a very careful delineation between goodwill and other intangible assets. Acquired research and development costs, if present, are immediately expensed. Other intangible assets include marketing-related intangibles (e.g., trademarks), customer-related intangibles (e.g., customer lists), contract-based intangibles (e.g., licensing and royalty agreements), and technology-based intangibles (e.g., computer software and patented technology). Goodwill is numerically defined as the difference between the amount paid for an acquired subsidiary and the fair market value of its individual net assets (assets minus liabilities). *Goodwill* represents the difference between the value of the enterprise as a totality and the fair market value of the individual assets and liabilities thereof. Goodwill might therefore be defined as the excess earning power of the acquisition.

Tests of Impairment. The basic impairment test after acquisition would compare (a) the fair market value of the acquisition against (b) the historical cost of the net assets plus goodwill at an annual measurement date after acquisition. If (a) is greater than (b), no impairment has occurred. However, if (b) is greater than (a), goodwill is impaired and the impaired amount is written off as a loss appearing above income from continuing operations.[15] The loss cannot exceed the recorded amount of goodwill, nor can goodwill, once written off, be restored. If circumstances merit it, tests of impairment should be done more frequently than annually.

The reporting unit for the impairment test would be done in accordance with SFAS No. 131 on segmental reporting and, therefore, done in line with how management itself assesses its reporting segments. A reporting unit would be an operating segment of the firm or possibly one level below, known as a component. A *component* would be a reporting unit if separable financial and operating information is available and the operating segment regularly reviews that information. Two or more components of an operating segment can be combined if they have similar economic characteristics. On occasion, the acquired entity might be broken apart for segmental reporting purposes or it might be combined with an already-owned entity. These situations might entail an allocation of goodwill between (or among) segmental units.

Of more significance is the question of how to measure the fair market value of the reporting unit when the impairment test is made. If shares of the reporting unit are still being traded, this might give both a representationally faithful and highly verifiable measure of fair market value of the segment.[16] In the absence of a market value stemming from quoted security prices, a discounted cash flow determination of estimated future cash flows might be used or even multiples of revenues or incomes of the unit.[17] Clearly these latter measures might have deficiencies of both representational faithfulness and verifiability.

For the value of the net assets of the acquisition or reporting unit, a fair value estimate of the individual net assets at the impairment test date was desired, but this method was considered too costly.[18] Hence the Board settled for a purchase price allocation (which basically means historical cost) for the reporting unit, including intangibles and goodwill to be measured against the fair market value of the reporting unit as an entity.

Finally, in the event of the sale of an acquired subsidiary, any goodwill attributable to the subsidiary must go off the books.[19]

Evaluating SFAS No. 142

The FASB's conception of goodwill as an asset with indefinite life but subject to impairment tests is a not unrealistic conception of this type of intangible. Indeed, there has been a long-held view going back many years that goodwill should not be amortized.[20] The problem with SFAS No. 142 is that it smacks of a quid pro quo: Since SFAS No. 141 closed out poolings, SFAS No. 142 may have been designed to provide a sop to firms for losing poolings.[21] Indeed Abraham Briloff, a retired professor from Baruch College of the City University of New York and a long-time critic of the FASB has stated, "The FASB has given the store away. . . . The FASB has capitulated to the pragmatic world of the companies that want to provide the highest level of earnings numbers they can generate."[22]

One also wonders if write-off manipulations might arise because the impairment rules are generally going to generate soft numbers with low verifiability (although AOL, the purchaser of Time Warner, wrote off $54 billion dollars of goodwill). SFAS No. 142 also goes beyond international accounting standards (Chapter 10), which require a finite life for goodwill. Despite questions and trepidations, SFAS No. 142 does provide a more theoretically satisfying interpretation than its predecessor, APB Opinion No. 17.

The New Entity Approach

Another possible method of accounting for a business combination is to regard the combined enterprise as an entirely new entity. This approach results in the use of current values for the assets and liabilities of all the separate entities. The reason for such an approach would be that the business combination results in a substantially new accounting entity. In other words, more is involved than merely one entity purchasing and integrating another into its own operation. The very nature of the combination may be such that an entirely new operation has come into existence. This approach to accounting for business combinations is not used in practice (except for statutory mergers), but it was identified as a possibility in the 1976 FASB discussion memorandum on business combinations.

In effect, it appears that SFAS No. 157 on fair value measurement or its successor will eventually bring about the new entity approach. However, there are still other possibilities, such as proportionate consolidation.

Proportionate Consolidation

Another method of consolidation that has been proposed is called *proportionate consolidation* (also called *pro rata* consolidation). As its name implies, consolidation of assets and liabilities occurs only to the extent of the stock acquired by the parent. A simple example, as shown in Exhibit 18.2, compares consolidation accounting with the proportionate consolidation approach, where Parent Company has acquired 80% of Sub Company at book value.

In the proportionate consolidation, only part of assets and liabilities acquired is consolidated. The implicit assumption in full consolidation is that the combinor controls all of the combinee's assets and liabilities. Only the proportion of assets actually acquired, as represented by the stock purchase, is consolidated under proportionate consolidation. One major advantage of proportionate consolidation discussed by Bierman is that an arbitrary distinction at the 50% point where control is assumed does not exist under proportionate consolidation.[23] Thus, Exhibit 18.2 could have been just as easily set up to reflect a 40% interest in Sub Company as opposed to the 80% actually used. Theoretically, one could use proportionate consolidation throughout the ownership range. Proportionate consolidation would thus be an example of rigid uniformity. It would be analogous to capitalizing all long-term leases rather than employing the capital versus operating lease distinction with an arbitrary potential break at the 75% of estimated economic life point. There may be a relatively low percentage of ownership where proportionate consolidation is not used and the fair value approach

Exhibit 18.2   Comparison of Consolidation Accounting With Proportionate Consolidation

	Parent Company	*Sub Company*	*Consolidation*	*Proportionate Consolidation*
Assets	$10,000	$6,000	$16,000	14,800[a]
Investment in 80% of Sub Company	$4,000[c]	–	–	–
Total	$14,000	$6,000	$16,000	$14,800
Liabilities	$6,000	$1,000	$7,000	$6,800[b]
Stockholders' equity	8,000	5,000	8,000	8,000
Minority interest	–	–	1,000	–
Total	$14,000	$6,000	$16,000	$14,800

[a] $10,000 + .8($6,000) = $14,800
[b] In this example, the investee was acquired at book value, which is also assumed to equal market value. As with full consolidation, proportionate consolidation would value assets and liabilities at the acquired (market) value, which may result in goodwill appearing on the proportionately consolidated balance sheet.
[c] $6,000 + .8($1,000) = $6,800

is employed with the stock investment shown as a current asset. This would be analogous to capitalizing all leases except for those with a life of a year or less.

Another possible advantage of proportionate consolidation is that the minority interest category does not arise. Minority interest has appeared in consolidations as a liability, between liabilities and stockholders' equity, and as an element of stockholders' equity.[24] However, the predominant view, as well as positions taken by FASB in the conceptual framework and a recent discussion memorandum, takes the viewpoint that minority interest is part of owners' equity.[25]

Minority interests can also be created in what has been called an *equity carve-out*. The equity carve-out arises when a combinor sells a portion of its interest in a combinee or dilutes its interest through an initial public offering of the subsidiary. Carve-out gains, under Staff Accounting Bulletin No. 51 of the SEC, can either be taken directly to owners' equity or booked as nonoperating income.[26] Whether this unusual choice will continue to be allowed remains to be seen, particularly in light of SFAS No. 130 on comprehensive income.

The question remains, however, as to whether proportionate consolidation would be more useful than the present approaches. Bierman generally sees proportionate consolidation as being useful, but a report by the AICPA Special Committee on Financial Reporting rejected proportionate consolidation on the grounds that users in their surveys preferred disaggregated data showing the risks and opportunities of the separate segments.[27] According to the report, separate information about segments is a key to usefulness, regardless of whether the equity method or full consolidation is being used. One of the problems with proportionate consolidation is that, despite less than 100% ownership, the combinor may well have virtually complete control of the combinee's net assets and would thus understate the controlling power of the combinor if proportionate consolidation were used. Proportionate consolidation remains, nevertheless, an interesting idea that might be combined with adequate segmental disclosure.[28]

Research on Pooling and Purchase Accounting

Earlier in the chapter we stated that pooling of interests accounting was viewed as an important motivation for business combinations. A FASB survey found that 66% of enterprises having entered into poolings believed that the combinations would not have occurred if purchase accounting had been required.[29] As would be expected, there is considerable evidence that the probability of pooling increased the larger the potential goodwill was, owing to the adverse impact of goodwill upon earnings.[30] On the other hand, purchase accounting would be more likely if the firm's assets need to be increased to avoid violating leverage-based debt covenants.[31] Pooling of interests generally produces more favorable financial statements than purchase accounting because combined assets are not revalued. Pooled financial statements would thus report higher income since depreciation, cost of goods sold, etc. would *not* be calculated on the basis of higher valued assets, nor would there be any amortization of the purchase differential (goodwill). In addition, return on investment would be greater owing to both a higher income level and a lower asset base.

Research has also been conducted to determine the attitude of financial statement users toward the two accounting methods. Interestingly, the two methods have been favored about equally. A FASB survey found that 40% preferred pooling of interests; 45%, purchase accounting; and 15%, a new accounting basis for both combinor and combinee.[32] Another survey of financial analysts found 46.7% preferred purchase accounting and 43.3% favored pooling of interests.[33] Although some academic researchers have taken a very critical stance on pooling of interests, it is interesting to see that the method has had a following with financial analysts.[34] *Accounting Trends and Techniques* reported that approximately 89% of combinations were accounted for as purchases.[35]

Finally, there has been some limited research to determine how the two accounting methods affect the security price of the combinor company. One study found no evidence that pooling accounting caused higher stock prices. In other words, the stock market did not appear to be fooled by the higher income reported under the pooling method.[36] This finding is consistent with capital market research regarding the sophistication of users of accounting information. However, in an experimental study involving 113 buy-side analysts, researchers found that analysts' price judgments were lower for purchases than for poolings, which generally goes against the idea of the market "seeing through" the bookkeeping applied to the transaction.[37]

What insight does empirical research give into the purchase/pooling question? Management seems to prefer pooling because of its favorable financial statement effect. However, security price research has generally shown that the market is not fooled or deceived by book profits arising solely from the way in which business combinations are accounted for. If the market is not fooled, one could argue that it makes no difference which method is used, so long as the method is disclosed. This is the efficient-market school of thought. Yet, if it really makes no difference, why bother having two methods of accounting for similar but subtly different phenomena, since it has proved difficult to specify the relevant circumstances that would justify the two very different accounting methods? Thus, eliminating pooling in SFAS No. 141 seems to be in line with both theoretical insights and empirical research.

The Equity Method

The equity method of accounting for investments in equity securities is used whenever the investor has the ability to exercise significant influence over the investee. If the investor's investment does not establish control (that is, ownership is not greater than 50%), consolidated financial statements are not required. Rather, what is frequently referred to as a *one-line consolidation* takes place: The investment account is used to reflect the investor's underlying book value of equity in the investee. Many of the mechanical adjustments that are required for consolidated financial statements (e.g., recognition and amortization of goodwill) are also required for a one-line consolidation—except that only the net effect of those adjustments is reported in the investment account rather than a consolidated reporting of all of the individual accounts actually involved.[38] Thus, the income statement under equity accounting is the same as if consolidated reporting had been used (after deducting minority interest in consolidated income). However, because of the absence of effective control, the investee's assets and liabilities are not reported as if they are owned outright as occurs with consolidated reporting. Rather, the investment account simply mirrors the net change in investee book value.

The investment is recorded at cost plus transaction costs. At the time of the investment, the investor must determine if more (or less) was paid than the underlying book value acquired. For example, assume P Company purchased 25% of S Company's voting stock for $100,000 when S Company's book value was $300,000. P Company paid $25,000 over the underlying book value of S Company ($100,000 – [$300,000][.25] = $25,000). An attempt should be made to determine what specific assets of S Company are undervalued; however, as is more often the case, the $25,000 is arbitrarily assumed to be attributable to goodwill and would have been amortized over a maximum of 40 years as allowed by APB Opinion No. 17. As with consolidations, goodwill in equity method situations would not be written off but would be subject to impairment.

Two events must be recorded in the investment account for each reporting period: (a) proportionate share of investee's income or loss for the period and (b) proportionate share of investee's cash dividend for the period. The investor's proportionate share of the investee's net income is recorded as a debit to the investment account and a credit to income from equity investments. The investor's proportionate share of the investee's cash dividends is recorded as a debit to cash and a credit to the investment account. Intercompany profits and losses are eliminated, and other adjustments typically made in consolidation also are recorded. The result is that one line on the balance sheet, the investment account, and one line on the income statement, the income from equity investments account, are reported as if consolidation had occurred.

In terms of both relevance and representational faithfulness, one may question the usefulness of the equity method. The investment account represents neither the cost nor the market value of that investment. Moreover, one cannot determine from the income statement the actual amount of dividends received from investments.

The lack of information under the equity method and the preference for proportionate consolidation is confirmed by Bauman.[39] The move toward fair values in SFAS No. 157 spells the virtual death knell for the equity method. APB Opinion No. 18 on the equity method is listed in SFAS No. 157 as a pronouncement in Appendix D that refers to fair value, but no further action against the equity method was taken there. However, the end is clearly in sight for the equity method.

The Fair Value Method

SFAS No. 115 replaced SFAS No. 12 where no significant influence exists in equity investments. The fair value approaches for shares classified as either trading securities or available-for-sale securities have already been discussed in Chapter 11. Fair value is readily determinable where sales price is available on SEC-registered exchanges or is published by recognized national publication systems for over-the-counter securities.[40] Foreign securities have readily determinable fair values when they are traded in markets similar to American markets if fair value is used. If fair value is not readily determinable, the investment would be carried at cost with income being credited for dividends received.

There are a plethora of valuation methods now in existence for intercorporate stock investments. Market value applies where no significant influence exists and market values are readily determinable for investments of approximately 20% or less. Increases or decreases in market value may go through income or comprehensive income, depending on management's intention to sell them in the near term. The adjusted cost basis applies where the equity method is deemed appropriate for investments of under 50%. Historical costs apply under poolings for both the combinor's statement alone and consolidated statements. Assets and liabilities of the combinee are brought forward at the combinee's historical cost. Where consolidations are employed using the purchase method, the combinor's acquisition price is used, which will include purchased goodwill if applicable. Whether all of these different valuation approaches are justified is an interesting question. SFAS No. 115 could yet have influence on equity and consolidation accounting.

Defining the Reporting Entity

SFAS No. 94, in justifying mandatory consolidation for *all* majority-owned investments, reiterated the rationale of ARB 51:

> The purpose of consolidated statements is to present, primarily for the benefit of the shareholders and creditors of the parent company, the results of operations and the financial position of a parent company and its subsidiaries essentially as if the group were a single company with one or more branches or divisions. There is a presumption that consolidated statements are more meaningful than separate statements and that they are usually necessary for a fair presentation when one of the companies in the group directly or indirectly has a controlling financial interest in the other companies.[41]

Thus, the FASB maintains that consolidated reporting is the most appropriate way to report, but this is little more than an assertion or presumption. At the heart of the consolidation issue is a deeper question concerning the definition of the reporting entity. To its credit, the FASB recognized this and in 1986 added the question of the reporting entity to its agenda (although the Board also made clear in doing so that it was not reopening the purchase-pooling debate). However, SFAS No. 94 was issued *before* any conclusion was reached concerning the reporting entity, which undermines the logic of that standard. Consolidation reporting presumes, then, that the accounting fiction of a group entity is more meaningful than defining the reporting entity in legal terms: that is, as the parent company alone, perhaps supplemented with the separate financial statements of other companies that are majority owned.

So SFAS No. 94 simply asserts, rather than demonstrates, that consolidated reporting (and the fictional accounting entity thus created) is more relevant to investors than are separate entity statements in which the reporting entity is the legal entity. The usefulness of consolidated reports has been questioned by Walker.[42] He rejects the claim that consolidated income statements provide a better basis for reporting parent company income than do parent company statements alone. From the complementary predictive standpoint, he rejects the contention that consolidated income statements, along with the income statements of subsidiary companies, provide a better basis for predicting the earnings of those subsidiaries than the subsidiaries' income statements alone.

The preceding discussion suggests that the consolidation question should not be reduced to a question of whether it is the right or only way of reporting. Rather, consolidation is a useful way of summarizing overall results *as if* an affiliated group were one legal entity. But such a method necessarily fails to report on the *real* separate legal entities, and for this reason there is bound to be a loss of information with respect to the separate legal entities.[43] SFAS No. 94 recognizes that consolidated statements do cause a loss of detail through the aggregation process. In fact, a number of studies have found that disaggregated data (by product line) are more useful in forecasting earnings and in valuing the firm.[44] Hence, the AICPA Special Committee on Financial Reporting, with its emphasis on the importance of disaggregated data, is in concurrence with these studies, which resulted in SFAS No. 131.

Consider the situation in which there are *no* cross-guarantees of debt between a parent company and its majority-owned (subsidiary) companies. In this situation, consolidated statements are misleading with respect to the debt situation of the parent company because the parent's assets are completely sheltered from any liability claims of the subsidiaries' debt holders. Indeed, this is one motivation for establishing a subsidiary structure as opposed to a divisional structure for the firm.

A simple example will illustrate the problem. Assume a 60%-owned subsidiary with assets of $2,000,000 and liabilities of $1,000,000 and a parent company with assets of $2,000,000 (excluding its investment in the subsidiary) and liabilities of $1,000,000. On a parent-only basis, which is the *legal* situation with respect to parent company debt, the ratio of debt to assets is 38.5% (parent debt of $1,000,000 divided by parent assets of $2,000,000 plus the parent's 60% equity in the *net* assets of $1,000,000). But on a consolidated basis, the ratio increases to 50% (parent debt of $1,000,000 plus subsidiary debt of the same amount divided by parent assets of $2,000,000 plus subsidiary assets of $2,000,000). These relationships are illustrated in Exhibit 18.3.

Of course, when there are cross-guarantees of debt, it follows that consolidated statements are *more* informative than separate entity statements. It should also be borne in mind that the opposite situation can also arise: Debts could be fully guaranteed by the investor in an unconsolidated investee with mention only in the footnotes. Indeed, there is some evidence that cross-guarantees of debt may have, at least in part, led to the voluntary adoption of consolidated reporting before it was required by regulation.[45]

The point that emerges here is simply that it is naive to presume consolidated reporting is always, under all conditions, preferable to reporting of the separate legal entities. Yet, this is exactly how consolidated statements have come to be viewed in the United States. Consolidated reporting emerged in the early 1900s in response to the growth of holding (parent) companies, and consolidated statements had already been substituted for parent-only statements by the time the Securities Acts of 1933 and 1934 were passed.[46] By contrast, holding companies and consolidation accounting came onto the British scene at the time of an already-existing regulatory framework, the British Companies Acts. As a result, consolidated reporting did not substitute for parent-only statements but was required as a *supplement* to them. In fact, parent-only statements are still required, and separate subsidiary

Exhibit 18.3   Debt-to-Asset Ratios Under Separate, Consolidated, and Proportionate Consolidation Approaches

	Parent	Subsidiary	Consolidated	Proportionate Consolidation
Assets	$2,000,000	$2,000,000	$4,000,000	$3,200,000
Investment in subsidiary	600,000			
Total assets	$2,600,000	$2,000,000	$4,000,000	$3,200,000
Liabilities	1,000,000	1,000,000	2,000,000	1,600,000
Minority interest			400,000	
Shareholders' equity	1,600,000	1,000,000	1,600,000	1,600,000
Total equities	$2,600,000	$2,000,000	$4,000,000	$3,200,000
Debt-to-asset ratio	38.5%		50%	50%

NOTE: For the consolidated entity, the investment in the subsidiary was eliminated against the subsidiary's shareholders' equity, with the balance becoming minority interest.

company statements can still be reported in lieu of consolidation, although consolidation is virtually the universal way of reporting subsidiary companies.

Furthermore, there are moves afoot to extend consolidated reporting. Whether the FASB will broaden the definition of *control* and require consolidation below 50% ownership is an open question. Nevertheless, new and interesting proposals have been forthcoming. King and Lembke would extend full consolidation based on control to nonownership situations such as leasing all of the assets of another firm under a long-term noncancellable lease and in certain unincorporated joint venture situations, for example.[47] They would introduce proportionate consolidation in situations in which control is less clear-cut, such as joint ventures with shared control, where the operations of the investor and investee are related.[48] King and Lembke would use the equity method where the investor has a beneficial financial interest (a financial interest in the investee's assets or profits as well as being a direct beneficiary of its operations or assets) and can "significantly influence or jointly control the investee on a continuing basis."[49] In situations of less-than-equity control, they would use the cost method, but SFAS No. 115 on market values had not yet appeared. King and Lembke are attempting to extend representational faithfulness to intercorporate investments by means of extending the span of finite uniformity. While their approach might yield financial reporting dividends, provided that adequate controls could be put on their combinatorial criteria, the question of which way to go relative to defining the reporting entity has still not been satisfactorily answered.

Translation of Foreign Operations

Translation of foreign-based operations and holdings into U.S. dollars has been addressed by all three standard-setting bodies. The Committee on Accounting Procedure (CAP) issued two

Accounting Research Bulletins (ARBs) on the subject (4 and 43); the Accounting Principles Board (APB) issued APB Opinion No. 6 and discussed the subject at length in 1971 but did not issue a pronouncement; and the FASB has issued three SFASs (Nos. 1, 8, and 52). The accounting issue is how to report foreign-currency-denominated operations in consolidated financial statements that are expressed in U.S. dollars. Hence, exchange rate differentials are critical.

The Bretton Woods Agreement of 1944 essentially set up a system of what might be termed "controlled floating exchange rates" for those nations that were signatories to the agreement. Fluctuations of exchange rates were allowed within certain limits with monetary actions such as monetary authorities buying or selling gold or foreign exchange that was intended to maintain the allowable range of fluctuation. The Bretton Woods Agreement collapsed in 1971, resulting in much freer and more volatile exchange rate fluctuations since that time. This development has heightened the importance of how translation of foreign-based operations should be handled.

What determines the exchange rate between currencies of different countries? Exchange rates are assumed to be the result of two factors: (1) different nominal interest rates arising from differences in expected inflation rates occurring in different countries and (2) the ratio of the relative prices of a common "market basket" of goods and services of two particular countries as expressed by the price level of one country divided by the price level of the second country.[50] Purchasing power parity—constancy of the price level ratio between different currencies—was expected to be stable, but it now appears that purchasing power parity does not hold in either the short-run or the long-run.[51] Both as a result of different expected rates of inflation in different countries and the lack of purchasing power parity, there is an instability in foreign exchange rates that has the potential to create large translation gains and losses. Hence, what exchange rate to use and how to dispose of the differential resulting from the translation process become key questions.[52]

There are numerous approaches to the translation of foreign operations, but all stem from the basic orientation one adopts. A *U.S. dollar orientation* requires an enterprise to account for foreign operations as if those operations actually occurred in U.S. dollars. That is, foreign-currency-denominated assets, liabilities, revenues, and expenses are reported as if originally recorded in U.S. dollars. On the other hand, a *foreign currency orientation* recognizes that the foreign operations occurred in a foreign currency and that those operations may not affect U.S. dollars; therefore, accounting should be consistent with the foreign-currency economic impact of the operations. Foreign-currency-denominated assets, liabilities, revenues, and expenses are assumed to be measured in the foreign currency but are translated to U.S. dollars for reporting purposes.[53] Consistent with the foreign orientation is the notion that exchange rate changes do not affect operations or cash flows until the net assets are exchanged. Therefore, the effects of changing exchange rates should not be reported in income until the net assets are exchanged.

SFAS No. 8

SFAS No. 8 and previous standards were consistent with the U.S. dollar orientation. The *temporal* method of translation was required by SFAS No. 8: All balance sheet items that were carried at current or future exchange prices (for example, monetary assets and liabilities, inventories at market price, and investments at market price) were translated at the current exchange rate, while items carried at past prices (for example, fixed assets) were translated at exchange rates existing at the time the item was acquired (that is, the historical exchange rate). Income statement items were translated at the average exchange rate for the reporting period—except that items related to balance sheet accounts that were translated at historical exchange rates (for example, cost of goods sold and depreciation) were also translated at the historical rates. The exchange adjustment, the amount required to balance the statements owing to different translation rates, was reported each period on the income statement as an exchange gain or loss.[54] This complex translation was necessary to convert foreign currency account balances to their U.S. dollar equivalent—that is, to arrive at the same dollar amount as if dollars had been used as the accounting basis all along.

SFAS No. 8 was faithful to the historical cost accounting model, but from an economic viewpoint it produced illogical results. For example, assume a Swiss subsidiary of a U.S. enterprise borrows $100 million in Swiss francs to finance the construction of a plant that costs $120 million in Swiss francs. Swiss franc revenues generated from use of the new plant will be used to retire the Swiss franc debt; therefore, no U.S. dollars will be used. If the franc appreciates 10% against the U.S. dollar, the liability would be written up to $110 million and an "accounting loss" of $10 million would be reported in the consolidated financial statements in accordance with SFAS No. 8. Because the cost of the plant is translated at the historical rate, however, no recognition would be given to the fact that the plant may be "worth" more in terms of its future net revenue stream in francs that will be used to retire the debt.

The preceding transaction may be viewed economically in two ways: (1) A gain of $2 million occurred because the building is "worth" $12 million more, while the debt owed is only $10 million more; or (2) no gain or loss occurred because the Swiss subsidiary is self-contained and its operations do not affect the U.S. parent's cash flows, nor do exchange rate changes affect the subsidiary's cash flows. As can be seen, accounting numbers produced by SFAS No. 8, although faithful to the historical cost model, did not necessarily reflect the perceived economic impact of the foreign operations.

A number of empirical studies were made of the economic impact of SFAS No. 8 on American multinational enterprises. Although the studies were directed to many facets of the subject, the only aspect that was found to have any possible impact dealt with foreign exchange risk and management policies regarding hedging of foreign currency exposures. Foreign currency exposure may be defined as either accounting or economic exposure. *Accounting exposure* is the exposure to exchange gains and losses resulting from translating foreign-currency-denominated financial statements into U.S. dollars (for example, the $10 million we have just been considering). *Economic exposure* is the exposure to cash flow changes resulting from dealings in foreign-denominated transactions and commitments (for example, the need to use more U.S. dollars to settle a foreign-currency-denominated debt).

In general, accounting exposure does not affect foreign currency cash flows, nor does it affect reporting currency cash flows (that is, U.S. dollars). Rather, it results in "paper" debits and credits. An example is the translation of the $110 million liability of the preceding example; it would result in reporting a $10 million loss but would not affect either Swiss franc or U.S. dollar cash flows. As a result, accounting exposures can lead to economic conse-quences: Noncash flow gains and losses can result in actions to eliminate their effect on income. On the other hand, economic exposure does directly affect consolidated cash flows. An example would be if the $110 million Swiss franc debt were settled using U.S. dollars rather than Swiss francs.

Many studies found that multinational enterprises adopted policies of minimizing account-ing exposure through hedging activities.[55] Unfortunately, accounting exposure and economic exposure frequently were opposite; for example, there might be a large potential accounting gain or loss with little if any cash flow implications (economic exposure). The result, then, was that many enterprises were risking cash resources through forward exchange contracts to hedge a noncash exposure, creating a real (economic) exposure. Those enterprises, in essence, were transferring a foreign exchange loss under SFAS No. 8 into an interest cost and simultaneously risking greater economic exposure.

SFAS No. 52

In May 1978, the FASB requested comments from constituents regarding the first 12 SFASs. Eighty-eight percent of the comments received requested that the Board reconsider SFAS No. 8. The primary complaints about SFAS No. 8 were similar to those illustrated in the pre-ceding example: Exchange gains and losses are reported, when from an economic viewpoint the reverse had occurred.

SFAS No. 52 changes drastically the means of accounting for foreign currency operations. It adopts a functional currency orientation rather than a U.S. dollar orientation. The *functional currency* is the currency of the subsidiary's "primary economic environment," where cash is primarily received and spent.[56]

If the foreign entity's currency is the functional currency, net income is measured in the foreign currency and then restated into dollars at the average exchange rate for the period. All balance sheet items are translated at the current exchange rate at the end of the period. Any exchange adjustment resulting from translating balance sheet and income statement items at different exchange rates is displayed as a separate component of stockholders' equity, not as a gain or loss on the income statement, thus leading to a situation of nonarticulation prior to the passage of SFAS No. 130 on comprehensive income.

The objective of translation under SFAS No. 52, then, is to avoid reporting (a) accounting exchange gains and losses when an economic gain or loss has not occurred and (b) foreign-currency-denominated operations as if they had occurred in U.S. dollars.[57] Thus, if the results of foreign-currency-denominated operations will not affect U.S. dollar cash flows, no exchange gain or loss is recorded. Moreover, assets, liabilities, revenues, and expenses that are denomi-nated in a foreign currency are measured in that currency and then translated to U.S. dollars. Bartov found a significant positive association between currency translation adjustments and changes in stock prices for enterprises where the functional currency is the foreign currency but no relation where the U.S. dollar is the functional currency (these latter firms would still be using the temporal method tantamount to SFAS No. 8).[58]

The key question brought up in SFAS No. 52 involves determination of the functional cur-rency. The FASB has stated that where an enterprise's operations are "relatively self-contained and integrated within a particular country, the functional currency generally would be the currency of that country."[59] This would not always be the case, however, particularly if the foreign operations are a mere extension of the operations of the parent. SFAS No. 52 does not provide "unequivocal" criteria for determining the functional currency, but it does provide extensive guidelines. The six guidelines or economic factors do have, as the discussion in the standard indicates, a differential cash flow orientation:

1. Cash flow indicators

   a. Foreign currency—Cash flows related to the foreign entity's individual assets and liabilities are primarily in the foreign currency and do not directly impact the parent company's cash flows.

   b. Parent's currency—Cash flows related to the foreign entity's individual assets and liabilities directly impact the parent's cash flows on a current basis and are readily available for remittance to the parent company.

2. Sales price indicators

   a. Foreign currency—Sales prices for the foreign entity's products are not primarily responsive on a short-term basis to changes in exchange rates but are determined more by local competition or local government regulation.

   b. Parent's currency—Sales prices for the foreign entity's products are primarily responsive on a short-term basis to changes in exchange rates; for example, sales prices are determined more by worldwide competition or by international prices.

3. Sales market indicators

   a. Foreign currency—There is an active local sales market for the foreign entity's products, although there also might be significant amounts of exports.

   b. Parent's currency—The sales market is mostly in the parent's country, or sales contracts are denominated in the parent's currency.

4. Expense indicators

   a. Foreign currency—Labor, materials, and other costs for the foreign entity's products or services are primarily local costs, even though there also might be imports from other countries.

   b. Parent's currency—Labor, materials, and other costs for the foreign entity's products or services, on a continuing basis, are primarily costs for components obtained from the country in which the parent company is located.

5. Financing indicators

   a. Foreign currency—Financing is primarily denominated in foreign currency, and funds generated by the foreign entity's operations are sufficient to service existing and normally expected debt obligations.

   b. Parent's currency—Financing is primarily from the parent or other dollar-denominated obligations, or funds generated by the foreign entity's operations are not sufficient to service existing and normally expected debt obligations without the infusion of additional funds from the parent company. Infusion of additional funds from the parent company for expansion is not a factor, provided funds generated by the foreign entity's expanded operations are expected to be sufficient to service that additional financing.

6. Intercompany transactions and arrangements indicators

   a. Foreign currency—There is a low volume of intercompany transactions, and there is not an extensive interrelationship between the operations of the foreign entity and the parent company. However, the foreign entity's operations may rely on the parent's or affiliates' competitive advantages, such as patents and trademarks.

b.   Parent's currency—There is a high volume of intercompany transactions and there is an extensive interrelationship between the operations of the foreign entity and the parent company. Additionally, the parent's currency generally would be the functional currency if the foreign entity is a device or shell corporation for holding investments, obligations, intangible assets, etc. that could readily be carried on the parent's or an affiliate's books.[60]

SOURCE: FASB Statement No. 52, Foreign Currency Translation. Used with permission of FASB.

The FASB research report by Evans and Doupnik found that the six criteria provided adequate guidance for determining the functional currency. Furthermore, the respondents to the study agreed very strongly that the standard works well.[61] Of the six indicators, the four that were most heavily weighted were the first four discussed above.[62] Only a small percentage of the participants had difficulty in determining the functional currency in many cases. In terms of the extent of numbers of functional currencies that had to be determined, the maximum number was in the lower 50s and the mean number was 14.[63] Hence, determining the functional currency as well as actually doing the translating can be an extremely significant problem.

If the functional currency of a foreign operation is judged to be U.S. dollars, a different approach is taken. For example, if a foreign subsidiary of a U.S. parent is, in reality, an extension of the parent (that is, it is nothing more than a sales branch selling the U.S. parent's products and remitting the sales proceeds to the U.S. parent), then although the subsidiary's records are kept in a foreign currency, the functional currency is the U.S. dollar, and the accounting records must be converted into U.S. dollars. This is called *remeasurement* and is done by following the approach in SFAS No. 8 discussed previously. As a result, exchange gains and losses arising from translation from the currency of record into the functional currency would be recognized on the income statement. Thus, in certain situations, SFAS No. 52 will result in the same reporting as SFAS No. 8.[64]

Although remeasurement may appear inconsistent with the approach adopted in SFAS No. 52, it is entirely consistent on theoretical grounds. The theory behind the functional currency concept is that some foreign subsidiaries are self-contained and that exchange rate fluctuations affect neither them nor their U.S. parent companies until cash is exchanged. On the other hand, however, if the functional currency is really the U.S. dollar, the presumption is that the foreign operation is not self-contained but rather an extension of the parent. Consequently, exchange rate fluctuations will affect cash flows and should be reported on the income statement as was done under SFAS No. 8. Remeasurement in SFAS No. 52 is an example of finite uniformity involving present magnitudes.

A problem does occur with the functional currency concept and the use of current exchange rates whenever the functional currency is too unstable to be used as a measurement base. This problem is referred to as the *"disappearing asset problem"* and is present when the functional currency is experiencing rapid inflation much in excess of that experienced in the reporting currency. For example, assume an Argentine subsidiary purchased a fixed asset in December 1974 when the Argentina peso–U.S. dollar exchange rate was $.20. The asset cost

20,000,000 pesos and would be translated as $4,000,000. By September 1982, the exchange rate was .000040; thus, the asset would be translated at $800.

At least three approaches are available for accounting for the disappearing asset problem. It could be ignored—so the asset would be translated at $800. The original exposure draft leading up to SFAS No. 52 adopted this position, but most of the comment letters received by the FASB objected. In the second exposure draft, the FASB proposed to adjust cost of the asset in pesos for the effects of changing prices and translate the adjusted amount at the current exchange rate. Although this approach probably is sound theoretically, it too met with considerable objection because it would result in introducing onto U.S. consolidated financial statements something that is not permitted for changes in prices denominated in U.S. dollars. Finally, in SFAS No. 52, the FASB specified that in highly inflationary economies (defined as those with a cumulative inflation rate of approximately 100% over three years), the U.S. dollar should be used as if it were the functional currency. Translations, therefore, are similar to the SFAS No. 8 approach, and fixed assets are translated at the historical rate (for example, $.20 in the preceding example).

IASB Standards

IFRS 3 succeeded IAS 22. It is fairly similar to SFAS Nos. 141 and 142. Pooling, as in the United States, is no longer allowed. IFRS 3, being more principles-based than FASB standards, does not have quantitative measures for consolidation. Instead IFRS 3 requires "obtaining control" of the combinee. IFRS 3, in line with SFAS No. 142, prohibits amortization of goodwill, requiring instead a write-off of any impaired goodwill.

For the IAS, accounting policies of the subsidiary must conform to those of the parent, with disclosures made if this is not the case. FASB is more lenient, not having this policy. IFRS 3 requires that minority interests be included in owners' equity, whereas under U.S. GAAP, minority interests can appear in either liabilities or equity.

Improving Accounting Standards

The new entity approach might be used with the present order of finite uniformity. If it is not, proportionate consolidation should be carefully considered, because it gives a generally useful rigid uniformity solution to the awkward FASB finite uniformity approach to consolidation. A lower cutoff point, such as 10%, could also be instituted for marketable security investments that are not consolidated.

Summary

SFAS Nos. 141 and 142 have brought extremely important changes to intercorporate equity investments. Pooling of interests—a method with no theoretical justification—is now history. Goodwill now has an indefinite life but is subject to impairment. Whether the change to goodwill is a sop or trade-off for the elimination of pooling is an interesting question.

There are problems with both fair value and equity methods. Whether unrealized market value changes under fair value accounting go directly to income or to comprehensive income is a question of management intent, a dubious distinction, though preferable to the dichotomy prior to SFAS No. 130. The equity method lacks representational faithfulness inasmuch as the book value of intercorporate investments accounted for under the equity method is an artificially constructed accounting attribute that has no market referent.

In foreign currency translation, we trace the change from SFAS No. 8 to SFAS No. 52. Some, but not all, of the problems of conflicts between accounting exposure and economic exposure have been eliminated by the move to SFAS No. 52.

The new entity approach views *all* of the assets and liabilities of the newly formed enterprise at their current value. Proportionate consolidation would be a rigid uniformity approach to the problem, but it is not without drawbacks.

Special purpose entities (SPEs) (Appendix 18-A) have been around for many years, but they burst into prominence in 2001 with the Enron scandal and have now been succeeded by variable interest entities (VIEs). Many questions need to be answered relative to when and whether consolidation should occur, when revenues should be recognized, and the propriety of recognizing gains and losses. In fact, the whole issue of the identity of the enterprise, of which the SPE is one small part, still remains to be resolved.

APPENDIX 18-A: Special Purpose Entities, Variable Interest Entities, and the Downfall of Enron

Special Purpose Entities (SPEs)

Special purpose entities were created solely to carry out an activity or series of transactions directly related to a specific purpose. Because SPEs were designed to conduct just one well-defined activity, it was relatively easy to attract a group of investors to invest in an SPE because the cash flows and the risks involved were well understood. Therefore, investors might have preferred to invest in an SPE with well-defined risks and returns than in other investments. For this reason, SPEs had been used for decades as a preferred form of financing arrangements, leasing arrangements, and sales/transfers of illiquid or poor performing assets.

Current accounting rules for consolidation of investments require an assumption of control. Since the structure of an SPE was such that the sponsoring company presumably did not have control (i.e., control rested with the outside equity investors), the sponsoring company did not have to consolidate the SPE on its books as long as the parent did not own more than 97% of the SPE (the famous 3% rule). This obviously flies in the face of the concept of control espoused in the notion of consolidation. Hence, this provided one of the obvious advantages of using an SPE. There were other advantages to using SPEs, such as the ability to moderate risk by transferring the economic risk and rewards of assets to a nonconsolidated third party while retaining use of the assets. There were also tax advantages. In fact, in many SPE transactions, the tax benefits alone were likely to outweigh any maintenance costs associated with the SPE.

Variable Interest Entities (VIE)

The abuse of SPEs by firms such as Enron has left a very bad taste in the public's mouth. Hence the FASB addressed this issue in Interpretation No. 46 (all paragraph numbers refer to that document).[65] The first thing the FASB did was change the name of the arrangement from *special purpose entity* to *variable interest entity* (VIE).

The crux of the interpretation broadens the requirements for consolidating variable interest entities. Previously, as little as a 3% equity interest by an outside investor allowed the controlling enterprise to avoid consolidation. The minimum investment to avoid consolidation has been raised to 10% in para. 9. This still allows companies to move large amounts of debt off the balance sheet and allows consolidation to be avoided if the equity investment in the VIE is sufficient to cover estimated losses.

However, consolidation criteria move to a new arena in the interpretation. An enterprise will consolidate a VIE if it would "receive a majority of the (variable interest) entity's losses if they occur, receive a majority of the (variable interest) entity's expected residual returns if they occur, or both" (para. 14). If there is a split between enterprises sharing losses and residual returns, the losses predominate relative to the issue of which enterprise should consolidate. A direct or an indirect ability to make major decisions for the variable interest entity is a good determinant for whether an enterprise is expected to absorb losses or receive residual gains.

Expected losses and expected residual gains are briefly illustrated in Appendix A of the interpretation. Both involve the use of expected values. These future amounts are discounted to present value using the interest rate for risk-free investments in accordance with Statement of Financial Accounting Concepts No. 7 of the conceptual framework.

This interpretation for determining who is to consolidate VIEs is extremely cumbersome. Depending on who is doing the calculating, we suspect that it would be possible for no firm to do the consolidating or for more than one firm to be consolidating the same VIE. This arises because there could be considerable differences in how future cash flows are estimated, weighted, and discounted (verifiability).

Interpretation 46 R

The FASB revised Interpretation 46 with 46 R, which came out in December 2003.[66] Interpretation 46 R adds further depth to the earlier version. As with Interpretation 46, the minimum investment to consolidation remains at 10%. In addition, consolidation must occur if equity investors:

- Do not participate in decision making by means of voting their stock
- Do not share in returns generated by the entity
- Do not absorb any of the VIE's losses
- Do not share in the expected residual returns of the VIE[67]

A Final Accounting of Enron's Accounting

By now, just about everyone is familiar, to one degree or another, with the Enron debacle. The late chairman of the board (Kenneth Lay) of the company insisted that Enron's downfall was created by a classic run on its stock triggered by short sellers and other Wall Street characters.[68] Such is not the case. Now that the Enron dust has almost settled, we can very fairly say that this was a company living in an accounting and financial fairyland. In turn, the unrealistic accounting led to insurmountable real hazards.

Bennett Stewart has given us a succinct analysis of Enron's situation, which he distilled into three problems.[69] First, the firm became a middleman in the natural gas market, acting between buyers and sellers of the commodity. The contracts entered into were long-term contracts where profits and losses should have been recognized over the lives of the various contracts, in line with accrual accounting. Instead, the entire amount of profit was taken into income in the year contracts were signed, creating huge phantom profits.

Second, huge managerial bonuses were paid on book income. This created a huge real cash outflow based on illusory profits. The bonuses were tempered only by earnings-per-share targets.

Third was the decision to allow the finance department to become a profit center, a strange decision that opened the door to many strange transactions. Perhaps principal among these was the decision to set up numerous SPEs—as many as 3,500 of them—with names sounding as if they were lifted from children's comic books or birds of prey (e.g., Whitewing, Osprey, and Nighthawk). These SPEs were used, of course, to remove debt from Enron's balance sheet.

Enron's actions have led to many consequences, some of which are still unfolding. Replacing SPEs with VIEs can be laid—no pun intended—at Enron's door. Also, the company can claim a fair share of the credit for the enacting of Sarbanes-Oxley (Chapter 3), which could lead to changes in the initial public offerings (IPOs) market.[70] And this says nothing about the financial and human suffering of Enron employees and shareholders, which may continue far into the future.

QUESTIONS

1. Are there relevant circumstance differences between purchase and pooling of interests? Explain.

2. The logic of pooling rests heavily on the assumption that no substantive economic transaction occurs between the combinor and stockholders of the combinee. Evaluate this assumption.

3. Why may companies not be indifferent to purchase and pooling accounting, and what do we know about this issue from research studies?

4. Why would proportionate consolidation result in rigid uniformity for intercorporate equity investment accounting?

5. Compare proportionate consolidation with capitalizing of all leases extending beyond a year, another example of rigid uniformity.

6. The equity method reports neither the investor's cost nor the market value of the investment. Do you believe the equity method provides useful information? Why or why not?

7. Compare the present system involving consolidation, equity method, and fair value accounting for intercorporate equity investments with finite uniformity as it exists in lease accounting.

8. What is meant by the term *one-line consolidation?* What differences occur in financial statements when a one-line consolidation rather than full consolidation is used?

9. What are some reasons that consolidated reports are thought to be relevant?

10. Discuss the limitations of consolidated financial statements and why dual reporting (consolidated and separate entity statements) as well as other forms of disaggregated reporting, such as SFAS No. 131, make sense.

11. Why does the FASB's reporting entity project logically precede any conclusion regarding consolidated financial reporting?

12. Describe the implicit assumption made in SFAS No. 94 about the reporting entity.

13. What is push-down accounting? What problems would arise in connection with the implementation?

14. How are minority interests handled in consolidations?

15. What is an equity carve-out?

16. Distinguish among sell-offs, spin-offs, split-offs, and split-ups.

17. Why does the elimination of poolings (SFAS No. 141) and the indefinite life of goodwill subject to impairment (SFAS No. 142) represent a possible "quid pro quo"?

18. Why does the elimination of poolings improve representational faithfulness and comparability?

19. What are the main issues surrounding the special purpose entity and its successor, the variable interest entity?

20. What are the differences between a foreign currency orientation and a U.S. dollar orientation regarding the translation of foreign currency operations?

21. How do accounting exposure and economic exposure differ?

22. Why would balance sheets prepared under SFAS No. 8 lack additivity?

23. Why does SFAS No. 52 provide an example of finite uniformity in terms of the use of remeasurement?

24. What is the disappearing asset problem?

25. What does the term *functional currency* mean?

CASES, PROBLEMS, AND WRITING ASSIGNMENTS

1. Examine the 2001 and 2002 annual reports for a corporation having a financial subsidiary. (Your instructor may suggest a corporation on the SEC's EDGAR Web site: www.sec.gov/edgarhp.htm). Determine the effect of SFAS No. 94 on operating ratios, profitability ratios, liquidity ratios, and leverage ratios.

2. The following items pertain to a parent company and its 60%-owned subsidiary at year end. There are no cross-guarantees of debt between the parent and subsidiary.

	Parent	Subsidiary
Current assets	$500,000	$1,000,000
Noncurrent assets (excluding subsidiary investment)	5,000,000	2,000,000
Current liabilities	750,000	250,000
Noncurrent liabilities	2,000,000	750,000
Revenues	1,700,000	1,500,000
Expenses	1,600,000	900,000
Dividends	100,000	600,000

Required:

Explain and illustrate how consolidated reporting using the previous data can be misleading.

3. Acquirer Company bought Servile Company for $5,000,000 on January 2, 2004. The fair market value of the individual net assets was $3,500,000. In succeeding years, the fair market value of Servile's costs and goodwill were as follows:

Year	Fair Market Value of Servile	Cost of Servile's Net Assets and Goodwill
2005	$7,000,000	$7,100,000
2006	7,300,000	6,700,000
2007	8,000,000	9,300,000

Required:

a. What amount of goodwill should be recognized as a result of the acquisition of Servile in 2004?
b. Determine the amounts of the goodwill write-offs (if any) in 2005, 2006, and 2007.

4. Why do the six criteria or guidelines for determining the functional currency in SFAS No. 52 provide a good example of finite uniformity?

CRITICAL THINKING AND ANALYSIS

1. If you had to choose among the current method of consolidation for combinees where the combinor owns at least 50%, the new entity approach, or proportionate consolidation, which would you choose? Explain.

Notes

1. *Henry (2002, p. 68).*
2. *Ibid. (p. 64).*
3. *Ibid.*
4. *Moonitz (1944, pp. 22–44).*
5. *Khurana (1991) found evidence that equity values of firms that were already consolidating finance subsidiaries, as well as firms that had been using the equity method prior to SFAS No. 94, suffered declines of equity values after the appearance of SFAS No. 94. He attributes these declines to higher transaction costs for factors such as increased costs of borrowing and possibly increased contracting costs owing to modifications of incentive or compensation plans. Why firms that were already consolidating prior to SFAS No. 94 should be adversely affected is not entirely clear.*
6. *SFAS No. 94 was silent on how to account for unconsolidated majority-owned companies where control is temporary or control is effectively lacking. SFAS No. 94, para. 11, does continue the general disclosure requirement of APB Opinion No. 18, in which summarized balance sheet and income statement data are to be disclosed for material, unconsolidated subsidiaries.*
7. *Beatty and Hand (1992).*
8. *See FASB (1981b).*
9. *FASB (1976, para. 4).*
10. *Cumming and Mallie (1999, p. 77).*
11. *Altria (Phillip Morris) recently spun-off its Kraft Foods subsidiary. The company wanted to separate its tobacco and food divisions, perhaps attempting to minimize its asset holdings in light of lawsuits by smokers. When Phillip Morris acquired Kraft, the purpose was to diversify its asset holdings. See O'Connell and Hallinan (2007).*
12. *If the combinee continues to operate as a separate entity, its records are maintained on the basis of the combinee's own historical cost. A proposal (called* push-down *accounting) has been to carry the combinee's accounts at the purchase price paid by the combinor. See Thomas and Hagler (1988) for an assessment.*
13. *Nurnberg (2001) recommends showing a fuller accounting for the minority interest in the consolidated statement of retained earnings, including the opening minority interest plus its share of consolidated net income less its share of dividends.*
14. *FASB (2001a, paras. B44 and B46).*
15. *Beatty and Webber (2006) find evidence that some firms have been classifying goodwill impairment write-offs* below *income from continuing operations and even delaying write-downs. As might be expected, contracting (agency) considerations such as potential debt covenant violations and bonus arrangements often underlie these practices.*
16. *FASB (2001b, para. 23).*
17. *Ibid. (paras. 24 and 25).*

18. *Ibid. (para. B134). As might be expected, SFAS No. 157 on fair value measurements has brought some modifications to the measurement of fair values of assets. For further details, see Chapter 14.*

19. *Ibid. (para. 39).*

20. *See Walker (1953), for example.*

21. *See Weil (2000).*

22. *Ibid.*

23. *Bierman (1992, p. 6).*

24. *For a review, see Clark (1993).*

25. *See FASB (1985, para. 254, and 1990, para. 16).*

26. *For empirical analysis of the agency theory aspects of this choice, see Hand and Skantz (1998).*

27. *AICPA (1994, pp. 74–75).*

28. *For a comparison of the new entity approach (also called the* economic unit concept*), the purchase method, and proportionate consolidation, see Beckman (1995).*

29. *FASB (1976, para. 138).*

30. *Nathan and Dunne (1991, p. 319).*

31. *Ibid.*

32. *FASB (1976, para. 110).*

33. *Burton (1970, p. 75).*

34. *See Briloff (1967).*

35. *AICPA (1997, p. 52). This is also brought out by Ayers, Lefanowicz, and Robinson (2000) in their study of business combinations for the years 1992–1997.*

36. *Hong, Kaplan, and Mandelker (1978).*

37. *Hopkins, Houston, and Peters (2000).*

38. *For a history of the equity method, see Nobes (2002).*

39. *Bauman (2003).*

40. *FASB (1993, para. 3). See also FASB (1975a).*

41. *FASB (1987, para. 1).*

42. *Walker (1976 and 1978).*

43. *See Pendlebury (1980) and Francis (1986).*

44. *See Mohr (1983) for a summary of relevant empirical research and Kim (1987) for a theoretical development of the argument.*

45. *See Whittred (1986 and 1987), although Francis (1986) reports that less than 10% of New York Stock Exchange companies cross-guarantee debt.*

46. *Prior to 1982, the SEC did, in very limited instances, require supplemental parent-only statements. But this last gesture to dual reporting was dropped in ASR 302 (See SEC 1981).*

47. *King and Lembke (1994, p. 15).*

48. *Ibid. (p. 18).*

49. *Ibid. (p. 19).*

50. *See Houston (1989, pp. 26–27) for further details.*

51. *Ibid. (p. 31).*

52. *Beaver and Wolfson (1982), in a deductive analysis under the assumption of perfect and complete markets, show that only in a system in which current values are employed and translation occurs at current exchange rates will the results be both symmetrical and economically interpretable. The former is defined as a situation in which two "economically equivalent investments"—one in the foreign market and the other in the investment market— will lead to the same financial statement numbers when translation into a common currency is made. Economic interpretability occurs only if the balance sheet values are equal to the present value of future cash flows for all balance sheet elements. If historical cost elements are translated at the historical rate, the results will be symmetrical.*

If accounts kept on a historical cost basis are translated at the current rate, the results are neither economically interpretable nor symmetrical. The authors duly note the problems of extending their analysis to incomplete and imperfect markets, including imperfections in exchange rates themselves. However, Ziebart and Choi (1998, p. 407) note that even if markets are perfect and complete, unless the foreign exchange rate between the two countries is proportional to "the change in the ratio of the foreign price level to the domestic price level," the results will not be both symmetrical and economically interpretable.

53. *Ijiri (1995) suggests using a composite currency rather than the home country currency for consolidation where investment is not temporary. He shows that translation of investee currencies can lead to gains or losses that are not comparable among investors. The composite currency would be a blend of the individual currencies in the parent's investments and would be based on a desired investment holding mixture of currencies by the parent company.*

54. *Salatka (1989) examined early versus late adopters of SFAS No. 8 (FASB 1975a). Late adopters were generally smaller than early adopters, indicating that the latter had higher political costs (being larger,) whereas the former generally had higher contracting costs (tighter debt–equity ratios, working capital ratios, and interest coverage ratios).*

55. *See, for example, Evans, Folks, and Jilling (1978) and Shank, Dillard, and Murdock (1979).*

56. *FASB (1981a, para. 162). Duangploy and Owings (1997) discuss an alternative to functional currency called* multicurrency accounting *in which a separate set of accounts is kept for each foreign subsidiary in its own currency unit with the difference between assets and liabilities being translated at the spot conversion rate.*

57. *Collins and Salatka (1993) found that earnings measurement under SFAS No. 52 appeared to have a higher quality than under SFAS No. 8, as perceived by market participants.*

58. *Bartov (1997).*

59. *FASB (1981a, para. 6).*

60. *Ibid. (para. 42).*

61. *Evans and Doupnik (1986, pp. 7–8). Further evidence that the functional currency approach of SFAS No. 52 is working is provided by Kirsch and Evans (1994), whose evidence indicates that American firms do take into account regional differences of subsidiaries when determining the functional currency.*

62. *Evans and Doupnik (1986, p. 6).*

63. *Ibid. (p. 5).*

64. *For continuing problems with the foreign currency translation adjustment under SFAS No. 52, see Louis (2003).*

65. *FASB (2003a).*

66. *FASB (2003b).*

67. *Ratcliffe (2005, p. 75).*

68. *Koppel (2006).*

69. *Stewart (2006).*

70. *Ip, Scannell, and Solomon (2007) point out that many believe that Sarbanes-Oxley is responsible for declining listings on the New York Stock Exchange, but many foreign exchanges are likewise tightening their rules and losing listings. One reason for this situation is that private-equity firms are making many acquisitions and taking firms private.*

References

American Institute of Certified Public Accountant (1994). *Improving Business Reporting—A Customer Focus: Meeting the Information Needs of Investors and Creditors.* AICPA.

——— (1997). *Accounting Trends and Techniques.* AICPA.

Ayers, Benjamin, C. E. Lefanowicz, and J. R. Robinson (March 2000). "The Financial Statement Effects of Eliminating the Pooling-of-Interests Method of Acquisition Accounting," *Accounting Horizons*, pp. 1–19.

Bartov, Eli (Winter 1997). "Foreign Currency Exposure of Multinational Firms," *Contemporary Accounting Research*, pp. 623–652.

Bauman, Mark (2003). "The Impact and Valuation of Off-Balance Sheet Activities Concealed by Equity Method Accounting," *Accounting Horizons* (December 2003), pp. 303–314.

Beatty, Ann, and J. Weber (May 2006). "Accounting Discretion in Fair Value Estimates: An Examination of SFAS 142 Goodwill Impairments," *Journal of Accounting Research*, pp. 257–288.

Beatty, Randolph, and John Hand (Fall 1992). "The Causes and Effects of Mandated Accounting Standards: SFAS No. 94 as a Test of the Level Playing Field Theory," *Journal of Accounting, Auditing & Finance*, pp. 509–530.

Beaver, William H., and Mark A. Wolfson (Autumn 1982, Pt. II). "Foreign Currency Translation and Changing Prices and Perfect and Complete Markets," *Journal of Accounting Research*, pp. 528–550.

Beckman, Judy (1995). "The Economic Unit Approach to Consolidated Financial Statements: Support From the Financial Economics Literature," *Journal of Accounting Literature*, pp. 1–23.

Bierman, Harold, Jr. (December 1992). "Proportionate Consolidation and Financial Analysis," *Accounting Horizons*, pp. 5–17.

Briloff, Abraham J. (July 1967). "Dirty Pooling," *Accounting Review*, pp. 489–496.

Burton, John C. (1970). *Accounting for Business Combinations*. Financial Executives Research Foundation.

Clark, Myrtle (June 1993). "Evolution of Concepts of Minority Interest," *Accounting Historians Journal*, pp. 59–78.

Collins, Daniel, and William Salatka (Fall 1993). "Noisy Accounting Earnings Signals and Earnings Response Coefficients: The Case of Foreign Currency Accounting," *Contemporary Accounting Research*, pp. 119–159.

Cumming, John, and Tina Mallie (February 1999). "Accounting for Divestitures: A Comparison of Sell-Offs, Spin-Offs, Split-Offs, and Split-Ups," *Issues in Accounting Education*, pp. 75–97.

Duangploy, Orapin, and G. Owings (1997). "The Compatibility of Multicurrency Accounting with Functional Currency Accounting," *International Journal of Accounting* (Vol. 32, No. 4), pp. 441–462.

Evans, Thomas G., and Timothy S. Doupnik (1986). *Determining the Functional Currency Under Statement 52*. FASB.

Evans, Thomas G., William R. Folks, Jr., and Michael Jilling (1978). *The Impact of Financial Accounting Standard No. 8 on the Foreign Exchange Risk Management Practices of American Multinational Firms: An Economic Impact Study*. FASB.

Financial Accounting Standards Board (1975a). Statement of Financial Accounting Standards No. 8, *Accounting for the Translation of Foreign Currency Transactions and Foreign Currency Financial Statements*. FASB.

———— (1975b). Statement of Financial Accounting Standards No. 12, *Accounting for Certain Marketable Securities*. FASB.

———— (1976). FASB Discussion Memorandum, *An Analysis of Issues Related to Accounting for Business Combinations and Purchased Intangibles*. FASB.

———— (1981a). Statement of Financial Accounting Standards No. 52, *Foreign Currency Translation*. FASB.

———— (1981b). Interpretation No. 35, *Criteria for Applying the Equity Method of Accounting for Investment in Common Stock*. FASB.

———— (1985). Statement of Financial Accounting Statements No. 6, *Elements of Financial Statements: A Replacement of FASB Concepts Statement No. 3* (incorporating an amendment of FASB Concepts Statement No. 2). FASB.

———— (1987). Statement of Financial Accounting Standards No. 94, *Consolidation of All Majority-Owned Subsidiaries*. FASB.

—— (1990). FASB Discussion Memorandum, *An Analysis of Issues Related to Distinguishing Between Liability and Equity Instruments and Accounting for Instruments With Characteristics of Both.* FASB.

—— (1993). Statement of Financial Accounting Standards No. 115, *Accounting for Certain Investments in Debt and Equity Securities.* FASB.

—— (2001a). Statement of Financial Accounting Standards No. 141, *Business Combinations.* FASB.

—— (2001b). Statement of Financial Accounting Standards No. 142, *Goodwill and Other Intangible Assets.* FASB.

—— (2003a). Interpretation No. 46, *Consolidation of Variable Interest Entities.* FASB.

—— (2003b). Interpretation No. 46 R, *Consolidation of Variable Interest Entities.* FASB.

Francis, Jere R. (Autumn 1986). "Debt Reporting by Parent Companies: Parent-Only Versus Consolidated Statements," *Journal of Business Finance and Accounting,* pp. 393–403.

Hand, John R. M., and T. Skantz (December 1998). "The Economic Determinants of Accounting Choices: The Unique Case of Equity Carve-Outs Under SAB 51," *Journal of Accounting and Economics,* pp. 175–203.

Henry, David (2002). "Mergers: Why Most Big Deals Don't Pay Off," *Business Week* (October 14), pp. 60–70.

Hong, H., R. Kaplan, and G. Mandelker (January 1978). "Pooling vs. Purchase: The Effects of Accounting for Mergers on Stock Prices," *Accounting Review,* pp. 31–47.

Hopkins, Patrick, R. W. Houston, and M. F. Peters (July 2000). "Purchase, Pooling, and Equity Analysts' Value Judgments," *Accounting Review,* pp. 257–281.

Houston, Carol Olson (1989). "Foreign Currency Translation Research: Review and Synthesis," *Journal of Accounting Literature,* pp. 19–29.

Ijiri, Yuji (1995). "Global Financial Reporting Using a Composite Currency: An Aggregation Theory Perspective," *International Journal of Accounting* (Vol. 30, No. 2), pp. 95–106.

Ip, Greg, K. Scannell, and D. Solomon (2007). "In Call to Deregulate Business, a Global Twist," *Wall Street Journal* (January 25), pp. A1 and A17.

Khurana, Inder (July 1991). "Security Market Effects Associated With SFAS No. 94 Concerning Consolidation Policy," *Accounting Review,* pp. 611–621.

Kim, Jae-Oh (1987). "Segmental Disclosures and Information Content of Earnings Announcements: Theoretical and Empirical Analysis" (PhD diss., University of Iowa).

King, Thomas E., and Valdean Lembke (1994). "An Examination of Financial Reporting Alternatives for Associated Enterprises," *Advances in Accounting* (Vol. 12), pp. 1–30.

Kirsch, Robert J., and Thomas G. Evans (1994). "The Implementation of SFAS 52: Did the Functional Currency Approach Prevail?" *International Journal of Accounting* (Vol. 29, No. 1), pp. 20–33.

Koppel, Nathan (2006). "Lay Says 'Classic Run on Bank' Ruined Enron," *Wall Street Journal* (April 25), pp. C1 and C4.

Louis, Henock (October 2003). "The Value Relevance of the Foreign Translation Adjustment," *Accounting Review,* pp. 1027–1047.

Mohr, R. (Spring 1983). "The Segmental Reporting Issue: A Review of Empirical Research," *Journal of Accounting Literature,* pp. 39–71.

Moonitz, Maurice (1944). *The Entity Theory of Consolidated Statements.* American Accounting Association.

Nathan, Kevin, and Kathleen Dunne (Winter 1991). "The Purchase-Pooling Choice: Some Explanatory Variables," *Journal of Accounting and Public Policy,* pp. 309–323.

Nobes, Christopher (2002). "An Analysis of the International Development of the Equity Method," *Abacus* (Vol. 38, No. 1), pp. 16–44.

Nurnberg, Hugo (June 2001). "Minority Interest in the Consolidated Retained Earnings Statement," *Accounting Horizons,* pp. 119–146.

O'Connell, Vanessa, and Joseph Hallinan (2007). "Smoke Clears for Kraft Spinoff," *Wall Street Journal* (January 26), p. A7.

Pendlebury, M. (Spring 1980). "The Application of Information Theory to Accounting for Groups of Companies," *Journal of Business Finance and Accounting*, pp. 105–117.

Ratcliffe, Thomas (December 2005). "To Consolidate or Not," *Journal of Accountancy*, pp. 75–79.

Salatka, William (February 1989). "The Impact of SFAS No. 8 on Equity Prices of Early and Late Adopting Firms: An Events Study and Cross-Sectional Analysis," *Journal of Accounting and Economics,* pp. 35–69.

Securities and Exchange Commission (1981). Accounting Series Release No. 302, *Separate Financial Statements Required by Regulation S-X* (November 6). SEC.

Shank, John K., Jesse F. Dillard, and Richard J. Murdock (1979). *Assessing the Economic Impact of FASB No. 8*. Financial Executives Research Foundation.

Stewart, Bennett (2006). "The Real Reasons Enron Failed," *Journal of Applied Corporate Finance* (Vol. 18, No. 2), pp. 116–119.

Thomas, Paula B., and J. Larry Hagler (September 1988). "Push Down Accounting: A Descriptive Assessment," *Accounting Horizons*, pp. 26–31.

Walker, George (February 1953). "Why Purchased Goodwill Should Be Amortized on a Systematic Basis," *Journal of Accountancy*, pp. 210–216.

Walker, Robert G. (December 1976). "An Evaluation of Information Conveyed by Consolidated Statements," *Abacus*, pp. 77–115.

——— (1978). *Consolidated Statements: A History and Analysis*. Arno Press.

Weil, Jonathan (2000). "FASB Backs Down on Goodwill-Accounting Rules," *Wall Street Journal* (December 7), pp. A2 and A6.

Whittred, Greg (September 1986). "The Evolution of Consolidated Financial Reporting in Australia," *Abacus*, pp. 103–120.

——— (December 1987). "The Derived Demand for Consolidated Financial Reporting," *Journal of Accounting and Economics*, pp. 259–285.

Ziebart, David, and J-H Choi (1998). "The Difficulty of Achieving Economic Reality Through Foreign Currency Translation," *International Journal of Accounting* (Vol. 33, No. 4), pp. 403–414.

Further Readings

Accounting Principles Board (1970a). APB Opinion No. 16, *Business Combinations*. AICPA.

——— (1970b). APB Opinion No. 17, *Intangible Assets*. AICPA.

——— (1971). APB Opinion No. 18, *The Equity Method of Accounting for Investments in Common Stock*. AICPA.

Name Index

Subject Index

About the Authors

Harry I. Wolk has a BS in economics from the Wharton School of the University of Pennsylvania and MBA and PhD degrees from Michigan State University. He is the author or co-author of approximately 25 journal articles, including publications in the *Accounting Review, Journal of Accounting Research, Accounting Horizons,* and the *International Journal of Accounting*. He has been the principle author of all seven editions of *Accounting Theory: Conceptual Issues in a Political and Economic Environment*. He previously taught at the University of Wisconsin–Milwaukee and was Aliber Professor of Accounting at Drake University, where he taught for over 30 years. He also visited Creighton University, where he was John P. Begley Professor of Accounting. He is a member of the American Accounting Association and Financial Executives International, where he has been president of the Iowa Chapter. Outside of accounting, his interests lie in following national and world affairs closely, listening to classical music, and following the fortunes of the Boston Red Sox, Boston Celtics, and the New England Patriots.

James L. Dodd, Aliber Distinguished Professor of Accounting at Drake University, holds a BS in accounting from California State University–Fresno, an MBA from the University of South Alabama, and a PhD from the University of Georgia, with a major in accounting and a minor in information systems. Before entering academe, Dr. Dodd worked in shipbuilding and aircraft-engine and diesel-engine filtration industries for 15 years. His assignments at Litton, Teledyne, and Cummins included international experiences in industrial engineering, capital budgeting, profit planning, product pricing, cost accounting, long-range systems planning, and accounting controllerships at plant and corporate levels. He is a Fulbright Scholar alumnus, participating in academic exchanges with Norway (1999–2000) and Iceland (2007). His current teaching and research interests are in areas involving accounting theory, fraud examination, and international accounting. He is a member of the American Accounting Association, American Institute of CPAs, Association of Certified Fraud Examiners, and Fulbright Alumni Association.

John J. Rozycki, associate professor of finance at Drake University, holds a BS in biology from King's College, an MBA from the University of Scranton, and a PhD from Penn State University, major in finance. Before pursuing his doctoral education, he worked in the health care planning and telecommunications industries. He teaches corporate finance and equity valuation. His professional interests are in equity and business valuation, corporate capital allocation decisions, financial planning, financing decisions, and financial statement analysis. He is a member of the CFA Institute, the CFA Society of Iowa, the Financial Management Association, and the Midwest Finance Association. He is a CFA charterholder. He was born in Wilkes-Barre, Pennsylvania, and is married with two sons. He is a member of the board of directors of Hospice of Central Iowa and is active in his church. He enjoys the outdoors.